Frank Wood
B.Sc.(Econ.), F.C.A.

THIRD EDITION

Business Accounting 2

With contributions from
J. M. Coy, A.A.C.C.A., A.C.I.S.
J. Townsley, B.Com., F.C.A.

Longman
London and New York

Longman Group Limited London

*Associated companies, branches and representatives
throughout the world*

*Published in the United States of America
by Longman Inc., New York*

© Frank Wood 1968
© Longman Group Limited 1973; 1979

First published 1968
Second edition 1973
Fourth impression 1977
Third edition 1980

British Library Cataloguing in Publication Data

Wood, Frank
  Business accounting.
  2. – 3rd ed
  1. Accounting
  I. Title II. Coy, John M III. Townsley, Joseph
  657   HF5635   78–40874

ISBN 0–582–41562–4

Printed and bound by Richard Clay (The Chaucer Press) Ltd.,
Bungay, Suffolk.

Contents

For the contents of Volume One see over page

VOLUME ONE

Contents

Preface to the Third Edition

This is the second volume of the textbook. It completes the coverage for examinations such as the professional foundation examinations: London Chamber of Commerce Intermediate and Higher Stages: Royal Society of Arts Stage II and most of Stage III; and for the General Certificate of Education Advanced Level.

John Coy, M.Sc., A.C.C.A., A.C.I.S., wrote chapters 42, 47 and 48, and Joe Townsley, B.Com., F.C.A., contributed chapters 45 and 46. At the time they acted as co-authors simply because I was ill and unable to meet the deadlines for production of the book. I now look back, and consider it a fortunate accident that these two friends of mine became involved with my books. I also owe a debt of gratitude to Eddie Cainen. A.C.C.A., for his untiring interest in my work.

At the time of writing, the problems of 'Accounting for Inflation are being considered by the professional bodies. It would be misleading if the chapter on this topic from the second edition was revised on the basis of mere conjecture on my part. Accordingly the chapter has been dropped from this edition.

Appendix 48.1 and Appendix 58.1 were not in the second edition. They are designed to help the reader tackle the examination(s) for which he/she is entered. All of the questions in the second edition have been retained, using the same numbers for the questions. Extra questions have been added to chapters 45, 47 and 48.

I wish to acknowledge the permission to use past examination papers granted by the Associated Examining Board, the Welsh Joint Education Committee, the Institute of Chartered Accountants in England and Wales, the Association of Certified Accountants, the Institute of Cost and Management Accountants, the Chartered Institute of Secretaries and Administrators, the Institute of Bankers, the Northern Counties Technical Examinations Council, the Royal Society of Arts. the London Chamber of Commerce, the Union of Educational Institutions, the Union of Lancashire and Cheshire Institutes, and the East Midland Educational Union.

FRANK WOOD
Autumn 1978

28

The Valuation of Stock

To the general public accounting often seems to imply a precision down to the last penny. A firm will usually know the exact amount of debtors or creditors, or the exact amount spent on wages or other expenses, and this gives the appearance of precision in all matters connected with accounting. In fact this is only true of some parts of accounting. A re-examination of the chapter on depreciation in Volume 1 will illustrate a part of accounting dealing with provisions for depreciation which are normally nothing more than sheer guesswork.

Precision is also lacking when stock is valued at the end of each financial year. This does not necessarily mean a lack of precision in actually counting the number of items in stock. In all but the very smallest businesses there will often be errors in checking the quantities in stock. There will be human errors unless everything is double-checked, and the cost of doing this is often not worth while for many items of small value. Then there will be defects in such aids to checking quantities as weighing machines or liquid measures, even though the margin of error may be very small. The real lack of precision exists in giving one indisputable value to the total quantity of stock.

It is possible to state that J. Smith is a debtor for £155 and to be perfectly correct. In this case there is only one correct figure. With stock valuation there is usually a whole spectrum of possible figures. The one chosen will depend on the attitudes and opinions of those whose responsibility it is to value stock.

Up to this point it has been assumed, for the sake of simplicity, that the stock of unsold goods at the end of each financial year is valued at cost. This might appear to be an easy task to be undertaken by the management of the firm. It is, however, far from the truth. Even if 'cost' was the only measure of the value of stock, it will be shown that 'cost' can have many different meanings attached to it.

Assume that a firm has just completed its first financial year and is about to value stock at cost price. It has dealt in only one type of good. A record of the transactions is as follows:

Bought		£	Sold		£
January	10 at £30 each	300	May	8 for £50 each	400
April	10 at £34 each	340	November	24 for £60 each	1,440
October	20 at £40 each	800			
	40	1,440		32	1,840

Still in Stock at 31 December, 8 units.

The total figure of purchases is £1,440 and that of sales is £1,840. The trading account for the first year of trading can now be completed if the closing stock is brought into the calculations. This brings to light the question as to exactly which eight units of stock remain on hand. If each of the units bought had cost exactly the same, then the question would not matter from an accounting point of view. However, the three lots of purchases were bought at different prices. The cost of the goods unsold therefore rests on exactly which goods are taken for this calculation. They are most probably eight of the October purchases, but they could well be eight of the April or January purchases instead, or else be some of each of these purchases. If it is the type of good which is subject to a fairly speedy deterioration because of age, then obviously a great deal of attention will be given to ensure that goods are issued or sold in chronological order. There are, however, many types of goods which do not suffer undue deterioration in the short term, and it will not matter vitally to the firms as to which items are sold first.

Therefore many firms will not know when the units in stock at the end of the financial year were purchased. Even if they could, many firms would not take the trouble of finding this out, nor would they want to incur the cost involved in obtaining the information. The valuation of stock therefore becomes one of an accounting custom rather than one based on any scientific facts. In accounting what matters is not which units were actually sold, but instead rests on the surmise of which units were 'deemed' to have been sold.

Three accounting methods of stating which goods were sold are now listed. It must not be thought that the list is comprehensive.

1. *First In, First Out* (abbreviated as FIFO, this 'shorthand' term often being used).

The first goods received are deemed to be the first to be issued. With this method, using the data already given, the stock figure at 31 December would be calculated as follows:

	Received	Issued	Stock after each transaction		
				£	£
January	10 at £30 each		10 at £30 each		300

	Received	Issued	Stock after each transaction	£	£
April	10 at £34 each		10 at £30 each	300	
			10 at £34 each	340	640
May		8 at £30 each	2 at £30 each	60	
			10 at £34 each	340	400
October	20 at £40 each		2 at £30 each	60	
			10 at £34 each	340	
			20 at £40 each	800	1,200
November		2 at £30 each			
		10 at £34 each			
		12 at £40 each			
		——			
		24	8 at £40 each		320
		==			

2. *Last In, First Out* (abbreviated as LIFO)

With this method, as each issue of goods is made they are deemed to be from the last lot of goods received prior to that date, and where the last lot received are insufficient to meet the issue then the balance is deemed to come from the next previous lot received still available. The stock figure at 31 December becomes £240.

	Received	Issued	Stock after each transaction	£	£
January	10 at £30 each		10 at £30 each		300
April	10 at £34 each		10 at £30 each	300	
			10 at £34 each	340	640
May		8 at £34 each	10 at £30 each	30	
			2 at £34 each	68	368
October	20 at £40 each		10 at £30 each	300	
			2 at £34 each	68	
			20 at £40 each	800	1,168
November		20 at £40 each			
		2 at £34 each			
		2 at £30 each	8 at £30 each		240
		——			
		24			
		==			

3. *Average Cost*

With each receipt of goods the average cost of goods held in stock is recalculated. Any subsequent issue is then made at that price until a further receipt of goods necessitates the average cost of goods held being recalculated. This shows a stock at 31 December of £296.

	Received	Issued	Average cost per unit of stock held	Number of units in stock	Total value of stock
			£		£
January	10 at £30		30	10	300
April	10 at £34		32	20	640
May		8 at £32	32	12	384
October	20 at £40		37	32	1,184
November		24 at £37	37	8	296

Stock Valuation and the Calculation of Profits

Using each of the three methods already described, the Trading Accounts would appear:

Trading Account for the year ended 31 December 19—

	Methods				Methods		
	1	2	3		1	2	3
	£	£	£		£	£	£
Purchases	1,440	1,440	1,440	Sales	1,840	1,840	1,840
Less Closing Stock	320	240	296				
Cost of Goods Sold	1,120	1,200	1,144				
Gross Profit	720	640	696				
	1,840	1,840	1,840		1,840	1,840	1,840

The amount of profits calculated is therefore always dependent on the basis on which the stock has been valued.

Profits as a Periodic Calculation

While it is true to say that the profits calculated for any year will differ if other bases were used for stock valuation purposes, it must be borne in mind that the total profits over the whole life-span of the business will be the same irrespective of which basis is used at the end of each intervening year.

An illustration of this can now be shown. Assume that a business commences without any stock and terminates its activities four years later, the stock then in hand being taken over by the purchaser of the business for £2,000. A record of the sales and purchases, together with two possible stock valuations for each year, are as follows:

	Year 1	Year 2	Year 3	Year 4
	£	£	£	£
Sales (excluding the sale of the final stock)	5,000	7,000	8,000	9,000
Purchases	4,000	5,000	6,200	7,500
Stock valuations:				
Basis (a)	800	1,000	1,500	
Basis (b)	500	800	1,100	

Trading Account

Stock valuation: basis (a)

	Years						Years			
	1	2	3	4			1	2	3	4
	£	£	£	£			£	£	£	£
Opening Stock	—	800	1,000	1,500	Sales		5,000	7,000	8,000	9,000
Add Purchases	4,000	5,000	6,200	7,500						
	4,000	5,800	7,200	9,000						
Less Closing Stock	800	1,000	1,500	2,000						
	3,200	4,800	5,700	7,000						
Gross Profit	1,800	2,200	2,300	2,000						
	5,000	7,000	8,000	9,000			5,000	7,000	8,000	9,000

Stock valuation: basis (b)

	Years						Years		
---	1	2	3	4		1	2	3	4
	£	£	£	£		£	£	£	£
Opening Stock	—	500	800	1,100	Sales	5,000	7,000	8,000	9,000
Add Purchases	4,000	5,000	6,200	7,500					
	4,000	5,500	7,000	8,600					
Less Closing Stock	500	800	1,100	2,000					
	3,500	4,700	5,900	6,600					
Gross Profit	1,500	2,300	2,100	2,400					
	5,000	7,000	8,000	9,000		5,000	7,000	8,000	9,000

Adding the profits together basis (*a*) shows £1,800+£2,200+£2,300 +£2,000=£8,300, while basis (*b*) shows £1,500+£2,300+£2,100 +£2,400=£8,300.

Different Meanings of 'Cost'

Dealing in the first instance with a retailing business, the word 'cost' may well mean just the actual cash paid to the supplier. However, where the retailer has paid separately for carriage inwards on the items bought, then he should undoubtedly treat this as part of the cost. Some firms will in addition add an amount representing the cost of storing the goods prior to resale, other firms will ignore such expenses for stock valuation purposes. Even firms who do bring in an amount for storage expenses will differ in the ways that they calculate it. There is no way that is laid down and adhered to by all firms.

With a manufacturing firm the problem becomes even more complex. It is permissible to value stocks of goods manufactured by the firm either at prime cost or at production cost or at some point in between. The difference between the prime cost and production cost is made up of factory indirect expenses. Where these indirect expenses are small relative to the prime cost the difference in the profits calculated may also be small, but the greater the relative indirect expenses then the greater the difference in profit calculations. An example of this can be seen in Exhibits 28.1 and 28.2.

Exhibit 28.1

A firm manufactures its own goods for resale. In its first year of trading it has incurred £10,000 for prime cost of goods completed and £2,000 for factory indirect expenses. There was no work in progress at the end of the year. The number of units made was 1,000 and the number sold was 800 at £20 each.

The directors wish to know what the profit calculations would be (*a*) if prime cost was taken as the stock valuation basis, and (*b*) if production cost was taken.

Trading Account for the year ended . . .

	(a)	(b)		(a)	(b)
	£	£		£	£
Production Cost of Goods b/d from Manufacturing Account	12,000	12,000	Sales	16,000	16,000
Less Closing Stock (see following calculations)	2,000	2,400			
	10,000	9,600			
Gross Profit	6,000	6,400			
	16,000	16,000		16,000	16,000

Closing Stock (a) $\dfrac{\text{Units in Stock}}{\text{Total Produced}} \times$ Prime Cost

$$= \frac{200}{1,000} \times £10,000 = £2,000$$

(b) $\dfrac{\text{Units in Stock}}{\text{Total Produced}} \times$ Production Cost

$$= \frac{200}{1,000} \times £12,000 = £2,400$$

Exhibit 28.2

All the facts are the same as in Exhibit 28.1 except that in this case the prime cost is £2,000 and the factory indirect expenses are £10,000.

Trading Account for the year ended . . .

	(a)	(b)		(a)	(b)
	£	£		£	£
Production Cost of Goods b/d from Manufacturing Account	12,000	12,000	Sales	16,000	16,000
Less Closing Stock (see following calculations.	400	2,400			
	11,600	9,600			
Gross Profit	4,400	6,400			
	16,000	16,000		16,000	16,000

Closing Stock (a) $\dfrac{\text{Units in Stock}}{\text{Total Produced}} \times$ Prime Cost $= \dfrac{200}{1,000} \times £2,000 = £400$

(b) Same as in Exhibit 28.1 = £2,400

Reduction to Net Realisable Value

When the cost of the stock, using the applicable method, has been determined, it is necessary to ascertain whether any part of such costs will not be recouped when the goods are sold. To do this the cost is compared with the 'net realisable value', this term meaning the amount that would be received from the sale of stock after deducting all expenditure to be incurred on or before disposal. If the net realisable value is less than the cost, then the stock valuation is reduced to the net realisable value instead of cost.

This is obviously the application of the accounting convention of conservatism, already discussed in Chapter 7 in Volume 1. A somewhat exaggerated example will show the necessity for this action. Assume that an art dealer has bought only two paintings during the financial year ended 31 December 19–8. He starts off the year without any stock, and then buys a genuine masterpiece for £6,000, selling this later in the year for £11,500. The other painting is a fake, but he does not realise this when he buys it for £5,100, only to discover during the year that in fact he had made a terrible mistake and that the net realizable value is £100. The fake remains unsold at the end of the year. The trading accounts, Exhibit 28.3, would appear as (*a*) if stock is valued at cost, and (*b*) if stock is valued at net realisable value.

Exhibit 28.3

Trading Account for the year ended 31 December 19–8

	(*a*)	(*b*)		(*a*)	(*b*)
	£	£		£	£
Purchases	11,100	11,100	Sales	11,500	11,500
Less Closing Stock	5,100	100			
	6,000	11,000			
Gross Profit	5,500	500			
	11,500	11,500		11,500	11,500

Method (*a*) ignores the fact that the dealer had a bad trading year owing to his skill being found wanting in 19–8. If this method were used, then the loss on the fake would reveal itself in the following year's trading account. Method (*b*), however, realises that the loss really occurred at the date of purchase rather than at the date of sale. Following the convention of conservatism accounting practice chooses method (*b*).

Stock Groupings and Valuation

It has already been seen that the valuation normally takes the lower or cost or net realisable value. This can be further interpreted in three different ways and each way is an acceptable one for accounting purposes.

1. **The Aggregate Method.** The whole of the stock at cost is compared with the whole of the stock at the net realisable value. The lower of these two figures is then used.

2. **The Category Method.** Similar or interchangeable articles are put together into categories. Then the cost and net realisable values for each category are compared, and the lower of these two figures for each category is then taken. For one category it may well be the cost figure, while for another category it will be the net realisable figure. The figures chosen for each category are then added together to give the total valuation.

3. **The Article Method.** The cost and net realisable value are compared for each article and the lower figure taken. These lower figures are then added together to give the total valuation. It must be stressed that an article means a type of good, so that if there are 50 units of an article in stock and that should the lower figure be £5 for one unit of an article, then the stock valuation for this item will be shown as £250.

Exhibit 28.4

From the following data the different stock figures can be calculated

Stock at 31 December 19–8

Article	Different categories	Cost	Net realisable value
		£	£
1	A	10	8
2	A	12	15
3	A	30	40
4	B	18	17
5	B	15	13
6	B	26	21
7	C	41	54
8	C	36	41
9	C	42	31
		230	240

Aggregate Method

The lower of the totals of the cost column or the net realisable value column. The choice is between £230 and £240, therefore £230 is chosen.

Category Method

	Cost	Net realisable value
Category A	£10+£12+£30=£52	£8+£15+£40=£63
Category B	£18+£15+£26=£59	£17+£13+£21=£51
Category C	£41+£36+£42=£119	£54+£41+£31=£126

The valuation is therefore £52+£51+£119=£222.

Article Method

Taking the lower figure for each article.

£8+£12+£30+£17+£13+£21+£41+£36+£31=£209

This business could therefore legitimately take any of these three figures for stock valuation.

Reduction to Replacement Price

In other businesses it may well be important to pay attention to the price at which stock could be replaced, if such a price is less than cost. This will be particularly applicable where there is uncertainty as to net realisable value; where the selling prices are based on current replacement prices; or where there is a desire to recognise uneconomic buying or production.

The stock may therefore in this case be stated as the lowest of (a) cost, (b) net realisable value, or (c) replacement price.

Some other Bases in Use

Some other businesses such as tea and rubber producing companies have a custom of valuing stocks at the prices realised subsequent to the balance sheet date less only selling costs.

Retail businesses often estimate the cost of stock by calculating it in the first place at selling price, and then deducting the normal margin of gross profit on such stock. Adjustment is made for items which are to be sold at other than normal selling prices.

Where the standard costing is in use the figure of standard cost is frequently used.

Factors affecting the Stock Valuation Decision

Nearly all that has been written in this chapter is in accordance with the Accounting Standards of the Institute of Chartered Accountants in England and Wales. These recommendations are followed by the vast majority of firms in these countries. The only method contained in this chapter which is not in the recommendations is the LIFO method. This has been felt to be well worth mentioning as there are certain advantages to be gained by using it. The recommendations do state that the over-riding consideration applicable in all circumstances is the need to give a 'true and fair view' of the state of the affairs of the undertaking as on the Balance Sheet date and of the trend of the firm's trading results. There is, however, no precise definition of 'true and fair view'; it obviously rests on the judgement of the persons concerned. It would be necessary to study the behavioural sciences to understand the factors that affect judgement. However, it should be possible to state that the judgement of any two persons will not always be the same in the differing circumstances of various firms.

In fact, the only certain thing about stock valuation is that the convention of consistency should be applied, i.e. that once adopted, the same basis should be used in the annual accounts until some good reason occurs to change it. A reference should then be made in the final accounts as to the effect of the change on the reported profits, if the amount involved is material.

It will perhaps be useful to look at some of the factors which cause a particular basis to be chosen. The list is intended to be indicative rather than comprehensive, and is merely intended as a first brief look at matters which will have to be studied in depths by those intending to make a career in accountancy.

1. Ignorance. The personalities involved may not appreciate the fact that there is more than one possible way of valuing stock.

2. Convenience. The basis chosen may not be the best for the purposes of profit calculation but it may be the easiest to calculate. It must always be borne in mind that the benefits which flow from possessing information should be greater than the costs of obtaining it. The only difficulty with this is actually establishing when the benefits do exceed the cost, but in some circumstances the decision not to adopt a given basis will be obvious.

3. Custom. It may be the particular method used in a certain trade or industry.

4. Taxation.
(a) The whole idea may be to defer the payment of tax for as long as possible. Because the stock figures affect the calculation of profits on which the tax is based the lowest possible stock figures may be taken to show the lowest profits up to the Balance Sheet date.
(b) Some bases are not acceptable for taxation purposes in the United Kingdom, an example being the LIFO method although it is now widely used in the U.S.A. It may be considered not worth while to have to recalculate the stock figure for taxation purposes after

having calculated the stock figure for the financial accounts. In this case the method chosen would be one that was acceptable for accounting purposes and for taxation purposes in addition.

(c) A sole trader or partnership may wish to minimise the taxation liability. Some methods of valuing stock tend to bring about wider variations in profit calculations than other methods. This may well be something to avoid for taxation purposes.

Exhibit 28.5

Simplifying the income tax situation, suppose that a man does not pay tax if profits are less than £800 per annum, while if he does make more than £800 he will pay tax at a low rate of 10 per cent on the next £300 and 40 per cent on all profits above that. In the two years under consideration assume that he earns £2,400. Suppose that stock basis (a) show profits of £800 in the first year and £1,600 in the second year, and that stock basis (b) shows profits of £1,200 in each year.

	Basis (a)			
	Year 1		Year 2	
	£		£	£
Profits	800		1,600	
Less Not taxable	800		800	
Taxable	Nil		800	
Tax payable	Nil		£300 at 10% = 30	
			£500 at 40% = 200	
			Total tax bill	230

	Basis (b)			
	Year 1		Year 2	
	£	£	£	£
Profits	1,200		1,200	
Less Not taxable	800		800	
Taxable	400		400	
Tax payable	£300 at 10% = 30		£300 at 10% = 30	
	£100 at 40% = 40		£100 at 40% = 40	
		70		70

Total tax bill £140

It is indeed unfortunate that accounting for taxation purposes has often usurped the more important purpose of accounting, namely that of providing information on which decisions can be made as to the best use of resources. Basis (a) may well have been the best one to use for resource allocation purposes, but obviously basis (b) is the best one for these two years from the viewpoint of taxation liability. It illustrates the fact that to use one set of financial accounts for all purposes is often quite invalid. What is needed is the construction of different accounting statements for different purposes.

The resources available to a business should be utilised to the best possible advantage in keeping with the aims of the firm. There is obviously a 'best' way of allocating resources so that the assets are used to their greatest advantage. For instance, it would be rather unwise if a firm were to carry unnecessary stocks and so deplete its bank balance that valuable discounts were lost by the firm owing to its inability to pay its creditors promptly. Conversely, it would also be unwise if the firm was to run its stocks down to a dangerously low level just to keep money lying idle in its bank account, and lose customers because the insufficiency of stocks meant that their orders could not be satisfied. The accountants should therefore provide the information on which decisions can be made to obtain the better allocation of resources. This cannot be done if the figures supplied by the accountant are useless for the purpose. It will often be true that the replacement cost of an asset will be a more useful piece of information to the decision-maker than the original cost of an asset. The accountant should therefore be willing to abandon his cost concept for this purpose and supply information relevant to the decision-maker's needs. For instance, the manager of a football team for which player A cost £400,000 six months ago but has since broken a leg and is unlikely to ever play again, and for which player B cost only a £10 signing-on fee six months ago and has since been capped for England, will surely not use the original cost prices of the players to make any decisions on their future playing careers.

5. *The capacity to borrow money or to sell the business at the highest possible price.* The higher the stock value shown, then the higher will be the profits calculated to date, and therefore at first sight the business looks more attractive to a buyer or lender. Either of these considerations may be more important to the proprietors than anything else. It may be thought that businessmen are not so gullible, but all businessmen are not necessarily well acquainted with accounting customs. In fact, many small businesses are bought, or money is lent to them, without the expert advice of someone well versed in accounting.

6. *Remuneration purposes.* Where someone managing a business is paid in whole or in part by reference to the profits earned, then one basis may suit him better than others. He may therefore strive to have that basis used to suit his own ends. The owner, however, may try to follow another course to minimise the remuneration that he will have to pay out.

7. *Lack of information*. If proper stock records have not been kept, then such bases as the average cost method or the LIFO method may not be calculable.

8. *Advice of the Auditors*. Many firms use a particular basis because the auditors advised its use in the first instance. If a different auditor is appointed he may well advise that a different basis be used.

The Conflict of Aims

The list of some of the factors which affect decisions is certainly not exhaustive, but it does illustrate the fact that stock valuation is usually a compromise. There is not usually only one figure which is true and fair, there must be a variety of possibilities. Therefore the desire to borrow money, and in so doing to paint a good picture by being reasonably optimistic in valuing stock, will be tempered by the fact that this may increase the tax bill. Stock valuation is therefore a compromise between the various ends for which it is to be used.

Work in Progress

The valuation of work in progress is subject to all the various criteria and methods used in valuing stock. Probably the cost element is more strongly pronounced than in stock valuation, as it is very often impossible or irrelevant to say what net realisable value or replacement price would be applicable to partly finished goods. Firms in industries such as those which have contacts covering several years have evolved their own methods.

Goods on Sale or Return

Quite often goods are supplied by a manufacturer (or a wholesaler) to a retailer on the basis of 'sale or return'. This means that should the retailer sell the goods, then he will incur liability for them to the manufacturer. Failing his being able to sell the goods he will then return them to the manufacturer, having incurred no liability for the goods. This is true where part of the goods are sold by the retailer and part are returned, the only goods being payable for to the manufacturer being those which were sold.

There is no one way of accounting for such activities. All that can be said is that the goods are not effectively sold to the retailer until he in turn has sold them to someone else. It is only then that the manufacturer's sales figures should be increased. Such goods still unsold by the retailer at the financial year end are not part of the retailer's stock, they are part of the manufacturer's stock and should be treated as such.

Sometimes the manufacturer's sales figures includes goods which are on sale or return, and which the retailer himself has not yet sold. Where this happens adjustments are needed for the Final Accounts.

Exhibit 28.6

A manufacturer's year end is 31 December 19–7. When he sends goods on sale or return to retailers he charges them out as ordinary sales. The following details are relevant to his end of year position:

	£
Stock (at factory) at cost 31 December 19–7	10,400
Sales (including goods on sale or return £15,000 of which £3,000 have not yet been sold by the retailer)	60,000
Debtors at 31 December 19–7 (including goods booked out on sale or return)	8,800

The goods sent on sale or return were at cost price plus 25 per cent for profit (mark-up).

The figures needed for the Final Accounts are:

	£
Sales	60,000
Less Goods on sale or return still unsold	3,000
	57,000
Debtors	8,800
Less Charges for goods on sale or return in respect of goods not sold	3,000
	5,800

Stocks:	£	£
At the factory (at cost)		10,400
Add Goods in customers' hands on sale or return (selling price)	3,000	
Less Profit content (20 per cent of selling price)	600	2,400
		12,800

From the retailer's point of view, goods on sale or return are not purchases until he actually incurs liability for them, i.e. he sells the goods. Neither do they constitute part of his stock, as they belong to the manufacturer.

Stocktaking and the Balance Sheet Date

It is often thought by students that the actual physical counting of stock all takes place after the close of business on the last day of the financial period. This could well be done in some small businesses with only a few items of a limited number of different types of stock. Other businesses will have hundreds, or even thousands, of different types of stock, and each type of stock may consist of thousands of items Stocktaking in such a case will have to be spread over a period.

At one time it was very rare for the auditors to attend at stocktaking time as observers. The professional accounting bodies now encourage the auditors to be present if at all possible. Some financial year ends are so popular with firms that it would be impossible for a representative of the auditors to be present at all the stocktakings, or even a reasonable number of them, if they were all held at the same time. The practice has started to grow up of the stocktaking being held in large firms at some time before the financial year end, the stock records (not being part of the double entry system of financial accounts) from then to the end of the financial year being relied upon to show the stock as the Balance Sheet date. Naturally this would not be done where it was felt that the stock records could not be relied upon, and various sample checks would be carried out to try to ensure that all was in order. This technique has the advantage, other than that of the auditors attending the stocktaking, of enabling the Balance Sheet to be published at a date ealier than would be normal if all stocktaking was done at the Balance Sheet date.

In many other firms stocktaking takes place after the financial year end, and calculations are needed to work out the stock at the Balance Sheet date. Exhibit 28–6 shows just such a calculation.

Exhibit 28.6

Bloom Ltd has a financial year which ends on 31 December 19–7. The stocktaking is not in fact done until 8 January 19–8. When the items in stock on that date are priced out, it is found that the stock value amounted to £28,850. The following information is available about transactions between 31 December 19–7 and 8 January 19–8:

  (i) Purchases since 31 December 19–7 amounted to £2,370 at cost.
 (ii) Returns inwards since 31 December 19–7 were £350 at selling price.
(iii) Sales since 31 December 19–7 amounted to £3,800 at selling price.
(iv) The selling price is always made up of cost price+25 per cent= selling price.

Bloom Ltd
Computation of stock as on 31 December 19–7

		£
Stock (at cost)		28,850
Add Items which were in stock on 31 December 19–7 (at cost)		
	£	
Sales	3,800	
Less Profit content (20 per cent of selling price)	760	3,040
		31,890

Less Items which were not in stock on 31 December 19–7 (at cost)

	£	£	
Returns Inwards	350		
Less Profit content (20 per cent of selling price)	70	280	
Purchases (at cost)		2,370	2,650
Stock in Hand as on 31 December 19–7			29,240

Stock Levels

One of the most common faults found in the running of businesses is that too high a level of stock is maintained. It is not the purpose of this book to deal with this in any detail, but merely to point out the dangers of carrying too much stock.

Generalisation is always dangerous, for the scope and variety of businesses is unlimited. For many firms the danger attached to running out of a particular item of stock can be very high indeed. Imagine a motor car manufacturer who ran out of stock of driving wheels. He would not be able to despatch any cars until new stock of this item was received.

The whole of the various items in stock should be scrutinized. In the case of a motor car manufacturer this consists of several thousand parts which go together in the assembly of a car, whereas for other firms the items will be very few indeed. For each item there should be established:

(a) A maximum stock level beyond which the stock should not be allowed to rise.

(b) A minimum stock level below which it would be highly undesirable for the stock to fall.

Looking at the problem simply, suppose that an item has a minimum stock level of 100 units. The firm uses 50 units per week, and it takes 6 weeks for the supplier to deliver an order. This means that 300 units will be used whilst waiting for the order to be delivered, i.e. 6 weeks × 50 units = 300. The order for 300 units must therefore be placed at the date when stock reaches 400 units, for by the time the delivery takes place 300 units will have been used, and stock will have fallen to 100 units. For each item of stock there should therefore be established:

(c) A re-order stock level. This is the level at which an order should be sent to the supplier, so that stock will be received before the stock in hand of the item falls below the minimum stock level.

Of course, this is looking at the problem very simply indeed. There are many factors to be considered besides those mentioned, such as quantity discounts, the cost of money tied up in stock, warehousing costs and so on. If you proceed further in your studies into a more detailed knowledge of *Business Mathematics* you will find that there are various mathematical techniques to assist in this field.

For a lot of firms in certain industries, it will be found on investigation that the bulk of the stock used consists of a relatively few items. Take a publisher as an instance who has 1,000 different titles which he publishes. Of these titles 50 may be best-sellers accounting for, say, a total of 2 million sales per annum, whilst the other 950 titles may sell only ½ million copies between them. It is obvious therefore that in this firm the highest priority be given to stocking the best-sellers. If a best-seller runs out of stock at a peak time, e.g. before Christmas in the case of novels bought as Christmas presents, the sales lost forever could be considerable. If a low-selling book ran out of stock the loss would normally be relatively small.

A considerable number of firms that have problems of the shortage of finance will find that they can help matters by having a sensible look at the amounts of stock they hold. It would be a very rare firm indeed which, if they had not investigated the matter previously, could not manage to let parts of their stock run down. As this would save spending cash on items not really necessary, this cash could be better utilised elsewhere.

Conclusion to the Chapter

It is not possible in a book of this type to give the arguments for and against the use of different stock bases. Any 'potted' version would probably be more misleading than it would be useful. There is a danger of thinking that the arguments for and against can be summarised in a few words. Many experts have argued on behalf of or against the bases described in this chapter, and there is no universal agreement as to which is the best one. Economists and operational research teams are often astounded by the lack of any 'scientific' approach. All that can be said here is that firms would be well advised to rethink their stock valuation procedures in terms of obtaining information from which they can derive the greatest possible benefit, and wherever possible to use different stock figures to serve different purposes.

Exercises

Note: **Questions numbered without the suffix 'A' have answers at the back of this book.**

28.1. The following details are available to you concerning the activity of a manufacturing firm:

		Units
1st year.	Opening Stock	500
	Sales	1,000

		Units
	Produced	800
	Closing Stock	300
2nd year.	Opening Stock	300
	Sales	1,000
	Produced	1,400
	Closing Stock	700
3rd year.	Opening Stock	700
	Sales	1,000
	Produced	800
	Closing Stock	500

There was no work in progress at the end of any of these years. For each of the years the prime cost of each unit produced was £1, while the production cost of each unit was £2. The selling price of all units was £3 each. You are required to:

(a) Draw up the Trading Account for each year if the stock was valued at prime cost.

(b) Draw up the Trading Account for each year if the stock was valued at production cost.

(c) Which method would you advise if income tax was the main consideration and all profits under £800 per annum were free of tax, while profits above that figure were taxable at the rate of 40 per cent.

(d) What is the main factor contributing to different reported profits under (a) and (b) above.

28.2. Uni Form Ltd, which manufactures a standard product, classifies its expenses as being fixed, varying in direct proportion to production or varying directly with sales. The company had no finished stocks at 1 January 19–6, and there was no work in progress at either 1 January or 31 December 19–6.

The items relating to production and sales for 19–6 were:

	£
For the production of 60,000 units:	
Raw Materials Consumed	180,000
Direct Wages	285,000
Indirect Wages (fixed)	36,000
Factory Expenses—(fixed)	24,000
(variable)	15,000

	£
Proceeds of sale of 50,000 units	550,000
Expenses (not included above) to be charged to	
Profit and Loss Account—(fixed)	36,000
(variable)	24,000

You are required to prepare statements showing:

(a) the valuation of the 10,000 units of finished stock at 31 December 19–6
 (i) at factory cost,
 (ii) including only the variable elements in factory cost;

(b) the net profit or loss for the year adopting your valuation of stock under (a) (ii) above;

(c) what the net profit or loss would have been if, by spending an extra £5,000 on advertising, the whole of the year's output had been sold at the normal selling price.

(*Associated Examining Board 'A' Level*)

28.3. At the end of a company's first financial year on 31 December 19–5, the directors of your firm ask you to ascertain the stock figure. The following information is presented to you.

	Purchases				Items sold		Net realisable value at 31 December 19–5
Item 1	January	500 at	£5	each	July	200	
	September	300 „	£6	„	October	350	£5½ each
Item 2	March	100 „	£2	„	April	50	
	November	200 „	£3	„	December	100	£3⅓ „
Item 3	June	600 „	£10	„	July	500	
	September	400 „	£12	„	October	100	£15 „
Item 4	April	200 „	£16	„	June	150	
	October	200 „	£18	„	November	50	£14 „
Item 5	October	1,000 „	£12	„			
	November	800 „	£10	„	December	1,200	£9 „
Item 6	January	200 „	£4	„			
	July	400 „	£5	„	September	500	£7 „

You are also told that there are three distinct groups or categories of items, Group A being items 1 and 2, Group B being items 3 and 4, and Group C being items 5 and 6.

You inform the directors that it is possible to arrive at more than one stock figure. The directors thereupon ask you to give them the various figures that are possible using the following bases:

(a) First In, First Out Method;
(b) Last In, First Out Method;

and applying the Aggregate, Category and Article methods to each of these bases. Show all your workings clearly.

28.4. You are preparing the accounts of P. Snow for the year ended 31 March 19–3. In carrying out your investigation of the books for that purpose you find that all invoices relating to sales and purchases and credit notes bearing dates in March 19–3 had been entered in the books but that such documents bearing dates in April 19–3 had been dealt with as though they related to the year commencing 1 April 19–3.

It had been impossible to actually take stock until 5 April 19–3, and the summary of the stock sheets showed the value of the total stock at cost at that date to be £16,420.

The rate of gross profit earned was 20 per cent on selling prices.
You find that:

1. For the period 1 April 19–3, to 4 April 19–3, sales and sales returns were £730 and £85 respectively and all the invoices and credit notes relating thereto bore dates in April 19–3.

2.   Suppliers had sent in goods during the four days to 4 April 19–3, invoices relating to such bearing dates in March 19–3 amounted in total to £340 and those bearing dates in April 19–3 to £180.

3.   An item of 200 articles priced at £0·875 each had been extended as £100.

4.   The total of one stock sheet amounting to £300 had not been carried to the summary and the total of another, namely 150, had been included in the summary as £180.

5.   Goods to the value of £325 at selling price had been sent, prior to 31 March 19–3, to a customer on approval. No entries as regards this transaction had been made in the books and neither were the goods included in the stock.

Show how you would arrive at the figure for stock to be inserted in the accounts for the year ended 31 March 19–3.

(Association of Certified Accountants)

28.5. Blacks Ltd made up their Annual Accounts to 31 December 19–1, and had prepared draft accounts to this date.

It was impossible to take a physical inventory of the stock until 5 January 19–2, on which date the total stock, as shown by the summary of the stock sheets, was £31,410, valued at cost. The rate of gross profit earned was $33\frac{1}{3}$ per cent on selling price.

Your audit disclosed the following:

1.   Goods to the value of £840 had been received from suppliers during the four days 1 to 4 January 19–2 of which £360 related to goods the invoices for which were dated December 19–1, and which had been included in creditors.

2.   Sales for the period 1 to 4 January 19–2 were £1,860, the relevant invoices for which were all dated January 19–2. Out of these sales, goods to the value of £90 were returned on 2 January and the necessary credit note had been issued on that date.

3.   A subtotal of £680 had been carried to stock summary as £860.

4.   One stock sheet overcast by £100 and one undercast by £50.

5.   The stock included an item of 600 articles priced at £1 per dozen which had been extended in error as £1 each.

6.   Goods, selling price £480, had been sent to Whites Ltd on approval. Not taken into stock nor any entries in the books.

7.   Sales credit notes to the value of £660 issued prior to 31 December 19–1, had been omitted in error from the books.

8.   The stock included goods value £360 held for processing and were in fact the property of Browns Ltd. These goods had been invoiced to Blacks Ltd and had been included both in purchases and creditors.

9.   It had been agreed to take back from Colours Ltd goods which had been invoiced to them for £510 but which, at 31 December 19–1 had not been returned nor had any credit note been issued.

You are required to prepare a statement showing the amount at which stock should be included in the Accounts to 31 December 19–1.

(Institute of Chartered Accountants)

Note: The following questions with the suffix 'A' do not have answers given at the back of this book.

28.6A. You are given the following details of a manufacturing firm:

		Units
Year 1	Opening Stock	800
	Sales	4,900
	Produced	5,200
	Closing Stock	1,100
Year 2	Opening Stock	1,100
	Sales	8,000
	Produced	9,200
	Closing Stock	2,300
Year 3	Opening Stock	2,300
	Sales	10,000
	Produced	9,400
	Closing Stock	1,700

There was no work in progress at the end of any of these years. In each year the prime cost per unit produced was £3, whilst the production cost of each unit was £5. The selling price of all units was £6 each. You are required to:

(a) Draw up a Trading Account for each year if the stock was valued at prime cost.

(b) Draw up a Trading Account for each year if the stock was valued at production cost.

(c) Advise as to the method you would think most suitable, assuming that the main factor was to keep the tax bill for these years to a minimum. Assume that there is no tax on the first £3,000 each year, whilst 30 per cent of the excess above that is taken in tax.

28.7A. You are the owner of a firm which has just completed its first year of trading. Looking at your figures of Sales and Purchases you see the following:

	Purchases			*Items sold*		*Net realisable value at 31 December 19–6*
Item A	January	1,000 at	£4 each	March	800	
	October	300 ,,	£5 ,,	November	200	£5·40 each
Item B	February	400 ,,	£7 ,,	May	100	
	November	200 ,,	£8 ,,	December	150	£9 ,,
Item C	April	600 ,,	£9 ,,	June	400	
	December	500 ,,	£10 ,,			£11 ,,
Item D	February	1,000 ,,	£14 ,,	April	700	
	May	600 ,,	£16 ,,			£12 ,,
Item E	January	600 ,,	£17 ,,	March	500	
	August	500 ,,	£18 ,,	October	200	£17·50 ,,
Item F	October	700 ,,	£22 ,,	December	500	£24 ,,

The items fall into three different categories. Items A and B, Items C and D and Items E and F.

Calculate the various figures that are possible using the following bases:

(a) First In, First Out Method,
(b) Last In, First Out Method,

and applying the Aggregate, Category and Article Methods to each of these bases. Show your workings.

28.8A. You are taking stock at your business as at 31 December 19–7. The actual date on which the stock was taken was 7 January 19–8. The stock sheets show a total of £85, 980 at cost as on that date. You are to adjust this figure to find the stock as at 31 December 19–7.

The rate of gross profit was 25 per cent on selling price.

On further scrutiny you find:

(a) Goods received after 1 January and for which invoices bear the date of January amounted to £3,987.
(b) You notice that one of the stock sheets has been added up to give a total of £4,897 instead of £4,798.
(c) Goods selling at £480 had been sent to a customer on 'sale or return' during December. These had not been sold by the customer, and they had been omitted from the stock figures.
(d) An item of 360 items priced at £1·60 each had been extended on the stock sheets as £420.
(e) Goods had been returned to suppliers amounting to £98 during the first week of January.

28.9A. England Ltd make up their accounts to 31 December each year. The valuation of the stock, at cost, as at 31 December 19–8 was not attempted until 11 January 19–9 when a physical stock check revealed a total per stock sheets of £198,444 at cost.

Further investigation revealed that:

(a) All goods are sold at a uniform profit of 50 per cent on cost.
(b) Sales for the period 1 January 19–9 to 11 January 19–9, and for which goods had been despatched, amounted to £6,960.
(c) One stock sheet was undercast by £50 and another one overcast by £1,000.
(d) An extension of 660 articles at £0·80 each was shown as £560.
(e) The stock figure includes goods held on approval £3,000 and for which no invoices had been received, nor were the goods to be kept by England Ltd.
(f) A total at the bottom of one page, £105,680 had been carried forward to the next page as £106,850.

Calculate the figure of stock for the final accounts as at 31 December 19–8.

29

Further Methods of Providing for Depreciation

In Chapter 10 of Volume 1 the Straight-line and Reducing Balance methods of making provisions for depreciation were discussed in detail. This chapter is concerned with some further methods of making provisions for depreciation. It must not be thought that this chapter will complete an examination of all the different methods in use. Providing for depreciation is a matter of apportioning the cost of a fixed asset over its useful life with a firm, and it was pointed out in Volume 1 that there is no 'true' way of doing this; the methods used are purely accounting customs. It is therefore quite possible to devise one's own method of providing for depreciation. If it stands up to the test of common sense and does not distort the reported trading results of the firm, then the specially devised method will often be more applicable than those commonly used. There is therefore no limit to the number of different depreciation provision methods.

This chapter deals in some detail with the Revaluation method, the Depreciation Sinking Fund method, and the Endowment Policy method. Some other methods are discussed in outline only. There is no information easily available of the number of firms in the United Kingdom using particular provision methods. It would, however, seem likely that the Revaluation method is widely used for certain kinds of assets, while the Depreciation Sinking Fund method and the Endownment Policy method are not now used to any great extent, at least in the private sector of industry.

1. The Revaluation Method

There are some fixed assets for which it is inappropriate, or not worth while, to calculate depreciation provisions in a formal way, whereby each asset has to be identifiable and accurate records kept of its location and adjusting entries made when the asset is put out of use by the firm. Examples of these assets are loose tools such as spanners, screwdrivers, small drills, etc., in an engineering works, or barrels, bottles and crates in a brewery. A fixed asset such as a spanner or a barrel may be capable of a long life but its use may well be short-lived. Some will be lost, others stolen, some broken or damaged through ill-use, and all of these facts will not be reported to management. Even if an accounting system could be devised to throw up such wastage of assets the operation of the system could well, except in a few instances, cost more than the savings to be gained from it. A spanner costing less than £1 and which is used infrequently, could well last for seven years. If the Straight Line or Reducing Balance methods were in use, then theoretically a calculation would have to be made of the over-depreciation or under-depreciation provided on the asset when it is put out of use, and an adjusting entry made to correct the accounts. With such an asset it is clearly not worth while to make accounting entries in such a fashion. In addition some firms may well make their own tools, etc., and it might be difficult and costly to keep elaborate records for each small tool made.

To provide a solution at a reasonable cost the Revaluation method of calculating depreciation provisions is used. The method used is simply that the assets are valued at the start of the period, the additions increase the value and then the assets are revalued at the end of the period. The amount of the decrease in value shows the amount by which the asset is deemed to have depreciated. This is now illustrated in Exhibit 29.1 by reference to a firm which uses metal crates.

Exhibit 29.1

The firm starts in business on 1 January 19–6.

	£
In its first year it buys crates costing	800
Their estimated value at 31 December 19–6	540
Crates bought in the year ended 31 December 19–7	320
Estimated value of all crates in hand on 31 December 19–7	530
Crates bought in the year ended 31 December 19–8	590
Estimated value of all crates in hand on 31 December 19–8	700

Crates

19–6		£	19–6		£
Dec 31 Cash (during the year)		800	Dec 31 Profit and Loss		260
			„ 31 Stock c/d		540
		800			800

19–7		£	19–7		£
Jan 1 Stock b/d		540	Dec 31 Profit and Loss		330
Dec 31 Cash (during the year)		320	” 31 Stock c/d		530
		860			860

Crates

19–8			19–8		
Jan 1 Stock b/d		530	Dec 31 Profit and Loss		420
Dec 31 Cash (during the year)		590	„ 31 Stock c/d		700
		1,120			1,120

19–9		
Jan 1 Stock b/d		700

Profit and Loss Account for the year ended 31 December

	£
19–6 Use of crates	260
19–7 Use of crates	330
19–8 Use of crates	420

The balance of the Crates Account at the end of each year is shown as a fixed asset in the Balance Sheet.

In an engineering firm the cost of wages and materials used in making loose tools may or may not be known. If it is known the cost should be charged to the Loose Tools Account. If not known, the Loose Tools Account cannot be charged with the cost of such additions, and may well appear to reveal an appreciation in the value of tools rather than depreciation. The appreciation would be transferred to the credit of the Manufacturing Account (or shown as a deduction on the debit side). The different treatment makes no difference to the calculated profit as can now be shown in Exhibit 29.2.

Exhibit 29.2

	£
At 1 January 19–7 loose tools valued at	800
During the year the cost of all raw materials used in the factory amounted to	10,000
The cost of all wages in the factory was	20,000
At 31 December 19–7 the loose tools are valued at	1,000

However, in the Loose Tools Account and Manufacturing Account shown as (A) it is known that materials £300 and wages £400 have been used in making loose tools, while in the accounts lettered (B) this information is not known.

Loose Tools (A)

19–7		£	19–7		£
Jan 1 Stock b/d		800	Dec 31 Manufacturing		
Dec 31 Transfer from wages		400	Account		500
„ 31 Transfer from Materials		300	„ 31 Stock c/d		1,000
		1,500			1,500

19–8
Jan   1 Stock b/d   1,000

Manufacturing Account (A) for the year ended 31 December 19–7

	£
Materials (i.e. *less* transfer £300)	9,700
Wages (i.e. *less* transfer £400)	19,600
Use of Loose Tools	500

The total effective debits are therefore £19,600+£9,700+£500 =£29,800

Loose Tools (B)

19–7		£	19–7		£
Jan 1	Stock b/d	800	Dec 31 Stock c/d		1,000
Dec 31	Manufacturing Account	200			
		1,000			1,000

19–8
Jan   1 Stock b/d   1,000

Manufacturing Account (B) for the year ended 31 December 19–7

	£		£
Materials	10,000	Increase in the value of	
Wages	20,000	loose tools	200

The total of effective debits is £10,000+£20,000−£200=£29,800.

In both cases (A) and (B) the Balance Sheet on 31 December 19–7, will show a fixed asset of Loose Tools £1,000.

Some firms show the stock of such assets in the same way as the stock of goods or raw materials. Give the information in Exhibit 19.2 it would appear as Manufacturing Account (C) which now follows.

Manufacturing Account (C) for the year ended 31 December 19–7

	£
Materials	10,000
Wages	20,000
Add Stock of Loose Tools on 1 January 19–7	800
	30,800
Less Stock of Loose Tools on 31 December 19–7	1,000
	29,800

Here again the total effective debits amount to £29,800.

Manufacturing Account (A) gives the most useful information as it shows the cost of using tools during 19–7. In the other Manufacturing Accounts all that is known is that the estimated value of loose tools has risen by £200. This by itself is a relatively meaningless piece of information. Suppose that it was possible to hire loose tools instead of owning them, and that this could be done at a cost of £300 per year. Manufacturing Account (A) would show that tool hire would be the cheaper method, assuming that the experience in 19–7 was typical. The other Manufacturing Accounts would not reveal this figure for comparison. However, like most accounting statements it is only one measure to be taken into account when making a business decision. Other factors may well be: (a) What will the reactions of the firm's own toolmakers and of their trade unions? (b) Could our own tools cost less if our methods were changed? (c) How long will it take to renew any tool when required? (d) What provisions are made for normal replacements? (e) Would it make the firm too dependent on the firm of tool hirers?

In Volume 1 it was stated that accountants had given up attempting to regard depreciation as a fall in value, yet this method appears to be reverting back to a 'value' concept. The fact that this method is called the Revaluation method is perhaps somewhat unfortunate in this respect. The 'value' to be carried forward is in fact the reappraised figure of the costs which should be carried forward to the following period. The 'value' is thus the 'unapportioned cost value'. Expediency and custom will play a large part in any such valuation. It would be quite ludicrous for a firm with several thousand barrels of the same size to have any sort of scientific appraisal of every barrel at the end of each financial period with the object of placing a valuation on it. It would more likely be found that the number of barrels would be counted in some way and then multiplied by an amount which the management considered reflected the average value of all the barrels.

The dairy herd belonging to a farmer is one of his fixed assets. Like all other fixed assets depreciation should be provided for, but during the early life of an animal it will probably be appreciating in value only to depreciate later. The task of calculating the cost of an animal becomes almost impossible if it has been born on the farm, reared on the farm by grazing on the pasture land and from other foodstuffs, some grown by the farmer and others bought by him. Expediency therefore takes over and the Revaluation method is used, the livestock being brought into account in the same way as stocks of goods. The cost factor being such an elusive one for many animals has led to the general practice being observed of valuing livestock at the price that the animals would fetch if sold at market. This therefore is an exception to the general rules regarding fixed assets being shown at cost price.

2. The Depreciation Sinking Fund Method

None of the methods dealt with have set out specifically to arrange for funds to be available for the replacement of an asset at the end of its estimated useful life with a firm. The objective of these methods has been the apportioning of the cost of an asset over various accounting periods.

The method now being considered is an attempt to achieve both of these objectives. This is probably an outdated concept except under special circumstances. There is a need not just to budget for the replacement of fixed assets when necessary but also for additions of fixed assets and for achieving a desired level of bank funds and of working capital. This comes within the wider scope of budgetary control.

The method involves the investment of cash outside the business. The aim is to make the regular investment of money which, together with the accumulated interest or dividends, is sufficient to finance the replacement of the asset when it is put out of use by the firm. The exact achievement of the aim is not an easy one because of one or more of the following reasons:

(a) When the time arrives for the replacement of the asset, even if the type of asset has not changed, prices may well have risen. A more unlikely assumption in recent years is that the price may have fallen.

(b) The asset may have become obsolete and will be replaced by something quite unlike it in construction or cost.

(c) The asset may have a longer or a shorter life than expected.

(d) Changes in the taxation system may affect the dividends or interest received and the amount received on sale of the investment.

(e) The market value of the investment may rise or fall, so that the realised value may differ considerably from that expected when the original scheme was drafted.

The example used in Exhibit 29.3 is an ideal one in that it conforms exactly to the original plan, none of the points (a) to (e) will apply.

Before calculations become too involved a simple proposition can be examined. As each period's interest (or dividend) is received, then that amount is immediately reinvested. Apart from the reinvestment of interest the other money taken for investment is to be an equal amount each period. This being so, if the money is to be invested at 5 per cent per annum, and the cost of the asset is £500 to be replaced in five years' time, then how much should be taken for investment each year? If £100 was taken each year for five years, then this would amount to more than £500 because of the interest and of the interest on the reinvested interest. Most readers will recognise this as money being invested as compound interest. Therefore something less than £100 per annum is needed. The exact amount can be calculated by the use of the compound interest formula. Chapter 46 illustrates how the amount needed can be calculated. As these calculations are left until later in the book, a summarised set of tables is now shown to help the student at this stage.

Annual Sinking Fund Instalments to Provide £1

Years	3%	3½%	4%	4½%	5%
3	0·323530	0·321933	0·320348	0·318773	0·317208
4	0·239028	0·237251	0·235490	0·233744	0·232012
5	0·188354	0·186481	0·184627	0·182792	0·180975
6	0·154597	0·152668	0·150761	0·148878	0·147017
7	0·130506	0·128544	0·126609	0·124701	0·122819
8	0·112456	0·110476	0·108527	0·106609	0·104721
9	0·098433	0·096446	0·094493	0·092574	0·090690
10	0·087230	0·085241	0·083291	0·081378	0·079504

The table gives the amount required to provide £1 at the end of the relevant number of years. To provide £1,000 multiply by 1,000, to provide for £4,986 multiply by 4,986.

Exhibit 29.3

A five-year lease is bought on 1 January 19–1 for £10,000. An option is obtained whereby the lease can be renewed on 1 January 19–6 for five years under identical terms. The firm therefore decides to set aside an equal annual amount which, together with interest reinvested immediately, will provide £10,000 on 31 December 19–5. According to the table £0·180975 invested annually will provide £1 in five years' time. Therefore £0·180975 × 10,000 will be needed annually=£1,809·75. This is the amount charged as depreciation in the Profit and Loss Account for each year and credited to the Depreciation Fund Account. An identical amount is then invested, the credit entry being in the Cash Book while the debit entry is in the Depreciation Fund Investment Account.

Depreciation Fund

	£			£
		19–1		
		Dec 31	Profit and Loss	1,809·75
		19–2		
		Dec 31	Cash: Interest	
19–2			(5% of £1,809·75)	90·49
Dec 31 Balance c/d	3,709·99	„ 31	Profit and Loss	1,809·75
	3,709·99			3,709·99
		19–3		
		Jan 1	Balance b/d	3,709·99
		Dec 31	Cash: Interest	
19–3			(5% of £3,709·99)	185·49
Dec 31 Balance c/d	5,705·23	„ 31	Profit and Loss	1,809·75
	5,705·23			5,705·23

			19–4		
			Jan 1	Balance b/d	5,705·23
			Dec 31	Cash: Interest	
19–4				(5% of £5,705·23)	285·26
Dec 31	Balance c/d	7,800·24	„ 31	Profit and Loss	1,809·75
		7,800·24			7,800·24

			19–5		
			Jan 1	Balance b/d	7,800·24
			Dec 31	Cash: Interest	
19–5				(5% of £7,800·24)	390·01
Dec 31	Lease now written off	10,000·00	„ 31	Profit and Loss	1,809·75
		10,000·00			10,000·00

Depreciation Fund Investment

19–1		£			£
Dec 31	Cash	1,809·75			
19–2					
Dec 31	Cash (see note A)	1,900·24			
19–3					
Dec 31	Cash (see note B)	1,995·24			
19–4			19–5		
Dec 31	Cash (see note C)	2,095·01	Dec 31	Cash: Sale of Investment	7,800·24
		7,800·24			7,800·24

Notes
Cash invested

	A	B	C
	£	£	£
The yearly instalment	1,809·75	1,809·75	1,809·75
Add Interest received reinvested immediately	90·49	185·49	285·26
	1,900·24	1,995·24	2,095·01

Lease

19–1		£	19–5		£
Jan 1	Cash	10,000	Dec 31	Depreciation Fund —expired lease written off	10,000

New Lease

19–6		£
Jan 1	Cash	10,000

The instalment for 19–5 is not in fact invested, nor is the interest received on 31 December 19–5 reinvested. The money to renew the lease is required on 1 January 19–6, and there is not much point (even if it was possible, which would very rarely hold true) in investing money one day only to withdraw it the day afterwards. The amount required to renew the lease is £10,000 and is available from the following sources:

	£
Dec 31 19–5 Sale of investment	7,800·24
„ 31 19–5 Interest received but not reinvested	390·01
„ 31 19–5 The fifth year's instalment not invested	1,809·75
	10,000·00

On reflection the reader may well question the validity of this method of providing for depreciation. The asset in Exhibit 29.3 cost £10,000 and was valueless at the end of five years. Therefore the depreciation amounted to £10,000, yet in the Profit and Loss Account there has been charged £1,809·75 for each of five years=£9,048·75. The fact is that only the net depreciation provision has been charged, after allowing for interest received on the investment. It would be normal for investment income to be shown as a credit in the Profit and Loss Account, yet this method credits the Depreciation Fund Account instead. What has appeared as:

Profit and Loss Account for the Five Years to 31 December 19–5

	£
Depreciation (5 × £1,809·75)	9,048·75

Profit and Loss Account for the Five Years to 31 December 19–5

	£		£
Depreciation (5 × £1,809·75)	9,048·75	Interest on Investments not entered in Profit and	
Depreciation not entered in Profit and Loss Account since it is cancelled out by Interest on Investments also not entered	951·25	Loss Account which cancels out part of depreciation provisions	951·25

3. The Depreciation Sinking Fund with Endowment Policy

The main difference between this and the method described already is that instead of buying securities a form of endowment policy is taken out to mature at the end of the asset's expected useful life. The insurance company will quote the amount of premium required. Another difference is that with the other Depreciation Fund method the money is invested at the end of each period, whereas the premium is payable on the endowment policy on the first day of each period.

Exhibit 29.4

A five-year lease is bought for £500 on 1 January 19–1. An endowment policy is taken out for £500 to mature on 31 December 19–5, the annual premium being £90. The lease is renewed for £500 on 1 January 19–6.

Depreciation Fund

19–5		£	19–1		£
Dec 31	Lease written off	500	Dec 31	Profit and Loss	90
			19–2		
			Dec 31	Profit and Loss	90
			19–3		
			Dec 31	Profit and Loss	90
			19–4		
			Dec 31	Profit and Loss	90
			19–5		
			Dec 31	Profit and Loss	90
			" 31	Endowment Policy —interest factor transferred	50
		500			500

Endowment Policy

		£			£
19–1			19–5		
Jan 1	Cash	90	Dec 31	Cash (policy	
19–2				matures)	500
Jan 1	Cash	90			
19–3					
Jan 1	Cash	90			
19–4					
Jan 1	Cash	90			
19–5					
Jan 1	Cash	90			
Dec 31	Interest factor— transferred to Depreciation Fund	50			
		500			500

Lease

		£			£
19–1			19–5		
Jan 1	Cash	500	Dec 31	Depreciation Fund: lease written off	500

New Lease

		£
19–6		
Jan 1	Cash	500

4. Other Methods

(a) Depletion Unit Method

With fixed assets such as mines or quarries the depreciation is often based on the quantity of raw materials extracted compared with the estimated total quantity available. For instance, if a firm bought for £5,000 a small mine which had an expected capacity of 1,000 tons of ore, then for each ton extracted during an accounting period the firm would provide for depreciation of the asset by £5 (expected average depreciation cost per ton).

(b) Machine Hour Method

With a machine the depreciation provision may be based on the number of hours that the machine was operated during the period compared with the total expected running hours during the machine's life with the firm. A firm which bought a machine costing £2,000 having an expected running life of 1,000 hours, and no scrap value, could provide for depreciation of the machine at the rate of £2 for every hour it was operated during a particular accounting period.

Investment Grants and Depreciation

Government grants are paid towards approved capital expenditure such as for certain types of buildings and new machinery and plant, assuming that the firms are situated in certain areas of the U.K. needing assistance. They are made to encourage such firms to invest in certain new assets. Before the introduction of the grants the government's encouragement had been by the means of a reduction in the taxation liability of a firm.

The question therefore arises as to the method of showing the receipt in the accounts of a firm. The Institute of Chartered Accountants in England and Wales has recommended the use of either of the following methods:

1.   The receipt be credited to the asset account thus reducing the price at which the asset is shown in the books. Any depreciation of the asset will then be on the net figure. If the grant is a material item, then the description of the asset in the Balance Sheet should disclose that the grant has been deducted.

2.   The receipt is credited to an Investment Grant Account. Each year an amount is transferred to the credit of the Profit and Loss Account at a rate consistent with the depreciation charge on the relevant asset. The balance on the account at the end of each financial period is to be shown on the Capital and Liabilities side of the Balance Sheet.

The use of these two methods is shown in Exhibit 29.5.

Exhibit 29.5

A firm buys machinery for £1,000 on 1 January in the year ended 31 December 19–6 and receives a grant of 40 per cent on 1 July 19–6. The machinery is depreciated at the rate of 25 per cent per annum on the straight-line basis, assuming no salvage value.

Method 1
Machinery

19–6		£	19–6		£
Jan 1	Cash	1,000	July 1	Cash (grant)	400
			Dec 31	Balance c/d	600
		1,000			1,000
19–7					
Jan 1	Balance b/d	600			

Profit and Loss Account for the year ended 31 December 19–6

	£	
Provision for Depreciation	150	(and so on each year until the asset has been depreciated by £600)

Balance Sheet as at December 19–6

	£	£
Machinery	600	
Less Depreciation	150	450

Method 2

Machinery

19–6	£
Jan 1 Cash	1,000

Investment Grant

19–6		£	19–6		£
Dec 31	Profit and Loss	100	July 1 Cash		400
„ 31	Balance c/d	300			
		400			400
			19–7		
			Jan 1 Balance b/d		300

Profit and Loss Account for the year ended 31 December 19–6

	£
Provision for Depreciation	250 (and so on each year until the asset has been depreciated by £1,000)
	Proportion of Investment Grant 100.

Balance Sheet as at 31 December 19–6

	£		£	£
Investment Grant	300	Machinery	1,000	
		Less Depreciation	250	750

It can be seen that the net effect of £450 on the Balance Sheet is the same with both methods.

Exercises

29.1. On 1 January 19–6 Prefab Ltd acquired for £3,000 the lease of some factory premises of which five years were unexpired. To amortise this lease over the five years and to provide for renewal it was decided to set up a sinking fund by taking annual instalments out of profits and investing cash of the same amount at 5 per cent compound interest.

Taking 0·180975 as the annual instalment required to produce £1 in five years, write up the sinking fund account and the investment account for the whole period, showing the closing entries, using decimals throughout.

(*Association of Certified Accountants*)

29.2. A firm both buys loose tools and also makes some itself. The following data is available concerning the years ended 31 December 19–4, 19–5, and 19–6.

19–4		£
Jan 1	Stock of Loose Tools	1,250
	During the year:	
	Bought loose tools from suppliers	2,000
	Made own loose tools: the cost of wages of employees being £275 and the materials cost £169	
Dec 31	Loose Tools valued at	2,700

19–5		
	During the year:	
	Loose tools bought from suppliers	1,450
	Made own loose tools: the cost of wages of employees being £495 and the materials cost £390	
Dec 31	Loose Tools valued at	3,340

19–6		
	During the year:	
	Loose tools bought from suppliers	1,890
	Made own loose tools: the cost of wages of employees being £145 and the materials cost £290. Received refund from a supplier for faulty tools returned to him	88
Dec 31	Loose Tools valued at	3,680

You are to draw up the Loose Tools Account for the three years, showing the amount transferred as an expense in each year to the Manufacturing Account.

Note: The following questions with the suffix 'A' do not have answers at the back of this book.

29.3A. On 1 January 19–2 Booker Ltd acquired the lease of its factory premises for five years for £8,000. It was decided to amortise this over five years by the use of a sinking fund. Annual instalments were to be taken out of profits and invested in securities of 5 per cent, compounded annually.

£0·180975 is the amount required, invested at 5 per cent compounded, to produce £1 after five years.

Write up the sinking fund account and the investment account for the whole period, showing the closing entries.

29.4A. A firm both buys tools and make them for itself. The following information is available to you for the year ended 31 December 19–5, 19–6 and 19–7.

19–5		£
Jan 1	Stock of Tools	3,890
	Bought during the year 19–5	1,570
	Own Tools made: Cost of wages	705
	Cost of materials	500
Dec 31	Tools valued at	5,020

19–6

During the year:		
Bought during 19–6		1,990
Own Tools made: Cost of wages		908
Cost of materials		486
Dec 31 Tools valued at		4,950

19–7

During the year:		
Bought during 19–7		3,665
Own Tools made: Cost of wages		1,290
Cost of materials		880
Dec 31 Tools valued at		6,868

Write up the Tools Account for the three years, showing the figure transferred each year to the Manufacturing Account.

30

Branch Accounts

From an accounting point of view, a firm which has branches is either one which keeps all the financial accounts at the head office, or it is one where each branch maintains its own full accounting system.

1. Where the Head Office Maintains all the Accounts

The purpose behind the accounts is not merely to record transactions so that changes in assets, liabilities or capital can be calculated but also attempts wherever possible to keep a check by remote control as to whether or not the firm is being defrauded of goods or cash. For a firm with branches this is obviously of utmost importance. Some multiple shops have over a thousand branches scattered all over Great Britain. The managers who run the businesses are thus handling considerable amounts of money and goods, and the actual feeling of not being able to be seen continually by the head office staff may well induce the manager or his staff, into feeling that they could misappropriate large sums of cash or goods without being found out.

The solution of the problem will differ as between firms. One firm with several branches which only sold Rolls-Royce cars could keep control easily, because the number of cars bought and sold would be relatively few, and the location of each car could be traced with very little effort. The opposite of this would be a grocery firm with hundreds of branches selling numerous different lines of goods. To keep a check on each jar of jam or bag of sugar is clearly uneconomic even if it could be done, and not many customers would be happy to wait at the cashier's desk while all the reference numbers on the goods sold were recorded.

The accounting solution to this is extremely simple in its basic form. This is to translate all the transactions at the branch into selling prices. Taking a small branch as an example, and given various pieces of information, it is possible to calculate the closing stock, if wastages, breakages and pilfering by customers are ignored.

	£
Stock on hand at 1 January—at selling price	500
January—Goods sent to the Branch by the Head Office—at selling price	4,000
January—Sales by the Branch—obviously at selling price	3,800

The calculation of the closing stock becomes:

	£
Opening Stock 1 January (selling price)	500
Add Goods sent to the Branch (selling price)	4,000
Goods which the Branch had available for sale (selling price)	4,500
Less Goods Sold (selling price)	3,800
Closing Stock at 31 January should therefore be (selling price)	700

An allowance will be made for wastages, breakages and pilferages, this being based on experience. For instance, it may be normal to allow a figure of 1 per cent of goods sent to the branch to cover those items, therefore an actual stock at selling price of £700 less £40 (1 per cent of £4,000)=£660 would be tolerated. An actual stock of less than £660 would call for investigation. The allowance may well differ as between branches, for instance in Uptown the pilferage rate may be very small whereas in Lowtown there may be a high incidence of pilferages. An oil firm with branches (e.g. petrol stations) situated in many countries will obviously allow more for evaporation of petrol in hot climates than it will in cold climates. Experience and common sense are the only guides.

If a manager, or one of his staff, is suspected of fraud, then the policy of the firm will dictate the action to be taken. It may involve the transfer of the manager to another branch to see whether or not the deficiencies cease at the old branch and restart at his new branch. A branch which only transfers managers when they are suspected of fraud will, of course, merely put the man on his guard. Some firms therefore transfer managers fairly frequently, but accounting needs should always be the servant of the firm and not the master.

It may well have occurred to the reader that the manager could say that the stock was a certain figure even though it was not true. For instance, a manager who has stolen £1,000 in goods or cash may try to cover this up by overstating his stock by £1,000. To counteract this many firms will carry out spot inspections of stock. This means that representatives of the firm may call at the branch without notifying the manager in advance and conduct a stocktaking. Then they will compare the actual stock with the stock calculated as follows—all items being shown at selling price—

1. Stock per the branch manager at the date of the last stocktaking by the branch.
2. Add goods received by branch since the date of (1).
3. Less sales since the date of (1).

4. Less allowances for wastages, etc.
5. The stock should be equal to $(1+2)-(3+4)$.

The knowledge that such spot checks are carried out will act as a deterrent to showing false stock figures.

The head office will normally insist that all branches will bank its full cash takings each day. The money will be paid into a local bank, and special paying-in slips will be used so that the amount deposited will be transferred through the banking system into the firm's main bank account at the head office's bank. Each entry will be coded so that the head office will be able to tell quickly if a branch is not banking its takings. Cash payments made by the branch will be kept on a basis similar to the petty cash imprest system, with the head office reimbursing the amount spent at regular intervals.

(a) The Double Column System

At regular intervals, obviously at least once a year, but usually more frequently, the head office may draft a Trading and Profit and Loss Account for each branch. The Trading Account can be shown with two columns, one in which goods sent to the branch or in stock are shown at cost price, i.e. the normal basis for any business. This column is therefore part of a normal Trading Account for the branch. The other column will show all Trading Account items at selling price. This is the column where deficiencies in trading can be compared with the normal deficiency allowed for wastages, pilferages, etc. It is not a part of the double entry recording; it is a memorandum column for control purposes only.

Exhibit 30.1

This is drafted up from the following details for a firm which sells goods at a uniform mark-up of $33\frac{1}{3}$ per cent profit on cost price:

	£
Stock 1 Jan 19–8 (at cost)	1,200
Goods sent to the Branch during the year (at cost)	6,000
Sales (selling price)	7,428
Stock 31 Dec 19–8 (at cost)	1,500
Allowance for wastage, etc., 1 per cent of Sales	
Expenses	1,000

As the actual deficiency of £172 exceeds the amount to be tolerated, i.e. 1 per cent of £7,428=£74 approximately, this means that an investigation will be made.

This method is suitable where all the sales are for cash, there being no sales on credit.

Branch Trading and Profit and Loss Account for the year ended 31.12.19–8

	At selling price		Sales	At selling price	
	£	£		£	£
Stock 1 Jan 19–8	1,600	1,200	Sales	7,428	7,428
Goods from Head Office	8,000	6,000	Deficiency (difference)		172
	9,600	7,200			
Less Stock 31 Dec 19–8	2,000	1,500			
	7,600	5,700			
Gross Profit c/d		1,728			
	7,600	7,428		7,600	7,428
Expenses		1,000	Gross Profit b/d		1,728
Net Profit		728			
		1,728			1,728

(b) The Stock and Debtors System

Where a branch also sells goods on credit terms then further refinements are necessary to ensure that the control element applies also to debtors. This system can either be operated on the basis that the control element is built in as part of the double entry effected, or else as memoranda columns so far as the stock is concerned. The method using memoranda columns would certainly appear to have all the benefits of simplicity and ease of operation, and is the one to be preferred in practice. The fully integrated method does, however, seem to be preferred by examiners, perhaps this is because this method is indicative of the way that will be illustrated of calculating gross profits using profit margins only.

Using the following basic data, Exhibit 30.2 shows the records where the memoranda method is used, while Exhibit 30.3 shows the records where the fully integrated method is in use.

Data: A branch sells all its goods at a uniform mark-up of 50 per cent profit on cost price. Credit customers are to pay their accounts direct to the head office.

		£
First day of the period—		
Stock (at cost)	A	2,000
Debtors	B	400
During the period—		
Goods sent to the Branch (at cost)	C	7,000
Sales—Cash	D	6,000

Sales—Credit		E	4,800
Cash remitted by Debtors to Head Office		F	4,500
At the close of the last day of the period—			
Stock (at cost)		G	1,800
Debtors		H	700

The letters A to H beside the figures have been inserted in order that the entries in Exhibit 30.3 can be more easily understood. The entries for each of the above items will have the relevant letter shown beside it.

Exhibit 30.2

Memoranda Columns in Use
Branch Stock

	Selling price memo. only			Selling price memo. only	
	£	£		£	£
Stock b/fwd.	3,000	2,000	Sales: Cash	6,000	6,000
Goods Sent	10,500	7,000	Credit	4,800	4,800
Gross Profit to			Stock c/d	2,700	1,800
Profit and Loss		3,600			
	13,500	12,600		13,500	12,600
Stock b/d	2,700	1,800			

Branch Debtors

	£		£
Balances b/fwd	400	Cash	4,500
Branch Stock	4,800	Balance c/d	700
	5,200		5,200
Balance b/d	700		

Goods Sent to Branches

	£		£
Transfer to Head Office		Branch Stock	7,000
Trading Account	7,000		

Cash Book

	£
Branch Stock—Cash Sales	6,000
Branch Debtors	4,500

The branch Stock Account is thus in effect a Trading Account, and is identical to the type used in the Double Column System. In addition, however, a Branch Debtors Account is in use.

The balance of the Goods Sent to Branches Account is shown as being transferred to the Head Office Trading Account. This figure is deducted from the purchases in the Head Office Trading Account, in order that goods bought for the branch can be disregarded when the gross profit earned by the head office is being calculated.

The fully integrated system introduces the idea that the gross profit earned by a firm can be calculated by reference to profit margins only. A simple example illustrates this point. Assume that a self-employed travelling salesman sells all his goods at cost price plus 25 per cent for profit. At the start of a week he has £4 stock at cost, he buys goods costing £40, he sells goods for £45 (selling price) and he has goods left in stock at the end of the week which had cost him £8. A normal Trading Account based on this data is shown below.

Trading Account for the week ended . . .

	£		£
Opening Stock	4	Sales	45
Add Purchases	40		
	44		
Less Closing Stock	8		
Cost of Goods Sold	36		
Gross Profit	9		
	45		45

This could, however, also be shown as:

	£
Profit made when opening stock is sold	1
Profit made when purchases are sold	10
Profit made when all goods are sold	11
But he still has left unsold goods (cost £8) on which the profit still has to be realised	2
Therefore profit realised	9

This could be expressed in account form as:

Salesman's Adjustment Account

		£			£
Gross Profit		9	Unrealised Profit b/fwd		1
Unrealised Profit c/d		2	Goods Bought		10
		11			11

The fully integrated system uses such a form of adjustment account. Goods sent to the branch are shown at cost price in an account for that purpose, while the Branch Stock Account is shown at selling price. To show one entry at selling price and the other at cost would mean that debit amounts would not equal credit amounts, thus violating double entry principles. To rectify this a Branch Adjustment Account is opened and the profit loading on the goods is recorded to preserve the equality of amounts of debit and credit entries. The Branch Stock Account by being entirely concerned with selling prices acts as a control upon stock deficiencies, while the Branch Adjustment Account shows the amount of gross profit earned during the period. In the example seen worked out in Exhibit 30.3 a stock deficiency does not exist. The action required when such a deficiency arises is demonstrated later in this chapter.

Exhibit 30.3

Branch Stock (Selling Price)

		£			£
Balance b/fwd	A	3,000	Sales: Cash	D	6,000
Goods sent to Branch	C	10,500	Credit	E	4,800
			Balance c/d	G	2,700
		13,500			13,500
Balance b/d	G	2,700			

Branch Debtors (Selling Price)

		£			£
Balances b/fwd	B	400	Cash	F	4,500
Branch Stock	E	4,800	Balances c/d	H	700
		5,200			5,200
Balances b/d	H	700			

Goods Sent to Branches (Cost Price)

		£			£
Transfer to Head Office Trading Account		7,000	Branch Stock	C	7,000

Branch Adjustment (Profit Loading)

		£			£
Gross Profit to Profit and Loss		3,600	Unrealised Profit b/fwd	A	1,000
Unrealised Profit c/d	G	900	Branch Stock—goods sent	C	3,500
		4,500			4,500
			Unrealised Profit b/d	G	900

The opening and closing stocks are shown in the Branch Stock Account at selling price. However, the Balance Sheet should show the stock at cost price (if for simplicity the fact that the net realisable value etc., may be lower, then cost can be ignored). The previous Balance Sheet should therefore have shown stock at cost £2,000. This is achieved by having a compensating £1,000 credit balance brought forward in the Branch Adjustment Account, so that the debit balance of £3,000 in the Branch Stock Account, when it comes to being shown in the Balance Sheet, has the £1,000 credit balance deducted to show a net figure of £2,000. Similarly, at the close of the period the balance sheet will show stock at £1,800 (Branch Stock debit balance £2,700 less Branch Adjustment credit balance £900).

The Fully Integrated System — Further Considerations

(a) *Returns*. Goods may be returned—

  (i) From the branch stock to the head office.
 (ii) From the branch debtors to the branch stock.
(iii) From the branch debtors to the head office.

To show the entries needed look at a firm which sells goods at cost plus 25 per cent profit, and according to the categories stated the following goods were returned, all prices shown being selling prices: (i) £45, (iii) £75, (iii) £15. The entries needed are:

Branch Stock (Selling Price)

		£			£
Returns from Debtors	(ii)	75	Returned to Head Office	(i)	45

Branch Adjustment (Profit Loading)

		£
Returns from Branch	(i)	9
Returns from Debtors	(iii)	3

Goods Sent to Branches (Cost Price)

		£
Returns from Branch	(i)	36
Returns from Debtors	(iii)	12

Branch Debtors (Selling Price)

		£
Returns to Branch	(ii)	75
Returns to Head Office	(iii)	15

Entries (ii) both being in accounts shown at selling price were two in number, i.e. £75 Dr and £75 Cr Entries (i) and (iii) each needed entries in three accounts, (i) being £45 Cr and £9 Dr and £36 Dr, (iii) being £15 Cr and £12 Dr and £3 Dr.

(b) Different Physical and Book Stock Figures

It has been assumed so far that the stock figures according to the accounts have been exactly the same as the actual stocks on hand. This will rarely be true, as there are almost bound to be errors made in selling prices, giving wrong change in cash sales, breakages, wastages, pilferages, or it could perhaps be that goods have been sold at a different profit mark-up from that which is normal in the business.

The stock to be carried forward in the Branch Stock Account is, however, the selling price of the actual stock on hand. The difference between the actual stock and the unadjusted balance on the stock account will normally be a deficiency of stock. The converse would only apply where goods had been sold at higher than normal profit mark-up. A deficiency of stock is entered by crediting the difference to the Branch Stock Account and debiting a similar amount to the Branch Adjustment Account. The converse applies to an excess of stock.

To understand why this should be so, a firm's accounts can be seen where a deficiency of stock exists.

Exhibit 30.4

A firm with one branch has a uniform mark-up of 50 per cent. The following details are known:

	£
Opening Stock—at selling price	1,800
Goods sent to the Branch—at selling price	6,000
Sales by the Branch—at selling price	6,300
Closing Stock—per actual stocktaking—at selling price	1,350

Branch Stock (Selling Price)

	£		£
Balance b/fwd	1,800	Sales	6,300
Goods sent to Branch	6,000	Deficiency (difference between the two sides of the account)	150
		Balance c/d	1,350
	7,800		7,800
Balance b/d	1,350		

Branch Adjustment (Profit Loading)

	£		£
Branch Stock (deficiency)	150	Unrealised Profit in Opening Stock b/fwd	600
Gross Profit to Profit and Loss	2,000	Goods sent to Branch	2,000
Unrealised Profit in Closing Stock c/d	450		
	2,600		2,600
		Unrealised Profit in Stock b/d	450

Suppose an ordinary Trading Account had been drafted, it would have appeared:

Trading Account for the Period ...

	£		£
Opening Stock	1,200	Sales	6,300
Add Goods from Head Office	4,000		
	5,200		
Less Closing Stock	900		
	4,300		
Gross Profit	2,000		
	6,300		6,300

Thus the profit calculated by the normal method and the Branch Adjustment method remains the same. The fact that the Adjustment Account is charged with the full selling price of the stock deficiency is because the gross profit part of the deficiency, £50, had already been taken into account in the £2,000 credited to the Adjustment Account, as it has not been realised it must be cancelled. In addition, the cost of the stock deficiency, £100, is a charge when calculating the gross profit, e.g. goods breakages mean less gross profit.

Missing Figures

It is the common practice of many examiners to omit certain figures when giving details for questions using the Stock and Debtors system. The student is entitled in such a case to assume that where one figure is missing in an account, then that figure may be taken to be the difference between the totals of the two sides.

2. Where Each Branch Maintains Full Accounting Records

This would very rarely be found in a firm with many branches, it is more common in a firm with just one or two or a few branches, and is particularly relevant where the branch is large enough to warrant a separate accounting staff being employed.

A branch cannot operate on its own without resources, and it is the firm that provides these in the first instance. The firm will want to know how much money it has invested in each branch, and from this arises the concept of Branch and Head Office Current Accounts. The relationship between the branch and the head office is seen as that of a debtor/creditor identity. The current accounts are medias where the branch is shown as a debtor in the head office records, while the head office is shown as a creditor in the branch records. This is purely for expediency, because as the branch and the head office both belong to the same firm it is apparent that a firm cannot owe money to itself.

The current accounts are used for those transactions that are concerned with supplying resources to the branch or in retrieving resources. For such transactions full double entry records are needed both in the branch records and also in the head office records, i.e. each item will be recorded twice in each set of records. Some transactions will, however, concern the branch only, and these will merely need two entries in the branch records and none in the head office records. Exhibit 30.5 shows several transactions and the records needed.

Exhibit 30.5

A firm with its head office in London opened a branch in Manchester. The following transactions took place in the first month:

A Opened a bank account at Manchester by transferring £1,000 from the London bank account.

B Bought premises in Manchester, paying by cheque drawn on the London bank account, £5,000.

C Manchester bought a motor van, paying by cheque £600 from its own bank account.

D Manchester bought fixtures on credit from V. Ryan Ltd, £900.

E London supplied a machine valued at £250 from its own machinery.
F Manchester bought goods from suppliers, paying by cheque on its own account, £270.
G Manchester's cash sales banked immediately in its own bank account, £3,000.
H Goods invoiced at cost to Manchester during the month by London (no cash or cheques being paid specifically for these goods by Manchester), £2,800.
I A cheque is paid to London by Manchester as general return of funds, £1,800.
J Goods returned to London by Manchester—at cost price, £100.

The exact dates have been deliberately omitted. It will be seen later that complications arise because of differences in the times of transactions. Each transaction has been identified by a capital letter. The relevant letter will be shown against each entry in the accounts.

Head Office Records (in London)
Manchester Branch Current Account

		£			£
Bank	A	1,000	Bank	I	1,800
Bank—Premises	B	5,000	Returns from Branch	J	100
Machinery	E	250			
Goods sent to Branch	H	2,800			

Bank

		£			£
Manchester Branch	I	1,800	Manchester Branch	A	1,000
			Manchester Premises	B	5,000

Machinery

		£
Manchester Branch	E	250

Goods Sent to Branch

		£			£
Returns from Branch	J	100	Manchester Branch	H	2,800

Branch Records (in Manchester)
Head Office Current Account

		£			£
Returns	J	100	Bank	A	1,000
Bank	I	1,800	Premises	B	5,000
			Machinery	E	250
			Goods from Head Office	H	2,800

Bank

		£				£
Head Office	A	1,000	Motor Van	C		600
Cash Sales	G	3,000	Purchases	F		270
			Head Office	I		1,800

Premises

		£
Head Office	B	5,000

Motor Van

		£
Bank	C	600

Fixtures

		£
V. Ryan Ltd	D	900

V. Ryan Ltd

			£
		Fixtures	D	900

Machinery

		£
Head Office	E	250

Purchases

		£
Bank	F	270

Sales

			£
		Bank	G	3,000

Goods from Head Office

		£			£
Head Office	H	2,800	Head Office—returns	J	100

It can be seen that items C, D, F and G are entered only in the Manchester records. This is because these items are purely internal transactions and are not concerned with resources flowing between London and Manchester.

Profit or Loss and Current Accounts

The profit earned by the branch (or loss incurred by it) does not belong to the branch. It belongs to the firm and must therefore be shown as such. The head office represents the central authority of the firm and profit of the branch should be credited to the Head Office Current Account, any loss being debited.

The branch will therefore draw up its own Trading and Profit and Loss Account. After agreement with the head office the net profit will then be transferred to the credit of the Head Office Current Account. The head office in its own records will then debit the Branch Current Account and credit its own Profit and Loss Account. Taking the net profit earned in Exhibit 30.5 as £700, the two sets of books would appear thus:

Head Office Records (in London)
London Profit and Loss Account

	£
Net Profit earned by the Manchester Branch	700

Manchester Branch Current Account

	£		£
Bank	1,000	Bank	1,800
Bank: Premises	5,000	Returns from Branch	100
Machinery	250		
Goods sent to Branch	2,800		
Net profit to main Profit and Loss Account	700	Balance c/d	7,850
	9,750		9,750
Balance b/d	7,850		

Branch Records (in Manchester)
Manchester Profit and Loss Account

	£
Net Profit carried to the Head Office Current Account	700

Head Office Current Account

	£		£
Returns to Head Office	100	Bank	1,000
Bank	1,800	Premises	5,000
		Machinery	250
		Goods from Head Office	2,800
Balance c/d	7,850	Profit and Loss Account	700
	9,750		9,750
		Balance b/d	7,850

The Combined Balance Sheet

After the Trading and Profit and Loss Accounts have been drawn up a Balance Sheet is required for the whole firm. The branch will send its trial balance to the head office which will add the assets in its own trial balance to those in the branch trial balance to give the total for each type of asset to be shown in the Balance Sheet, and a similar procedure will be carried out for the liabilities.

In the trial balances the Head Office Current Accounts will be a debit balance while the Branch Current Accounts will be a credit balance, e.g. the two figures of £7,850 in the London and Manchester books. These therefore cancel out and are not shown in the combined Balance Sheet. This is in order, as the two balances do not in fact represent assets or liabilities, but are merely a measure of the resources at the branch.

Items in Transit

It was stated earlier that the timing of transactions raised complications. Obviously a cheque sent by a Manchester branch one day would probably arrive in London the next day, while goods sent from London to Manchester, or returned from Manchester to London, could well take longer than that. Both the head office and the branch will have entered the transactions at the dates of remittance or receipt, and as the remittance from one place will occur on one day and the receipt occur at the other place on another day, then where items are in transit at the end of a financial period each set of records will not contain identical figures. This will mean that the balances on the current accounts will not be equal to one another.

It is, however, necessary to have identical amounts of balances on the current accounts so that they will cancel out when the combined Balance Sheet is prepared. As the two sets of records contain some figures which are different from each other they must somehow be reconciled so that the balances carried down are the same. Which set of figures are to be altered? The answer is one of expediency. It would be normal to find the most experienced accountants at the head office, and therefore the amendments should all be made in the head office books, instead of leaving it to junior accountants at the branches who would be more likely to make mistakes. Also if there are several branches the problems of communicating specific instructions to several accountants some distance away make it easier for all amendments to be made at the head office.

Exhibit 30.6 is for the second month of the business shown in Exhibit 30.5. However, whereas there were no items in transit at the end of the first month, this does not hold true at the conclusion of the second month.

Exhibit 30.6

Head Office Records (showing current accounts only)

	£
Goods sent to Branch	3,700
Cheques received from Branch	2,950
Returns received from Branch	440
Branch Records	
Goods received from Head Office	3,500
Cheques sent to Head Office	3,030
Returns sent to Head Office	500

It may be assumed that the net profit as shown by the Profit and Loss Account of the branch is £800.

Branch Records (in Manchester)
Head Office Current Account

	£			£
Bank	3,030	Balance b/fwd		7,850
Returns to Head Office	500	Goods from Head Office		3,500
Balance c/d	8,620	Net Profit		800
	12,150			12,150
		Balance b/d		8,620

Head Office Records (in London)
Manchester Branch Current Account

		£			£
Balance b/fwd		7,850	Bank	B	2,950
Goods sent to Branch	A	3,700	Returns received	C	440
Net Profit		800			

At this point the following items are observed to be in transit at the end of the period (these should be confirmed to ensure that they are not merely errors in accounting records):

1. Goods sent to the branch amounting to £200 (£3,700–£3,500).
2. Cheques sent by the branch amounting to £80 (£3,030–£2,950).
3. Returns from the branch amounting to £60 (£500–£440).

(A) needs amending to £3,500. This is done by crediting the account with £200.

(B) needs amending to £3,030. This is done by crediting the account with £80.

(C) needs amending to £500. This is done by crediting the account with £60.

As these are items in transit they need to be taken to the period in which they arrive, i.e. the next month. This is effected by carrying them down as balances into the next period. The Branch Current Account will now be completed.

It may appear at first sight to be rather strange that all the items in transit are shown as debit balances. However, it must be appreciated that goods (including returns) and money in transit are assets of the firm at the end of a financial period. That they are in transit is merely stipulating that the assets are neither at the head office nor at the branch but are somewhere else. Assets are always shown as debit balances and there is no reason why it should be different just because they have not reached their destination on a certain date.

Manchester Branch Current Account

	£		£
Balance b/fwd	7,850	Bank	2,950
Goods sent to Branch	3,700	Returns Received	440
Net Profit	800	Goods in Transit c/d	200
		Cheques in Transit c/d	80
		Returns in Transit c/d	60
		Balance c/d	8,620
	12,350		12,350
Balance b/d	8,620		
Goods in Transit b/d	200		
Cheques in Transit b/d	80		
Returns in Transit b/d	60		

All of these four balances are shown in the trial balance. When the combined Balance Sheet is being prepared the balance of the two current accounts, i.e. in this case £8,620, will cancel out as it is a debit balance in one trial balance and a credit balance in the other. The goods in transit £200 and the returns in transit £60, both being goods, are added to the stock in the Balance Sheet. This is because stock is made up of the following items:

At the end of the second month:

	£
Stock at London	
Add Stock at Manchester	
Add Stocks in Transit (£200+£60)	260
Total Stock	

Similarly, the balance for cheques or remittances in transit is added to the bank balances at London and Manchester.

	£
Bank Balance at London	
Add Bank Balance in Manchester	
Add Remittances in Transit	80

This is rather like a man who has £14 in one pocket and £3 in another. He takes a £5 note from the pocket containing the larger amount and is transferring it to his other pocket when someone asks him to stay perfectly still and calculate the total cash in his possession. He therefore has:

	£
Pocket 1	9
Pocket 2	3
Cash in Transit	5
Total Cash	17

Exhibit 30.7

Trial Balances as at 29 February 19–8

	London Head Office		Manchester Branch	
	Dr	Cr	Dr	Cr
	£	£	£	£
Premises	10,000		5,000	
Machinery	2,000		400	
Fixtures	3,100		1,400	
Motor Vans	1,500		900	
Closing Stocks	3,800		700	
Debtors	1,100		800	
Bank	12,200		600	
Head Office Current Account				8,620
Branch Current Account	8,620			
Goods in Transit	200			
Cheques in Transit	80			
Returns in Transit	60			
Creditors		1,300		1,180
Capital Account as at 1 Jan 19–8		37,860		
Net Profit for the two months (Branch £1,500+Head Office £2,000)		3,500		
	42,660	42,660	9,800	9,800

Using the figures already given in Exhibit 30.6, but adding some further information, trial balances for London Head Office and the Manchester Branch are now shown in Exhibit 30.7 after the Profit and Loss accounts have been drawn up for the second month.

The combined Balance Sheet can now be drawn up.

Balance Sheet as at 29 February 19–8

	£	£		£	£
Capital			*Fixed Assets*		
Balance at 1 Jan			Premises		15,000
19–8	37,860		Machinery		2,400
Add Net Profit:			Fixtures		4,500
London	2,000		Motor Vans		2,400
Manchester	1,500	41,360			
					24,300
Current Liabilities			*Current Assets*		
Creditors		2,480	Stocks	4,760	
			Debtors	1,900	
			Bank	12,880	19,540
		43,840			43,840

Notes:

	£		£
Stocks: London	3,800	Bank: London	12,200
Manchester	700	Manchester	600
In Transit		In Transit	80
(£200+£60)	260		
	4,760		12,880

Foreign Branch Accounts

The treatment of the accounts of foreign branches is subject to only one exception from that of branches in the United Kingdom. This is concerned with the fact that when the trial balance is drawn up by the branch then this will be stated in a foreign currency. To amalgamate these figures with the United Kingdom figures will mean that the foreign branch figures will have to be translated into British currency.

There are rules for general guidance as to how this can be done. These are the ones which the examiner will expect a student to observe in an examination. It must be stressed that in practice these rules should not be slavishly observed, as in certain circumstances the reported trading results of firms would be seriously distorted. Some firms have therefore devised their own adaptations of these rules.

The amount of a particular currency which one can obtain for another currency is known as the exchange rate. Taking an imaginary country with a currency called chips, there might be a general agreement that the exchange rate should stay at about 5 chips to equal £1. At certain times the exchange rate will exactly equal that figure, but due to all sorts of economic reasons it may well be 5·02 chips to £1 on one day and 4·97 chips to £1 several days later. In addition, some years ago there may have been an act of devaluation by one of the countries involved; the exchange rate could well have then been 3 chips to £1. To understand more about exchange rates and devaluation the reader of this book would be well advised to read a relevant economics textbook.

It is clear, however, that all items in the trial balance should not be converted to British currency on the basis of the exchange rate ruling at the date of the trial balance. The rules have been devised in an attempt to bring about conversion into British currency so as not to distort reported trading results.

Now for the rules:

1.
(a) Fixed assets at the exchange rate ruling when the assets were bought. If fixed assets have been bought on different dates, then different rates will have to be used for each separate purchase.
(b) Depreciation on the fixed assets at the same rate as the fixed assets concerned.

2. Current assets and current liabilities—at the rate ruling at the date of the trial balance.

3. Opening stock in the Trading Account—at the rate ruling at the previous Balance Sheet date.

4. Goods sent by the head office to the branch, or returns from the branch—at the actual figures shown in the Goods sent to Branches Account in the head office books.

5. Trading and Profit and Loss Account items, other than depreciation, opening and closing stocks, or goods sent to or returned by the branch —at the average rate for the period covered by the accounts.

6. The Head Office Current Account—at the same figures as shown in the Branch Current Account in the head office books.

When the conversion of the figures into British currency is completed, the totals of the debit and credit sides of the British currency trial balance will not normally be equal to one another. This is due to different exchange rates being taken for conversion purposes. A balancing figure will therefore be needed to bring about the equality of the totals. For this purpose a Difference on Exchange Account will be opened and a debit entry made therein if the lesser total is on the debit side of the credit side. When the head office redrafts the Profit and Loss Account any debit balance on the Difference on Exchange Account should be transferred to it as an expense. A credit balance on the Difference on Exchange Account should, however, be treated as a reserve and shown on the Capital and Liabilities side of the Balance Sheet.

Exhibit 30.8

An example of the conversion of a trial balance into British currency is now shown. The branch is in Flavia, and the unit of currency is the Flavian dollar. The exchange rates needed are:

(a) On 1 January 19–3, 10 dollars= £1
(b) On 1 January 19–5, 11 dollars=£1
(c) On 1 January 19–8, 17 dollars=£1
(d) On 31 December 19–8, 15 dollars=£1
(e) If no further information were given the average rate for 19–8 would have to be taken as $(c)+(d)\div2$, i.e. 16 dollars=£1. This is not an advisable procedure in practice, the fact that the average has been calculated from only two readings could mean that the average calculated might be far different from a more accurate one calculated from a larger number of readings.

Trial Balance as on 31 December 19–8

	Dr (dol.)	Cr (dol.)	Exchange rates	Dr £	Cr £
Fixed Assets:					
Bought 1 Jan 19–3	10,000		10 =£1	1,000	
Bought 1 Jan 19–5	8,800		11 =£1	800	
Stock 1 Jan 19–8	6,800		17 =£1	400	
Expense Accounts	8,000		16 =£1	500	
Sales		32,000	16 =£1		2,000
Goods from Head Office	21,900		£ per account in Head Office books	1,490	
Head Office Current Account		43,000	£ per account in Head Office books		3,380
Debtors	9,000		15 =£1	600	
Creditors		4,500	15 =£1		300
Bank	15,000		15 =£1	1,000	
	79,500	79,500		5,790	5,680
Difference on Exchange Account					110
				5,790	5,790

The stock at 31 December 19–8 is 12,000 dollars. When the Trading Account is drawn up this will be converted at 15 dollars=£1, i.e. £800.

Exercises

30.1. Octopus Ltd, whose head office is at Cardiff, operates a branch at Swansea. All goods are purchased by head office and invoiced to and sold by the branch at cost plus 33⅓ per cent.

Other than a sales ledger kept at Swansea, all transactions are recorded in the books at Cardiff.

The following particulars are given of the transactions at the branch during the year ended 28 February 19–7:

	£
Stock on Hand, 1 March 19–6, at invoice price	4,400
Debtors on 1 March 19–6	3,946
Stock on Hand, 28 February 19–7, at invoice price	3,948
Goods sent from Cardiff during the year at invoice price	24,800
Credit Sales	21,000
Cash Sales	2,400
Returns to Head Office at invoice price	1,000
Invoice value of goods stolen	600
Bad Debts written off	148
Cash from Debtors	22,400
Normal loss at invoice price due to wastage	100
Cash Discount allowed to Debtors	428

You are required to write up the Branch Stock Account and Branch Total Debtors Account for the year ended 28 February 19–7, as they would appear in the head office books.

(*Institute of Chartered Accountants*)

30.2. L.G.D. Ltd, a London trading company, has a branch in Brighton.

All purchases are made by the head office and goods sent to the branch are invoiced to the branch at selling price, which is 20 per cent above cost. All sales by the branch are on credit terms. Branch expenses are paid by head office and all cash received by the branch is remitted to head office. All branch transactions are recorded in the head office books.

The balances, relating to the branch, in the head office ledger on 1 April 19–4, were as follows:

	£
Branch Stock Account (stock at branch, at invoice price to branch)	3,600
Branch Adjustment Account	600
Branch Debtors (amounts owing by branch customers)	2,575

Transactions during the year to 31 March 19–5 were:

	£
Goods sent to Branch (at invoice price to the branch)	32,460
Returns from Branch to Head Office (at invoice price to branch)	642
Branch sales	33,780
Returns from customers to Branch	354

	£
Cash received from Branch Debtors	32,848
Discounts allowed to Branch Debtors	1,415
Branch Expenses Paid	4,027

The branch stock at 31 March 19–5 (at invoice price to the branch) was £1,962.

There were no expenses outstanding at 31 March 19–5, and none had been paid in advance.

You are required to show the accounts relating to the branch (including the branch profit and loss account), in the ledger of the head office, for the year to 31 March 19–5.

(*Chartered Institute of Secretaries*)

30.3. A Co Ltd has a branch in Manchester at which a full set of books are kept. At the end of the year the following is a summary of the transactions between the branch and the head office as recorded in the latter's books:

	£
Balance due from Branch at 1 January	20,160
Cash received from Branch	30,000
Goods supplied to Branch	23,160
Goods returned by Branch	400
Expenses paid on behalf of Branch	6,000

At 30 June the branch Profit and Loss Account showed a net profit of £3,500.

(*a*) Show the above items as they would appear in the ledger of the head office.
(*b*) How can any resulting balance from these figures be proved, and what does it indicate?

(*East Midland Educational Union*)

30.4.

	Head office books		Branch books	
	Dr	Cr	Dr	Cr
	£	£	£	£
Capital		15,844		
Drawings	4,800			
Fixed Assets	9,400		3,200	
Head Office Current Account				3,314
Branch Current Account	3,910			
Stock-in-Trade (1 July 19–5)	3,571		1,206	
Purchases	37,276			
Goods sent to Branch		9,987		
Goods received from Head Office			9,706	
Sales		38,813		13,712
Trade Debtors and Trade Creditors	912	4,107	381	
Salaries and Wages	5,116		1,612	
Rent, Rates and Insurance	1,547		536	
General Expenses	418		74	
Bank and Cash Balances	1,801		311	
	68,751	68,751	17,026	17,026

F. T. Jay owns a retail business comprising a main store in Ilfield and a branch store at Loston. All goods are purchased by the head office in Ilfield and goods sent out to the branch are invoiced at cost price.

The trial balances already shown were extracted as at 30 June 19–6.

For the purpose of preparing final accounts the following information is available:

(i) Stock-in-trade at 30 June 19–6: head office £4,109 and branch £1,362. The branch stock (£1,362) does not include goods in transit.

(ii) Head office makes a charge of £300 against the branch for administrative services.

(iii) Goods, at cost £281, sent by head office to the branch on 30 June 19–6 and entered in head office books on that date were received at the branch on 2 July 19–6 and entered in the branch books on the latter date.

(iv) A cheque for £315 sent by the branch to head office on 30 June 19–6 did not arrive at head office until 2 July 19–6 and was entered in the head office books on that date.

(v) Depreciation on fixed assets is to be provided at 10 per cent.
Prepare:

(a) The Trading and Profit and Loss Accounts (in columnar form) for the year ended 30 June 19–6 of (i) the main store and (ii) the branch store.

(b) The general Balance Sheet of the business as at 30 June 19–6.

(c) The Head Office Current Account as it would appear in the branch books after the closing entries have been made.

(d) A Trial Balance showing the balances remaining in the branch books after all the closing entries have been made.

(*Associated Examining Board 'A' Level*)

30.5. Packer and Stringer were in partnership as retail traders sharing profits and losses: Packer three-quarters, Stringer one-quarter. The partners were credited annually with interest at the rate of 6 per cent per annum on their fixed capitals; no interest was charged on their drawings.

Stringer was responsible for the buying department of the business. Packer managed the head office and Paper was employed as the branch manager. Packer and Paper were each entitled to a commission of 10 per cent of the net profits (after charging such commission) of the shop managed by him.

All goods were purchased by head office and goods sent to the branch were invoiced at cost.

The following was the trial balance as on 31 December 19–4:

	Head office books		Branch books	
	Dr	Cr	Dr	Cr
	£	£	£	£
Drawings Accounts and Fixed Capital Accounts:				
Packer	2,500	14,000		

	Head office books		Branch books	
	Dr	Cr	Dr	Cr
	£	£	£	£
Stringer	1,200	4,000		
Furniture and Fittings, at cost	1,500		1,100	
Furniture and Fittings, provision for depreciation as on 31 December 19–3		500		350
Stock on 31 December 19–3	13,000		4,400	
Purchases	37,000			
Goods sent to Branches		18,000	17,200	
Sales		39,000		26,000
Provision for doubtful debts		600		200
Branch and Head Office Current Accounts	6,800			3,600
Salaries and Wages	4,500		3,200	
Paper, on account of commission			240	
Carriage and Travelling Expenses	2,200		960	
Administrative Expenses	2,400			
Trade and General Expenses	3,200		1,800	
Sundry Debtors	7,000		3,000	
Sundry Creditors		5,800		400
Bank Balances	600			1,350
	81,900	81,900	31,900	31,900

You are given the following additional information:

 (i) Stocks on 31 December 19–4, amounted to: head office £14,440, branch £6,570.
 (ii) Administrative expenses are to be apportioned between head office and the branch in proportion to sales.
 (iii) Depreciation is to be provided on furniture and fittings at 10 per cent of cost.
 (iv) The provision for doubtful debts is to be increased by £50 in respect of head office debtors and decreased by £20 in the case of those of the branch.
 (v) On 31 December 19–4 cash amounting to £2,400, in transit from the branch to head office, has been recorded in the branch books but not in those of head office, and on that date goods invoiced at £800, in transit from head office to the branch, had been recorded in the head office books but not in the branch books.

Any adjustments necessary are to be made in the head office books.
You are required to:

(a) prepare Trading and Profit and Loss Accounts and the Appropriation Account for the year ended 31 December 19–4, showing the net profit of the head office and branch respectively,
(b) prepare the Balance Sheet as on that date, and
(c) show the closing entries in the Branch Current Accounts giving the make-up of the closing balance.
Income tax is to be ignored.

(Institute of Chartered Accountants)

30.6A. Norsea Ltd has a head office in Hull, and operates a branch in Grimsby.

All purchases are made by the head office and goods for the branch are invoiced at selling price, being cost price plus 50 per cent.

On 30 April 19–8 stock of goods at the branch, at selling price, amounted to £4,020 and debtors £1,652.

During the year ended 30 April 19–9 the following transactions took place at the branch:

	£
Cash sales	25,200
Credit sales	18,000
Cash discounts allowed to debtors	452
Cash received from debtors	17,156
Debts written off as bad	149
Goods received by the branch at selling price	45,000
Goods returned to head office at selling price	420

On 30 April 19–9 stock of goods at the branch, at selling price, amounted to £5,250.

You are required to write up the ledger accounts in the head office books to record the above transactions, and compute the branch gross profit for the year ended 30 April 19–9.

(*Institute of Chartered Accountants*)

30.7A. Stainless Ltd operates from a head office in London and a branch at Leeds, where separate books are kept. The company makes up its accounts to 31 December in each year.

Goods sent to the branch by head office are charged at cost plus 10 per cent. Other than the sales to branch, head office sales are made at a uniform gross profit of 25 per cent on selling price. Leeds sales are all made at a uniform gross profit to the branch of 20 per cent on selling price.

You are given the following relevant information regarding the year ended 31 December 19–7:

1. Expenses paid during the year:

	London	Leeds
	£	£
Wages	6,415	2,418
Selling expenses	4,220	1,610
Overhead expenses	2,991	2,021

2. Overhead expenses accrued:

31 December 19–6	249	156
31 December 19–7	416	82

3. Purchases at head office totalled £97,680, and sales, included £44,000 invoiced to Leeds branch, were £119,000.

4. In addition to goods received from head office the Leeds branch had purchased goods from outside suppliers amounting to £9,200. On 31 December 19–7, there were goods in transit from head office at an invoice price of £3,400 which were not received by the branch until 3 January 19–8.

5. Sales at Leeds were £60,000 and discounts allowed to customers during the year amounted to £910.

6. The stocks on hand on 31 December 19–6 had been £17,250 at London and

£7,500 at Leeds, being cost to the branch. The stock at Leeds included stock invoiced by head office at £5,600. On 31 December 19–7, the stock at Leeds contained stock invoiced by head office amounting to £7,700.

You are required to prepare, in columnar form, the head office, branch and combined Trading and Profit and Loss Accounts for the year ended 31 December 19–7.

(*Institute of Chartered Accountants*)

30.8A. New Ventures Ltd, a trading company, opened a branch on 1 October 19–9. All purchases are made by the head office. Goods sent to the branch are invoiced at cost plus 25 per cent. A full double entry record of transactions is kept in the branch books. Some branch expenses are paid by head office and some by the branch.

The following trial balance was extracted from the head office books at 30 September 19–0:

	£	£
Fixed assets	42,000	
Branch current account	25,875	
Debtors and creditors	9,300	8,070
Balance at bank	12,300	
Head office stock at cost (1 October 19–9)	13,200	
Purchases	126,240	
Sales		106,860
Goods sent to branch at cost plus 25 per cent		68,250
Profit and loss account balance at 1 October 19–9		9,000
General expenses (Head Office only)	23,265	
Issued share capital		60,000
	252,180	252,180

No entries had been made in the Head Office books for cash in transit from the branch to Head Office on 30 September 19–0, £2,580. This item had, however, been reflected in the balances shown below, which were extracted from the branch books at the same date. No entries had been made in the branch books for goods in transit on that date from head office to branch (£2,250 at invoice price) or for expenses paid in September 19–0 by head office on behalf of the branch £555, but these transactions were included in head office balances shown above.

In addition to the balances which can be deducted from the information given above, the following balances appeared in the branch books on 30 September 19–0:

	£
General expenses	14,925
Sales	76,050
Debtors	1,080
Creditors (excluding head office)	1,470
Fixed Assets	13,800
Balance at Bank	2,205

Stocks at 30 September 19–0 were valued as follows:

	£
Head Office (at cost)	14,100 (excluding goods in transit)
Branch (at cost to Head Office)	6,300 (excluding goods in transit)

You are required to:

1.   Prepare Trading and Profit and Loss Accounts in columnar form for the Head Office and Branch separately for the year ended 30 September 19-0. A balance sheet is not required.

2.   Prepare the branch current account in the Head Office books on the assumption that the Head Office makes the adjustments for all items in transit.
Note: Ignore depreciation and taxation.

(*Associated Examining Board, G.C.E. 'A' level*)

30.9A. L. R., a trader, commenced business on 1 January 19-9, with a head office and one branch.

All goods were purchased by the head office and goods sent to the branch were invoiced at a fixed selling price of 25 per cent above cost. All sales, both by the head office and the branch, were made at the fixed selling price.

The following trial balance was extracted from the books at the head office at 31 December 19-9.

Trial Balance

	£	£
Capital		52,000
Drawings	1,740	
Purchases	123,380	
Sales		83,550
Goods sent to branch (at selling price)		56,250
Branch current account	24,550	
Fixed assets	33,000	
Debtors and creditors	7,980	11,060
General expenses	8,470	
Balance at bank	3,740	
	202,860	202,860

No entries had been made in the head office books for cash in transit from the branch to head office at 31 December 19-9, £1,000.

When the balances shown below were extracted from the branch books at 31 December 19-9, no entries had been made in the books of the branch for goods in transit on that date from head office to branch, £920 (selling price).

In addition to the balances which can be deduced from the information given above, the following balances appeared in the branch books on 31 December 19-9:

	£
Fixed assets	6,000
General expenses	6,070
Debtors	7,040
Creditors (excluding head office)	1,630
Sales	51,700
Balance at bank	1,520

When stock was taken on 31 December 19-9, it was found that there was no shortage at the head office, but at the branch there were shortages amounting to £300, at selling price.

You are required to prepare trading and profit and loss accounts (i) for head office, and (ii) for the branch, as they would have appeared if goods sent to the branch had been invoiced at cost, and a balance sheet of the whole business as on 31 December 19–9.

Head Office and branch stocks are to be valued at cost.

Ignore depreciation of fixed assets.

(*Chartered Institute of Secretaries*)

30.10A. EG Company Limited, a manufacturing business, exports some of its products through an overseas branch whose currency is 'florins', which carries out the final assembly operations before selling the goods.

The trial balances of the head office and branch at 30 June 19–8 were:

	Head office		Branch	
	£	£	'Fl.'	'Fl.'
Freehold buildings at cost	14,000		63,000	
Debtors/creditors	8,900	9,500	36,000	1,560
Sales		104,000		432,000
Authorised and issued capital		40,000		
Components sent to branch		35,000		
Head office/branch accounts	60,100			504,260
Branch cost of sales			360,000	
Depreciation provision, machinery		1,500		56,700
Head office cost of sales (including goods to branch)	59,000			
Administration costs	15,200		18,000	
Stock at 30 June 19–8	28,900		11,520	
Profit and loss account		2,000		
Machinery at cost	6,000		126,000	
Remittances		28,000	272,000	
Balance at bank	4,600		79,200	
Selling and distribution costs	23,300		28,800	
	220,000	220,000	994,520	994,520

The following adjustments are to be made:

1. The cost of sales figures include a depreciation charge of 10 per cent per annum on cost for machinery.

2. A provision of £300 for unrealised profit in branch stock is to be made.

3. On 26 June 19–8 the branch remitted 16,000 'Fl.'; these were received by the head office on 4 July and realised £1,990.

4. During May a branch customer in error paid the head office for goods supplied. The amount due was 320 'Fl.' which realised £36. It has been correctly dealt with by head office but not yet entered in the branch books.

5. A provision has to be made for a commission of 5 per cent of the net profit of the branch after charging such commission, which is due to the branch manager.

The rates of exchange were:

At 1 July 19–7	10 'Fl.'=£1
At 30 June 19–8	8 'Fl.'=£1
Average for the year	9 'Fl.'=£1
On purchase of buildings and machinery	7 'Fl.'=£1

You are required to prepare, for internal use:

(a) detailed operating accounts for the year ended 30 June 19–8;
(b) combined head office and branch balance sheet as at 30 June 19–8;
(c) the branch account in the head office books, in both sterling and currency, the opening balance on 1 July 19–7 being £25,136 (189,260 'Fl.').

Taxation is to be ignored.

(*Institute of Cost and Management Accountants*)

30.11A. O.T.L. Ltd commenced business on 1 January 19–0. The head office is in London and there is a branch in Highland. The currency unit of Highland is the crown.

The following are the trial balances of the head office and the Highland branch as at 31 December 19–0:

	Head office		Highland branch	
	£	£	crowns	crowns
Branch account	65,280			
Balances at bank	10,560		66,000	
Creditors		21,120		92,400
Debtors	18,480		158,400	
Fixed assets (purchased 1 January 19–0)	39,600		145,200	
Head office account				316,800
Profit and loss account (net profit for the year)		52,800		79,200
Issued share capital		86,400		
Stocks	26,400		118,800	
	160,320	160,320	488,400	488,400

The trial balance of the head office was prepared before any entries had been made in respect of any profits or losses of the branch.

Remittance from head office to branch and from branch to head office were recorded in the books at the actual amounts paid and received.

The rates of exchange were:

On 1 January 19–0	5 crowns = £1
Average rate for year 19–0	4·4 crowns = £1
On 31 December 19–0	4 crowns = £1

Required:

1. The trial balance of the Highland branch as at 31 December 19–0, in sterling.

2. The closing entries, as at 31 December 19–0, in the Branch account in the books of the head office.

3. A summary of the balance sheet of O.T.L. Ltd as at 31 December 19–0.

Ignore depreciation of fixed assets.
Ignore taxation.

(*Chartered Institute of Secretaries*)

31

Container Accounts

A container is anything in which goods are contained. This may consist of a packet containing cigarettes, a large wooden crate containing tractor parts, or a barrel containing beer. Some will be returnable by the purchaser after use, an obvious example being the beer-barrel, while others such as the cigarette packet will be disposed of at will by the customer. The returnable containers will often be subject to a deposit being charged to the customer, a refund being allowed when the container is returned in good condition to the supplier.

In suppliers' books it is therefore convenient to divide containers into those which are (1) not chargeable to the customers, and (2) where a deposit charge is made to the customer.

1. *Containers not Charged to Customers*

Many containers will be treated as manufacturing expenses, e.g. cigarette packets, sugar bags or tin cans containing fruit. Theoretically they are a distribution expense if the contents and the containers are regarded as being two distinct items, and as such would be chargeable to the Profit and Loss Account, but really the containers for such items are an integral part of the goods sold and are therefore chargeable to the Manufacturing Account. On the other hand, returnable wooden crates in which goods are delivered would be chargeable to the Profit and Loss Account.

There will normally be a stock of containers in hand at the end of each accounting period. Exhibit 31.1 shows an account for cartons in which salt is packed for sale.

Exhibit 31.1

	£
Stock of containers 1 January 19–6	100
Containers bought in the year ended 31 December 19–6	2,800
Stock of containers 31 December 19–6	300

Containers

19–6		£	19–6		£
Jan 1	Stock b/d	100	Dec 31	Manufacturing	
Dec 31	Cash (during the			Account	2,600
	year)	2,800	„ 31	Stock c/d	300
		2,900			2,900
19–7					
Jan 1	Stock b/d	300			

For returnable containers on which deposits are not charged the question of whether or not accurate statistical records would be kept would depend on the nature and value of the containers. It would not be normal for a milk roundsman to keep accurate records of the number of bottles returnable by each household. The records he does keep are concerned with the amount of money collectible for milk supplied. He would soon notice, however, if a substantial number of bottles was not returned by a particular household. Simple observation would therefore suffice for this purpose.

2. Containers on which Deposits are Charged to Customers

There are containers which many purchasers would not return if they were not charged with a deposit refunded only on return. These are obviously containers which require more than a marginal effort to return, or those which could be put to alternative uses. The deposit chargeable must therefore be sufficient to discourage the purchaser from keeping the containers after use, but should not be so great as to deter him from buying the goods in the first place. In some instances a time limit is fixed within which the container is to be returned to obtain a cancellation of the deposit charged. Common sense must however prevail, as it would be unwise to refuse refunds of deposits in circumstances which could bring about a worsening in the firm's relationship with customers it wished to retain.

Accounting must therefore fulfil two needs, (a) it must enable some form of check on the stock of containers, and (b) it must reveal the amount of deposit returnable to customers. This can be satisfied, for (a) a Containers Stock Account can be kept, and for (b) a Containers Suspense Account may be opened.

Chapter 29 has already illustrated the need for the depreciation of containers to be provided normally by the Revaluation method. The Container Stock Account will therefore provide for the depreciation element by the process of revaluing the containers at the end of each accounting period. Each container account may also include, in addition to the £ columns, further columns for quantities and for the monetary rates at which the transactions are carried out.

Exhibit 31.2

A new firm, Duncan and Co, sells its goods in crates on which a deposit is chargeable to the customer, a credit being allowed on their return within three months.

During the year ended 31 December 19–5:

(A) 50 crates were bought for £3 each.

(B) 180 crates were sent to customers, these being charged to their accounts at £4 deposit each. You may well wonder how 180 crates can be sent out when only 50 have been bought by Duncan and Co. The fact is that the figure of 180 consists of recounting the same crates, as they are sent out and returned several times each year. However, during the year 180 debits of £4 each have been made in customers' accounts.

(C) 150 crates were returned by customers, credits being entered in their accounts for £4 each.

(D) 10 crates were kept by customers beyond the three months' limit, and they therefore forfeited their right to return them to obtain a refund of the deposit.

(E) 2 crates were damaged and were sold for £1 each.

On 31 December 19–5 the following facts are relevant:

(F) There were 20 returnable crates with customers.

(G) There were 18 crates at Duncan and Co's warehouse.

The stock of crates at 31 December 19–5 are to be valued at £2 each to provide for depreciation through usage.

The identifying letters (A) to (G) are shown against the recorded transactions in the accounts that now follow.

Containers Stock

	Rate	Quan- tity	£			Rate	Quan- tity	£
			£					£
19–5				19–5				
Dec 31 Cash (during the year) (A)	3	50	150	Dec 31 Containers Suspense: kept by customers (D)	4	10	40
				„ 31 Cash: damaged crates (E)	1	2	2
				„ 31 Profit and Loss: Cost of container usage			32
				„ 31 Stock: c/d In Warehouse (G)	2	18	36
				At Customers (F)	2	20	40
		50	150			50	150

19–6
Jan 1 Stock b/d

		Rate	Quantity	
In Warehouse (G)		2	18	36
At Customers (F)		2	20	40

Containers Suspense

		Rate	Quantity	£	£			Rate	Quantity	£	£
19–5						19–5					
Dec 31	Sales Ledger: crates credited to customers' accounts on return (C)	4	150		600	Dec 31	Sales Ledger: crates charged to customers' accounts (B)	4	180		720
„ 31	Containers Stock: kept by customers (D)	4	10		40						
„ 31	Deposits on crates returnable c/d (F)	4	20		80						
				180	720					180	720
						19–6					
						Jan 1	Deposits on crates returnable b/d (F)	4	20		80

The Balance Sheet will show the balances in the following manner:

Duncan & Co
Balance Sheet as at 31 December 19–5

	£		£
Containers Suspense— deposits returnable	80	Crates—at valuation	76

Sometimes containers are charged out to customers at an initial price greater than that allowed on their return. The difference therefore represents a hiring charge. If the same data is taken as in Exhibit 31.2 but instead of £4 being allowed on return this had been restricted to £3 instead, then the accounts would have appeared as follows:

Containers Stock

		Rate	Quan-tity	£			Rate	Quan-tity	£
		£		£			£		£
19–5					19–5				
Dec 31	Cash (during the year)	3	50	150	Dec 31	Containers Suspense: kept by customers	3	10	30
„ 31	Profit and Loss: Profit on container usage			138	„ 31	Cash: damaged crates	1	2	2
					„ 31	Containers Suspense: Hiring charge			180
					„ 31	Stock: c/d			
						In Warehouse	2	18	36
						At Customers	2	20	40
			50	288				50	288
19–6									
Jan 1	Stock b/d								
	In Warehouse	2	18	36					
	At Customers	2	20	40					

Containers Suspense

		Rate	Quan-tity	£			Rate	Quan-tity	£
		£		£			£		£
19–5					19–5				
Dec 31	Sales Ledger: crates credited to customers' accounts on return		150	450	Dec 31	Sales Ledger: crates charged to customers' accounts	4	180	720
„ 31	Containers Stock: kept by customers	3	10	30					
„ 31	Containers Stock: Hiring charge			180					
„ 31	Deposits on crates returnable	3	20	60					
			180	720				180	720
					19–6				
					Jan 1	Deposits on crates returnable b/d	3	20	60

The Balance Sheet would have appeared in the following manner:

Duncan & Co
Balance Sheet as at 31 December 19–5

	£		£
Current Liabilities			
Containers Suspense—		Crates—at valuation	76
deposits returnable	60		

Exercises

31.1. D. Clark's manufactures are sold in boxes which are returnable. They are charged out to customers at £8 each and credit of £6 is given for each box returned within two months. For the purpose of the annual accounts, the value of boxes in the factory and those in customers' hands, which had been invoiced within two months, was taken as being £1·5 each. The quantities of these on 31 January 19–3 were 600 and 4,000 respectively.

The following were the transactions as regards boxes during the year ended 31 January 19–3:

Purchases—5,000 at £2 each.
Invoiced to customers—17,000.
Returned by customers—14,000.
450 could no longer be used and were sold, realising £100.

The number of boxes invoiced after 30 November 19–3 and still in customers' hands on 31 January 19–4 was 6,200.

Write up the accounts in the books of D. Clark to record these transactions and to show the profit on boxes and the quantities involved.

31.2. A company makes a charge to its customers for cases in which the product is delivered. If they are returned in good condition within two months a refund is made.

At the start of the year there were 9,600 cases in stock at the company's warehouse and 6,100 in the hands of customers supplied within the previous two months. The company bought 18,000 new cases during the year and following a dispute with a supplier returned 4,000 new cases for which a credit note of £11,610 was received. At 31 December 19–6 there were still in the hands of customers 4,800 supplied during the previous two months.

During the year 19–6, 47,600 cases were sent to customers and 43,100 returned by them. The company scrapped 3,500 damaged cases and sold the timber for £55. A physical check of cases in stock at 31 December 19–6 revealed an unaccounted deficit of 420 cases.

New cases cost £3 each
Charged out to customers at £5 each
Credited on return at £4 each
Valued for stocktaking at £2 each

Show the accounts in the books for 19–6 to record the above, and the balances of cases, in quantities and values at 31 December 19–6.

You are entitled to deduce the following missing information from the details above:

(a) The number of cases kept by customers over the two-month limit for returning them.

(b) The number of cases in the warehouse on 31 December 19–6.

31.3A. K.R.R. Ltd sells goods in containers which are charged to customers at 20p each. Customers are credited with 12½p for each container returned within four months.

On 31 December 19–7, there were 1,580 containers on the company's premises and 5,520 containers, the time limit for the return of which had not expired, were held by customers.

During 19–8:

(i) K.R.R. Ltd purchased 8,700 containers for 10p each.

(ii) 26,460 containers were charged to customers.

(iii) 23,720 containers were returned by customers and credited to them.

On 31 December 19–8, customers held 6,000 containers, the time limit for the return of which had not expired.

For purposes of the annual accounts of K.R.R. Ltd, all stocks of containers on the company's premises and returnable containers in the possession of customers are valued, at 10p each.

You are required to show the container stock account and the container trading account for the year 19–8. These accounts should be provided with additional memorandum columns in which quantities are to be shown.

(Chartered Institute of Secretaries and Administrators)

31.4A. The G Company supplies gas in expensive containers which are returnable after use. These containers cost £20 each and are charged out to customers on sale or return within six months at £26 each. Provided they are returned within the six months period they are credited at £23 each. As each container is returned it is inspected and overhauled at a cost of £2.

At the end of the year the company values all returnable containers in customers hands and containers held in stock at £16 each.

You are advised that:

	At the beginning of the year	At the end of the year
Containers held by the company	2,760	3,144
Returnable containers held by customers	4,790	2,910

During the year 3,100 new containers were purchased, 20,620 were invoiced to customers and 17,960 were returned. On inspection 260 required additional repairs costing £325 and 56 had to be sold as scrap for £60.

From the information given above prepare:

(a) returnable containers suspense account;

(b) an account showing the profit or loss on dealings in containers.

(Institute of Cost and Management Accountants)

32

Royalty Accounts

In some classes of business the owner of some form of privilege or monopoly can allow other firms to utilise this right, the owner being remunerated by reference to the extent which it has been used. The name given to payments for certain of these rights is 'royalty'. Instances of payments of royalties are as follows:

(*a*) For the extraction of minerals from the ground.
(*b*) The publisher of a book remunerating the author.
(*c*) For the use of a patent.

Where the remuneration is simply a case of a fixed amount per unit of use the accounting necessary is quite straightforward. The payer of the royalty will simply charge it as an expense in a Royalty Account.

Complications start to appear when a certain minimum amount is payable per annum even though the actual use of the right may result in a lesser figure for royalties. Such agreements are commonly found in the case of mining and quarrying. These agreements are understandable because of the desire of the owner to be certain of a minimum income. Without a minimum amount the lack of activity on the part of the user would result in a small income for the owner. Carried to extremes no activity would result in no income. On the other hand, the user would probably feel aggrieved if he not only had to pay the minimum amount in a period of low activity but also have to pay the full amount in a period of high activity. The part of the minimum amount not represented by use of the right, in the case of a mine, is known as 'short workings'. It is very often found that royalty agreements provide for such short workings to be carried forward to reduce royalties payable in future years where the activity results in the royalties being in excess of the minimum agreed amount. A limit is usually set upon the number of years for which such short workings can be carried forward for this purpose. Once the final date has been reached, such short workings are then irrecoupable. Exhibit 32.1 illustrates such a case.

Exhibit 32.1

The lessor of a mine is to pay £1 for each ton of ore extracted. The minimum rent is to be £400 per annum. Any payments for short workings are recoupable only in the two years following that in which they occurred. The following table shows the effect of extraction figures contained in column (*a*). As the minimum rent is £400, then obviously column (*b*) must never show a figure of less than £400.

Year	(a) Tons extracted	(b) Payable	(c) Short workings carried forward	(d) Short workings recouped	(e) Short workings now irrecoupable
	£	£	£	£	£
1	420	420			
2	310	400	90		
3	560	470		90	
4	280	400	120		
5	440	400	80	40	
6	450	400		50	30
7	780	780			

Notes:

Column (*c*) shows the value of the short workings at the end of each year which can still be set off against future royalties. £120 is carried forward at the end of year 4, of this £40 is set off against the royalties for year 5, leaving £80 carried forward at the end of year 5.

Column (*e*). The £120 short workings originating in year 4 are partly recouped by £40 in year 5 and £50 in year 6. The remaining £30 can no longer be recouped as the time limit of two years following the year of origin comes into play. The £30 cannot therefore be carried forward to year 7, so that it is in year 6 that it is shown as being irrecoupable.

The short workings carried forward can in fact be likened to the pre-payment of an expense. The minimum amount exceeds the actual royalties, therefore the excess is in effect a prepayment of royalties.

All of the accounting calculations have now been made, the only action necessary is that the table is to be translated into double entry terms. This now follows. It is assumed that the financial year is the same as the calendar year and that the landlord is paid on the last day of each year.

Royalties

		£			£
Year 1			Year 1		
Dec 31	Landlord	420	Dec 31	Operating Account (A)	420
Year 2			Year 2		
Dec 31	Landlord	310	Dec 31	Operating	310

Royalties

	£			£
Year 3			Year 3	
Dec 31 Landlord	560		Dec 31 Operating	560
Year 4			Year 4	
Dec 31 Landlord	280		Dec 31 Operating	280
Year 5			Year 5	
Dec 31 Landlord	440		Dec 31 Operating	440
Year 6			Year 6	
Dec 31 Landlord	450		Dec 31 Operating	450
Year 7			Year 7	
Dec 31 Landlord	780		Dec 31 Operating	780

Short Workings

	£			£
Year 2			Year 3	
Dec 31 Landlord	90		Dec 31 Landlord (recouped amount)	90
Year 4			Year 5	
Dec 31 Landlord	120		Dec 31 Landlord (recouped amount)	40
			Year 5	
			Dec 31 Balance c/d	80
	120			120
Year 6			Year 6	
Jan 1 Balance b/d	80		Dec 31 Landlord (recouped amount)	50
			„ 31 Profit and Loss—amount now irrecoupable	30
	80			80

Landlord

	£			£
Year 1			Year 1	
Dec 31 Cash	420		Dec 31 Royalties	420

| | *Landlord* | | | |
	£			£

Year 2			Year 2		
Dec 31	Cash	400	Dec 31	Royalties	310
			,, 31	Short Workings	90
		400			400
Year 3			Year 3		
Dec 31	Short Workings—		Dec 31	Royalties	560
	recouped	90			
,, 31	Cash	470			
		560			560
Year 4			Year 4		
Dec 31	Cash	400	Dec 31	Royalties	280
			,, 31	Short Workings	120
		400			400
Year 5			Year 5		
Dec 31	Short Workings—		Dec 31	Royalties	440
	recouped	40			
,, 31	Cash	400			
		440			440
Year 6			Year 6		
Dec 31	Short Workings—		Dec 31	Royalties	450
	recouped	50			
,, 31	Cash	400			
		450			450
Year 7			Year 7		
Dec 31	Cash	780	Dec 31	Royalties	780

Operating Account for the year(s) ended 31 December . . . (extracts)

		£
Year 1	Royalties	420
Year 2	,,	310
Year 3	,,	560
Year 4	,,	280
Year 5	,,	440
Year 6	,,	450
Year 7	,,	780

Profit and Loss Account for the year(s) ended 31 December . . . (extracts)

	£
Year 6 Irrecoupable Short Workings Written off (B)	30

Balance Sheet(s) as at 31 December (extracts)
Current Assets

	£
Year 2 Short Workings Recoupable	90
Year 4 Short Workings Recoupable	120
Year 5 Short Workings Recoupable	80

Notes:
(A) The term Operating Account is used. This could instead be called a Working Account or a similar name could be used; in the case of a manufacturer it would be Manufacturing Account. Where royalties are paid per unit of use they can be seen to be an example of what in costing would be called a direct expense.

(B) The irrecoupable short workings can hardly be charged to an Operating Account, as they are an expense connected with non-operation.

It must not be thought that the method described is the only one by which the double entry can be carried out. Obviously the various methods finish up with the same answers eventually, it is merely the ways by which these answers are worked out that are different.

Exercises

32.1. Smoker, who had patented a tobacco filter, granted to Piper & Co a licence for seven years to manufacture and sell the filter on the following terms:
  (i) Piper & Co to pay a royalty of £1 for every 100 filters sold with a minimum payment of £1,000 per annum. Calculations to be made annually as on 31 December, and payment on 31 January.
  (ii) If, for any year, the royalties calculated on filters sold amount to less than £1,000, Piper & Co may set off the deficiency against royalties payable in excess of that sum in the next two years.

The number of filters sold were:
Year to 31 December
19–1	60,000
19–2	80,000
19–3	120,000
19–4	140,000

You are required to show the ledger accounts recording the above transactions in respect of royalties in the books of Piper & Co, which are closed annually on 31 December.

(Institute of Chartered Accountants)

32.2. J.B. owned the patent rights for a bottle opener. On 1 April 19–2 he granted R.S. & Co Ltd a licence for ten years to manufacture and sell the bottle opener on the following terms:

(i) R.S. & Co Ltd were to pay J.B. a royalty of £0·05 for each opener sold.
(ii) The minimum royalty for each of the first three years covered by the licence was to be £500.
(iii) If royalties on openers sold amounted to less than £500 R.S. & Co Ltd were entitled to deduct the deficiency from royalties in excess of that sum payable in respect of each of the first three years of the agreement.
(iv) After the first three years royalties were to be payable on the actual number of bottle openers sold each year.
(v) Accounts were to be settled to 31 March in each year.

The numbers of bottle openers sold in the first four years were as follows:

Year ended 31 March
19–3	8,600
19–4	9,800
19–5	10,900
19–6	10,500

Show the accounts relating to the above transactions in the books of R.S. & Co Ltd for the first four years of the agreement.

(Associated Examining Board 'A' Level)

32.3. Shipton, who had patented an automatic door closer, granted Doors Ltd a licence for ten years to manufacture and sell the closer on the following terms:

(i) Doors Ltd to pay a royalty of £1 for every closer sold with a minimum payment of £500 per annum. Calculations to be made annually as on 31 December and payment to be made on 31 January.
(ii) If, for any year, the royalties calculated on closers sold amount to less than £500, Doors Ltd may set off the deficiency against royalties payable in excess of that sum in the next two years.

With effect from the end of the second year the agreement was varied and a minimum annual payment of £400 was substituted for £500, the other terms of the annual agreement remaining unchanged.

The numbers of the closers sold were:

Year ended 31 December
19–2	200
19–3	400
19–4	600
19–5	500

You are required to show the ledger accounts recording the above transactions in respect of royalties in the books of Doors Ltd which are closed annually on 31 December.

(Institute of Chartered Accountants)

32.4A. Laurie Ltd (sand and gravel merchants) entered into an agreement to purchase from Sands Ltd over a period of five years such quantities of sand as they might require from time to time and which they were to extract from a sand pit belonging to Sands Ltd on the following terms:

1.   Laurie Ltd to pay a royalty of 10p per ton for all material extracted with a minimum rent of £2,000 per annum.

2.   If, for any of the first three years, the royalties on sand extracted fall short of the minimum rent, the short fall is to be set off against any royalties payable in excess of the rent for those three years.

3.   The following quantities were extracted:

	Tons
First year	4,000
Second year	16,000
Third year	28,000

Prepare the ledger accounts recording these transactions in the books of Laurie Ltd, assuming that the payments due for any year were made during the following year.

Income Tax is to be ignored.

(*Association of Certified Accountants*)

32.5A. Close, who had patented an automatic dish washer, granted Sinks Ltd a licence for ten years to manufacture and sell the washer on the following terms:

1.   Sinks Ltd to pay a royalty of £1 for every washer sold with a minimum payment of £5,000 per annum. Calculations to be made annually as on 31 December and payment to be made on 31 January.

2.   If, for any year, the royalties calculated on washers sold amount to less than £5,000, Sinks Ltd may set off the deficiency against royalties payable in excess of that sum in the next two years.

As from the commencement of the third year the agreement was varied, and a minimum annual payment of £4,000 was substituted for £5,000, the other terms of the agreement remaining unchanged.

The number of washers sold were:

Year ended 31 December
19–6	2,000
19–7	4,000
19–8	6,000
19–9	5,000

You are required to prepare the following ledger accounts recording the above transactions in respect of royalties in the books of Sinks Ltd which are closed annually on 31 December:

(*a*)   royalties account,
(*b*)   short workings account, and
(*c*)   the account of Close.

(*Institute of Chartered Accountants*)

32.6A. White, who manufactures fasteners, uses leased machines for this purpose.
   The terms of the lease for each machine provide that:

1. The lessee should pay a royalty of £5 for every 100 fasteners produced.

2. The minimum royalty should be £500 per annum.

3. The lessee could recoup in the second year any short workings in the first year of leasing the machine.

Details in respect of three machines leased were as follows:

Machine Number	1	2	3
Date lease commenced	1 Jan. 19–4	1 Jan. 19–5	1 Jan. 19–6
Production of fasteners:			
Year ended 31 December			
19–4	8,000	—	—
19–5	15,000	10,200	—
19–6	17,400	9,600	8,900
19–7	18,100	12,400	7,400

You are required to show the ledger accounts recording the above transactions in respect of royalties in the books of White, which are closed annually on 31 December.

(*Institute of Chartered Accountants*)

33

Hire Purchase and Payments by Instalments

When goods are bought under a hire purchase agreement, the legal title to the goods does not pass to the purchaser until every instalment has been paid and a small amount, usually included in the last payment, is paid which legally exercises an option to buy the goods. Thus to buy on hire purchase is legally to hire the goods until a certain time, when an option can be exercised to take over the legal title to the goods. Normally the hire purchaser is not compelled to complete the transaction. If he so wishes he may return the goods and not pay any further instalments. He will, however, forfeit the right to have any of his previous instalments repaid to him. On default the seller can reclaim the goods, subject to certain provisions of the Hire Purchase Acts.

In contrast to this are credit sales payable by instalments, in which the absolute ownership passes immediately to the purchaser. The seller cannot reclaim the goods, but can sue for the unpaid instalments. There is also a class of sale known as a 'conditional sale agreement', which legally has some of the characteristics of both hire purchase and credit sale transactions.

A book on Hire Purchase Law should be studied for the precise legal position of the three types of sales payable for by instalments. From the accounting point of view the three types have a great deal in common. The total amount payable for the asset is made up of (*a*) the cash price, this being the amount that would have been payable if payment has been made immediately on acquisition instead of being paid for by instalments, and (*b*) the interest element. A firm would not normally sell goods for exactly the same price to customer (i) who is being given two years to pay for the goods by regular instalments, than they would to customer (ii) who is to pay immediately for the goods. Therefore customer (i) will have to pay something extra to compensate the selling firm for extra administration expenses, the risk element of default by the purchaser, and the loss of working capital for a period of time. The rate of interest should therefore be fixed so that it is adequate to cover these items.

Exhibit 33.1

A car which had a cash sale price of £500 might have a hire purchase price of £600 calculated as follows:

	£
Cash Price	500
Add Hire Purchase Interest—10 per cent of £500 for two years	100
Hire Purchase Price	600

Payable by 24 monthly instalments of £25 each.

Substitute the words 'credit sale' or 'conditional sale' for the words 'hire purchase' and the facts apply to these other two cases.

Of course, requirements concerning deposits and lengths of repayment allowed change with various governmental attempts to control the economy. If a deposit of £100 had been required, the agreement for the car may have been as follows:

Exhibit 33.2

	£
Cash Price	500
Add Hire Purchase Interest—10 per cent of £400 for two years	80
Hire Purchase Price	580

Deposit of £100 paid, therefore the interest is only calculated on the actual amount owing, i.e. £500−£100=£400. Payment is completed by 24 monthly instalments of £20 each.

From this point in the chapter the items dealt with will be goods bought and sold on hire purchase. The accounting treatment of credit sale and conditional sale items can well be exactly the same as for hire purchase items. Therefore in each of the examples the substitution of 'credit sale' or 'conditional sale' would convert the method from being one used only for hire purchase.

Hire Purchaser's Books

Because of the restriction on the resale of goods bought on hire purchase the goods normally bought by a firm are in the nature of fixed assets. There are those who maintain that as the legal title to the goods does not pass until the final payment has been made, then it is wrong to bring the full cash price into the books until this has been done. This would seem to be an extreme view in most cases, and one which should normally be avoided. The vast majority of firms enter into hire purchase agreements with the intention of honouring them. Hire purchase is nothing more than the means of financing the purchase of a fixed asset. To capitalise only the proportion of the cash price actually paid is a case of the convention of conservatism being carried to extremes. It is also misleading to anyone who is interested in the analysis of the Balance Sheet, as the fixed assets which have been used to win the profits are not fully represented. This method will not therefore be used in this book.

The main problem is that of splitting the amount actually paid between that which refers to hire purchase interest and that which refers to a reduction in the amount of the cash price still owing. Hire purchase interest is normally the cost of borrowing money which is used to buy a fixed asset. Like the cost of borrowing money generally, such as bank overdraft interest or loan interest, it is revenue expenditure and should therefore be charged to the Profit and Loss Account. The cash price is the actual cost of the asset itself; the fact that the asset is bought on hire purchase has no relevance as far as the asset itself is concerned. The extra money paid for hire purchase is due, not to the asset itself but because the firm did not possess the amount of liquid resources available at the time of purchase to pay for the asset immediately. The cash price is therefore capital expenditure and will have to be shown accordingly in the Balance Sheet. If the hire purchase agreement was begun and terminated in the same accounting period, then the apportioning of the amount actually paid between hire purchase interest and the cash price would be a simple matter. If a car was bought for a total hire purchase price of £96, being cash price £90 and hire purchase interest £6, and this was paid by six monthly instalments of £16 each, then the Cash Book would show credits of £96 in all and the debits would be £90 in the Motor Car Account and £6 in the Hire Purchase Interest Account. Either an intermediate account called a Hire Purchase Account could be used to which the £96 would be debited, and the £90 and the £6 then transferred to the relevant accounts, or else with every credit of £16 in the Cash Book the debits could be made of £1 in the Hire Purchase Interest Account and of £15 in the Motor Car Account. The full cash price of £90 would still show in the Balance Sheet, because the purchase is completed before the year end.

On the other hand, where the agreement is not started and completed within the accounting period, then the separation of the interest from the proportion of the cash price paid is not a simple matter. The aim is to show the full cash price of the asset in the Balance Sheet. If not fully paid for, then the amount owing will have to also be shown in the Balance Sheet as being owed. This is similar to any asset bought which has not been paid for at the Balance Sheet date. However, the liability to be shown is not the amount of the hire purchase price that is to be paid, but is instead confined to the part of the cash price which still has to be paid. The hire purchase interest which has to be paid in the future is not a liability of the firm at that point in time. Interest is essentially based on the time factor and is only charged in the Profit and Loss Account when it accrues. Therefore future hire purchase interest will only be chargeable as an expense during the years when it accrues, and is not chargeable in this year's Profit and Loss Account. This is rather like saying that if premises were bought they would be shown as an asset in the Balance Sheet, and that if they were only partly paid for, then the liability would also be shown in the Balance Sheet, but revenue expenditure such as rates will only appear in the accounts, and therefore in the Balance Sheet as a liability as it falls due.

How accurately this can be done depends on whether or not the 'true' running rate of interest is known. In Exhibit 33.3 below the rate of interest is stated to be 10 per cent per annum. This interest is only payable on the amounts actually owing from time to time, i.e. the interest is calculated on the reducing balance owed. On the other hand, if the interest is calculated as a percentage rate of the original amount owing, then this is not a 'true' running rate of interest. An example of this is in Exhibit 31.1 where a car is bought for £500 and the interest chargeable is said to be 10 per cent. The 10 per cent for two years was calculated by reference to the £500, the original amount owing. However, after each instalment has been paid the amount of the £500 still owing will fall. The 'true' running rate of interest refers to the interest rate per annum which would have to be applied to each reducing balance so as to bring the amount owing down to zero after the payment of the last instalment.

The accurate calculation of the 'true' rate is quite involved, but there is a method used which is satisfactory for normal use by a firm which does not have substantial dealings in hire purchase and where repayment is by equal instalments. The formula for this is:

$$\frac{\text{Nominal rate*} \times 2 \times \text{Number of instalments}}{\text{Number of instalments} + 1} = \text{True rate of interest}$$

* Nominal rate means the interest applied to the original amount owing, e.g. in the case just mentioned the nominal rate was 10 per cent. The true rate was therefore:

$$\frac{10 \times 2 \times 24}{24 + 1} = \frac{480}{25} = 19 \cdot 2 \text{ per cent}$$

The 'true' rate is thus considerably more than the nominal rate.

The accuracy of the method of calculating the 'true' rate can now be tested.

Exhibit 33.3

A car is bought on hire purchase on 1 January 19–5, the price being as follows:

	£
Cash Price	300
Add Interest—6⅔ per cent per annum (nominal rate) for three years	60
	360

Repayable by three annual instalments of £120, payable on 31 December of each year.

$$\text{True rate of interest} = \frac{6\frac{2}{3} \times 2 \times 3}{3+1} = \frac{40}{4} = 10 \text{ per cent per annum}$$

	£
Proof: Cash Price	300
Add Interest 19–5. 10 per cent of £300	30
	330
Less paid 31 December 19–5	120
	210
Owing 1 January 19–6	210
Add Interest 19–6. 10 per cent of £210	21
	231
Less paid 31 December 19–6	120
	111
Owing 1 January 19–7	111
Add Interest 19–7	11·1
	122·1
Less paid 31 December 19–7	120
Owing 1 January 19–8	—
Error in approximating 'true' rate of interest	2·1

Therefore in considering financing operations one must consider like with like. It is no use comparing the nominal rate of interest offered by one organization against the 'true' rate offered by another. Comparison can only be achieved by data calculated on the same basis, and therefore the two rates should be expressed as 'true' rates. An example of this is the bank overdraft on which interest is expressed in 'true' interest terms, while a personal bank loan is in 'nominal' rate terms. Hire purchase interest rates, especially in the retail field, are usually expressed in nominal rate terms.

The necessary accounts needed can now be considered.

Exhibit 33.4

1. True Rate of Interest Known. Equal Instalments

A machine is bought for £3,618 hire purchase price from Suppliers Ltd on 1 January 19–3, being paid for by three instalments of £1,206 on 31 December of 19–3, 19–4 and 19–5. The cash price is £3,000. The true rate of interest is 10 per cent. (For convenience all figures are rounded off, fractions of pounds are not shown.)

Machinery

19–3			£
Jan 1 Suppliers Ltd	(A)	3,000	

Suppliers Ltd

19–3			£	19–3			£
Dec 31 Bank	(B)	1,206		Jan 1 Machinery	(A)	3,000
„ 31 Balance c/d	(D)	2,094		Dec 31 H.P. Interest	(C)	300
		3,300				3,300
19–4				19–4			
Dec 31 Bank	(B)	1,206		Jan 1 Balance b/d	(D)	2,094
„ 31 Balance c/d	(D)	1,097		Dec 31 H.P. Interest	(C)	209
		2,303				2,303
19–5				19–5			
Dec 31 Bank	(B)	1,206		Jan 1 Balance b/d	(D)	1,097
				Dec 31 H.P. Interest	(C)	109
		1,206				1,206

Hire Purchase Interest

19–3			£	19–3			£
Dec 31 Suppliers Ltd	(C)	300		Dec 31 Profit and Loss	(E)	300
19–4				19–4			
Dec 31 Suppliers Ltd	(C)	209		Dec 31 Profit and Loss	(E)	209
19–5				19–5			
Dec 31 Suppliers Ltd	(C)	109		Dec 31 Profit and Loss	(E)	109

Provision for Depreciation: Machinery

			19–3			£
			Dec 31 Profit and Loss	(F)	600
			19–4			
			Dec 31 Profit and Loss	(F)	600
			19–5			
			Dec 31 Profit and Loss	(F)	600

Balance Sheets as at 31 December

		£	£	£
19–3	Machinery (at cost)		3,000	
	Less Depreciation	600		
	„ Owing on Hire Purchase Agreement	2,094		
			2,694	
				306
19–4	Machinery (at cost)		3,000	
	Less Depreciation to date	1,200		
	„ Owing on Hire Purchase Agreement	1,097		
			2,297	
				703
19–5	Machinery (at cost)		3,000	
	Less Depreciation to date		1,800	
				1,200

Description of entries:

(A) When the asset is acquired the cash price is debited to the asset account and the credit is in the supplier's account.

(B) The instalments paid are credited to the Bank Account and debited to the supplier's account.

(C) The interest is credited to the supplier's account for each period as it accrues, and debited to the expense account, later to be transferred to the Profit and Loss Account for the period (E).

(D) The balance carried down each year is the amount of the cash price still owing.

(F) Depreciation provisions are calculated on the full cash price, as the depreciation of an asset is in no way affected by whether or not it has been fully paid for.

The Balance Sheet consists of balance (A) the cash price, less balance (F) the amount of the cash price apportioned as depreciation, less balance (D) the amount of the cash price still owing at each Balance Sheet date.

2. True Rate of Interest Known. Unequal Instalments

Sometimes the cash price portion is repaid by equal instalments, while the interest portion is paid as it accrues. As the interest falls due, the proportion of the cash price owing on which the interest is based is being reduced each year, thus it will be obvious that the total repayments will be different for each accounting period.

Assuming that the same details applied as in (1), but that £1,000 was to be paid off the cash price each year, plus the whole of the interest as it accrued, then Suppliers Ltd Account would appear as follows:

Exhibit 33.5

Suppliers Ltd

19–3		£	19–3		£
Dec 31	Bank	1,300	Jan 1	Machinery	3,000
„ 31	Balance c/d	2,000	Dec 31	H.P. Interest (10 per cent of £3,000)	300
		3,300			3,300
19–4			19–4		
Dec 31	Bank	1,200	Jan 1	Balance b/d	2,000
„ 31	Balance c/d	1,000	Dec 31	H.P. Interest (10 per cent of £2,000)	200
		2,200			2,200
19–5			19–5		
Dec 31	Bank	1,100	Jan 1	Balance b/d	1,000
			Dec 31	H.P. Interest (10 per cent of £1,000)	100
		1,100			1,100

All the ways in which the debit and credit entries were made in (1) will be repeated in this case. The only difference will be that the figures will be governed by the transfers now to be effected from Suppliers Ltd Account.

Where the rate of interest expressed on the hire purchase agreement was a nominal rate, many firms have not known how to determine the 'true' rate, or else have just not bothered to calculate it. They have either (a) apportioned the interest equally on a time basis, for instance in (1) the total interest is £618, and some firms will have apportioned this as £206 for each year, or (b) have used an approximation of the average cash price owing. By this method the interest would have been apportioned as follows:

Cash price is £3,000, therefore it is assumed that this is paid off equally at £1,000 per annum. The average amount then outstanding is expressed as a ratio of the average amounts outstanding for the other years.

	Average amount outstanding. Owing at start of year + owing at end of year divided by 2	Proportion of interest	Amount credited as interest in the supplier's account for the year
19–3	$\frac{£3,000 + £2,000}{2} = £2,500$	$\frac{£2,500}{£4,500} \times £618 =$	£343

	Average amount outstanding. Owing at start of year+ owing at end of year divided by 2	Proportion of interest	Amount credited as interest in the supplier's account for the year
19–4	$\dfrac{£2,000+£1,000}{2}=£1,500$	$\dfrac{£1,500}{£4,500}\times£618=$	£206
19–5	$\dfrac{£1,000+£0}{2}=£500$	$\dfrac{£500}{£4,500}\times£618=$	£69
	£4,500		£618

Interest on money borrowed is affected by (i) the amount owing from time to time, and (ii) the time factor. Method (1) recognises this, while (a) takes only the time factor into account and ignores completely the fact that interest is dependent on the different amounts owing, and (b) is an attempt to take both (i) and (ii) into consideration, but uses a rule of thumb method which is not reasonably accurate.

It is fairly obvious that large firms will not rely to any great extent on the financing of the purchase of fixed assets by normal hire purchase. The interest costs of a bank overdraft or of a bank loan will often be considerably less than the normal interest costs under hire purchase. The smaller firms which rely on hire purchase, perhaps because of inability to obtain funds from the bank, or simply because management does not properly compare interest costs, will not have such sophisticated accounting methods.

The Seller's Books

There are a considerable number of ways of drawing up the final accounts of a business which sells goods on hire purchase and of calculating the amounts to be shown therein. The methods chosen should be suitable for the particular firm and needs obviously vary. There is a vast gulf between the old-established firm which sells quality goods to well-known reputable customers, and the back-street firm which sells cheap, easily breakable goods, to anyone without enquiring very deeply as to the customer's creditworthiness.

It can, however, be stipulated that the interest earned from hire purchase sales is earned because money is owed to the firm for a period of time. The interest that should be credited to the Trading Account is therefore the amount which has accrued during the period covered by the account.

On the other hand the profit made on the goods sold is usually either:

(a) Treated as being profit of the firm entirely in the period in which it was first sold to the purchaser, i.e. when the agreement was entered into and the goods delivered to him.

(b) A proportion of the profits is brought into the Trading Account, this being in the ratio which the cash actually received during the period bears to the total cash receivable.

It is inappropriate in a book at this level to go into intricate details of the methods used in practice by firms. With firms that have many hire purchase transactions the methods of apportioning interest and profit are often ones of expediency, exact accuracy often being too costly to achieve. Therefore in an examination the examiner's instructions should always be carried out, he may be envisaging such a situation. The fact that the examinee may disagree with the method used is irrelevant for this purpose.

Exhibit 33.6 shows the accounts needed by a firm with two departments, one department uses method (a), while the other department uses method (b).

Exhibit 33.6

A. Phelps started business on 1 January 19–5. He sold washing machines of a uniform type which cost him £90 each, for a cash price of £120, and also on hire purchase terms for £140, being payable by a deposit of £20 followed by three instalments of £40 each on the first, second and third anniversaries of the date of the contract. The total price of £140 included compound interest at 10 per cent on the reducing balance owed (calculated after each year's payment) of the normal cash price. It is assumed that the sales were evenly spread over the year.

He also sold food mixers of a uniform type on hire purchase only. These required an initial deposit of £6 followed by 12 quarterly instalments of £2 each over a period of three years. The cost of the food mixers was £18 each.

The following trial balance was extracted as on 31 December 19–5:

	£	£
Capital: Cash Introduced		50,000
Fixed Assets	10,000	
Hire Purchase Sales—Washing Machines (200 at £140 each)		28,000
Cash Sales—Washing Machines (50 at £120 each)		6,000
Cash collected from hire purchasers of food mixers (1,000 mixers sold)		9,600
Debtors	24,000	
Purchases—Washing Machines (350 at £90)	31,500	
Purchases—Food Mixers (1,200 at £18)	21,600	
Bank	8,900	
Creditors		6,400
Salaries and General Expenses	4,000	
	100,000	100,000

It was decided to take credit, in the annual accounts, for the normal gross profit (excluding interest) on washing machines sold to customers and to apportion the interest on a time basis.

In view of the large number of transactions in food mixers, and the difficulty of apportioning the interest, it was decided to adopt for this section of the business the alternative method of taking credit for the profit, including interest, on food mixers only in proportion to the cash collected.

Stocks were valued at cost, being washing machines (100) £9,000, and food mixers (200) £3,600.

The following accounts demonstrate the methods used. The letters (A) to (H) refer to the narratives which follow the accounts and are needed to explain those items that are not self-evident.

Washing Machines Trading Account for the year ended 31 December 19–5

		£			£
Purchases		31,500	Cash Sales		6,000
Less Stock		9,000	Hire Purchase Sales		
			—at Cash Prices	(A)	24,000
Cost of Goods Sold		22,500	Hire Purchase		
Gross Profit		8,500	Interest	(C)	1,000
		31,000			31,000

Washing Machines–Interest Suspense

		£			£
Trading Account— 10% per annum on £20,000 for six months	(C)	1,000	Hire Purchase Sales —Interest included in Hire Purchase Price	(B)	4,000
Interest not yet earned c/d	(D)	3,000			
		4,000			4,000

Washing Machines—Hire Purchase Sales

		£			£
Interest Suspense— 200 × £20	(B)	4,000	Debtors		28,000
Trading Account— Cash Price of Sales	(A)	24,000			
		28,000			28,000

(A) As the interest factor of profit is being calculated separately the cash price of goods sold on hire purchase is transferred so that the goods factor of profit can be dealt with.

(B) The whole interest factor is transferred to the suspense account.

(C) The apportionment of the interest earned in this period is now calculated. For simplicity it has been stated that the sales were spread evenly throughout the year. This means that the average time that money was owing was six months. The interest of 10 per cent per annum is based on the part of the cash price owing. As only the deposits of £20 were paid in this year the balance of £100 of the cash price was therefore owing for each machine, i.e. 200 machines=£20,000. As this money had been owed for six months on average, then the interest is £20,000 for six months at the rate of 10 per cent per annum=£1,000. This now needs transferring to the Trading Account as it constitutes part of this year's profit.

Of course, if the sales have not been spread evenly over the year, then the interest earned would have been different. If most of the sales had taken place at the start of the year the average time that each £100 was owing would be greater than six months, if most of the sales had taken place at the end of the year, then each £100 would have been owing for an average time of less than six months. It all depends on the facts. Calculations must therefore be based on the facts in each firm.

(D) When the goods have been sold on hire purchase the total hire purchase price has been debited to each customer's account. However, of the £4,000 total hire purchase interest, £3,000 still has to be earned and is accordingly carried forward to the next accounting period. As the figure of debtors includes this amount, then the debtors need to be shown net in the Balance Sheet after the deduction of the unearned interest.

Food Mixers Trading Account for the year ended 31 December 19–5

		£			£
Purchases		21,600	Sales at Hire Purchase		
Less Stock		3,600	Price	(E)	30,000
Cost of Goods Sold		18,000			
Provision for					
Unrealised Profit	(F)	8,160			
Gross Profit c/d		3,840			
		30,000			30,000

(E) As the interest factor and the profit on goods factor are not being separated for profit calculations, there is no need to show them separately.

(F) The provision for unrealised profit is debited to the Trading Account, and will be credited to a Provision for Unrealised Profit

Account. At the end of each accounting period the provision will need adjusting, sometimes it will have to be increased, this will be done by debiting the Trading Account and crediting the Provision Account. At other times the provision will need reducing, this will necessitate the debiting of the Provision Account and the crediting of the Trading Account. It will now be seen to work in a similar manner to a Bad Debts Provision Account, the main difference being that provision for unrealised profits affects the Trading Account while provision for bad debts affects the Profit and Loss Account instead. Also, like the bad debts example, the balance of the Provision for Unrealised Profit Account is deducted from the instalments owing in the Balance Sheet.

The provision is calculated thus:

$$\frac{\text{Cash yet to be collected}}{\text{Total Cash collectible from the Sales}} \times \text{Total Gross Profit (incl. interest)}$$

$$= \frac{20,400}{30,000}(G) \times \pounds12,000 \ (H) = \pounds8,160$$

Profit and Loss Account for the year ended 31 December 19–5

	£		£
Salaries and General Expenses	4,000	Gross Profits b/d	
Net Profit	8,340	On Washing Machines	8,500
		On Food Mixers	3,840
	12,340		12,340

Balance Sheet as at 31 December 19–5

	£	£		£	£
Capital			Fixed Assets		10,000
Cash Introduced	50,000		*Current Assets*		
Add Net Profit	8,340		Stocks	12,600	
		58,340	Hire Purchase Instalments		
Current Liabilities			not yet due	£	
Creditors		6,400	Washing Machines	24,000	
			Less Provisions for		
			Interest not due	3,000	
					21,000
			Food Mixers	20,400	
			Less Provision for		
			Unrealised Profit	8,160	
				12,240	
			Bank	8,900	
					54,740
		64,740			64,740

(G) The £20,400 is found by taking the total cash collectible from the sales less the amount already collected: i.e. £30 × 1,000=£30,000 *less* £9,600 (see trial balance)=Cash yet to be collected £20,400.

(H) This figure is found by taking the profit for each food mixer (including interest) and multiplying by the number of units sold. Hire purchase price £30 *less* cost £18=£12 profit (including interest) per unit. 1,000 units sold, therefore £12 × 1,000=£12,000 total profit.

Repossessions

If in the accounts shown, some of the people buying food mixers had defaulted on their payments and the goods had been repossessed, then this would need special accounting treatment. The sums paid by the customers would have been forfeited by them. On the other hand, the repossessed items taken back into stock are not new and will therefore have to be revalued accordingly.

The Food Mixer Trading Account can now be reconstructed if, in addition to the transactions already described, a further 10 food mixers on which a total of £8 each had been paid were repossessed, (i.e. 1,010 sold originally, 10 of these being repossessed later). On 31 December 19–5 they were not valued at cost, i.e. £18 each, but were valued as being worth £13 each.

Food Mixers Trading Account for the year ended 31 December 19–5

	£		£
Purchases	21,600	Sales at Hire Purchase	
Less Stock (I)	3,550	Price	30,000
		Instalments Received on	
Cost of Goods Sold	18,050	Repossessions	80
Provision for Unrealised			
Profit	8,160		
Gross Profit	3,870		
	30,080		30,080

(I) The final stock is now made up of:

	£
Unsold Items—190 × £18	3,420
Items Repossessed—10 × £13	130
	3,550

The gross profit is now £3,870. This can be explained as follows:

	£	£
(i) Original profit		3,840
Additional transactions—		
Received instalments 10 × £8	80	
Loss of value—cost *less* new value £18—£13=£5 × 10	50	
Therefore additional profit	—	30
Revised Profit		3,870

Exercises

33.1. A taxi-hire concern purchased vehicles on the H.P. system over a period of three years paying £846 down on 1 January 19–3, and further annual payments of £2,000 due on 31 December 19–3, 19–4 and 19–5.

The cash price of the vehicle was £6,000, the vendor company charging interest at 8 per cent per annum on outstanding balances.

Show the appropriate ledger accounts in the hire purchaser's books for the three years and how the items would appear in the balance sheet at 31 December 19–3; depreciation at 10 per cent per annum on the written down value is to be charged and interest calculated to the nearest £.

(*Union of Lancashire and Cheshire Institutes*)

33.2. On 1 January 19–3 J. Robson bought a machine (cash price £1,046) from X.Y. & Co Ltd on the following hire purchase terms. Robson was to make an immediate payment of £300 and three annual payments of £300 on 31 December in each year. The rate of interest chargeable is 10 per cent per annum.

Robson depreciates this machinery by 10 per cent on the diminishing balance each year.

(*a*) Make the entries relating to this machine in Robson's ledger for the year 19–3, 19–4 and 19–5. (All calculations are to be made to the nearest £.)
(*b*) Show how the item machinery would appear in the Balance Sheet as at 31 December 19–3.

(*Associated Examining Board—'A' Level*)

33.3. A firm was acquiring two cars under hire purchase agreements, details of which are as follows:

Registration Number	UE 452	XA 300
Date of Purchase	20 June 19–4	31 January 19–5
Cash Price	£850	£910
Deposit	£94	£118
Interest (deemed to accrue evenly over the period of the agreement)	£108	£144

Both agreements provided for payment to be made in thirty-six equal monthly instalments commencing on the last day of the month following purchase.

On 1 August 19–5 vehicle UE 452 became a total loss. In full settlement on 10 August 19–5:

(i) an insurance company paid £700 under a comprehensive policy, and
(ii) the hire purchase company accepted £500 for termination of the agreement.

The firm prepared accounts annually to 28 February and provided depreciation on a straight line basis at a rate of 20 per cent for motor vehicles, with a full year's depreciation in the year of purchase, no depreciation being provided in the year of disposal.

All instalments were paid on the due dates.

You are required to record these transactions in the following accounts:

(a) Motor Vehicles,
(b) Depreciation, and
(c) Hire Purchase Company,
(d) Assets Disposal,

carrying down the balances as on 28 February 19–6.
(*Institute of Chartered Accountants*)

33.4. S. Corner started business on 1 October 19–5 selling washing machines of one standard type on hire purchase terms. During the year to 30 September 19–6 he purchased machines at a uniform price of £60 and sold 950 machines at a total price under hire purchase agreements of £100 per machine, payable by an initial deposit of £30 and 10 quarterly instalments of £7.

The following trial balance was extracted from Corner's books as at 30 September 19–6.

	£	£
Capital		38,000
Drawings	2,000	
Fixed Assets	5,000	
Purchases	60,000	
Cash collected from Customers		41,800
Rent, Rates and Insurance	2,250	
Wages	4,300	
General Expenses	5,135	
Balance at Bank	5,315	
Sundry Trade Creditors		4,200
	84,000	84,000

The personal accounts of customers are memorandum records (i.e. they are not part of the double entry system).

Corner prepares his annual accounts on the basis of taking credit for profit (including interest) in proportion to cash collected from customers.

Prepare Corner's Hire Purchase Trading Account and a Profit and Loss Account for the year ended 30 September 19–6 and a Balance Sheet as at that date.

Ignore depreciation of fixed assets.
(*Associated Examining Board 'A' Level*)

33.5A. A firm was acquiring two lorries under hire purchase agreements, details of which are as follows:

Registration Number	NOL 862	NOM 760
Date of purchase	31 May 19–6	31 October 19–6
Cash price	£1,800	£2,400

Deposit	£312	£480
Interest (deemed to accrue evenly over the period of the agreement)	£192	£240

Both agreements provided for payment to be made in twenty-four monthly instalments commencing on the last day of the month following purchase.

On 1 September 19–7, vehicle NOL 862 became a total loss. In full settlement on 20 September 19–7:

(i) an insurance company paid £1,250 under a comprehensive policy, and
(ii) the hire purchase company accepted £600 for the termination of the agreement.

The firm prepared accounts annually to 31 December and provided depreciation on a straight line basis at a rate of 20 per cent per annum for motor vehicles, apportioned as from the date of purchase and up to the date of disposal.

All instalments were paid on the due dates.

The balance on the Hire Purchase Company Account in respect of vehicle NOL 862 is to be written off.

You are required to record these transactions in the following accounts, carrying down the balances as on 31 December 19–6, and 31 December 19–7:

(a) Motor Vehicles on Hire Purchase,
(b) Provision for Depreciation of Motor Vehicles,
(c) Motor Vehicles Disposals, and
(d) Hire Purchase Company.

(*Institute of Chartered Accountants*)

33.6A. On 30 September 19–7, B. Wright, who prepares final accounts annually to 30 September, bought a motor lorry on hire purchase from the Vehicles and Finance Co Ltd. The cash price of the lorry was £3,081. Under the terms of the hire purchase agreement, Wright paid a deposit of £1,000 on 30 September 19–7, and two instalments of £1,199 on 30 September, 19–8 and 19–9. The hire vendor charged interest at 10 per cent per annum on the balance outstanding on 1 October each year. All payments were made on the due dates.

Wright maintained the motor lorry account at cost and accumulated the annual provision for depreciation, at 25 per cent on the diminishing balance method, in a separate account.

You are required to:

(i) prepare the following accounts as they would appear in the ledger of B. Wright for the period of the contract:

(a) Vehicles and Finance Co Ltd.
(b) Motor Lorry on hire purchase.
(c) Provision for depreciation of motor lorry.
(d) Hire purchase interest payable.

(ii) show how the above matters would appear in the balance sheet of B. Wright at 30 September 19–8.

The Vehicles and Finance Co Ltd prepares final accounts annually to 30 September, on which date it charges B. Wright with the interest due.

Make calculations to the nearest £.

33.7A. R.J. commenced business on 1 January 19–8. He sells refrigerators, all of one standard type, on hire-purchase terms. The total amount, including interest, payable for each refrigerator, is £300. Customers are required to pay an initial deposit of £60, followed by eight quarterly instalments of £30 each. The cost of each refrigerator to R.J. is £200.

The following trial balance was extracted from R.J.'s books as on 31 December 19–8.

Trial Balance

	£	£
Capital		100,000
Fixed assets	10,000	
Drawings	4,000	
Bank overdraft		19,600
Creditors		16,600
Purchases	180,000	
Cash collected from customers		76,500
Bank interest	400	
Wages and salaries	12,800	
General expenses	5,500	
	£212,700	£212,700

850 machines were sold on hire-purchase terms during 19–8.

The annual accounts are prepared on the basis of taking credit for profit (including interest) in proportion to the cash collected from customers.

You are required to prepare the hire purchase trading account, and the profit and loss account for the year 19–8 and balance sheet as on 31 December 19–8.

Ignore depreciation of fixed assets.

Show your calculations.

(Chartered Institute of Secretaries and Administrators)

33.8A. On 1 January 19–6, F Limited commenced business selling goods on hire-purchase. Under the terms of the agreements, an initial deposit of 20 per cent is payable on delivery, followed by four equal quarterly instalments, the first being due three months after the date of sale.

During the year sales were made as follows:

	Cost price	*H.P.* sales price
	£	£
10 January	150	225
8 March	350	525
12 May	90	135
6 July	200	300
20 September	70	105
15 October	190	285
21 November	160	240

The goods sold in July were returned in September and eventually sold in November for £187 cash. All other instalments are paid on the due dates.

It may be assumed that:

(a) gross profit and interest are credited to profit and loss account in the proportion that deposits and instalments received bear to hire purchase price; or

(b) the cost is deemed to be paid in full before any credit is taken for gross profit and interest.

You are to prepare for the first year of trading, a hire-purchase trading account compiled firstly on assumption (a) and secondly on assumption (b) and give the relevant balance sheet entries under each assumption.

Workings should be clearly shown.

(*Institute of Cost and Management Accountants*)

34

Limited Companies: General Background

A very brief introduction was made to the accounts of limited companies in Chapter 27 of Volume 1. It was intended to show some of the basic outlines of the Final Accounts of limited companies to those people who would be finishing their studies of accounting with the completion of Volume 1. This volume now carries the study of limited companies accounting to a more advanced stage.

The Acts of Parliament now governing limited companies are the Companies Act 1948, and its amending acts, the Companies Act 1967 and the Companies Act 1976. These acts, when cited, should be shown as the 'Companies Acts 1948 to 1976'. The 1967 act brought in special provisions relating to insurance companies, banks, shipping companies and moneylenders. As this volume is concerned with basic principles, these special provisions will be ignored. They are better left until such time as the student has reached a more advanced stage in his studies.

The Companies Acts 1948 to 1976 are the descendants of modern limited liability company legislation which can be traced back to the passing of the Companies Act 1862. This act was a triumph for the development of the limited liability principle which had been severely restricted since the so-called 'Bubble Act' of 1720, this latter act being the remedy for a multitude of spectacular frauds perpetrated behind the cloak of limited liability. Not until 1862 was general prejudice overcome, and the way paved for the general use of the limited liability principle which is now commonplace. Company law therefore consists of the Companies Acts 1948 to 1976, together with a considerable body of case law which has been built up over the years. It must be borne in mind that there are still a number of Chartered Companies in existence which were incorporated by Royal Charter, such as the Hudson's Bay Company, or else which were formed by special Acts of Parliament, such as the Mersey Docks and Harbour Board.

The Companies Acts also cover:

(a) Companies with unlimited liability. These are very rarely met in practice. For instance, in 1966 out of 28,500 new company registrations in Great Britain only fifty-seven were unlimited companies.

The fact that unlimited companies were needed was because it was the only way in which more than twenty people (or ten in a banking business) could carry on business together without limitation of liability. This meant that persons who were not allowed by law to form themselves into limited liability companies, could only combine together to run businesses with more than twenty participants if they turned themselves into an unlimited liability company. The 1967 Act rendered the unlimited company formed for this purpose somewhat obsolete, since it exempted partnerships of solicitors, accountants and members of a recognised stock exchange from any limitation on the number of partners. In addition, the Board of Trade may by regulation extend this exemption to other types of partnerships. Such powers will be reserved for members of other professional bodies. For reasons of possible taxation benefits some of the unlimited companies may well turn themselves into partnerships.

(b) Companies limited by guarantee, which may or may not have a share capital. Such a company is one formed by a society where no trading capital is needed, but the interests of the creditors must be protected. Each member of the company guarantees to pay a stated sum if the company has to be liquidated (comes to an end by being wound up) during his term of membership, or within a year after relinquishing his membership.

These two types of company, (a) and (b), are relatively unimportant, and therefore any future reference to a 'limited company' or merely a 'company' will refer to limited liability companies of the normal type.

The outstanding feature of a limited company is that, no matter how many individuals have bought shares in it, yet it is treated in its dealings with the outside world as if it were a person in its own right, it is said to be a separate 'legal entity'. Just as the law can create this separate legal person, then so also can it eliminate it, but its existence can only be terminated by using the proper legal procedures. Thus the identity of the shareholders in a large concern may be changing daily as shares are bought and sold by different people. On the other hand, a small private company may have the same shareholders from when it is incorporated (the day it legally came into being), until the date when liquidation is completed (the cessation of a company, often known also as 'winding up' or being 'wound up'). A prime example of its identity as a separate legal entity is that it may sue its own shareholders, or in turn be sued by them.

The legal formalities by which the company comes into existence can be gleaned from any textbook on Company Law. It is not the purpose of this book to discuss Company Law in any great detail, this is far better left to a later stage of one's studies. As companies must, however, comply with the law, the essential Company Law concerning accounting matters will be dealt with in this book as far as is necessary. This is not a book in which company accounts should be discussed in great detail.

What is important is that the basic principles connected with company accounts can be seen in operation. In order that the student may not be unduly confused, points which very rarely occur, or on which the legal arguments are extremely involved and may not yet have been finally settled, will be left out completely or merely mentioned in passing. This means that some generalisations will bear closer scrutiny when accounting studies reach a more advanced stage.

Each company is governed by two documents, known as the Memorandum of Association and the Articles of Association, generally referred to as the 'memorandum' and the 'articles'. The memorandum consists of five clauses, which contain the following details:

(1) The name of the company.

(2) The part of the United Kingdom where the registered office will be situated.

(3) The objects of the company.

(4) A statement (if a limited liability company) that the liability of its members is limited.

(5) Details of the share capital which the company is authorised to issue.

The memorandum is said to be the document which discloses the conditions which govern the company's relationship with the outside world.

The principle of limited liability underlying clause 4 has been of the utmost importance in industry and commerce. It is inconceivable that large business units, such as Imperial Chemical Industries Ltd or Great Universal Stores Ltd, could have existed except for a very few instances. The investor in a limited company, who therefore buys shares in it, is a shareholder, the most he can lose is the money he has paid for the shares, or where he has only partly paid for them, then he is also liable for the unpaid part in addition. With public companies, where their shares are dealt in on a Stock Exchange, he can easily sell them whenever he so wishes. The sale of a share in a private company is not so easily effected.

The fact that the shares issued to the members constitute the capital of the company means that the creditors, and the members, are entitled to regard the capital as continually existing. It is not returnable to members as the result of a mere whim, the creditors would certainly be aggrieved if the members could have limited liability and then have their share capital repaid to them whenever they so desired. Like most people they would certainly draw their money out if they were allowed to do so every time they stood a chance of losing it. This would seriously prejudice the chance of the creditors being paid in full if the company started losing money. The return of capital to the shareholders is only allowed in certain cases; these will be shown later in the book. Of course there is nothing to stop a shareholder from selling his shares to another person who will then become a shareholder himself. This, however, is money passing from one person to another outside the company; what it most certainly is not is the return of capital from the company to the shareholder.

On the other hand, while the capital is not normally returnable to the shareholders during the life of the company, it would be ridiculous if they were also denied access to the profits earned by the company. The desire to obtain an income is the basic reason for buying shares. Therefore the profits are treated separately, as they are normally payable to the shareholders, or are partly held back by the company to help finance the expansion of the firm or for other reasons to be shown in a later chapter. Unlike sole traders or partnerships, where profits can be added to the capital accounts, in a company, the profits and the capital are kept quite separate.

When the profits are shared out between the shareholders, then this is known as a dividend. The profits which can be so utilised must therefore constitute a dividend fund. In none of the Companies Acts has a direct reference been made to the dividend fund. It has always been left to the judges to decide what should, and what should not, be allowed to increase or reduce the dividend fund. This has led to a considerable number of cases referring to whether or not certain items could be placed into the dividend fund, or whether in fact they could be ignored in calculating the fund. To a student at this stage the mere recital of the law cases, and the decisions made, would only cloud the issue. In fact, at the present time the judge's decision on the constitution of the dividend fund is often based on how a rational businessman might act in a certain set of circumstances. Therefore to really understand the law relating to dividends, one must read the full reports of the law cases to see the ways in which the judge's mind has worked on each separate case. It is a grave mistake to read a statement such as 'dividends cannot be paid while there is an adverse balance on the Profit and Loss Appropriation Account' and to think that this must always be true. Every case is different, and it must therefore be judged on the facts which may be completely unlike any situation in any other case which has arisen previously. On the other hand, there are problems which are alike in almost every respect except for one very small difference, and it could be this difference which makes one firm able to place some income into the dividend fund while the other firm will not be allowed to do so.

Besides the Memorandum of Association every company must also have Articles of Association. Just as the memorandum governs the company's dealings with the outside world, the articles govern the relationships which exist between the members and the company, between one member and the other members, and other necessary regulations. The Companies Act 1948, in the first schedule attached to it, has a model set of articles known as Table A. A company may, if it so wishes, have its articles exactly the same as Table A, commonly known as 'adopting Table A', or else adopt part of it and have some sections altered. The adoption of the major part of Table A is normal for most private companies. In accounting textbooks, unless stated to the contrary, the accounting examples shown are usually on the basis that Table A has been adopted.

Table A lays down regulations concerning the power of the directors of the company. On the other hand, the company may draft its own regulations for the powers of directors. Any such regulations are of the utmost importance when it is realised that the legal owners of the business, the shareholders, have entrusted the running of the company to the directors. The shareholders' own rights are largely limited to attending Annual General Meetings and having voting rights thereat, although some shares do not carry voting rights. The Companies Acts make the keeping of proper sets of accounting records and the preparation of Final Accounts compulsory for every company. In addition the accounts must be audited, this being quite different from a partnership or a sole trader's business where an audit is not compulsory at all.

With the passing of the Companies Act 1967, all companies having limited liability, whether they are private or public companies, have to send a copy of their Final Accounts, drawn up in a prescribed manner, to the Registrar of Companies. The classification of 'exempt private company' was abolished in the 1967 Act. Chapter 41 is concerned with stating the accounting requirements of the Companies Acts.

The Companies Act 1976, which received the Royal Assent on 15 November 1976, did not come into operation as on that day. Only a few sections came into operation, whilst the remaining sections have been put into effect as and when needed.

The shares of most of the public companies are dealt in on one or other of the recognised Stock Exchanges. The shares of private companies cannot be bought and sold on any Stock Exchange, as this would contravene the requirements for the company being recognised as a 'private' company. The sale and purchase of shares on the Stock Exchanges has no effect on the accounting entries made in the company's books. The only entry made in the company's books when a shareholder sells all, or some, of his shares to someone else, is to record the change of identity of the shareholders. The price at which shares were sold does not enter into the company's books. While no accounting entries are necessary, probably apart from a small charge being made to the shareholder to compensate the company for administrative expenses in recording the change of identity caused by the share transfer and the completion of certain legal documents by the company, the price of the shares on the Stock Exchange has repercussions on the financial policy of the company. If some new shares are to be issued, the fact at what price they are to be issued will be largely dependent on the Stock Exchange valuation. If another firm is to be taken over by the company, part of the purchase price being by the means of shares in the company, then the Stock Exchange value will also affect the value placed upon the shares being given. A takeover bid from another firm may well be caused because the Stock Exchange value of the shares has made a takeover seem worthwhile. It must be recognised that the Stock Exchanges are the 'second-hand market' for a company's shares. The company does not actually sell (normally called 'issue') its shares by using the Stock Exchange as a selling place. The company issues new shares directly to the people who make application to it for the shares at the times when the company has shares available for issue. The company does not sell to, or buy from, the Stock Exchanges. This means that the shares of a public company sold and bought on Stock Exchanges are passing from one shareholder to another person who will then become a shareholder. Apart from the effect upon the financial policies of the firm the double entry accounts of the company are not affected.

Chapter 40 contains the details whereby the shares of a company may be made into 'stock'. Thus 500 Ordinary Shares of £1 each may be made into £500 Stock. The dividends paid on the shares or the stock would be the same, and the voting powers would also be the same. Apart from administrative convenience there is really no difference between shares and stock.

Classes of Shares

The main classes of shares are Ordinary shares and Preference shares. Unless clearly stated in the memorandum or articles of association Preference shares are assumed to be of the cumulative variety already described in Chapter 27.

There are also a variety of other shares. The rights attaching to these shares are purely dependent on the skill and ingenuity of the draftsman of the memorandum and articles of association. An entirely new type of share may be created provided it does not contravene the law.

The shares which carry the right to the whole of the profits remaining after the Preference shares (and any other fixed dividend shares) have been paid a dividend are often known as the equity share capital or as 'equities'.

35

The Issue of Shares and Debentures

The Issue of Shares

In the case of public companies a new issue of shares can be very costly indeed, and the number of shares issued must be sufficient to make the cost worthwhile. However, for simplicity, so that the principles are not obscured by the difficulties of grappling with large amounts, the numbers of shares shown as issued in the illustrations that follow will be quite small.

Shares can be issued being payable for (a) immediately on application, or (b) by instalments. The first instances will be of shares being paid for immediately. Issues of shares may take place on the following terms connected with the price of the shares:

(i) Shares issued at par. This would mean that a share of £1 nominal value would be issued for £1 each.

(ii) Shares issued at a premium. In this case a share of £1 nominal value would be issued for more than £1 each, say for £3 each.

(iii) Shares issued at a discount. Shares each of £5 nominal value might be issued for £3 each.

This will all seem rather strange at first. How can a £1 share, which states that value on the face of it, be issued for £3 each, and who would be foolish enough to buy it? On the other hand, surely there would be a queue of people waiting to buy a £5 share for £3 each. The reasons for this apparently strange state of affairs stems from the somewhat peculiar method in England and Wales of always having the Share Capital Accounts at the nominal value of the shares, irrespective of how much the shares are worth or how much they are issued for. To illustrate this, the progress of two firms can be looked at, firm A and firm B. Both firms started in business on 1 January 19–1 and issued 1,000 ordinary shares each of £4 nominal value at par. Ignoring any issue expenses, the Balance Sheets on that date would appear:

Firms A Ltd and B Ltd

Balance Sheet as at 1 January 19–1

	£		£
Ordinary Share Capital	4,000	Bank	4,000

Five years later, on 31 December 19–5, the Balance Sheets show that the companies have fared quite differently. It is to be assumed here, for purposes of illustration, that the Balance Sheet values and any other interpretation of values happen to be identical.

£4,000 capital is needed by firm A Ltd, and this is to be met by issuing more ordinary shares. Suppose that another 1,000 ordinary shares of £4 nominal value each are issued at par. Column (*a*) shows the Balance Sheet before the issue, and column (*b*) shows the Balance Sheet after the issue has taken place.

A Ltd Balance Sheets (Solution 1) as at 31 December 19–5

	(*a*)	(*b*)		(*a*)	(*b*)
	£	£		£	£
Ordinary Share			Fixed and Current		
Capital	4,000	8,000	Assets (other than		
Profit and Loss	6,000	6,000	bank)	9,000	9,000
			Bank	1,000	5,000
	10,000	14,000		10,000	14,000

Now the effect of what has happened can be appreciated. Before the new issue there were 1,000 shares. As there were £10,000 of assets and no liabilities, then each share was worth £10. After the issue there are 2,000 shares and £14,000 of assets, so that now each share is worth £7. This would be extremely disconcerting to the original shareholders who see the value of each of their shares fall immediately by £3. On the other hand, the new shareholder who has just bought shares for £4 each sees them rise immediately to be worth £7 each. Only in one specific case would this be just, and that is where each original shareholder buys an equivalent number of new shares. Otherwise this obviously cannot be the correct solution. What is required is a price which is equitable as far as the interests of the old shareholders are concerned, and yet will attract sufficient applications to provide the capital required. As in this case the Balance Sheet value and the real value are the same, the answer is that each old share was worth £10 and therefore each new share should be issued for £10 each. The Balance Sheets will now appear:

A Ltd Balance Sheets (Solution 2) as at 31 December 19–5

	(a)	(b)		(a)	(b)
	£	£		£	£
Ordinary Share Capital			Fixed and Current		
(at nominal value)	4,000	8,000	Assets (other than		
Share Premium			bank)	9,000	9,000
(see note below)		6,000	Bank	1,000	11,000
Profit and Loss	6,000	6,000			
	10,000	20,000		10,000	20,000

Thus in (a) above 1,000 shares own between then £10,000 of assets =£10 each, while in (b) 2,000 shares are shown as owning £20,000 of assets=£10 each. Both the old and new shareholders are therefore satisfied with the bargain that has been made.

Note: The Share Premium shown on the left-hand side of the Balance Sheet is needed, ignoring for a moment the legal requirements to be complied with in company Balance Sheets, simply because the Balance Sheet would not balance without it. If shares are stated at nominal value, but issued at another price, the actual amount received increases the bank balance, but the Share Capital shown is increased by a different figure. The Share Premium therefore represents the excess of the cash received over the nominal value of the shares issued.

The other firm, B Ltd, has not fared so well. It has, in fact, lost money. The accumulated losses are reflected in a debit balance on the Profit and Loss Appropriation Account as shown in the following Balance Sheet (c). It can be seen that there are £3,000 of assets to represent the shareholders, stake in the firm of 1,000 shares, i.e. each share is worth £3 each. If more capital was needed 1,000 more shares could be issued. From the action taken in the previous case it will now be obvious that each new share of £4 nominal value will be issued for its real value of £3 each. The Balance Sheets will appear:

B Ltd Balance Sheets (correct solution) as at 31 December 19–5

	(c)	(d)		(c)	(d)
	£	£		£	£
Ordinary Share			Fixed and Current		
Capital	4,000	8,000	Assets (other than		
			bank)	2,000	2,000
			Bank	1,000	4,000
			Discounts on Shares		
			(see note below)		1,000
			Profit and Loss—		
			Debit Balance	1,000	1,000
	4,000	8,000		4,000	8,000

Once again, as the share capital is shown at nominal value, but the shares issued at a different figure, the difference being Discounts on Shares must be shown on the right-hand side of the Balance Sheet in order that the Balance Sheet may balance. It is, of course, not actually an asset, it is merely a balancing figure needed because the entries already made for an increase in the Ordinary Share Capital and the increase in the bank balance have been at different figures. The figure for Discounts on Shares therefore rectifies the double entry 'error'.

For the purpose of making the foregoing explanations easier it was assumed that Balance Sheet values and other values were the same. This is very rarely true for all the assets, and in fact there is more than one other 'value'. A Balance Sheet is a historical view of the past based on records made according to the firm's interpretation and use of accounting concepts and conventions. When shares are being issued it is not the historical view of the past that is important, but the view of the future. Therefore the actual premiums and discounts on shares being issued is not merely a matter of Balance Sheet values, but on the issuing company's view of the future and its estimate of how the investing public will react to the price at which the shares are being offered.

The actual double entry accounts can now be seen.

1. Shares Payable in Full on Application

The issue of shares in illustrations (i), (ii) and (iii) which follow are based on the Balance Sheets that have just been considered.

(i) Shares issued at par.
1,000 ordinary shares with a nominal value of £4 each are to be issued. Applications, together with the necessary money, are received for exactly 1,000 shares. The shares are then allotted to the applicants.

Bank

		£			
Ordinary Share Applicants	(A)	4,000			

Ordinary Share Applicants

		£			£
Ordinary Share Capital	(B)	4,000	Bank	(A)	4,000

Ordinary Share Capital

					£
			Ordinary Share Applicants	(B)	4,000

It may appear that the Ordinary Share Applicants Account is unnecessary, and that the only entries needed are a debit in the Bank Account and a credit in the Ordinary Share Capital Account. However, applicants do not always become shareholders; this is shown later. The applicant must make an offer for the shares being issued, accompanied by the necessary money, this is the application. After the applications have been vetted the allotments of shares are made by the company. This represents the acceptance of the offer by the company and it is at this point that the applicant becomes a shareholder. Therefore (A) represents the offer by the applicant, while (B) is the acceptance by the company. No entry must therefore be made in the Share Capital Account until (B) happens, for it is not until that point that the share capital is in fact in existence. The Share Applicants Account is therefore an intermediary account pending allotments being made.

(ii) Shares issued at a premium.
1,000 Ordinary Shares with a nominal value of £4 each are to be issued for £10 each (see A Ltd previously). Thus a premium of £6 per share has been charged. Applications and the money are received for exactly 1,000 shares.

Bank

	£		
Balance b/fwd	1,000		
Ordinary Share Applicants	10,000		

Ordinary Share Applicants

		£		£
Ordinary Share Capital	(A)	4,000	Bank	10,000
Share Premium	(B)	6,000		
		10,000		10,000

Share Premium

		£
Ordinary Share Applicants	(B)	6,000

Ordinary Share Capital (A Ltd)

		£
Balance b/fwd		4,000
Ordinary Share Applicants	(A)	4,000

Note: (A) is shown as £4,000 because the share capital is shown at nominal value and not as total issued value. (B) The £6,000 share premiums must therefore be credited to a Share Premium Account to preserve double entry balancing.

(iii) Shares issued at a discount.
1,000 Ordinary Shares with a nominal value of £4 each are to be issued for £3 each (see B Ltd previously). Thus a discount of £1 per share is being allowed. Applications and the money are received for exactly 1,000 shares.

Bank

	£		
Balance b/fwd	1,000		
Ordinary Share Applicants	3,000		

Ordinary Share Applicants

	£		£
Ordinary Share Capital	4,000	Bank	3,000
		Discounts on Shares	1,000
	4,000		4,000

Ordinary Share Capital

			£
		Balance b/fwd	4,000
		Ordinary Share Capital	4,000

Discounts on Shares

	£		
Ordinary Share Applications	1,000		

(iv) Oversubscription and undersubscription for shares.
When a public company invites investors to apply for its shares it is obviously very rare indeed if in fact the applications for shares equal exactly the number of shares to be issued. Where more shares are applied for than are available for issue, then the issue is said to be 'oversubscribed'. Where fewer shares are applied for than are available for issue, then the issue has been 'undersubscribed'.

With a brand-new company a minimum amount is fixed as being necessary to carry on any further with the running of the company. If the applications are less than the minimum stated, then the application monies must be returned to the senders. This does not apply to an established company. If therefore 1,000 shares of £1 each are available for issue, but only 875 shares are applied for, then only 875 will be issued, assuming that this is above the fixed minimum figure. The accounting entries will be in respect of 875 shares, no entries being needed for the 125 shares not applied for, as this part does not represent a transaction.

The opposite of this is where the shares are oversubscribed. In this case some sort of rationing is applied so that the issue is restricted to the shares available for issue. The process of selecting who will get how many shares depends on the policy of the firm. Some firms favour large shareholders because this leads to lower administrative costs. Why the cost will be lower will be obvious if the cost of calling a meeting of two companies each with 20,000 shares is considered. H Ltd has 20 shareholders with an average holding of 1,000 shares each. J Ltd has 1,000 shareholders with an average holding of 20 shares each. They all have to be notified by post and given various documents including a set of the final accounts. The cost of printing and sending these is less for H Ltd with 20 shareholders than for J Ltd with 1,000 shareholders. This is only one example of the costs involved, but it will also apply with equal force to many items connected with the shares. Conversely, the directors may prefer to have more shareholders with smaller holdings, one reason being that it decreases the amount of voting power in any one individual's hands. The actual process of rationing the shares is then a simple matter once a policy has been agreed. It may consist of scaling down applications, of drawing lots or some other chance selection, but it will eventually bring the number of shares to be issued down to the number of shares available. Excess application monies will then be refunded by the company.

An issue of shares where 1,000 ordinary shares of £1 nominal value each are to be issued at par payable in full, but 1,550 shares are applied for, will appear as follows:

Bank

	£		£
Ordinary Share Applicants	1,550	Ordinary Share Applicants (refunds)	550

Ordinary Share Applicants

	£		£
Bank	550	Bank	1,550
Ordinary Share Capital	1,000		
	1,550		1,550

Ordinary Share Capital

			£
		Ordinary Share Applicants	1,000

Issue of Shares payable by Instalments

The shares considered so far have all been issued as paid in full on application. Conversely, many issues are made which require payment by instalments. These are probably more common with public companies than with private companies.

The various stages, after the initial invitation has been made to the public to buy shares by means of advertisements (if it is a public company), etc., are as follows:

(A) Applications are received together with the application monies.

(B) The applications are vetted and the shares allotted, letters of allotment being sent out.

(C) The excess application monies from wholly unsuccessful, or where the application monies received exceed both the application and allotment monies required, and partly unsuccessful applicants, are returned to them. Usually, if a person has been partly unsuccessful, his excess application monies are held by the company and will reduce the amount needed to be paid by him on allotment.

(D) Allotment monies are received.

(E) The next instalment, known as the first call, is requested.

(F) The monies are received from the first call.

(G) The next instalment, known as the second call, is requested.

(H) The monies are received from the second call.

This carries on until the full number of calls have been made, although there is not usually a large number of calls to be made in an issue.

The reasons for the payments by instalments becomes obvious if it is realised that a company will not necessarily require the immediate use of all the money to be raised by the issue. Suppose a new company is to be formed, it is to buy land, erect a factory, equip it with machinery and then go into production. This might take two years altogether. If the total sum needed was £1,000,000, the allocation of this money could be:

Ordinary Share Capital

	£
Cost of land, payable within 1 month	200,000
Cost of buildings, payable in 1 year's time	300,000
Cost of machinery, payable in 18 months' time	200,000
Working capital required in 2 years' time	300,000
	1,000,000

The issue may therefore well be on the following terms:

	Per cent
Application money per share, payable immediately	10
Allotment money per share, payable within 1 month	10
First call, money payable in 12 months' time	30
Second call, money payable in 18 months' time	20
Third call, money payable in 24 months' time	30
	100

The entries made in the Share Capital Account should equal the amount of money requested to that point in time. However, instead of one Share Applicants Account, this is usually split into several accounts to represent the different instalments. For this purpose application and allotment are usually joined together in one account, the Application and Allotment Account, as this cuts out the need for transfers where excess application monies are held over and set off against allotment monies needed. When allotment is made, and not until then, an entry of £200,000 (10 per cent + 10 per cent) would be made in the Share Capital Account. On the first call an entry of £300,000 would be made in the Share Capital Account, likewise £200,000 on the second call and £300,000 on the third call. The Share Capital Account will therefore contain not the monies received, but the amount of money requested. Exhibit 35.1 now shows an instance of a share issue.

Exhibit 35.1

A company is issuing 1,000 7 per cent Preference Shares of £1 each, payable 10 per cent on application, 20 per cent on allotment, 40 per cent on the first call and 30 per cent on the second call. Applications are received for 1,550 shares. A refund of the money is made in respect of 50 shares, while for the remaining 1,500 applied for, an allotment is to be made on the basis of 2 shares for every 3 applied for (assume that this will not involve any fractions of shares). The excess application monies are set off against the allotment monies asked for. The remaining requested instalments are all paid in full. The letters by the side of each entry refer

Bank

		£			£
Application and Allotment:			Application and		
Application monies	(A)	155	Allotment refund	(C)	5
Allotment monies					
(£1,000 × 20% *less*					
excess application					
monies £50)	(B)	150			
First call	(F)	400			
Second call	(H)	300			

Application and Allotment

			£				£
Bank—refund of				Bank	(A)		155
application monies	(C)		5	Bank	(B)		150
Preference Share Capital	(B)		300				
			305				305

First Call

			£				£
Preference Share Capital	(E)		400	Bank	(F)		400

Second Call

			£				£
Preference Share Capital	(G)		300	Bank	(H)		300

7 per cent Preference Share Capital

		£				£
			Application and			
			Allotment	(B)		300
			First Call	(E)		400
Balance c/d		1,000	Second Call	(G)		300
		1,000				1,000
			Balance b/d			1,000

If more than one type of share is being issued at the same time, e.g. preference shares and ordinary shares, then separate Share Capital Accounts and separate Application and Allotment Accounts and Call Accounts should be opened.

Forfeited Shares

Sometimes, although it is probably fairly rare in recent times, a shareholder fails to pay the calls requested from him. The Articles of Association of the company will probably provide that the shareholder will have his shares forfeited, provided that certain safeguards for his protection are fully observed. In this case the shares will be cancelled, and the instalments already paid by the shareholder will be lost to him.

After the forfeiture, the company may reissue the shares, unless there is a provision in the Articles of Association to prevent it. There are certain conditions as to the prices at which the shares can be reissued. These are that the amount received on reissue plus the amount received from the original shareholder should at least equal (*a*) the called-up value where the shares are not fully called up, or (*b*) the nominal value where the full amount has been called up.

Exhibit 35.2

Take the same information as that contained in Exhibit 35.1, but instead of all the calls being paid, Brunt, the holder of 100 shares, fails to pay the first and second calls. He had already paid the application and allotment monies on the required dates. The directors conform to the provisions of the Articles of Association and (A) Brunt is forced to suffer the forfeiture of his shares. (B) The amount still outstanding from Brunt will be written off. (C) The directors then reissue the shares at 75 per cent of nominal value to J. Davies. (D) Davies pays for the shares.

First Call

	£			£
Preference Share Capital	400	Bank		360
		Forfeited Shares	(B)	40
	400			400

Second Call

	£			£
Preference Share Capital	300	Bank		270
		Forfeited Shares	(B)	30
	300			300

7 per cent Preference Share Capital

		£			£
Forfeited Shares	(A)	100	Application and Allotment		300
Balance c/d		900	First Call		400
			Second Call		300
		1,000			1,000
			Balance b/d		900
Balance c/d		1,000	J. Davies	(C)	100
		1,000			1,000
			Balance b/d		1,000

Forfeited Shares

		£			£
First Call	(B)	40	Preference Share Capital	(A)	100
Second Call	(B)	30			
Balance c/d		30			
		100			100
J. Davies (see following note)		25	Balance b/d		30
Balance c/d		5			
		30			30
			Balance b/d		5

Bank

		£
First Call (£900 × 40%)		360
Second Call (£900 × 30%)		270
J. Davies	(D)	75

J. Davies

	£			£
Preference Share Capital	100	Bank	(D)	75
		Forfeited Shares (discount on reissue) see following note		25
	100			100

The transfer of £25 from Forfeited Shares Account to J. Davies Account is needed because the reissue was entered in Preference Share Capital Account and Davies Account at nominal value, i.e. following standard practice of a Share Capital Account being concerned with nominal values, but Davies was not to pay the full nominal price. Therefore the transfer of £25 is needed to close his account.

The balance of £5 on the Forfeited Shares Account can be seen to be: Cash Received from original shareholder on application and allotment £30 + from Davies £75 = £105. This is £5 over the nominal value so that the £5 appears as a credit balance. This is usually stated to be either transferred to a Profit on Reissue of Forfeited Shares Account, but it really cannot be thought that this is followed in practice for small amounts. More normally it would be transferred to the credit of a Share Premium Account.

Calls in Advance and in Arrear and the Balance Sheet

At the Balance Sheet date some shareholders will not have paid all the calls made, these are collectively known as calls in arrear. On the other hand, some shareholders may have paid amounts in respect of calls not made by the Balance Sheet date. These are calls in advance.

The normal practice is to show any calls in arrear, being a debit balance, as a deduction from the called-up portion of the share capital while the calls in advance, being a credit balance, is added as a separate item after the calls in arrear have been deducted.

A typical example might be as follows:

Balance Sheet (Capital and Liabilities side)

	£	£	£
Issued Share Capital			
10,000 Ordinary Shares of £4 each,			
£3 called-up	30,000		
Less Calls in Arrear	180		
		29,820	
Add Calls in Advance		50	
			29,870

Rights Issues

The costs of making a new issue of shares can be quite high. A way to reduce the costs of raising new long-term capital in the form of issuing shares may be by way of a rights issue. To do this the company circularises the existing shareholders, and informs them of the new issue to be made and the number of shares which each one of them is entitled to buy of the new issue. In most cases the shareholder is allowed to renounce his rights to the new shares in favour of someone else. The issue is usually pitched at a price which will make the rights capable of being sold, i.e. if the existing shareholder does not want the shares he can renounce them to A who will give him £x for the right to apply for the shares in his place, a right that A could not otherwise obtain. If any shareholder does not either buy the shares or transfer his rights, then the directors will usually have the power to dispose of such shares not taken up by issuing them in some other way.

Debentures

A debenture is a bond, acknowledging a loan to a company, usually under the company's seal, which bears a fixed rate of interest. Unlike shares, which normally depend on profits out of which to appropriate dividends, debenture interest is payable whether profits are made or not.

A debenture may be redeemable, i.e. repayable at or by a specified date. Conversely they may be irredeemable, redemption only taking place when the company is eventually liquidated, or in a case such as when the debenture interest is not paid within a given time limit.

People lending money to companies in the form of debentures will obviously be interested in how safe their investment will be. Some debentures are given the legal right that on certain happenings the debenture holders will be able to take control of specific assets, or of the whole of the assets. They can then sell the assets and recoup the amount due under their debentures, or deal with the assets in ways specified in the deed under which the debentures were issued. Such debentures are known as being secured against the assets, the term 'mortgage' debenture often being used. Other debentures have no prior right to control the assets under any circumstances. These are known as 'simple' or 'naked' debentures.

The Issue of Debentures

The entries for the issue of debentures are similar to those for shares. It would, however, certainly not be the normal modern practice to issue debentures at a premium. If the word 'debentures' appears instead of 'share capital', then the entries in the accounts would be identical.

Shares of no Par Value

It can be seen that the idea of a fixed par value for a share can be very misleading. For anyone who has not studied accounting, it may well come as a shock to them to find that a share with a par value of £1 might in fact be issued for £5. If the share is dealt in on the Stock Exchange he might find a £1 share selling at £10 or even £20, or equally well may sell for only 10p.

Another disadvantage of a par value is that it can give people entirely the wrong impression of the activities of a business. If a par value is kept to, and the dividend based on that, then with a certain degree of inflation the dividend figure can look excessive. Many trade union leaders would howl with disapproval if a dividend of 100 per cent was declared by a company. But is this so excessive? Exhibit 35.3 gives a rather different picture.

Exhibit 35.3

Jordan buys a share 40 years ago for £1. He is satisfied with a return of 5 per cent on his money. With a 5 per cent dividend he could buy a certain amount of goods which will be called x. Forty years later to buy that amount of goods, x, he would need (say) 20 times as much money. Previously 5p would have bought x, now it would take 100p. To keep his dividend at the same level of purchasing power he would need a dividend now of 100 per cent, as compared with the 5 per cent he was receiving 40 years ago.

In the United States of America, Canada and Belgium, and even in a developing country such as Ghana, no par value is attached to shares being issued. A share is issued at whatever price is suitable at the time, and the money received is credited to a Share Capital Account.

Exercises

35.1. A limited company has a nominal capital of £120,000 divided into 120,000 Ordinary Shares of £1 each. The whole of the capital was issued at par on the following terms:

	Per share
Payable on Application	£0·125
Payable on Allotment	£0·25
First Call	£0·25
Second Call	£0·375

Applications were received for 160,000 shares and it was decided to allot the shares on the basis of three for every four for which applications had been made. The balance of application monies were applied to the allotment, no cash being refunded. The balance of allotment monies were paid by the members.

The calls were made and paid in full by the members, with the exception of a member who failed to pay the first and second calls on the 800 shares allotted to him. A resolution was passed by the directors to forfeit the shares. The forfeited shares were later issued to D. Regan at £0·9 each.

Show the ledger accounts recording all the above transactions, and the relevant extracts from a Balance Sheet after all the transactions had been completed.

35.2. Badger Ltd has an authorised capital of £100,000 divided into 20,000 ordinary shares of £5 each. The whole of the shares were issued at par, payments being made as follows:

	£
Payable on Application	0·5
Payable on Allotment	1·5
First Call	2·0
Second Call	1·0

Applications were received for 32,600 shares. It was decided to refund application monies on 2,600 shares and to allot the shares on the basis of two for every three applied for. The excess application monies sent by the successful applicants is not to be refunded but is to be held and so reduce the amount payable on allotment.

The calls were made and paid in full with the exception of one member holding 100 shares who paid neither the first nor the second call and another member who did not pay the second call on 20 shares. After requisite action by the directors the shares were forfeited. They were later reissued to B. Mills at a price of £4 per share.

You are to draft the ledger accounts to record the transactions.

35.3A. The authorised and issued share capital of Cosy Fires Ltd was £75,000 divided into 75,000 ordinary shares of £1 each, fully paid. On 2 January 19–7, the authorised capital was increased by a further 85,000 ordinary shares of £1 each to £160,000. On the same date 40,000 ordinary shares of £1 each were offered to the public at £1·25 per share payable as to £0·60 on application (including the premium), £0·35 on allotment and £0·30 on 6 April 19–7.

The lists were closed on 10 January 19–7, and by that date applications for 65,000 shares had been received. Applications for 5,000 shares received no allotment and the cash paid in respect of such shares was returned. All the shares were then allocated to the remaining applicants pro rata to their original application, the balance of the monies received on application being applied to the amounts due on allotment.

The balances due on allotment were received on 31 January 19–7, with the exception of one allottee of 500 shares and these were declared forfeited on 4 April 19–7. These shares were re-issued as fully paid on 2 May 19–7, at £1·10 per share. The call due on 6 April 19–7 was duly paid by the other shareholders.

You are required:

1. To record the above-mentioned transactions in the appropriate ledger accounts, and

2. To show how the balances on such accounts should appear in the company's Balance Sheet as on 31 May 19–7.
(*Association of Certified Accountants*)

35.4A. Applications were invited by the directors of Grobigg Ltd for 150,000 of its £1 ordinary shares at £1·15 per share payable as follows:

	Per share
On application on 1 April 19–8	£0·75
On allotment on 30 April 19–8	
(including the premium of £0·15 per share)	£0·20
On first and final call on 31 May 19–8	£0·20

Applications were received for 180,000 shares and it was decided to deal with these as follows:

1. To refuse allotment to applicants for 8,000 shares.

2. To give full allotment to applicants for 22,000 shares.

3. To allot the remainder of the available shares pro rata among the other applicants.

4. To utilise the surplus received on applications in part payment of amounts due on allotment.

An applicant, to whom 400 shares had been allotted, failed to pay the amount due on the first and final call and his shares were declared forfeit on 31 July 19–8. These shares were re-issued on 3 September 19–8 as fully paid at £0·90 per share.

Show how the transactions would be recorded in the company's books.
(*Association of Certified Accountants*)

36

Redemption of Redeemable Preference Shares and of Redeemable Debentures

Redemption of Redeemable Preference Shares

The principle of limited liability is one which is conducive to the confidence aspect of investing, with the consequent effect on the ability to form large organisations. It has, on the other hand, often been suspected by creditors who have feared that they might be defrauded by unscrupulous individuals hiding behind the cloak of limited liability. Thus, it used to be the law, that once a share was issued it stayed issued unless the court approved some special scheme for the reduction of capital or of its repayment to the shareholders. While a share was in existence it was of course represented by assets on the other side of the Balance Sheet (if such items as Discounts on Shares Accounts or a debit balance on the Profit or Loss Appropriation Account can be temporarily ignored for the purposes of the argument), and in the event of liquidation the creditors would have the right to claim such assets before the shareholders. During the nineteenth century the limited company was achieving respectability, and to do this the interest of the creditors was of paramount importance.

However, with changing conditions came a change in the law governing companies. The Companies Act 1929 introduced a completely new concept. It permitted a company, if its articles so authorised it, to issue preference shares which could be redeemed (bought back from the shareholders by the company) at a later date according to terms laid down. The need that this was to fill was for companies which might require a large amount of capital initially, but which would not need such a large amount indefinitely as accumulated profits would take its place. In addition, a company might need funds for expansion, these funds also being no longer required as soon as sufficient accumulated profits had been built up.

The creditors were not forgotten however, and this is still evidenced by the presence of Section 58 of the Companies Act 1948, which has remained unchanged as far as this item is concerned by the amending act of 1967. This section contains various safeguards for creditors. It is perhaps instructive to look at the possible effects on a company's affairs if redeemable preference shares could be redeemed without any safeguards being in existence. The following Balance Sheet (A) of C. Goulden Ltd shows that the liquid position of the company is very weak, and could easily lead to the company needing to be wound up in the near future. Balance Sheet (B) shows the position if the shares were redeemed at par.

G. Goulden Ltd
Balance Sheets

	(A)	(B)		(A)	(B)
	£	£		£	£
Ordinary Share			Fixed Assets	8,000	8,000
Capital	5,000	5,000	Stock	300	300
Redeemable			Debtors	200	200
Preference Shares	2,000	—	Bank	2,500	500
Profit and Loss					
Account	100	100			
Creditors	3,900	3,900			
	11,000	9,000		11,000	9,000

Obviously the directors could normally have foreseen that the company would very likely have to be wound up. They could therefore have salvaged as much as they could for the redeemable preference shareholders, by redeeming the shares. If the fixed assets and the stock are of little saleable value, then there would only be the bank balance of £500 plus the proceeds from the debtors as the main assets against which the £3,900 creditors could claim. This means that the creditors would have suffered severely because the shares had been redeemed. If the redemption had not taken place there would have been £2,000 extra in the bank to meet the creditors' claims.

The safeguards that the law insists on (Section 58, Companies Act 1948) may be summarised as follows:

1. Redeemable preference shares can only be redeemed when they are fully paid.

2. There must be either:

(*a*) A new issue of shares to provide the funds for redemption.
(*b*) Sufficient distributable profits must be available (i.e. a large enough credit balance on the Profit and Loss Appropriation Account), which could be diverted from being used up as dividends to being treated as used up for the purpose of redeeming the redeemable preference shares. Therefore, when shares are redeemed other than by out of the proceeds of a new issue, then, and only then, the amount of distributable profits treated as used up by the nominal value of the shares redeemed is transferred to an account called a Capital Redemption Reserve Fund. Thus the old Share Capital will equal the total of the new Share Capital plus the Capital

Redemption Reserve Fund. The process of diverting profits from being usable for dividends means that the non-payment of the dividends leaves more cash in the firm against which the creditors could claim if necessary.

3. Where a premium is paid on redemption, e.g. a £4 redeemable preference share being redeemed for £5, then the source of the bank funds used for payment of the premium must be traced, and the source is deemed to be:

(a) The Share Premium Account, if one exists.
(b) Failing the existence of a Share Premium Account, or should that account be insufficient for the purpose, then the Profit and Loss Appropriation Account balance is deemed to be the source.

When the source has been established according to these rules, then that account must be reduced by an equal amount to the premiums paid. The Companies Acts do not force a company to utilise the Share Premium Account first, it is merely the normal accounting practice not to use the Profit and Loss Appropriation Account balance until the whole of the Share Premium Account has been used.

There are several permutations of possible happenings in a redemption of redeemable preference shares. The main ones are now to be seen in Exhibits 36.1 to 36.6, inclusive, which follow. The whole of each set of transactions are taken as being started and finished within one day. Each Balance Sheet has three columns on each side. The Before column simply means the Balance Sheet as it existed before the transactions took place, while the After column shows it after the transactions have been completed. The column headed + or − shows the additions to, or the deductions from, the balances in the various accounts shown in the Before Balance Sheets. In each exhibit the transactions will be described, each transaction having a signifying letter. By the side of the items in the + or − column will also be a letter which refers to the transactions already described by that letter.

Exhibit 36.1

Balance Sheets

	Before	+ or −	After		Before	+ or −	After
	£	£	£		£	£	£
Ordinary Share				Other Assets	10,000		10,000
Capital	5,000	+2,000(A)	7,000	Bank	1,000	+2,000(A)	
Redeemable Preference						−2,000(B)	1,000
Share Capital	2,000	−2,000(B)	—				
Capital Redemption							
Reserve Fund	—	—	—				
Profit and Loss	1,000		1,000				
Creditors	3,000		3,000				
	11,000		11,000		11,000		11,000

Shares are redeemed at par, a new issue of ordinary shares being made for the purpose.

(A) 2,000 Ordinary Shares of £1 each are issued at par, cash being received immediately.

(B) The whole of the 2,000 redeemable preference shares of £1 each are now redeemed at par.

Exhibit 36.2

The shares are redeemed at par, with no new issue of shares to provide funds for the purpose. Therefore an amount equal to the nominal value of the shares redeemed must be transferred from the Profit and Loss Appropriation Account to a Capital Redemption Reserve Fund.

(A) 2,000 Redeemable preference shares of £1 each are redeemed at par.

(B) The transfer from the Profit and Loss Appropriation Account to the Capital Redemption Reserve Fund takes place.

Balance Sheets

	Before	+ or −	After		Before	+ or −	After
	£	£	£		£	£	£
Ordinary Share				Other Assets	7,700		7,700
Capital	5,000		5,000	Bank	5,100	−2,000(A)	3,100
Redeemable Preference							
Share Capital	2,000	−2,000(A)	—				
Capital Redemption							
Reserve Fund	—	+2,000(B)	2,000				
Profit and Loss	2,800	−2,000(B)	800				
Creditors	3,000		3,000				
	12,800		10,800		12,800		10,800

Exhibit 36.3

The shares are redeemed at par, being partly out of the proceeds of a new issue and partly by using up some of the Profit and Loss Appropriation Account balance. The amount transferred from the Profit and Loss Appropriation Account to the Capital Redemption Reserve Fund is therefore equal to the nominal amount of the shares redeemed not covered by the proceeds of the new issue.

(A) 1,200 Ordinary Shares of £1 are issued at par being paid for immediately.

(B) 2,000 redeemable preference shares of £1 each are redeemed at par.

(C) The part of the shares redeemed not covered by the proceeds of the new issue is £800. This has to be transferred from the Profit and Loss Appropriation Account to the Capital Redemption Reserve Fund.

Balance Sheets

	Before	+ or −	After		Before	+ or −	After
	£	£	£		£	£	£
Ordinary Share				Other Assets	7,700		7,700
Capital	5,000	+1,200(A)	6,200	Bank	5,100	+1,200(A)	
Redeemable Preference						−2,000(B)	4,300
Share Capital	2,000	−2,000(B)	—				
Capital Redemption	—	+ 800(C)	800				
Profit and Loss	2,800	− 800(C)	2,000				
Creditors	3,000		3,000				
	12,800		12,000		12,800		12,000

Exhibit 36.4

The redeemable preference shares are redeemed at a premium of 20 per cent. There is no new issue of shares. The Share Premium Account has a large enough balance to cover the premium on redemption.

(A) 2,000 redeemable preference shares of £1 each are redeemed (the nominal value portion).

(B) Payment of the premium of 20 per cent on redemption. This is being shown separately here to show the effect more clearly. In point of fact these will not be paid by cheques separate from (A), both (A) and (B) being added together to give the amounts needed for each cheque.

(C) The transfer of the nominal value of the redeemed shares from the Profit and Loss Appropriation Account to the Capital Redemption Reserve Fund.

Balance Sheets

	Before	+ or −	After		Before	+ or −	After
	£	£	£		£	£	£
Ordinary Share				Other Assets	8,200		8,200
Capital	5,000		5,000	Bank	5,100	−2,000(A)	
Redeemable Preference						−400(B)	2,700
Share Capital	2,000	−2,000(A)	—				
Capital Redemption							
Reserve Fund	—	+2,000(C)	2,000				
Share Premium	500	−400(B)	100				
Profit and Loss	2,800	−2,000(C)	800				
Creditors	3,000		3,000				
	13,300		10,900		13,300		10,900

Exhibit 36.5

The redeemable preference shares are redeemed at a premium of 10 per cent. There is no Share Premium Account. No new shares are issued.

(A) 2,000 redeemable preference shares of £1 each are redeemed at a premium of 10 per cent. (The payment out of the bank is the full amount of the nominal value of the shares plus the premium.)

(B) Transfer of the nominal value of the shares redeemed to the Capital Redemption Reserve Fund from the Profit and Loss Appropriation Account.

Balance Sheets

	Before	+ or −	After		Before	+ or −	After
	£	£	£		£	£	£
Ordinary Share				Other Assets	7,700		7,700
Capital	5,000		5,000	Bank	5,100	−2,200(A)	2,900
Redeemable Preference							
Share Capital	2,000	−2,000(A)	—				
Capital Redemption							
Reserve Fund	—	+2,000(B)	2,000				
Profit and Loss	2,800	−200(A)					
		−2,000(B)	600				
Creditors	3,000		3,000				
	12,800		10,600		12,800		10,600

Exhibit 36.6

The redeemable preference shares are redeemed at a premium of 25 per cent. There is an issue of an equivalent number of ordinary shares at a premium of 5 per cent. However, the Share Premium Account is insufficient to cover the premiums on redemption.

(A) 2,000 Ordinary Shares of £1 each issued at a premium of 5 per cent.

(B) 2,000 redeemable preference shares are redeemed at a premium of 25 per cent.

(C) The Share Premium Account opening balance £50, plus the share premium on the ordinary shares £100, is deemed to be the source of funds out of which the premium on the shares redeemed has been paid. As this amounts to 25 per cent of £2,000=£500, it wipes out the Share Premium Account. The remainder of £350 must therefore be deemed to come from the Profit and Loss Appropriation Account.

Balance Sheet

	Before	+ or −	After		Before	+ or −	After
	£	£	£		£	£	£
Ordinary Share				Other Assets	7,750		7,750
Capital	5,000	+2,000(A)	7,000	Bank	5,100	+2,100(A)	4,700
Redeemable Preference						−2,500	
Share Capital	2,000	−2,000(B)	—			(B&C)	
Capital Redemption							
Reserve Fund	—		—				
Share Premium	50	+100(A)					
		−500(C)	—				
Profit and Loss	2,800	−350(C)	2,450				
Creditors	3,000		3,000				
	12,850		12,450		12,850		12,450

Redemption of Redeemable Preference Shares and Journal Entries

As the redemption is one of the types of transactions which should be journalised, it is therefore not surprising if examiners require the journal entries to be shown rather than the actual entries in the accounts. This is a constant source of trouble for students. However, if the reader has been able to understand the entries made in the Balance Sheets in Exhibits 36.1 to 36.6 inclusive, then the journal entries should not cause undue trouble. To revise basic accounting entries, the accounts for assets, liabilities and capital in the books are increased $(+)$ and reduced $(-)$ in the following manner:

Debit Side	Liabilities		Credit Side
Reduce	−	Increase	+

Debit Side	Capital		Credit Side
Reduce	−	Increase	+

Debit Side	Assets		Credit Side
Increase	+	Reduce	−

Therefore to take Exhibit 36.3 as an example, look at the location of the $+$ and the $-$ signs in the Balance Sheet and compare with the accounts $+$ and $-$ just shown. It should now be easily possible to state which accounts are being reduced or increased, and to understand whether this involves debit or credit entries. The Journal entries will now be shown in Exhibit 36.7.

Exhibit 36.7

The Journal

		Dr	Cr
		£	£
(A)	Bank	1,200	
	Ordinary Share Capital		1,200
	1,200 Ordinary Shares of £1 each issued at par		
(B)	Redeemable Preference Share Capital	2,000	
	Bank		2,000
	Payment of cheques to redeem the shares		

	The Journal	Dr	Cr
		£	£
(C)	Profit and Loss Appropriation Account	800	
	Capital Redemption Reserve Fund		800
	Portion of nominal value of shares redeemed not covered by proceeds of new issue		

It is therefore a matter of translating the details in Exhibit 36.3 into the Journal style of Exhibit 36.7. For many people it will be easier to draft a working paper as in Exhibit 36.3, and then to translate it into Journal form. Thinking in terms of Balance Sheet layout is often not unduly difficult for students, but relatively fewer students can visualise transactions in Journal form.

Redemption of Debentures

Unless they are stated to be irredeemable, debentures are redeemed according to the terms of the issue. The necessary funds to finance the redemption may be from:

(*a*) An issue of shares or debentures for the purpose.

(*b*) The liquid resources of the company.

Resembling the redemption of redeemable preference shares, when the redemption is financed as in (*a*), no transfer of profits from the Profit and Loss Appropriation Account to a Reserve Account is needed. However, when financed as in (*b*) it is good accounting practice, although not legally necessary, to divert profits from being used as dividends by transferring an amount equal to the nominal value redeemed from the debit of the Profit and Loss Appropriation Account to the credit of a Reserve Account.

Redemption may be effected:

1. By annual drawings out of profits.

2. By purchase in the open market when the price is favourable, i.e. less than the price which will have to be paid if the company waited until the last date by which redemption has to be carried out.

3. In a lump sum to be provided by the accumulation of a sinking fund.

These can now be examined in more detail.

1. *Regular Annual Drawings out of Profits*

(i) When redeemed at a premium.

In this case the source of the bank funds with which the premium is paid should be taken to be (*a*) Share Premium Account, or if this does not exist, or the premium is in excess of the balance on the account, then any

part not covered by a Share Premium Account is deemed to come from
(*b*) The Profit and Loss Appropriation Account. Exhibit 36.8 shows
the effect of a Balance Sheet where there is no Share Premium Account,
while Exhibit 36.9 illustrates the case when a Share Premium Account
is in existence.

Exhibit 36.8

Starting with the Before Balance Sheet, £400 of the debentures are
redeemed at a premium of 20 per cent.

Balance Sheets

	Before	+ or −	After		Before	+ or −	After
	£	£	£		£	£	£
Share Capital	10,000		10,000	Other Assets	12,900		12,900
Debenture Redemption				Bank	3,400	−480(A)	2,920
Reserve	—	+400(A)	400				
Debentures	2,000	−400(A)	1,600				
Profit and Loss	4,300	−400(B)					
		− 80(A)	3,820				
	16,300		15,820		16,300		15,820

Exhibit 36.9

Starting with the Before Balance Sheet, £400 of the debentures are
redeemed at a premium of 20 per cent.

Balance Sheets

	Before	+ or −	After		Before	+ or −	After
	£	£	£		£	£	£
Share Capital	10,000		10,000	Other Assets	13,500		13,500
Share Premium	600	− 80(A)	520	Bank	3,400	−480(A)	2,920
Debenture Redemption							
Reserve	—	+400(B)	400				
Debentures	2,000	−400(A)	1,600				
Profit and Loss	4,300	−400(B)	3,900				
	16,900		16,420		16,900		16,420

In both Exhibits 36.8 and 36.9 the Debenture Redemption Reserve
Account is built up each year by the nominal value of the debentures
redeemed each year. When the whole issue of debentures has been
redeemed, then the balance on the Debenture Redemption Reserve
Account should be transferred to the credit of a General Reserve
Account. It is, after all, an accumulation of undistributed profits.

(ii) Redeemed—originally issued at a discount.
The discount originally given was in fact to attract investors to buy the
debentures, and is therefore as much a cost of borrowing as is debenture
interest. The discount therefore needs to be written off during the life

of the debentures. It might be more rational to write it off to the Profit and Loss Account, but in fact accounting custom, as permitted by law, would first of all write it off against any Share Premium Account or, secondly, against the Profit and Loss Appropriation Account.

The amounts written off can be calculated either as:

(a) Equal annual amounts over the life of the debentures.
(b) In proportion to the debenture debt outstanding at the start of each year. Exhibit 36.10 shows such a situation.

Exhibit 36.10

£30,000 debentures are issued at a discount of 5 per cent. They are repayable at par over five years at the rate of £6,000 per annum.

Year	Outstanding at start of each year	Proportion written off		Amount
	£			£
1	30,000	$\frac{30}{90} \times £1,500$	=	500
2	24,000	$\frac{24}{90} \times £1,500$	=	400
3	18,000	$\frac{18}{90} \times £1,500$	=	300
4	12,000	$\frac{12}{90} \times £1,500$	=	200
5	6,000	$\frac{6}{90} \times £1,500$	=	100
	90,000			1,500

2. Redeemed by Purchase in the Open Market

A sum equal to the cash actually paid on redemption should be transferred from the debit of the Profit and Loss Appropriation Account to the credit of the Debenture Redemption Reserve Account. The sum actually paid will of course have been credited to the Cash Book and debited to the Debentures Account.

Any discount (or profit) on purchase will be transferred to a Reserve Account. Any premium (or loss) on purchase will be deemed to come out of such a Reserve Account, or if no such account exists or it is insufficient, then it will be deemed to come out of the Share Premium Account. Failing the existence of these accounts any loss must come out of the Profit and Loss Appropriation Account. It may seem that purchase would not be opportune if the debentures had to be redeemed at a premium. However, it would still be opportune if the premium paid was not as high as the premium to be paid if the final date for redemption was awaited.

3. By Means of a Sinking Fund

First of all the Sinking Fund and the Sinking Fund Investment Account

are built up as with the Depreciation Sinking Fund method.
  Finally the entries are:

Debit Bank Account } With the sale of the
Credit Sinking Fund Investment Account } investments

Debit Debentures Account } With the cheques paid on redemption
Credit Bank Account } of the debentures

  At this point the account now open is the Sinking Fund Account with a credit balance. This credit balance is now transferred to the credit of a General Reserve Account. Compare this with the similar stage of the Depreciation Sinking Fund, which then had a credit balance on the Sinking Fund Account and a debit balance on the Old Asset Account. The Sinking Fund Account balance was then transferred to extinguish the Old Asset Account balance. Therefore the redemption of a liability by this method leaves eventually a higher credit balance in the General Reserve Account, while the replacement of an asset leaves no balances, if the Bank Account is ignored.

  Sometimes debentures bought in the open market are not cancelled, but are kept 'alive' and are treated as investments of the sinking fund. The annual appropriation of profits is credited to the Sinking Fund Account, while the amount expended on the purchase of the debentures is debited to the Sinking Fund Investment Account. Interest on such debentures is debited to the Profit and Loss Account and credited to the Sinking Fund Account, thus the interest, as far as the Sinking Fund Account is concerned, is treated in the same fashion as if it was cash actually received by the firm from an outside investment. The sum then expended on investments will then be equal to the annual appropriation + the interest on investments actually received + the interest on debentures kept in hand.

Exercises

36.1. The following is the summarised Balance Sheet of Britain Ltd at 31 March 19–6:

Balance Sheet

	£		£
Issued Capital:		Fixed Assets	11,750
Ordinary Shares of £1		Stock	3,400
each	10,000	Debtors	1,400
Redeemable Preference		Bank	5,200
Shares of £1 each	3,000		
Share Premium Account	550		
Profit and Loss Account	7,200		
Current Liabilities	1,000		
	21,750		21,750

The following transactions occur on 1 April 19–6:

1.   1,800 shares of £1 each are issued at a premium of 5 per cent, these being paid for immediately. The proceeds are to be used in redeeming the preference shares.

2.   All the redeemable preference shares are redeemed at a premium of 25 per cent.

3.   £8,000 7 per cent debentures are issued at a discount of 3 per cent. One-third of the discount is to be written off immediately.

You are required to draw up the revised Balance Sheet as at 1 April 19–6 after the above transactions have been completed. Show all workings.

36.2. A company with an issued capital of £20,000 8 per cent redeemable preference shares of £1 each fully paid and 300,000 ordinary shares of £1 each fully paid had a credit balance of £36,000 on the Profit and Loss Account and adequate cash resources. It was decided to redeem the preference shares at a premium of 10 per cent per share out of profits.

Make the necessary entries by means of the journal. (Cash transactions are to be journalised.)

(*Associated Examining Board 'A' Level*)

36.3. Change Limited has an issued share capital of 65,000 7 per cent redeemable cumulative preference shares of £1 each and 450,000 ordinary shares of £0·5 each. The preference shares are redeemable at a premium of 7½ per cent on 1 August 19–7.

As on 31 July 19–7, the company's Balance Sheet, showed the following position:

	£		£
Issued Share Capital:		Sundry Assets	346,000
65,000 7 per cent		Investments	17,500
Redeemable Cumulative		Balance at Bank	30,000
Preference Shares of £1			
each, fully paid	65,000		
450,000 Ordinary Shares			
of £0·5 each, fully paid	225,000		
Profit and Loss Account	46,000		
Sundry Creditors	57,500		
	393,500		393,500

In order to facilitate the redemption of the preference shares, it was decided:

1.   to sell the investments for £15,000;

2.   to finance part of the redemption from company funds, subject to leaving a balance on Profit and Loss Account of £10,000; and

3.   to issue sufficient ordinary shares at a premium of 25 per cent per share to raise the balance of funds required.

The preference shares were redeemed on the due date, and the issue of ordinary shares was fully subscribed.

You are required to prepare:

(a) the necessary journal entries to record the above transactions (including cash); and

(b) the Balance Sheet as on completion.

(*Institute of Chartered Accountants*)

36.4. The following items appeared in the Balance Sheet of A.B. and Co Ltd as on 31 December 19–5.

	£	£
Share Capital		
75,000 Ordinary Shares of £1 each, fully paid	75,000	
25,000 6 per cent Redeemable Preference Shares of £1 each, fully paid	25,000	
		100,000
Revenue Reserves:		
General	40,000	
Profit and Loss Account	30,000	
		70,000

On 1 January 19–6, the company resolved:

  (i) to issue 25,000 Ordinary Shares of £1 each at a premium of 25 per cent in order to finance the redemption of the 6 per cent Redeemable Preference Shares;

 (ii) to redeem the Preference Shares at a premium of 17½ per cent per share; and

(iii) to make a bonus issue of two Ordinary Shares, £1 each, for every three shares held by the existing Ordinary Shareholders.

Write up the accounts of the company to record the above transactions (the issue referred to in (i) above being wholly subscribed and paid up), and show how the items would appear in the company's Balance Sheet after they had been effected.

(*Union of Lancashire and Cheshire Institutes*)

36.5. Oaken Ltd issued £100,000 6 per cent debentures at par ten years previously redeemable at 101 on 31 December 19–1. Under the terms of a debenture trust deed a sinking fund had been built up by annual appropriations out of profits which were invested, together with any income which had arisen on the fund, in gilt-edged investments on 31 December in each year. The trustees have power to purchase, for immediate cancellation, any debentures available at a market price below par and to realise sinking fund investments for this purpose.

On 1 January 19–1, there were the following balances:

1.   Debentures outstanding £80,000.

2.   Sinking Fund Account £79,350 represented by an equivalent amount of gilt-edged securities standing in the books at cost.

During the twelve months ended 31 December 19–1, the undernoted transactions took place:

1.   On 30 June the half-year's debenture interest to date was paid.

2.   On 1 July £5,000 debentures were purchased in the market at 99 and cancelled. To provide funds for this purchase investments costing £5,650 were sold and realised £5,500.

3.   Interest was received on the sinking fund investments amounting to £3,850 which was not invested in view of the impending sale of the investments of the fund.

4. On 28 December £72,100 was received representing the proceeds of sale of the remaining investments of the sinking fund.

5. On 31 December the debentures were repaid together with the half-year's interest thereon.

You are required to write up the following ledger accounts for the twelve months ended 31 December 19–1:

(a) 6 per cent Debentures;
(b) Sinking Fund; and
(c) Sinking Fund Investments.

Ignore income tax.
(*Institute of Chartered Accountants*)

36.6. In 1953, Alpha Ltd issued £200,000 6 per cent Debentures at par which were redeemable at 102 on 30 June 19–4. Annual appropriations had been made out of profits to a Sinking Fund set up under the terms of the debenture trust deed. The appropriations were invested annually on 30 June together with the Sinking Fund investment income received in the year ended on that date. The trustees have power to purchase, for immediate cancellation, any debentures available at a market price below par, and to realise investments of the Sinking Fund for this purpose.

The following balances appeared in the company's books on 1 July 19–3:

(i) Sinking Fund Account £117,490, represented by investments at cost of an equal amount.

(ii) 6 per cent Debentures £120,000.

The undermentioned transactions took place during the year ended 30 June 19–4:

1. Half-year's debenture interest to 31 December 19–3 was paid on that date.

2. Investments costing £9,750 were sold, and realised £10,050 on 1 January 19–4 in order to provide funds for purchase of debentures. On the same date, £10,000 debentures were purchased at 98 (inclusive of expenses) on the market, and cancelled.

3. The remaining investments of the Fund were sold, and the proceeds amounting to £110,200 were received on 29 June 19–4.

4. Income amounting to £6,950 received in the year from the Sinking Fund investments was not invested in view of the impending debenture redemption.

5. On 30 June 19–4, the debentures were repaid together with the half-year's interest thereon.

You are required to write up the following ledger accounts for the year ended 30 June 19–4:

(a) 6 per cent Debentures, showing capital and interest entries;
(b) Sinking Fund Investments;
(c) Sinking Fund; and
(d) Debenture Redemption.

Ignore income tax.
(*Institute of Chartered Accountants*)

36.7A. Change Limited has an issued share capital of 65,000 7 per cent redeemable cumulative preference shares of £1 each and 450,000 ordinary shares of £0·5 each. The preference shares are redeemable at a premium of $7\frac{1}{2}$ per cent on 1 August 19–7.

As on 31 July 19–7, the company's Balance Sheet showed the following position:

	£		£
Issued Share Capital:		Sundry Assets	346,000
65,000 7 per cent		Investments	17,500
Redeemable Cumulative		Balance at Bank	30,000
Preference Shares of £1			
each, fully paid	65,000		
450,000 Ordinary Shares			
of £0·5 each, fully paid	225,000		
Profit and Loss Account	46,000		
Sundry creditors	57,500		
	393,500		393,500

In order to facilitate the redemption of the preference shares, it was decided:

1. To sell the investments for £15,000.

2. To finance part of the redemption from company funds, subject to leaving a balance on Profit and Loss Account of £10,000.

3. And to issue sufficient ordinary shares at a premium of $12\frac{1}{2}$p per share to raise the balance of funds required.

The preference shares were redeemed on the due date, and the issue of ordinary shares was fully subscribed.

You are required to prepare:

(a) The necessary journal entries to record the above transactions (including cash).

(b) And the Balance Sheet as on completion.

(*Institute of Chartered Accountants*)

36.8A. On 30 April 19–6, the summarised Balance Sheet of Craft Ltd showed the following position:

	£	£		£
Share Capital:			Fixed Assets	429,000
7 per cent Redeemable			Current Assets	200,000
Preference Shares			Balance at Bank	204,000
of £1 each	120,000			
Ordinary Shares				
of £1 each	280,000			
		400,000		
General Reserve		80,000		
Profit and Loss Account		226,000		
		706,000		
Current Liabilities		127,000		
		833,000		833,000

On 1 May 19–6, the following transactions took place:

1. The redeemable preference shares were repaid at a premium of 10p per share, and

2. £150,000 7½ per cent Debentures 19–0/–2 were issued at £98 per centum.

You are required to show:

(a) the necessary ledger accounts (including cash) to record the above transactions, and

(b) the summarised Balance Sheet of the company as it would appear immediately after completion.

(*Institute of Chartered Accountants*)

36.9A. The following is a summary of the Balance Sheet of E.T.E. Ltd as on 31 March 19–8:

Balance Sheets

	£		£	£
Issued Share Capital		Fixed Assets		360,000
300,000 Ordinary				
Shares of £1 each	300,000	Current Assets		
60,000 7 per cent		Stocks and		
Redeemable Preference		Debtors	58,500	
Shares of £1 each	60,000	Balance at Bank	31,500	
				90,000
	360,000			
Profit and Loss Account	51,000			
Current Liabilities	39,000			
	450,000			450,000

On 1 April 19–8, the company:

1. Redeemed the preference shares, at a premium of 10p per share.

2. Issued £15,000 7½ per cent debentures, at par.

3. Issued, at par, a number of ordinary shares of £1 each.

The shares and debentures were fully paid up in cash on 1 April.

The number of ordinary shares issued was such as to ensure that, after compliance with the requirements of the Companies Acts in regard to the redemption of preference shares, the credit balance on the profit and loss account would be £9,000.

You are required to show:

(i) the entries in the company's cash book and ledger in respect of the above transactions, and

(ii) a summary of the company's balance sheet as it would appear immediately after the completion of the above.

(*Chartered Institute of Secretaries and Administrators*)

36.10A. Fox Ltd issued £275,000 6¼ per cent Debentures at par in 19–8 which were redeemable eleven years later at 103 on 30 September 19–9. In accordance with provisions in the debenture trust deed, annual appropriations had been made out of profits to a Sinking Fund, to provide for the redemption of the debentures. The appropriations had been invested annually on 30 September together with the Sinking Fund investment income received in the year ended on that date.

On 1 October 19–8, the following balances appeared in the company's books:

1.   Sinking Fund Account £173,570 represented by investments (at cost) amounting to a similar figure.

2.   6¼ per cent Debentures £180,000 (balance remaining after cancellations authorized by the Trust Deed). During the year ended 30 September 19–9, the undermentioned transactions had taken place:

(i) On 31 March 19–9, a half-year's debenture interest was paid.
(ii) The Sinking Fund investments were sold, and the proceeds amounting to £185,640 were received on 12 September 19–9.
(iii) The income from Sinking Fund investments received during the year amounted to £11,200 and was not invested but retained in view of the impending redemption of the debentures.
(iv) The debentures were repaid on 30 September 19–9, together with the half-year's interest due thereon.

You are required to write up the following accounts for the year ended 30 September 19–9, as they would appear in the ledger:

(i) 6¼ per cent Debentures,
(ii) Sinking Fund Investments,
(iii) Sinking Fund,
(iv) Debenture Redemption, and
(v) Debenture Interest.

  Ignore income tax.
(*Association of Certified Accountants*)

36.11A. Robin Ltd issued £350,000 7 per cent Debentures in 19–7, which were redeemable at a premium of 3 per cent ten years later on 31 December 19–7.

When the debentures were issued, it was provided that annual appropriations were to be made out of profits to a Sinking Fund to provide for their redemption, and that the appropriations be invested outside the company annually on 31 December, together with the Sinking Fund investment income received in the year ended on that date.

During the life of the debentures, the trustees were empowered to purchase for immediate cancellation any debentures available on the open market below redemption price, and to finance the purchase by selling Sinking Fund investments.

On 1 January 19–7, the balance on the Sinking Fund Account amounted to £209,650, represented by an equal amount of investments at cost. The debentures in issue at that date amounted to £220,000.

During the year ended 31 December 19–7, the following transactions took place:

1.   On 2 January 19–7, investments costing £19,500 were sold, realising the sum of £21,040, and on the same date £20,600 debentures were purchased at 101 (including expenses) and cancelled.

2. The half-year's debenture interest was paid on 30 June 19-7.

3. The income on Sinking Fund investments received during the year amounting to £10,500 was retained in cash pending the redemption of the debentures.

4. The balance of the Sinking Fund investments were sold and the proceeds amounting to £215,690 were received on 14 December 19-7.

5. The debentures were repaid on 31 December 19-7, together with the interest due to date.

You are required to write up the ledger accounts (excluding the cash book) necessary to record the above transactions for the year ended 31 December 19-7. (*Institute of Chartered Accountants*)

37

Limited Companies Taking Over Other Businesses

Limited companies will often take over other businesses which are in existence as going concerns. The purchase considerations may either be in cash, by giving the company's shares to the owners, by giving the company's debentures, or by any combination of these three factors.

It must not be thought that because the assets bought are shown in the selling firm's books at one value that the purchasing company must record the assets taken over in its own books at the same value. The values shown in the purchasing company's books are those values at which the company is buying the assets, such values being frequently quite different than those shown in the selling firm's books. As an instance of this, the selling firm may have bought premises many years ago for £1,000 but they may now be worth £5,000. The company buying the premises will obviously have to pay £5,000 and it is therefore this value that is recorded in the buying company's books. Alternatively, the value at which it is recorded in the buying company's books may be less than that shown in the selling firm's books. Where the total purchase consideration exceeds the total value of the identifiable assets then such excess is the goodwill, and will need entering in a Goodwill Account in the purchasing company's books. Should the total purchase consideration be less than the values of the identifiable assets, then the difference would be entered in a Capital Reserve Account.

Before the accounting entries necessary to record the purchase of a going business are looked at, it must be pointed out that such recording of the transactions is the simple end of the whole affair. The negotiations that take place before agreement is reached, and the various strategies undertaken by the various parties is a study in itself. The accounting entries are in effect the 'tip of the iceberg', i.e. that part of the whole affair which is seen by the eventual reader of the accounts.

Taking over a Sole Trader's Business

It is easier to start with the takeover of the simplest sort of business unit, that of a sole trader. Some of the Balance Sheets shown will be deliberately simplified so that the principles involved are not hidden behind a mass of complicated calculations.

Exhibit 37.1

Earl Ltd is to buy the business of M. Kearney. The purchase consideration is to be £6,000 cash, the company placing the following values on the assets taken over—Machinery £3,000, Stock £1,000. The goodwill must therefore be £2,000, because the total price of £6,000 exceeds the values of Machinery £3,000 and Stock £1,000 by the sum of £2,000. The company's Balance Sheets will be shown before and after the take-over, it being assumed that the transactions are all concluded immediately.

M. Kearney
Balance Sheet

	£		£
Capital	3,000	Machinery	1,700
		Stock	1,300
	3,000		3,000

Earl Ltd
Balance Sheet(s)

	Before	+ or −	After		Before	+ or −	After
	£	£	£		£	£	£
Share Capital	20,000		20,000	Goodwill		+2,000	2,000
Profit and Loss	5,000		5,000	Machinery	11,000	+3,000	14,000
				Stock	5,000	+1,000	6,000
				Bank	9,000	−6,000	3,000
	25,000		25,000		25,000		25,000

Exhibit 37.2

Suppose the purchase had been made instead by issuing 7,000 shares of £1 each at par to Kearney. The goodwill would then be £7,000−assets taken over £4,000 = £3,000. The Balance Sheets of Earl Ltd would be:

Earl Ltd
Balance Sheets

	Before	+ or −	After		Before	+ or −	After
	£	£	£		£	£	£
Share Capital	20,000	+7,000	27,0	Goodwill		+3,000	3,000
Profit and Loss	5,000		5,00	Machinery	11,000	+3,000	14,000
				Stc	5,000	+1,000	6,000
				Bank	9,000		9,000
	25,000		32,000		25,000		32,000

Exhibit 37.3

If the purchase had been made by issuing 5,000 shares of £1 each at a premium of 50 per cent, then the total consideration would have been worth £7,500, which, if the assets of £4,000 are deducted leaves good-will of £3,500. The Balance Sheets would then be:

Earl Ltd
Balance Sheet(s)

	Before	+ or −	After		Before	+ or −	After
	£	£	£		£	£	£
Share Capital	20,000	+5,000	25,000	Goodwill		+3,500	3,500
Share Premium		+2,500	2,500	Machinery	11,000	+3,000	14,000
Profit and Loss	5,000		5,000	Stocks	5,000	+1,000	6,000
				Bank	9,000		9,000
	25,000		32,500		25,000		32,500

Exhibit 37.4

Now if the purchase had been made by the issue of 1,000 shares of £1 each at a premium of 40 per cent, £3,000 worth of 7 per cent debentures at par and £4,000 in cash, then the total purchase consideration would be shares valued at £1,400, debentures valued at £3,000 and cash £4,000, making in all £8,400. The assets are valued at £4,000, the goodwill must be £4,400. The Balance Sheets would appear:

Earl Ltd
Balance Sheet(s)

	Before	+ or −	After		Before	+ or −	After
	£	£	£		£	£	£
Share Capital	20,000	+1,000	21,000	Goodwill		+4,400	4,400
Share Premium		+ 400	400	Machinery	11,000	+3,000	14,000
Profit and Loss	5,000		5,000	Stocks	5,000	+1,000	6,000
Debentures		+3,000	3,000	Bank	9,000	−4,000	5,000
	25,000		29,400		25,000		29,400

In each of Exhibits 37.1 to 37.4 it has been assumed that all trans-actions were started and completed within a few moments. The fact is that an intermediary account would be created but then closed almost immediately when the purchase consideration was handed over. Taking Exhibit 37.3 as an example, there will be a credit in the Share Capital Account and in the Share Premium Account, and debits in the Goodwill, Machinery and Stock Accounts. Nevertheless, shares cannot be issued to goodwill, machinery or stocks. They have, in fact, been issued to M. Kearney. This means that there should have been an account for M. Kearney, but that the balance on it was cancelled on the passing of the purchase consideration. The actual accounts for Exhibit 37.3 were as follows in the books of Earl Ltd:

Share Premium

	£
M. Kearney	2,500

Share Capital

	£		£
Balance c/d	25,000	Balance b/fwd	20,000
		M. Kearney	5,000
	25,000		25,000
		Balance b/d	25,000

Profit and Loss

			£
		Balance b/fwd	5,000

Goodwill

	£		
M. Kearney	3,500		

Machinery

	£		£
Balance b/fwd	11,000		
M. Kearney	3,000	Balance c/d	14,000
	14,000		14,000
Balance b/d	14,000		

Stock

	£		£
Balance b/d	5,000		
M. Kearney	1,000	Balance c/d	6,000
	6,000		6,000
Balance c/d	6,000		

(In actual fact the £1,000 would probably be entered in the Purchases Account. It does, however, obviously increase the actual amount of stock.)

Bank

	£		
Balance b/fwd	9,000		

M. Kearney

	£		£
Consideration Passing:		Assets Taken Over	
Share Capital	5,000	Goodwill	3,500
Share Premium	2,500	Machinery	3,000
		Stock	1,000
	7,500		7,500

Some accountants would have preferred to use a Business Purchase Account instead of a personal account such as that of M. Kearney.

Sometimes the company taking over the business of a sole trader not only pays a certain amount for the assets but also assumes responsibility for paying the creditors in addition. Take the case of a sole trader with assets valued at Premises £5,000 and Stock £4,000. To gain control of these assets the company is to pay the sole trader £11,000 in cash, and in addition the company will pay off creditors £1,000. This means that the goodwill is £3,000, calculated as follows:

	£		£
Paid by the company to gain control of the sole trader's assets:			
Cash to the Sole Trader			11,000
Cash to the Sole Trader's Creditors			1,000
		£	12,000
The Company receives Assets			
Premises		5,000	
Stock		4,000	
			9,000
Excess paid for Goodwill			3,000

Partnership Business taken over by a Limited Company

The entries are the same as for those of taking over a sole traders' business, with the exception that there will be a personal account for each partner. There are, however, difficulties about the distribution of shares as between the partners when the balances on their Capital Accounts are not in the same ratio with one another as their profit-sharing ratios. This is, however, better left to a more advanced stage of studies in accounting.

The partnership will, of course, show a Realization Account in its own books. The total purchase consideration will be credited to the Realization Account and debited to the company's personal account. The discharge of the purchase consideration will close the partnership books.

The Takeover of a Limited Company by another Limited Company

One company may take over another company by one of two methods:

1. By buying all the assets of the other company, the purchase consideration being by cash, shares or debentures. The selling company may afterwards be wound up, the liquidators either distributing the purchasing company's shares and debentures between the shareholders of the selling company, or else the shares and debentures of the buying company may be sold and the cash distributed instead.

2. By giving its own shares and debentures in exchange for the shares and debentures of the selling company's share and debenture holders. Exhibit 37.5 is an illustration of each of these methods.

Exhibit 37.5

The following are the Balance Sheets of three companies as on the same date.

	R Ltd	S Ltd	T Ltd		R Ltd	S Ltd	T Ltd
	£	£	£		£	£	£
Share Capital				Buildings	13,000	—	1,000
(£1 shares)	18,000	3,000	5,000	Machinery	4,000	2,000	1,000
Profit and Loss	2,000	1,000	4,000	Stock	3,000	1,000	2,000
Current				Debtors	2,000	1,000	3,000
Liabilities	3,000	2,000	1,000	Bank	1,000	2,000	3,000
	23,000	6,000	10,000		23,000	6,000	10,000

R takes over S by exchanging with the shareholders of S two shares in R at a premium of 10 per cent for every share they hold in S.

R takes over T by buying all the assets of T, the purchase consideration being 12,000 £1 shares in R at a premium of 10 per cent, and R will pay off T's creditors. R values T's assets at Buildings £2,000, Machinery £600, Stock £1,400, Debtors £2,500, and the Bank is £3,000, a total of £9,500.

R's deal with the shareholders of S means that R now has complete control of S Ltd, so that S Ltd becomes what is known as a subsidiary company of R Ltd, and will be shown as an investment in R's Balance Sheet.

On the other hand, the deal with T has resulted in the ownership of the assets resting with R. These must therefore be added to R's assets in its own Balance Sheet. As R has given 12,000 £1 shares at a premium of 10 per cent plus taking over the responsibility for creditors £1,000, the total purchase consideration for the assets taken over is £12,000+£1,200 (10 per cent of £12,000)+£1,000 = £14,200. Identifiable assets as already stated are valued at £9,500, therefore the goodwill is £14,200−£9,500 = £4,700.

The distinction between the acquisition of the two going concerns can be seen to be a rather fine one. With S the shares are taken over, the possession of these in turn giving rise to the ownership of the assets. In the books of R this is regarded as an investment. With T the actual assets and liabilities are taken over so that the assets now directly belong to R. In the books of R this is therefore regarded as the acquisition of additional assets and liabilities and not as an investment (using the meaning of 'investment' which is used in the Balance Sheets of companies). The Balance Sheet of R Ltd therefore becomes:

R Ltd
Balance Sheet

	Before	+ or −	After		Before	+ or −	After
	£	£	£		£	£	£
Share Capital	18,000	+(S) 6,000		Goodwill		+(T) 4,700	4,700
		+(T)12,000 = 36,000		Buildings	13,000	+(T) 2,000	15,000
Share Premium		+(S) 600		Machinery	4,000	+(T) 600	4,600
		+(T) 1,200 = 1,800		Investment in			
Profit and Loss	2,000		2,000	S at cost	.	+ 6,600	6,600
Current				Stock	3,000	+(T) 1,400	4,400
Liabilities	3,000	+(T) 1,000	4,000	Debtors	2,000	+(T) 2,500	4,500
				Bank	1,000	+(T) 3,000	4,000
	23,000		43,800		23,000		43,800

No entry is necessary in the books of S Ltd, as it is merely the identity of the shareholders that has changed. This would be duly recorded in the register of members, but this is not really an integral part of the double entry accounting system.

If, however, T Ltd is now liquidated, then a Realization Account must be drawn up and the distribution of the shares (or cash if the shares are sold) to the shareholders of T Ltd must be shown. Such accounts would appear as follows:

Books of T Ltd
Realization

	£		£
Book Values of Assets		R Ltd: Total Purchase	
Disposed Of:		Consideration	14,200
Buildings	1,000		
Machinery	1,000		
Stock	2,000		
Debtors	3,000		
Bank	3,000		
Profit on Realization			
transferred to Sundry			
Shareholders	4,200		
	14,200		14,200

Share Capital

	£		£
Sundry Shareholders	5,000	Balance b/fwd	5,000

Profit and Loss

	£		£
Sundry Shareholders	4,000	Balance b/fwd	4,000

Creditors

	£		£
R Ltd—taken over	1,000	Balance b/fwd	1,000

R Ltd

	£		£
Realization:		Creditors	1,000
Total Consideration	14,200	Sundry Shareholders:	
		12,000 £1 shares	
		received at premium	
		of 10 per cent	13,200
	14,200		14,200

Sundry Shareholders

	£		£
R Ltd; 12,000 £1 shares		Share Capital	5,000
at premium of 10 per cent	13,200	Profit and Loss	4,000
		Profit on Realization	4,200
	13,200		13,200

It can be seen that the items possessed by the sundry shareholders have been transferred to an account in their name. These are (i) the share capital which obviously belongs to them, (ii) the credit balance on the Profit and Loss Account built up by withholding cash dividends from the shareholders, and (iii) the profit on realization which they, as owners of the business, are entitled to take. As there were 5,000 shares in T Ltd, and 12,000 shares have been given by R Ltd, then each holder of 5 shares in T Ltd will now be given 12 shares in R Ltd to complete the liquidation of the company.

The Exchange of Debentures

Sometimes the debentures in the company taking over are to be given in exchange for the debentures of the company being taken over. This may be straightforward on the basis of £100 debentures in company A in exchange for £100 debentures in company B. However, the problem often arises where the exchange is in terms of one of both sets of debentures being at a discount or at a premium. The need for such an exchange may be two-fold:

(a) To persuade the debenture holders in company B to give up their debentures some form of inducement may be needed, such as letting them have A's debentures at a discount even though they may well be worth the par value.

(b) There may be a difference in the debenture interest rates. For instance, a person with a £100 7 per cent debenture would not normally gladly part with it in exchange for a £100 6 per cent debenture in another company. The first debenture gives him £7 a year interest, the second one only £6 a year. Thus the debenture in the second company may be issued at a discount to redeem the debenture in the first company at a premium. As the amount of interest is only one factor, there are also others such as the certainty of the debenture holder regaining his money if the firm had to close down, the precise terms of the exchange cannot be based merely on arithmetical calculations of interest rates, but it is one of the measures taken when negotiating the exchange of debentures.

Exhibit 37.6

(i) D Ltd is to give the necessary debentures at a discount of 10 per cent necessary to redeem £9,000 debentures in J Ltd at a premium of 5 per cent. The problem here is to find exactly what amount of debentures must be given by D Ltd.

Answer: Total nominal value of debentures in J Ltd to be redeemed (exchanged) $\times \dfrac{\text{Redeemable value of each £100 debenture of J Ltd}}{\text{Issue value of each £100 debenture of D Ltd}}$

= Total nominal value of D Ltd to be issued

= £9,000 $\times \frac{105}{90}$ = £10,500

Thus, to satisfy the agreement, debentures of D Ltd of a total nominal value of £10,500 are issued at a discount of 10 per cent to the debenture holders of J Ltd.

(ii) H Ltd is to give the necessary debentures at par to redeem £5,000 debentures in M Ltd at a premium of 4 per cent.

£5,000 $\times \frac{104}{100}$ = Debentures of £5,200 nominal value are given by H Ltd at par

Profit (or Loss) prior to Incorporation

Quite frequently companies take over businesses from a date which is actually before the company was itself incorporated. It could be that two persons enter into business and start trading with the intention of running the business as a limited company. However, it takes more than a few days to attend to all the necessary formalities before the company can be incorporated. Obviously it depends on the speed with which the formation is pushed through and the solution of any snags which crop up. When the company is in fact incorporated it may enter into a contract whereby it adopts all the transactions retrospectively to the date that the firm, i.e. with two persons it was a partnership, had started trading. This means that the company accepts all the benefits and disadvantages which have flowed from the transactions which have occurred. The example used was that of a brand-new business; it could well have been an old-established business that was taken over from a date previous to incorporation.

Legally a company cannot earn profits before it comes into existence, i.e. is incorporated, and therefore to decide what action will have to be taken such profits will first of all have to be calculated. Any such profits are of a capital nature and must be transferred to a Capital Reserve Account, normally titled Pre-Incorporation Profit Account or Profit Prior to Incorporation Account. That this should be so is apparent if it is realized that though the actual date from which the transactions have been adopted falls before the date of incorporation, yet the price at which the business is being taken over is influenced by the values of the assets, etc., at the date when the company actually takes over, i.e. the date of incorporation. Suppose that Doolin and Kershaw start a business on 1 January with £1,000 capital, and very shortly afterwards Davie and Parker become interested as well, and the four of them start to form a company in which they will all become directors, Davie and Parker to start active work when the company is incorporated. The company is incorporated on 1 May 19–5 and the original owners of the business, Doolin and Kershaw, are to be given shares in the new company to compensate them for handing over the business. If they know, not necessarily with precision, that the original £1,000 assets will have grown to net assets of £6,000, then they most certainly would not part with the business to the company for £1,000. Ignoring goodwill, they would want £6,000 of shares. Conversely, if the net assets will shrink to £400, then would Davie and Parker be happy to see £1,000 of shares handed over? This means that the price at which the business is taken over is dependent at the expected value at date of the company incorporation, and not at the value at the date on which the company is supposed to take over. Taking the case of the increase in net assets to £6,000 the £5,000 difference is made up of profits. If these profits could be distributed as dividends, then in effect the capital payment of £6,000 in shares is being part used up for dividend purposes. This is in direct contradiction to the normal accounting practice of retaining capital intact (the accountant's meaning of 'capital' and not the meaning given to 'capital' by the economist). The £5,000 profits must therefore be regarded as not being available for dividends. They are thus a capital reserve.

Although the profit cannot be regarded as free for use as dividends, any such loss can be taken to restrict the dividends which could be paid out of the profits made after incorporation. This is the convention of conservatism once again coming into play, and if the price paid on take-over was misjudged and a high figure was paid, only to find out later that a loss had been made, then the restriction of dividends leads to the capital lost being replaced by assets held back within the firm. Alternatively the amount of the pre-incorporation loss could be charged to a Goodwill Account, as this is also another way of stating that a higher price has been paid for the assets of the firm than is represented by the value of the tangible assets taken over.

It is possible for the profits up to the date of incorporation to be calculated quite separately from those after incorporation. However, the cost of stocktaking, etc., may be felt to be not worth while merely to produce accounts when in fact the accounts could be left until the normal financial year end. This is invariably the case in examination questions. Therefore when the accounts for the full financial year are being made up, they will consist of profits before and after incorporation. The accounts must therefore be split to throw up the two sets of profit (or loss), so that distinction can be made between those profits usable, and those not usable, for dividend purposes. There is no hard-and-fast rule as to how this shall be done. Known facts must prevail, and where an arbitrary apportionment must be made it should meet the test of common sense in the particular case. Exhibit 37–7 shows an attempt to calculate such profits.

Exhibit 37.7

Slack and King, partners in a firm, are to have their business taken over as from 1 January 19–4 by Monk Ltd which is incorporated on 1 April 19–4. It was agreed that all profits made from 1 January 19–4 should belong to the company, and that the vendors be entitled to interest on the purchase price from 1 January to date of payment. The purchase price was paid on 30 April 19–4, including £1,600 interest. A Profit and Loss Account is drawn up for the year ended 31 December 19–4. This is shown as column (X). This is then split into, before incorporation, shown as column (Y), after incorporation, being column (Z). The methods used to apportion the particular items are shown after the Profit and Loss Account, the letters (A) to (I) against the items being the references to the notes. These particular methods must definitely not be used in all cases for similar expenses, they are only an indication of different methods of apportionment. The facts and the peculiarities of each firm must be taken into account, and no method should be slavishly followed. Assume for this example that all calendar months are of equal length.

Monk Ltd
Profit and Loss Account for the year ended 31 December 19–4

		(X) Total	(Y) Before	(Z) After		(X) Total	(Y) Before	(Z) After
		£	£	£		£	£	£
Partnership Salaries	(B)	1,000	1,000		Gross Profit (A)	38,000	8,000	30,000
Employees Remuneration	(C)	12,000	3,000	9,000				
General Expenses	(C)	800	200	600				
Commission on Sales	(D)	1,700	200	1,500				
Distribution Expenses	(E)	1,900	400	1,500				
Bad Debts	(F)	100	20	80				
Bank Overdraft Interest	(G)	200		200				
Directors' Remuneration	(H)	5,000		5,000				
Directors' Expenses	(H)	400		400				
Debenture Interest	(H)	500		500				
Depreciation	(C)	1,000	250	750				
Interest Paid to Vendors	(I)	1,600	1,200	400				
Net Profit:		11,800						
Transferred to Capital Reserves			1,730					
Carried down to the Appropriation Account				10,070				
		38,000	8,000	30,000		38,000	8,000	30,000

Notes:

(A) For the three months to 31 March Sales amounted to £40,000, and for the remaining nine months they were £150,000. Gross profit is at a uniform rate of 20 per cent of selling price throughout the year. Therefore the gross profit is apportioned (Y) 20 per cent = £8,000, and (Z) 20 per cent of £150,000 = £30,000.

(B) The partnership salaries of the vendors, Slack and King, obviously belong to (Y), because that is the period of the partnership.

(C) These expenses, in this particular case, have accrued evenly throughout the year and are therefore split on the time basis of Y three-twelfths, Z nine-twelfths.

(D) Commission to the salesmen was paid at the rate of $\frac{1}{2}$ per cent on sales up to 31 March, and 1 per cent thereafter. The commission figure is split:

$$(Y) \tfrac{1}{2} \text{ per cent of £40,000} = 200$$
$$(Z) 1 \text{ per cent of £150,000} = 1,500$$
$$\overline{1,700}$$

(E) In this particular case (but not always true in every case) the distribution expenses have varied directly with the value of sales. They are therefore split:

(Y) $\dfrac{\text{Y Sales}}{\text{Total Sales}} \times \text{Expenses} = \dfrac{40,000}{190,000} \times £1,900 = \frac{4}{19} \times £1,900 = £400$

(Z) $\dfrac{\text{Z Sales}}{\text{Total Sales}} \times \text{Expenses} = \dfrac{150,000}{190,000} \times £1,900 = \frac{15}{19} \times £1,900 = £1,500$

(F) The bad debts were two in number:
(i) In respect of a sale in January, the debtor dying penniless in March, £20.
(ii) In respect of a sale in June, the debtor being declared bankrupt in December, £80.

(G) The bank account was never overdrawn until June, so that the interest charged must be for period (Z).

(H) Only in companies are such expenses as Directors' Salaries, Directors' Expenses and Debenture Interest to be found. These must naturally be shown in period (Z).

(I) The interest paid to the vendors was due to the fact that the company was receiving all the benefits from 1 January but did not in fact pay any cash for the business until 30 April. This is therefore in effect loan interest which should be spread over the period it was borrowed, i.e. three months to (Y) and 1 month to (Z).

Exercises

37.1. D.Q.N. Ltd was incorporated on 31 December 19–3 with a nominal capital of 25,000 ordinary shares of £1 each. On 1 January 19–4, the company took over all the assets of E.E., a trader. The balance sheet of E.E., as on 31 December 19–3 was as follows:

Balance Sheet

	£			£
Capital	10,125	Motor Vehicles		2,800
Trade Creditors	4,360	Furniture and Fittings		770
Bank Overdraft	685	Stock-in-Trade		6,385
		Trade Debtors	5,415	
		Less Provision for		
		Bad Debts	200	
				5,215
	15,170			15,170

It was agreed that the assets appearing in the above balance sheet are there shown at fair valuations. The purchase price was fixed at £20,000 and the company discharged it by paying off E.E.'s bank overdraft, by the issue to E.E. of 10,000 ordinary shares at par, and by a cash payment to E.E. The company undertook no responsbility in regard to the trade creditors of E.E.

On 1 January 19–4, the company issued 15,000 shares, at par, for cash, which was paid up in full on that day.

During the year 19–4, no entries were made in the company's books in regard to the acquisition of E.E.'s business, except for receipts and payments of cash. The company kept no personal accounts for debtors or creditors.

The following trial balance was extracted from the company's books as at 31 December 19–4:

	£	£
Share Capital		15,000
Payment to E.E.	9,315	
Payment in settlement of E.E's Overdraft	685	
Cash received from E.E.'s Debtors		5,300
Payments to Trade Creditors	52,730	
Freehold Property	7,500	
Cash received from Trade Debtors		64,180
Wages and Salaries	6,420	
Rates and Insurances	270	
General Expenses	4,040	
Balance at Bank	3,520	
	84,480	84,480

At 31 December 19–4, £3,930 was owing to trade creditors, and £6,150 was due to the company from trade debtors; stock-in-trade was valued at £7,115 and rates and insurance paid in advance amounted to £50. There were no outstanding expenses. No discounts were allowed or received during the year. A provision of £560 is to be made for depreciation of motor vehicles. Ignore depreciation of furniture and fittings.

You are required to prepare the trading and profit and loss account for the year 19–4 and a summary of the balance sheet as on 31 December 19–4.

Ignore taxation.

(Chartered Institute of Secretaries and Administrators)

37.2. Bestways Ltd was incorporated on 1 April 19–5 to take over the business of R. S. Best as from 1 January 19–5.

The company took over assets and liabilities at the following valuations:

Assets: Stock £9,800; Sundry Trade Debtors £11,550; Freehold Premises £25,000; Motor Vehicles £3,600.
Liabilities: Sundry Trade Creditors £7,950.

and agreed to pay £10,000 for goodwill.

The company had an authorized capital of £100,000 divided into 10,000 8 per cent preference shares of £1 each and 180,000 ordinary shares of £0·5 each.

All of the preference shares, valued at par, were issued to R. S. Best and the balance of the purchase price paid in cash on 2 April 19–5.

On 1 April the company issued 80,000 ordinary shares at £0·625 per share payable in full on application. These shares were taken up and paid in full.

In August 19–5 the company purchased additional motor vehicles for £2,100.

The net profit for the year 1 January to 31 December 19–5 was £16,240 *after* providing £1,425 for depreciation on motor vehicles. £4,120 of this net profit was calculated as attributable to the period 1 January 19–5 to 31 March 19–5.

On 31 December 19–5, in addition to the balances arising from the above the following balances appeared in the books of the company.

	£	£
Cash in Hand and Balance at Bank	19,011	
Sundry Trade Debtors	14,306	
Provision for Bad Debts		700
Sundry Trade Creditors		8,406
Stock	11,104	
Preference Share Dividend	800	
Preliminary Expenses	850	

The directors decided to transfer £4,000 to reserve and to recommend a dividend of 12 per cent on the ordinary shares.

(a) Show, by means of journal entries, including those for receipts and payments of cash:
(i) the purchase of and payment for Best's business;
(ii) the issue of capital by the company.
(b) Prepare the Appropriation Account of the company for the year ended 31 December 19–5 and a Balance Sheet as at that date.

Ignore taxation.
(Associated Examining Board 'A' Level)

37.3. Engineers Ltd agreed to acquire the goodwill and assets, other than cash, of Metals Ltd as on 31 January 19–5.

A summary of the Balance Sheet of Metals Ltd as on 31 January 19–5 was as follows:

	£		£
Share Capital in £1		Goodwill	5,000
Ordinary Shares, fully paid	50,000	Land, Buildings and	
General Reserve	18,000	Plant	67,000
Profit and Loss Account	9,000	Stock	10,400
8 per cent Debentures	10,000	Debtors	3,800
Creditors	2,000	Cash	2,800
	89,000		89,000

The consideration payable by Engineers Ltd was agreed as follows:

1. A cash payment equivalent to £0·5 for every £1 ordinary share in Metals Ltd.

2. The issue of 80,000 £1 ordinary shares, fully paid, in Engineers Ltd, having an agreed value of £1·25 per share.

3. The issue of such an amount of fully-paid 6 per cent debentures of Engineers Ltd at 96 as is sufficient to discharge the 8 per cent debentures of Metals Ltd at 120.

The liabilities of Metals Ltd, other than the debentures, were discharged by that company.

When computing the agreed consideration the directors of Engineers Ltd valued the land, buildings and plant at £115,000, the stock at £9,000 and the debtors at the amount stated on the Balance Sheet of Metals Ltd, subject to an allowance of 5 per cent to cover doubtful debts.

On the sale of its assets Metals Limited went into voluntary liquidation, the ordinary shareholders receiving cash and ordinary shares in Engineers Ltd as repayment of their capital in Metals Ltd.

You are required to draft the journal entries:

(a) to record the acquisition in the books of Engineers Ltd; and
(b) to close off the books of Metals Ltd.

Ignore the cost of liquidating Metals Ltd.
(Institute of Chartered Accountants)

37.4. X Ltd and Y Ltd agreed to amalgamate. A new company, XY Ltd, was formed to take over all the assets and liabilities of X Ltd and Y Ltd at the date of the balance sheets shown below.

	X Ltd	Y Ltd		X Ltd	Y Ltd
	£	£		£	£
Issued Share Capital			Goodwill	—	3,000
in £1 shares	50,000	20,000	Freehold Premises	38,000	15,000
General Reserve	7,000	—	Stock	15,000	2,000
Profit and Loss			Debtors	7,000	1,500
Account	2,850	—	Balance at Bank	4,850	—
Creditors	5,000	3,000	Profit and Loss		
Bank Overdraft	—	1,000	Account	—	2,500
	64,850	24,000		64,850	24,000

For the purpose of the amalgamation: Goodwill of X Ltd was agreed at £5,000 and that of Y Ltd was regarded as valueless; freehold premises were revalued at the following amounts: X Ltd £45,000, Y Ltd £17,000; the stock of Y Ltd was reduced by obsolete items amounting to £425 and it was agreed that 5 per cent be allowed for doubtful debts in respect of both companies.

The purchase price of X Ltd and Y Ltd was discharged by the issue by XY Ltd of £1 shares valued at £1·25.

You are required to:

(a) submit your workings of how many shares in XY Ltd would be received by:
(i) the holder of 1,000 shares in X Ltd
(ii) the holder of 100 shares in Y Ltd

and

(b) draft the balance sheet of the new company, XY Ltd, as it would appear on completion of the amalgamation.

Ignore formation expenses.
(Associated Examining Board 'A' Level)

37.5. Bowling Ltd and Green Ltd propose to sell their businesses to a new company being formed for that purpose.

The summarized Balance Sheets as on 31 December 19–6, and profits of the companies for the past three years are as follows:

	Bowling Ltd	Green Ltd		Bowling Ltd	Green Ltd
	£	£		£	£
Ordinary Shares of £1 each	60,000	25,000	Freehold Property (at cost)	36,000	12,000
Capital Reserve	—	15,000	Plant and machinery (at cost)		
General Reserve	39,000	12,000	*less* depreciation	32,000	18,000
Profit and Loss Account	11,000	16,000	Investment (at cost)	—	10,000
Creditors	21,580	12,680	Stock-in-Trade	11,100	8,950
			Debtors	8,800	6,400
			Balance at Bank	43,680	25,330
	131,580	80,680		131,580	80,680

	Bowling Ltd	Green Ltd
	£	£
Net profits for the years ended:		
31 December 19–4	17,450	10,760
31 December 19–5	19,340	12,290
31 December 19–6	21,470	14,450

You are also given the following relevant information:

(1) It is agreed:

(i) that the properties and plant and machinery be re-valued as follows:

	Bowling Ltd	Green Ltd
	£	£
Freehold Property	44,800	14,400
Plant and Machinery	30,570	17,095

(ii) that the value of stocks be reduced by 10 per cent and a provision of 12½ per cent be made on debtors for bad and doubtful debts.

(iii) that goodwill be valued at two years' purchase of the average annual trading profits of the past three years, after deducting a standard profit of 10 per cent on the net trading assets, before revaluation or adjustment, on 31 December 19–6.

(2) Profits of Green Ltd include £600 income from the investment in each of the three years. The market value of the investment as on 31 December 19–, was £10,000.

You are required to prepare a statement showing how you would arrive at the value per share of the ordinary shares in:

(a) Bowling Ltd; and
(b) Green Ltd.
(Institute of Chartered Accountants)

37.6. On 1 April 19–2 Smith and Brown Co Ltd was incorporated to take over an existing business and to continue it from that date as a limited company. For the year ended 31 December 19–2 the total turnover amounted to £100,000. This turnover divides as follows: From 1 January to 31 March £20,000 and £80,000 for the remaining nine months.

The accounts for the whole year showed a gross profit of £30,000 and total expenditure of £19,800 for the year. This expenditure includes directors' fees of £600.

What proportion of the profits should be regarded as being earned prior to incorporation, taking turnover as a basis, and what is the profit subsequent to incorporation?

(East Midland Educational Union)

37.7 Checkers Ltd was incorporated on 1 April 19–5 and took over the business Black and White, partners, as from 1 January 19–5. It was agreed that all profits made from 1 January should belong to the company and that the vendors should be entitled to interest on the purchase price from 1 January to date of payment. The purchase price was paid on 31 May 19–5 including £1,650 interest.

The following is the Profit and Loss Account for the year to 31 December 19–5:

	£		£
Salaries of Vendors	1,695	Gross Profit	28,000
Wages and General Expenses	8,640		
Rent and Rates	860		
Distribution Expenses	1,680		
Commission on Sales	700		
Bad Debts	314		
Interest paid to Vendors	1,650		
Directors' Remuneration	4,000		
Directors' Expenses	515		
Depreciation: £			
Motors 1,900			
Machinery 575			
	2,475		
Bank Interest	168		
Net Profit	5,303		
	28,000		28,000

You are given the following information:

1. Sales amounted to £20,000 for the three months to 31 March 19–5 and £50,000 for the nine months to 31 December 19–5. Gross Profit is at a uniform rate of 40 per cent of selling price throughout the year, and commission at a rate of 1 per cent is paid on all sales.

2. Salaries of £1,695 were paid to the vendors for their assistance in running the business up to 31 March 19–5.

3. The Bad Debts written off are:

(*a*) A debt of £104 taken over from the vendors.
(*b*) A debt of £210 in respect of goods sold in August 19–5.

4. On 1 January 19–5 motors were bought for £7,000 and machinery for £5,000. On 1 March 19–5 another motor van was bought for £3,000, and on 1 October 19–5 another machine was added for £3,000. Depreciation has been written off motors at 20 per cent per annum, and machinery 10 per cent per annum.

5. Wages and general expenses and rent and rates accrued at an even rate throughout the year.

6. The bank granted an overdraft in June 19–5.
   Assuming all calendar months are of equal length.

(a) Set out the Profit and Loss Account in columnar form, so as to distinguish between the period prior to the company's incorporation and the period after incorporation.

(b) To state how you would deal with the profit prior to incorporation.

(c) To state how you would deal with the results prior to incorporation if they turned out to be a net loss.

37.8. Switch formed a limited company called Switch Ltd to take over his existing business as from 1 January 19–6, but the company was not incorporated until 1 April 19–6. No entries relating to the transfer of the business were entered in the books, which were carried on without a break until 31 December 19–6.

On 31 December 19–6 the following trial balance was extracted from the books:

	£	£
Stock on 1 January 19–6	4,294	
Sales		27,930
Purchases	19,678	
Carriage Outwards	165	
Travellers' Commission	615	
Office Salaries	1,664	
Office Expenses	240	
Rent and Rates	164	
Capital Account, Switch, on 1 January 19–6		20,000
Director's Salary	1,500	
Fixed Assets	12,500	
Current Liabilities		3,166
Current Assets (other than stock)	10,120	
Preliminary Expenses	156	
	51,096	51,096

You are also given the following information:

1. Stock on 31 December 19–6 amounted to £3,542.

2. The purchase consideration was agreed at £25,000 to be satisfied by the issue of 25,000 ordinary shares of £1 each.

3. The gross profit margin is constant and the monthly average of sales in January, November and December is double the monthly average for the remaining months of the year.

4. The preliminary expenses are to be written off.

5. You are to assume that carriage outwards and travellers' commission vary in direct proportion to sales.

You are required to prepare Trading and Profit and Loss Accounts for the year ended 31 December 19–6, apportioning between the periods before and after incorporation, and a Balance Sheet as on that date. Ignore depreciation.
(Institute of Chartered Accountants)

37.9. The following is the summarized Balance Sheet of Wilkinson Co Ltd.

	£		£
Issued Share Capital:			
10,000 Ordinary Shares		Goodwill	4,000
of £1 each	10,000	Sundry Assets	45,000
General Reserve	14,000		
Profit and Loss Balance	6,000		
5 per cent Debentures	10,000		
Sundry Creditors	9,000		
	49,000		49,000

The assets are valued at their balance sheet figure but Goodwill is revalued at £5,000.

The average profit available for the Ordinary Shares each year is £4,000. It is considered that a fair yield on Ordinary Shares would be 10 per cent per annum.

Calculate the value of the shares—showing step by step calculations with written indication of steps taken—by:

(i)   the Asset basis method; and
(ii) the Yield basis method.
       Ignore depreciation.
(East Midland Educational Union)

37.10. On 31 December 19–6 Breeze Ltd acquired all the assets, except the investments, of Blow Ltd.

The following are the summaries of the Profit and Loss Accounts of Blow Ltd for the years 19–4, 19–5 and 19–6:

	19–4	19–5	19–6		19–4	19–5	19–6
	£	£	£		£	£	£
Motor Expenses	1,860	1,980	2,100	Trading Profits	22,050	25,780	25,590
Depreciation of Plant &				Investment Income	290	340	480
Machinery	4,000	3,200	2,560	Rents Received	940	420	—
Bank Overdraft Interest	180	590	740	Profit on Sale of Property		4,800	
Wrapping Expenses	840	960	1,020				
Preliminary Expenses							
written off	—	690	—				
Net Profit	16,400	23,920	19,650				
	23,280	31,340	26,070		23,280	31,340	26,070

The purchase price is to be the amount on which an estimated maintainable profit would represent a return of 25 per cent per annum.

The maintainable profit is to be taken as the average of the profits of the three years 19–4, 19–5 and 19–6, after making any necessary adjustments.

You are given the following information:

(i)   The cost of the plant and machinery was £20,000. It is agreed that depreciation should have been written off at the rate of 12½ per cent per annum using the straight line method.

(ii) A form of new plastic wrapping material introduced on to the market means that wrapping expenses will be halved in future.

(iii) By a form of long-term rental of motor vehicles, it is estimated that motor expenses will be cut by one-third in future.

(iv) Stock treated as valueless at 31 December 19–3 was sold for £1,900 in 19–5.

(v) The working capital of the new company is such that an overdraft is not contemplated.

(vi) Management remuneration has been inadequate and will have to be increased by £1,500 a year in future.

You are required to set out your calculation of the purchase price. All workings must be shown. In fact, your managing director, who is a non-accountant, should be able to decipher how the price was calculated.

37.11. Acquisition Ltd was formed on 1 January 19–5, with an authorized share capital of 100,000 ordinary shares of £1 each, 20,000 shares were issued for cash at a premium of £0·25 per share and are fully paid up.

No other transactions took place until 1 April 19–5, when Acquisition Ltd agreed to buy the assets (including goodwill) and assume the liabilities of Box Ltd and Cox Ltd for a total of 80,000 shares of £1 each in Acquisition Ltd.

For the purpose of determining the premium at which the shares in Acquisition Ltd were to be issued, fixed and current assets and liabilities are to be taken at their book amounts; goodwill is to be determined on the basis of two and a half times the average profits of the past three years, after deducting a standard profit of 10 per cent on capital employed as shown by the accounts of the companies concerned as on 31 March 19–5.

The summarized Balance Sheets of Box Ltd and Cox Ltd as on 31 March 19–5 showed the following:

	Box Ltd	Cox Ltd		Box Ltd	Cox Ltd
	£	£		£	£
Issued Share Capital:			Fixed Assets	45,000	29,000
£1 shares, fully paid	31,000	33,500	Current Assets	25,000	61,000
Profit and Loss Account	19,000	1,500			
Current Liabilities	20,000	55,000			
	70,000	90,000		70,000	90,000

	Box Ltd	Cox Ltd
	£	£
Trading profits have been: Year ended 31 March 19–3	7,050	5,500
Year ended 31 March 19–4	8,800	6,400
Year ended 31 March 19–5	8,900	6,850

You are required:

(a) to calculate the number of shares to be issued by Acquisition Ltd to the shareholders in Box Ltd and Cox Ltd respectively, stating the ratio thereof to their former holdings, and

(b) to prepare the Balance Sheet of Acquisition Ltd to show the position immediately after the undertakings of Box Ltd and Cox Ltd have been purchased.

(Institute of Chartered Accountants)

37.12A. AB Ltd, an established company with a paid up capital of £120,000, issued a further 30,000 ordinary shares of £1 each payable £0·5 on application and £0·7 (including a premium of £0·2) on allotment.

Applications were received for 36,000 shares on 7 January 19–9. The directors proceeded to allotment on 10 January on which date the excess application money was refunded. All the allotment money was received on 15 January.

On 1 February, 19–9, AB Ltd took over all the assets, except the balance at bank, and all the liabilities, except the debentures, of Downturn Ltd, for a price of £84,000. This was discharged by payment of the whole proceeds of the January share issue and the issue of £1 ordinary shares in AB Ltd, valued at £1·20 each, in respect of the balance.

Balance Sheet of Downturn Ltd, as at 31 January 19–9

	£		£	£
Share Capital:		Fixed Assets:		
£1 Ordinary Shares	85,000	Goodwill		8,000
less Debit Balance on Profit		Freehold Property		30,000
and Loss Account	7,000	Equipment		40,000
	78,000			78,000
Debentures	10,000	Current Assets:		
Current Liabilities	12,000	Stock	17,000	
		Debtors	4,000	
		Balance at Bank	1,000	
				22,000
	100,000			100,000

Give
(i) the journal entries (without narrations) including bank items, to record the January share issue in the books of AB Ltd, and
(ii) the realization account, bank account and sundry shareholders' account to show the closing of the ledger of Downturn Ltd.

(Associated Examining Board—G.C.E. 'A' level)

37.13A. Olde Ltd and Tyred Ltd agree to amalgamate, and NEW Co Ltd was formed to take over all the assets (other than the bank balances) and liabilities of Olde Ltd and Tyred Ltd, at the date of their balance sheets shown below

	Olde Ltd	Tyred Ltd		Olde Ltd	Tyred Ltd
	£	£		£	£
Share Capital:			Fixed Assets:		
Ordinary Shares			Goodwill	10,000	—
of £1 each:			Freehold Property	30,000	10,000
Fully-paid	75,000	—	Equipment	10,000	20,000
75p paid	—	30,000	Current Assets:		
General Reserve	4,000	—	Stocks	20,000	15,100
Profit and Loss			Trade Debtors	11,400	5,000
Account	1,450	17,100	Bank Balances	3,750	1,000
Trade Creditors	4,700	4,000			
	85,150	51,100		85,150	51,100

The following revaluations were agreed for the purpose of the amalgamation:

	Olde Ltd	Tyred Ltd
	£	£
Goodwill	8,000	5,000
Freehold property	45,600	19,000
Trade debtors	11,100	4,900

The NEW Co Ltd was registered with an authorized capital of £200,000 in ordinary shares of £1 each. It issued 20,000 shares for cash at par and the whole amount due was received. Preliminary expenses of £1,700 were paid.

The purchase consideration due to Olde Ltd and to Tyred Ltd was discharged by the issue of £1 ordinary shares in NEW Co Ltd at par.

You are required to:

(a) submit your calculations of what the holder of 100 shares in Olde Ltd and the holder of 100 shares in Tyred Ltd would respectively receive from the liquidation of their companies (ignoring expenses of liquidation);

(b) prepare the balance sheet of NEW Co Ltd incorporating all the relevant items from the information given above. The balance sheet need not be in published form but attention should be paid to presentation and layout.

(Associated Examining Board—G.C.E. 'A' level)

37.14A. The summarized Balance Sheet of Takeover Ltd as on 30 June 19–8 showed the following position:

	£		£
Issued Share Capital:		Fixed Assets	125,000
£1 Shares, Fully Paid	100,000	Current Assets	50,000
Profit and Loss Account	50,000		
Current Liabilities	25,000		
	175,000		175,000

Takeover Ltd agreed to buy the assets, and assume the liabilities, of Little Ltd and of Titch Ltd as on 1 July 19–8, for a total consideration of 90,000 shares of £1 each in Takeover Ltd.

The summarized Balance Sheets of Little Ltd and Titch Ltd as on 30 June 19–8 showed the following:

	Little Ltd	Titch Ltd		Little Ltd	Titch Ltd
	£	£		£	£
Issued Share Capital:			Fixed Assets	50,000	30,000
£1 Shares, Fully Paid	50,000	15,000	Current Assets	29,000	14,000
Profit and Loss Account	10,000	5,000			
Current Liabilities	19,000	24,000			
	79,000	44,000		79,000	44,000

You are also given the following relevant information:

1. It is agreed that the fixed and current assets be re-valued as follows:

	Little Ltd	Titch Ltd
	£	£
Fixed Assets	55,000	34,400
Current Assets	23,800	13,000

2. Goodwill is to be valued at four years' purchase of the average profits of the past three years after deducting a standard profit of 12½ per cent on capital employed on 30 June 19–8, before adjustment or revaluation.

3. Trading profits have been:

Year ended 30 June	Little Ltd	Titch Ltd
	£	£
19–6	9,900	6,200
19–7	12,750	6,600
19–8	15,000	7,150

You are required:

(a) to calculate the number of shares to be issued by Takeover Ltd to the shareholders in Little Ltd and Titch Ltd respectively, stating the ratio thereof to their former holdings, and

(b) to prepare a summarized Balance Sheet of Takeover Ltd showing the position immediately after the acquisitions.

(*Institute of Chartered Accountants*)

37.15A. CJK Ltd was incorporated on 15 December 19–9 with an authorized capital of 200,000 ordinary shares of £0·2 each to acquire as at 31 December 19–9 the businesses of C K, a sole trader, and RP Ltd, a company.

From the following information you are required to prepare:

(a) the realization and capital accounts in the books of C K and RP Ltd showing the winding up of these two concerns;

(b) the journal entries to open the books of CJK Ltd, including cash transactions and the raising of finance;

(c) the balance sheet of CJK Ltd after the transactions have been completed.

The balance sheet of C K as at 31 December 19–9 is as follows:

Balance Sheet

	£		£
Capital	16,000	Freehold premises	8,000
Creditors	3,200	Plant	4,000
		Stock	2,000
		Debtors	5,000
		Cash	200
	19,200		19,200

The assets (excluding cash) and the liabilities were taken over at the following values: freehold premises £10,000, plant £3,500, stock £2,000, debtors £5,000 less a bad debt provision of £300, goodwill £7,000, creditors £3,200 less a discount provision of £150. The purchase consideration, based on these values, was settled by the issue of shares at par.

The balance sheet of RP Ltd as at 31 December 19–9 is as follows:

Balance Sheet

	£		£
Share capital:		Freehold premises	4,500
10,000 shares at £0·4 each	4,000	Plant	2,000
Revenue surplus	2,500	Stock	1,600
Creditors	1,500	Debtors	3,400
Bank overdraft	3,500		
	11,500		11,500

The assets and liabilities were taken over at book value with the exception of the freehold premises which were revalued at £5,500. The purchase consideration was a cash payment of £1 and three shares in CJK Ltd at par in exchange for every two shares in RP Ltd.

Additional working capital and the funds required to complete the purchase of RP Ltd were provided by the issue for cash of:

(i)   10,000 shares at a premium of £0·3 per share;
(ii) £8,000 7 per cent Debenture Stock at 98.

The expenses of incorporating CJK Ltd were paid, amounting to £1,200.
(Institute of Cost and Management Accountants)

37.16A. *Tables Ltd*

	£		£
Issued share capital:		Net assets	67,000
5 per cent Preference		(Assets minus liabilities)	
Shares of £1 each	9,000		
Ordinary Shares of £1 each	30,000		
Revenue reserves	28,000		
	67,000		67,000

Chairs Ltd

	£		£
Issued share capital:		Net assets	57,000
7½ per cent Preference		(Assets minus liabilities)	
Shares of £1 each	10,000		
Ordinary Shares of £1 each	40,000		
Revenue reserves	7,000		
	57,000		57,000

The above summarized balance sheets of Tables Ltd and Chairs Ltd at 31 December 19–6:

The dividends proposed on the ordinary share capital of the companies in 19–6 were £6,000 for Tables Ltd and £4,000 for Chairs Ltd. These amounts, together with proposed dividends for the year on the preference shares, were included among liabilities in the balance sheets of the companies at 31 December 19–6.

On 1 January 19–7, the two companies amalgamated to form a new company, Furniture Ltd, which took over the net assets of Tables Ltd and Chairs Ltd at that date.

Shares were issued by Furniture Ltd to the former shareholders of Tables Ltd and Chairs Ltd as consideration for the surrender of their interests in those companies.

The shares were allocated on the following basis:

1. The ordinary and preference dividends payable by Furniture Ltd for 19–7 are intended to be the same as the total amount of dividends payable by Tables Ltd and Chairs Ltd for 19–6, and shares in Furniture Ltd were allocated to ensure that former shareholders in both Tables Ltd and Chairs Ltd receive the same amounts of dividends from Furniture Ltd for 19–7 as they receive for 19–6.

2. The former preference shareholders of Tables Ltd and Chairs Ltd were issued with 6 per cent preference shares of £1 each, at par, in Furniture Ltd.

3. The former ordinary shareholders of Tables Ltd and Chairs Ltd were issued with ordinary shares of £1 each, at par, in Furniture Ltd. It is intended that the *rate* of dividend on the ordinary share capital of Furniture Ltd shall be 8 per cent in 19–7.

The net assets of the amalgamated companies are to be valued in the accounts of Furniture Ltd at an amount equal to that company's total share capital.

Prepare the balance sheet of Furniture Ltd at 1 January 19–7, after these transactions have taken place. Divide the share capital section of the balance sheet between shares issued to former shareholders of Tables Ltd and shares issued to former shareholders of Chairs Ltd.

(Institute of Bankers)

37.17A. The Balance Sheet of Hubble Ltd as at 31 May 19–0 is shown below.

Hubble Ltd

	£	£		£	£
Authorized Share Capital:			Fixed Assets:		
650,000 Ordinary Shares			Freehold Premises		
of £1 each		650,000	at Cost		375,000
			Plant and Machinery		
Issued Share Capital:			at Cost		
400,000 Ordinary Shares			*Less* Depreciation		
of £1 each Fully Paid		400,000	£48,765		101,235
Profit and Loss Account		180,630	Motor Vehicles		
			at Cost		
		580,630	*Less* Depreciation		
Current Liabilities:			£1,695		6,775
Trade Creditors	63,200				
Bank Overdraft	38,175				483,010
		101,375	Current Assets:		
			Stock in Trade	102,550	
			Debtors	96,340	
			Cash in Hand	105	
					198,995
		682,005			682,005

Hubble Ltd agreed to purchase at this date the Freehold Premises, Plant and Machinery and Stock of A. Bubble at agreed valuations of £100,000, £10,000 and £55,000, respectively. The purchase price was to be fully settled by the issue to Bubble of 120,000 Ordinary Shares of £1 each in Hubble Ltd, and a cash payment to Bubble of £25,000. Bubble was to collect his debts and to pay his creditors.

Hubble Ltd sold one of its own premises prior to taking over Bubble for £75,000 (cost £55,000) and revalued the remainder at £400,000 (excluding those acquired from Bubble).

You are required to:

(a) Show the journal entries, including cash items, in the books of Hubble Ltd to give effect to the above transactions, and
(b) Show the Balance Sheet of Hubble Ltd after completing them.

(Association of Certified Accountants)

37.18A. From the following information you are required to:

(a) prepare a statement apportioning the unappropriated profit between the pre-incorporation and post-incorporation period, showing the basis of apportionment;
(b) show the share capital and profits on the balance sheet of the company as at 31 March 19–0.

VU Limited was incorporated on 1 July 19–9 with an authorized share capital of 60,000 ordinary shares of £1 each, to take over the business of L and Sons as from 1 April 19–9.

The purchase consideration was agreed at £50,000 for the net tangible assets taken over, plus a further £6,000 for goodwill.

Payment was satisfied by the issue of £30,000 8 per cent Debentures and 26,000 ordinary shares both at par, on 1 August 19–9. Interest at 10 per cent per annum on the purchase consideration was paid up to this date.

The company raised a further £20,000 on 1 August 19–9 by the issue of ordinary shares at a premium of £0·25 per share.

The abridged profit and loss account for the year to 31 March 19–0 was as follows:

	£	£
Sales:		
1 April 19–9 to 30 June 19–9	30,000	
1 July 19–9 to 31 March 19–0	95,000	
		125,000
Cost of Sales for the Year	80,000	
Depreciation	2,220	
Directors' Fees	500	
Administration Salaries and Expenses	8,840	
Sales Commission	4,375	
Goodwill Written Off	1,000	
Interest on Purchase Consideration, Gross	1,867	
Distribution Costs (60 per cent variable)	6,250	
Preliminary Expenses written off	1,650	
Debenture Interest, Gross	1,600	
Proposed Dividend on Ordinary Shares	7,560	
		115,862
Unappropriated Profit carried forward		9,138

The company sells one product only, of which the unit selling price has remained constant during the year, but due to improved buying the unit cost of sales was reduced by 10 per cent in the post-incorporation period as compared with the pre-incorporation period.

Taxation is to be ignored.

(Institute of Cost and Management Accountants)

37.19A. Rowlock Ltd was incorporated on 1 October 19–8 to acquire Rowlock's mail order business, with effect from 1 June 19–8.

The purchase consideration was agreed at £35,000 to be satisfied by the issue on 1 December 19–8 to Rowlock or his nominee of:

20,000 Ordinary Shares of £1 each, fully paid, and £15,000 7 per cent Debentures.

The entries relating to the transfer were not made in the books which were carried on without a break until 31 May 19–9.

On 31 May 19–9 the trial balance extracted from the books is as overleaf.

	£	£
Sales		52,185
Purchases	38,829	
Wrapping	840	
Postage	441	
Warehouse Rent and Rates	921	
Packing Expenses	1,890	
Office Expenses	627	
Stock on 31 May 19–8	5,261	
Director's Salary	1,000	
Debenture Interest (gross)	525	
Fixed Assets	25,000	
Current Assets (other than stock)	9,745	
Current Liabilities		4,162
Formation Expenses	218	
Capital Account—Rowlock, 31 May 19–8		29,450
Drawings Account—Rowlock	500	
	85,797	85,797

You also ascertain the following:

1. Stock on 31 May 19–9 amounted to £4,946.

2. The average monthly sales for June, July and August were one-half of those for the remaining months of the year. The gross profit margin was constant throughout the year.

3. Wrapping, postage and packing expenses varied in direct proportion to sales, whilst office expenses were constant each month.

4. Formation expenses are to be written off.
   You are required to prepare the Trading and Profit and Loss Account for the year ended 31 May 19–9 apportioned between the periods before and after incorporation, and Balance Sheet as on that date.
   (Institute of Chartered Accountants)

38

Taxation in Accounts

This chapter is concerned with the entries made in the accounts of firms in respect of taxation. It is not concerned with the actual calculations of the taxes. Taxation legislation is now extremely complex and contains many exceptions to the general rules applicable to companies. It is impossible in a book at this level to delve into too many of the complications, and it should therefore be appreciated that, as far as companies are concerned though the facts in this chapter apply to the great majority of limited companies, there are in fact some other complications in a small minority of cases.

Taxation can be split between:

1. Direct taxes, payable to the Inland Revenue, this being the government department responsible for the calculation and collection of the taxes. For a company these taxes are corporation tax and income tax.

2. Value Added Tax, abbreviated as VAT. This has been dealt with in Volume 1.

1. Limited Companies + Corporation Tax and Income Tax

The tax which limited companies suffer is known as Corporation Tax. It is legally an appropriation of profits, it is not an expense, and it should therefore be shown in the Profit and Loss Appropriation Account. Two law cases, many years ago, did in fact settle any arguments as to whether it was an expense or appropriation, both cases being decided in favour of the view that it was an appropriation of profits.

When a company makes profits, then such profits are assessable to corporation tax. It does not mean that corporation tax is payable on the net profits as shown in the accounts. What it does mean is that the corporation tax is assessable on the profit calculated after certain adjustments have been made to the net profit shown according to the Profit and Loss Account. These adjustments are not made in the actual accounts, they are made in calculations performed quite separately from the drafting of Final Accounts. Suppose that K Ltd has the following Profit and Loss Account:

K Ltd Profit and Loss Account for the year ended 31 March 19-8

	£		£
General Expenses:	30,000	Gross Profit b/d	100,000
Depreciation Provision			
Machinery	20,000		
Net Profit	50,000		
	100,000		100,000

The depreciation provision for machinery is the accounting figure used for the financial accounts. It is not usually the same figure as that allowed by the Inland Revenue for the depreciation of the machinery. The allowances made for depreciation by the Inland Revenue are known as 'capital allowances'. These are calculated on rules which usually vary at one point or another from the methods applied by the company in determining depreciation provisions. A detailed study of a textbook on taxation would be necessary to see exactly how capital allowances are calculated. In some fairly rare cases, hardly ever found in large or medium-sized concerns but probably more common in very small firms, the capital allowances are calculated and the financial provision for depreciation is taken at the same figure. In the case of K Ltd assume that the capital allowances amount to £27,000, and that the rate of corporation tax is 50 per cent on assessable profits. The calculation of the corporation tax liability would be:

	£
Net Profit per the Financial Accounts	50,000
Add Depreciation provision not allowed as a deduction for corporation tax purposes	20,000
	70,000
Less Capital Allowances	27,000
Adjusted Profits assessable to corporation tax	43,000

As the corporation tax is assumed to be at the rate of 50 per cent of assessable profits, the corporation tax liability will be £43,000 × 50 per cent = £21,500. Sometimes the adjusted profits are greater than the net profits shown in the financial accounts, but may equally well be less. This illustrates the fact that it is relatively rare for the external observer to be able to calculate the corporation tax payable merely by knowing the net profit made by the company. In fact, there are also other items than depreciation provisions that need adjusting to find the correct assessable profits for corporation tax purposes. All that is needed here is the understanding that profit per the Profit and Loss Account is normally different from assessable profit for corporation tax calculations.

The rate of corporation tax is fixed by the Chancellor of the Exchequer in his budget, normally presented to Parliament in March/April of each year. There have been budgets in other months of the year, but it is normal practice for the April budget to fix corporation tax rates. This rate is to be applied to the assessable profits of companies earned during the twelve months to 31 March before the budget. If the Chancellor announced in April 19–8 that the rate was to be 50 per cent, then this refers to each company's adjusted profits for the government financial year 1 April 19–7 to 31 March 19–8. Likewise, if in April 19–4 the corporation tax rate was announced as 45 per cent, then this would refer to profits from 1 April 19–3 to 31 March 19–4. A company whose financial year end is not 31 March will therefore span two governmental financial years.

Example

Company T Ltd. Adjusted profits for the year ended 31 December 19–7, £160,000.
Rate of corporation tax for the government financial year ended 31 March 19–7, 50 per cent.
Rate of corporation tax for the government financial year ended 31 March 19–8, $52\frac{1}{2}$ per cent.
The corporation tax liability will be:

	£
Three months profit from 1 January 19–8 to 31 March 19–7,	
$\frac{3}{12} \times £160,000 = £40,000$ at 50 per cent	20,000
Nine months profit from 1 April 19–7 to 31 December 19–7,	
$\frac{9}{12} \times £160,000 = £120,000$ at $52\frac{1}{2}$ per cent	63,000
	83,000

Corporation Tax – When Payable

1. Mainstream Corporation Tax

This depends on when the company first started trading.

(a) Companies trading before 1 April 1965
Mainstream corporation tax is payable annually on 1 January. To find when it has to be paid on the adjusted profits for a firm's financial year, the simple, but rather peculiar, way of doing it is to find the next 6 April following the firm's financial year end, and then the 1 January following that particular 6 April is the date on which the tax is due.

Example

(i)   Firm's year ended 31 March 19–3. Mainstream corporation tax payable 1 January 19–4.
(ii) Firm's year ended 30 April 19–3. Mainstream corporation tax payable 1 January 19–5.
(iii) Firm's year ended 30 June 19–6. Mainstream corporation tax payable 1 January 19–8.
(iv) Firm's year ended 31 December 19–7. Mainstream corporation tax payable 1 January 19–9.

It might appear that a mistake has been made by the author. (i) shows a gap of nine months between the end of the firm's financial year end and the date for payment of corporation tax, (ii) shows twenty months, (iii) reveals eighteen months, and (iv) is twelve months. The reasons for this rather strange timing for tax payments cannot be fully appreciated unless a full study of taxation is undertaken. The reasons are bound up with the tax laws which were in existence before corporation tax was first introduced.

(*b*) *Companies starting trading from 1 April 1965 onwards*

Mainstream corporation tax is due for payment nine months after the company's financial year end.

Every company is not so prompt as to have its accounts submitted to the Inland Revenue, and to have its corporation tax liability agreed before the due date for the payment of the tax arrives. In both cases (*a*) and (*b*) the tax is due for payment one month after the making of the assessment (the bill for the corporation tax), if such an assessment is made later than the due date mentioned in (*a*) and (*b*).

For the rest of this chapter, unless mentioned otherwise, corporation tax will be assumed to be at the rate of 50 per cent for the purposes of illustration. In fact companies with relatively small profits often pay at a lower rate than companies with larger profits.

2.   *Advance Corporation Tax*

When a dividend is paid by the company, a sum equal to a fraction of that figure must be paid to the Inland Revenue by the company. The fraction to be found will depend on the standard rate of income tax in operation at the time.
The fraction will be found thus:

$$\frac{\text{Standard rate of income tax}}{100 - \text{standard rate}}$$

Therefore, if the standard rate of income tax is 33 per cent, the fraction will be $\dfrac{33}{100-33} = \dfrac{33}{67}$. For the sake of simplicity in working, the standard rate of income tax will always be assumed for this purpose to be 30 per cent, so that the fraction will be $\dfrac{30}{100-30} = \dfrac{3}{7}$. This will make the arithmetic rather easier to attempt. This is *not* deducted from the dividend, the dividend is paid in full, it is merely that this advance payment is *equal* to $\frac{3}{7}$ of the dividend paid, and is payable to the Inland Revenue within 3 months of the payment of the dividend to the shareholder.

An illustration will now be used to summarise the payment situation.

Exhibit 38.1

In the year to 31 March 19–5 a company has adjusted profits of £100,000 on which it must suffer corporation tax at the rate of 50 per cent. It pays a dividend of £42,000 in that year.

	£	£
Advance Corporation Tax payable:		
£42,000 × $\frac{3}{7}$		18,000
Corporation Tax liability:		
£100,000 × 50 per cent	50,000	
Less Advance Corporation Tax	18,000	
Mainstream Corporation Tax payable at the due date		32,000
Total Corporation Tax paid		50,000

There is however one restriction on the amount of advance corporation tax payment that can be set off against the mainstream corporation tax payment. The mainstream corporation tax payment must equal at least 20 per cent of the taxable profits, and consequently the amount of advance corporation tax which can be set off against that year's corporation tax is restricted accordingly. This is shown in Exhibit 38.2.

Exhibit 38.2

	£	£	£
Taxable Profits	50,000		
Dividend Paid	49,000		
Advance Corporation Tax £49,000 × $\frac{3}{7}$			21,000
Corporation Tax Liability £50,000 × 50 per cent		25,000	
Less Advance Corporation Tax (restricted) (A)		15,000	
Mainstream Corporation Tax payable at the due date			10,000
Total Corporation Tax Paid			31,000

Although normally £21,000 would be deducted it would mean that the mainstream corporation tax would have been £4,000 (i.e. £25,000−£21,000). The figure of £4,000 would be less than 20 per cent of the taxable profits, and this just would not be allowed. As £10,000 is 20 per cent of the taxable profits of £50,000 the figure allowed as an advance payment per (A) is the amount needed so that the Corporation Tax liability less (A) equals £10,000. The amount of restricted advance corporation tax which would be allowed is therefore £15,000. The surplus advance corporation tax paid, i.e. £21,000−£15,000 = £6,000 can be set off against the corporation tax for the past two periods or carried forward and set off against future corporation tax liability.

Corporation Tax owing at the Balance Sheet Date

Any Corporation Tax owing at the balance sheet date is quite simply shown as a current liability on the balance sheet.

Income Tax

As already stated, companies do not pay income tax, instead they suffer corporation tax. In the case of sole traders income tax is not directly connected with the business, as the calculation of it depends on whether the sole trader is married or not, the number of dependants that he may have and their ages, the amount and type of other income received by him, etc. It should therefore be charged to the Drawings Account.

The income tax charged upon a partnership is also subject to the personal situation of the partners. The actual apportionment of the tax between the partners must be performed by someone who has access to the personal tax computations, it most certainly is not apportioned in the partners' profit-sharing ratios. When the apportionment has been made each partner should have the relevant amount debited to his Drawings Account.

Sole traders and partnerships are not liable to corporation tax.

Income tax does, however, come into the accounts of limited companies in that the company, when paying charges such as debenture interest or some sorts of royalties, will deduct income tax from the amount to be paid to the debenture holder or royalty owner. This figure of income tax is then payable by the company to the Inland Revenue. This means simply that the company is acting as a tax collector on behalf of the Inland Revenue. Suppose the company has 1,000 different debenture holders, then it is far easier for the Inland Revenue if the company pays only the net amount (i.e. the amount of debenture interest less income tax) due to each debenture holder and then pays the income tax deducted, in one figure, to the Inland Revenue. This saves the Inland Revenue having to trace 1,000 debenture holders and then collect the money from them. It obviously cuts down on the bad debts that the Inland Revenue might suffer, it makes it more difficult to evade the payment of income tax, and all this plus the fact that it makes it cheaper for the Inland Revenue to administer the system.

For the rest of this book it will be assumed that the standard rate of income tax is 30 per cent. This rate will obviously differ from time to time. In addition where an individual has a high income he/she will pay rates of income tax which will exceed 30 per cent. However, a company will deduct income tax at the standard rate, even though individual debenture holders may have to pay income tax at higher rates, or indeed pay no income tax at all.

This means that if a company had 8 per cent debentures amounting to £100,000 then, assuming that the debenture interest was payable in one amount, cheques amounting to a total of £5,600 (8 per cent of £100,000 = £8,000 less 30 per cent income tax, £2,400 = £5,600), will be paid to the debenture holders. A cheque for £2,400 will then be paid to the Inland Revenue by the company. Assume that debenture holder AB is liable on his income to income tax at the rate of 30 per cent, and that he receives interest of £70 net (i.e. £100 gross less income tax £30), on his debenture of £1,250 then he has already suffered his rightful income tax by deduction at the source, He will thus not get a further bill from the Inland Revenue for the £30 tax, he has already suffered the full amount due by him, and the company will have paid the £30 income tax as part of the total income tax cheque of £2,400.

On the other hand debenture holder CD may not be liable to income tax because his income is low, or that he has a large number of dependants or other such circumstance for which he obtains liability from having to pay any income tax. If he has a debenture of £1,000 he will receive a cheque for interest amounting to £56 (i.e. £80 gross less income tax £24). As he is not liable to income tax, but as £24 of his money has been included in the total cheque paid by the company to the Inland Revenue of £2,400, then he will be able to claim a refund of £24 from the Inland Revenue. Such a claim is made direct to the Inland Revenue, the company has nothing to do with the refund.

With another debenture holder, EF, this person is liable to a very high rate of income tax, say 75 per cent, on his income. If he has a debenture of £25,000, then the company will pay a cheque to him of £1,400 (£2,000 gross less income tax £600). In fact he is really liable to £1,500 income tax £2,000 at 75 per cent) on this income. As £600 income tax has been taken from him and handed over by the company, included in the total cheque of £2,400 income tax paid to the Inland Revenue by the company, then eventually the Inland Revenue will send an extra demand for income tax of £900 (£1,500 liable less £600 already paid). The company will have nothing to do with this extra demand.

Of course, a company may well have bought debentures or own royalties, etc., in another company. This may mean that the company not only pays charges, such as debenture interests, but also receives similar items from other companies. The company will receive such items net after income tax has been deducted. When the company both receives and pays such items, it may set off the tax already suffered by it from such interest, etc., received against the tax collected by it from its own charges, just paying the resultant net figure of income tax to the Inland Revenue.

The figures of charges to be shown as being paid or received by the company in the company's own Profit and Loss Account are the gross charges, i.e. the same as they would have been if income tax had never been invented. An exhibit will now be used to illustrate this more clearly.

Exhibit 38.3

RST Ltd has 7 per cent debentures amounting to £10,000 and has bought a £4,000 debenture of 10 per cent in a private company, XYZ Ltd. During the year cheques amounting to £490 (£700 less 30 per cent) have been paid to debenture holders, and a cheque of £280 (£400 less 30 per cent) has been received from XYZ Ltd. Instead of paying over the £210 income tax deducted on payment of debenture interest, RST Ltd waits until the cheque is received from XYZ Ltd, and then pays a cheque for £90 (£210 collected by it less £120 already suffered by deduction by XYZ Ltd) to the Inland Revenue in settlement.

Debenture Interest Payable

	£		£
Cash	490	Profit and Loss	700
Income Tax	210		
	700		700

Unquoted Investment Income*

	£		£
Profit and Loss	400	Cash	280
		Income Tax	120
	400		400

Income Tax

Unquoted Investment Income	120	Debenture Interest	210
Cash	90		
	210		210

*N.B. Interest or dividends from a private company are known as unquoted investment income. The word 'unquoted' arises because a private company cannot have its shares 'quoted' on a stock exchange, i.e. the shares and debentures of a private company cannot be dealt in on the stock exchange.

It may well have been the case that, although the income tax had been deducted at source from both the payment out of the company, and the amount received, no cash has been paid specifically to the Inland Revenue by the company by the balance sheet date. This means that the balance of £90 owing to the Inland Revenue will be carried down as a credit balance and will be shown under Current Liabilities in the balance sheet.

Corporation Tax and the Imputation System

When a dividend is paid by a company, this is done without any specific deduction of tax of any kind from the dividend payment. However, the dividend has been paid out of the balance of profits remaining after corporation tax has been charged. In addition, although this has not been deducted specifically from the dividend cheques, a sum equal to $\frac{3}{7}$ of the dividend has to be paid as Advance Corporation Tax. The final part of what is called the Imputation System is that the recipient of the dividend is entitled to a tax credit. The tax credit will equal $\frac{3}{7}$ of the actual amount of the dividend received.

This works out in this way. An individual, not a company, who has 700 shares of £1 each in a company will receive a dividend cheque for £70 if the company pays a dividend of 10 per cent on its shares. When he declares the income on his tax return he will have to show the figure of the actual income received plus a tax credit equal to $\frac{3}{7}$ of that figure, i.e. in this case £70$+\frac{3}{7}$ of £70 = £100. Assuming an income tax rate of 30 per cent he would normally have to pay £30 income tax on this income of £100, but he is able to set off the tax credit he is entitled to, making a liability of nil. On the other hand, if his personal reliefs are such that he would not have to pay any income tax at all, then he will be able to get a refund of the £30 tax credit from the Inland Revenue. If his income is so great that he has to pay a higher rate of income tax than 30 per cent, then the Inland Revenue will send him a tax demand for the extra income tax.

When it comes to companies buying shares in other companies there are a few differences. Some terminology is necessary here. 'Franked Investment Income' consists of the dividend received, plus the tax credit, by a UK resident company from another UK resident company. A 'Franked Payment' is a dividend, plus the relevant advance corporation tax, payable by a UK resident company. During the accounting period the company will set the tax portion of the franked investment income against the tax portion of the franked payment, and will pay only the balance as advance corporation tax. This means that if company A pays a dividend of £3,500 then normally it would have to pay advance corporation tax of £1,500 ($\frac{3}{7}$ of £3,500). If then company A recives a dividend from company B of £560, there will also be a tax credit of £240 ($\frac{3}{7}$ of £560). The amount of advance corporation tax will therefore be restricted to £1,500$-$£240 = £1,260. In the relatively rare instance where the franked investment income exceeds the franked payment, then the excess of the tax portion of the income can be set off against the advance corporation tax payable in the next accounting period.

Although the payments of advance corporation tax are affected as stated, the full payment of corporation tax liability will be affected only as regards the allocation of it between the advance corporation tax part and the mainstream part. The dividends shown as being proposed or as being receivable are shown in the profit and loss and appropriation accounts at the actual figures paid or received. There is thus no form of double entry made for the tax credit, this just does not come into the final accounts at all. Exhibit 38.4 now illustrates the various items discussed so far in this chapter.

Exhibit 38.4

The following are relevant to GB Ltd for the year ended 31 December 19–7.

(a) There are 8 per cent debentures amounting to £20,000. The debenture interest was paid on 31 December less income tax of 30 per cent.

(b) GB Ltd had bought debentures of £5,000 in a private company giving debenture interest at the rate of 9 per cent. A cheque for the year's interest, less income tax at the rate of 30 per cent, is received on 31 December 19–7.

(c) Any income tax owing to the Inland Revenue has not been paid before the year-end.

(d) A dividend of 25 per cent is proposed for the year 19–7 on the 100,000 ordinary shares of £1 each.

(e) GB Ltd had bought 30,000 ordinary shares of £1 each in HH Ltd a public company quoted on the stock exchange in 19–4. On 30 November 19–7 HH Ltd declares and pays a dividend of 14 per cent.

(f) The corporation tax liability for the year 19–7 is expected to be £40,000.

GB Ltd Profit and Loss Account for the year ended
31 December 19–7 (extracts)

		£			£
Debenture Interest	(a)	1,600	Quoted Investment Income	(e)	4,200
			Unquoted Investment Income	(b)	450
Net Profit carried down					

	£		£
Corporation Tax based on Profits of the Year	(f) 40,000	Net Profit brought down	
Proposed Ordinary Dividend of 25 per cent	(d) 25,000		
Balance carried to next year			

Balance Sheet as at 31 December 19–7 (extracts)

	£
Current Liabilities:	
Proposed Ordinary Dividends	(d) 25,000
Corporation Tax Payable	(f) 40,000
Income Tax Owing (a) £480 – (b) £135	345

Deferred Taxation

Quite frequently the profits on which the corporation tax is assessable and the profits per the accounts are markedly different. This is especially the case when tax regulations from time to time allow free depreciation of assets, i.e. a far greater amount will be given as capital allowances than would be shown as depreciation in the Profit and Loss Account. This can mean a relatively small amount of corporation tax payable for this year, even though the accounting profits would suggest a much higher figure.

The difference between these two figures would be best shown as an extra charge in the Profit and Loss Appropriation Account, and credited to a Deferred Taxation Account. In the balance sheet the balance in the Deferred Taxation Account should not be put with Reserves or with current liabilities, for it is neither of these. It should instead be shown as a separate item immediately above Current Liabilities in the Balance Sheet.

Thus the accounting net profit for the year might be £250,000, but because of the company being able to claim extra capital allowances when compared with depreciation charges, the taxable profits are £140,000. The rate of corporation tax is taken as being 50 per cent. This means that corporation tax chargeable will be £140,000 × 50 per cent = £70,000. The deferred taxation charge should therefore be £250,000 – £140,000 = £110,000 at 50 per cent = £55,000.

Profit and Loss Appropriation Account for the year ended . . .

	£		£
Corporation Tax	70,000	Net Profit brought down	250,000
Deferred Taxation	55,000		

Balance Sheet as at . . .

	£
Deferred Taxation	55,000
Current Liabilities:	
Corporation Tax owing	70,000

Exercises

38.1. BG Ltd has a trading profit for the year ended 31 December 19–7, before dealing with the following items, of £50,000. You are to complete the Profit and Loss Account and Appropriation Account and show the balance sheet extracts.

(*a*) The standard rate of income tax is taken as being 30 per cent.
(*b*) BG Ltd had £40,000 of 9 per cent debentures. It sent them cheques for debenture interest for the year less income tax on 31 December 19–7.
(*c*) BG Ltd had bought £10,000 of 11 per cent debentures in another company. It received a year's interest, less income tax, on 30 December 19–7.
(*d*) No cheque has been paid to the Inland Revenue for income tax.
(*e*) BG Ltd had bought 15,000 ordinary shares of £1 each in MM Ltd. MM Ltd paid a dividend to BG Ltd of 20 per cent on 30 November 19–7.
(*f*) BG Ltd had a liability for Corporation Tax, based on the profits for 19–7, of £24,000.
(*g*) BG proposed a dividend of 30 per cent on its 70,000 ordinary shares of £1 each, out of the profits for 19–7.
(*h*) Transfer £5,000 to General Reserve.
(*i*) Unappropriated profits brought forward from last year amounted to £9,870.

38.2A. KK Ltd has a trading profit, before dealing with any of the undermentioned items, for the year ended 31 December 19–9 of £200,000. You are to complete the Profit and Loss and Appropriation Account for the year and balance sheet extracts as at the end of the year.

(*a*) The standard rate of income tax is taken as being 30 per cent.
(*b*) KK Ltd has bought £80,000 of 10 per cent debentures in another company. KK Ltd receives its interest, less income tax, for the year on 15 December 19–9.
(*c*) KK has issued £150,000 of 8 per cent debentures, and pays interest, less income tax for the year on 20 December 19–9.
(*d*) No cheque has been paid to the Inland Revenue for income tax.
(*e*) KK Ltd has a liability for Corporation Tax, based on the year's profits for 19–9, of £97,000.
(*f*) KK Ltd owns 60,000 ordinary shares of £1 each in GHH Ltd, and receives a cheque for the dividend of 20 per cent in November 19–9.
(*g*) KK Ltd proposed a dividend of 15 per cent on the 100,000 ordinary shares of £1 each, payable out of the profits for 19–9.
(*h*) Transfer £20,000 to General Reserve.
(*i*) Unappropriated profits brought forward from last year amounted to £19,830.

39

Provisions, Reserves and Liabilities

A 'provision' is an amount written off or retained by way of providing for depreciation, renewals or diminution in value of assets; or retained by way of providing for any known liability of which the amount cannot be determined with 'substantial' accuracy. This therefore covers such items as Provisions for Depreciation. A 'liability' is an amount owing which can be determined with substantial accuracy.

Sometimes, therefore, the difference between a provision and a liability hinges around what is meant by 'substantial' accuracy. Rent owing at the end of a financial year would normally be known with precision, this would obviously be a liability. Legal charges for a court case which has been heard, but for which the lawyers have not yet submitted their bill, would be a provision. The need for the distinction between liabilities and provision will not become obvious until Chapter 41, where the requirements of the Companies Acts regarding disclosures in the Final Accounts are examined.

A 'Revenue Reserve' is where an amount has been voluntarily transferred from the Profit and Loss Appropriation Account by debiting it, thus reducing the amount of profits left available for cash dividend purposes, and crediting a named Reserve Account. The reserve may be for some particular purpose, such as a Foreign Exchange Reserve Account created just in case the firm should ever meet a situation where it would suffer loss because of devaluation of a foreign currency, or it could be a General Reserve Account.

Such transfers are, in fact, an indication to the shareholders that it would be unwise at that particular time to pay out all the available profits as dividends. The resources represented by part of the profits should more wisely and profitably be kept in the firm, at least for the time being. Revenue Reserves can be called upon in future years to help swell the profits shown in the Profit and Loss Appropriation Account as being available for dividend purposes. This is effected quite simply by debiting the particular Reserve Account and crediting the Profit and Loss Appropriation Account.

A General Reserve may be needed because of the effect of inflation. If the year 19–3 a firm needs a working capital of £4,000, the volume of trade remains the same for the next three years but the price level increases by 25 per cent, then the working capital requirements will now be £5,000. If all the profits are distributed the firm will still only have £4,000 working capital which cannot possibly finance the same volume of trade as it did in 19–3. Transferring annual amounts of profits to a General Reserve instead of paying them out as dividends is one way to help overcome this problem. On the other hand it may just be the convention of conservatism asserting itself, with a philosophy of 'it's better to be safe than sorry', in this case to restrict dividends because the funds they would withdraw from the business may be needed in a moment of crisis. This is sometimes overdone, with the result that the firm has excessive amounts of liquid funds being inefficiently used, whereas if they were paid out to the shareholders, who after all are the owners, then the shareholders could put the funds to better use themselves.

This then leaves the question of the balance on the Profit and Loss Appropriation Account, if it is a credit balance. It is a Revenue Reserve? There is no straightforward answer to this, the fact that it has not been utilized for dividend purposes could mean that it has been deliberately held back and as such could be classified as a Revenue Reserve. On the other hand, there may be a balance on the account just because it is inconvenient to pay dividends in fractions of percentages.

A Capital Reserve is normally quite different from a Revenue Reserve. It is a reserve which it not available for transfer to the Profit and Loss Appropriation Account to swell the profits shown as available for cash dividend purposes. Most Capital Reserves can never be utilized for cash dividend purposes; notice the use of the word 'cash', as it will be seen later that Bonus Shares may be issued as a 'non-cash' dividend.

The ways that Capital Reserves are created must therefore be looked at.

1. Created in Accordance with the Companies Acts

The Companies Acts state that the following are Capital Reserves and can never be utilized for the declaration of dividends payable in cash.

(a) Capital Redemption Reserve Fund. See Chapter 36.
(b) Share Premium Account. See Chapter 35.

2. Created by Case Law

It would be dangerous to try to establish in a few words the rules laid down by various decisions given in many cases concerning what was and what was not a 'profit', and whether such a 'profit' could or could not be utilized for cash dividend purposes. The law involved is very complex, and even the type of business carried on affects the legality or otherwise of utilizing a 'profit' for cash dividend purposes, and the law is very uncertain on some points.

The following can be stipulated:

(a) The profit must be realized. The mere increase in value of an asset without it being sold is not distributable as cash dividends.

(b) A surplus must exist after a revaluation of all the other assets. Therefore a profit of £10,000 on the sale of one asset cannot be paid out as cash dividends if the other assets are overvalued by £11,000.

(c) There must be nothing in the Articles of Association to forbid such a distribution.

3. In Accordance with Accounting Custom

Accounting custom, as evidenced by the recommendations of the Institute of Chartered Accountants in England and Wales, state that although some reserves are legally distributable, they can be regarded by the directors, if so desired, as capital reserves. Such a reserve can be shown as a capital reserve in one Balance Sheet and as a revenue reserve in the next.

An example of such a reserve is a Fixed Assets Replacement Reserve. Reference has already been made to the effect of inflation on working capital. Similarly, the replacement of fixed assets may require a greater sum than the original cost. If the cost of a fixed asset with a life of four years was £8,000, but the replacement price will be £10,000, then there will normally be £8,000 charged as depreciation over the four years. This reduces the recorded net profits by a similar amount which in turn means that the profits available for distribution is also reduced by £8,000. However, it is clear that it would be unwise to treat the rest of the profits as being available for dividend purposes as if the firm wishes to maintain the same volume of business, and replace the fixed assets when necessary, it needs an extra £2,000 retained in the business to finance the extra fixed assets cost. Ignoring an inflow of new capital the company must finance this extra cost by reducing the amount available for dividends. To signify to the shareholders that this is the purpose of the retention, transfers to a total of £2,000 over the four years can be made to a Fixed Assets Replacement Reserve.

The Companies Acts 1967

This act abolished the need to distinguish in the Balance Sheet between those reserves which were capital reserves and those which were revenue reserves. This was normally shown by grouping the two types of reserves under the headings of 'Capital Reserves' and 'Revenue Reserves'. It does not mean that the nature of the reserves have changed, it merely means that there is no need to identify the two types separately.

The act states that the reserves shall be classified under headings appropriate to the company's business. No doubt many firms will still stick to the previous method already shown. It does, however, mean that the groupings can be made more intelligible to the non-accountant. Some suggested headings for grouping reserves are:

Reserves

Required by Law
Recommended by the Directors

Reserves

Compulsorily Required
Set Aside Voluntarily

Reserves

Subject to Restrictions on Use
Usable at the Company's Option

Capital Reserves put to Use

The capital reserves which are not legally necessary can be utilized for cash dividend purposes, or for bonus issues of shares, or for absolutely any use not specifically forbidden by the Companies Acts, on the directors' recommendations, provided that in certain cases such as the reduction of capital, proper authority is obtained.

The ones created by law, be it statute or case law, can be dealt with only in accordance with the Companies Acts. The following description of the action which can be taken assumes that in fact the articles of association are the same as Table A for this purpose, and that therefore there are no provisions in the articles to prohibit any such actions.

(a) Capital Redemption Reserve Fund (for creation, see Chapter 36)

(i) To be applied in paying up unissued shares of the company as fully-paid shares. These are commonly called 'bonus shares', and are dealt with in Chapter 40.
(ii)' Can be reduced only in the manner as to reduction of share capital (see Chapter 40).

(b) Share Premium Account (for creation, see Chapter 35)

(i) The same provision referring to bonus shares as exists with the Capital Redemption Reserve Fund.
(ii) Writing off preliminary expenses.
(iii) Writing off expenses and commission paid on the issue of shares or debentures.
(iv) In writing off discounts on shares or debentures issued (for creation of these accounts, see Chapter 35)
(v) Providing any premium payable on redemption of redeemable preference shares or debentures.

(c) Profits prior to Incorporation (for creation, see Chapter 37)

These can be used for the issuing of bonus shares, in paying up partly paid shares, or alternatively they may be used to write down goodwill or some such similar fixed asset.

(d) Created by Case Law

These can be used in the issue of bonus shares or in the paying up of partly paid shares.

The Increase and Reduction of the Share Capital of Limited Companies

Alteration of Capital

A limited company may, if so authorized by its articles, and the correct legal formalities are observed, alter its share capital in any of the following ways:

1. Increasing its share capital by new shares, e.g. increase Authorized Share Capital from £5,000 to £15,000.

2. Consolidate and divide all or any of its share capital into shares of larger amount than its existing shares, for instance to make 5,000 Ordinary Shares of £1 each into 1,000 Ordinary Shares of £5 each.

3. Convert all or any of its paid-up shares into stock, and reconvert that stock into shares of any denomination, e.g. 10,000 Ordinary Shares of £1 each made into £10,000 Ordinary Stock.

4. Subdivide all, or any, of its shares into shares of smaller denominations, e.g. 1,000 Ordinary Shares of £6 each made into 2,000 Ordinary Shares of £3 each, or 3,000 Ordinary Shares of £2 each, etc.

5. Cancel shares which have not been taken up. This is 'diminution' of capital, not to be confused with reduction of capital described later in the chapter. Thus a firm with an Authorized Capital of £10,000 and an Issued Capital of £8,000 can alter its capital to be Authorized Capital £8,000 and Issued Capital £8,000.

Bonus Shares

If the articles give the power, and the requisite legal formalities are observed, the following may be applied in the issuing of bonus shares:

1. The balance of the Profit and Loss Appropriation Account.

2. Any other revenue reserve.

3. Any capital reserve.

This thus comprises all of the reserves.

The reason why this should ever be needed can be illustrated by taking a somewhat exaggerated example, shown in Exhibit 40.1.

Exhibit 40.1

A firm, Better Price Ltd, started business fifty years ago with 1,000 Ordinary Shares of £1 each and £1,000 in the bank. The firm has constantly had to retain a proportion of its profits to finance its operations, thus diverting them from being used for cash dividend purposes. Such a policy has conserved working capital.

The firm's Balance Sheet as at 31 December 19-7 is shown as:

Better Price Ltd

Balance Sheet as at 31 December 19–7
(before bonus shares are issued)

	£		£
Share Capital	1,000	Fixed Assets	5,000
Reserves (including Profit		Current Assets *less*	
and Loss Appropriation		Current Liabilities	5,000
balance)	9,000		
	10,000		10,000

If in fact an annual profit of £1,500 was now being made, this being 15 per cent on capital employed, and £1,000 could be paid annually as cash dividends, then the dividend declared each year would be 100 per cent, i.e. a dividend of £1,000 on shares of £1,000 nominal value. It is obvious that the dividends and the share capital have got out of step with one another. Employees and trade unions may well become quite belligerent, as owing to the lack of accounting knowledge, or even misuse of it, it might be believed that the firm was making unduly excessive profits. Customers, especially if they are the general public, may also be deluded into thinking that they were being charged excessive prices, or, even though this could be demonstrated not to be true because of the prices charged by competitors, they may well still have the feeling that they were somehow being duped.

In point of fact, an efficient firm in this particular industry or trade may well be only reasonably rewarded for the risks it has taken by making a profit of 15 per cent on capital employed. The figure of 100 per cent for the dividend is due to the very misleading custom in the United Kingdom of calculating dividends in relationship to the nominal amount of the share capital.

If it is considered, in fact, that £7,000 of the reserves could not be used for dividend purposes, due to the fact that the net assets should remain at £8,000, made up of Fixed Assets £5,000 and working capital £3,000, then besides the £1,000 Share Capital which cannot be returned to the shareholders there are also £7,000 reserves which cannot be rationally returned to them. Instead of this £7,000 being called reserves, it might as well be called capital, as it is needed by the business on a permanent basis.

To remedy this position, as well as some other needs less obvious, bonus shares were envisaged. The reserves are made non-returnable to the shareholders by being converted into share capital. Each holder of one Ordinary Share of £1 each will receive seven bonus shares (in the shape of seven ordinary shares) of £1 each. The Balance Sheet, if the bonus shares had been issued immediately, would then appear:

Better Price Ltd
Balance Sheet as at 31 December 19–7
(after bonus shares are issued)

	£		£
Share Capital (£1,000+ £7,000)	8,000	Fixed Assets	5,000
Reserves (£9,000–£7,000)	2,000	Current Assets *less* Current Liabilities	5,000
	10,000		10,000

When the dividends of £1,000 per annum are declared in the future, they will amount to $\dfrac{£1,000}{£8,000} \times \dfrac{100}{1} = 12\cdot5$ per cent. This will cause less disturbance in the minds of employees, trade unions, and customers.

Of course the issue of bonus shares may be seen by any of the interested parties to be some form of diabolical liberty. To give seven shares of £1 each free for each one previously owned may be seen as a travesty of social justice. In point of fact the shareholders have not gained at all. Before the bonus issue there were 1,000 shares that owned between them £10,000 of net assets. Therefore, assuming just for this purpose that the book 'value' is the same as any other 'value', each share was worth £10. After the bonus issue each previous holder now has eight shares for every one share he held before. If he had owned one share only, he now owns eight shares. He is therefore the owner of $\frac{8}{8,000}$ part of the firm, i.e. a one-thousandth part. The 'value' of the net assets are £10,000, so that he owns £10 of them, so his shares are worth £10. This is exactly the same 'value' as that applying before the bonus issue was made.

It would be useful to, in addition, refer to other matters for comparison. Anyone who had owned a £1 share fifty years ago, then worth £1, would now have (if he was still living after such a long time) eight shares worth £8. A new house of a certain type fifty years ago might have cost £x, it may now cost £$8x$, the cost of a pint of beer may now be y times greater than it was fifty years ago, a packet of cigarettes may be z times more and so on. Of course, the firm has brought a lot of trouble on itself by waiting so many years to capitalize reserves. It should have been done by several stages over the years.

This is all a very simplified, and in many ways an exaggerated version. There is, however, no doubt that misunderstanding of accounting and financial matters have caused a great deal of unnecessary friction in the past and will probably still do so in the future. Yet another very common misunderstanding is that the assumption the reader was asked to accept, namely that the Balance Sheet values equalled 'real values', is often one taken by the reader of a Balance Sheet. Thus a profit of £10,000 when the net assets book values are £20,000 may appear to be excessive, yet in fact a more realistic value of the assets may be saleable value, in which case the value may be £100,000.

The accounting entries necessary are to debit the Reserve Accounts utilized, and to credit a Bonus Account. The shares are then issued and the entry required to record this is to credit the Share Capital Account and to debit the Bonus Account. The Journal entries would be:

The Journal

	Dr	Cr
	£	£
Reserve Account(s) (show each account separately)	7,000	
Bonus Account		7,000
Transfer of an amount equal to the bonus payable in		
fully-paid shares		
Bonus Account	7,000	
Share Capital Account		7,000
Allotment and issue of 7,000 shares of £1 each, in satisfaction		
of the bonus declared		

Reduction of Capital

1. *Where Capital is not Represented by Assets*

Any scheme for the reduction of capital needs to go through the legal formalities via the shareholders and other interested parties, and must receive the consent of the court. It is assumed that all of this had been carried out correctly.

Capital reduction means in fact that the share capital, all of it if there is only one class such as ordinary shares, or all or part of it if there is more than one class of shares, has been subjected to a lessening of its nominal value, or of the called-up part of the nominal value.

Thus:

(a) A £4 share might be made into a £3 share.
(b) A £5 share might be made into a £1 share.
(c) A £3 share, £2 called up, might be made into a £1 share fully paid up.
(d) A £5 share, £3 called-up, might be made into a £3 share £1 called up. And any other variations.

Why should such a step be necessary? The reasons are rather like the issue of bonus shares in reverse. In this case the share capital has got out of step with the assets, in that the share capital is not fully represented by assets. Thus Robert Ltd may have a Balance Sheet as follows:

Robert Ltd
Balance Sheet as at 31 December 19–7

	£		£
Ordinary Share Capital		Net Assets	30,000
10,000 Ordinary Shares of			
£5 each fully paid	50,000		
Less Debit Balance—			
Profit and Loss Account	20,000		
	30,000		30,000

The net assets are shown at £30,000, it being felt in this particular firm that the book value represented a true and fair view of their 'actual value'. The company will almost certainly be precluded from paying dividends until the debit balance on the Profit and Loss Appropriation Account has been eradicated and a credit balance brought into existence. Some firms, in certain circumstances, may still pay a dividend even though there is a debit balance, but it is to be assumed that Robert Ltd is not one of them. If profits remaining after taxation are now running at the rate of £3,000 per annum, it will be more than seven years before a dividend can be paid. As the normal basic reason for buying shares is to provide income, although there may well enter another reason such as capital appreciation, the denial of income to the shareholders for this period of time is serious indeed.

A solution would be to cancel, i.e. reduce, the capital which was no longer represented by assets. In this case there is £20,000 of the share capital which can lay no claim to any assets. The share capital should therefore be reduced by £20,000. This is done by making the shares into £3 shares fully paid instead of £5 shares. The Balance Sheet would become:

Robert Ltd
Balance Sheet as at 31 December 19–7

	£		£
Ordinary Share Capital	30,000	Net Assets	30,000
	30,000		30,000

Now that there is no debit balance on the Profit and Loss Appropriation Account the £3,000 available profit next year can be distributed as dividends.

Of course, the firm of Robert Ltd is very much a simplified version. Very often both preference and ordinary shareholders are involved and sometimes debenture holders as well. Even creditors occasionally sacrifice part of the amount owing to them, the idea being that the increase in working capital so generated will help the firm to achieve prosperity, in which case the creditors hope to enjoy the profitable contact that they used to have with the firm. The whole of these capital reduction schemes are matters of negotiation between the various interested parties. For instance, preference shareholders may be quite content for the nominal value of their shares to be reduced if the rate of interest they receive is increased. As with any negotiation the various parties will put forward their points of view and discussions will take place, until eventually a compromise solution is arrived at. When the court's sanction has been obtained, the accounting entries are:

(a) For amounts written off assets.
   Debit Capital Reduction Account.
   Credit Various Asset Accounts.
(b) For reduction in liabilities (e.g. creditors).
   Debit liability accounts.
   Credit Capital Reduction Account.
(c) The reduction in the share capital.
   Debit Share Capital Accounts (each type).
   Credit Capital Reduction Account.
(d) If a credit balance now exists on the Capital Reduction Account.
   Debit Capital Reduction Account (to close).
   Credit Capital Reserve.

It is very unlikely that there would ever be a debit balance on the Capital Reduction Account, as the court would very rarely agree to any such scheme which would bring about that result.

2. Where Some of the Assets Are No Longer Needed

Where some of the firm's assets are no longer needed, probably due to a contraction in the firm's activities, a company may find itself with a surplus of liquid assets. Subject to the legal formalities being observed, in this case the reduction of capital is effected by returning cash to the shareholders, i.e.:

(i) Debit Share Capital Account (with amount returnable).
   Credit Sundry Shareholders.
(ii) Debit Sundry Shareholders.
   Credit Bank (amount actually paid).

Such a scheme could be objected to by the creditors if it affected their interests.

Exercises

40.1 The following is the summarized Balance Sheet of Traders Ltd as on 31 December 19-4.

Balance Sheet

Issued Share Capital:	£	Fixed Assets:	£	£
160,000 Ordinary Shares of £0·5 each, fully paid	80,000	Freehold Premises		71,000
24,000 6½ per cent Redeemable Preference Shares of £1 each, fully paid	24,000	Furniture and Fittings *less* Provision for Depreciation	15,000 5,000	10,000
Profit and Loss Account	37,000	Current Assets:		
5 per cent Debentures	16,000	Stock-in-Trade		43,200
Current Liabilities	63,000	Debtors		39,650
		Investments		15,000
		Balance at Bank		41,150
	220,000			220,000

On 1 January 19–5:

(i) Freehold premises had been revalued at £120,000 and were written up in the books to that amount.

(ii) A bonus dividend out of the surplus created by the revaluation of the premises was declared and satisfied by the issue to ordinary shareholders of one ordinary £0·5 share, as fully paid, for every two shares held.

(iii) Additional furniture and fittings £2,000 were installed. These were purchased on credit from Shop Fitters Ltd.

(iv) The investments were sold for £13,750.

(v) The redeemable preference shares were redeemed at par.

(vi) The debentures were repaid at a premium of 2 per cent.

You are required:

(a) to show (by means of Journal entries) the entries in respect of the above matters;

(b) to set out the Balance Sheet as on 1 January 19–5 after completion of the above.

Note: Assume that the company had no transactions on 1 January 19–5 other than those mentioned above.

(Associated Examining Board 'A' Level)

40.2. Deflation Ltd, which had experienced trading difficulties, decided to reorganize its finances.

On 31 December 19–5 a final trial balance extracted from the books showed the following position:

	£	£
Share Capital, authorized and issued:		
150,000 6 per cent Cumulative Preference Shares of £1 each		150,000
200,000 Ordinary Shares of £1 each		200,000
Share Premium Account		40,000
Profit and Loss Account	114,375	
Preliminary Expenses	7,250	
Goodwill (at cost)	55,000	
Trade Creditors		43,500
Debtors	31,200	

	£	£
Bank Overdraft		51,000
Leasehold Property (at cost)	80,000	
„ „ (provision for depreciation)		30,000
Plant and Machinery (at cost)	210,000	
„ „ (provision for depreciation)		62,500
Stock in Hand	79,175	
	577,000	577,000

Approval of the Court was obtained for the following scheme for reduction of capital:

1. The preference shares to be reduced to £0·75 per share.

2. The ordinary shares to be reduced to £0.125 per share.

3. One £0·125 ordinary share to be issued for each £1 of gross preference dividend arrears; the preference dividend had not been paid for three years.

4. The balance on share premium account to be utilized.

5. Plant and machinery to be written down to £75,000.

6. The profit and loss account balance, and all intangible assets, to be written off.

At the same time as the resolution to reduce capital was passed, another resolution was approved restoring the total authorized capital to £350,000, consisting of 150,000 6 per cent cumulative preference shares of £0·75 each and the balance in ordinary shares of £0·125 each. As soon as the above resolutions had been passed 500,000 ordinary shares were issued at par, for cash, payable in full upon application.

You are required:

(a) to show the journal entries necessary to record the above transactions in the company's books, and

(b) to prepare a Balance Sheet of the company, after completion of the scheme.

(Institute of Chartered Accountants)

40.3. The Balance Sheet of Planners Ltd on 31 March 19–6 was as follows:

Balance Sheet

	£		£	£
Issued Share Capital:		Goodwill		20,000
120,000 Ordinary Shares		Fixed Assets		100,000
of £1 each	120,000			
50,000 6 per cent				120,000
Cumulative Preference		Current Assets:		
Shares of £1 each	50,000	Stock	22,000	
		Work in		
	170,000	Progress	5,500	
Less Profit and Loss		Debtors	34,000	
Account Debit Balance	40,000	Bank	17,500	
				79,000
	130,000	Capital Expenses:		
6 per cent Debentures	50,000	Formation Expenses		1,000

Balance Sheet

	£		£	£
Current Liabilities:				
Creditors	20,000			
	200,000			200,000

The dividend on the preference shares is £9,000 in arrears. A scheme of reconstruction was accepted by all parties and was completed on 1 April 19–6.

A new company was formed, Budgets Ltd, with an authorized share capital of £200,000, consisting of 200,000 ordinary shares of £1 each. This company took over all the assets of Planners Ltd. The purchase consideration was satisfied partly in cash and partly by the issue, at par, of shares and debentures by the new company in accordance with the following arrangements:

1. The creditors of the old company received, in settlement of each £10 due to them, £7 in cash and three fully paid ordinary shares in the new company.

2. The holders of preference shares in the old company received seven fully paid ordinary shares in the new company to every eight preference shares in the old company and three fully paid ordinary shares in the new company for every £5 of arrears of dividend.

3. The ordinary shareholders in the old company received one fully paid share in the new company for every five ordinary shares in the old company.

4. The holders of 6 per cent debentures in the old company received £40 cash and £60 6 per cent debentures issued at par for every £100 debenture held in the old company.

5. The balance of the authorised capital of the new company was issued at par for cash and was fully paid on 1 April 19–6.

6. Goodwill was eliminated, the stock was valued at £20,000 and the other current assets were brought into the new company's books at the amounts at which they appeared in the old company's balance sheet. The balance of the purchase consideration represented the agreed value of the fixed assets.

You are required to show:

(a) The closing entries in the Realisation Account and the Sundry Shareholders Account in the books of Planners Ltd.

(b) To show your calculation of:
   (i) The Purchase Consideration for the Assets, and (ii) the agreed value of the fixed assets.

(c) The summarised balance sheet of Budgets Ltd as on 1 April 19–6.

40.4. On 31 March 19–6 the following was the Balance Sheet of R.S.T. Ltd:

Balance Sheet

Authorized Capital:	£	£	Fixed Assets:	£	£
50,000 7 per cent Preference Shares of £1 each	50,000		Goodwill and Trade Marks as valued	75,000	
700,000 Ordinary Shares of £0·5 each	350,000		Plant and Machinery (at cost *less* depreciation)	71,600	
		400,000	Furniture and Fittings (at cost *less* depreciation)	4,200	
					150,800
Issued and Fully Paid Capital:					
50,000 7 per cent Preference Shares of £1 each	50,000		Current Assets:		
			Stock-in-Trade	56,950	

Balance Sheet

	£	£		£	£
400,000 Ordinary			Sundry Debtors	21,700	
Shares of £0·5 each	200,000		Cash in Hand	50	
		250,000			78,700
Capital Reserve		16,000			
		266,000			
Deduct Profit and Loss					
Account (debit balance)		61,300			
		204,700			
Current Liabilities:					
Sundry Creditors		10,600			
Bank Overdraft		14,200			
		229,500			229,500

The following scheme of capital reduction was sanctioned by the Court and agreed by the shareholders:

(i) Preference shares were to be reduced to £0·75 each.

(ii) Ordinary shares were to be reduced to £0·2 each.

(iii) The capital reserve was to be eliminated.

(iv) The reduced shares of both classes were to be consolidated into new ordinary shares of £1 each.

(v) An issue of £50,000 8 per cent Debentures at par was to be made to provide fresh working capital.

(vi) The sum written off the issued capital of the company and the capital reserve to be used to write off the debit balance of the Profit and Loss Account and to reduce fixed assets by the following amounts:

	£
Goodwill and trade marks	70,000
Plant and machinery	15,000
Furniture and fittings	2,200

(vii) The bank overdraft was to be paid off out of the proceeds of the debentures which were duly issued and paid in full.

A further resolution was passed to restore the authorized capital of the company to 400,000 ordinary shares of £1 each.

Prepare journal entries (cash transactions to be journalized) to give effect to the above scheme and draw up the Balance Sheet of the company after completion of the scheme.

(Associated Examining Board 'A' Level)

40.5A. The summarized Balance Sheet of Optimists Ltd at 31 December 19–9 was as follows:

	£		£
Issued Capital:			
75,000 6 per cent		Freehold Premises	30,000
Preference Shares of		Plant	105,000
£1 each	75,000	Stock	32,000
150,000 Ordinary Shares		Debtors	35,000
of £1 each	150,000	Development Expenditure	37,500
Creditors	60,000	Cash at Bank	3,000
		Profit and Loss Account	42,500
	285,000		285,000

A capital reduction scheme has been sanctioned under which the 75,000 preference shares are to be reduced to £0·75 each, fully paid, and the 150,000 ordinary shares are to be reduced to £0·10 each, fully paid.

Development expenditure and the debit balance on Profit and Loss Account are to be written off, the balance remaining being used to reduce the book value of the plant.

Prepare the journal entries recording the reduction scheme and the balance sheet as it would appear immediately after the reduction. Narrations are not required in connection with journal entries.

(Associated Examining Board—G.C.E. 'A' level)

40.6A. Depression Ltd decided to reorganize its structure following a period of adverse trading conditions.

The Balance Sheet of the company as on 31 December 19–9 showed the following:

	£	£		£	£
Share Capital			Fixed Assets:		
Authorized and Issued:			Goodwill, at Cost		55,000
200,000 8 per cent			Freehold Property, at Cost		60,000
Cumulative Preference			Leasehold Property, at Cost	140,000	
Shares of £1 each		200,000	Less Depreciation	18,000	
300,000 Ordinary Shares					122,000
of £0·5 each		150,000	Plant and Machinery,		
Share Premium Account		5,000	at Cost	220,000	
		———	Less Depreciation	60,000	
		355,000			160,000
9 per cent Debenture					397,000
(secured on Freehold					
Property	60,000		Quoted Investment, at Cost		40,000
Add Accrued Interest	2,700				
	———	62,700	Current Assets:		
Creditors		85,000	Stock	30,000	
Bank Overdraft		96,000	Debtors	60,000	
					90,000
			Preliminary Expenses		2,500
			Profit and Loss Account		69,200
		———			———
		598,700			598,700

Note: Preference dividends are four years in arrear.

Subsequent to approval by the Court of a scheme for the reduction of capital, the following steps were taken:

1. The preference shares were reduced to £0·75 per share, and the ordinary shares to £0·10 per share. After reduction the shares were consolidated into £1 shares. The authorized capital was restored to 200,000 8 per cent cumulative preference shares and 150,000 ordinary shares, both of £1 each.

2. One new ordinary share of £1 was issued for every £4 of gross preference dividend arrears.

3. The balance on share premium account was utilized.

4. The debenture holder took over the freehold property at an agreed figure of £75,000 and paid the balance to the company after deducting the amount due to him.

5. Plant and machinery was written down to £140,000.

6. Quoted investment was sold for £32,000.

7. Goodwill, preliminary expenses, debts of £8,600, and obsolete stock of £10,000 were written off.

8. A contingent liability for which no provision had been made was settled at £7,000 and of this amount £6,300 was recovered from the insurers.

You are required:

(a) to show the journal entries necessary to record the above transactions in the company's books, and

(b) to prepare a Balance Sheet, after completion of the scheme.

(*Institute of Chartered Accountants*)

40.7A The balance sheet of SAD Limited as at 30 June 19–0 was as follows:

	£		£
Share Capital; authorized,		Freehold Land and	
issued and fully paid:		Buildings	34,000
100,000 6 per cent Cumul-		Plant	96,000
ative Preference Shares	100,000	Tools and Dies	27,300
300,000 Ordinary Shares		Investments	15,000
at £0·5 each	150,000	Current Assets:	
	———	Stocks	42,500
	250,000	Debtors	53,400
Less Profit and Loss Account:		Research and Develop-	
Debit Balance	98,000	ment Expenditure	18,000
	———		
	152,000		
7 per cent £			
Debentures 60,000			
Interest due 4,200			
	64,200		
Bank Overdraft, secured on			
freehold land and buildings			
and plant	20,000		
Creditors	50,000		
	———		———
	286,200		286,200

The scheme of reorganization detailed below has been agreed by all the interested parties and approved by the Court.

You are required to prepare:

(a) the journal entries recording the transactions in the books, including cash; and

(b) a balance sheet of the company as at 1 July 19–0 after completion of the scheme.

1. The following assets are to be revalued as shown below:

	£
Plant	59,000
Tools and Dies	15,000
Stock	30,000
Debtors	48,700

2. The research and development expenditure and the balance on profit and loss account are to be written off.

3. A piece of land recorded in the books at £6,000 is valued at £14,000 and is to

be taken over by the debenture holders in part repayment of principal. The remaining freehold land and buildings are to be revalued at £40,000.

4.   A creditor for £18,000 has agreed to accept a second mortgage debenture of 10 per cent per annum secured on the plant for £15,500 in settlement of his debt. Other creditors totalling £10,000 agree to accept a payment of £0·85 in the £1 for immediate settlement.

5.   The investments, at a valuation of £22,000, are to be taken over by the bank.

6.   The ascertained loss is to be met by writing down the ordinary shares to £0.05 each and the preference to £0.80 each. The authorized share capital to be increased immediately to the original amount.

7.   The ordinary shareholders agree to subscribe for two new ordinary shares at par for every share held. This cash is all received.

8.   The costs of the scheme are £3,500. These have been paid and are to be written off. The debenture interest has also been paid.

(Institute of Cost and Management Accountants)

41

The Final Accounts of Limited Companies for Internal Use and for Publication

The reader has in fact been partly prepared for the drafting of a limited company's Balance Sheet by the ways in which certain items have already been shown in a sole trader's or a partnership's Balance Sheet. The attempt has been made in this book to standardize Balance Sheet presentation as far as possible in firms in the private sector of industry and commerce.

When a company draws up its own Final Accounts, purely for internal use by the directors and the management, then it can draft them in any way which is considered most suitable. Drawing up a Trading and Profit and Loss Account and Balance Sheet for the firm's own use is not necessarily the same as drawing up such accounts for examination purposes. If a firm wishes to charge something in the Trading Account which perhaps in theory ought to be shown in the Profit and Loss Account, then there is nothing to prevent the firm from doing so. The examinee, on the other hand, must base his answers on accounting theory and not on the practice of his own firm.

Even if the firm does draw up its internal Final Accounts strictly adhering to accounting theory, these are not necessarily the ones which are going to be published, i.e. sent to each shareholder, the Registrar of Companies and perhaps (in the case of a public company) published in the Press. The Companies Act 1967 lays down the minimum requirements for disclosure. Any firm can, if it so wishes, show more than the minimum information required, but it is solely a matter for the company concerned. Many firms take the attitude that the less its rivals know about them, then so much the better. Such firms will keep to the minimum requirements. In examinations it is to be assumed that only the minimum information is to be given. Probably the Balance Sheet of a company is the easiest to start with.

Published Balance Sheets

Schedule 2 of the Companies Act 1967 lays down the minimum information to be disclosed. The amount of information needed, if it was all shown on the fact of the Balance Sheet itself, would make that document a very cumbersome one indeed. The practice has grown up of showing certain types of information in notes attached to the Balance Sheet, a reference to the note being made against the item actually included in the Balance Sheet, e.g. Capital Reserves (note 3). Note 3 will then give full details of the Capital Reserves. It is purely a matter for the discretion of the company as to which items it will deal with in this way.

The 1967 Act which increased the details to be shown has undoubtedly led to a greater proliferation of notes containing the required information. It would be possible here to merely reprint a copy of the second schedule of the Act, leaving it to the reader to decide which are the important points, and also to interpret the language of the Act. This would, however, be rather unfair to the student at this stage, although he would be expected at a later date to possess a facility in reading various acts and interpreting the language used in Statute Law. At this juncture the student's knowledge of the law may be marginal, and therefore the author has attempted to summarize the Act, using the simplest language possible and omitting items which are not normally of very great importance. The reader must therefore realize that this is not a full exposition of the Second Schedule.

The following items must be shown, either on the face of the Balance Sheet or by additional notes attached to it.

1. The Authorized Share Capital.

2. The Issued Share Capital—showing the amount called up.

3. The Share Premium Account.

4. Shown under separate headings so far as they are not written off:

(a) The preliminary expenses.
(b) Issue and commission expenses of shares and debentures.
(c) Discounts on Debentures.
(d) Discounts on Shares.

5. Shown under separate headings:

(a) Fixed assets.
(b) Current assets.
(c) Assets that are neither fixed nor current. An example would be debts not due within twelve months of the Balance Sheet date.

6. Fixed assets.

(a) To be stated at cost or valuation.
(b) Aggregate depreciation to date of Balance Sheet must be shown.
(c) This part expected to be by way of notes. Where any fixed assets are shown at valuation other than cost, then the company should disclose the years of the valuations and the values applicable to each year, so far as they are known to the directors.
    In the year which the fixed asset is revalued the company must

give particulars of the valuers or their qualifications, and of the bases of valuation used by them.

The total movements during the year on fixed assets other than investments have to be disclosed. Land (and this may well include buildings) has to be divided up between freeholds, long leases and short leases.

Capital expenditure authorized by the directors, if material, as well as that contracted for, must be shown.

An illustration of a note of the movement in Fixed Assets can be given as:

Plant and Machinery	Cost	Depreciation	Net
Balance as at 1 January 19–7	50,000	20,000	30,000
Less Disposals	6,000	5,000	1,000
	44,000	15,000	29,000
Additions	10,000		10,000
			39,000
Depreciation for the year 19–7		7,000	−7,000
	54,000	22,000	32,000

It should be realised that the agove note of the movements are all at book values. Profits and losses on disposals are taken to the Profit and Loss Account by the usual methods.

(d) The details just shown as (c) do not refer to goodwill, patents or trade marks.

(e) Where depreciation has not been calculated by reference to the Balance Sheet value, then this must be stated.

7. Aggregate reserves and provisions (other than depreciation provisions which are shown against fixed assets) must be shown, if material.

8. If a material change in a reserve or a provision is made, and such a change is not shown in the published Profit and Loss Account, then the Balance Sheet, or a note attached to the Balance Sheet, must give details.

9. The following items must be shown:

(a) 'Quoted' investments. This means investments that are dealt in on a recognized Stock Exchange. The market value of the investments at the Balance Sheet date must be shown as a note.

(b) 'Unquoted' investments. These are investments obviously not dealt in on a recognized Stock Exchange.

(c) in on a recognized Stock Exchange.

(d) Loans not repayable within five years.

(e) Loans which will not be fully repaid within five years.

For both (d) and (e) particulars of rates of interest and terms of repayment.

10. The method of the computation of stock and work in progress if the amount is material.

A Balance Sheet suitable for publication is now shown. It will be shown first in the conventional form and then in a more modern vertical form. Chapter 42 should be consulted for further details of the vertical presentation of Balance Sheets.

F.G.Z. Ltd

Balance Sheet as at 31 March 19–8

	£		Cost or valuation £	Depreciation to date £	Net £
Share Capital:		Fixed Assets:			
Authorised: 200,000 Ordinary		Buildings, at			
Shares of £1 each	200,000	Valuation (note 1)	80,000	—	80,000
		Machinery, at Cost			
		(note 2)	30,000	10,000	20,000
Issued: 130,000 Ordinary Shares of		Motor Vehicles, at			
£1 each fully paid	130,000	Cost	18,000	7,000	11,000
			128,000	17,000	111,000
Reserves Legally Required:					
Capital Redemption Reserve Fund	8,000				
Recommended by Directors:	£	Investments:			
General Reserve	35,000	Quoted: at Cost			
Profit and Loss	2,000 37,000	(market value £15,689)		10,000	
	175,000	Unquoted: at Cost		4,000	
7 per cent Debentures	20,000				14,000
		Current Assets:			
Current Liabilities	£	Stock and Work in Progress			
Corporation Tax: Payable		(note 3)		43,000	
1 January 19–9	8,000	Debtors		48,000	
Creditors	10,000	Cash		1,000	
Bank Overdraft	6,000				92,000
	24,000	Preliminary Expenses			2,000
	219,000				219,000

Notes:

1. The buildings were valued by a firm of chartered surveyors on 31 March 19–6.

2. During the year fixed assets at a total cost of £5,000 were bought, none being sold. The depreciation provision for those bought during the year amounted to £600.

3. Stock and Work in Progress have been valued at prime cost.

F.G.Z. Ltd
Balance Sheet as at 31 march 19–8

Assets Employed	Cost or Valuation	Depreciation to date	Net
	£	£	£
Fixed Assets:			
Buildings, at Valuation (note 1)	80,000	—	80,000
Machinery, at Cost (note 2)	30,000	10,000	20,000
Motor Vehicles, at Cost	18,000	7,000	11,000
	128,000	17,000	111,000
Investments:			
Quoted: at Cost (market value £15,689)		10,000	
Unquoted: at Cost		4,000	
			14,000
Current Assets:			
Stock and Work in Progress (note 3)		43,000	
Debtors		48,000	
Cash		1,000	
			92,000
Total Assets Employed			217,000

			£
Financed by:			
Shareholders—Out of 200,000 Ordinary Shares of £1 each 130,000 have been issued			130,000
Reserves—Legally Required: Capital Redemption Reserve Fund			8,000
		£	
Recommended by Directors:			
General Reserve		35,000	
Profit and Loss		2,000	
			37,000
			175,000
Less Debit Balance not represented by Assets:			
Preliminary Expenses			2,000
Net Worth			173,000
Seven per cent Debentures			20,000
Current Liabilities:			
		£	
Corporation Tax: Payable 1 January 19–9		8,000	
Creditors		10,000	
Bank Overdraft		6,000	
			24,000
			217,000

The Profit and Loss Accounts of Companies

As with the Balance Sheets, there are certain regulations in the Second Schedule to the Companies Act 1967 referring to the information which must be shown in the Profit and Loss Account for publication purposes. The most important of these are:

1.   Provisions for depreciation.

2.   Debenture interest, and interest on the loans which must be disclosed in the Balance Sheet.

3.   The amount charged for corporation tax.

4.   Amounts respectively provided for redemption of share capital or for redemption of loans.

5.   Changes in provisions, other than depreciation provisions, if material.

6.   To show separately the income from quoted investments and the income from unquoted investments.

7.   If material, the expenses for the hire of plant and machinery.

8.   Dividends paid and proposed.

9.   The auditors' remuneration, this includes their expenses.

10. Directors' total remuneration, including pensions. (In a note accompanying the accounts there must be given an analysis of the directors' remuneration in the manner described in the Act. This also applies to executives earning over £10,000 per annum.)

The following shall be shown by way of note, if not otherwise:

(a) The turnover for the financial year, and the method by which it is arrived at. Subject to the fact that it need not be stated if the turnover does not exceed £250,000.
(b) Material profits or losses from activities not usually undertaken by the company, or exceptional profits of a non-recurrent nature.
(c) Any material effect caused by a change in the basis of accounting.

Conventional Form of a Trading and Profit and Loss Account of a Limited Company

A company may have the following Trading and Profit and Loss Account:

Block Ltd

Trading and Profit and Loss Account for the year ended 31 March 19–8

	£			£
Stock 1 April 19–7	5,000	Sales	(A)	65,000
Add Purchases	40,000			
	45,000			
Less Stock 31 March 19–8	6,000			
Cost of Goods Sold	39,000			
Gross Profit c/d	26,000			
	65,000			65,000
Wages and Salaries	11,000	Gross Profit b/d		26,000
Rent and Rates	1,000	Income from quoted		
General Trade Expenses	2,000	investments		400*
Debenture Interest	300*	Income from unquoted		
Auditors' Remuneration	200*	investments		100*
Directors' Remuneration	5,000*			

Provision for Depreciation:

	£			
Machinery	1,500			
Motor Vehicles	1,200			
		2,700*		
Net Profit c/d		4,300*		
		26,500		26,500

Corporation Tax based on			Balance brought	
the profits of the year	2,000*		forward from last year	3,000*
Proposed ordinary			Net Profit b/d	4,300*
dividend of 10 per cent	2,500*			
Transfer to General				
Reserve	500*			
Balance carried forward				
to next year	2,300*			
	7,300			7,300

Items marked * have to be shown in the published Profit and Loss Account. It should be noted that the term 'Profit and Loss Account' includes the Profit and Loss Appropriation Account.

(A) To be shown as a note, if not otherwise. The published Profit and Loss Account should preferably be shown in vertical form, and this would certainly be expected by examiners. Block's published account would therefore appear as follows:

Block Ltd

Profit and Loss Account for the year ended 31 March 19–8

		£
Profit for the year before taxation		4,300
(After taking into account the undermentioned charges and income)		
Charges:	£	
Debenture Interest	300	
Auditors' Remuneration	200	
Directors' Remuneration	5,000	
Depreciation	2,700	
Income from:		
Quoted Investments	400	
Unquoted Investments	100	
Less Corporation Tax based on the profits of the year		2,000
Profit for the year after taxation		2,300
Add Unappropriated Profits brought forward from last year		3,000
Profits available for appropriation		5,300
Less Appropriations:		
Proposed Ordinary Dividend of 10 per cent	2,500	
Transfer to General Reserve	500	
		3,000
Unappropriated Profits carried forward to next year		2,300

It must not be thought that there is only one way of drafting Profit and Loss Accounts for publication. So long as the information required by law is shown there is no limit as to the possible variations of style of presentation. Chapter 42 looks further into the question of vertical presentations of accounting statements.

Directors' Report

A directors' report has to be attached to the Balance Sheet. Note that it is not part of the Balance Sheet itself. The 1967 Act considerably increased the details which need to be shown. As it is not part of the accounts the following brief details will give an indication of some of the essential information which has to be given.

1. Proposed dividend. ⎫ Also shown in the Profit and

2. Proposed transfers to reserves. ⎬ Loss Account.

3. The market value of the land (and this is expected to include buildings) if it differs substantially from the Balance Sheet value.

4. The directors' ownership of shares and debentures in the company.

5. Where the company carries on two or more classes of business, then they must be described and the split of turnover and profit before tax must be shown. This does not include companies whose turnover does not exceed £250,000.

6. The average number of employees on the payroll throughout the year, and their aggregate remuneration for the year.

7. Political or charitable contributions where they total more than £50.

8. The value of goods exported from the United Kingdom during the year, except for companies whose turnover is less than £250,000 a year.

There are, in fact, many difficulties connected with the interpretation of the 1967 Act. It will probably take some years before they are satisfactorily resolved.

41.1. The following trial balance was extracted from the books of Fiddlems Ltd, as on 31 March 19–4. The authorized capital consists of 100,000 ordinary shares of £1 each and 30,000 5 per cent preference shares of £1 each.

	£	£
Ordinary Share Capital		100,000
Preference Share Capital Issued (£20,000 shares fully paid)		20,000
Sales		160,800
Purchases	110,670	
Stock-in-Trade, 31 March 19–3	29,145	
Preference Dividend, paid 30 September 19–3	500	
Provision for bad debts, 31 March 19–3		600
Investment Income		1,000
Wages and Salaries	16,328	
Motor Expenses	5,895	
Motor Vehicles (cost £18,000)	9,240	
Debtors and Creditors	28,370	25,650
Rates and Insurance	1,217	
Freehold Properties (at cost)	88,000	
Profit and Loss Account Balance at 31 March 19–3		6,954
Directors' Remuneration	3,000	
Bad Debts	770	
Unquoted Investments (at cost)	5,800	
General Expenses	7,890	
Balance at Bank	8,179	
	315,004	315,004

You are given the following information:
(a) Stock-in-Trade, 31 March 19–4, £32,630.
(b) The provision for bad debts is to be increased to £750.
(c) The directors have decided to recommend a dividend of 10 per cent on the ordinary share capital.
(d) Provide for depreciation of motor vehicles at 20 per cent of cost.
(e) Insurance paid in advance, 31 March 19–4, £78.
(f) Wages outstanding on 31 March 19–4, £220.
(g) £3,000 to be transferred from the profits to General Reserve.

(h) An extension to the office block was built during the year by the firm's own workmen, the cost of their labour, £420, is included in wages account. The materials, costing £1,180, were from the company's stocks—no entry has been made in the books.

(i) Ignore Taxation.

You are required to:

(a) Prepare a Trading and Profit and Loss Account for the year ended 31 March 19–4, and a Balance Sheet as on 31 March 19–4.

From your answer to (a)

(b) Ascertain the

(i) Working Capital,   (ii) Members' Equity.

Explain the significance of each.

41.2. L. & Y. Matthews Ltd are in business as wholesalers. From the information given below prepare the Trading, Profit and Loss Accounts and Appropriation Account of L. & Y. Matthews Ltd for the year ended 31 March 19–7 and a Balance Sheet at that date.

Trial Balance—31 March 19–7

	Dr	Cr
	£	£
Issued Share Capital:		
20,000 Ordinary Shares of £1 each		20,000
5,000 8 per cent Cumulative Preference Shares of £1 each		5,000
Purchases	61,450	
Sales		75,210
Stock 1 April 19–6	6,024	
Returns	320	410
Carriage Inwards	630	
Carriage Outwards	470	
Warehouse Wages	1,716	
Heating and Lighting	730	
Rates	1,200	
Repairs and Maintenance	648	
Office Salaries	972	
Fixtures and Fittings (at cost)	8,000	
Office Equipment (at cost)	900	
Motor Vans (at cost)	4,000	
Provisions for Depreciation 31 March 19–6:		
Fixtures and Fittings		3,000
Office Equipment		250
Motor Vans		2,000
Discounts	265	120
Directors' Fees	600	
Directors' Salaries	1,800	
Advertising	120	
Premises at Cost	15,000	
Share Premium Account		2,000
Interim Dividends—Preference	200	
Interim Dividends—Ordinary	1,000	
General Reserve		2,000
Debtors and Creditors	8,050	5,120

Trial Balance—31 March 19–7

	Dr	Cr
	£	£
Profit and Loss Balance—31 March 19–6		2,320
Cash at Bank	3,335	
	117,430	117,430

Notes:

(a) Stock 31 March 19–7, £7,434.

(b) Electricity bill outstanding £70; Rates prepaid £240; Office salaries owing £28; Wages owing £84.

(c) Heating and Lighting, Rates, and Repairs and Maintenance are to be allocated $\frac{7}{8}$ to the Warehouse and $\frac{7}{8}$ to the Office.

(d) Depreciate Motor Vans at 25 per cent on the reducing balance system and Fixtures and Fittings and Office Equipment at 10 per cent on cost.

(e) Transfer £1,000 to General Reserve.

(f) Provide for the final Preference Dividend and for a recommended final Ordinary Dividend of 15 per cent.

(g) The authorized capital of the company consists of 25,000 Ordinary shares of £1 each and 10,000 Preference shares of £1 each.

Ignore Taxation.

(Northern Counties Technical Examinations Council)

41.3. The accountant of A. and B. Ltd asks you for help in finalizing the accounts as at 31 March 19–7, which have been prepared in the following form:

Debits		*Credits*	
	£		£
Fixtures	200	Purchases Creditors	888
Debtors	1,245	Debenture	500
Stock	980	Capital originally	
Bank	144	contributed	4,500
Freehold Premises	2,400	Expense Creditors	120
Plant	1,500	Profits Retained	1,173
Pre-Payments and Sundry			
Items	712		
	7,181		7,181

This statement has been prepared from the company's double-entry bookkeeping system. After an exhaustive examination concerning the basis on which the statement is prepared you note down that the following matters require some attention:

1. The company is involved in a legal dispute and if judgement is given against it a liability of £150 is estimated to become payable.

2. Fixtures, premises and plant were all purchased five years prior to the balance sheet, on 1 April 19–2, at costs of £300, £3,200 and £3,000 respectively.

3. Prepayments and sundries consist of:

	£	£
Payments in advance	115	
Goods taken for personal use equally by A. and B. directors of the company	500	
Payment for stock still in supplier's hands	97	
	—	712

4. Bank balance represents the amount shown on the bank statement as at 31 March 19–7, but does not take into account the following cheques issued and charges made on the dates indicated:

	£
27 March Motor-car for use in business (including tax and insurance for 19–7 of £40)	500
28 March Payment to purchases creditor	78
31 March Bank charges	26
	—
	604

5. Stocks of £980 include an item valued at £120 which has been sold already to a customer for £180 but which was being stored for him. The customer has already paid a deposit of £20 prior to 31 March 19–7, but no amount is included in either debtors or creditors in respect of this sale transaction.

6. Debtors consist of:

	£
Owing by customers (including £100 considered as bad)	1,520
Less Owing to customers	210
	1,310
5 per cent Bad debts allowance	65
	1,245

7. No allowance has been made for the 5 per cent interest due on the debenture for the year to 31 March 19–7.

Required:

(a) A concise statement of how you would deal with each of these seven matters. State any necessary assumptions you have made in dealing with items.

(b) A revised Balance Sheet in good style.

Ignore taxation.

(Chartered Institute of Secretaries and Administrators)

41.4. Just before being dismissed the accountant of a company presented the following 19–4 accounts for the consideration of the board of directors. The meeting had to be postponed pending the completion of a revised set of accounts, which will clearly show the income for 19–4 and the position at 31 December 19–4, and which does not contain the errors of the accountant's version.

You are asked to prepare the revised set of accounts, paying attention to clarity of presentation and making any assumptions that you consider to be necessary.

Trading and Profit and Loss Account for 19–4
(as submitted by the accountant)

	£	£		£
Administrative Expenses:			Opening Stocks (at	
(Payments in 19–4			1 January 19–4)	20,000
plus In advance at			Cash Sales	19,200
1 January 19–4)	8,000		Cash Received in 19–4	
(*plus* In advance at			from Credit Customers	77,100
31 December 19–4)	2,000		Sales Debtors at 31	
		10,000	December 19–4	8,000
Debenture Interest		300		
Capital Charges for 19–4				
Depreciation of				
Fixed Assets	4,500			
Purchases of				
Fixtures—19–4	750			
		5,250		
Closing Stocks (at 31				
December 19–4)		15,000		
Directors'				
Remuneration		3,200		
Purchases of Stocks				
during year		70,000		
Selling Expenses—				
paid in 19–4	6,000			
Less Owing at 31				
December 19–4	1,000			
Plus Owing at 1				
January 19–4	Nil			
		5,000		
Discounts Received		1,700		
Sales Debtors at 1				
January 19–4		6,000		
Corporation Tax		2,500		
Dividends for 19–4		1,500		
Bad Debts:				
Provision for present				
Debtors (5 per cent of				
£8,000)—no provision				
has been made in				
previous year		400		
		120,850		
Difference—being				
apparent profit for				
19–4		3,450		
		124,300		124,300

Balance Sheet, 31 December 19–4
(as submitted by the accountant)

Debits	£	Credits	£	£
Cash	5,300	Ordinary Shares		30,000
Debtors	8,000	Unappropriated Profits:		
Freehold Land and		Balance at 1 January 19–4	10,600	
Buildings (at cost)	20,000	Balance for 19–4	3,450	
Payments in Advance	2,000			14,050
Plant and Fixtures		Liabilities, Reserves and		
(at cost)	29,250	Provisions:		
		Purchases Creditors	15,400	
		Selling Expenses due	1,000	
		Dividends and Debenture		
		Interest	1,800	
		Corporation Tax	2,500	
		Depreciation (including		
		19–4 charge)— £		
		Buildings 5,000		
		Plant and		
		Fixtures 8,000		
			13,000	
				33,700
		6 per cent Debentures		5,000
		Contingent liability—in		
		respect of bills discounted		2,000
	64,550			
*Difference—being				
excess of credits				
over debits	20,200			
	84,750			84,750

*I presume that this must be the 'goodwill' of the business.
(Chartered Institute of Secretaries and Administrators)

41.5. Peat Fires Ltd was incorporated on 1 January 19–4 and on that day issued for cash:

1. 20,000 Ordinary shares of £1 each, at par;

2. 8,000 6 per cent Preference shares of £1 each, at a premium of 5 per cent.

3. £6,000 5 per cent Debentures, at a discount of 2 per cent.
    All amounts due to the company in respect of the above issues were received on 1 January 19–4.

The Company paid preliminary expenses, £360, on 1 January 19–4, and purchased fixed assets, for cash, as follows:

	£
On 1 January 19–4	15,000
On 1 July 19–4	10,000

During the year 19–4, in addition to the above receipts and payments, the company received £53,620 for cash sales and on account of credit sales and paid £43,730 to trade creditors on account of purchases, £8,850 for wages and salaries, £4,250 for general expenses and £150 in respect of debenture interest for the six months to 30 June. All receipts were paid into the bank and all payments were made by cheque. Discounts allowed amounted to £670 and discounts received to £590.

At 31 December 19–4 stock-in-trade was valued at £8,200, trade debtors amounted to £7,450 and £6,340 was owing to trade creditors.

Provision for depreciation of the fixed assets is to be made at the rate of 10 per cent per annum.

One quarter of the preliminary expenses is to be written off to the Profit and Loss Account.

Provision is to be made for the dividend on the Preference shares for the year 19–4, but no dividend on the Ordinary shares is proposed.

You are required to prepare a Trading and Profit and Loss Account for the year 19–4 and a Balance Sheet (not necessarily in a form for publication) as on 31 December 19–4.

Ignore taxation.

(Institute of Bankers)

41.6. Jaydee Ltd was formed on 1 January 19–4, to take over the business assets and liabilities of J. Dixon at an agreed price of £10,000, which was settled by the issue at par of 8,000 Ordinary shares of £1 each and the balance in cash. The authorized share capital of the company is £25,000—15,000 Ordinary shares of £1 each and 10,000 7 per cent Preference shares of £1 each. 2,000 Ordinary shares were issued to the public at par and 8,000 Preference shares at a premium of 10 per cent—all these shares were fully paid up. J. Dixon was appointed general manager at an annual salary of £1,600.

Other ledger balances at 31 December 19–4 were:

	£		£
Goodwill	5,000	Rates, Insurances, etc.	410
Trade Debtors	8,250	Stock—1 January	2,610
Trade Creditors	4,543	Purchases	9,204
Freehold Premises	8,000	Sales	20,120
Fixtures	3,000	Bank and Cash	3,169
6 per cent Debentures	3,000	Debenture Interest (to	
Wages and Salaries	4,914	30 June)	90
Discounts Allowed	76	Preliminary Expenses	540
		General manager (salary	
		to 30 September)	1,200

Notes:

(i) At 31 December 19–4 Stock was valued at £2,986, Wages due, but unpaid, were £40 and Rates paid in advance were £35.

(ii) The Preliminary Expenses are to be written off over three years.

(iii) Provision for bad debts is to be made equal to 2 per cent of Debtors and depreciation on Fixtures at 10 per cent is to be charged.

(iv) Provision is to be made for dividend on the Preference shares and for Ordinary Dividend at 8 per cent (ignore tax).

(v) Transfer £1,000 to General Reserve.

Prepare Trading and Profit and Loss Accounts for the year ended 31 December 19–4, and Balance Sheet as on that date.

(Union of Lancashire and Cheshire Institutes)

41.7. The following trial balance was extracted from the books of Rockbound Ltd as on 31 December 19–6:

	£	£
Issued Share Capital (30,000 ordinary shares of £1 each)		30,000
Balance on Trading Account (gross profit)		22,150
Stock-in-Trade, 31 December 19–6 (at cost)	8,412	
Motor Vans	1,020	
Trade Debtors and Trade Creditors	9,018	7,363
Freehold Property (at cost)	27,500	
Wages and Salaries (including director's salary, £3,000)	8,275	
Loan		12,000
Investments	1,450	
Profit and Loss Account—		
Balance at 1 January 19–6		2,481
Balance at Bank	4,980	
Office and Administration Expenses	9,267	
Selling Expenses	4,072	
	73,994	73,994

The authorized capital of the company is £40,000, in shares of £1 each. You are informed that:

1. During December 19–6, the company:

(a) repaid the loan of £12,000, with interest accrued thereon, £250;

(b) sold all its investments for £1,283; and

(c) issued the remainder of its authorised capital, at a premium of 10 per cent, and received the whole amount in cash.

The proceeds of the sale of the investments and of the issue of shares were paid into a special bank account opened for the purpose, and the cheque for the repayment of the loan (with interest) was drawn on this account. The balance on this bank account at 31 December 19–6, £33, has not been included in the trial balance and no entries have been made in the company's ledger in regard to these matters.

2. During December 19–6, part of the company's stock in trade was destroyed by fire. It is expected that the full cost of this stock will be recovered from the insurance company, but the claim has not yet been lodged. Calculations made for purposes of the claim show that the cost of the goods sold during 19–6 was £78,225 and that total sales for the year amounted to £104,300.

3. The balance on the motor vans account (£1,020) represents the book value on 1 January 19–6, of an old van, £320, plus a payment of £700 on 2 January, for a new van. The vendor of the new van took over the old van, in part settlement, at a valuation of £250.

4. Depreciation is to be provided in respect of the new van, at 20 per cent of cost.

Prepare the company's Profit and Loss Account for the year 19–6, and Balance Sheet as on 31 December 19–6.

Ignore taxation.

(Institute of Bankers)

41.8. The following trial balance was extracted from the books of M. Campbell Ltd as on 31 January 19–7.

	£	£
Bills Payable and Receivable	1,128	10,190
Bank and Cash Balances	88,540	
Quoted Investments (market value £12,950)	10,326	
Share Capital: Authorised and Issued 200,000		
Ordinary Shares of £1 each fully paid		200,000
6 per cent Preference Shares of £1 each		100,000
Debtors and Creditors	176,940	163,510
Profit and Loss Account as at 1 February 19–6		76,834
Provision for Depreciation:		
Buildings		56,800
Motor Lorries		7,380
Motor-cars		2,832
Machinery and Plant		24,794
Office Furniture		2,132
Office Furniture and Fittings	5,900	
Machinery and Plant	70,800	
Motor-cars	8,720	
Motor Lorries and Trailers	22,740	
Freehold Buildings	157,000	
7 per cent Debentures		24,000
Capital Redemption Reserve Fund		60,000
Discounts on Shares Account	8,000	
Formation Expenses	6,292	
Loans to Directors	4,000	
Debenture Interest Received (net)		980
Debenture Interest (net)	1,176	
Bad Debts Provision		1,250
Provision for Discounts on Debtors		800
Directors' Remuneration	15,000	
General Expenses	32,872	
Insurances	2,498	
Rent and Rates	14,728	
Stock 1 February 19–6	276,946	
Salaries	37,872	
Wages (Productive)	76,328	
Purchases	458,832	
Sales		751,136
Preference Dividend paid	6,000	
	1,482,638	1,482,638

Notes at 31 January 19–7:

1. Stock £303,484.

2. Depreciate (Straight-line Method) Motor Lorries 20 per cent, Machinery

12½ per cent, Cars 20 per cent, Office Furniture 10 per cent.

3.   Directors decide (i) to transfer £2,000 to Debenture Redemption Reserve, (ii) to write off all formation expenses, (iii) propose ordinary dividend of 20 per cent.

4.   Assume that the standard rate of income tax is 30 per cent.

5.   Directors' remuneration to be accrued £3,000.

6.   The bad debts provision is to be changed to £1,140.

7.   The provision for discounts on debtors is to be changed to £830.

8.   Corporation tax based on the year's profits is estimated at £34,000.

9.   Accrue auditors' remuneration (fixed by directors) of £500.

You are to prepare a Trading and Profit and Loss and Appropriation Account for the year ended 31 January 19–7,

(a)   for internal use,
(b)   for publication.

Also a Balance Sheet for publication as at 31 January 19–7.

41.9. The following trial balance was extracted from the books of Better Gears Ltd as on 31 March 19–6:

	£	£
Sales		189,363
Purchases	134,163	
Wages and Salaries	19,377	
Stock 1 April 19–5	14,444	
Royalties—gross (Trading A/c)	1,800	
Delivery Expenses Outwards	1,549	
General Expenses	3,563	
Debenture Interest (gross)	1,100	
10 per cent Debentures		11,000
Investment Income:		
From Unquoted Investments		565
From Debenture Interest from other companies		1,045
Unquoted Investments (at cost)	3,000	
Debentures held in other companies	7,490	
Preliminary Expenses	1,500	
Share Premium		5,000
Machinery and Plant	137,000	
Land and Buildings	255,000	
Motor Vehicles	29,000	
Fixtures and Fittings	16,800	
Provision for Depreciation:		
Machinery		32,590
Land and Buildings		74,360
Motors		11,493
Fixtures		6,250
Capital Redemption Reserve Fund		15,000
Debenture Redemption Reserve		3,500
General Reserve		5,200
Profit and Loss Account as at 31 March 19–5		14,890

	£	£
Debtors and Creditors	18,590	13,210
Bad Debts Provision		205
Income Tax		557
Share Capital—Authorized and Issued (£1 Ordinary Shares)		200,000
Suspense Account		115
Bank		60,033
	644,376	644,376

Notes at 31 March 19–6:

1. Stock £51,246.

2. Depreciate Machinery 10 per cent, Buildings 5 per cent, Motors 20 per cent, Fixtures 2½ per cent, all on a straight-line basis.

3. Suspense account is sale of a machine on 31 December 19–5 for £115. It was bought 8½ years previously for £1,000.

4. The Income Tax balance is as follows:

Income Tax

Tax deducted from Interest		Tax deducted from charges	
Received (£1,045 × 30%)	£313	(£1,800 + £1,100 × 30%)	£870

5. Directors decide (*a*) to transfer £1,000 to debenture redemption reserve (*b*) to provide for final dividend of 12½ per cent.

6. Assume income tax at rate of 30 per cent.

7. Increase bad debts provision to £250.

8. Accrue directors' remuneration £7,000.

9. Corporation tax based on the year's profits estimated at £7,000. Prepare the company's Trading and Profit and Loss Account,

(*a*) for internal use,
(*b*) for publication.

Also the Balance Sheet for publication purposes.

41.10A. Manufacturers Ltd has an authorized share capital of £500,000 made up of 100,000 6 per cent redeemable preference shares of £1 each and 400,000 ordinary shares of £1 each.

All the preference shares, which are redeemable at par between 1 January 19–4, and 31 December 19–6, have been issued and are fully paid.

250,000 of the ordinary shares have been issued and fully called, but there are calls in arrear of £600.

Apart from those arising from the above the following were the balances in the company's ledger, after the preparation of the manufacturing account, at 31 March 19–9.

	£	£
Plant and Machinery 31 March 19–8, at Cost	190,000	
Additions to Plant and Machinery during the year, at Cost	20,000	
General Reserve		28,000
Share Premium Account		24,000
Stock of Finished Goods 31 March 19–8	41,600	

	£	£
Manufacturing Account—factory cost of finished goods produced	216,000	
Balance at Bank	32,000	
Trade Debtors	75,000	
Provision for Doubtful Debts		2,000
Sales		314,000
Sales Returns	15,400	
Freehold Land and Buildings, at Valuation in 19–7	161,340	
Leasehold Properties	28,000	
Unquoted Investments at Cost	21,200	
Reserve arising on Revaluation of Freeholds		80,000
General Expenses	42,000	
Auditors' Remuneration	1,050	
Directors' Remuneration	14,210	
Preliminary Expenses	1,000	
Income from Investments		1,000
Profit and Loss Account, balance at 31 March 19–8		32,220
Preference Dividend paid for the year ended 31 March 19–9	6,000	
Provision for Depreciation of Plant and Machinery to 31 March 19–9		58,250
Work in progress 31 March 19–9	35,400	
Stocks of Raw Materials 31 March 19–9	20,000	
Current Liabilities		37,330
Goodwill and Patents at Cost	6,000	

Notes:

(a) Depreciation of the leasehold properties has to be provided for in respect of the year to 31 March 19–9. There are two leasehold properties: one, which cost £19,000 and had a book value of £15,000 in 19–8, expires in 1995 and is to be depreciated by £500; the other, which cost £15,000 and had a 19–8 book value of £13,000, expires in 2030 and is to be depreciated by £400.

(b) No adjustment had been made for general expenses accrued of £1,300 at 31 March 19–9.

(c) £2,000 is to be written off goodwill and patents.

(d) The directors propose a dividend of £15,000 on the ordinary shares.

(e) The provision for doubtful debts is to be adjusted to £2,500.

(f) The stock of finished goods at 31 March 19–9 was valued at £40,000.

(g) The directors' valuation of the unquoted investments at 31 March 19–9 was £22,000.

(h) At 31 March 19–9, the company had entered into contracts for capital expenditure amounting to £12,000, and the value of capital expenditure authorized by the directors but not yet contracted for was estimated at £30,000.

(i) The investments are regarded as long-term investments.

You are required to prepare the company's trading and profit and loss account for the year ended 31 March 19–9, and the balance sheet as at that date.

The balance sheet should comply with the requirements of the Companies Acts 1948 to 1967 (so far as the information given permits), and be so arranged as to show the amounts of the shareholders' funds and the working capital, i.e. net current assets.

Pay particular attention to layout and presentation.
Ignore taxation.
(Associated Examining Board—G.C.E. 'A' level)

41.11A. The following trial balance was taken from the ledger of Newly Ltd at 31 December 19–8, after the preparation of the trading account:

	£	£
Ordinary Shares of £1 each, fully paid		80,000
6 per cent Redeemable Preference Shares of £1 each, fully paid		30,000
7 per cent Debentures—Redeemable in 1990		16,000
Share Premium Account		10,000
General Reserve		13,000
Sales of £350,000 gave a Gross Profit of		78,000
Stock at 31 December 19–8	34,000	
Dividends from Quoted Investments		2,000
Staff Salaries and Wages	34,000	
Preference Dividend paid	1,800	
General Expenses	3,900	
Directors' Fees	3,000	
Directors' Salaries	8,000	
Debenture Interest	560	
Goodwill at Cost	30,000	
Freehold Property at Valuation in 19–7	82,000	
Freehold Property purchased in February 19–8, at Cost	20,000	
Quoted Investments at Cost	21,000	
Equipment at Cost	80,000	
Trade Debtors	15,000	
Provision for Doubtful Debts		430
Trade Creditors		35,000
Bank Overdraft		5,500
Interest on Bank Overdraft	260	
Cash in Hand	410	
Surplus arising on Revaluation of Freeholds		15,000
Provision for Depreciation of Equipment at 1 January 19–8		42,000
Profit and Loss Account Balance at 1 January 19–8		7,000
	333,930	333,930

Notes:
(a) Adjustment has to be made for auditors' fees and expenses for 19–8 of £500, depreciation of equipment at 10 per cent on cost, general expenses accrued of £200 at 31 December 19–8 and for the debenture interest due at that date; a provision of £700 is to be carried forward for doubtful debts.
(b) The directors' emoluments were:

	Fees	Salary
	£	£
Mr X	1,000	2,500
Mr Y	750	3,000
Mrs Y	500	—
Mr Z	750	2,500

724

(c) The directors propose that £5,000 be written off goodwill, £3,000 be transferred to general reserve and an ordinary dividend of £0·05 a share be declared.
(d) The Company has an authorized share capital of £200,000 made up of 150,000 ordinary shares of £1 and 50,000 preference shares of £1.
(e) The quoted investments had a market value of £25,000 at 31 December 19–8.
(f) The preference shares must be redeemed at par between 1 January 19–4, and 31 December 19–7.

From the above information prepare, in a form which complies (so far as the above information permits) with the minimum requirements of the Companies Acts 1948 to 1967:

(i) a profit and loss account, which starts with the net profit, before crediting investment income and before deducting appropriations; and
(ii) a balance sheet at 31 December 19–8, so designed as to show clearly the shareholders' funds and the working capital.

Submit your calculation of the net profit for (i) above.
Ignore taxation.

(Associated Examining Board—G.C.E. 'A' level)

41.12A. F. Faith has an Authorized Capital of 100,000 £16 per cent Preference Shares and 200,000 Ordinary Shares of £0·5 each.
On 31 May 19–0 the following balances appear in the books:

	Dr	Cr
	£	£
Bank Current Account	12,040	
Bank Interest and Charges	460	
Bank Loan		68,000
Consultant (fee unpaid)		500
Debtors and Creditors	170,000	135,500
Depreciation Fund for Machinery and Plant, 31 May 19–9		10,000
Directors' Remuneration: Fees; £1,000 Other: £8,500	9,500	
Fixed Assets as valued ten years previously on 31 May 19–0, plus additions at cost to 31 May 19–9:		
Freehold Property	84,000	
Machinery and Plant	24,500	
Additions to Fixed Assets during year ended 31 May 19–0:		
Machinery and Plant	17,500	
General Reserve		49,500
Goodwill as valued by the directors ten years previously in 19–0	15,000	
Investments at Cost	5,000	
Profit and Loss Account, 31 May 19–9		33,000
Share Capital: Issued and Fully Paid-up:		
50,000 Preference Shares		50,000
200,000 Ordinary Shares		100,000

	Dr	Cr
	£	£
Stocks	154,500	
Trading Surplus for year ended 31 May 19–0		46,000
	492,500	492,500

There are the following items not yet entered in the books:

(a) Dividends accrued on Investments £600,
(b) Managing Director's Commission £2,500.

The directors decide to:

(c) Commence to write off Goodwill by reducing it by £3,000.
(d) Increase Depreciation Fund for Machinery and Plant by £4,000.
(e) Increase General Reserve by £5,000.
(f) Make a Provision for Bad Debts of 5 per cent of the Debtors, and one for Discounts Allowable of 5 per cent of the net amount of the Debtors.
(g) Pay one year's Dividend on the Preference Shares and recommend payment of a Dividend on the Ordinary Shares of 8 per cent.

The Consultant's Fee, the Managing Director's Commission, and the Dividend on the Preference Shares are all paid on 31 May 19–0.

The market value of the Investments is £11,000.

Prepare Profit and Loss Account for the year ended 31 May 19–0, and Balance Sheet as at that date.

Ignore taxation.

(Welsh Joint Education Committee—G.C.E. 'A' level)

41.13A. The following trial balance was extracted from the books of Wholesale Ltd at 31 December 19–6:

Trial Balance

	£	£
Bank Balance	5,455	
Creditors		6,125
7 per cent Debentures		6,000
Debtors	10,500	
Directors' Salaries	4,700	
Discount on issue of Debentures	240	
Furniture and Fittings	8,900	
Goodwill	5,000	
Gross Profit on Trading		29,950
Motor Vehicles at Cost	22,500	
Motor Vehicle Disposal Account		350
Provision for Depreciation of Motor Vehicles		7,300
Preliminary Expenses	435	
Provision for Corporation Tax on Profits of 19–5		1,360
Profit and Loss Account at 31 December 19–5		7,030
Rent, Salaries and Expenses	16,745	
Share Capital (authorized and issued):		
25,000 Ordinary Shares of £1 each		25,000
5,000 6 per cent Preference Shares of £1 each		5,000

Trial Balance

	£	£
Share Premium Account		6,000
Stock-in-trade 31 December 19–6, at Cost	19,640	
	94,115	94,115

You are given the following information:

1. On 1 January 19–6, a motor vehicle which cost £1,500 on 1 January 19–2 was sold for £350. Entries for this amount have been made to the bank and motor vehicle disposal accounts, but no entries were made in 19–6 in relation to this vehicle. Depreciation is provided on motor vehicles at 20 per cent on cost, but no amount has yet been provided for the current year.

2. A provision for bad and doubtful debts is to be created, equal to 4 per cent of the debtors shown in the trial balance.

3. Provision is to be made for corporation tax at 40 per cent on chargeable profits of £4,200 for the year ended 31 December 19–6.

4. The debentures were issued on 31 December 19–6, and no interest has accrued.

5. Those items which the law permits to be charged against share premium account are to be written off, out of the balance of that account.

6. The directors have proposed a dividend of 5 per cent on the ordinary share capital for the year 19–6.

7. A customer is suing the company for breach of contract, and is claiming £4,000 damages.

Prepare the profit and loss account for the year 19–6 and the balance sheet at 31 December 19–6, set out to conform (so far as the information permits) with the requirements of the Companies Acts 1948 and 1967.

Ignore depreciation of furniture and fittings.
(Institute of Bankers)

41.14A. H.L.Y. was incorporated in December 19–6, and issued 50,000 ordinary shares of £1 each, at a premium of £0·10 each. These shares were fully paid up in cash on 31 December 19–6, and the company commenced business on 1 January 19–7.

H.L.Y. Ltd paid preliminary expenses £400 and paid £40,000 for fixed assets, which were retained throughout the year 19–7. In January 19–7, H.L.Y. Ltd acquired the whole issued share capital of F.S.H. Ltd (22,000 ordinary shares of £1 each) at a valuation of £1·25 per share. The purchase consideration was satisfied by the issue of 25,000 fully paid ordinary shares in H.L.Y. Ltd.

In March 19–7, H.L.Y. Ltd lent £10,000, free of interest, to F.S.H. Ltd.

F.S.H. Ltd was wound up and, after paying all creditors in full, the liquidator on 30 June 19–7, made a first and final payment, on account of share capital, to H.L.Y. Ltd amounting to £34,000.

The net trading profit of H.L.Y. Ltd for the year 19–7 amounted to £12,650, after charging £6,000 for depreciation of fixed assets.

Except for £9,470 owing to trade creditors, all purchases and expenses (other than depreciation) were paid in cash and all sales were for cash.

On 31 December 19–7, stock in trade amounted to £11,230 at cost.

You are required:

(a) to show your calculation of the net trading receipts of H.L.Y. Ltd for the year 19–7;

(b) to prepare a summary of the company's cash account for the year 19–7; and

(c) to set out the balance sheet of the company (not necessarily in a form for publication) at 31 December 19–7.

Ignore taxation.

(Chartered Institute of Secretaries and Administrators)

41.15A. The following is the trial balance of W.Z.D. Ltd, as on 30 September 19–8.

	£	£
Authorized and Issued Share Capital		
(37,500 ordinary shares of £1 each, fully paid)		37,500
Stock, 30 September 19–7	8,000	
Purchases	92,500	
Sales		127,500
Debtors	21,000	
Properties, at Cost	50,000	
Provision for Depreciation of Leasehold Properties to		
30 September 19–7		1,800
Motor vans: as at 30 September 19–7, at Cost	1,500	
Net payment for new van	450	
	1,950	
Provision for depreciation of motor vans to		
30 September 19–7		900
Rents receivable		2,430
Directors' Emoluments	16,000	
6 per cent Debentures (issued in 19–0)		10,000
Interest on Debentures and Bank Overdraft	640	
Investments (acquired in 19–3) at Cost	4,500	
Investment Income		270
Bank Overdraft		485
Trade Creditors		10,715
General Administration Expenses	11,710	
Profit and Loss Account: Balance at 30 September 19–7		14,700
	206,300	206300

1. Stock in trade at 30 September 19–8, at cost, £9,500.

2. The properties consist of freeholds, £39,000, and two leaseholds, as follows:

(i) Cost £6,000, on 1 October 19–4, four years ago, for 60 years from that date.

(ii) Cost £5,000, on 1 October 19–2, 16 years ago, for 50 years from that date.

The total market value of all the properties on 30 September 19–8, was £72,500.

3. There are three directors, A., B., and C., who shared the emoluments: A. one-half, B. and C. one-quarter each.

4. On 1 October 19–7, a motor van (cost £500 on 1 October 19–4) was traded in, at a valuation of £175, in part settlement of the price (£625) of a new van. Depreciation has been and is to be provided at the rate of 20 per cent per annum, of cost.
5. The item 'Investments £4,500' consists of £1,000 7 per cent debentures in a public company (cost £1,000) and ordinary shares in a private company. The current market value (stock exchange quotation) of the debentures is £1,000; the directors estimate that the current value of the shares is £2,000, but have decided to make no provision for depreciation.
6. The company's own debentures are redeemable at par on 30 September 19–5, and are secured by a floating charge on the assets of the company.

Required:

A profit and loss account for the year to 30 September 19–8, and a balance sheet as on that date. The profit and loss account and balance sheet should comply (so far as the information permits) with the requirements of the Companies Acts 1948–1967, showing, in the form of footnotes, any information required by the Act, not otherwise disclosed, including any matters required to be stated in the directors' report. The profit and loss account should be divided into sections and any items the disclosure of which is *not* required by law are to be shown in the first section.

Ignore taxation.
(Chartered Institute of Secretaries and Administrators)

41.16A. From the information given you are required to prepare:
(*a*) the balance sheet of XY Ltd, a public company, as at 31 December 19–0, giving the minimum information required by the Companies Acts 1948 and 1967, together with the necessary notes required by the Acts;
(*b*) statement showing how the profit and loss account balance has been computed;
(*c*) statement showing how depreciation has been computed.

XY Ltd had an authorized capital of 50,000 8 per cent cumulative preference shares of £1 each and 800,000 ordinary shares of £0·25 each.

The trial balance at 31 December 19–0 was as follows:

	£	£
8 per cent Cumulative Preference Shares		50,000
Ordinary Shares of £0·25 fully paid		100,000
Share Premium		5,000
Buildings	40,000	
Plant	65,000	
Vehicles	8,000	
Doubtful Debt provision		3,500
Patents at Cost (£10,000), *less* amounts written off	9,000	
Debtors and Creditors	36,000	19,000
Corporation Tax on 19–9 Profits		18,000
Investments at Cost:		
Quoted (market value £22,000)	20,500	
Unquoted (directors' valuation £13,600)	12,500	
Tax Reserve Certificates	25,000	
Plant Replacement Reserve		12,000
Stock	52,000	
Profit and Loss Account, Balance at 1 January		6,000

	£	£
Profit for the year		47,000
Bank Overdraft		7,500
	268,000	268,000

Further information is given below.

1. The buildings, plant and vehicles accounts are made up as under.

		Buildings £	Plant £	Vehicles £
19–0				
1 January	To Cost	45,000	87,212	23,500
31 December	To Additions at Cost	5,000	18,000	3,000
		50,000	105,212	26,500
19–0				
1 January	By Depreciation provided	10,000	39,000	13,500
31 December	By proceeds of Sale			5,000
	By Profit and Loss Account, book value of plant scrapped		1,212	
		10,000	40,212	18,500
19–0				
31 December	Balance	40,000	65,000	8,000

2. The plant scrapped was purchased on 1 January 19–6 for £2,000 and the vehicles sold on 31 March 19–0 cost £10,666 on 1 January 19–7.

3. The Corporation Tax assessment for 19–9 has been agreed at £17,300.

4. The following provisions and appropriations are to be made:

		£
(i)	Corporation Tax	21,000
(ii)	Increased Cost of plant replacement	5,000

(iii) Depreciation:

Buildings	2½ per cent of cost
Plant	10 per cent on written down value at end of year
Vehicles	25 per cent on written down value at end of year

(iv) Preference dividend of 8 per cent and ordinary dividend of 7 per cent

(Institute of Cost and Management Accountants)

41.17A. From the following information you are required to prepare the profit and loss account and balance sheet as at 31 December 19–9, in accordance with the requirements of the Companies Acts 1948 and 1967 together with the notes required thereto.

Comparative figures, directors' report and audit report are not required. Calculation of pre-tax profit should be shown.

1. AB Ltd Trial Balance—31 December 19–9

	£	£
Ordinary Share Capital, authorized and issued:		
400,000 Ordinary Shares of £1 fully paid		400,000

	£	£
Debenture Redemption Reserve		60,000
Capital Reserve		210,000
Retained Profits		120,000
£300,000 8 per cent Debentures 19–8/19–8		
(redeemable at £30,000 per annum)		213,000
Land at Cost	55,000	
Buildings at Cost	230,000	
Plant and Machinery at Cost	430,000	
Debtors (including £320,000 trade)	355,000	
Stocks and work-in-progress	535,000	
Tax Equalization Reserve		25,000
Corporation Tax on 19–8 Profits		65,000
Unquoted Investments	70,000	
Trading Profit 19–9		262,000
Investment Income		6,000
Provision for Depreciation 31 December 19–8:		
Buildings		82,000
Plant		148,000
Provision for Doubtful Debts		5,000
Interim Dividend	16,000	
Cash at Bank	6,800	
Royalties	5,000	
Creditors		126,000
Debenture Interest	19,200	
	1,722,000	1,722,000

2.   Land with a book value of £15,000 was sold for £45,000 on 30 November 19–9, and the cash proceeds credited to the land account. It is estimated that a capital gains liability of £13,000 will arise. The remainder of the land has been professionally valued at £135,000 but the necessary entries have still to be made in the books.

3.   During the year £30,000 debentures were redeemed at a price of 90 per £100 debenture, the cost being debited against the debentures outstanding. These are not available for re-issue.

4.   On 31 December 19–9, a contract was signed to dispose of a product line and the brand name for a sum of £47,000 including stocks with a book value of £44,000.

5.   Corporation Tax on the 19–8 profits has been agreed at £71,000.

6.   The following provisions are to be made:

		£
(a)	Depreciation: Buildings	25,000
	Plant	46,000
(b)	Directors' Fees (chairman £1,500)	4,000
(c)	Auditors' Remuneration	1,500
(d)	Corporation Tax on 19–9 profits	73,000
(e)	Increased Bad Debt Provision to 2½ per cent of the Trade Debtors.	
(f)	Compensation to a Director for Loss of Office	6,000

7.   The tax equalization provision is to be increased by   3,000

8. Turnover for the year totalled £1,556,000 including exports of £273,000.
9. The Directors valued the Trade Investment at £76,000.
10. Profits were shown after charging Directors' Remuneration of £11,000.
11. Capital Expenditure commitment at 31 December 19–9 totalled £76,000 of which £35,200 was covered by firm orders on suppliers.
12. Proposed Final Dividend was 8 per cent.

41.18A. The following trial balance has been extracted from the records of Benders Ltd as on 31 March 19–1:

	£	£
Profit and Loss Account balance at 31 March 19–0		2,000
Sales		400,000
Cost of Goods Sold	280,000	
Wages and Salaries	25,000	
Trade Expenses	23,000	
Debenture Interest (net)	700	
10 per cent Debentures		10,000
Ordinary Shares (shares of £1 each)		100,000
7 per cent Preference Shares (shares of £1 each)		40,000
Share Premium		100,000
Buildings at Cost	100,000	
Plant and Machinery at Cost	120,000	
Motor Vehicles at Cost	60,000	
Provisions for Depreciation as at 31 March 19–0:		
Plant and Machinery		28,000
Motor Vehicles		11,000
Stock-in-Trade as at 31 March 19–0	40,000	
Debtors and Creditors	78,000	62,000
Directors' Remuneration	11,000	
Bank	15,300	
	753,000	753,000

Adjustments are needed for the following items when the final accounts are drafted for the year:

(a) Provisions for depreciation are to be made: Motor Vehicles 20 per cent, Plant and Machinery 15 per cent, in both cases the straight line method is to be used.
(b) Assume that the standard rate of Income Tax is 30 per cent.
(c) Accrue audit fees of £300.
(d) The buildings have been revalued by the directors at a figure of £170,000 on 31 March 19–1. The increase in value is to be credited to a Capital Reserve Account.
(e) The preference dividend for the year ended 31 March 19–1 was paid on 15 April 19–1.
(f) Corporation Tax, based on the year's profits, is estimated at £11,000.
(g) The directors propose that a dividend of 14 per cent on the ordinary shares be paid.
(h) You are required to draft a Profit and Loss Account for the year ended 31 March 19–1 and a Balance Sheet as at that date in a form suitable for publication.

42

Vertical Presentation of Accounting Statements

In this chapter, an alternative to the traditional form of Profit and Loss Account and Balance Sheet is considered. For many years, both statements have been presented in ledger form. The tendency today is to abandon the two-sided approach, and to present the information as a narrative or vertical-styled statement. Thus, instead of looking at figures on the left-hand and the right-hand sides of a statement, the eye commences to take in information at the top, and then travels downwards in more or less a straight line to the final figure.

Exhibit 42.1 shows the conventional Profit and Loss Account, and Exhibit 42.2 shows the same information in vertical form. It will also be noticed that alternative terms are in use throughout this chapter. For example, the term 'Income Statement' has been used instead of 'Profit and Loss Account', and 'Operating Statement' instead of 'Manufacturing, Trading and Profit and Loss Account'.

Exhibit 42.1
(Conventional form)

Trading and Profit and Loss Account for year ended . . .

	£		£
Cost of Sales	60	Sales	100
Gross Profit c/d	40		
	100		100
Expenses:		Gross Profit b/d	40
(detailed)	x		
	x		
	x		
	15		
Net Profit	25		
	40		40

Exhibit 42.2
(Vertical form)

Income Statement for year ended . . .

	£	*(Effect on net worth)*
Sales	100	+
Cost of Sales	60	−
Gross Margin	40	+
Overhead:		
(detailed)	x	−
	x	−
	x	−
	15	−
Net Profit	25	+

In effect the traditional layout is 'twisted' ninety degrees anti-clockwise, and the left-hand figures (debits or minuses) are deducted from the right-hand figures (credits or pluses). The final figure is the resultant plus (+) to the net worth of the business. Some important reasons for preferring the style as in Exhibit 42.2 are:

(a) Persons who are unaccustomed to the historical system of debits and credits can understand the modern statement more easily. Such persons often include shareholders, employees, technical staff, and others concerned with production and sales. Sometimes key management staff are completely ignorant of the work and statements produced by the accounting staff, and they naturally view with suspicion inferences conveyed by complicated statements written in unfamiliar language.

(b) Comparison one year with another is greatly facilitated if the statements are in vertical form. Two or more years' past figures can be added to the statement by simply including additional columns: again, budgeted or standard costs can be shown and variances (differences) much more readily discerned.

(c) From a student's point of view, a good deal of time is saved if the two-sided approach (which often necessitates a number of sections balanced off and carried down) is discarded. It is also important to notice that examiners encourage, and in the case of published statements often insist on, the use of vertical statements;

(d) In manufacturing concerns, all statements concerning costs and production are in vertical form for simplicity and ease of understanding, and for ease of comparison with prior production periods, budgets or standards. It is logical that all financial statements dealing with stages beyond production costs should similarly be in vertical form;

(e) Today, the recording of business transactions is frequently not in the traditional two-sided form. Machine book-keeping, punched cards and computers have revolutionized the method and style of recording, but without damaging the principles of double-entry book-keeping. It is therefore unrealistic to perpetuate old-fashioned presentation when an alternative form is superior. It must be remembered that the purpose of accounting statements is to convey information accurately and simply—particularly to those unversed in accounting skills.

Exhibit 42.3

(Conventional form)

Balance Sheet at . . .

	£	£		Cost	Accumulated Depreciation	Net
				£	£	£
Capital:			Fixed Assets:			
At . . .		2,800	Premises	2,000	300	1,700
Undrawn Profits		1,000	Fittings	500	200	300
Net Worth		3,800		2,500	500	2,000
Current Liabilities:			Current Assets:			
Creditors	1,100		Stock		1,000	
Expenses Owing	100		Debtors		1,000	
		1,200	Bank		1,000	
						3,000
		5,000				5,000

Exhibit 42.3 indicates the conventional Balance Sheet, and the vertical approach is outlined in Exhibit 42.4.

The above are simple examples of the two major financial statements, but they are sufficient to convey the general idea. Style and terminology vary considerably according to the outlook and favoured definitions adopted by the accountants concerned. Of course, disclosure must in any case conform with the requirements of the companies acts in force, and full use is often made of the right to disclose certain information by way of notes to the accounts. For examination purposes, this practice is not recommended; it is better, if possible to show the information on the face of the accounts. Many accountants emphasize the capital employed and (according to their definition of capital employed) may have a layout different to that shown in Exhibit 42.4. These are shown as 42.5 and 42.6.

Exhibit 42.4

(Vertical form)

Financial Position Statement at . . .

ASSETS EMPLOYED	Cost	Accumulated Depreciation	Net
Fixed Assets:	£	£	£
Premises	2,000	300	1,700
Fittings	500	200	300
	2,500	500	2,000

Current Assets:		
Stock	1,000	
Debtors	1,000	
Bank	1,000	
		3,000
Total		5,000

FINANCED BY		
Capital	2,800	
Undrawn Profits	1,000	
Net worth		3,800
Current Liabilities:		
Creditors	1,100	
Expenses Owing	100	
		1,200
		5,000

Exhibit .42.5

(Variation in form)

CAPITAL EMPLOYED	£
Share Capital	x
Retained Profits	x
Shareholders Net Worth	x
Long-term Loans	x
Total Capital Employed	x

EMPLOYMENT OF CAPITAL

		£	
Current Assets:			
Stocks		x	
Debtors		x	
Bank		x	x
Less			
Current Liabilities:			
Creditors		x	
Corporation Tax		x	
Dividends		x	x
Net working Capital			x

	Cost	Depreciation	Net	
	£	£	£	
Fixed assets:				
Premises	x	x	x	
Plant	x	x	x	
	x	x	x	x
				x

Or again, some managements prefer to emphasize the shareholders' capital employed; in which case the long-term loans are deducted from the fixed assets—possibly on the grounds that long-term finance is normally used for long-term expansion of capacity. Exhibit 42.6 shows this variation.

Exhibit 42.6

(Variation in form)

NET ASSETS EMPLOYED

	£	£
Current Assets:		
Stocks		x
Debtors		x
Bank		x
		x
Deduct		
Current Liabilities:		
Creditors	x	
Corporation Tax	x	
Dividends	x	
		x
Working Capital		x

	Cost	Depreciation	Net
	£	£	£
Fixed Assets:			
Premises	x	x	x
Plant	x	x	x
	x	x	x

Deduct		
Long-term loan	x	x
		x

FUNDED BY

Shareholders Issued and paid up Share Capital	x
Retained Profits	x
	x

Alternatively, the working capital is added to the fixed assets, and the long-term loans deducted from this subtotal.

A fuller example of company year-end statements now follows. The statements are for internal use and will require editing for publication. By way of practice, the reader should prepare the statements for publication in accordance with the 1967 Companies Act—assuming such figures as are necessary in addition to the data given in Exhibit 42.7.

Exhibit 42.7

(Vertical form)

Dolce Vita Company Ltd
Operating Statement for year ended . . .

	£	£
Sales:		500,000
Production cost—		
Materials consumed	110,000	
Direct labour	200,000	
Prime cost	310,000	
Factory overhead:		
Indirect labour	40,000	
Services	10,000	
Power	5,000	
Depreciation—Premises	15,000	
Plant	20,000	
	90,000	
		400,000
Factory Margin		100,000

Dolce Vita Company Ltd
Operating Statement for year ended . . .

	£	£
Overheads:		
Selling and Distribution		
Director's Salary	5,000	
Salaries	10,000	
Commissions	5,000	
Expenses	5,000	
Depreciation—Vehicles	5,000	
Advertising	10,000	
		40,000
Administration and Occupancy:		
Directors' Salaries	8,000	
Salaries	5,000	
Expenses	4,000	
Directors' Fees	1,000	
Audit	1,000	
Heat, Light, Insurance, Repairs	5,000	
Depreciation—Fittings, etc.	1,000	
		25,000
Financial:		
Debenture Interest	7,000	
Discounts Allowed	3,000	
		10,000
		75,000
Net Operating Profit before Corporation Tax		25,000
Corporation Tax		12,000
Profit after Corporation Tax		13,000
Proposed Dividends (20 per cent)		10,000
Retained this year		3,000
Brought forward		47,000
Total Retained Profits carried forward		50,000

Dolce Vita Company Ltd
Financial Position Statement at . . .

ASSETS EMPLOYED

	Cost £	Depreciation £	Net £
Fixed assets:			
Premises	190,000	90,000	100,000
Plant	100,000	60,000	40,000
Vehicles	20,000	10,000	10,000
	310,000	160,000	150,000

Current Assets:	£	£
Stocks	60,000	
Debtors	25,000	
Bank and Cash Balances	15,000	
		100,000
Total Assets Employed		250,000

FINANCED BY

Shareholders—Share Capital Subscribed		50,000
Retained Profits		50,000
Net Worth		100,000
7 per cent Debentures (secured)		100,000
Current Liabilities:		
Creditors	28,000	
Taxation	12,000	
Proposed Dividend	10,000	
		50,000
		250,000

Notes:

1. Contracts for capital expenditure not included in the accounts amount to approximately £18,000.

2. The authorised capital is 100,000 shares of £1 each.

3. The stocks are at cost, and include raw materials £30,000 and work in process (alternative name for work in progress) £10,000.

Exercises

42.1. Present in 'narrative' (vertical) form only the following balance sheet figures of Supreme Co Ltd as at 31 December.

Authorized Capital 100,000 6 per cent Preference shares of £1 each and 100,000 Ordinary shares of £1 each. Issued Share Capital 60,000 6 per cent Preference shares of £1 each and 50,000 £1 Ordinary shares of £1 each; Debtors £20,000; 4,000 5 per cent Debentures of £10 each; Balance at Bank and Cash in Hand £15,000; Factory Buildings (cost £110,000) £100,000; Creditors £4,000; Stock £15,000; Goodwill at cost £10,000; Machinery at cost £12,000; Depreciation of Machinery—Depreciation accumulated Fund £1,000. Profit and Loss Balance is missing and is to be calculated and shown therein.

(East Midland Educational Union)

42.2. Take the Balance Sheet given as an answer to Exercise 41.8, and redraft in vertical form.

42.3. Take the Balance Sheet given as an answer to Exercise 41.9, and redraft in vertical form.

42.4A. The following is taken from the balance sheet of a large enterprise in the distributive sector of Industry. Redraft the balance sheet in narrative form. The company has been in existence for sixty-nine years.

Z Limited
Balance Sheet at 31 March 19–8 (in thousands of £)

	Auth:	Issued:		Cost or Valuation	Deprecia- tion	Net Book Value
	£	£		£	£	£
Share Capital:			Fixed Assets:			
Ordinary Shares of			Properties	145,050	3,793	141,257
£0·25 each	54,100	53,859	Fixtures and			
			Equipment	12,366	2,112	10,254
Reserves:				157,416	5,905	151,511
Surplus on Revaluation of Properties		22,738				
Retained Profits		41,858				
Ordinary Shareholders' Interests		118,455	Current Assets:			
Preference Share Capital:			Stock—at the lower of			
10 per cent Cumulative			Cost or Replacement Value		23,574	
Preference Shares of £1	350	350	Debtors and Prepayments		4,908	
7 per cent Cumulative			Cash and Short Term			
Preference Shares of £1	1,000	1,000	Deposits		20,298	
	1,350	119,805				48,780
7 per cent First Mortgage			Investments:			
Debenture Stock		37,500	Quoted (Market Value			
			£9,184,000)		2,341	
Current Liabilities:			Unquoted (Directors'			
Creditors and Accrued			Valuation £458,000)		252	
Charges	17,604					2,593
Corporation Tax	16,350					
Proposed Dividend (final)	11,625					
		45,579				
		202,884				202,884

42.5A. Manus Ltd has an authorized share capital of £500,000 made up of 100,000 6 per cent Redeemable Preference Shares of £1 each and 400,000 ordinary shares of £1 each. All the preference shares, which are redeemable at par between 1 January 19— and 31 December 19—, have been issued and are fully paid.

250,000 of the ordinary shares have been issued and fully called, but there are calls in arrear of £600.

Apart from those arising from the above, the following were the balances in the company's ledger, after the preparation of the manufacturing account at 31 March Year 9.

	£	£
Plant and machinery 31 March, at cost Year 9	190,000	
Additions to plant during the year at cost	20,000	
General Reserve		28,000
Share premium account		24,000
Stock of finished goods 31 March Year 8	41,600	
Manufacturing account—factory cost of finished goods produced	216,000	
Balance at bank	32,000	
Trade debtors	75,000	
Provision for doubtful debts		2,000
Sales		314,000
Sales returns	15,400	

	£	£
Freehold land and buildings at valuation in Year 7	161,340	
Leasehold properties	28,000	
Unquoted investments at cost	21,200	
Reserve arising on revaluation of freeholds		80,000
General expenses	42,000	
Auditors' remuneration	1,050	
Directors' remuneration	14,210	
Preliminary expenses	1,000	
Income from investments		1,000
Profit and Loss Account balance 31 March Year 8		32,220
Preference dividend paid for the year	6,000	
Plant and machinery depreciation provision to 31 March Year 9		58,250
Work in progress 31 March Year 9	35,400	
Raw materials stock 31 March Year 9	20,000	
Trade creditors and accruals		37,330
Goodwill and patents at cost	6,000	

Notes:

1.   Depreciation for the leasehold properties has to be provided for in respect of the year to 31 March Year 9. There are two properties: one, which cost £19,000 and had a book value last year of £15,000, expires in 26 years' time and is to be depreciated by £500; the other, which cost £15,000 and had a book value last year of £13,000, expires in 61 years' time and is to be depreciated by £400.

2.   No adjustment has been made for general expenses accrued of £1,300 at 31 March Year 9.

3.   £2,000 is to be written off goodwill and patents.

4.   The directors propose a dividend of £15,000 on the ordinary shares.

5.   The provision for doubtful debts is to be adjusted to £2,500.

6.   The stock of finished goods at 31 March Year 9 was valued at £40,000.

7.   The directors' valuation of the unquoted investments at 31 March Year 9 was £22,000.

8.   At 31 March Year 9, the company had entered into contracts for capital expenditure amounting to £12,000, and the value of capital expenditure authorized by the directors' but not yet contracted for was estimated at £30,000.

9.   The investments are regarded as long-term investments.

You are required to prepare the company's Trading and Profit and Loss Account for the year ended 31 March Year 9, and the Balance Sheet as at that date.

The Balance Sheet should comply with the requirements of the Companies Acts 1948 to 1967 (so far as the information given permits), and be arranged so as to show the amounts of the shareholders' funds and the working capital, i.e. net current assets.

Pay particular attention to layout and presentation.

Ignore taxation.

43

Investment Accounts

It is possible to envisage a situation where the only external investment made by a firm is in the form of money in an account with a Savings Bank, which had (say) an interest rate of 5 per cent per annum. Interest is calculated to 31 December each year and a cheque for the interest is sent to the account holder to arrive on 31 December. Such a type of account adhering to these dates would be very rare in practice. However, with such an account the accounting entries needed by the investing firm would be very simple indeed. If £400 was invested by a firm in such an account on 1 January 19–4 and eventually withdrawn on 31 December 19–7, then assuming that the firm's financial year was equated with the calendar year, the Cash Book for each year would be debited with £20 while each year's Investment Income Account would be credited with £20. The balance of the Investment Income Account, £20, would be transferred to the credit side of the Profit and Loss Account for each of the years ended 31 December 19–4, 19–5, 19–6 and 19–7. On the withdrawal of the £400 the Cash Book would be debited with £400 and the credit entry would be made in the Investment Account, thereby cancelling the original debit entry made when the cash was invested.

Most investments, however, are not of this sort, and have complicating factors. Investments can be divided into two main classes, government stocks and investments in limited companies, the latter may take the form of shares, stock or debentures. In this chapter government stocks will be dealt with first. Taxation will be ignored until it is mentioned specifically.

Government Stocks

With United Kingdom government stock the price is always quoted for that of £100 nominal value. Prices on the Stock Exchange will vary in accordance with supply and demand. Thus Treasury 3 per cent Stock may be shown as 45. This means that on the Stock Exchange the price for £100 nominal value of the stock was £45. The purchaser of the stock will receive interest at the rate of £3 each year as interest payable is always based on the nominal value and not the Stock Exchange value.

Interest is payable at regular intervals depending on the stock concerned. Taking a government stock which carried interest at 5 per cent per annum, interest may be payable quarterly on 31 March, 30 June, 30 September and 31 December. Imagine that a man was willing to sell stock of £1,200 nominal value at 80, i.e. for £960 (£80 for £100 nominal value, therefore £80 × 12 = £960 for £1,200 nominal value). The purchaser is to receive the whole of the next interest on 31 March, this being £1,200 at 5 per cent per annum for three months = £15. The seller has received interest up to 31 December, the day before he sold the stock. Ownership of stock and ownership of interest have therefore both been on the same time scale. If market conditions do not change, consider the case of a man who is to sell the stock on 1 February, and the purchaser was still to receive all of the £15 interest on 31 March. The seller will not want to sell at the same price, for as January's interest is not to be received by him, the ownership of the stock and the right to receive interest have moved on to a different time scale. The seller is not now merely selling stock, he is also selling the right to one month's interest in addition. He would therefore now want £960 + one month's interest £5 = £965. When the purchaser pays £965 he will want to record the purchase in his own books. He will accordingly split this price as to £960 paid for the stock, a capital item, and the cost of income £5. When the full quarter's interest £15 is received, the £5 cost will be deducted in the income calculation leaving net income for the period as £10. This accords with the evidence, as two months' ownership for February and March is worth £1,200 × 5 per cent per annum × two months = £10. The seller would also apportion the selling price £1,205 as to £1,200 for the stock and £5 for the interest. The £5 interest would then be shown as investment income in his books. This is, in fact, saying that where the interest is bought and sold as part of a total price, then interest received is not equal to interest accrued. The apportionment of cost and selling price is the way by which investment income can be equated with the duration of the ownership of the investment, i.e. fifteen months' ownership should show fifteen months' investment income.

Where the price of the stock does not include the right to the next instalment of interest it is stated to be *ex div* or e.d.; this stands for excluding dividend. Where it does include the right to receive the next instalment of interest, irrespective of how long the stock has been owned it is known as *cum div*, meaning including dividend. All prices are *cum div* unless stated specifically to be *ex div*.

Because of the necessity to keep income separate from the capital cost of the investment, each Investment Account has a column for income and a column for capital. In addition a column is used to show the nominal value of the stock, this being used for convenience and does not form part of the double-entry system. Brokerage charges and stamp duties are part of the capital cost of the investment and are included in the cheque paid to the firm's stockbrokers. Brokerage charges on sale are deducted from the cheque remitted by the stockbrokers for the sale proceeds, so that as the sale price is brought in net they have been effectively charged.

Exhibit 43.1

Brent Ltd bought £10,000 3 per cent Government Stock at 40 *ex div* on 1 January 19–6, the cheque for the stock £4,000 plus brokerage charges £100 being £4,100. The interest is received on 31 March, 30 June, 30 September and 31 December 19–6. During 19–7 interest is received on 31 March, and all the stock is sold for 43 *cum div* on 31 May, the cheque being £4,190, made up of £4,300 total proceeds *less* £110 brokerage charges. The financial year end of Brent Ltd is 31 December.

The following shows the entries in the Investment Account for the years ended 31 December 19–6 and 19–7.

Investment—3 per cent Government Stock

		Nominal	Income	Capital			Nominal	Income	Capital
		£	£	£			£	£	£
19–6					19–6				
Jan 1	Cash	10,000		4,100	Mar 31	Cash		75	
Dec 31	Investment Income				Jun 30	,,		75	
	to Profit and Loss		300		Sep 30	,,		75	
					Dec 31	,,		75	
					, 31	Balance c/d	10,000		4,100
		10,000	300	4,100			10,000	300	4,100

Investment—3 per cent Government Stock

		Nominal	Income	Capital				Nominal	Income	Capital
		£	£	£				£	£	£
19–7					19–7					
Jan 1	Balance b/d	10,000		4,100	Mar 31	Cash			75	
Dec 31	Investment Income				May 31	,,	(A)	10,000	50	4,140
	to Profit and Loss		125			Sale Proceeds				
,, 31	Profit on sale to									
	Profit and Loss			40						
		10,000	125	4,140				10,000	125	4,140

(A) As the stock is sold *cum div*, Brent Ltd is therefore including in the selling price the value of two months' interest for April and May $= \frac{2}{12} \times 3$ per cent $\times £10,000 = £50$. The £4,190 sale price is accordingly apportioned £50 as to income and £4,140 as to capital.

To illustrate matters further, Exhibit 43.2 shows an investment where there are both extra purchases and sales of part of the investment.

Exhibit 43.2

On 1 January 19–4 Green Ltd bought £4,000 6 per cent Government Stock at £90, the cheque of £3,680 paid being £3,600 for the stock and £80 for the brokerage charges. Interest is receivable each year on 31 March, 30 June, 30 September, and 31 December.

Investment—6 per cent Government Stock

Dr

Date		Particulars	Ref	Nominal £	Income £	Capital £
19-4						
Jan	1	Cash		4,000		3,680
Dec	31	Investment Income to Profit and Loss			240	
				4,000	240	3,680
19-5						
Jan	1	Balance b/d		4,000		3,680
Jun	1	Adjustment for sale at *ex div* price	(B)		10	
Dec	31	Investment Income to Profit and Loss	(C)		115	
				4,000	125	3,680
19-6						
Jan	1	Balance b/d		1,000		920
Feb	1	Cash	(E)	5,000	25	4,345
Jun	1	Adjustment of purchase at *ex div* price	(F)	1,000		910
						5
Dec	31	Investment Income to Profit and Loss			370	
				7,000	395	6,180
19-7						
Jan	1	Balance b/d		7,000		6,180

Cr

Date		Particulars	Ref	Nominal £	Income £	Capital £
19-4						
Mar	31	Cash			60	
Jun	30	"			60	
Sep	30	"			60	
Dec	31	"			60	
Dec	31	Balance c/d		4,000		3,680
				4,000	240	3,680
19-5						
Feb	1	Cash Sale proceeds	(A)	1,000	5	945
Mar	31	Cash (£3,000 × 6% × 3 months)			45	
Jun	1	Cash Sale proceeds	(B)	2,000		1,710
"	1	Adjustment for sale at *ex div* price				10
"	30	Cash (£3,000 × 6% × 3 months)			45	
Sep	30	Cash (£1,000 × 6% × 3 months)			15	
Dec	31	Cash (£1,000 × 6% × 3 months)			15	
"	31	Profit and Loss—Loss on Sale of Investments				95
"	31	Balance c/d	(D)	1,000		920
				4,000	125	3,680
19-6						
Mar	31	Cash (£6,000 × 6% × 3 months)			90	
Jun	1	Adjustment of purchase at *ex div* price	(E)		5	
"	30	Cash (£6,000 × 6% × 3 months)			90	
Sep	30	Cash (£7,000 × 6% × 3 months)			105	
Dec	31	Cash (£7,000 × 6% × 3 months)			105	
"	31	Balance c/d		7,000		6,180
				7,000	395	6,180

On 1 February 19–5 £1,000 nominal value of the stock is sold *cum div*, the net proceeds being £950.

1 June 19–5, £2,000 nominal value sold *ex div*, net proceeds after brokerage being £1,710.

1 February 19–6, £5,000 nominal value bought *cum div*, the cost including brokerage being £4,370.

1 June 19–6, £1,000 nominal value bought *ex div*, cost including brokerage being £910.

On page 745 is the Investment Account in Green's books for the financial years ended 31 December 19–4, 19–5 and 19–6. Taxation is ignored.

Notes:

(A) The sale proceeds £950 represent the sale of the right to one month's interest, £1,000 × 6 per cent per annum for one month = £5, plus the right to the actual stock itself. This must therefore be the balance of the net sale proceeds, £950 − £5 = £945.

(B) The sale at an *ex div* price means that Green Ltd will receive interest for June on this £2,000 of stock even though the stock itself had passed out of Green Ltd's ownership. The actual net sale price is therefore £1,270, which is made up of £1,710 actually received plus £10 for the right to one month's interest retained. This is adjusted by debiting the Income column with £10 to cancel the income which was not equated with ownership, and crediting the Capital column with £10 representing the actual reduction in the sale price caused by selling at an *ex div* price. Note (C) will illustrate the validity of debiting the income column, as without this entry the amount of investment income transferred to the Profit and Loss Account would not agree with the facts relating to the duration of the investment and the rate of interest.

(C) The correctness of this can be proved if the interest actually accrued during ownership is calculated:

		£
6 per cent per annum on £4,000 for one month	=	20
6 per cent per annum on £3,000 for four months	=	60
6 per cent per annum on £1,000 for seven months	=	35
		115

(D)

		£	£
Cost of £1,000 nominal value of stock £3,680 × ¼	=	920	
Sold on 1 February 19–5 for		945	25 profit
Cost of £2,000 nominal value of stock £3,680 × ½	=	1,840	
Sold on 1 June 19–5 for (adjusted net sale price)		1,720	120 loss
			95 net loss

(E) The stock bought on 1 June 19–6 for £910 *ex div* meant that June's ownership would not bring in any interest on this stock. The price paid for the stock would have been reduced by the amount of June's interest, i.e. £1,000 at 6 per cent per annum for one month = £5. The true price paid therefore was £915. This is represented by a debit of £5 in the Capital column, while a credit of £5 in the Income column is made to show that ownership of fixed interest stock does in fact bring in a return of interest in accordance with the length of ownership.

(F) This can be proved to be correct.

		£
£1,000 at 6 per cent per annum for one month	=	5
£6,000 at 6 per cent per annum for four months	=	120
£7,000 at 6 per cent per annum for seven months	=	245
		370

Investment in Limited Companies

In the cases where stocks, shares or debentures carry a fixed rate of interest the treatment is the same as with Government Stocks. However, where the investment is not of the fixed interest type, e.g. ordinary shares, the next dividend receivable is not known on purchase or sale. On the declaration of the next dividend an adjustment can be made, so that the account will contain the same balances as it would have done if the next dividend had been known, and the necessary apportionments taken place at sale or purchase rather than wait until the dividend had been declared. In theory these adjustments should always be made, but in practice they are usually ignored where the purchase and sale of investments do not constitute the main business of the firm.

Exercises

43.1. The following transactions of Trust Ltd took place during the year ended 30 June 19–7:

19–6

1 July	Purchased £12,000 4 per cent Consolidated Loan (interest payable 1 February and 1 August) at 60½ *cum div*.
12 July	Purchased 2,000 ordinary shares of £0·5 each in Abee Ltd for £4,000.
1 August	Received half-year's interest on 4 per cent Consolidated Loan.
15 August	Abee Ltd made a bonus issue of three ordinary shares for every two held. Trust Ltd sold 2,500 of the bonus shares for £1 each.
1 October	Purchased 5,000 ordinary shares of £1 each in Ceedee Ltd at £0·775 each.

19–7

2 January	Sold £3,000 4 per cent Consolidated Loan at 61 *ex div*.
1 February	Received half-year's interest on 4 per cent Consolidated Loan.
1 March	Received dividend of 18 per cent on shares in Abee Ltd.
1 April	Ceedee Ltd made a 'rights' issue of one share for every two held at £0·5 per share. 'Rights' sold on market for £0·25 per share.
1 June	Received dividend of 12½ per cent on shares in Ceedee Ltd.

You are required to write up the relevant investment accounts as they would appear in the books of Trust Ltd for the year ended 30 June 19–7, bringing down the balances as on that date.

Ignore brokerage and stamp duty.

(Institute of Chartered Accountants)

43.2. On 31 March 19–5 the investments held by Jowetts of Mayfair Ltd included 6,000 Ordinary shares of £1 each fully paid in Composite Interest Ltd, such shares appearing in the books at £7,200. It is not the practice of Jowetts of Mayfair Ltd to make apportionments of dividends received or receivable.

Jowetts of Mayfair Ltd sold 1,000 shares on 31 May 19–5 for £1,965. On 20 September 19–5 Composite Interest Ltd:

(a) Issued by way of a bonus issue three fully paid shares for every five held on 31 August 19–5.

(b) It gave the right to shareholders to apply for one share for every two actually held on 31 August 19–5, the price to be £1·05 per share payable in full on application.

The shares issued under (a) and (b) were not to participate in the dividend for the year ended 31 August 19–5.

The bonus shares were received. For the rights issue 1,800 shares were taken up and paid for on 30 September 19–5. The rights on the remaining shares were sold for £0·3 per share, the money for this being received on 15 November 19–5.

On 17 December 19–5 Composite Interest Ltd declared and paid a final dividend of 20 per cent for the year ended 31 August 19–5, and on 15 March 19–6 an interim dividend of 5 per cent for the year ended 31 August 19–6.

Show the investment account for the year ended 31 March 19–6 as it would appear in the books of Jowetts of Mayfair Ltd.

Expenses of sale are to be ignored.

43.3A. Stag Ltd is an investment company making up its accounts to 31 December in each year.

The following transactions have been extracted from the company's records for 19–9.

19–9

1 January	Purchased 1,000 ordinary shares of £0·25 each in Bull Ltd at £1·75 per share.
12 February	Purchased £2,000 ordinary stock in Bear Ltd for £1,500.
1 March	Received dividend of 20 per cent on shares in Bull Ltd.
24 April	Bull Ltd made a bonus issue of one share for every four held.
2 May	Received dividend of 2½ per cent on ordinary stock in Bear Ltd.
10 May	Bull Ltd announced a rights issue of two ordinary shares for every five held on that date, at £1·25 per share. Rights sold on market for £0·5 per share.

1 August	Applied for £5,000 7¼ per cent Loan stock in Bear Ltd issued at £98 per cent, and payable half on application and the balance in two equal instalments on 1 October and 1 December. The application was successful.
16 September	Received dividend of 30 per cent on shares in Bull Ltd.
1 October	Paid instalment on loan stock in Bear Ltd.
20 November	Received dividend of 3 per cent on ordinary stock in Bear Ltd.
1 December	Paid final instalment on loan stock in Bear Ltd.

You are required to write up the accounts for the investments in Bull Ltd and Bear Ltd as they would appear in the books of Stag Ltd for the year ended 31 December 19–9, bringing down the balances as on that date.

Ignore stamp duty, brokerage and taxation.

(Institute of Chartered Accountants)

43.4.A. H.M. Ltd bought £10,000 nominal of Peatshire 6 per cent Loan Stock at 92 *cum div* on 30 April 19–8. Interest on the stock is paid half-yearly on 30 June and 31 December. £4,000 of the stock was sold at 94 *ex div* on 30 November 19–8.

H.M. Ltd prepares final accounts annually to 31 March.

Prepare the investment account in the company's ledger from the date of the purchase to 1 April 19–9.

Ignore brokerage, stamp duty and taxation and make apportionments in months.

(Associated Examining Board—G.C.E. 'A' level)

43.5A. On 1 April 19–7, F.R.Y. Ltd purchased 10,000 ordinary shares of £1 each, fully paid, in T.L.S. Ltd at a cost of £20,500.

On 1 September 19–7, T.L.S. Ltd declared and paid a dividend of 15 per cent on its ordinary shares for the year ended 30 June 19–7.

On 1 November 19–7, T.L.S. Ltd gave its members the right to subscribe for one ordinary share for every eight held on 1 November 19–7, at a price of £1·5 per share, payable in full on application.

On 15 November 19–7, F.R.Y. Ltd purchased for £0·4 per share the rights of another shareholder in T.L.S. Ltd to subscribe for 750 shares under the rights issue.

On 30 November 19–7 F.R.Y. Ltd applied and paid for all the shares in T.L.S. Ltd to which it was then entitled.

On 8 September 19–8, T.L.S. Ltd declared and paid a dividend for the year ended 30 June 19–8, of 15 per cent on all ordinary shares, including those issued in 1967.

On 1 October 19–8, F.R.Y. Ltd sold 4,500 ordinary shares in T.L.S. Ltd for £9,875.

The accounting year of F.R.Y. Ltd ends on 31 December.

F.R.Y. Ltd does not make apportionments of dividends received or receivable. When part of a holding of shares is sold, it is the practice of this company to calculate the cost of the shares sold as an appropriate part of the average cost of all the shares held at the date of the sale.

You are required to show the investment account in the books of F.R.Y. Ltd for the two years ended 31 December 19–7, and 31 December 19–8, bringing down the balance at the end of each year.

Ignore taxation.

(Chartered Institute of Secretaries and Administrators)

44

Contract Accounts

The span of production differs between businesses, and some fit into the normal pattern of annual accounts easier than others do. A farmer's accounts are usually admirably suited to the yearly pattern, as the goods they produce are in accordance with the seasons, and therefore repeat themselves annually. With a firm whose production span is a day or two the annual accounts are also quite suitable.

On the other hand, there are businesses whose work does not conform to a financial year's calculation of profits. Assume that a firm of contractors has only one contract being handled, and that is the total construction of a tunnel under the Irish Sea. This might take ten years to complete. Not until it is completed can the actual profit or loss on the contract be correctly calculated. However, if the company was formed especially with this contract in mind, the shareholders would not want to wait for ten years before the profit could be calculated and dividends paid. Therefore an attempt is made to calculate profits yearly. Obviously, most firms will have more than one contract under way at a time, and also it would be rare for a contract to take such a long time to complete.

For each contract an account is opened. It is, in fact, a form of Trading Account for each contract. Therefore if the firm has a contract to build a new technical college it may be numbered Contract 71. Thus a Contract 71 Account would be opened. All expenditure traceable to the contract will be charged to the Contract Account. This is far easier than ascertaining direct expenses in a factory, as any expenditure on the site will be treated as direct, e.g. wages for the manual workers on the site, telephone rental for telephones on the site, hire of machinery for the contract, wages for the timekeepers, clerks, etc., on the site.

The contractor is paid by agreement on the strength of architects' certificates in the case of buildings, or engineers' certificates for an engineering contract. The architect, or engineer, will visit the site at regular intervals and will issue a certificate stating his estimate of the value of the work done, in terms of the total contract price (the sale price of the whole contract). Thus he may issue a certificate for £10,000. Normally the terms governing the contract will contain a clause concerning retention money. This is the amount, usually stated as a percentage, which will be retained, i.e. held back, in case the contract is not completed by a stated date, or against claims for faulty workmanship, etc. A 10 per cent retention in the case already mentioned would lead to £9,000 being payable by the person for whom the contract was being performed.

The administration overhead expenses not traceable directly to the sites are sometimes split on an arbitrary basis and charged to each contract. Of course, if there was only one contract, then all the overhead expenses would quite rightly be chargeable against it. On the other hand if there are twenty contracts being carried on, any apportionment must be arbitrary. No one can really apportion on a 'scientific' basis the administration overhead expenses of the managing director's salary, the cost of advertising to give the firm the right 'image', the costs of running accounting machinery for the records of the whole firm, and these are only a few of such expenses. In a fashion similar to the departmental accounts principle in Chapter 25 it sometimes gives misleading results, and it is therefore far better left for the administrative overhead expenses which are obviously not chargeable to a contract to be omitted from the Contract Accounts. The surplus left on each Contract Account is thus the 'contribution' of each contract to administrative overhead expenses and to profit.

Exhibit 44.1

Contract 44 is for a school being built for the Blankshire County Council. By the end of the year the following items have been charged to the Contract Account:

	Contract 44
Wages—Labour on Site	£5,000
Wages—Foremen and Clerks on the Site	600
Materials	4,000
Sub-contractors on the Site	900
Other Site Expenses	300
Hire of Special Machinery	400
Plant Bought for the Contract	2,000

The entries concerning expenditure traceable direct to the contract are relatively simple. These are charged to the Contract Account. These can be seen in the Contract Account shown on the next page.

Architects' certificates have been received during the year amounting to £14,000, it being assumed for this example that the certificate related to all work done up to the year end. A retention of 10 per cent is to be made, and the Blankshire County Council has paid £12,600. The £14,000 has been credited to a holding account called an Architects' Certificates Account, and debited to the Blankshire County Council Account. The total of the Architects' Certificates Account now needs transferring to the Contract 44 Account. It is, after all, the 'sale' price of the work done so far, and the Contract Account is a type of Trading Account. The £12,600 received has been debited to the Cash Book and credited to Blankshire County Council's Account, which now shows a balance of £1,400, this being equal to the retention money.

The cost of the stock of the materials on the site unused is not included in the value of the architects' certificates and is therefore carried forward to the next year at cost price. The value of the plant at the end of the year is also carried forward. In this case the value of the cost of the plant not yet used is £1,400. This means that £2,000 has been debited for the plant and £1,400 credited, thus effectively charging £600 for depreciation. Assume that the stock of unused materials cost £800.

The Contract 44 Account will now appear:

Contract 44

	£		£
Wages—Labour on Site	5,000	Architects' Certificates	14,000
Wages—Foremen and Clerks		Stock of Unused	
on the Site	600	Materials c/d	800
Materials	4,000	Value of Plant c/d	1,400
Sub-contractors on the Site	900		
Other Site Expenses	300		
Hire of Special Machinery	400		
Plant Bought for the Contract	2,000		

The difference between totals of the two sides (Credit side £16,200, Debit side £13,200) can be seen to be £3,000. It would be a brave man indeed who would assert that the profit made to date was £3,000. The contract is only part completed, and costly snags may crop up which would dissipate any potential profit earned, or snags may have developed already, such as subsidence, which has remained unnoticed as yet. The convention of conservatism now takes over. The normal custom is, barring any evidence to the contrary, for the apparent profit (in this case £3,000) to have the following formula applied to it:

$$\text{Apparent profit} \times \tfrac{2}{3} \times \frac{\text{Cash received}}{\text{Work certified}} = \begin{array}{l}\text{Amount which can be utilized}\\\text{for dividends, etc.}\end{array}$$

In this case this turns out as $£3,000 \times \tfrac{2}{3} \times \dfrac{12,600}{14,000} = £1,800$.

There are variations on the formula under differing circumstances, but it is the formula which is usually propounded as being the most suitable.

Why two-thirds? Why not three-quarters? This is a fair question, and all that can be said is that the rule of thumb method devised years ago happened to be two-thirds. This was acceptable to accountants and businessmen. Just as technology has changed so also the two-thirds rule needs re-examination in a rapidly changing world. Modern techniques of building and engineering have undoubtedly minimized errors and snags compared with the past, therefore a much higher figure than two-thirds may now be quite justifiable.

The Contract 44 Account can now be completed:

Profit and Loss Account

	£
Profits from contracts:	
Contract 43	
Contract 44	1,800
Contract 45	

Balance Sheet (extracts)

	£		£
Profit reserve on Contract		Plant (Contract 44 part)	1,400
44	1,200	Stock (Contract 44 part)	800

Contract 44

	£		£
Wages—Labour on Site	5,000	Architects' Certificates	14,000
Wages—Foremen and Clerks		Stock of Unused	
on the Site	600	Materials c/d	800
Materials	4,000	Value of Plant c/d	1,400
Sub-contractors on the Site	900		
Other Site Expenses	300		
Hire of Special Machinery	400		
Plant Bought for the			
Contract	2,000		
Profit to the Profit and Loss			
Account	1,800		
Reserve (the part of the			
apparent profit not yet			
recognized as earned)	1,200		
	16,200		16,200
Stock of Unused Materials		Reserve b/d	1,200
b/d	800		
Value of Plant b/d	1,400		

In the case shown there has been an apparent profit of £3,000, but the action would have been different if instead of revealing such a profit, the Contract Account had in fact shown a loss of £3,000. In such a case it would not be two-thirds of the loss to be taken into account but the whole of it. Thus £3,000 loss would have been transferred to the Profit and Loss Account. This is in accordance with the convention of conservatism which states that profits may be underestimated but never losses.

It is in fact not always the case that an engineer or architect will certify the work done up to the financial year end. He may call several days earlier than the year end. The cost of work done, but not certified at the year end, will therefore need carrying down as a balance to the next period when certification will take place.

Exercises

44.1. Cantilever Ltd was awarded a contract to build an office block in London and work commenced at the site on 1 May 19–5.

During the period to 28 February 19–6, the expenditure on the contract was as follows:

	£
Materials Issued from Stores	9,411
Materials Purchased	28,070
Direct Expenses	6,149
Wages	18,493
Charge made by the Company for Administration Expenses	2,146
Plant and Machinery purchased on 1 May 19–5, for use at site	12,180

On 28 February 19–6 the stock of materials at the site amounted to £2,164 and there were amounts outstanding for wages £366 and direct expenses £49.

Cantilever Ltd has received on account the sum of £64,170 which represents the amount of Certificate No. 1 issued by the architects in respect of work completed to 28 February 19–6, after deducting 10 per cent retention money.

The following relevant information is also available:

1. the plant and machinery has an effective life of five years, with no residual value, and
2. the company only takes credit for two-thirds of the profit on work certified.

You are required:

(a) to prepare a contract account for the period to 28 February 19–6, and
(b) to show your calculation of the profit to be taken to the credit of the company's Profit and Loss Account in respect of the work covered by Certificate No. 1.

(Institute of Chartered Accountants)

44.2. The final accounts of Diggers Ltd are made up to 31 December on each year. Work on a certain contract was commenced on 1 April 19–5 and was completed on 31 October 19–6. The total contract price was £174,000, but a penalty of £700 was suffered for failure to complete by 30 September 19–6.

The following is a summary of receipts and payments relating to the contract:

	During 19–5	During 19–6
Payments:		
Materials	25,490	33,226
Wages	28,384	45,432
Direct Expenses	2,126	2,902
Purchase of Plant on 1 April 19–5	16,250	—

	During 19–5	During 19–6
Receipts:		
Contract Price (*less* penalty)	52,200	121,100
Sale, on 31 October 19–6, of all plant purchased on 1 April 19–5	—	4,100

The amount received from the customer in 19–5 represented the contract price of all work certified in that year less 10 per cent retention money.

When the annual accounts for 19–5 were prepared it was estimated that the contract would be completed on 30 September 19–6, and that the market value of the plant would be £4,250 on that date. It was estimated that further expenditure on the contract during 19–6 would be £81,400.

For purposes of the annual accounts, depreciation of plant is calculated, in the case of uncompleted contracts, by reference to the expected market value of the plant on the date when the contract is expected to be completed, and is allocated between accounting periods by the straight-line method.

Credit is taken, in the annual accounts, for such a part of the estimated total profit, on each uncompleted contract, as corresponds to the proportion between the contract price of the work certified and the total contract price.

You are required to prepare a summary of the account for this contract, showing the amounts transferred to profit and loss account at 31 December 19–5 and 31 December 19–6.

44.3A. Stannard and Sykes Ltd are contractors for the construction of a pier for the Seafront Development Corporation. The value of the contract is £300,000, and payment is by engineer's certificate subject to a retention of 10 per cent of the amount certified, this to be held by the Seafront Development Corporation for six months after the completion of the contract.

The following information is extracted from the records of Stannard and Sykes Ltd.

	£
Wages on site	41,260
Materials delivered to site by supplier	58,966
Materials delivered to site from store	10,180
Hire of Plant	21,030
Expenses charged to Contract	3,065
Overheads charged to Contract	8,330
Materials on site at 30 November 19–8	11,660
Work certified	150,000
Payment received	135,000
Work in progress at cost (not the subject of a certificate to date)	12,613
Wages accrued 30 November 19–8	2,826

You are to prepare the Pier Contract Account to 30 November 19–8, and to suggest a method by which profit could be prudently estimated.

(Associated of Certified Accountants)

44.4A. Cantilever Ltd was awarded a contract to build an office block in London and work commenced at the site on 1 May 19–5.

During the period to 28 February 19–6, the expenditure on the contract was as follows:

	£
Materials issued from stores	9,411
Materials purchased	28,070
Direct expenses	6,149
Wages	18,493
Charge made by the company for administration expenses	2,146
Plant and machinery purchased on 1 May 19–5, for use at site	12,180

On 28 February 19–6, the stock of materials at the site amounted to £2,164 and there were amounts outstanding for wages £366 and direct expenses £49.

Cantilever Ltd has received on account the sum of £64,170 which represents the amount of Certificate No. 1 issued by the architects in respect of work completed to 28 February 19–6, after deducting 10 per cent retention money.

The following relevant information is also available:

1.   the plant and machinery has an effective life of five years, with no residual value, and

2.   the company only takes credit for two-thirds of the profit on work certified.

You are required:

(a)   to prepare a contract account for the period to 28 February 19–6, and
(b)   to show your calculation of the profit to be taken to the credit of the company's Profit and Loss Account in respect of the work covered by Certificate No. 1.

(Institute of Chartered Accountants)

44.5A. You are required to prepare the contract account for the year ended 31 December 19–0, and show the calculation of the sum to be credited to the profit and loss account for that year.

On 1 April 19–0 MN Ltd commenced work on a contract which was to be completed by 30 June 19–1 at an agreed price of £520,000.

MN Ltd's financial year ended on 31 December 19–0, and on that day expenditure on the contract totalled £263,000 made up as under:

	£
Plant	30,000
Materials	124,000
Wages	95,000
Sundry expenses	5,000
Head office charges	9,000
	263,000

Cash totalling £195,000 had been received by 31 December 19–0 representing 75 per cent of the work certified as completed on that date, but in addition, work costing £30,000 had been completed but not certified.

A sum of £9,000 had been obtained on the sale of materials which had cost £8,000 but which had been found unsuitable. On 31 December 19–0 stocks of unused materials on site had cost £10,000 and the plant was valued at £20,000.

To complete the contract by 30 June 19–1 it was estimated that:

1.   the following additional expenditures would be incurred:

	£
Wages	64,000
Materials	74,400
Sundry expenses	9,000

2.   further plant costing £25,000 would be required;

3.   the residual value of all plant used on the contract at 30 June 19–1 would be £15,000;

4.   head office charges to the contract would be at the same annual rate plus 10 per cent.

It was estimated that the contract would be completed on time but that a contingency provision of £15,000 should be made. From this estimate and the expenditure already incurred, it was decided to estimate the total profit that would be made on the contract and to take to the credit of the profit and loss account for the year ended 31 December 19–0, that proportion of the total profit relating to the work actually certified to that date.

(Institute of Cost and Management Accounts)

45

Flow of Funds Statements

Most of the accounting statements described in the book so far have been concerned with evaluating profit or loss and with presenting a statement of assets, capital and liabilities. In this chapter the information that is presented in the Profit and Loss Account, and in the Balance Sheet, will be adjusted and reframed to give a particular emphasis to the sources and application of funds within the business. In practice, this will normally be treated as an analysis of the reasons for changes in either the firm's cash resources or its fund of working capital.

A small trader who buys goods for £100 and then sells them for £150 cash has generated cash funds of £50. This figure, however, will rarely be his profit. If he has to pay rent for the period of £8, and his motor van depreciates by £20, his profit will be only £22. To establish how much of the cash funds generated by the trader are retained in the business, any 'non-cash' expenses must be added back to the profit. But a 'non-cash' expense is not necessarily an expense which does not result in an outflow of cash. What it does mean is that the outflow of cash takes place in a period other than the one being considered. An outstanding example of this is the provision for depreciation. If a motor van is bought in year 1 for £1,000 and is immediately paid for, it involves an outflow of £1,000 cash in that year, but that amount is not in fact charged against the profit as an expense. The reader will realize that the depreciation provisions are the method of charging this 'expense'. Therefore the charge for depreciation in each of the years during which the van is in use do not involve actual cash being paid out in that particular year. In the case of the small trader being considered, assume that he had bought the motor van in a previous period. In this case depreciation £20 will be added back to the profit of £22 to give a total of £42 cash funds actually generated from trading.

It is absolutely vital for a firm not just to know what its profits are, but also to establish the sufficiency of its cash resources and of its working capital to meet its commitments at a future point in time. A reference page one of Volume 1 will show that this was one of the two main purposes of accounting; these were (a) to ascertain whether or not the firm is making a profit, and (b) would the firm be able to meet its commitments as they fell due and so not to have to close down owing to lack of funds. To meet the need of (b) many firms prepare a statement on the lines illustrated very simply for the small trader, weekly or monthly, and make projections (budgets) far into the future. Thus they have put their minds to calculating what the bank balances or working capital items are expected to be at future points in time. Then, if it becomes obvious that a bank overdraft will be needed, or that there should be an issue of shares or debentures to provide longer-term finance, this will be known some time in advance and all the necessary preparations can be made. Suddenly trying to obtain an overdraft, or to arrange an issue of shares, in a hurry are not the best possible conditions for financial success, and have spelt disaster for many a firm in the past. Maxims such as 'to be forewarned is to be forearmed' certainly are not out of place in the arranging of financial facilities. In most of the examples that follow the period is stated as the year, but the principles remain the same if it is done on a weekly or a monthly basis.

The sources from which business funds are received can now be summarized:

1. Trading, where the total income exceeds expenses requiring the use of cash or working capital.

2. The sale of assets or long-term investments.

3. The proceeds received from the issue of additional share capital or the introduction of new capital by the proprietor.

4. Proceeds from the issue of debentures or long-term loans.

As it is usually cash funds, meaning by this the cash and bank balances, or the working capital funds, that are highlighted by the use of flow of funds statements it is perhaps useful to consider these two aspects by first looking at how changes in the various items on a Balance Sheet affect the cash funds or the working capital.

Exhibit 45.1

These statements are looked at as though all the items in the Balance Sheet have had an immediate and direct effect upon the cash funds held, or to be held, by the business. Increases in Capital or Liabilities (which represent sources of funds into the business) usually increase cash, whereas increases in non-cash assets reduce cash. Examples from each column are given as follows: An increase in the shares issued means that cash will have been received by the firm during the year, thus increasing cash funds. An increase in creditors means that a delay has occurred in the firm making payment to them, thus temporarily keeping cash funds at a higher level than they would otherwise have been. An increase in stock, however, means that as this is deemed to be paid for, an outflow of cash will have been necessary for the purpose. An increase in fixed assets means a decrease in cash funds, while a reduction would mean that the sum received would swell cash funds.

Effect on Cash Funds
Balance Sheet as at . . .

	An increase in the following items changes cash	A decrease in the following items changes cash
Share Capital	+	−
Profit (adjusted to give cash effect)	+	−
Debentures and Loans	+	−
Current Liabilities (each separate item)	+	−
Fixed Assets	−	+
Current Assets (each separate item other than cash funds)	−	+
Cash Funds (there will be an increase (+) if there is overall a greater value of sources (+)s than applications (−)s and a reduction if more greater value (−)s than (+)s)	+or−	+or−

(+) represents an increase in cash (−) a reduction in cash

Exhibit 45.2

These statements are now looked at as though changes in the other items in the Balance Sheet had an immediate effect on the working capital. Increases in Capital or Long-Term Liabilities usually increase working capital, whereas increases in Fixed and other non-current assets reduce working capital. Remember that working capital is made up of current assets *less* current liabilities. Thus if creditors were reduced by being paid off, this would have no effect on the working capital, because both the bank balance and the creditors would be reduced by identical amounts, leaving the working capital at exactly the same figure.

Effect on Working Capital
Balance Sheet as at . . .

	An increase in the following items changes working capital	A decrease in the following items changes working capital
Share Capital	+	−
Profit (adjusted to give cash effect)	+	−
Debentures and Loans	+	−

Effect on Working Capital
Balance Sheet as at . . .

	An increase in the following items changes working capital	A decrease in the following items changes working capital
Fixed Assets	−	+
Working Capital (current assets less current liabilities)	+or−	+or−
(There will be an increase in working capital if there is a greater value of (+)s than (−)s and a reduction if a greater value of (−)s than (+)s)		

The two main flow of funds statements are therefore concerned with cash funds or with working capital. From the management point of view the cash position is usually of greatest importance, but to the shareholder the working capital statement is of greater relevance, since it cannot be so easily manipulated as the cash statement. For example, the cash picture could be deliberately distorted at the year end by allowing stocks to fall below a desirable level, so that the ratio of cash balances to creditors looked healthy. In point of fact the stock position may be decidedly unhealthy, but this is very often not detectable from looking at a Balance Sheet.

The objective is, however, the same in both cases of cash funds and working capital funds, and that is to ensure that a proper control is exercised over the assets of the firm, and to ensure that sufficient liquid funds are available when required. Statements relating to the source and application of funds have been recognized as of sufficient importance by the Accounting Standards Committee to warrant their inclusion as part of the audited accounts published by all major firms.

Without a sufficient supply of working capital a business finds itself unable to continue trading, in much the same way as the human body dies without an adequate supply of blood. The main interrelationships and flows of working capital for a manufacturing business are shown in Exhibit 45.3.

In the examples worked out in the rest of this chapter it will be seen that the Fund Statement is simply a convenient way of describing in concise form the changes which take place over a period of time in those accounts which directly influence working capital and cash flows. The examples are restricted to analyzing fund flows starting by taking the contribution from trading as a known quantity. It is sometimes useful to go beyond the profit to analyze the flows of revenues and expenses comprising the net flow of profit. However, for this particular book this detail is ignored, and the flows examined are those which would normally be discernable to the external analyst examining the published accounts of a company.

Exhibit 45.3

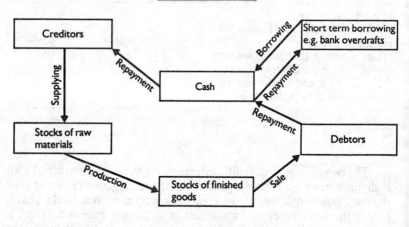

Working Capital Flow

Exhibit 45.4

J. Evans—Hot Dog Vendor
Balance Sheets as at

	31 December 19–1	31 December 19–2	Debit (applications)	Credit (sources)
	£	£	£	£
Capital Account	1,000	1,600		600
Loan Account	500	700		200
Trade Creditors	750	1,000		250
Expenses Owing	250	200	50	
	2,500	3,500		
Plant and Machinery	800	1,900	1,100	
Stock	700	800	100	
Debtors	950	600		350
Cash and Bank Balances	50	200	150	
	2,500	3,500	1,400	1,400

Analysis of changes (spanning the Debit and Credit columns)

Notes:

	£	£
1. Capital Account 31 December 19–1		1,000
Profit for the year		2,000
		3,000
Less Drawings		1,400
Capital Account 31 December 19–2		1,600
2. Plant and Machinery		
Balance at cost 31 December 19–1		1,300
Additions at cost in the year		1,500
		2,800
Depreciation up to and including 31 December 19–1	500	
Depreciation for the year ended 31 December 19–2	400	
		900
Balance on the Plant and Machinery Account 31 December 19–2		1,900

From the two Balance Sheets shown in the example an analysis of changes has been extended into columns headed Debit and Credit. Although this is not double entry accounting as such, it is useful to follow the double entry rules. The Credit column will include increases in capital and liability accounts or reductions in asset accounts. The debit column will include increases in asset accounts or reduction in capital or liability accounts. The differences extended into the analysis columns must of course total the same on the debit and credit sides. From these balances a preliminary statement can be prepared, although normally some adjustments will be necessary.

J. Evans—Hot Dog Vendor
Cash Flow Statement year ended 31 December 19–2

	£	£
Sources of Cash:		
Capital Account	600	
Loans	200	
Increase in Creditors	250	
Reduction in Debtors	350	
		1,400
Application of Cash:		
Reduction in Expenses Owing	50	
Increase in Plant and Machinery	1,100	
Increase in Stock	100	
		1,250
Increase in Cash and Bank Balances during the year		150

This statement is unsatisfactory because some important factors contributing to fund flows are not revealed. First the total against the Capital Account of £600 represents the balance of capital introduced, drawings and profit, all of which should be shown separately. In addition the increase shown for Plant and Machinery is the balance after depreciation has been deducted, and not the cost of the Plant and Machinery purchased. If these adjustments are made the statement would appear:

J. Evans—Hot Dog Vendor
Cash Flow Statement year ended 31 December 19–2

	£	£
Sources of Cash:		
Contribution from Trading (Net Profit £2,000+Non-cash Expenses, i.e. Depreciation £400)		2,400
Loans		200
Increase in Creditors		250
Reduction in Debtors		350
		3,200
Application of Cash:		
Proprietors' Drawings	1,400	
Reduction in Expenses Owing	50	
Additions to Plant and Machinery (£1,100+ Depreciation £400)	1,500	
Increase in Stock	100	
		3,050
Increase in Cash during the year		150

Exactly the same information can be combined in a different form to emphasize the change in working capital. In this form of statement all the differences in current asset and current liability accounts are grouped together to be explained in terms of changes in all the other assets, capital and liability accounts.

Working Capital Flow Statement

	£	£
Sources of Working Capital:		
Contribution from Trading		2,400
Loans		200
		2,600
Application of Working Capital:		
Proprietors' Drawings	1,400	
Additions to Plant and Machinery	1,500	
		2,900
Reduction in Working Capital during the year		300

The £300 reduction in working capital should be analyzed as follows:

	£	£
Increases in Working Capital:		
Reduction in expenses owing		50
Increase in Stock		100
Increase in Cash		150
		300
Reduction in Working Capital:		
Increase in trade creditors	250	
Reduction in debtors	350	
	—	600
Net reduction in working capital		300

This analysis should be attached to the Working Capital Flow Statement shown above.

In the case of limited companies the procedure for presenting flow of funds statement is basically the same as for the sole trader's accounts illustrated. It is usual to show dividends and taxation paid as separate applications of funds and to cancel out transfers from the Appropriation Account to Reserves, none of which alter cash or working capital in any way.

Example:

The Balance Sheets of Economy Ltd for 19–1 and 19–2 were as follows:

	19–1	19–2	Analysis of changes Debit	Analysis of changes Credit
	£	£	£	£
Share Capital	100,000	120,000		20,000
Share Premium Account	20,000	25,000		5,000
General Reserve	20,000	30,000		10,000
Profit and Loss Account	15,000	20,000		5,000
	155,000	195,000		
5 per cent Debentures	40,000	30,000	10,000	
Current Liabilities	35,000	30,000	5,000	
	230,000	255,000		

	19–1	19–2	Analysis of changes Debit	Credit
	£	£	£	£
Fixed Assets (cost *less* depreciation)	100,000	120,000	20,000	
Investments	40,000	30,000		10,000
Stock	60,000	80,000	20,000	
Debtors	20,000	18,000		2,000
Cash	10,000	7,000		3,000
	230,000	255,000	55,000	55,000

Abridged Profit and Loss Account for the year ending 19–2

	£	£
Trading Profit		36,500
Less: Depreciation	6,000	
Loss on Sale of Investments	1,000	
Premium on Redemption of Debentures	1,500	8,500
		28,000
Add: Profit on Sale of Fixed Assets		2,000
Net Profit for the year		30,000
Profits brought forward from last year		15,000
		45,000
Dividends paid on Shares	15,000	
Transfer to General Reserve	10,000	
		25,000
Profits carried foward		20,000

The following transactions had taken place during the year:

1. 20,000 £1 shares were issued for cash at a price of £25,000.
2. £10,000 of Debentures were redeemed. The company had to pay the Debenture holders a premium of £1,500, which required a total payment of £11,500.
3. The Changes of Fixed Assets were as follows:

	Cost	Depreciation	Net
	£	£	£
Balance at 19–1	150,000	50,000	100,000
Add: Assets Bought	31,000	—	31,000
	181,000	50,000	131,000
Less: Assets Sold	21,000	16,000	5,000
Depreciation for the year	—	6,000	6,000
Balance at 19–2	160,000	40,000	120,000

4. Investments with a book value of £10,000 were sold at a loss of £1,000 for £9,000 cash.

Before setting out the Cash or Fund Flow Statement we should link together certain items which are shown separately in the accounts. For example, our initial analysis of change shows Share Capital £20,000 and Share Premium £5,000. We know from the first note that these can be added together and shown as the 'proceeds of issue of shares' £25,000.

Note 2 shows us that debentures of £10,000 were redeemed with the payment of a premium shown in Profit and Loss Account of £1,500. The total cash required was £11,500. Note 3 covers both additions and sales of fixed assets. The additions are shown as being £31,000 and the sales at book value £5,000, the net change is thus £26,000 at book value. This is the amount in the analysis of change statement £20,000 adjusted by £6,000 depreciation for the year. The Profit and Loss Account however shows that a profit on sale of fixed assets of £2,000 was made. Linking this with the book value of sales £5,000 indicates that the cash proceeds of sale were £7,000.

The Loss on Sale of Investments can similarly be linked with the change in book value of Investments of £10,000 showing cash proceeds from sale of £9,000.

Finally, the payment of Dividends should be shown separately from Profit and Loss, and the effect of the transfer to Reserves cancelled out.

The results of these adjustments are incorporated with our initial analysis of change statement as follows:

	Analysis of changes		Adjustments				Final Analysis of change	
	Debit	Credit		Debit		Credit	Debit	Credit
Share Capital		20,000			(A)	5,000	—	25,000
Share Premium		5,000	(A)	5,000			—	—
General Reserve		10,000	(F)	10,000			—	—
Profit and Loss		5,000	(D)	2,000	(C)	6,000		36,500
					(E)	1,000		
					(B)	1,500		
					(F)	10,000		
					(G)	15,000		
Dividends			(G)	15,000			15,000	
5 per cent Debentures	10,000		(B)	1,500			11,500	
Current Liabilities	5,000						5,000	
Fixed Assets	20,000		(C)	6,000	(D)	2,000	31,000	7,000
Investments		10,000	(E)	1,000				9,000
Stock	20,000						20,000	
Debtors		2,000						2,000
Cash		3,000						3,000
	55,000	55,000		40,500		40,500	82,500	82,500

Adjustments
A Share Premium
B Premium on Debenture Redemption
C Depreciation
D Profit on Sale of Fixed Assets
E Loss on Sale of Investments
F General Reserve
G Dividend

Expressed as (i) a Cash Flow Statement and (ii) a Fund Flow (Working Capital) Statement, this would be set out:

Economy Ltd

Cash Flow Statement for the year 19–2

	£	£
Sources of Cash:		
Sale of Shares at a premium of £5,000	25,000	
Contribution from Trading (including		
Depreciation £6,000)	36,500	
Sale of Fixed Assets (book value £5,000)	7,000	
Sale of Investments (book value £10,000)	9,000	
Reduction in Debtors	2,000	
		79,500
Uses of Cash:		
Redemption of Debentures at a premium		
of £1,500	11,500	
Purchases of Fixed Assets	31,000	
Payment of Dividends	15,000	
Increase in Stock	20,000	
Reduction in Current Liabilities	5,000	
		82,500
Reduction in Cash Balance		3,000

Economy Ltd

Fund Flow (Working Capital) Statement for the year 19–2

	£	£
Sources of Working Capital:		
Sale of Shares at a premium of £5,000	25,000	
Contribution from Trading (including		
Depreciation £6,000)	36,500	
Sale of Fixed Assets	7,000	
Sale of Investments	9,000	
		77,500
Applications of Working Capital:		
Redemption of Debentures at a premium of £1,500	11,500	
Purchase of Fixed Assets	31,000	
Payment of Dividends	15,000	
		57,500
Increase in Working Capital		20,000
Increase in Working Capital:		
Increase in Stock	20,000	
Reduction in Current Liabilities	5,000	
		25,000
Reductions in Working Capital:		
Reduction in Debtors	2,000	
Reduction in Cash	3,000	
		5,000
Net increase in Working Capital		20,000

In summary the adjustments made were:

Premiums or Discounts on Issues and Redemptions of Shares or Debentures were adjusted so that the actual cash proceeds of sale or cash paid out on redemption is shown.

Profits or Losses on Sales of Fixed Assets or Investments were shown with the change in book value to give cash proceeds of sale. Additions were shown at cost.

Transfers to Reserves were cancelled out, since the primary source of funds is trading profit.

The Depreciation adjustment to profit is often in practice shown on the face of the statement which we have done as a note in the example. Depreciation is sometimes even shown quite separately as a source of funds, this we do not agree with since quite clearly the primary source of funds is from Trading.

The Statement of Standard Accounting Practice Number Ten issued in July 1975 on Statements of source and application of funds had the objective of establishing the practice of providing these statements as a part of audited accounts and to lay down a minimum standard of disclosure. The Standard requires that the statement be produced for businesses unless the turnover or gross income is less than £25,000. The Standard does not give any special guidance on the layout of the statement and simply indicates the minimum amount of information to be included. This information is as follows:

1. The profit or loss for the period.

2. Adjustments for items not influencing funds, e.g. depreciation.

    And where material:

3. Dividends paid.

4. Acquisitions and disposals of fixed and other non-current assets.

5. Funds raised by increasing or expended in repaying or redeeming medium or long term loans or the issued capital of the company.

6. Increase or decrease in working capital sub-divided into its components and showing movements in net liquid funds as one component. Net liquid funds is defined as cash at bank and in hand, and cash equivalents (e.g. investments held as current assets) less bank overdrafts and other borrowings repayable in less than one year of the accounting date.

7. If the accounts are those of a group then the statement will be based on the consolidated group accounts.

The explanatory note to the standard suggests that a minimum of 'netting off' should take place so that major items of sales and purchases of assets be shown separately and not in an aggregated lump sum. It is also required that comparative figures for the previous period be shown.

The Fund Flow (Working Capital) Statement for Economy Ltd shown earlier would comply with the form of the Standard. The reduction in Cash would be shown under a sub heading 'Net liquid funds' but in this example reduction in cash is the only item.

Forecasting the Future

While the historical analyses described so far in this chapter can provide useful information, it will frequently be of far greater importance to project the fund flows into the future. Thus the firm will be in a position to predict probable shortages or surpluses of funds, so that proper action can be taken in good time. This is best done on a monthly basis; the fact that there will be £5,000 cash funds available in twelve months' time may cloak the fact that there will be a shortage of £7,000 of cash funds some time during the year.

The following simplified example illustrates the method of preparing a cash budget. The firm's requirements of cash can be seen to vary considerably from month to month by examining the balance of surplus cash or the deficit of cash.

Exhibit 45.5

King and Keen start business on 1 January 19–1. The following estimates are made covering the first year's operations:

Credit Sales £10,000 per month for the first 6 months, thereafter £15,000 per month.
Materials bought on credit £6,000 per month for the first 6 months, thereafter £9,000 per month.
Wages £1,500 per month.
General Overhead Expenses £1,000 per month.
Rent £2,400 per annum, payable quarterly in advance.

King and Keen expect to allow three months' credit to their customers, it being assumed that all receipts will be on the last day of the month in which they can be received.

They expect to pay their creditors on the last day of the month following that in which they bought the goods. All other payments are assumed to also be on the last day of each month. There are no stocks of materials or goods.

They start with £10,000 in the bank.

Figures in brackets indicate minus quantities, this being fairly normal practice in accounting. The calculation is shown in Exhibit 45.6.

The divergence between cash funds required and the net profit figure can be seen from the figures of net profit for each month shown at the bottom of the schedule, thus net profits and cash surpluses or deficits bear no resemblance to one another. For illustration, January's profit has been worked out as:

	£	£
Sales		10,000
Less Purchases	6,000	
Wages	1,500	
Overheads	1,000	
Rent (per month)	200	
		8,700
Net Profit for January		1,300

The year's profit would be:

Profit & Loss Account for the year ending 31 December

	£	£
Sales		150,000
Less Purchases	90,000	
Wages	18,000	
Overheads	12,000	
Rent	2,400	122,400
Net Profit for the year		27,600

It is interesting also to look at the Balance Sheet at the end of December, which will show:

	£
Opening Capital	10,000
Add Profit for the Year	27,600
	37,600
Current Assets:	
Debtors (3 × £15,000)	45,000
Cash	1,600
	46,600
Less Current Liabilities	
Creditors	9,000
	37,600

A Cash Flow Statement for the year starting from 1 January Balance Sheet:

Capital £10,000   Cash £10,000

will show the difference between Profit and the change in cash.

Sources & Applications of Cash for the year ending 31 December

	£
Sources:	
Trading Profit	27,600
Increase in creditors	9,000
	36,600
Applications:	
Increase in Trade Debtors	45,000
Reduction in Cash (£10,000−£1,600)	8,400

This does not in fact mean that neither the cash balance nor the net profit figure are useful pieces of information, but it does show the complementary nature of the two analyses. Having examined the cash budget for the year, King and Keen will be able to arrange further supplies of funds at the right time. They will also be able to demonstrate to the lenders that they expect to have the ability to repay the loans by the end of the year, when they hope to have a cash surplus of £1,600.

In more detailed examples the acquisition of capital and loans and the expenditure on fixed assets will be of great importance. Where, for example, a company is planning a major expansion, it is very desirable to be planning for it several years in advance, in order to take advantage of favourable times in the Capital Market for raising capital. Five-year forecasts for this purpose are quite common.

Exercises

Extra questions for this edition have been inserted as numbers 45.13, 45.14, 45.15A and 45.16A. Answers to 45.13 and 45.14 are to be found at the back of the book.

45.1. The Balance Sheets of a sole trader for two successive years are given below. You are required to calculate the variation in working capital and to explain how the variation has arisen.

Balance Sheets—as on 31 December

	19–3	19–4		19–3	19–4
	£	£		£	£
Capital Account:			Land and Premises		
1 January	4,200	4,700	(cost £3,000)	2,600	2,340
Add Net Profit for			Plant and Machinery		
the year	1,800	2,200	(cost £2,000)	1,500	—
			(cost £3,000)	—	2,300
	6,000	6,900	Stocks	660	630
Deduct Drawings	1,300	1,500	Trade Debtors	1,780	1,260
			Bank	—	710
	4,700	5,400			
Trade Creditors	1,200	840			
Bank Overdraft	640	—			
Loan (repayable					
December 1970)	—	1,000			
	6,540	7,240		6,540	7,240

(Union of Lancashire and Cheshire Institutes)

45.2. After studying his 19–4 audited Balance Sheet (see below), a trader is unable to understand why, 'despite the fact that I have made a loss for that year (as compared with a profit for the previous year) and that my personal drawings are higher than in 19–3, my bank balance nevertheless shows a considerable increase over the year 19–4'.

You are asked to prepare for the trader a numerical statement based upon the Balance Sheet figures for 19–3 and 19–4, which shows why his accounting loss for 19–4 is £640.

19–3 Figures £	£	Capital	£	19–3 Figures £	19–3 Figures £	£	Fixed Assets	£	£
9,330		Opening Balance		9,300	4,980		At Cost, 1 Jan		6,730
1,340	(Profit)	Loss for Year		(640)	1,750		Additions in year		2,800
10,670				8,660	6,730				9,530
1,370		*Less* Drawings		1,810	1,927		*Less* Depreciation		2,880
9,300				6,850	4,803				6,650
1,000		Loan Current Liabilities:		2,500			Current Assets:		
		Sundry Creditors				3,960	Stocks	2,340	
	1,633		2,960			3,820	Debtors	1,960	
	620	Bank Overdraft	—			—	Bank	1,360	
2,283				2,960	7,780				5,660
12,583				12,310	12,583				12,310

(Chartered Institute of Secretaries and Administrators)

45.3. The Managing Director of your company is very perplexed as to the reasons why the firm's bank balance has fallen over the last year. You are to prepare a statement of sources and disposition of funds to help you explain the reasons to him.

The balances from the books were as follows:

	1 Janaury 19–5	31 December 19–5
	£	£
Ordinary Share Capital	300,000	350,000
General Reserve	120,000	140,000
Profit on Sale of Motor Vehicles		6,000
Profit and Loss Account:		
Balance brought forward	65,500	65,500
Profit for the year, after taxation, proposed dividend and transfer to general reserve		89,600
Debentures	50,000	200,000
Taxation	32,000	44,000
Proposed Dividend (19–4)	21,000	(19–5) 17,500
Creditors	174,000	65,200
	762,500	977,800

	£	£	£	£
Freehold Premises		220,000		235,000
Plant (at cost)	189,000		218,000	
Less Depreciation to date	75,000		91,000	
		114,000		127,000
Motor Vehicles (at cost)	45,000		51,000	
Less Depreciation to date	29,000		26,000	
		16,000		25,000
Investments (at cost)		115,000		180,000
Stock		35,500		69,900
Work in Progress		29,000		44,000
Debtors		114,500		294,600
Bank		118,000		2,000
Cash		500		300
		762,500		977,800

You also have access to the following information:

1. In the year motors costing £18,000 which had been depreciated by £11,000 were sold for £13,000.
2. Taxation paid during the year amounted to £29,000.

45.4. From the following information you are to prepare a statement of sources and application of funds (working capital).

Engineers Ltd

Comparative Balance Sheets at ...

(thousands of pounds)		31 December 19–1		31 December 19–2
	£	£	£	£
Share Capital—Ordinary shares		3,927		4,110
Revenue Reserves:				
General Reserve		621		639
Profit and Loss Account		12,186		13,332
6 per cent Debentures		1,587		1,659
Current Liabilities		3,417		3,774
		21,738		23,514
	£	£	£	£
Plant and Machinery	18,558		20,001	
Less Accumulated Depreciation	10,044		10,968	
		8,514		9,033
Goodwill, Patents, etc.		363		384
Investments (Long Term)		1,509		1,656
Current Assets:				
Cash		1,203		1,260
Other Current Assets		10,149		11,181
		21,738		23,514

*Trading and Profit and Loss Account for the year ended
31 December 19–2*

	£	£
Sales		38,208
Dividends for Investments		168
Other Income		234
		38,610
Less Expenses	31,332	
Depreciation	1,164	
Taxation	3,237	
		35,733
Net Profit		2,877
Add brought forward from last year		12,186
		15,063
Less Dividends		1,731
Balance carried forward		13,332

Plant and Machinery costing £300,000 with a written down value of £60,000 was sold for £90,000.

An investment in a subsidiary company was sold for £27,000. It had cost £9,000.

45.5. The following is a summary of the Trading and Profit and Loss Accounts of Blakes Ltd for the six months to 31 May 19–6 and a Balance Sheet as at that date:

Trading and Profit and Loss Account

	£		£
Stock	13,600	Sales	72,000
Purchases	55,980	Stock	11,980
Gross Profit	14,400		
	83,980		83,980
Wages and Salaries	5,800	Gross Profit	14,400
Administration expenses	3,600		
Net Profit	5,000		
	14,400		14,400

Balance Sheet

	£		£
Issued Share Capital		Fixed Assets	9,000
(Ordinary £1 shares)	10,000	Stock	11,980
Profit and Loss Account	15,070	Debtors	9,600
Trade Creditors	9,330	Bank	4,420
Administration Expenses			
outstanding	600		
	35,000		35,000

At a meeting of the directors the following forward projections for the six months to 30 November 19–6 were agreed to:

1.   Rate of gross profit to be reduced from 20 per cent to $16\frac{2}{3}$ per cent of Sales. The period of credit is to be increased from one month to two months, and it is expected that every customer will pay for the goods two months after the date of sale. It is expected that sales will be increased from £12,000 to £18,000 each calendar month.

2.   It is assumed that Blakes Ltd will pay for all purchases one month after purchase. The stock is to be increased to £20,000 by the end of September and is to remain at that figure.

3.   Wages and Salaries will be £1,100 per calendar month payable each month.

4.   Administration expenses will be £720 per calendar month, and it is expected that on the last day of each month there will be one month's expenses owing.

Exhibit 45.6

King and Keen
Cash Budget for the year ended 31 December 19-1

	Jan	Feb	Mar	Apl	May	Jun	Jul	Aug	Sept	Oct	Nov	Dec
Cash Sources:												
Collections from Debtors	—	—	—	10,000	10,000	10,000	10,000	10,000	10,000	15,000	15,000	15,000
Cash Uses:												
Payments to Creditors	—	6,000	6,000	6,000	6,000	6,000	6,000	9,000	9,000	9,000	9,000	9,000
Wages	1,500	1,500	1,500	1,500	1,500	1,500	1,500	1,500	1,500	1,500	1,500	1,500
Overheads	1,000	1,000	1,000	1,000	1,000	1,000	1,000	1,000	1,000	1,000	1,000	1,000
Rent	600			600			600			600		
	3,100	8,500	8,500	9,100	8,500	8,500	9,100	11,500	11,500	12,100	11,500	11,500
Opening Cash Balances at start of each month	10,000	6,900	(1,600)	(10,100)	(9,200)	(7,700)	(6,200)	(5,300)	(6,800)	(8,300)	(5,400)	(1,900)
+ Cash Sources	—	—	—	10,000	10,000	10,000	10,000	10,000	10,000	15,000	15,000	15,000
− Cash Uses	3,100	8,500	8,500	9,100	8,500	8,500	9,100	11,500	11,500	12,100	11,500	11,500
Closing Cash Balances at end of each month												
(A) If a Surplus	6,900											1,600
(B) If a Deficit		(1,600)	(10,100)	(9,200)	(7,700)	(6,200)	(5,300)	(6,800)	(8,300)	(5,400)	(1,900)	
Net Profit for each month	1,300	1,300	1,300	1,300	1,300	1,300	3,300	3,300	3,300	3,300	3,300	3,300

5.   The firm is to issue 5,000 Ordinary shares in September at a premium of 25 per cent payable in full on application. The issue is expected to be a success.

6.   Further finance is expected to be by bank overdraft. All sums received are to be paid into the bank and all payments made by cheque. No discounts will be received or allowed.

You are required to prepare a summary of the company's bank account for the six months, the Trading and Profit and Loss Account for the same period and a summary of the Balance Sheet as at the last day. Depreciate Fixed Assets at the rate of 10 per cent per annum.

45.6. Decanters Ltd was incorporated on 1 December 19–6. It is proposed to commence a trading business on 1 January 19–7 and the following plans and estimates for the six months to 30 June 19–7 have been made:

1.   On 1 January the company will acquire buildings at a cost of £40,000, machinery at a cost of £22,000 and fixtures at a cost of £4,000.

2.   Sales will be £50,000 in each month. The gross profit will be at a uniform rate of 30 per cent of selling price.

3.   Overhead expenses will amount to £9,600 in each month except March, when they will amount to £15,000. All expenses are to be paid on the last day of the month in which they are incurred.

4.   An initial stock of goods is to be bought on 1 January at a cost of £12,000, and subsequent purchasing is to be so arranged that the stock at the end of each month will amount to exactly £12,000 (at cost price).

5.   Trade creditors will be paid on the last day of the month in which the goods are bought. Payments for all sales will be received on the last day of the month after that in which the goods are sold.

6.   On 1 January the company will issue, at par, the minimum number of ordinary shares (to be paid up in full on that day) required to ensure that, on the basis of the above plans and estimates, the company will not borrow money at any time during the six months to 30 June 19–7.

You are required:

(a)   to prepare a summary of the company's bank account for each month and a trading and profit and loss account for the six months to 30 June 19–7.
(b)   a Balance Sheet as on 30 June 19–7 as they would appear if the company's transactions were in accordance with the above plans and estimates.

Note:
Ignore taxation and depreciation of fixed assets.

45.7A. The Balance Sheet of Haltman Ltd contained the following information:

	31 March 19–2	31 March 19–1
	£	£
Ordinary Shares	60,000	60,000
Preference Shares	24,000	—
Profit and Loss Account	45,600	36,000
Proposed Dividend	12,000	12,000
Taxation	14,880	13,600
Bank	4,800	—
Creditors	14,400	12,000
	175,680	133,600
Freehold Land and Buildings	65,280	16,000
Plant and Machinery	57,600	41,600
Stock	33,600	40,800
Debtors	19,200	24,000
Bank	—	11,200
	175,680	133,600

The Profit and Loss Account information is as follows:

	£	£
Trading Profit		240,000
Cost of Sales		153,600
		86,400
Expenses	40,000	
Depreciation:		
Plant and Machinery	8,000	
		48,000
		38,400
Taxation		14,880
		23,520
Preference Dividend	1,920	
Proposed Ordinary Dividend (20 per cent)	12,000	
		13,920
		9,600

You are required to prepare a Statement of Fund Flow (Working Capital) showing the sources from which funds became available and the way in which those funds have been used.

45.8A. Summarized balance sheets of Gryphon Ltd, for the year ended 31 December 19–1 and 31 December 19–2, appear below:

	19–1	19–2		19–1	19–2
	£	£		£	£
Share Capital	300,000	450,000	Buildings	300,000	300,000
Capital Reserves	150,000	—	Cash	43,440	4,860
Profit and Loss a/c	81,780	106,260	Debtors	86,100	98,300
Corporation Tax (future)	52,500	42,660	Plant*	189,600	222,960
Corporation Tax (current)	49,800	52,500	Stock	75,540	84,700
Creditors	60,600	59,400			
	694,680	710,820		694,680	710,820

*Movements on Plant Account.

	Cost	Depreciation	Net book value
	£	£	£
Balance at 31 December 19–1	327,000	137,400	189,600
Add Purchases			
Depreciation for the year	72,960	32,700	40,260
	399,960	170,100	229,860
Less Sales	65,400	58,500	6,900
Balance at 31 December 19–2	334,560	111,600	222,960

A profit of £12,000 on the sales of plant had been credited to the profit and loss account.

Account in as much detail as possible for the change in the cash balance between 31 December 19–1 and 31 December 19–2.

45.9A. The draft balance sheet and revenue account in respect of the year ended 31 March 19–2, together with comparative figures for the previous year, for the Z Co Ltd, are as shown below:

	31 March 19–1		31 March 19–2	
	£	£	£	£
Issued Share Capital:				
Ordinary Shares £1 each		75,000		100,000
Reserves:				
General	7,500		10,000	
Profit and Loss Account	14,500		21,000	
		22,000		31,000
		97,000		131,000

	31 March 19–1		31 March 19–2	
	£	£	£	£
Represented by:				
Fixed Assets		94,000		101,500
Additions		7,500		38,000
		101,500		139,500
Depreciation		9,000		15,000
		92,500		124,500
Current Assets:				
Stock	17,500		21,000	
Debtors	9,250		10,800	
Cash in hand	75		90	
Balance at Bank	3,025		4,910	
	29,850		36,800	
Less Current Liabilities:				
Trade Creditors	12,000		12,900	
Taxation	5,850		7,400	
Proposed Dividend	7,500		10,000	
		4,500		6,500
	25,350		30,300	
		97,000		131,000

Profit and Loss Account for year ended 31 March 19–2

	£	£
Trading Profit		26,400
After charging:		
Directors' Emoluments	16,000	
Depreciation	6,000	
Audit Fee	450	
Taxation		7,400
Profit After Taxation		19,000
Balance brought forward from 31 March 19–1		14,500
		33,500
Transfer to General Reserve	2,500	
Proposed Dividend 10 per cent (Gross)	10,000	
		12,500
		21,000

You are required to prepare:

(a) A Funds Statement (Working Capital),
(b) A Sources and Application of Cash Funds Statement for the year ended 31 March 19–2.

Buxton Ltd
Comparative Balance Sheets

	31 December 19–3	31 December 19–2
	£'(000)	£'(000)
Fixed Assets	1,400	960
Accumulated Depreciation	(240)	(180)
Inventories	880	720
Accounts Receivable	240	320
Provision for Doubtful Debts	(12)	(6)
Cash	120	102
	2,388	1,916
Ordinary Share Capital	1,800	1,200
Undistributed Profits	308	236
Taxation	100	120
Accounts Payable	180	360
	2,388	1,916

Income Statement, 19–3

Sales	1,600	
Investment Income	20	
Profit on Sale of Machine (1)	4	
		1,624
Operating Expenses and Taxes (2)		912
Net Profit for Year		712
Undistributed Profits Brought Forward		236
		948
Dividends	240	
Bonus issue of shares, one for every three held	400	
		640
Undistributed Profits Carried Forward		308

1. Machine sold for cash. It had cost £10,000, and its net book value at the time of sale was £4,000.

2. Includes depreciation, £66,000, and write-off of obsolete stocks, £8,000.

TAX   88 000.

Required:

- (a) Schedules of changes in working capital and Statement of Sources and Application of Funds for the year 19–3.
- (b) The Chairman of Buxton Ltd has asked you why cash has increased by only £18,000 during the year, while the net profit was £712,000. Briefly outline your answer to him.

45.11A. Mr Bode is considering setting up business to manufacture 'Grommits' and asks your advice on the financial implications of the proposal. He supplies you with the following information:

1.   He has £9,000 to invest in the business. His bank is willing to grant him an interest-free overdraft of up to £45,000.

2.   He will have to buy equipment costing £9,000 immediately he commences business. He will be required to pay £6,000 on delivery and the balance at the end of the third month. The equipment is expected to last five years.

3.   Each Grommit will require one pound (weight) of raw materials costing £0·75. Sufficient material will be purchased at the beginning of each month for the month's production; in addition, a reserve stock of 300 lb will be bought at the start and held throughout. The supplier will require payment in the month of purchase.

4.   The wage rate will be £1·20 per hour and each Grommit takes a man two hours to make. Wages will be paid in the month in which they are incurred.

5.   Production will commence immediately and sufficient Grommits will be produced each month for the following month's sales. They will be sold at £3·60 each and demand is expected to be:

	Units
Month 2	4,500
Month 3 and subsequent months	5,000

6.   Customers will be given one month's credit so that all sales in Month 2, for example, should be paid for by the end of Month 3.

7.   Other business expenses will be £1,500 a month, payable in the month in which they are incurred.

8.   Mr Bode will work full-time in the business. He plans to withdraw £300 cash each month for personal expenses.

Required:

(*a*)   A cash budget for the first four months clearly showing, month by month, the maximum overdraft required.

(*b*)   Briefly consider the profitability of Mr Bode's business.

45.12A. You intend to form a small limited company to manufacture a standard article. The initial finance will be provided by the sale of 80,000 £1 Ordinary Shares to yourself and fellow directors.

You will pay for 40,000 of the Shares in April, and the remainder will be received from your co-directors in May, £20,000, and in June, £20,000. Trading would commence on 1 April.

You approach the bank to enquire about overdraft facilities and are told that the bank will grant up to £48,000. If this amount is insufficient for the company's requirements you are prepared to make an interest-free loan of £20,000 but this must be repaid by the following 31 March.

You have made the following estimates and forecasts:

1.   the company will take a 5-year lease on an empty warehouse at an initial premium of £8,000 paid on 1 April, at a quarterly rental of £1,200 in advance payable on 1 April, and thereafter every quarter;

2. machinery would be obtained as under:

(a) costing £60,000 purchased in April, allowed two months to pay;

(b) deposit of £32,000 paid in April on machinery costing £88,000. Balance payable by four equal instalments on 1 April, together with interest at 10 per cent per annum on the balance outstanding since the last instalment was paid;

(c) costing £40,000 purchased in January to cope with anticipated increase in sales. One month's credit allowed;

(d) 10 per cent per annum depreciation to be charged for a full year on any plant in use at 31 March;

3. production will be 8,000 units per month until 31 December. In January, 9,600 units will be made and 12,000 per month thereafter. Production costs will be £8 each unit for materials and £4 each for wages and other variable expenses;

4. material suppliers will allow two months' credit on the first three months' supplies but thereafter will grant only one months' credit;

5. variable expenses will be paid for as they are incurred;

6. stocks, assumed to be all in a finished state, will be maintained at 20 per cent of the month's production—all stocks being cleared in the following month— and will be valued at £12 per unit;

7. fixed expenses will be £100,000 per annum, £8,000 paid monthly one month in arrear, the balance payable after the year end;

8. each article will sell for £20 per unit, customers paying during the month next but one following the month in which the sale is made. For sales made in January and subsequently 5 per cent cash discount will be allowed to customers paying within the month following sale and it is expected that half of the customers will take advantage of this. In addition, as from 31 January, selling price per unit will be reduced to £18 in attempt to boost sales;

9. it is assumed that all production not required to maintain stock levels will be sold in the month in which it is produced;

10. an interim dividend of 10 per cent will be paid on 31 December.

Required:

(a) A statement showing whether sufficient finance will be available, throughout the first year's trading, to meet the company's cash requirements, showing the month in which most finance will be needed;

(b) the estimated income statement and balance sheet at the end of the first year's trading.

N.B. All calculations in complete months and to nearest £.

Extra Questions for the Third Edition

45.13. The balance sheets of Boswell Ltd at 31 March 19–2 and 31 March 19–3, appear below:

	31 March			31 March	
	19–2	*19–3*		*19–2*	*19–3*
	£	£		£	£
Issued share capital	30,000	40,000	Freehold property,		
Profit and loss a/c	27,000	23,000	at cost	25,000	25,000
Corporation tax due:			Equipment (see note)	18,000	22,200
1 January 1973	6,000	—	Stock-in-trade	16,400	17,800
1 January 1974	—	4,000	Debtors	13,600	14,000
Creditors	12,000	13,000	Bank	2,000	1,000
	75,000	80,000		75,000	80,000

Note:
Equipment movements during the year ended 31 March 19–3 were:

	Cost	Depreciation	Net
	£	£	£
Balance at 31 March 19–2	30,000	12,000	18,000
Additions during year	9,000		
Depreciation provided during year		3,800	
	39,000	15,800	
Disposals during year	4,000	3,000	
Balance at 31 March 19–3	35,000	12,800	22,200

The company's summarized profit calculation for the year ended 31 March 19–3 revealed:

		£
Sales		100,000
Gain on sale of equipment		400
		100,400
Less		
cost of goods and trading expenses	86,600	
depreciation	3,800	
		90,400
Net profit		10,000
Corporation tax on profits of the year		4,000
Retained profit of the year		6,000

During the year ended 31 March 19–3 Boswell Ltd made a bonus issue of 10,000 £1 ordinary shares by capitalization from the profit and loss account.

Required:
A flow of funds statement for Boswell Ltd revealing the sources and applications of working capital during the year ended 31 March 19–3.

(Institute of Bankers)

45.14. D. Ltd intends to commence business as a retailer on 1 January 19–4. Initial requirements are expected to be fittings and equipment £500, and stocks £4,500. Goods are expected to be sold at 33⅓ per cent above cost. Expected sales are £3,000 per month for the first two months and £4,000 per month for remaining ten months. Three months' credit will be allowed on sales, and one month's credit is expected from suppliers of goods and equipment. Monthly expenses paid out in cash will be £800. This does not include exceptional expense items of £100 which will be paid in February and August. Stock will be replaced in full the month after materials are used.

You are required to:

(a) estimate the capital requirements of D. Ltd with the aid of a projected cash statement for 19–4. (Assume that an initial amount of £9,000 can be raised in the form of ordinary share capital, and any additional funds can be obtained in the form of a bank overdraft.)

(b) prepare a projected Profit Statement and Balance Sheet for 19–4. (Fittings and equipment depreciation is to be calculated at 20 per cent per annum, and taxation at 50 per cent of net profit.)

(c) comment on the projected results for 19–4. (The Managing Director of D. Ltd considers that a satisfactory return on capital is 10 per cent after interest and taxation.)

(*Certified Accountants*)

45.15A. The following statements are reproduced from the published accounts of two companies, Alpha and Beta.

Alpha Ltd

	19–4	19–3
	£s000	£s000
Source and Application of Group Funds		
Source of Funds		
Profit before taxation	3,241	2,662
Less: Profit of associated company	15	46
	3,226	2,616
Surplus on sale of goodwill, patents and trade marks	—	60
Depreciation	660	551
Sale of fixed assets	61	61
Government grants	26	6
	3,973	3,294
Application of Funds		
Capital expenditure	1,588	974
Additional working capital	1,297	1,026
Taxation	1,154	662
Dividends	531	279
	4,570	2,941

	19–4	19–3
	£s000	£s000
Source and Application of Group Funds		
Unrealized gains (loss)es arising from changes in exchange rates	73	153
	4,497	2,788
Increase (Decrease) in Group Funds	(524)	506

Note:
Group funds comprise bank and short term deposits, less short term borrowings.

Beta Ltd

	19–4	19–3
	£s000	£s000
Sources and Application of Group Funds		
Sources of Funds		
Retained profit (including minority interests)	5,866	9,248
Depreciation	15,214	18,319
Deferred tax	2,302	2,645
Internal cash flow	23,382	30,212
Loan capital	(774)	15,024
Bank overdrafts and loans repayable within one year	8,715	2,997
Increases in capital and share premium	1,515	—
Other	(951)	19
	31,887	48,252
Application of Funds		
Expenditure on fixed assets (net)	23,908	25,145
Increase in working capital	3,183	16,548
Increase in investments	2,864	5,059
Goodwill arising on acquisitions	1,932	1,500
	31,887	48,252

You are required to discuss critically and constructively these two statements having due regard for Statement of Standard Accounting Practice No. 10 (statement of source and application of funds). Your answer should deal with both presentation and interpretation.

(Institute of Chartered Accountants)

45.16A On 31 March 19–5 the Balance Sheet of Schubert Ltd, retailers of musical instruments, was as follows:

	£		£	£
Ordinary shares of £1 each		Equipment at cost	2,000	
fully paid	2,000	*Less* depreciation	500	
Unappropriated profit	1,000			1,500
Trade creditors	4,000	Stock		2,000
Proposed ordinary dividend	1,500	Trade debtors		1,500
		Balance at bank		3,500
	8,500			8,500

The company is developing a system of forward planning and on 1 April 19–5 supplies the following information:

1.

Month	Credit sales	Cash sales	Credit purchases
	£	£	£
March 19–5 (actual)	1,500	1,400	4,000
April 19–5 (budgeted)	1,800	500	2,300
May 19–5 (budgeted)	2,000	600	2,700
June 19–5 (budgeted)	2,500	800	2,600

2. All trade debtors are allowed one month's credit and are expected to settle promptly; the trade creditors are paid in the month following delivery.

3. On 1 April 19–5 all the equipment was replaced at a cost of £3,000; £1,400 was allowed on the old equipment and a net payment made of £1,600. Depreciation is to be provided at the rate of 10 per cent per annum.

4. The proposed dividend will be paid in June 19–5.

5. The following expenses will be paid:
   Wages £300 per month
   Administration £150 per month
   Rent £360 for year to 31 March 19–6 (to be paid in April 19–5).

6. The gross profit percentage on sales is estimated at 25 per cent.

   You are required to:

(a) prepare a cash budget for each of the months April, May and June 19–5,
(b) prepare a budgeted Trading and Profit and Loss Account for the three months ended 30 June 19–5, and
(c) explain the reasons for the difference between budgeted profitability and budgeted liquidity for the period.

(Institute of Chartered Accountants)

46

Discounting Techniques

This chapter is an introduction to those areas of business decision where interest is an important item for consideration. Interest is the charge for borrowing money or the return from lending it. In more general terms since money can be freely borrowed or lent it may be considered as the cost of using or holding money. Since interest charges vary with time it follows that the interest factor will be important when deciding on things involving money flows spread out over periods of time.

Few people would hesitate if offered £1,000 now or £1,000 in twelve months' time to accept £1,000 now. However, if the offer was £900 now, or £1,000 at the end of twelve months, the decision might well be different. The increment of £100 in the year is equivalent to interest of 11·1 per cent on the capital sum of £900. If the recipient could obtain a return of more than 11·1 per cent he would be wise to take the £900 immediately. If, however, he were unable to find an outlet at a higher rate of interest he may well be advised to take £1,000 at the end of the year.

As in other areas of accountancy the problem of uncertainty plays an important part in decisions where the interest factor is concerned. Many of the decisions which have to be made involve areas which cannot be precisely calculated. Forecasts of future cash flows from profits for example, or the future trends of interest rates, can never be exact. For this reason it is frequently argued that detailed calculations involving interest are a waste of time. While it is fair to say that the results given by the processes described in this chapter can never be more accurate than the information on which they are based, they do give a logical decision based on the facts as presented.

In order to understand the basis on which interest calculations are made, a brief summary is included in the chapter covering the more important formulae for the calculation of interest.

Simple Interest

Simple interest is the return on a capital sum for one period of time. In practice, simple interest rarely applies other than for short periods of one year or less. Expressed as a formula simple interest (Is) is

$$Is = P \times r \times t$$

where P is the amount of the principal capital sum, $r =$ the rate of interest, $t =$ the length of time.

Example. £200 invested for six months at 5 per cent per annum

$$Is = 200 \times \tfrac{5}{100} \times \tfrac{6}{12} = £5$$

The total amount of the principal capital sum plus interest identified as A can be expressed by adapting the formula:

$$A = P + (Prt)$$

or

$$A = P(1 + rt)$$

Example. What amount would £200 invested at 5 per cent per annum accumulate to at the end of six months?

$$A = 200 \left[1 + (\tfrac{5}{100} \times \tfrac{6}{12})\right] = £205$$

Present Value

By adapting the formula again it is possible to calculate the present value of a future sum where a given rate of interest is earned on the money. Present value is a term used widely in the context of this chapter and means the value at the present moment of future sums of money after allowing for interest. In our simple interest calculation the principal capital sum is the same as the present value. The present value is the principal capital sum which if it were invested now would accumulate at the given interest rate to the future amount which we have called A. The present value will, of course, be worth less than the future amount.

Since

$$A = P(1 + rt)$$
$$P = \frac{A}{(1 + rt)}$$

Example. You have the prospect of receiving £205 at the end of six months. What is the present value of this money if the current rate of interest is 5 per cent per annum?

$$P = \frac{205}{[1 + (\tfrac{5}{100} \times \tfrac{6}{12})]}$$
$$P = £200$$

Compound Interest

Compound interest is the return on, or increase in, a capital sum for more than one time period, assuming that at the end of each time period the return or increase (i.e. interest) is added to the capital sum at the end of that time period and earns a return in all subsequent periods.

Example. What would £100 invested at 5 per cent per annum compound interest accumulate to at the end of three years?

Using the simple formula developed previously:

$$P (1+r \times t) = A$$
End of Year 1 £100 $(1+0\cdot05\times1) = £105$
End of Year 2 £105 $(1+0\cdot05\times1) = £110\cdot25$
End of Year 3 £110·25 $(1+0\cdot05\times1) = £115\cdot7625$

Expressing the above calculations as a general formula would show:

End of Year 1	$P(1+rt)$
End of Year 2	$P(1+rt)(1+rt)$ or $P(1+rt)^2$
End of Year 3	$P(1+rt)(1+rt)(1+rt)$ or $P(1+rt)^3$

If n is taken as the number of periods during which the principal sum accumulates at interest and instead of using rt we use i as the rate of interest per time period, the compound interest formula can be written $A = P(1+i)^n$ (*note:* if the rate of interest is 5 per cent per annum and the time period is for three months $i = 5$ per cent $\times \frac{3}{12} = 1\cdot25$ per cent and $n = 3$).

Example. What would £500 invested at 6 per cent per annum accumulate to at the end of two years?

$$A = P(1+i)^n = 500(1+0\cdot06)^2 = £561\cdot8$$

In order to simplify calculations tables are available which show the amount to which £1 will accumulate at given rates of interest for different periods of time.

An example of a compound interest table is shown below and a more extensive one in the Appendix to this book. The figures shown by the tables can be checked as follows:

Example. To what amount would £1 accumulate in three years at 4 per cent per annum?

$$A = 1(1+0\cdot04)^3 = 1\cdot1249$$

Compound Sum of £1

Year	1%	2%	3%	4%	5%	6%	7%	8%	9%	10%
1	1·010	1·020	1·030	1·040	1·050	1·060	1·070	1·080	1·090	1·100
2	1·020	1·040	1·061	1·082	1·102	1·124	1·145	1·166	1·188	1·210
3	1·030	1·061	1·093	1·125	1·158	1·191	1·225	1·260	1·295	1·331
4	1·041	1·082	1·126	1·170	1·216	1·262	1·311	1·360	1·412	1·464
5	1·051	1·104	1·159	1·217	1·276	1·338	1·403	1·469	1·539	1·611

Reading from the table the figure shown against year 3 under the 4 per cent column is 1·125 (note that these tables are rounded to three places of decimals). This figure can be employed as a multiplier to calculate any required sums invested for three years at 4 per cent. Thus £400 for three years at 4 per cent would be—

$$£400 \times 1 \cdot 125 = £450$$

Present Value

As an extension of the basic formula it will often be important to know the present value of a future sum of money which has been invested at a given rate of compound interest for a known number of periods.

Since we know that

$$A = P \, (1+i)^n$$

then

$$P = \frac{A}{(1+i)^n}$$

Tables are commonly available to show the present value of an amount of £1 at various rates of interest over given periods of time. An example is included in the Appendix.

Example. Find the present value of £1,500 due at the end of four years at 6 per cent per annum interest:

$$P = \frac{A}{(1+i)^n} = \frac{1,500}{(1+0 \cdot 06)^4} = £1,188 \cdot 12$$

or using the tables

$$£1,500 \times 0 \cdot 792 = £1,188$$

This result can be tested by working out what sum £1,188 would accumulate to over four years at 6 per cent. The answer should be £1,500.

$$A = P \, (1+i) \; = 1,188 \cdot 12 \, (1+0 \cdot 06)^4 = £1,500$$

or using tables

$$£1,188 \times 1 \cdot 262 = £1,500$$

Annuities

An annuity is a series, or one of a series, of equal payments at fixed intervals. For example, rent payable every month, quarter or year, is one form of annuity. The term annuity originated in the field of insurance where in exchange for a lump sum payment or a series of premiums a regular payment would be made to the annuitant during his life. Regular payments such as rents or purchase by instalments occur frequently in business and it is, therefore, useful to know something about the calculation of annuities.

In practice there are a number of different kinds of annuity varying mainly in the details of when the regular payments are made, for example at the beginning or end of the period. In this chapter attention is centred entirely on the Ordinary Annuity in which the equal periodic payments occur at the end of the period. In practice, with a little thought it will be possible to handle most situations with a knowledge of how to calculate an Ordinary Annuity.

Formula for the Amount of an Ordinary Annuity

The amount of an annuity of £1 per period for three periods at 5 per cent interest might be determined as follows:

The first rent payment of £1 accumulates at 5 per cent interest for two periods and grows to:
$$£1 (1+0·05)^2 = £1·1025$$

The second rent payment of £1 accumulates at 5 per cent interest for one period and grows to: £1·05

The third rent is due at the end of the annuity period £1·00

These add up to £3·1525

To develop the formula for the annuity we need to examine the relationship between compound interest, and an annuity of the amount of the interest. If £1 is invested for two periods at 5 per cent interest we have shown above that it will accumulate to £1·1025. Deducting the original investment from this amount we are left with the compound interest on £1 for two periods as £0·1025. This amount is simply the amount of an annuity of 5 per cent of £1 for two periods at 5 per cent.

This can be set down as:
$$0·05 \times \text{Annuity} = 1 (1+0·05)^2 - 1$$
or
$$\text{Annuity} = 1 \frac{(1+0·05)^2 - 1}{0·05} = \frac{(1·05)^2 - 1}{0·05}$$

Substituting generalized letters into the formula
$$\text{Annuity} = R \frac{(1+i)^n - 1}{i}$$

Where R = the annuity per period.

As in previous examples tables are available calculated on the basis of £1 to assist calculations; see the Appendix.

Example. A company plans to invest £1,000 at the end of the year for each of the next five years at an interest rate of 5 per cent per annum. How much will have accumulated at the end of the fifth year?

$$£1,000 \frac{(1+0·05)^5 - 1}{·05} = £5,525·631$$

or using tables

$$£1,000 \times 5·526 = £5,526$$

It will frequently be useful to know the amount required by way of periodic rents to accumulate to a known future sum, for example when establishing a sinking fund.

It has already been established that where the amount of an annuity $= A$

$$A = R\frac{(1+i)^n - 1}{i}$$

$$R = \frac{Ai}{(1+i-)^n 1)}$$

Example. A company wishes to set aside equal annual amounts at the end of each year of the next four years, to accumulate to a fund of £5,000 for the replacement of assets. The amounts set aside will be invested at 6 per cent per annum interest. What amounts should be set aside?

$$R = \frac{Ai}{(1+i)^n - 1} = \frac{5,000\,(0 \cdot 06)}{(1 \cdot 06)^4 - 1} = £1,142 \cdot 9578$$

This figure can be proved correct by the table below worked (as would be normal) to the nearest £1.

	Deposit £	Interest £	Increase in fund £	Balance of fund £
End of year 1	1,143	—	1,143	1,143
End of year 2	1,143	69	1,212	2,355
End of year 3	1,143	141	1,284	3,639
End of year 4	1,143	218	1,361	5,000

If reference is made to Chapter 29 a table has been prepared showing the amounts required to be set aside annually to accumulate to an amount of £1. This can be proved by using the formula.

Example. What amount invested annually at 5 per cent per annum will provide £1 in five years time?

$$R = \frac{Ai}{(1+i)^n - 1} = \frac{1\,(0 \cdot 05)}{(1 \cdot 05)^5 - 1} = £0 \cdot 180975 \text{ (as per table)}$$

The Present Value of Annuities

It will often be necessary to calculate the present value of an annuity to evaluate a business problem. The present value of an annuity is the amount which if it were invested now at compound interest would be just sufficient to allow for the withdrawal of equal amounts (rents) at the end of a fixed number of periods. For example, we may wish to know whether to pay £135 cash now for a television or five instalments of £30 over the next two-and-a-half years instead. By converting the five instalments to a present cash value we can make direct comparison with the £135 cash price. If the present value of the annuity is more than £135 we should choose to pay cash. If, however, it comes to less than £135 the instalment method is cheaper. The result obtained will depend on the rate of interest used in the calculation.

The present value of an annuity will be equal to the sum of the present values of every individual rent payment. This can be illustrated in the above example, assuming an 8 per cent rate of interest. The calculation shows it better at this rate of interest to pay by instalment.

Period	£		Present Value Multiplier from Tables		£
1	30	×	0·962	=	28·86
2	30	×	0·925	=	27·75
3	30	×	0·889	=	26·67
4	30	×	0·855	=	25·65
5	30	×	0·822	=	24·66
					133·59

(*Note:* when taking a half-yearly period the annual rate of interest is halved. The multiplier is therefore from the 4 per cent column of the Present Value tables.)

The formula for finding the present value of an ordinary annuity is developed as follows:

Compound discount (equivalent to compound interest) is the amount by which the total investment at compound interest will exceed the original capital. On the basis of £1:

$$\text{Discount} = 1 - \frac{1}{(1+i)^n}$$

By the same process of argument that was used when developing the formula for an ordinary annuity, it can be shown that the compound discount on £1 at 5 per cent is equal to 5 per cent of the present value of an annuity of £1. Thus

$$i \times \text{Present Value} = 1 - \frac{1}{(1+i)^n}$$

$$\text{Present Value} = \left[\frac{1 - \frac{1}{(1+i)^n}}{i} \right]$$

Tables are given in the Appendix to show the present values of an annuity of £1.

Example (details per previous example). The present value of five half-yearly payments of £30 at 8 per cent per annum would be:

$$R \left[\frac{1 - \frac{1}{(1+i)^n}}{i} \right] = 30 \left[\frac{1 - \frac{1}{(1+0·04)^5}}{0·04} \right] = £133·57$$

or using the tables $30 \times 4·452 = £133·56$.

Finally, to prove that the present value of an annuity is the amount which if it were invested now at compound interest would be just sufficient to allow for the withdrawal of equal amounts at the end of a fixed number of periods, we can show that the present value of £133·57 just calculated would fulfil this condition for withdrawals of £30 over five half-yearly periods with interest at 8 per cent per annum.

		£	
Start		133·57	
Period 1	Interest	5·34	(133·57 at 8 per cent for 6 months)
	Payment	(30·00)	
Balance		108·91	
Period 2	Interest	4·35	
	Payment	(30·00)	
Balance		83·26	
Period 3	Interest	3·33	
	Payment	(30·00)	
		56·59	
Period 4	Interest	2·26	
	Payment	(30·00)	
Balance		28·85	
Period 5	Interest	1·15	
	Payment	(30·00)	
Balance		00·00	

Applications to Business Situations

The interest formulae which have been described in this chapter are useful over a wide range of business situations and accounting problems. While it will not be possible in this one chapter to examine in detail the whole range of applications, some of the more important ones are described. For convenience these can be dealt with under the following headings:

1. Finance Decisions relating to the borrowing and lending of money.

2. Investment Decisions related to the question of whether capital expenditure is justified by the probable future returns, and in the selection of alternatives.

3. Accounting problems of valuing assets and calculation of appropriations to sinking funds and depreciation.

Finance Decisions

When issuing shares, debentures or loans, a company will have to decide on the precise terms of the issue. It can choose whether they should be issued at par, at a premium or at a discount. It can in the case of redeemable preference shares, debentures or loans decide both on the rate of interest to be paid, and a date for redemption. While all the factors involved are complex and cannot be considered here, by applying interest calculations a proper decision can be made on the basis of financial costs.

Example. A company needs £500,000 cash for a ten-year period. The company's financial advisers have made the following offers:

> 7 per cent Ten-year debentures at 110
> 6 per cent Ten-year debentures at 100
> 5 per cent Ten-year debentures at 90

Repayment at par will be made at the end of ten years.

Which offer should be accepted on cost considerations alone?

In order to consider the cost of the various issues, each will have to be converted to its present value at the date of issue. In order to do this a rate of interest will have to be used in the calculations. For this example since 6 per cent is the rate when debentures are issued at par this will be assumed to be the Market rate of interest. The present value of the issues will comprise:

1. The present value of the interest payments to be made over ten years.

2. The present value of the capital repayment at the date of redemption ten years hence.

The nominal value of debentures issued will vary according to the terms of issue:

(*a*) 7 per cent Debentures at 110

$$\frac{£500,000}{1} \times \frac{100}{110} = £454,545 \left(\begin{array}{l} £ \\ Check\ 454,545 \\ Add\ 10\ per\ cent\ 45,455 \\ \overline{500,000} \end{array} \right)$$

(*b*) 6 per cent Debentures at 100

$$\frac{£500,000}{1} \times \frac{100}{100} = £500,000$$

(*c*) 5 per cent Debentures at 90

$$\frac{£500,000}{1} \times \frac{100}{90} = £555,556 \left(\begin{array}{l} Check\ 555,556 \\ Less\ 10\ per\ cent\ 55,556 \\ \overline{500,000} \end{array} \right)$$

The interest payments on the bonds sold will be:

£

(a) Nominal Value £454,545 at 7 per cent = 31,818
(b) Nominal Value £500,000 at 6 per cent = 30,000
(c) Nominal Value £555,556 at 5 per cent = 27,778

Calculation of the Present Value of the Capital Sum and Interest:

(a) 7 per cent Debentures   £
Capital Sum £454,545 at 6 per cent = £454,545 × 0·558 = 253,637
Interest of £31,818 at 6 per cent = £31,818 × 7·360   = 234,180

487,817

Appendix Present Value of £1 table = 0·558
Appendix Present Value of an Annuity of £1 table = 7·360

(b) 6 per cent Debenture   £
Capital Sum £500,000 at 6 per cent = £500,000 × 0·558 = 279,000
Interest of £30,000 at 6 per cent = £30,000 × 7·360   = 220,800

499,800

(c) 5 per cent Debenture   £
Capital Sum £555,556 at 6 per cent = £555,556 × 0·558 = 310,000
Interest of £27,778 at 6 per cent = £27,778 × 7·360   = 204,446

514,446

In this example, therefore, the 7 per cent debenture is the cheapest despite the fact that the annual interest charges are the highest. It is interesting to note, however, that if the period of the loan had been twenty years instead of ten years exactly the reverse situation would apply. The impact of taxation has been ignored.

Investment Decisions

One of the most important areas in which interest plays a role is where a decision has to be made about whether or not to invest business funds. In general no business wishes to invest money in a project unless the return or profit is considered to be sufficient. The decision as to whether a return is adequate in the light of the risks to be undertaken is a management and not an accounting decision. What the accountant should do is to show as accurately as he can the relationship between the cost of the project and the returns expected from it.

The comparison between a capital investment and the flow of funds which arise from that investment can be made in a number of ways. For example a company which has the opportunity to install a new machine costing £2,100 which will produce net income of £100 (after charging depreciation) per annum over three years and will then be scrapped without value, must decide whether the investment is a paying proposition. One common method would be to compare the average capital outlay with the average profit. In practice, firms interpret these things differently, but average capital will often be taken as the average of the opening and closing capital investment, i.e. $\frac{£2,100+0}{2} = £1,050$.

The average profit will usually be calculated by taking an arithmetic average of each year's profit. £100+£100+£100 = £300÷3 = £100.

The average profit expressed as a percentage of the average capital employed would then be:

$$\frac{£100}{£1,050} \times \frac{100}{1} = 9\cdot4 \text{ per cent}$$

The management of the company would then have to decide whether or not a 9·4 per cent return was adequate. This method of appraisal is often known as the Book Rate of Return Method.

Another method of assessing the information is to work out the time period in which the outlay on the project is recouped from the cash flows originating from it. The Cash Flow which arises from a project will rarely be exactly the same as the accounting profit. One main item of difference is depreciation. Cash outflow usually only takes place at the point when a fixed asset is bought and paid for. Depreciation is an allocation against profit of this original cost, over the assets life. After the initial purchase however no cash payments take place and depreciation can thus be called a non-cash expense. In this example the original outlay is £2,100 and the cash flows are:

Year 1	Profit £100+the non-cash expense Depreciation	£700 = £800
Year 2	,, £100 ,, ,, ,, ,,	£700 = £800
Year 3	,, £100 ,, ,, ,, ,,	£700 = £800

The original outlay of £2,100 would be recouped during year 3. Assuming cash flows evenly during the year it would take $2\frac{5}{8}$ years to recover the whole original outlay. Companies using this method, which is known as the 'Payback Method', have a standard time within which they expect to be paid back. If the Standard Payback period required was three years, then this project would be acceptable.

The Book Rate of Return Method ignored the cost of money over time and the value which can be placed on the results obtained is thereby considerably reduced. Let us assume that the company concerned has to pay on average for borrowing capital an amount equivalent to a 6 per cent rate of interest. Knowing this rate of interest it is possible to convert the future cash flows from the project to a present value at the start of the project. If the present values of the future cash values exceed the capital outlay it can be said that the project is worthwhile, or at least will yield a real profit. It is important to note that it is cash flows that matter when considering the cost of money over time and not profit as such. The profit figure includes many items which are allocated to a period quite independently of when the expense or revenue is paid or received.

The present values of the cash flows in the example are as follows:

Year	£		Multiplier from present value of £1 tables at 6 per cent		£
1	800	×	0·943	=	754·4
2	800	×	0·890	=	712·0
3	800	×	0·840	=	672·0
					2,138·4

(Note in this example the calculation could have been reduced by using the present value of an annuity table for an annuity of £800 for three years at 6 per cent—£800 × 2·673 = £2,138·4.)

By comparison with the outlay of £2,100 the project is worthwhile. The project has a net present worth of £38·04 which is the discounted value of the cash flows arising from the project £2,138·04 less the present worth of the capital outlays. So long as the present value of the cash flows exceeds the present value of the capital outlays thus giving a positive value to net present worth the project will be worthwhile. It must be noted, however, that if the company's cost of capital were only 1 per cent higher the present value would be £2,099 and the same project would be inadvisable. This is known as the Present Value Method.

The present value information may be assessed also as an index comparing the present value of the capital outlay with the present value of the other flows. In the example shown, the index would be $\frac{2,138·4}{2,100} = 1·018$. This is known as the profitability index. The profitability index may be useful in comparing projects. For example, an investment with capital outlay £100 may give rise to other flows with a net present value of £300. The index is 3·00. A comparable capital outlay of £1,000,000 may produce flows with present value 1,000,500 which is an index of 1·0005. Thus whilst the net present worth of the second project at £500 is higher than that of the first £300, the index shows that the ratio of return to capital outlay is better in the first project with an index of 3·00 compared to only 1·0005.

Another method of evaluating this information which is similar to the present value method just examined is one that seeks to find out which rate of interest would, if applied in the present value method, exactly equate the present value of the cash flows with the investment outlay. This can only be done by a trial and error process:

Year	Cash Flow	6 per cent		7 per cent	
	£		£		£
1	800	0·943	754·4	0·935	748·0
2	800	0·890	712·0	0·873	698·4
3	800	0·840	672·0	0·816	652·8
			2,138·4		2,099·2

When starting a problem of this sort from scratch it is necessary to choose two widely dispersed rates of interest in order to obtain an idea of where the final rate lies. For example, in the problem just examined we might have taken 5 per cent and 15 per cent. The present values from these rates would be £2,178 and £1,827 respectively and from this we could see that the solution will be nearer to the 5 per cent end. Notice that the higher the interest rate the lower will be the present value. By successive trials our answer will be located between 6 per cent and 7 per cent. Unfortunately, the number we are looking for does not happen to be a whole number. Often it will be sufficient to take the nearest whole number rate of interest which in our example would be 7 per cent. If a more exact rate is required it can be calculated by what is known as interpolation. Starting from the lower rate of interest of 6 per cent we add $\frac{38·4}{39·2}$ths of the 1 per cent difference between 6 per cent and the higher rate of 7 per cent. The denominator of 39·2 is the difference between 2138·4 and 2,099·2. The numerator of 38·4 is the difference between the present value at 6 per cent £2,138·4 and the required present value of £2,100.

$$6 \text{ per cent} + \frac{38·4}{39·2} \times 1 \text{ per cent} = 6·98 \text{ per cent}$$

This method of assessing projects is known as the Yield or Internal Rate of Return Method.

In comparing the results given by the different methods we have examined it can be seen that a discrepancy arises between the Book Rate of Return result at 9·4 per cent and the Yield result at 6·98 per cent. If the company's cost of capital were 7 per cent we should accept the project using the Book Rate of Return since that is higher. However, since the yield is only 6·98 per cent and the net present worth at 7 per cent is negative we should reject this project. By ignoring the cost of capital the Book Rate of Return is giving an incorrect result. The Present Value and Yield methods will give the same answer in all except a few special cases. The Payback Method is unsatisfactory because it ignores the total profit receivable from a project. If, for example, two projects are compared, both costing £1,000 but one yielding £500 per annum for three years and the other yielding £500 per annum for four years the payback period in both would be the same although the second alternative is clearly preferable. The payback method can be a useful supplement, however, to the present value or the yield methods for a company that is short of funds. If two projects give approximately the same yield, the one with quickest payback will be preferable.

So far in the example used the decision has been whether a project is worth while or not, based on its cost, and the expected returns from it. The same methods are equally useful in deciding between two or more alternative investments, the project giving the highest present value or yield being the most desirable. No mention has been made of the impact that taxation will have in investment decisions. Provided it is remembered that we are dealing with cash flows and the tax is included in the year in which it is actually paid or refunded, then no special problems arise. An approximation which is often employed is to assume that cash flows occur at the end or beginning of each period (rather than throughout the period as will happen in practice). Whilst this assumption is not usually likely to cause serious distortion, and simplifies calculation, for some purposes half-yearly or shorter periods may be used for discounting.

Example: Enterprise Ltd is considering two alternative investments for increasing its plant capacity.

	Project 1 5 years	Project 2 6 years
Project Life	£	£
Investment in Equipment (scrap value nil) at beginning of first year	70,000	120,000
Investment in Working Capital at beginning of first year (recoverable at the end of the projects life)	30,000	30,000
Estimated Profits before taxation		
Year 1	10,000	15,000
Remainder of life	20,000 per annum	27,000 per annum
Depreciation	14,000 per annum	20,000 per annum
Taxation in year of payment		
Year 2 (refund)	(2,000)	(3,000)
Remainder of life	6,000 per annum	7,000 per annum

The company estimate that its cost of capital is 10 per cent per annum. It will be assumed that cash flows arise at the end of the year unless otherwise stated.

Using the Present Value Method of appraisal, it is useful to set out the problem as shown on pages 703 and 704.

The solution to this problem shows that the Net Present Worth of Project (2) £44,795 is higher than that for Project (1) £27,722. On this criteria the company would choose Project (2) although Project (1) would be worthwhile if it were not an alternative. The Internal Rate of Return and the Profitability Index, however, are marginally higher for Project (1) than for Project (2). The directors will have to decide whether they prefer Project (2) with its higher Investment and Net Present

Project 1 (Outflows are shown in brackets)

	Year	0	1	2	3	4	5	Totals of columns 0–5
	Capital Flows							
	Equipment	(70,000)						
	Working Capital	(30,000)						
1	Total Capital Flow	(100,000)						
2	Discount Factors—10 per cent	1·00					0·621	
3 = 1×2	Discounted Capital Flow	(100,000)					18,630	(81,370)
	Other Flows							
	Profit		10,000	20,000	20,000	20,000	20,000	
	Depreciation		14,000	14,000	14,000	14,000	14,000	
	Taxation		—	2,000	(6,000)	(6,000)	(6,000)	
4	Total Other Flows		24,000	36,000	28,000	28,000	28,000	
5	Discount Factors		0·909	0·826	0·751	0·683	0·621	
6 = 4×5	Discounted Other Flows		21,816	29,736	21,028	19,124	17,388	109,092
7 = 3+6	Total Discounted Flow	(100,000)	21,816	29,736	21,028	19,124	36,018	27,722

Summary: Net Present Worth at 10 per cent interest £27,722.
Internal Rate of Return (yield) = 19·2 per cent (Net Present Worth at 18 per cent £3,022: at 20 per cent (£2,000).

Profitability Index = 1·341 $\left(\dfrac{109·092}{81·370}\right)$

Project 2 (Outflows are shown in brackets)

Year	0	1	2	3	4	5	6	Totals of Columns 0–6
Capital Flows								
Equipment	(120,000)							
Working Capital	(30,000)					30,000		
1 Total Capital Flow	(150,000)					30,000		
2 Discount Factors—10 per cent	1·00					0·564		
3 = 1 × 2	(150,000)						16,920	(133,080)
Other Flows								
Profit	—	15,000	27,000	27,000	27,000	27,000	27,000	
Depreciation	—	20,000	20,000	20,000	20,000	20,000	20,000	
Taxation	—	—	3,000	(7,000)	(7,000)	(7,000)	(7,000)	
4 Total Other Flows		35,000	50,000	40,000	40,000	40,000	40,000	
5 Discount Factors		0·909	0·826	0·751	0·683	0·621	0·564	
6 = 4 × 5		31,815	41,300	30,040	27,320	24,840	22,560	177,875
7 = 3 + 6 Total Discounted Flow	(150,000)	31,815	41,300	30,040	27,320	24,840	39,480	44,795

Summary: Net Present Worth at 10 per cent interest £44,795.

Internal Rate of Return (yield) = 18·97 per cent (Net Present Worth at 18 per cent £3,925: at 20 per cent £4,175).

Profitability Index = $1 \cdot 337 \left(\dfrac{177 \cdot 875}{133 \cdot 080} \right)$

Worth or Project (1) which with a smaller Investment and Net Present Worth but which has a slightly higher yield. The decision will take into account the resources available to the firm, the risks associated with the two projects, also the alternative investment opportunities which might be available for the £50,000 difference in capital investment.

The methods of appraisal discussed in this part of the chapter describe the discounted cash flow approach to investment decision taking. We have not, however, considered many of the practical problems which surround such decisions. For example, there are often great difficulties in estimating what future cash flows will be. There will also be considerable uncertainty associated with future estimates which may be hard to quantify. It is by no means easy to determine the appropriate rate of interest to use in the calculations. In general terms it may be said that the company's cost of capital should be used as the rate of interest for present value calculations, or as the minimum acceptable rate when the internal rate of return is assessed. This still leaves the problem of defining the company's 'cost of capital'. Above all, in most management decisions the problem of investment is complicated by the many interrelationships involved. One decision can have implications for very many different parts of the business and the best solution for all the different parts may be hard to arrive at. Despite these problems this method of assessment is very valuable because it requires a disciplined approach to estimating the results of investment and does not forget the importance of interest where cash flows are spread over several periods of time.

Accounting Problems

Depreciation

In Chapter 29 a description was included of the calculation of the equal amounts of depreciation required to be set aside each year in a sinking fund, to accumulate with interest to a given sum in the future. From the descriptions given in the earlier section in this chapter it should be apparent that this is nothing more than a straightforward annuity calculation.

Example. Facts as in Exhibit 3, Chapter 29.

Required: to find the amount of an annuity that will amount to £10,000 at the end of five years invested at 5 per cent per annum.

From Table 3 it can be seen that a £1 annuity will amount to £5·526 over five years. The annuity which will amount to £10,000 will therefore be

$$\frac{£10,000}{5\cdot526} = £1,810 \text{ (to the nearest whole £1)}$$

Alternatively the formula could have been employed as on page 694:

$$R = \frac{Ai}{(1+i)^n-1} = \frac{£10,000\,(0{\cdot}05)}{(1{\cdot}05)^3-1} = £1,810$$

The calculation can be proved as follows:

Year	Sinking Fund amount set aside	5 per cent Interest at	Total Depreciation	Cumulative total
	£		£	£
1	1,810	—	1,810	1,810
2	1,810	90	1,900	3,710
3	1,810	185	1,995	5,705
4	1,810	285	2,095	7,800
5	1,810	390	2,200	10,000

It is also possible to use the same calculation as a basis for allocating depreciation over the life of an asset without in fact investing funds, in sinking fund investments. The total depreciation column in the above table shows how the original cost of an asset costing £10,000 would be spread over its working life. (The appropriate rate of interest would be the return expected on the asset.)

Another depreciation method employing similar concepts to the sinking fund method is one, in fact, called the 'Annuity Method'. In this method besides the basic depreciation charge an additional cost is worked out and charged against profit.

This is an interest charge for using the asset during the year and is equal to the rate of return from the asset times the investment at the beginning of the year.

Example. Taking the facts as they were presented in the previous example the position would be:

Year	Book Value of Asset at beginning of year £	Basic Depreciation £	Interest on book value of assets using 5 per cent return £	Total depreciation including interest £
1	10,000	1,810	500	2,310
2	8,190	1,900	410	2,310
3	6,290	1,995	315	2,310
4	4,295	2,095	215	2,310
5	2,200	2,200	110	2,310
	10,000	1,550	11,550

In this example, since the rate of return on the asset is taken at the same rate as the interest used on the sinking fund method, the total depreciation charge works out to an equal amount each year. The interest on the book value of assets is a charge applying only within the business itself. It will be charged therefore as depreciation in one section of the Profit and Loss Account and credited in another, as interest received. The net effect is therefore the same as the sinking fund method of depreciation. Using T accounts to record the transactions the position shown would be:

Depreciation Fund

	Year		£
	1	A	1,810
	2	B	1,900
	3	C	1,995
	4	D	2,095
	5	E	2,200
			10,000

Internal Interest Revenue

Year		£	Year			£
1	Profit and Loss	500	1		A	500
2		410	2		B	410
3		315	3		C	315
4		215	4		D	215
5		110	5		E	110

Depreciation Expense

Year		£	Year		£
1	A	2,310	1	Profit and Loss	2,310
2	B	2,310	2		2,310
3	C	2,310	3		2,310
4	D	2,310	4		2,310
5	E	2,310	5		2,310

Profit and Loss Account (Extract)

Year 1

£	£
Depreciation Expense 2,310	Internal Interest 500

Year 2

£	£
Depreciation Expense 2,310	Internal Interest 410

Year 3

£	£
Depreciation Expense 2,310	Internal Interest 315

Year 4

£	£
Depreciation Expense 2,310	Internal Interest 215

Year 5

£	£
Depreciation Expense 2,310	Internal Interest 100

Both the sinking fund and the annuity methods of depreciation have taken account of the importance of the cost of money over time. The depreciation has been allocated over the life of the asset in a way which charges profits in the later years of the asset's life with a higher cost. This is not unreasonable if the asset concerned yields an equal profit over its life. This will be illustrated in the following example which uses basically the same facts that were illustrated in the earlier examples.

In order for the annuity method of depreciation to be applied, for this purpose it is necessary that the rate of return or interest used should be the one which discounts the future cash flow from profits to a present value equivalent to the original investment, i.e. the present value of an annuity of £2,310 for five years at 5 per cent = £10,000. In normal practice the investment figure of £10,000 and the cash flows of £2,310 would be known quantities. It would then be necessary by examination of the present value of annuity tables to establish that the rate of return was 5 per cent. (This figure would be used in subsequent calculations.)

Example. An asset costing £10,000 is to be depreciated over a five-year life in which the profit yielded is £2,310 per annum before depreciation. The following results are shown if straight-line depreciation is used.

Year	Asset at w.d.v. at beginning of year	Depreciation	Profit after depreciation	Profit as per cent assets at w.d.v.
	£	£	£	
1	10,000	2,000	310	3·1
2	8,000	2,000	310	3·87
3	6,000	2,000	310	5·17
4	4,000	2,000	310	7·75
5	2,000	2,000	310	15·5
		10,000	1,550	

It is clear that where straight-line depreciation is used the return on assets increases from 3·1 per cent to 15·5 per cent over the five years, without any alteration in efficiency of the business whatever. By comparison figures where sinking fund depreciation is employed are as follows:

Year	Asset at w.d.v. at beginning of year	Depreciation	Profit after depreciation	Profit as per cent assets at w.d.v.
	£	£	£	
1	10,000	1,810	500	5
2	8,190	1,900	410	5
3	6,290	1,995	315	5
4	4,295	2,095	215	5
5	2,200	2,200	110	5
		10,000	1,550	

The sinking fund and annuity methods in these circumstances are yielding an answer to one of the problems of depreciation accounting, namely the distortion of reported net profit in relation to the net assets employed. This was one of the problems mentioned in an earlier chapter relating to ratio analysis. Unfortunately, however, there is implicit in sinking fund and annuity methods an assumption that the cash flows, and correspondingly depreciation, occur evenly over the life of the asset. In practice, this rarely happens apart from items such as leases where the rents are exactly known.

Present Value

The theoretical answer to this problem lies in the use of the present value techniques already explored earlier in the chapter. Not only could the depreciation problem be solved but also that of the valuing of fixed assets. In order to solve the problem two things must be known, firstly the future cash flows which would originate from the asset, and secondly, the appropriate rate of interest representing cost of capital to the firm.

Example. A business expects cash flows from an investment costing £456·8 amounting to £200 per annum for three years. The company's cost of capital is 10 per cent.

The cash flows converted to present value at a rate of interest of 10 per cent would be:

Year		Present value factor	Present value
	£		£
1	200	0·909	181·8
2	200	0·826	165·2
3	200	0·751	150·2
			497·2

At the end of year 1 the Present Value of the Investment

$$= £200 \times 0·909 \quad £181·8$$
$$£200 \times 0·826 \quad £165·2$$
$$£347·0$$

At the end of year 2 the Present Value of the Investment

$$= £200 \times 0·909 \quad £181·8$$

The amount to be written off each year can be computed as follows:

Year	Present value at beginning of year	Present value at end of year	Reduction in present value
	£	£	£
1	497·2	347·0	150·2
2	347·0	181·8	165·2
3	181·8	—	181·8
			497·2

The reduction in present value figures incorporate both a charge for true depreciation, which would be the same as the present value figures of the cash flow each year, i.e. the capital cost expired in the year

Year	Depreciation
1	£181·8
2	£165·2
3	£150·2

together with an adjustment for the interest on the capital employed. The interest factor is shown as follows:

Year	Reduction in present value	Depreciation	Interest factor
	£	£	
1	150·2	181·8	+31·6
2	165·2	165·2	—
3	181·8	150·2	−31·6

These figures can be proved in detail in the following way:

Year	Present value of cash flows	Interest at 10 per cent	Present value + interest	Interest at 10 per cent	Present value + Interest	Interest at 10 per cent
	£	£	£	£	£	£
1	181·8	18·18				
2	165·2	16·52	181·72	18·17		
3	150·2	15·02	165·22	16·52	181·74	18·17
		49·72		34·69		18·17

Year 1 Interest Expense 18·1 Interest Revenue 49·7 = +31·6
Year 2 Interest Expense 34·7 Interest Revenue 34·7 = 0
Year 3 Interest Expense 49·7 Interest Revenue 18·1 = −31·6

In the accounts of the company this would be presented as follows:

Year	Flow	Cash Depreciation	Income before Interest	Interest Expense	Income	Interest Revenue	Net Income
	£	£	£	£	£	£	£
1	200	181·8	18·2	18·1	—	49·7	49·7
2	200	165·2	34·8	34·7	—	34·7	34·7
3	200	150·2	49·8	49·7	—	18·2	18·2

The Return on net assets would be equal each year as shown below:

Year 1 $\dfrac{\text{Net Income}}{\text{Net Whole Value of Asset}}$ $\dfrac{49\cdot7}{497\cdot2} = 10$ per cent

Year 2 $\dfrac{\text{Net Income}}{\text{Net Value of Asset}}$ $\dfrac{34\cdot7}{347\cdot0} = 10$ per cent

Year 3 $\dfrac{\text{Net Income}}{\text{Net Value of Asset}}$ $\dfrac{18\cdot2}{181\cdot8} = 10$ per cent

The Accounting entries to record the interest expense and revenue would be as shown in the T accounts below:

Interest Expense		Interest Revenue		Deferred Interest	
Year 1 18·1		Year 1 49·7	Year 1 31·6	—	
Year 2 34·7		Year 2 34·7	—	—	
Year 3 49·7		Year 3 18·1	—		Year 3 31·6

One important point has been overlooked in the analysis so far. It has been assumed that the assets should be valued in the accounts at the figure for the present value of future cash flows and depreciated accordingly. However, since this figure exceeds the cost value of the asset by £40·4 the method could be unacceptable where assets were required to be recorded at cost. In this circumstance it would be necessary to create a capital reserve for the amount of unrealized profit on revaluation of the asset. In the Balance Sheet this would be recorded as follows:

	£
Assets (valued on the basis of the Present Value of future Cash Flows)	497
Less Reserve for unrealized profits	40
Asset at Cost Value	457

The problem would arise at the end of the first and subsequent years of calculating the balance of unrealized profit. The way to do this is to calculate the interest rate that would exactly equate the future cash flows with the cost of the asset (as in the yield or discounted cash flow calculation). Trial and error methods give the following result:

Year	Cash Flow	Present Value Factor 15 per cent	Present Value
	£		£
1	200	0·870	174·0
2	200	0·756	151·2
3	200	0·658	131·6
			456·8

Having established that with a cost of capital of 15 per cent the present value of future cash flows would equal the cost of investment, the allocation of net income should be recalculated for the project using the 15 per cent interest rate.

This would amount to:

Year	Net Income at 15 per cent Interest
1	68·4
2	48·8
3	26·0
	143·2

If this is then compared with the net income with a 10 per cent rate of interest, the difference gives the expected profit that has been realized:

Year	Net Income at 15 per cent Interest	Net Income at 10 per cent Interest	Net Income Realised
	£	£	£
1	68	50	18
2	49	35	14
3	26	18	8
	143	103	40

At the end of year 1 the reserve for unrealised profit would be £22 and at the end of year 2 £8.

At the beginning of this section of the chapter the ideas put forward were described as a theoretical solution, since the uncertainty of predicting future cash flows creates great practical problems. The method nevertheless provides a most satisfactory model for the depreciation of assets. The depreciation charge is correctly spread out over the life of the asset in proportion to the return obtained from it, and proper allowance is made for the cost of money over time. Not only this but a valuation is placed upon the asset exactly related to the future returns expected from it, and the relationship between net profit and the net book value of the asset will not be distorted by the depreciation charge. The main value in understanding the present value method is as a standard for criticism of other methods, it also offers some useful advantages in the preparation of information for the management of a business.

Exercises

46.1. The managing director of your firm has obtained the terms on which three different firms would manufacture a special machine. These are:

Firm A	£2,000 payable on delivery
	£500 payable at the end of each of the following four years
	Total £4,000
Firm B	£1,000 payable on delivery
	£3,500 payable at the end of five years from delivery
	Total £4,500
Firm C	Nothing payable on delivery
	£800 at the end of each of the following four years
	£1,000 at the end of the fifth year after delivery
	Total £4,200

He says, obviously, the offer from Firm A is the best one. Would you agree with him or would you recommend one of the other offers, and if so, which one? You are required to show all your workings to substantiate your decision.

The average cost of capital to the firm is 6 per cent per annum.

46.2. Consider three investment projects A, B and C, all costing £300 to initiate, having a life of three years with income arising end-year on average, and the residual value of the assets being zero. Depreciation both for tax purposes and accounting purposes is on the straight-line basis of £100 per year. Tax is at the rate of 50 per cent and is levied and collected simultaneously at the end of each year. The details of earnings, depreciation, tax and profitability are given below:

Years	1	2	3
Project A	£	£	£
Gross Earnings	250	250	250
Depreciation	100	100	100
Profits before Tax	150	150	150
Tax at 50 per cent	75	75	75
Profits after Tax	75	75	75
Project B			
Gross Earnings	150	250	350
Depreciation	100	100	100
Profits before Tax	50	150	250
Tax at 50 per cent	25	75	125
Profits after Tax	25	75	125
Project C			
Gross Earnings	350	250	150
Depreciation	100	100	100
Profits before Tax	250	150	50
Tax at 50 per cent	125	75	25
Profits after Tax	125	75	25

(*a*) Calculate:
(i) The 'Payback Period' for each project.

(ii) The 'Rate of Return' (defined for this exercise as the ratio of average profit to average capital) for each project.

(iii) The 'Net Present Value' for each project; with a cost of capital of 10 per cent.

(b) If projects A, B and C were mutually exclusive indicate which one you would choose giving your reasons.

46.3. Some years ago a company purchased a lathe for £5,300. It now requires a major overhaul and the company is faced with two alternatives.

(a) To overhaul the machine for £3,250. At the end of five years it is estimated that the machine will be worth £600. Maintenance costs will be £250 per annum.

(b) To sell the machine for £2,000 and to replace it with a new machine costing £5,800. The saleable value of this machine in five years' time is expected to be £1,000. Maintenance costs will be £150 per annum.

Which alternative is preferable assuming both machines will perform identical work, and the company's cost of capital is 10 per cent?

Ignore taxation.

46.4. On 1 December 19–1 J. Smith acquires a building for £26,485, payable 20 per cent down and the balance in twenty equal annual instalments which are to include interest at 7 per cent on a compound annual basis. What equal instalments will have to be paid for the building?

46.5A. A man has the choice of investing £8,000 in one of two policies.

Policy 1 yields an income of £2,000 per year for 5 years then £1,000 per year for a further 5 years.

Policy 2 yields an income of £1,600 per year for the 10 years.

If the market rate of interest was 10 per cent what would you advise the man to do?

What would be the effect if the market rate of interest was 20 per cent?

46.6A. At the end of the year the Q Company must pay the Industrial Tools Corporation £6,000 against the unpaid balance for the cost of new tools. If the bank pays 8 per cent per annum interest compounded quarterly on deposits how much, to the nearest pound, should the company deposit at the beginning of the year so that the accumulated amount on deposit will meet the company's obligation?

46.7A. If instead of paying a lump sum, the manager of the Q company chooses to pay £1,440 quarterly, would the compound amount from the four quarterly deposits be sufficient to meet his £6,000 obligation?

46.8A. A research worker receives a grant of £15,000 to cover a project lasting 5 years. He invests the money at 5 per cent per annum, intending to withdraw equal amounts at the end of each year. How much can he withdraw on each occasion?

46.9A. A firm has to select between two investment projects, D and G. The relevant information is:

Cash inflows at year end	
Project D	Project G
1,500	900
1,800	600
1,500	600
1,200	600
900	300
	300

Project A costs £4,200, all incurred at the beginning of the period.

Project B cost £300 at the beginning of the period, and £300 at the end of each subsequent year. The present return on investment is 15 per cent.

Advise the firm as to which project should be undertaken.

46.10A. A client is considering buying a factory to make a new product which he has developed. He asks you which is the best method to use to assess the profitability and risk of the venture and says that he has heard of three methods, namely:
1. Discounted cash flow.
2. Return on investment.
3. The payback method.

You are required to explain briefly two of these methods of appraising capital expenditure and state the advantages and disadvantages of each.

(Institute of Chartered Accountants)

46.11A. A large insurance company is considering the installation of a computer which can be acquired on extended credit terms as follows:

	£
A payment on delivery of	8,100
A payment at the end of each of the next four years of	5,400
A final payment at the end of the 5th year of	6,300

As an alternative method, payment can be made in full on delivery, taking into account compound interest at 6 per cent per annum, tables for which provide the following data:
The amount required to produce an annuity of £1 for 4 years is £3·4651 and for 5 years £4·2124.
An annuity of £1 amounts to £4·3746 in 4 years and to £5·6371 in five years.
The present value of £1 payable 4 years hence is £0·79209 and 5 years hence £0·74726.
(a) What is the full amount payable on extended credit terms?
(b) Using the data provided calculate to two places of decimals the amount payable under the alternative method.
Ignore income tax.

(Association of Certified Accountants)

46.12A. The XYZ Co Ltd is considering the replacement of three of its present machines with a single machine which has just come on to the market. Consideration of this proposition has arisen because of the necessity to spend £5,000 on exceptional maintenance on the present machines. The three machines which would be replaced were purchased two years ago for £1,500 each, and are being depreciated over 12 years on a straight-line basis with an estimated final scrap value of £600 each. The current second hand market value of each of the machines is £1,000.

The annual operating costs for each of the existing machines are

	£	£
Material		60,000
Labour—1 operator at 1,800 hours		1,350
Variable Expenses		925
Maintenance (excluding any exceptional expenditure)		2,000
Fixed Expenses:		
Depreciation	75	
Fixed factory overhead absorbed	2,700	
		2,775

The new machine has an estimated life of 10 years and will cost £100,000 as follows:

	£
Purchase Price (scrap value in 10 years £4,500)	87,000
Installation Costs	13,000

The estimated annual operating costs for all the existing output on the new machine are:

	£	£
Material		162,000
Labour:		
2 operators at 1,500 hours	3,000	
1 operator's assistant at 1,500 hours	900	
		3,900
Variable Expenses		2,275
Maintenance		4,500
Fixed Expenses		
Depreciation	9,550	
Fixed Factory overhead absorbed	7,800	
		17,350

The company's cost of capital is 10 per cent and products are evaluated in rate of return terms. In addition to satisfying the profitability test, projects must also satisfy a financial viability test, in that they must pay for themselves within a maximum period of 5 years.

You are required to:

(a) Advise management on the profitability of this proposal by applying the discounted cash flow—Trial and Error Yield Technique.

(b) Subject the proposal to a financial viability test and

(c) Comment briefly on two other factors that could influence this decision.

Notes:

1. Taxation is to be ignored.

2. Assume that residual value is received on the last day of a machine's working life.

(*Association of Certified Accountants*)

46.13A. A firm can pursue two alternative policies:

(i) Invest £90,000 in a project which will yield £12,000 at the end of each of the following 20 years.

(ii) Invest the same sum in a project which will yield £21,000 at the end of each of the following 5 years and £6,000 for a further 15 years.

What would you advise the firm to do if the rate of interest used for discounting is (a) 5 per cent (b) 8 per cent assuming that it wishes to maximize net present value? Give the reason for your advice.

46.14A. A company is considering investment in a project, the details of which are shown below.

	£
Capital outlay at Base date	30,000
Expected life of machine purchased 4 years	
Estimated income receivable annually:	
Year 1	20,000
Year 2	20,000
Year 3	15,000
Year 4	10,000

You are required to state whether you consider the project should be undertaken where the return expected on capital invested is 10 per cent after deduction of taxation.

Taxation may be taken as 40 per cent on income; taxation allowances may be ignored for the purposes of your answer.

46.15A. The B.Z. Co owns a small subsidiary. The equipment of this subsidiary is outdated and costly to operate, which along with a falling off in demand for the product, is causing profits to decline.

The subsidiary's equipment could be modernized at a cost of £18,000. This would stabilize profits at £9,000 for the next two years, thereafter they could be expected to decline annually by £1,200. This modernization would not qualify for capital allowances.

An alternative is to replace the equipment and change production into a new 'growth' product. This re-equipment would cost £21,000 but would qualify for capital allowances of £6,000, £5,400, £3,600 and £3,000. It is predicted that the profits from the growth product would be £6,000, £6,600, £7,200, £8,400 and £9,600. The scrap value of the old equipment is £1,500.

The company uses a money rate of 6 per cent, which is increased by 4 per cent for new ventures. Assume corporation tax at 30 per cent payable a year in arrears.

Review these projects within a 5-year horizon and comment

Discount Factors:

Year	1	2	3	4	5	6
6 per cent	0·94	0·89	0·84	0·80	0·75	0·70
10 per cent	0·91	0·83	0·75	0·68	0·62	0·56

47

Interpretation of Accounts

To interpret means to put the meaning of a statement into simple terms for the benefit of a person. From a student's point of view interpretation of accounts entails broadly the following:

1.   Understanding the terms (language) of financial statements;

2.   Appreciating the relationship between one accounting figure and another in financial statements: thus, while there is no obvious relationship between sales income and interest on long-term loan, there is certainly some connection between sales on credit and discounts given to credit customers;

3.   Grasping the significance of the related figures: in other words, whether such related figures indicate a satisfactory state of affairs or otherwise;

4.   Making deductions;

5.   Preparing a report summarizing the deductions.

The importance of analyzing and interpreting financial statements stems from the establishment of the principle of limited liability in 1845 and the passing of a companies act in 1862. From this point on the limited company became the most important business unit and large-scale operations accelerated industrial and commercial growth. It will be recalled that some of the more important distinguishing features of the limited company are:

1.   Ownership by many (shareholders);

2.   Control by few (directors);

3.   Annual published statements of profit and financial position;

4.   In the case of liquidation, the limitation of liability to the amount, if any, unpaid on the owner's shares.

Creditors, formerly able to rely on personal knowledge of sole business owners or partners, their standing in the particular trade, and, in the event of bankruptcy their private assets as well as business assets, had to rely mainly on published financial statements to guide them when dealing with the larger public companies. Careful study of these financial statements became essential if credit was to be given at normal risk.

In the United States, credit-reporting agencies laid great emphasis on Balance Sheets being voluntarily supplied by companies seeking credit. Indeed, during the 1870s the Mercantile Agency stated bluntly that a refusal to supply Balance Sheets by any company other than those of the highest repute would be taken to indicate financial weakness. At about this time American and European bankers had begun to give full recognition to the value of systematic analysis and interpretation of financial statements.

Interested Parties

While it is perhaps true to say that trade creditors and bankers originally took the greatest interest in financial statements, the diagram Exhibit 47.1 illustrates the wider interest today. Some of these interests are now examined in greater detail.

Debenture Holders

The main interests of the debenture holders are:

1. The ability of the company to pay loan interest promptly;

2. A long-term interest in the arrangements to repay the loan eventually; and

3. Their security if the company gets into financial difficulties.

The profit performance and the liquid position answers the first interest; the conditions of the loan answers the second—for example, the contract may require the company to build up funds steadily over the period of the loan so as to ease repayment arrangements on maturity; and in return for accepting a moderate rate of annual interest, the debenture holders are usually offered security of all the company's assets in the event of failing to pay interest or defaulting on repayment of the loan.

Virtually this means that the debenture holders can suspend the directors' control and sell the company's assets in order to repay their loan and/or unpaid interest. On the other hand, these loans requiring, say, 7 per cent annual interest, are put to work by the directors and may very well earn profits for the company in the order of 10 to 20 per cent or even more. Such loans therefore represent a cheap form of finance. This fact is well appreciated by company top management and is further discussed under gearing.

Limited Company
Financial Statement Analysis and Interpretation

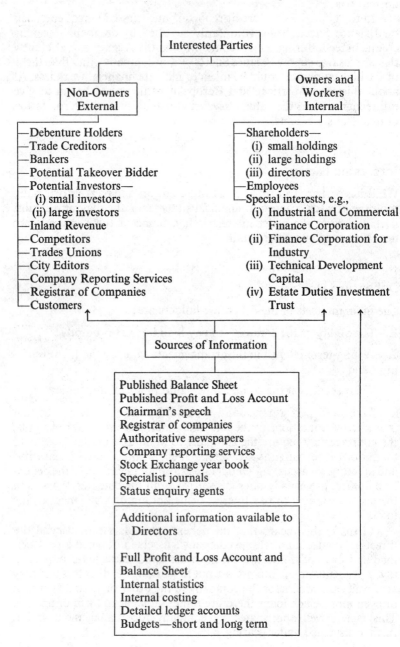

Interested Parties

Non-Owners External

—Debenture Holders
—Trade Creditors
—Bankers
—Potential Takeover Bidder
—Potential Investors—
  (i) small investors
  (ii) large investors
—Inland Revenue
—Competitors
—Trades Unions
—City Editors
—Company Reporting Services
—Registrar of Companies
—Customers

Owners and Workers Internal

—Shareholders—
  (i) small holdings
  (ii) large holdings
  (iii) directors
—Employees
—Special interests, e.g.,
  (i) Industrial and Commercial Finance Corporation
  (ii) Finance Corporation for Industry
  (iii) Technical Development Capital
  (iv) Estate Duties Investment Trust

Sources of Information

Published Balance Sheet
Published Profit and Loss Account
Chairman's speech
Registrar of companies
Authoritative newspapers
Company reporting services
Stock Exchange year book
Specialist journals
Status enquiry agents

Additional information available to
  Directors

Full Profit and Loss Account and
Balance Sheet
Internal statistics
Internal costing
Detailed ledger accounts
Budgets—short and long term

Trade Creditors

The most common business cycle follows this pattern:

Simple Profit-making Cycle

		Time in months
Step 1	Goods costing £100 purchased on credit	0
Step 2	The goods sold on credit for £150	$\frac{1}{2}$ (say)
Step 3	Trade creditor paid off—£100	1
Step 4	Debtor settles—£150 (month-end following month of sale)	2

Not until step 4 is the profit realized in cash and money is available to pay the trade creditor. But if the firm's reputation and its cash discounting policy is to be preserved, £100 less the discount must be paid before step 4 is reached. Therefore the business must possess enough funds to bridge the time interval between step 1 and step 4. This is the working capital which has been discussed in Volume 1. The point is, that not only must there be sufficient working capital to pay trade creditors and, of course, weekly and monthly business expenses, but also some of it must exist in liquid or near liquid form. The amount of working capital required in heavy engineering companies to cover the fairly long interval of time between buying raw materials, processing them into finished products, and the eventual receipt of cash from the sale of the products can well be considerable.

The ability to pay for credit purchases as they fall due is the measure of solvency, and it is this point which is of greatest interest to trade creditors. Thus they focus their attention on:

1. The current assets available to pay the current liabilities.

2. The make-up of the current assets and the estimated actual ability to pay their debts.

3. Who has priority of claim on the assets in the event of the company failing.

4. The earnings record and possible future expansion or contraction of business.

5. The policy and calibre of management.

A good illustration of the last two points is the danger of incautious expansion of business after a depression. Rapid expansion has often followed periods of economic stagnation. Sometimes large volumes of goods have been purchased on normal trade credit but sold on hire purchase terms. Unfortunately, the anxiety to boost sales in such conditions has often led to poor credit rating of customers and bad credit control. Huge losses by way of bad debts would then affect liquidity and many consumer goods businesses would be unable to settle their current liabilities. This in turn will have drastic effects on the original trade creditors.

Bankers

Short-term loans, mainly by bank overdraft, is a common way to obtaining finance. Bankers do not like to tie up their money for long periods, but the provision of overdraft facilities under suitable circumstances is an importance course of profit to them owing to the interest charged for the facility. When considering a request for a loan their main interests are:

1. For what purpose is the loan required and for how long.

2. What is the company's plan for repaying the loan.

3. What are the prospects of repayment in fact—in other words, is the trend of profit satisfactory as disclosed by several past years' financial statements.

4. What will the Bank's position be if the company fails, and who has prior rights on liquidation.

5. What is the calibre and policies of the management as disclosed by recent financial statements.

The Bank pays close attention to the liquidity position and, from an examination of the company's bank current account whether or not there is evidence of present overdrafts 'hardening' into permanency. The existence of prior rights of debenture holders and their security are studied. The value of the assets in the Balance Sheet are compared with their saleable value if sold under liquidation. If the overdraft facility is granted, the company's financial position is kept under constant review and the Bank's risk periodically considered in the light of published financial statements and other sources of information.

Potential Takeover Bidder

A potential takeover bidder is usually a large public company wishing to diversify its interests or to strengthen its position by vertical or lateral integration. Sometimes the bidder simply sees the takeover as a good business deal because he is able to offer a seemingly good price to the shareholders for their shares, whereas in fact the shareholders are not aware of the real value of their shares for a variety of reasons. For example, the stock exchange quotation before the bid may undervalue the shares; there may be assets in the Balance Sheet which are far below their real value if sold; again, the directors may be under-utilizing funds under their control—which if put to work in other ways might earn much more profit. The potential bidder is therefore particularly interested in:

1. The real value of assets as compared with the Balance Sheet value (the reader should now recall or revise all he has learned about depreciation policies and methods of stock valuation).

2. The financial and dividend policy of the directors and their effect on shareholder loyalties.

3. The stock exchange price of the shares compared with their Balance Sheet value and real value.

4. The existence of assets which, if sold, would realize large cash profits—for example, valuable land and buildings.

5. The existence of large cash balances or short-term loans disclosing excess liquidity and therefore under-utilization of resources.

Many directors have realized too late the danger of being too unmindful of their shareholders' interest and forgetting that companies are run for the benefit of shareholders and not for directors. Thus loyalty is lost and control passes into the hands of others. Sometimes they have paid too little attention to the employment of all assets to the full, and they have overlooked the astuteness and financial skills of persons who have access to published financial statements.

Interesting cases have included an attempt to take over a large brewing concern which had numerous valuable property in the shape of public houses, but which were earning a relatively small profit in relation to the value of the freehold properties; and an attempted takeover of a large textile concern which had (among other items of interest) large holdings of short-term investments earning only a small rate of return compared with other assets. This company had too much money and was not making good use of it.

Potential Investors + Small Holdings

There is a growing interest in channelling a flow of capital into industry through the savings of small investors, either individually or through investments trusts and unit trusts. In the case of an individual, he will often rely on his broker for advice rather than trust to his own judgement. Investors usually fall into two main classes, those who prefer a moderate income with some security of income and preference in the event of liquidation, and those who are prepared to speculate in return for higher income and other advantages. Both are primarily interested in the earnings performance of the company concerned and the ease with which the dividend can be paid out of profits. The speculative investor is often interested in the potential growth and consequent prospect of receiving bonus shares or preferential rights on share issues for cash. The potential investor pays particular attention to:

1. The trend of profits and sales over recent years.

2. Forecasts of expansion in the particular industry: reports and comments by authorititative newspapers and economists are often useful in this respect.

3. The yield on a proposed investment, and the possible yields from alternative investments.

4. The ease with which dividends can be paid from profits earned, and the probable certainty of future payments at the same or higher level of dividend currently reported.

5. The policy and calibre of the directors.

Potential Investors—Large Holdings

Buyers of large holdings (institutional investors) such as companies, merchant banks, unit trusts, investment trusts and insurance companies have experienced analysts on their staff to evaluate published financial statements. They chart the progress of companies over a period of years, using many of the ratios explained in this chapter, and paying particular attention to statistical and economic surveys relevant to the industry being studied. They are interested, naturally, in companies with good growth prospects consistent with financial stability, and the analysis is of a high order.

Existing Shareholders

Investors, both large and small, who have made their choice of company are naturally anxious to reap the rewards expected. Regrettably, many small investors show no interest beyond receiving their dividend which, if no less than in previous years, appears to satisfy them. Attendance at the annual general meeting is often sparse, and the published financial statements are all too often unceremoniously consigned to the dustbin. The complacency is sometimes thought to stem from lack of understanding of accountancy 'jargon' and difficult presentation of Profit and Loss Accounts and Balance Sheets. In order to overcome this there is a move towards issuing simplified statements supported by charts of one sort or another.

It is left to the institutional investor such as insurance companies, or those buying investments to provide income for the pensions funds of large firms, to bring pressure on directors in times of falling dividends or dividends not being proposed, or impending financial failure. Owners of large shareholdings have, of course, considerable interest in the progress of the company in which they have invested, and as mentioned previously have experienced staff continuously assessing the value of their investment and possible advantages of switching to other companies.

Employees

Interest varies among employees according to whether or not there is participation in the profits. A number of important companies operate profit sharing in the form of special employee shares which vary according to the profit earned each year. Probably government policy will encourage more worker participation in company control and this must obviously encourage interest in company progress as disclosed by its financial statements. On the other hand, there is often keen interest in the amount of dividend being paid to shareholders, particularly when workers have been refused increases in pay.

Directors

Apart from their shareholder position, the dominant interest of the directors should be that their company shall earn the maximum profit consistent with continuing financial stability and with a proper regard for changing economic conditions and employee, shareholder, and customer relations. Perhaps a better word than 'maximum' is 'optimum' because the profit earned in any one year may not be the greatest amount that could have been earned for the very reason that such profit would leave the company vulnerable from a future earnings or future financial point of view.

This concept of optimum profit is so important and is so inextricably bound up with cost control and budgetary control, that internal analysis and costing and budgetary techniques are dealt with in a separate chapter. The rest of this chapter is concerned with external analysis as indicated by the diagram on page 720 which also indicates some of the sources of information available to external analysts.

External Analysis

Remember that the traditional function of accounting is:

1.   To record business transactions.

2.   Periodically to prepare an income statement (Profit and Loss Account) which, subject to accounting conventions and limitations, attempts to measure the profit for the period.

3.   To draw up a financial position statement (Balance Sheet), at the end of the period.

These are past-history functions which must be done as a matter of law. On the basis that what happened in the past should be a guide to the future, previous years' published statements are analyzed and evaluated in order to form a view of the trend, which will in turn assist in deducing future results. This approach is termed 'dynamic analysis'.

In fact analysis and interpretation is a painstaking affair requiring a methodical approach; no one impression gained from one observed set of figures is conclusive; and common sense, careful cross-checking, and an aptitude for grasping the inference of figures in financial statements rather than the figures themselves, are likely to produce the most satisfactory results. It must also be remembered that in most cases there is no access to internal data. The audited statements, as augmented by the other sources of information mentioned previously, must form the 'hard-core' of the investigation. Very occasionally, even audited Balance Sheets have proved to be disastrously inaccurate and misleading. Cases in the High Courts have included deliberate manipulation of profits and current assets on the part of highly-placed company officials by inflating closing stocks. One bank advanced about a quarter of a million pounds on the strength of such a Balance Sheet. The subsequent failure of the company revealed the stock manipulation and the bank suffered large losses.

Two points stand out from the preceding discussion of interests, the earnings performance of a company and its solvency. These are now examined from a general point of view.

Earnings Performance

The dominant test on how well the directors have managed the assets under their control is the Return of Investment. The 'return' means the total available net profit after tax at the directors' disposal. The 'investment' means:

(i) Shareholders' paid up capital; or
(ii) (i) above plus all shareholders' reserves; or
(iii) (ii) above plus all long-term loans; or
(iv) (iii) above plus current liabilities

according to the viewpoint held. Another name for 'investment' could well be 'assets employed' since the purpose of obtaining finance in the shape of share capital, loans and short-term credit is to acquire assets of all kinds and to use those assets (employ them) to earn profits. Thus the dominant test could equally as well be described as 'Return on Assets Employed' or, more loosely, 'Return on Capital Employed'. But company Balance Sheets often disclose intangible assets such as goodwill and trademarks which may or may not have the value appearing therein. Therefore a modern concept of Return on Investment from the viewpoint of efficient use of finance uses the gross tangible assets as the Investment. Terminology is unfortunately not consistent in the many textbooks written on this topic.

Consider the simple financial position statement and income statement for a single year shown in Exhibit 47.2. (The figures have been shown very small to keep the discussion simple: the student may regard the Statements as being in £000s.)

Exhibit 47.2

Brite Ltd
Balance Sheet 31 December, Year 4
(Conventional style—published)

	Cost	Accumulated Depreciation	Net
	£	£	£

	£			
Authorized and Issued Share Capital:		Fixed Assets: Vehicles and		
Ordinary shares of £1	1,000	Fittings	2,000	1,000	1,000
Reserves:				
Share Premium	200	Current Assets:		
Profit and Loss Balance	800	Stocks	1,000	
		Debtors	500	
Net Worth	2,000	Bank and Cash	500	
6 per cent Debentures				2,000
(secured)	1,000	Patents and Trademarks		1,000
Current Liabilities	£			
Creditors	200			
Taxation	300			
Proposed Dividend	500			
	1,000			
	4,000			4,000

Income Statement (Profit and Loss Account) for the year ended 31 December, Year 4 (Modern style—published)

Further details of Trading— NOT *published*

		£		£
Sales Income		12,000	Sales Income	12,000
Cost of Sales and Overheads		10,200	Cost of Sales	8,000
	£	1,800	Gross Margin	4,000
Depreciation	440			
Directors' Salaries	100		Selling and Distribution	1,500
Debenture Interest	60	600	Administration and Occupancy	700
			Directors' Salaries	100
Profit before Tax		1,200	Depreciation	440
Taxation		300	Debenture Interest	60
Profit after Tax		900	Total Overhead	2,800
Proposed Dividend of 50 per cent		500	Net Profit before Tax	1,200
Retained Earnings this year		400		
Balance forward from last year		400		
Carried forward per Balance Sheet		800		

Taking Return on Investment as the criteria for measuring earnings efficiency, then:

$$\text{Return on Investment} = \frac{\text{Net Profit after Tax}}{\text{Gross Tangible Assets}} \times 100$$

$$= \frac{£900 \times 100}{3,000} = 30 \text{ per cent}$$

Alternatively the investment base might be:

(i) issued share capital: $\frac{£900}{1,000} \times 100 = 90$ per cent;

(ii) plus reserves: $\frac{£900}{2,000} \times 100 = 45$ per cent;

(iii) plus long-term loans: $\frac{£900}{3,000} \times 100 = 30$ per cent;

(iv) plus short-term credit: $\frac{£900}{4,000} \times 100 = 22 \cdot 5$ per cent.

From the assets employed point of view notice that—

(ii) above equals Net Assets (£4,000−£1,000−£1,000),
(iii) above equals Gross Assets minus Short-term Liabilities
(£4,000−£1,000)

and that among the gross assets there is £1,000 in respect of patents and trademarks. Whether or not these have a value of £1,000 is difficult to establish. The same point arises in the case of goodwill in a Balance Sheet. On the other hand there can be no doubt that preliminary and issue expenses not yet written off in the Balance Sheet is certainly not an asset being employed to earn profits. Thus it is probably best to use the gross tangible assets as the investment base, especially when the financial statements are not being examined from a pure shareholder point of view.

An added complication must be mentioned immediately, although dealt with later in the chapter. The Balance Sheet values at the end of the year have been used to compute the investment base. Although the data does not give last year's figures, the following alternatives might have been considered:

1. Beginning of the year values.

2. Average values computed in a number of different ways.

3. Instead of Balance Sheet values (going concern values and all the conventions of cost *less* accumulated depreciation based on cost, stock valuations, etc.) a computed value representing cost of fixed assets and stocks at replacement prices; in other words the finance required now to acquire assets similar to those in fact employed—but at today's prices. This sophisticated approach attempts to take into account inflation and

it may be important when trying to compare the performances of different companies in the same line of business but of differing ages. Thus one company may possess relatively new plant requiring high depreciation charges, or premises may be fairly new in one case and relatively old in another. These sophistications are properly left until a higher stage of study.

It is suggested, however, that at least some form of averaging is adopted and one commonly used by external analysts is that of adding the opening asset values to the closing values and dividing by two. This is a simple method and while certainly not scientific, it is better than taking beginning or ending values in isolation.

The return on investment can now be given further examination. The calculation of 30 per cent $\left(\dfrac{\text{net profit after tax}}{\text{gross tangible assets}} \times 100 \right)$ is an example of ratio analysis. A relationship has been expressed between two items—in this case an item from the Profit and Loss Account and items from the Balance Sheet. Relationships between two items from the same statement will be looked at later. This is again ratio analysis. Since, however, the above calculation is taken from a single period, it is an example of static ratio analysis. This is of little use except to an internal analyst who has access to pre-determined yardsticks to measure the static ratios against, and so, as previously mentioned, trend ratios must be established by taking a number of years' statements and observing the same ratios over a period of years (dynamic analysis).

If the sales income is available, the Return on Investment can be broken down into two principal factors thus:

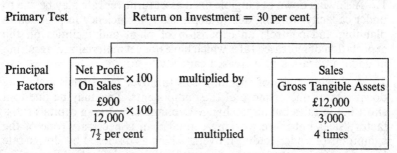

This is useful, since the principal factors highlight the percentage of profit made per £ of sales, and the volume of sales £ achieved by the assets employed. The volume of sales to assets employed is often termed 'asset turnover'. It will now be obvious that the return of 30 per cent could have been obtained in very many ways according to the business structure, policy and line of trade. Thus:

	Net profit per cent		*Asset turnover*	*Return*
(i) (say)	5%	×	6 times	30%
(ii) (say)	4%	×	7½ times	30%
(iii) (say)	10%	×	3 times	30%

The net profit depends on two major factors—

(a) the gross margin, which in turn depends on the sales income of the products *less* the purchase cost or production cost; and

(b) the various items of overhead (many of which are largely fixed) which must be paid for out of the gross margin (gross profit).

The analyst is clearly interested in changes in factors composing the net profit. Much vital information is often missing in published statements, and the reason for net profit changes may be difficult or impossible to establish without access to inside records. Similarly the overall asset turnover depends on a number of component turnover speeds such as:

(a) Fixed asset turnover rates which in turn can be further analyzed into individual rates for the items composing the fixed assets, such as plant and equipment.

(b) Current asset turnover rates which in turn can be further analyzed into individual rates for stocks and debtors.

A continuation of the diagram is now shown in Exhibit 47.3.

The object of this methodical approach is to try and give the answer to why a fall in earnings performance has occurred and to establish trends. The difficulty facing the external analyst with regards to 'why' has already been mentioned when discussing profit margin factors.

Asset Turnover Rates

1. A slowing down of tangible fixed asset turnover rate may be due to under capacity working due to depression; inefficiency in production planning and control; an expansion of plant and facilities on the expectation of increased sales which have not yet materialized, resulting in under-utilization of increased capacity.

2. A slowing down of current assets turnover rate signals a slowing down rate of one or more of the components. This may be due to a short fall in sales but an unchanged volume of working capital; satisfactory sales but more working capital than is necessary (one of the symptoms of under-trading); overstocking as disclosed by slower rate for stock; a lengthening of the production cycle; a building up of finished stocks; a longer period of credit given to debtors as disclosed by a slower rate for debtors' turnover.

It would be a mistake to think that quick dogmatic answers can be given in answer to the question 'why'—even with the most painstaking records of trend ratios. Every impression gained must be cross-checked with other evidence and at all times the absence of inside information must be taken into account. Nevertheless, valuable deductions can be made and unexpressed policies of the directors detected and gauged if the above approach is adopted.

Exhibit 47.3

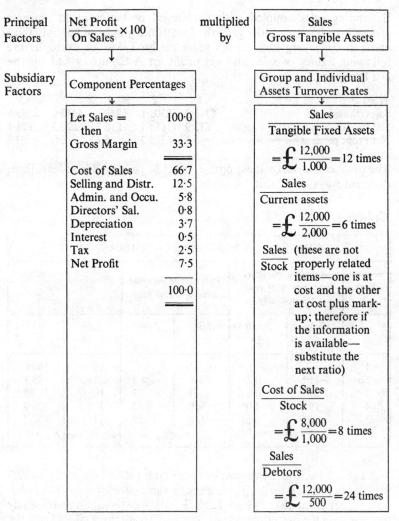

Principal Factors

$$\frac{\text{Net Profit}}{\text{On Sales}} \times 100$$

multiplied by

$$\frac{\text{Sales}}{\text{Gross Tangible Assets}}$$

Subsidiary Factors

Component Percentages

Let Sales =	100·0
then	
Gross Margin	33·3
Cost of Sales	66·7
Selling and Distr.	12·5
Admin. and Occu.	5·8
Directors' Sal.	0·8
Depreciation	3·7
Interest	0·5
Tax	2·5
Net Profit	7·5
	100·0

Group and Individual Assets Turnover Rates

$$\frac{\text{Sales}}{\text{Tangible Fixed Assets}}$$

$$= £\frac{12,000}{1,000} = 12 \text{ times}$$

$$\frac{\text{Sales}}{\text{Current assets}}$$

$$= £\frac{12,000}{2,000} = 6 \text{ times}$$

$\dfrac{\text{Sales}}{\text{Stock}}$ (these are not properly related items—one is at cost and the other at cost plus mark-up; therefore if the information is available— substitute the next ratio)

$$\frac{\text{Cost of Sales}}{\text{Stock}}$$

$$= £\frac{8,000}{1,000} = 8 \text{ times}$$

$$\frac{\text{Sales}}{\text{Debtors}}$$

$$= £\frac{12,000}{500} = 24 \text{ times}$$

Earnings Performance + Additional Aspects

Among other aspects of earnings performance which are now shortly discussed are:

1. Sales and income trends; cyclical companies.
2. Breakeven sales.
3. Earnings per share, price-earnings ratio and dividend policy.
4. Capital structure and gearing.
5. Fixed interest charges and earnings.

Sales and Income Trends

Expanding sales coupled with unchanged or better profit margins generally indicates healthy growth. Sometimes graphs or special tables assist in conveying such trends more easily. Take, for example, the following figures of sales and net profit for A Company Ltd for the last five years:

Years	1	2	3	4	5
Sales (thousands)	£313·9	£302·1	£323·1	£342·9	£363·8
Net Profit (thousands)	£15·9	£15·7	£16·5	£20·5	£21·1
Net Profit per cent	5·1	5·3	5·1	6·0	5·8

The trend conveyed by these figures could be presented in at least three different ways; see Exhibit 47.4.

Exhibit 47.4

A COMPANY LTD. FIVE-YEAR SURVEY OF SALES AND PROFIT					
Year	Absolute increase over previous year (thousands)		Percentage increase over previous year		Growth percentage in relation to base year	
	Sales £	Profit £	Sales	Profit	Sales	Profit
1					100·0	100·0
2	−11·8	−0·2	−3·8	− 1·3	96·2	98·7
3	21·0	0·8	7·0	5·1	103·0	103·8
4	19·8	4·0	6·1	24·2	109·2	128·9
5	20·9	0·6	6·1	2·9	115·9	132·7
	TABLE 1		TABLE 2		TABLE 3	

Table 3 discloses a five-year growth in sales of 15·9 per cent and 32·7 per cent in profit, whereas Table 2 shows successive increases over each year (apart from year 2) and Table 1 indicates the amount of yearly increase over the preceding year—year 2 apart. All three tables show the 'jump' in profits earned in year 4.

Investors are interested in identifying companies whose earnings fluctuate as business conditions change. In times of depression such companies experience falling profits and their share prices tend to drop on anticipation of lower dividends. Before this happens, investors switch to companies offering more stable earnings. On the other hand, when an 'upswing' of the economy is expected, investors tend to switch back to the original company while the shares are at a low price and thus hope to reap the benefit of revived or increasing dividends; an improved yield on the shares; and possibly capital gains on sale of the shares when the price has risen sufficiently on the stock exchange.

Identification of cyclical companies is assisted by graphing sales and costs over a period of years and by charting a value for break-even sales. The first graph, Exhibit 47.5, helps to show the sensitivity of the company's profit to sales volume; the second, Exhibit 47.6, pinpoints (very roughly) that volume of sales at which the company neither makes a profit nor suffers loss.

Exhibit 47.5

Sensitivity of Profits to changes in volume of Business
Data: Y Company Limited.

Year	Sales	Profit	Total Costs
1	£50,000	Loss £2,000	£52,000
2	70,000	8,000	62,000
3	40,000	Loss 13,000	53,000
4	90,000	21,000	69,000
5	65,000	10,000	55,000

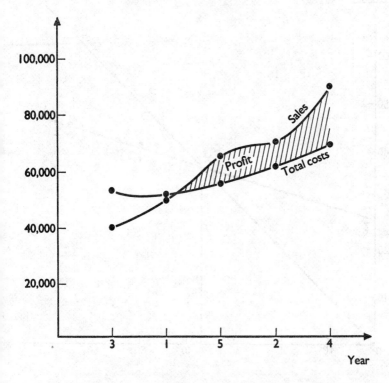

In Exhibit 47.5, the smallest sales figure and the corresponding total costs for same year are plotted first; then the next smallest sales figure and corresponding total costs are plotted and so on. Thus the order of plotting for both sales and total costs is year 3, year 1, year 5, year 2

and finally year 4. The sales plots and the total costs plots are then joined up by hand as accurately as possible. The sensitivity of Y Company's profits to varying sales volumes is thus brought out more clearly than by mere inspection of figures.

Exhibit 47.6

Break-Even by Charting

Data: T Company Limited.

Year	Sales	Profit	Total Costs
1	£55,000	£13,000	£42,000
2	65,000	20,000	45,000
3	50,000	9,000	41,000
4	45,000	6,000	39,000
5	60,000	17,000	43,000

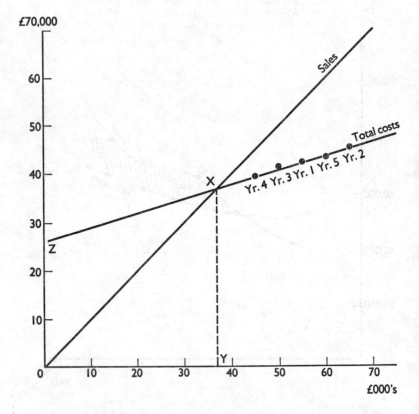

In the case of T Company, Exhibit 47–6, the sales line is drawn as a straight line from zero to £70,000. The lowest sales figure is then taken (£45,000) and correlated with the total cost for those sales (£39,000), and *one* point plotted and endorsed with the year (year 4). Then the second lowest sales figure is taken (£50,000) and its corresponding total costs (£41,000) and a second point is plotted and so on. A line of best fit—that is, as many points above the line as below it—is drawn with a ruler. Where the line intersects the sales line (X on the chart) denotes the break-even point. A perpendicular dropped to the base discloses the value in £ of the break-even point to be approximately £37,000. At this volume of sales, T Company makes no profit nor suffers any loss. Additionally, where the line of best fit cuts the vertical axis of the graph (Z on the chart) an approximate value for fixed over-heads of the company can be read—in this case about £26,000.

Further mention of the above charts and techniques is made in the next chapter dealing with internal analysis, evaluation and costing.

Earnings per Share, Price-Earning Ratio, Dividend Policy

Investors and potential investors are particularly interested in the total net profit earned in the year which would have been received if the directors had paid it all out as dividend. This is calculated as the profit earned per share. Such an amount compared with what the directors have in fact paid out per share gives an indication of the dividend policy of the directors.

Secondly, an investor must constantly review the yield he is in fact receiving from his investment, most particularly when he has had to pay, for example, £3 on the stock exchange to obtain a £1 share in a popular company. Clearly if the directors of that company declare a dividend of 30 per cent, the yield to the investor is only 10 per cent.

To sum up then, an investor is interested in the amount earned per share and the amount paid per share—but above all he views both these points in relation to the amount he has had to pay to obtain the shares in the first place, that is the market price. The same remarks apply to a potential investor. Reverting to the published statements for Brite Ltd, you will note that the available profit for year 4 is £900. The directors have recommended a dividend amounting to £500, and £400 has been retained. If a market price for Brite Ltd shares at the date of the Balance Sheet is assumed to be £2 per share, the above discussion would then read:

Earnings per share $\dfrac{£900}{1,000 \text{ shares}}$ = 90 per cent

Dividends per share $\dfrac{£500}{1,000 \text{ shares}}$ = 50 per cent

Market price per share at year end   £2

Price-earnings ratio at year end   = Total market value of shares: Earnings,
    $1,000 \times £2 = £2,000$ £900
    = 2·2 to 1 (approx.)

Dividend yield on market price at year end as a per cent = £ $\dfrac{500}{2,000}$ = 25 per cent

The student should now look up some actual published results and stock exchange quotations, and reason out why, if there was such a company as Brite Ltd with a price-earnings ratio of 2·2 to 1, potential investors would probably have a heart attack in the rush to buy its shares.

Capital Structure, Gearing

The manner in which a company is financing its assets is termed capital structure. Most company balance sheets disclose that the assets at the Balance Sheet date are owned by:

  (i) debenture holders, for money lent to the company; they have first priority in case of failure (if secured against the assets);
 (ii) creditors, largely for goods and materials contained in the 'Stock' on the Balance Sheet; they have second claim on liquidation; and
(iii) shareholders, for money subscribed in exchange for shares, and for undrawn profits and other reserves; they have residual claim on any surplus after prior claims have been met in full.

It is of interest to compare the amounts that each of the above parties have at risk at the Balance Sheet date. A reasonable assumption might be that those who stand to gain the most in times of prosperity should have the most at risk. This assumption should mean that the ordinary shareholders should be expected to have most at risk. This by no means always happens in actual fact.

The proportions in which class (i) and class (iii) above share the risk is termed 'gearing'. Since funds from long-term lenders are usually cheaper than shareholders' funds, the gearing has a profound effect on profits after tax. In times of depression the gearing can be the cause of company failure. Exhibit 47.7 illustrates the points.

Exhibit 47.7

Classes (i) and (iii)	D Company Ltd	E Company Ltd
Capital Structure:	£	£
Ordinary Share Capital	400,000	100,000
Retained Profits	100,000	100,000
Ordinary Shareholders' Risk	500,000	200,000
8 per cent Debentures	100,000	400,000
Total Long-term Funds Employed	600,000	600,000
Ratio of Fixed Funds (Debentures) to Equity (ordinary shareholders) Funds	1 to 5	4 to 2
Ratio of Fixed Funds to Equity Capital	1 to 4	4 to 1
Gearing	Low	High

Trading Results	D Company Ltd			E Company Ltd		
	£	£	£	£	£	£
Profit	72,000	54,000	36,000	72,000	54,000	36,000
Debenture Interest	8,000	8,000	8,000	32,000	32,000	32,000
	64,000	46,000	28,000	40,000	22,000	4,000
Tax (say 50 per cent)	32,000	23,000	14,000	20,000	11,000	2,000
Available Profit Earned for Ordinary Share- holders	32,000	23,000	14,000	20,000	11,000	2,000
Earnings Rate on Ordinary Capital	8%	5·75%	3·5%	20%	11%	2%
Ratio of D Co. Available Profit to that of E Co	1·6 to 1 2·09 to 1 7 to 1					

Notice that a drop in profits of 50 per cent (£72,000 to £36,000) just more than halves D Company's available profit but reduces that of E Company by ninety per cent to £2,000. This is because E Company is *high geared*; it is using more fixed funds than 'risk' funds. There is therefore a tendency for investors to disfavour the high-geared company when the economy is depressed. The converse holds good when business is buoyant; the speculative investor stands a very good chance of high rewards; for example, if E Company in boom periods produced a profit of £132,000, then, after debenture interest deduction of £32,000 and tax of £50,000, the profit earned for the ordinary shareholder would be £50,000 and therefore a very high dividend is possible.

Fixed Interest Charges and Earnings

The ease with which a company can pay its fixed interest is important. Failure to pay interest means that control passes to the debenture holders who may force a sale of assets to satisfy their claims, with all the attendant bad publicity and losses on enforced sales.

The capacity to pay interest is tested by dividing the interest payment into the profits after tax plus the interest paid giving an 'interest times covered' ratio. This is not an absolutely accurate test owing to the incidence of taxation and its legal computation regarding debenture interest, but it is near enough for external analysis purposes. Capital structure, gearing and interest 'times covered' as applicable to Brite Ltd, year 4, now follow:

Brite Ltd, Year 4

Capital Structure:		%
net Total Assets *minus* Current Liabilities		100·0

then

Ordinary Share Capital	=	33·3
Reserves	=	33·3
Risk Capital (Equity)		66·7
Long-term Loans		33·3
		100·0

Gearing:
Fixed Funds to Risk Funds—

(a) on Risk Capital	= £1,000 to £1,000
	= 1 to 1 = equal geared
(b) on Total Risk Funds	= £1,000 to £2,000
	= 1 to 2 = low geared

Interest 'times covered':	
Profit after Tax	£900
Add Interest Paid	60
	960

$$\text{Times covered} \pounds\frac{960}{60} = 16 \text{ times}$$

It can be seen that Brite Ltd is a low-geared company; its annual interest payment is amply covered sixteen times; and that the shareholders have twice as much risk as the debenture holders, or a 'debt/equity' ratio of 1 to 2 (50 per cent).

The second topic of outstanding interest can now be dealt with—the ability of a company to pay its way from day to day.

Solvency

Working capital is the excess of current assets over current liabilities. The excess is sometimes termed 'net working capital'. If there is no excess or if the excess is not sufficiently liquid, creditors' accounts cannot easily be paid as they fall due. Short-term creditors are therefore vitally interested in changes of working capital and in unexpressed policies of the directors. It is not unreasonable to suppose that if a company is making substantial profits, its financial position must be secure. This is often far from the case. Indeed, it has been said that as many firms fail for doing too much business as for doing too little.

Major causes of working capital difficulties are:

1. Increasing the volume of business by relying too much on short-term credit. Consider the case of F Company Ltd, which doubled its business operations in a single period:

F Company Ltd		
	Year 4	*Year 3*
	£	£
Sales	800,000	400,000
Current Assets	400,000	200,000
Current Liabilities	320,000	120,000
Net Working Capital	80,000	80,000
Net Working Capital as a Percentage of Sales	20%	20%
Current Ratio	1·25 to 1	1·66 to 1

The volume (£80,000) of net working capital remains the same although business operations have doubled. This is one aspect of what is known as 'overtrading'. The ratio net working capital to sales draws attention to this potential danger spot. The current ratio, which is the ratio of current assets to current liabilities, shows the weakening financial position by a fall from 1·66 to 1·25. If this fall persists in the next year, the company is clearly heading for a crisis. It would have been safer to finance the expansion with at least some long-term funds.

2. Using the cash generated by profit-making for:

(a) purchasing fixed assets;
(b) repaying long-term liabilities;
(c) paying-out excessive dividends

and thus depleting working capital. A movement of cash statement termed 'Flow of Funds Statement', which is dealt with in Chapter 45 is a valuable aid for detecting the above policies.

3. A lengthening of the working capital cycle due to overstocking, carrying obsolete stock, bottlenecks in production, poor credit control and the like. Turnover speeds for stocks and debtors has already been mentioned in the discussion on earnings performance.

In order to focus attention on the make-up of the current assets two further ratios are in common use:

1. The Liquid or Quick Ratio: which is (current assets *less* stocks) to current liabilities.

2. The Acid Test Ratio: which is (current assets *less* stocks *less* Debtors and prepayments *less* any other non-liquid asset) to current liabilities. This ratio generally means bank, cash and quickly realizable investments to current liabilities.

Terminology varies considerably; for example, the quick ratio is often taken to mean current assets *less* stocks *less* prepayments to current liabilities. Some writers use 'acid test' instead of the term 'quick'. Whether or not the bank overdraft is included as part of the current liabilities depends on the degree of permanency of the facility. Liquidity ratios for Brite Ltd are now computed:

Brite Ltd, Year 4, Analysis

Schedule I: Liquidity ratios

	£	
Current Assets	2,000	
Current Liabilities	1,000	
Net Working Capital	1,000	
Current Ratio	2 to 1	(£2,000 to £1,000)
Liquid Ratio	1 to 1	(£1,000 to £1,000)
Acid Test Ratio	0·5 to 1	(£500 to £1,000)

Schedule II: Stock turnover speed

	£	
Cost of Sales	8,000	
Average Stock	1,000	(year-end figure taken)
Turnover speed for year	8 times	
Turnover speed in days	46 days	(365 days ÷ by 8)

Schedule III: Debtor collection speed

	£	
Credit Sales	12,000	
Average Debtors	500	(year-end figure taken)
Turnover speed for year	24 times	
Turnover speed in days	16 days	(365 days ÷ by 24)

Schedule IV: Calculation of working capital cycle in days

From Schedule II: average days to convert stock into sales	46 days
From Schedule III: average days to collect cash from debtors	16 days
Average working capital cycle in days	62 days

A further example of liquidity analysis for G Company Ltd covering a three-year period, and incorporating the simple averaging of assets employed mentioned earlier, is now given.

G Company Ltd

Data

	Year 4 £	Year 3 £	Year 2 £	Year 1 £
Current Assets:				
Stock	1,000	600	500	300
Debtors	600	500	400	250
Bank and Cash	50	150	200	
	1,650	1,250	1,100	
Current Liabilities:				
Creditors	750	550	300	
Tax	400	200	200	
Proposed Dividends	100	100	100	
	1,250	850	600	
Sales (all credit)	3,500	3,000	2,500	
Cost of Sales	2,800	2,400	2,000	
Gross Margin	700	600	500	

G Company Ltd, Three-Year Analysis

Schedule I: Liquidity ratios

	Year 4 £	Year 3 £	Year 2 £
Current Assets	1,650	1,250	1,100
Current Liabilities	1,250	850	600
Net Working Capital	400	400	500
Current Ratio	1·3 to 1	1·47 to 1	1·83 to 1
Liquid Ratio	0·52 to 1	0·76 to 1	1·0 to 1

Schedule II: Stock turnover speed

	£	£	£
Cost of Sales	2,800	2,400	2,000
Opening Stock	600	500	300
Closing Stock	1,000	600	500
Average Stock (opening plus closing divided by 2)	800	550	400
Turnover speed for year	3·5 times	4·4 times	5 times
Turnover speed in days	105 days	83 days	73 days

Schedule III: Debtor collection speed

	£	£	£
Credit Sales	3,500	3,000	2,500
Opening Debtors	500	400	250
Closing Debtors	600	500	400
Average Debtors (opening plus closing divided by 2)	550	450	325
Turnover speed for year	6·36 times	6·7 times	7·7 times
Turnover speed in days	58 days	55 days	48 days

Schedule IV: Calculation of working capital cycle in days

Average days to convert stock into sales (Schedule II)	105 days	83 days	73 days
Average days to collect cash from debtors (Schedule III)	58	55	48
Average working capital cycle	163 days	138 days	121 days

The picture conveyed by the above analysis is that of financial resources being strained by business expansion. Despite a vigorous growth in sales, this company is heading for financial trouble unless the unfavourable trends can be reversed. Whether or not the stock and debtor policies are due to deliberate intention on the part of the directors is not known. If they have increased the range of goods, and extended more credit to debtors in order to encourage an expansion of business, then additional finance must be obtained to support the expansion. Further investigation into the movements of cash generated by profits would be important.

The important matter of 'yardsticks' has been left until last. The reasons have been discussed why the return on investment and working capital analysis are important, and an indication has been made of some of the ways to evaluate earnings performance and working capital strength. The problem is:

(a) What percentage should the Return on Investment be?
(b) Is there a 'right' ratio for current ratio and liquid ratio?
(c) How long should the working capital cycle be?

As may be suspected, there is no 'right' answer to any of these questions. Earnings performance varies from industry to industry and also within any one industry. Working capital requirements differ enormously according to trade, complexity of process and custom. It must also be remembered that, although trade creditors like to see the current ratios as high as possible, a very high ratio could well mean idle cash balances or persistent undertrading; that a high stock turnover rate could indicate loss of sales due to carrying too low a stock or too limited a range of items; that a very short collection period for debtors could result in loss of customers through denying sufficient or unjustifiable credit.

A possible solution is for the external analyst to check his results with other companies in the same line of business, and of similar size and structure. Specialist concerns, such as the Centre for Interfirm Comparison Ltd, collate a number of companies' operating ratios, for the benefit of the trade concerned. Board of Trade statistics and published material in financial and economic journals are often useful.

Five tentative points are offered:

1. Many American companies expect a return on investment of 20 per cent from their overseas companies.

2. An acid test ratio (bank, cash and quickly realizable short-term investments to current liabilities) greater than 0·5 to 1 often means idle resources.

3. Adverse trends within an established company signal a departure from its own 'norm'. This is more important than comparison with other companies.

4. Year-end stock and debtors in the Balance Sheet may be a long way removed from the true average figures. Simple averaging using the opening and closing Balance Sheet figures may be somewhat nearer the true averages.

5. As Balance Sheets and Profit and Loss Accounts show the results of past transactions they are always out of date to some extent when published.

Exercises

Extra questions for this edition have been inserted as numbers 47.11, 47.12 and 47.13. Answers to these are to be found at the back of the book.

47.1. The Balance Sheet of AB Co Ltd shows the following figures:

AB Co Ltd Balance Sheet Figures

	£		£
Issued Ordinary Capital	152,000	Debtors	20,000
Cash in Hand and Bank	30,000	Provision for Bad Debts	2,000
Fixed Assets	113,000	Stock of Finished Goods	35,000
Creditors	20,000	Stock of Raw Material	12,000
Accruals	4,000	Work in Progress	5,000
Debentures:		General Reserve	8,000
24,000 £1		Profit and Loss App.	
5 per cent Debentures	24,000	Account	5,000

(i) Prepare a Balance Sheet in vertical or 'Narrative' form.
(ii) What is the Liquid Ratio?
(iii) What is the Current Ratio?
(iv) What is the Working Capital?

(East Midland Educational Union)

47.2. The following is a summary of the final accounts of Ritchie Ltd for the year ending 31 December 19–5.

Trading and Profit and Loss Accounts

	£	£
Net Sales		960,000
Stock 1 January 19–5	36,000	
Purchases	808,000	
	844,000	
Stock 31 December 19–5	44,000	
Cost of Goods Sold		800,000
Gross Profit		160,000
Selling and Administration Expenses		80,000
Net Profit before Tax		80,000

Balance Sheet

Capital and Reserves	£	*Assets*	£
Ordinary Shares	400,000	Fixed Assets	380,000
Revenue Reserves	100,000	Current Assets:	
Current Liabilities	80,000	Stock	44,000
		Debtors	120,000
		Cash	36,000
	580,000		580,000

From the above information calculate (showing your workings):

(a) Rate of stock turnover.
(b) Working capital ratio.
(c) Debtor's turnover and average credit period taken.
(d) Return on total assets employed.
(e) Return on equity interest in the assets.

(Northern Counties Technical Examinations Council)

47.3. The following are the summarized Trading and Profit and Loss Accounts for the year 19–6 and the Balance Sheet, on 31 December 19–6 of Case Ltd and Box Ltd.

Trading and Profit and Loss Accounts

	Case £	Box £		Case £	Box £
Stock 1 January 19–6	48,000	8,000	Sales	360,000	360,000
Purchases	319,000	324,000	Stock 31 December 19–6	52,000	12,000
Gross Profit	45,000	40,000			
	412,000	372,000		412,000	372,000

Trading and Profit and Loss Accounts

	Case £	Box £		Case £	Box £
			Gross Profit	45,000	40,000
Overhead Expenses	16,200	17,600			
Net Profit	28,800	22,400			
	45,000	40,000		45,000	40,000

Balance Sheets

	Case £	Box £		Case £	Box £
Issued Share Capital	100,000	100,000	Fixed Assets	127,800	107,500
Reserves	80,000	16,000	Stock	52,000	12,000
Profit and Loss Account	60,000	24,000	Debtors	40,000	24,000
Creditors	63,800	40,500	Bank	84,000	37,000
	303,800	180,500		303,800	180,500

You are required:

(a) To set out and complete a table in the following form:

	Case Ltd	Box Ltd
Stockturn		
Debtor Ratio (in months)		
Creditor Ratio (in months)		
Current Ratio		
Return on Equity interest in the Assets		
Liquid Ratio		
Gross Profit as percentage of Sales		
Working Capital		
Return on Total Assets Employed		

You may assume that the stock of each company has been built up from the amount at 1 January to the amount at 31 December at an even rate during the year. In relation to the liquid ratio, trade debtors are to be treated as liquid assets.

(b) To describe briefly the conclusions to be drawn from a comparison of the above ratios and percentages relating to C Ltd with those relating to B Ltd. You are to assume that both companies sell the same kind of products in similar markets.

All calculations should be carried to two decimal places.

47.4A. A Poodle Parlour Proprietor has an option of buying two types of coats specially designed for poodles as follows:

	Dog Coat	Dog Coat
	A	B
	£	£
Cost Price	8	12
Probable selling price	10	20

He estimates that his expenses of dealing in these coats, quite apart from the finance required to buy them, will amount to £200, and that he requires a profit of at least £200 on this particular venture.

Calculate:

(a) how many of Coat A he would have to sell to recover his expenses of £200; and

(b) if he did not buy Coat A, how many of Coat B he would have to sell to recover his expenses of £200; and

(c) if he bought an equal quantity of each coat, the number of each type he would have to sell to recover his expenses of £200 and provide the desired profit.

47.5A. From the following incomplete statement calculate:

(a) the cost of sales
(b) the overhead.

Income statement

	£
Sales	14,000
Gross margin	2,800
Net profit	700

and prepare the complete information in the form of component percentages.

47.6A. From the following information, calculate:

(a) sales to capital employed ratio; and
(b) the capital employed for each business.

	Business	Business
	A	Z
	£	£
Sales	20,000	30,000
Net Profit	1,000	3,000
	per cent	per cent
Return on capital employed achieved	20	20

47.7A. Cassius and Claudius both started up business at the same time, but they were completely independent of each other and operated in different towns. At the end of the first year, their income statements were:

	Claudius	Cassius
	£	£
Sales	10,000	5,000
Cost of Sales	5,000	2,000

	Claudius	Cassius
	£	£
Gross Margin	5,000	3,000
Overhead	3,000	1,000
	2,000	2,000

Their financial position statements showed that they had both employed total assets of £5,000.

Who was the more efficient businessman?

47.8A. David Evans had started business on 1 January Year 1, with his cash savings of £1,200 and premises, given to him by his father, valued at £4,700.

Two years later when his cash and balance at bank was only £90 he asks you whether he has been making any profit and, if so, to explain where it has gone.

You ascertain that at 31 December Year 2, Evans' stock valued at cost price amounted to £1,700 and he had debtors of £260; at the same time he had creditors of £190 as well as a mortgage on the premises of £500. It was agreed that the premises should be depreciated by 2 per cent per annum on cost and that a van he had bought on 7 January Year 1, for £600 should be written down by £100 for each year.

Evans' withdrawals from the business for private purposes were estimated at: Year 1 £960, and Year 2 £1,450. You also found that in February, Year 2 Evans had received a legacy of £200 which he had paid into the business bank account.

You are required to prepare:

(i) a statement of Evans' profit or loss for the two-year period to 31 December Year 2.
(ii) an assets variation statement showing the sources and applications of funds during the two years.

47.9A. The following is a summary of the final accounts of F.T.A. Ltd, Timber Merchants, for the year ended 31 December Year 5, and the Balance Sheet at that date, together with the prior year's figures:

Trading and Profit and Loss Account
for year ended 31 December

	Year 5	Year 4
	£	£
Sales	23,220	19,550
Cost of Sales	18,576	15,249
Gross Margin	4,644	4,301
Discount Received	104	302
	4,748	4,603
Wages	1,020	1,120
Overheads	1,670	1,563
Debenture Interest	200	—
Directors' Fees	460	460

	Year 5	Year 4
	£	£
Bad Debts	260	220
Depreciation	335	360
	3,945	3,723
Profit before Tax	803	880
Balance from last year	1,000	1,186
	1,803	2,076

		Year 5		Year 4
Formation Costs	76		76	
Preference Dividend	500		500	
Transfer to Reserve	—		500	
		576		1,076
		1,227		1,000

Balance Sheet at 31 December

			Year 5		Year 4
		£	£	£	£
Goodwill at Cost			11,000		11,000
Tangible Fixed Assets:	Cost	Deprn.			
Premises	13,400	1,860	11,540		11,840
Equipment	600	283	317		352
				11,857	12,192
	14,000	2,143			
Current Assets:					
Stock			3,625		4,620
Debtors *less* Provision			4,610		5,684
Bill Receivable			5,295		660
Bank and Cash			146		—
				13,676	10,964
Formation Costs				—	76
Assets Employed:				36,533	34,232

Funded by:					
Share Capital:	*Authorized and Issued:*				
Ordinary Shares of £0·5 each			15,000		15,000
5 per cent Preference Shares of £1 each			10,000		10,000
				25,000	25,000
Reserves:					
General Reserve			1,000		1,000
Retained Profit			1,227		1,000
				2,227	2,000
				27,227	27,000

	Year 5		Year 4
	£	£	£	£
5 per cent mortgage debentures		4,000		—
Current Liabilities:				
Creditors	3,131		2,960	
Bills Payable	2,075		1,872	
Debenture Interest	100		—	
Bank Overdraft	—		2,400	
		5,306		7,232
		36,533		34,232

Required:

(i) Calculate the percentage of gross profit on Sales for both years.

(ii) Suggest two possible reasons for any difference between these two percentages.

(iii) Prepare a Statement showing the increase in the company's funds during the year and the manner in which such increase has been applied.

47.10A. The Balance Sheets of P. Hedges Ltd at 31 December Year 14 and 31 December Year 15, are as under:

P. Hedges Ltd
Balance Sheets

	31 December Year 14	31 December Year 15
	£	£
Issued Capital (£1 shares)	50,000	80,000
Share Premium		6,000
Surplus on Revaluation of Property		10,000
Profit and Loss Balance	20,000	16,000
6 per cent Debentures	10,000	
Creditors	12,000	14,000
Bank Overdraft	17,000	
	109,000	126,000

	31 December Year 14		31 December Year 15	
	£	£	£	£
Freehold Property, Cost		30,000		40,000 (Revalued)
Plant and Machinery:				
Cost	60,000		70,000	
Depreciation to Date	20,000		28,000	
		40,000		42,000
Stock		20,000		19,000
Debtors		19,000		23,000
Balance at Bank				2,000
		109,000		126,000

Required:

Discuss the progress of the company during Year 15, so far as it can be deduced from these two balance sheets.

47.11. Joe Loss has a retail merchandising business in soft furnishings. You are present at a monthly management meeting held shortly after the preparation of draft accounts for the year ended 31 December 19–5, part of which is reproduced below as exhibit A.

Mr Loss expressed surprise at the meeting at which the accounts were produced insofar that, although the sales had increased by 20 per cent over 19–4, the gross margin was the same for both years. Mr Loss hands you Exhibit A without comment but endorses on the exhibit the following note:

'In order to arrive at the selling price, the strict procedure laid down is to mark up on cost 22½ per cent; e.g., if the cost of a bale of curtaining is £100, the selling price is (£100 +22½ per cent)= £122·50. This policy has been strictly adhered to during 19–4 and 19–5.'

Mr Loss asks you to look into the matter.

Required:

Write a short report to Mr Loss giving five possible reasons for the discrepancy between the gross margin based on his figures in his note, and the figures shown by exhibit A; include three reasons which, if occurring in 19–4 would automatically affect the gross margin for 19–5 by the same amount.

Exhibit A

	31 December 19–4	31 December 19–5
	£	£
Opening stock at cost	220,000	300,000
Purchases	2,080,000	2,450,000
Available stock	2,300,000	2,750,000
Closing stock at cost	300,000	250,000
Cost of sales	2,000,000	2,500,000
Gross margin	500,000	500,000
Sales	2,500,000	3,000,000

47.12. Abridged data for a chain of foodstores and for a motorcycle manufacturing concern is given below:

	Foodstores	Motor Cycle Concern
	£ millions	£ millions
Sales	500	125
Net operating profit	20	20
Fixed assets	50	40
Current assets	50	75
Current liabilities	50	30
Loans	—	20
Net worth	50	65

Required:
(a) Complete a table (work to 2 decimal places) in the following form:

	FOODSTORES	MOTOR CYCLE CONCERN
1. Return on Investment using total assets employed as the investment base		
2. Net profit margin (as a per cent)		
3. Asset turnover rate per annum		
4. Current Ratio		
5. Return on Shareholders' Capital Employed		

(b) Comment on the implication of the differences between the two concerns as revealed in part (a).

(*Institute of Bankers adapted*)

47.13. Minards Limited trades in musical instruments, Hi-Fi equipment, and cassette tapes. Good profits have been made over recent years and income statements (as per extracts given below) for years 31 March 19–5 and 19–6 disclosed gross margins of £159,300 and £166,200 respectively.

The Managing Director is not particularly happy about the results for 19–6 and has asked for a short report. Assuming that you are at present working in the Finance Department of the company and that your senior has passed the matter on to you—

1. Calculate an accounting ratio for each year which will reveal the extent of the problem; and
2. Write a Report not exceeding 150 words in length to the Managing Director stating five possible reasons for the difference in the ratio between these two years; and
3. Make any recommendations which you consider may assist in localizing such difference.

Extract from Income Statement

	£ 19–5	£ 19–6
Opening stock	25,000	38,000
Purchases	278,700	318,300
Available stock	303,700	356,300
Closing stock	38,000	22,500
Cost of sales	265,700	333,800
Sales	425,000	500,000
Gross margin	159,300	166,200

48

Profit Control: including Budgeting, Costing and Internal Analysis

Aim of Business Management

In a free enterprise, the aim of business managers is to make the maximum profit without jeopardizing the long-term interests and stability of the enterprise—in other words, the *optimum* profit. Basically, as was shown in the preceding chapter, this means:

1. Achieving an acceptable return on investment.

2. Maintaining adequate working capital and preserving the ability to settle short-term creditors with reasonable promptness.

3. Paying proper attention to the 'image' of the enterprise, and giving reasonable consideration to the interests of shareholders, long-term lenders and customers.

These objectives place a heavy responsibility on top management. In a large enterprise the managing director must recruit key personnel of the right calibre and outlook to help him to achieve the optimum profit. Teamwork is essential, and it has been found that the most effective way to achieve the above is to forecast sales and production activity in advance; record and measure actual events against the forecast at short intervals; and take corrective action during the year so as to achieve the forecast as nearly as possible. This process of planning, recording, reporting and taking action, together with special studies showing the probable financial results of alternative courses of action, is termed management accounting. Exhibit 48.1 shows the typical 'team' and areas of responsibility for a manufacturing concern of medium size (with which this chapter is largely concerned).

Exhibit 48.1

Organizational Structure—Manufacturing Concern

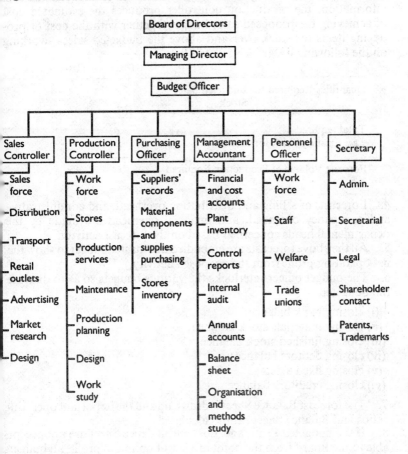

Budgetary Control

Briefly, the procedure is as follows:

1. About three to four months before the current year-end, the Budget Office issues all available information concerning top management policies and plans for the future to the various controllers and managers, and initiates the planning for the coming year.

2. The sales controller, with the aid of market surveys, trend and statistical studies, forecasts sales in physical units and value.

3. These are studied by the production controller, and assuming he has the production capacity available, he forecasts quantities of materials and labour hours and probable production overheads to produce the forecast volume. If the present capacity is too small, or if there are other

limiting factors such as materials shortage or specialist labour shortage, then urgent high-level discussions must be held to resolve the difficulties or to adjust the budget for sales. With the aid of financial and cost information, the production controller produces the estimated cost of achieving the proposed sales budget together with the cost of producing items for stock over and above the budgeted sales—working on the following lines:

	Units	Cost
Quantities Required for Budgeted Sales	x	
,, ,, Stock	x	
Total required	x	
Less Existing Stock for Sale	x	
Forecast Volume of Production Required	x	£x

4.   Forecasts of selling and distribution overhead, and administrative and occupancy overhead, and financial overhead are made by the departmental heads concerned based on the forecast activity.

5.   All the above forecasts are embodied in a master budget to show the net operating profit from the proposed activity.

6.   The budget officer interlocks the various budgets so as to disclose the budgeted—

  (i) closing bank balance;
 (ii) closing materials stock balance;
(iii) closing finished stock balance;
(iv) closing debtors balance;
 (v) closing fixed assets;
(vi) closing creditors balance.

7.   The forecast Balance Sheet is drawn up and the important operating ratios and Balance Sheet ratios calculated.

8.   If the budgeted Profit and Loss and Balance Sheet are not acceptable to the Board from the point of view of optimum profit, all budgets are referred back to the 'team' for alternative proposals.

9.   When the overall forecast is acceptable to the Board, it is broken down into short-term periods of, say, one month, and then issued to the controllers and managers as firm budgets for the coming year.

10. As soon as the year starts, sales, production costs and overheads are recorded with the same detail as was contained by the budgets.

11. At short intervals, usually monthly, actual results are compared with the budgets and:

(*a*) reported to top management, with
(*b*) sectional reports to the appropriate departmental heads and section leaders.

In many cases, weekly reports concerning material usage and labour efficiency are made to the production controller who passes on the information right down to the factory floor for action as necessary.

12. The reports should show:

(a) actual results for the period and cumulatively to-date;
(b) budgeted results;
(c) variances (differences) from the budgets;
(d) explanations for all important deviations from budgets;
(e) as an additional 'yardstick' for comparison, last year's cumulative actual results up to the same date;
(f) comments and suggestions.

13. As a result of the above reporting, actions authorized by top management are implemented with a view to:

(a) exploiting favourable deviations from the budgets; and
(b) minimizing the effects of unfavourable deviations.

The above system of control is generally referred to as 'budgetary control'.

Master Budget and Balance Sheet

Exhibit 48–2 shows how the various budgets are reflected in the forecast Profit and Loss Account and Balance Sheet. The former is often referred to as the 'Master Budget'.

In some cases the management accountant also acts as the budget officer. In any case, all controllers and managers and section leaders can expect considerable help from the management accountant when they are compiling their budgets for costs and revenues. It should not be thought, however, that the management accountant overshadows all other departmental heads. The modern view is to avoid imposing targets on departmental heads, but rather to encourage them to make their own forecasts with the help of accounting and costing information from past efforts. In this way, all departmental heads and key staff become involved in the technique of forward planning and working in harmony with each other, in an effort to produce a single master plan acceptable to the board of directors. Of course, wildly inaccurate forecasting cannot be passed over for very long. If, over a period of three years for example, persistent inaccuracies are experienced, the departmental heads and section leaders responsible must make way in favour of those who have a better aptitude for forecasting.

Ratios: (re Exhibit 48.2). The following ratios would be calculated:

1. Forecast return on investment (see preceding chapter);
2. Principal factors: profit margins
   asset turnover rates
3. Forecast working capital;
   Forecast—current ratio
   　　　　—liquid ratio
   　　　　—other ratios and yardsticks.

Exhibit 48.2

Forecast Operating Statement for the year ending . . .

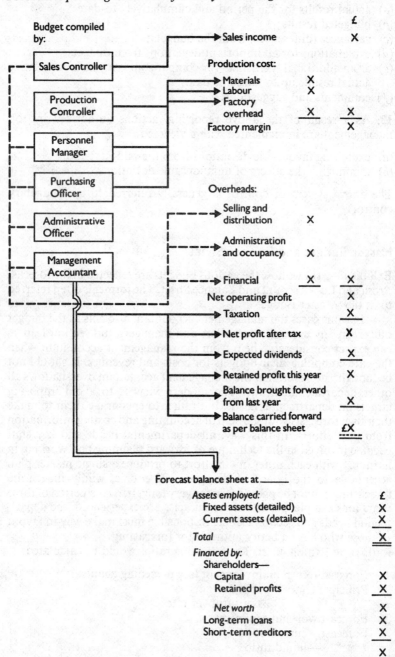

Budget compiled by:		£
Sales Controller	Sales income	X
	Production cost:	
Production Controller	Materials	X
	Labour	X
Personnel Manager	Factory overhead	X
	Factory margin	X
Purchasing Officer		
	Overheads:	
Administrative Officer	Selling and distribution	X
	Administration and occupancy	X
Management Accountant	Financial	X
	Net operating profit	X
	Taxation	X
	Net profit after tax	X
	Expected dividends	X
	Retained profit this year	X
	Balance brought forward from last year	X
	Balance carried forward as per balance sheet	£X

Forecast balance sheet at _____

	£
Assets employed:	
Fixed assets (detailed)	X
Current assets (detailed)	X
Total	X
Financed by:	
Shareholders—	
Capital	X
Retained profits	X
Net worth	X
Long-term loans	X
Short-term creditors	X
	X

4. Forecast book value per share and risk ratios.

In respect of Exhibit 48.2, notice:

(*a*) The vertical presentation of accounting information;
(*b*) The cost of sales in a manufacturing concern is the production cost of what has been sold, made up of—

 (i) materials used up in making the product;
 (ii) labour in actually making the product;
(iii) factory overhead, meaning costs which are difficult to assign to any specific product direct, but essential for efficient production to proceed at all, and which include the following—Indirect labour such as supervision, inspection, foremen; Factory services such as maintenance, repairs, lighting, heating, planning, production control and costing, internal transport, plant and crane facilities, welfare and canteen services, etc.

Further mention of factory overhead is made when costing is discussed later in this chapter.

(*c*) The selling, distribution, administrative, occupancy and financial budgets are prepared in great detail. For example, the selling and distribution overhead would be supported by schedules prepared for every section of this function showing:

 (i) sales staff salaries;
 (ii) commissions;
 (iii) sales office expenses in detail;
 (iv) advertising expenditure;
 (v) research staff salaries and expenses;
 (vi) distribution staff wages and salaries;
 (vii) drivers' bonuses, overtime, expenses;
(viii) vehicle expenses showing—petrol and oil, insurances and licences, road taxes, repairs and depreciation.

(*d*) Every budget has an impact on the bank balance. The way in which the budgets react are brought out in a finance budget. The monthly movements of money in and out of the business are of vital interest to the executive controlling the finances.

An example of forecasting using very simple figures now follows. It is given in schedule form so that the effect of each budget on the closing Balance Sheet can easily be followed. More detail is then given under the heading 'short-term problems within the budget year'.

Elphick Ltd operates a system of budgetary control. In October of year 7 the Balance Sheet (conventional form) at the year end, 31 December, was expected to be as follows:

Balance Sheet at 31 December, Year 7

	£	£		Cost £	Depreciation £		Net £
			Fixed Assets:				
Share Capital Balance	G	2,000	Plant	1,000	500	A	500
Profit and Loss	H	300	Fittings, etc.	500	100	B	400
		——	Vehicles	500	200	C	300
Net Worth		2,300		——	——		——
				2,000	800		1,200
Current Liabilities:							
Creditors	I	200					
Tax	J	200	Current Assets:				
Dividend	K	100	Stocks		D	500	
		——	Debtors		E	500	
		500	Bank		F	600	
						——	
							1,600
		2,800					2,800

A forecast sale of 500 products valued at £5,000 was made for year 8. Budgets were prepared under the general guidance of the budget officer and the effects of these budgets are summarized in Exhibits 48.3 and 48.4.

Evaluation

Profitability

Return on Investment   per cent
Net Profit on Sales   per cent
Sales: Assets Employed Ratio
Various Assets Turnover Rates and Ratios as called for by management.

Solvency

Net Working Capital
Current Ratio
Liquid Ratio
Acid Test Ratio and any other ratios as called for by top management
Risk, Book Value of Share, and other observations.

Some Problems within the Budget Year

Liquidity

In seasonal businesses, factory production and sales are often out of step. Thus, a factory may be steadily producing cough lozenges which will not really start to sell until the autumn and winter months. Until the cash flows in from sales, there could be problems of temporary cash shortages. A solution could be by way of overdraft facilities to finance

Exhibit 48.3

Schedule showing budget totals for year 8 and closing Balance Sheet totals.

	Detail	Profit and Loss £	Creditors £	Tax £	Dividends £	Fixed Assets £	Depreciation £	Raw Materials Stock £	Debtors £	Bank £
Balance forward from opening Balance Sheet		(see below)	200	200	100	2,000	800	500	500	600
Budgets										
1. Sales	Forecast Sales Income (all credit)	+5,000							+5,000	
	Estimated Receipts								-4,500	+4,500
2. Materials Cost	Forecast Purchases (all credit)		+1,100					+1,100		
	Forecast Consumption	1,000						-1,000		
	Estimated Payments to Creditors		-900							-900
3. Labour Cost	Forecast Payments	2,000								-2,000
4. Factory Overhead	Forecast Payments	-200								-200
	Depreciation (Plant)	-200					+200			
	Factory Margin	1,600								
5. Selling and Distribution Overhead	Forecast Payments	600								-600
	Depreciation (Vehicles)	200					+200			
6. Administration and Occupancy Overhead	Forecast Payments	-200								-200
	Depreciation (Fixtures, etc.)	-100					+100			
	Net Operating Profit	500								
7. Taxation	Forecast Provision	-300		+300						
	Net Profit after Tax	200								
8. Dividends	Forecast Dividends	-100			+100					
	Profits Retained this year	100								
	Brought forward—Opening Balance Sheet	300								
	Carried forward per Closing Balance Sheet	400								
9. Finance	Tax Payments during year			-200						-200
	Dividend Payment during year				-100					-100
	All other closing balances per Closing Balance Sheet		400	300	100	2,000	1,300	600	1,000	900
	Balance Sheet Reference Letter	H.I.	I.I.	J.I.	K.I.	A.B.C.I.	A.B.C.I.	D.I.	E.I.	F.I.

Exhibit 48.4

Master Budget and Financial Position

Elphick Ltd

Forecast Operating Statement for year ended 31 December, Year 8 — Forecast Balance Sheet at 31 December, Year 8

	£	£			Cost £	Depreciation £		Net £
Sales		5,000	Assets employed					
Production Cost:			Fixed Assets:					
Materials	1,000		Plant		1,000	700	A.1.	300
Labour	2,000		Fittings, etc.		500	200	B.1.	300
Overhead	200		Vehicles		500	400	C.1.	100
Depreciation	200	400	3,400					
					2,000	1,300		700
Factory Margin		1,600						
			Current Assets:					
Selling and Distribution			Stock	D.1.	600			
Overhead:			Debtors	E.1	1,000			
Sundry	600		Bank	F.1	900			
Depreciation	200							2,500
		800						
Administration and Occupancy			Total					3,200
Overhead:								
Sundry	200		Financed by					
Depreciation	100		Shareholders—Capital			G.1.	2,000	
		300	—Retained Profits			H.1.	400	
		1,100						
			Net Worth					2,400
			Short-term creditors					
Net Operating Profit		500	(Current Liabilities)					
Taxation		300	Trade Creditors	I.1.	400			
			Taxation	J.1.	300			
Net Profit after Tax		200	Proposed Dividends	K.1.	100			
Dividends		100						800
Profit Retained this year		100						
Balance brought forward		300						
Balance carried forward as per Balance Sheet		400						3,200

production for short periods. The case for such overdraft facilities is much stronger if backed by a realistic budget which forecasts the temporary shortage of funds month by month. One of the reasons for breaking down the budget into short periods of a month (or even less) is to view the impact of the proposed plans on the monthly bank balance. Naturally, a bank manager will be impressed by a budget only if it is well founded, and not merely 'hopeful'. He will generally look for a record of sound forecasting and achievement in past periods.

Again, top management decisions to buy fixed assets during a financial year may seriously affect liquidity. Unless fresh long-term finance is obtained, such purchases can only come out of existing bank balances generated by past and current profits. Similarly, decisions to increase stocks or lengthen debtor collection periods decrease liquidity.

Peak Production Periods

Sometimes the budgeted sales and stocks for particular months outstrip the production capacity available. A difficult decision faces top management. Either:

(a) Production capacity must be enlarged permanently; this could mean additional factory premises and plant if there is no further space in existing premises. Most managements are cautious before deciding to expand capacity permanently. For one thing, the capital outlay is high and may involve the issuing of share capital or debentures. For another, unless the increased total capacity is kept reasonably fully productive, the financial return will be poor. In other words permanent increased sales must be a fair certainty before permanent expansion can be considered.

Or,

(b) Shift working or overtime working must be organized if the budgeted sales and stocks are to stand. This means a larger work force for short periods or overtime working with existing operatives and staff. Either case may involve the business in difficulties with trades unions, and if overtime working is agreed upon, the overtime premium (time and a half, etc.) must be borne in mind. The extra cost does not increase the value of products and must be borne out of profits from sales.

Or,

(c) Possibly some sub-contracting may have to be considered with a reduction of operating margins of profit offsetting additional profits from extra sales.

Storage

Problems of storing finished stocks sometimes occur with all the attendant risks of deterioration, pilfering, etc. Decisions on acquiring additional storage facilities, costs of storage, minimum levels of stocks to be held, etc., must all be faced.

The above illustrates one of the greatest advantages of budgeting, in that problems of all types are spotlighted before they occur, thus allowing time for action to be taken or for budgets to be drastically revised.

Short-Period Budgets within the Budget Year

In order to illustrate the general form in which the budgets are drawn up, and to demonstrate the impact of a proposed budget on the bank balance, the proposed activity, for Elphick Ltd for budget year 8 now follows in Exhibit 48.5. Notice that the No. 1 Sales Budget and the No. 2 Production Budget deal in the main with the number of units sold or produced, and need converting into £ figures to be able to incorporate them into the other budgets.

Discussion of the Detailed Budgets

It will be appreciated that certain features have been deliberately simplified. For example:

1. The company does not have problems of partly finished products. Apparently the stocks in the Balance Sheet are stocks of materials.

2. No stocks of finished products are held at the year end.

3. The production pattern is high from February to July, and is very low at the end of the year, apparently due to running down stocks of finished goods to zero at 31 December each year.

4. The sales are high from April to September and quite low for all other months. This emphasizes the seasonal demand for the company's products which, according to (3) above, is met by a concentrated production effort for half the year.

5. The above two points illustrate the deep problems caused by uneven production and sales. A study of the financial budget discloses the impact of the proposed policies on the bank balance. Production controllers generally prefer even production throughout the year, even though this means finished stock-piling during the months of low sales activity. The policies envisaged in the foregoing detailed budgets would almost certainly lead to a clash of opinions. Severe labour problems could be expected.

6. Additionally, plant facilities would be under-utilized for half the year—although still depreciating in value.

7. The materials purchasing programme is disjointed.

8. The pattern of settling suppliers' accounts is somewhat haphazard. Since payments are within the control of a company, some sort of consistency in the pattern of payments can be expected in actual fact.

9. The estimated receipts from credit sales is also somewhat haphazard. Again, it is usually possible to establish an average collection pattern.

In addition to the problems of the workforce and usage of factory

Exhibit 48.5

Elphick Ltd – detailed budgets

No. 1 Sales Budget — Budget year 8 — Prepared by . . . . . .

	Jan	Feb	Mar	Apr	May	Jun	Jul	Aug	Sep	Oct	Nov	Dec	Total
Units, U	10	30	40	50	50	60	50	50	50	40	40	30	500
Value, £	100	300	400	500	500	600	500	500	500	400	400	300	5,000
Closing Stock Required (in units), U	30	50	60	60	60	60	60	50	40	30	11	Nil	Nil

No. 2 — Budget year 8 — Prepared by . . . . . .

	Jan	Feb	Mar	Apr	May	Jun	Jul	Aug	Sep	Oct	Nov	Dec	Total
Units: as per Sales Budget, U	10	30	40	50	50	60	50	50	50	40	40	30	500
Closing Stock	30	50	60	60	60	60	60	50	40	30	10	Nil	Nil
	40	80	100	110	110	120	110	100	90	70	50	30	500
Opening Stock	Nil	30	50	60	60	60	60	60	50	40	30	10	Nil
Production Required, U	40	50	50	50	50	60	50	40	40	30	20	20	500

No. 3 Production Cost Budget — Budget year 8 — Prepared by . . . . . .

	Jan	Feb	Mar	Apr	May	Jun	Jul	Aug	Sep	Oct	Nov	Dec	Total
Materials, Cost, £	80	100	100	100	100	120	100	80	80	60	40	40	1,000
Labour Cost, £	160	200	200	200	200	240	200	160	160	120	80	80	2,000
Total, £	240	300	300	300	300	360	300	240	240	180	120	120	3,000

864

No. 4 Overheads Budget

Budget year 8   Prepared by · · · · · ·

	Jan	Feb	Mar	Apr	May	Jun	Jul	Aug	Sep	Oct	Nov	Dec	Total
Factory:													
Expenses. £	17	17	16	17	17	16	17	17	16	17	17	16	200
Depreciation, £	16	17	17	16	17	17	16	17	17	16	17	17	200
Selling:													
Expenses, £	20	30	40	50	60	80	70	70	60	50	40	30	600
Depreciation, £	17	16	17	17	16	17	17	16	17	17	16	17	200
Administration:													
Expenses, £	16	17	17	17	16	17	17	16	17	17	16	17	200
Depreciation, £	9	8	8	9	8	8	9	8	8	9	8	8	100
Total. £	95	105	115	126	134	155	146	144	135	126	114	105	1,500

No. 5 Materials Budget

Budget year 8   Prepared by · · · · · ·

	Jan	Feb	Mar	Apr	May	Jun	Jul	Aug	Sep	Oct	Nov	Dec	Total
Opening Stock. £	500	520	550	600	640	670	670	670	670	650	630	620	500
Purchases. £	100	130	150	140	130	120	100	80	60	40	30	20	1,100
Issue (No. 3). £	600	650	700	740	770	790	770	750	730	690	660	640	1,600
	80	100	100	100	100	120	100	80	80	60	40	40	1,000
Closing Stock. £	520	550	600	640	670	670	670	670	650	630	620	600	600

No. 6 Creditors Budget | Budget year 8 | Prepared by ....

	Jan	Feb	Mar	Apr	May	Jun	Jul	Aug	Sep	Oct	Nov	Dec	Total
Opening Balance, £	200	140	190	270	360	470	560	580	530	480	450	420	200
Purchases, No. 5, £	100	130	150	140	130	120	100	80	60	40	30	20	1,100
	300	270	340	410	490	590	660	660	590	520	480	440	1,300
Payments, £	160	80	70	50	20	30	80	130	110	70	60	40	900
Closing Balance, £	140	190	270	360	470	560	580	530	480	450	420	400	400

No. 7 Debtors Budget | Budget year 8 | Prepared by ....

	Jan	Feb	Mar	Apr	May	Jun	Jul	Aug	Sep	Oct	Nov	Dec	Total
Opening Balance, £	500	400	600	800	1,000	1,300	1,600	1,700	1,800	1,700	1,500	1,300	500
Sales (No. 1), £	100	300	400	500	500	600	500	500	500	400	400	300	5,000
	600	700	1,000	1,300	1,500	1,900	2,100	2,200	2,300	2,100	1,900	1,600	5,500
Reipts, £	200	100	200	300	200	300	400	400	600	600	600	600	4,500
Closing Balance, £	400	600	800	1,000	1,300	1,600	1,700	1,800	1,700	1,500	1,300	1,000	1,000

No. 8 Finance Budget	Jan	Feb	Mar	Apr	May	Jun	Jul	Aug	Sep	Oct	Nov	Dec	Total
					Budget year 8							Prepared by	
Receipts:													
Debtors (No. 7), £	200	100	200	300	200	300	400	400	600	600	600	600	4,500
Payments:													
Creditors (No. 6), £	160	80	70	50	20	30	80	130	110	70	60	40	900
Labour (No. 3), £	160	200	200	200	200	240	200	160	160	120	80	80	2,000
Overhead Expenses—													
Factory (No. 4), £	17	17	16	17	17	16	17	17	16	17	17	16	200
Selling (No. 4), £	20	30	40	50	60	80	70	70	60	50	40	30	600
Administration (No. 4), £	16	17	17	17	16	17	17	16	17	17	16	17	200
Tax paid	200												200
Dividends paid		100											100
	573	444	343	334	313	383	384	393	363	274	213	183	4,200
Opening Balance, £	600	227	−117	−260	−294	−407	−490	−474	−467	−230	96	483	
" Overdraft, £													
Receipts	200	100	200	300	200	300	400	400	600	600	600	600	
	800	327	83	40	−94	−107	−90	−74	133	370	696	1,083	
Payments	573	444	343	334	313	383	384	393	363	274	213	183	
Closing Balance, £	227	−117	−260	−294	−407	−490	−474	−467	−230	96	483	900	
" Overdraft, £													

space and plant, the detailed budgets have thrown up short-term liquidity problems. Thus:

			£
February month-end:	Bank Deficit	..	117
March	,,	..	260
April	,,	,,	294
May	,,	,,	407
June	,,	,,	490
July	,,	,,	474
August	,,	,,	467
September	,,	,,	230

Clearly, adequate arrangements must be made by the financial controller if the company is not to become embarrassed for several months of the year.

It is worth remembering that a study of year-end Balance Sheets alone by no means discovers important events and trends during the financial year. In this example, if the budgeted proposals were permitted to operate, there is no indication of severe liquidity problems in certain months. Only a note of bank interest charges would highlight the fact that the bank account had been overdrawn during the year (assuming the problem had been met in this way).

Cost Accounting and Reporting Variances from Budget

The next step in the technique of budgetary control is to record the costs of the products made in the factory and report (at short intervals) on the differences (variances) between actual costs and budgeted costs. This poses the difficult problem in a manufacturing concern of 'what is cost'? Take the case of the desk at which many a college student sits. It is composed of:

1. The wooden surface made of nine-ply and measuring, say, 3 feet by 2 feet, grooved to take pen and pencil, and with a circular hole to act as an inkwell recess.

2. The legs are formed of two tubular steel lengths bent in the shape of an inverted capital U, bolted to the wooden surface by four fixing bolts.

3. The legs have rubber bushes on them to save floor scratching and to reduce noise.

The 'cost' of such a desk could be:

	£	Identifying letter
(i) Six square feet of nine-ply cut to size at £0·2 per square foot	1·2	M

(ii) Machine power to groove and drill out inkwell recess—6 minutes at £1·5 per hour	0·15	FO
(iii) Machine operator's time—6 minutes at £0·5 per hour	0·05	L
Cost at this stage	1·4	
(iv) Two lengths tubular steel ready bent and drilled	0·45	M
(v) Four fixing bolts	0·1	M
(vi) Four rubber bushes	0·025	M
(vii) Assembly time 6 minutes at	0·25	L
Unit Cost on above basis	2·0	
Planned Selling price	4·0	
Contribution to Overheads and Profit	2·0	

Clearly, if the costing proceeded as above and there were no variations from the planned costs, then each desk made and sold would yield £2 gross margin towards paying all other overhead and providing a profit. If 10,000 desks were made and sold the margin would be £20,000 and the year's effort might be shown as follows:

Units Produced		10,000	*Unit direct cost*
Units Sold		10,000	
		£	£
Sales		40,000	4·0
Direct Cost of Sales:			
Materials (total M = £1·775 × 10,000)		17,750	1·775
Labour (total L = £0·075 × 10,000)		750	0·075
Factory Variable Overhead (total FO = £0·15 × 10,000)		1,500	0·15
		20,000	2·0
		£	£
Margin		20,000	2·0
All other overheads:	£		
Factory	5,000		
Selling, etc.	4,000		
Administration, etc.	3,000		
		12,000	
Net Operating Profit before Tax		8,000	

The costing philosophy indicated above is known as direct costing. An alternative term in use is marginal costing. When using this approach to costing, the only items which 'qualify' for inclusion in the cost of a product are those costs which will be incurred if the product is made at all. Taking the desk example above, and putting the philosophy simply, then: (continued on page 871)

Exhibit 48.6A

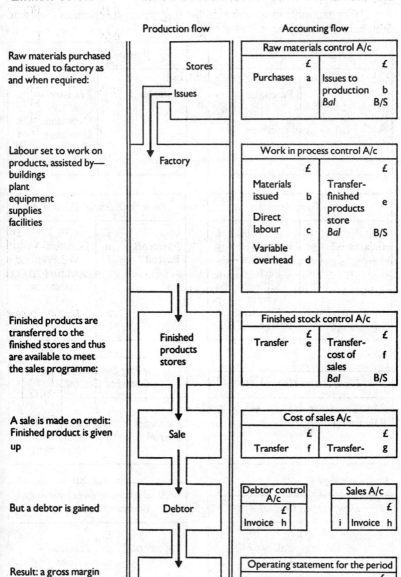

Exhibit 48.6B

Other accounts maintained in the fully integral system of Cost and Financial Accounting

Creditors Control A/c		
£		£
	Purchases	a

Payrolls Control A/c		
	£		£
Total Paid	j	Transfers—	
		W.I.P.	c
		Overhead	k
		Overhead	l
		Overhead	m

Bank A/c		
	£		£
Balance b/f		Payrolls	j
		Overheads—	
		Factory	n
		Selling	o
		Admin.	p
		Financial	q
		Balance c/f B/S	

Factory Overhead Control A/c		
	£		£
Payments	n	Transfers—	
Payroll	k	W.I.P.	d
		Operating	
		Statement	r

Fixed Assets Control A/c		
£		£
Balance b/f		

Selling and Distribution Overhead Control A/c		
	£		£
Payments	0	Transfers—	
Payroll	I	Operating	
		Statement	s

Depreciation Control A/c		
£		£
	Balance b/f	

Administration and Occupancy Overhead Control A/c		
	£		£
Payments	p	Transfers—	
Payroll	m	Operating	
		Statement	t

Share Capital A/c		
£		£
	Balance b/f	

Financial Overhead Control A/c		
	£		£
Payments	q	Transfers—	
		Operating	
		Statement	u

```
              Operating Statement for the period
                         (Continued)
                                              £        £
        Factory Margin                                 £
                                                       ⎯

        Other Overhead:
           Factory                            r
           Selling and Distribution           s
           Administration and Occupancy       t
           Financial                          u        £
                                              ⎯
        Net Operating Profit before Tax                £
                                                       ⎯
```

(a) If one desk is made, it will cost £2.
(b) If the desk is not made, then no materials will be used, and the labour force will be sacked, and there will be no cost for machine power. And therefore;
(c) The concern will save £2.

Before discussing this and other costing philosophies, it will be shown how, in an efficient concern, the accounting records follow the flow of work through the factory. Such a system is known as flow accounting, and the costing and financial records are fully integrated. This means that costing is not permitted to proceed divorced from the financial accounts. In the author's view, if reliance is to be placed on costs, then such costs must form the basis of the financial accounts. Exhibit 48.6A shows the production flow and how the products are costed under direct costing. The accounting records in Exhibit 48.6B are in T form, and the double entry may be followed more easily by identifying a debit as an alphabetical letter, and then locating the same letter as a credit in the other appropriate account. For example, purchases of raw material are debited (a) to raw materials control account and credited (a) to creditors control account. The operating statement (or Profit and Loss Account) shows the direct costing approach.

The Balance Sheet is constructed from the following accounts:

Appropriate Ledger Account	Balance Sheet Item
Raw Materials Control—Closing Balance	Stocks—Raw Materials
Work in Process Control—Closing Balance	—Work in Process
Finished Stock Control—Closing Balance	—Finished Stocks
Debtor Control—Closing Balance	Debtors
Bank—Closing Control	Bank
Creditors Control—Closing Balance	Creditors

There is, of course, an absolute necessity to maintain subsidiary records to 'back up' certain accounts. These are:

Subsidiary Records	Controlled by
Raw materials inventory—detailed	Raw materials control

movements of each item in stock	account
Work in process records—detailed costs of batches of products or individual jobs or processes	Work in process control account
Finished stock inventory—detailed movements of finished stock or completed jobs	Finished stock control account
Individual debtor records	Debtor control account
Individual creditor records	Creditors control account
Plant inventory—details of every item, with subsection for balance sheet classification	Fixed Assets control account and Depreciation control account
Factory overhead detailed records— classified into variable, semi-variable, and constant expense	Factory overhead control account
Selling and distribution overhead detailed records—similarly classified if necessary	Selling and distribution overhead control account
Administration and occupancy overhead detailed records—similarly classified if necessary	Administration and occupancy overhead control account
Financial overhead detailed records	Financial overhead control account

Variable and Non-Variable Overhead

Variable overhead means an item of expense which moves in sympathy with the volume of production. In the example, power was chosen to illustrate this point. If one desk was made, the cost of power used would be £0·15; if two desks were made, the cost would be £0·3; thus power moves in direct ratio to the production activity. This is practically saying that the cost of this particular item of overhead is within the control of those persons in charge of production activity in the factory, and they can be identified as being responsible for this cost being incurred at all. It is therefore logical that a serious attempt should be made to report any variance between budgeted cost and actual cost of power (assuming the budgeted cost of £0·15 has been forecast by the production controller and accepted by top management).

On the other hand, there are many items of expense which do not vary (within reason) with the production activity. Examples are store men's salaries, depreciation of machinery—this will occur whether the factory is producing at full capacity or not—works office salaries. A great deal of non-factory overhead is reasonably constant and will be incurred irrespective of production activity and sales activity. Direct costing infers that all such constant or unavoidable expense must be borne out of whatever margins is produced by the actual sales won in the accounting period.

This is not to say that there should be no control of constant overhead. What is suggested is that there must be a serious attempt to separate the variable from non-variable overhead, so that the main effort of reporting deviations from the budgeted costs is concentrated on the variable items and made the subject of weekly or even daily reporting to those persons responsible. The most sophisticated method devised so far is that of standard costing. This means virtually that, instead of budgeting on the basis of the immediate past information and standard of efficiency, the budgeting is on the basis of what it ought to cost if the concern is reasonably efficient. It is one thing to forecast costs in the light of what it has cost before and then measure variances; it is quite another to measure variances from what it ought to cost on the basis of reasonably attainable efficiency.

Reasonable attainable efficiency is established by work studies and pilot runs. This is very expensive and it also needs wholehearted co-operation from the factory personnel and workforce, but once installed offers a most effective tool of control. Not all businesses are suitable for such sophistication, and in many cases the cost would be unwarranted. In such cases, budgetary control is still very effective even though unaided by standard costing, and the distinction of variable from non-variable expense is in any case vital if the forecasting is to be reasonably accurate. Taking the case of the desks once again, if a forecast of 9,000 desk sales was made, then:

			£
Sales	9,000 at £4		36,000
Direct Cost, £2			18,000
Margin			18,000
All other Non-variable Overhead (say)			
		£	
Factory—as before		5,000	
Selling—as before		4,000	
Administration—as before		3,000	
			12,000
Forecast Net Profit before Tax			6,000

Full or Absorption Costing

Full costing means that all factory overhead whether variable or constant is absorbed into the product cost.

Assume that the factory was capable of producing 11,000 desks a year, but that anticipated annual production would be 10,000. This means that 11,000 represents full capacity usage, but that planned capacity usage would be about 90 per cent. Further assume that with a usage between 80 and 100 per cent the non-variable factory overhead is £5,000 (as in the previous examples). Now below 80 per cent capacity usage it may be possible to reduce certain factory overhead. For example, the factory could probably do with only four inspectors instead of five. A graph of such a cost behaviour would be:

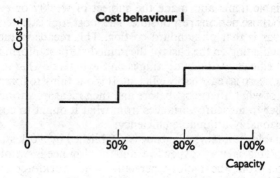

Power, on the other hand, being largely proportionate to any capacity usage, presents a different cost behaviour pattern, thus:

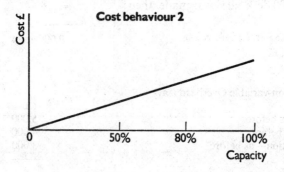

Still different in behaviour is factory overhead such as the production controller's salary. Even sizeable 'jumps' in capacity usage is not likely to affect his salary. The cost behaviour pattern in this case is:

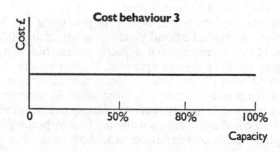

Despite the differences in cost behaviour, full costing seeks to allocate all factory overhead to production, and under such philosophy, the unit cost and year's results would be:

		10,000	Unit cost, etc,
Units Produced		10,000	
Units Sold		10,000	
		£	£
Sales		40,000	4·5
Production Cost:			
Materials		17,750	1·775
Labour		750	0·075
Prime Cost		18,500	1·85
Factory Overhead (£1,500 plus £5,000)		6,500	0·65
Total Production Cost		25,000	2·5
Gross profit		15,000	1·5
Other Overheads:	£		
Selling, etc.	4,000		
Administration, etc.	3,000		
		7,000	
Net Operating Profit before Tax		8,000	

Exhibit 48.7

	Units	Units	Difference 1 Unit
Annual Rate of Production	10,000	10,001	
Production Cost:	£	£	£
Variable—Materials	17,750	17,751·775	1·775
—Labour	750	750·075	0·075
—Overhead	1,500	1,500·15	0·15
	20,000	20,002·0	2·0
Other Overhead:			
Non-variable—Factory,	5,000	5,000	—
—Selling, etc.	4,000	4,000	—
—Administration, etc.	3,000	3,000	—
	12,000	12,000	—
Total Cost	32,000	32,002	2

It might be thought that there is nothing to choose between the two costing philosophies. The full year's results show a profit of £8,000 in both cases—although the unit cost is £2·5—under full costing as opposed to £2 under direct costing. In fact, there are powerful reasons why direct costing should receive the more serious consideration. Consider Exhibit 48.7.

The cost of producing one more unit in the same time span is £2, no more or less. Yet a unit cost of £2·5 has been produced under full costing! An inexperienced management might very well be misled by such a unit cost. Thus, if a sales forecast of 9,000 units at £4 each was made, then the comparison in Exhibit 48.8 is revealing.

Exhibit 48.8

Forecast of Profit to Management

Full costing			*Direct costing*		
		Units			*Units*
Production		9,000	Production		9,000
		£			£
Sales	9,000 units	36,000	Sales	9,000 units	36,000
Production Cost			Direct Cost		
(Unit Cost × 9,000			(Direct Cost × 9,000		
£2·5 × 9,000)		22,500	£2 × 9,000)		18,000
'Gross Profit'		13,500	Margin		18,000
Other Overhead:			Non-variable Overhead:		
	£			£	
Selling, etc.	4,000		Factory	5,000	
Administration,			Selling	4,000	
etc.	3,000		Administration	3,000	
		7,000			12,000
Forecast Profit		6,500			6,000
Profit Overstated		500			

In other words, the unit cost of £2·5 under full costing holds good only when the rate of production is 10,000 units in a given interval of time. For any other rate of production in the same interval of time, this particular unit cost is not appropriate. Compare this with the direct cost per unit which remains at £2 per unit irrespective of variations in the level of output.

When production and sales are out of step, and there are considerable variations in the year-end stock of finished products (and partly finished products), the actual profit reported under the two costing philosophies will be different. Assume the following data in Exhibit 48.9 for the desk-making factory:

Year	Production	Sales	*(Variable costs, selling price, other overhead all as before)*
1	10,000 units	9,000 units	
2	11,000 „	9,000 „	
3	9,000 „	12,000 „	

Assume also that the business closed down at the end of year 3.

In year 1 the cost accountant decided that since the expected average rate of production per annum would be 10,000 units, he would spread the constant factory overhead of £5,000 over 10,000 and allocate £0·5 to each unit. He was therefore a 'full cost' advocate. The profits that he reported over the 'life' of the concern are given below, with alternative profits that would be reported if direct costing had been chosen:

Exhibit 48.9

					Full costing	Direct costing
					£	£
				Sales	36,000	36,000
Year 1		(A)	(B)	(C)		
		Vari-	*Con-*			
		able	*stant*	*Total*		
		costs	*costs*	*costs*		
	Units	£	£	£		
Opening Stock	—	—	—	—		
Production	10,000	20,000	12,000	32,000		
Available	10,000	20,000	12,000	32,000		
Closing Stock	1,000	2,000	500	2,500		
	9,000	18,000	11,500	29,500	29,500	18,000
Margin						18,000
Less all Non-variable Costs						12,000
Profits Reported					6,500	6,000

					£	£
Year 2				Sales	36,000	36,000
		(A)	(B)	(C)		
	Units	£	£	£		
Opening Stock	1,000	2,000	500	2,500		
Production	11,000	22,000	12,000	34,000		
Available	12,000	24,000	12,500	36,500		
Closing Stock	3,000	6,000	1,500	7,500		
	9,000	18,000	11,000	29,000	29,000	18,000
Margin						18,000
Less all Non-variable Costs						12,000
Profits Reported					7,000	6,000

	Units	(A) £	(B) £	(C) £	£	£
Year 3					Sales 48,000	48,000
Opening Stock	3,000	6,000	1,500	7,500		
Production	9,000	18,000	12,000	30,000		
Available	12,000	24,000	13,500	37,500		
Closing Stock	—	—	—	—		
	12,000	24,000	13,500	37,500	37,500	24,000
Margin						24,000
Less all Non-variable Costs						12,000
Profits Reported					10,500	12,000

Summary

	Full costing		Direct costing	
	Profits £	Year-end stocks £	Profits £	Year-end stocks £
Year				
1	6,500	2,500	6,000	2,000
2	7,000	7,500	6,000	6,000
3	10,500	—	12,000	—
Total	24,000		24,000	

Although the total profits under the two systems will be the same over the life of the concern, the annual reporting shows considerable variations. Furthermore, notice that:

Year		Full costing	Direct costing
1	Sales 9,000 units	Profit 6,500	Profit 6,000
2	Sales 9,000 units	,, 7,000	,, 6,000

It is often very difficult to explain to non-accountants that, even when costs and selling prices remain unchanged, an identical sales effort (of in our case 9,000 units) produces two different profits. It is even possible to have reduced sales and show an increased profit under full costing, owing to the incidence of postponing the charging of constant factory overhead until the stock in which the costs are 'suspended' is sold. Under direct costing, such overhead is written off against the margin achieved by the sales effort, and the closing stock is valued at direct cost only. Since profit is made only when a sale takes place, and since there can be no profit in producing merely for stock, then to carry forward factory overhead which is a constant charge on the profits is unrealistic.

Another reason for favouring the direct costing approach, is the way in which it assists in evaluating the effects of various alternative courses of action, and in giving the correct answers to important questions. Supposing the business management asks the following questions:

(a) How far can sales of desks fall before we start sustaining losses with our present size and costs?

(b) What will the profit be if we sell 7,500 desks at present costs and selling prices?

(c) Suppose we drop the selling price to £3·75 and we were able to sell 10,000 desks; what will the profit be then?

These and other searching questions can be answered if there has been a serious attempt to separate variable costs from other costs, as is required by the direct costing approach. The answers can be given by mathematical calculations, but perhaps the easiest way to appreciate the effect of decisions is to construct what is called a break-even chart. Exhibit 48.10 shows a break-even chart for the hypothetical desk-making company based on the prices and costs used in the above examples. The procedure is:

1. Choosing suitable scales, draw the horizontal axis to represent capacity of production, and the vertical axis to represent costs and sales income.

2. Plot variable costs at—

(a) £0 when sales activity is nil;
(b) £20,000 when sales activity is 10,000 units;

Draw a graph line to join up the two points.

3. Draw constant costs line £12,000 *above and parallel* to the variable cost line. Thus at 10,000 units sold the point will be (£20,000+ £12,000) = £32,000, and for nil sales activity it will be £12,000. The line just drawn is the total cost line.

4. Draw the sales income graph line from £0 at nil sales activity to £40,000 at 10,000 units sold.

Where the sales line intersects the total cost line is the point at which there is neither profit or loss—that is, the break-even point. Drop a perpendicular from the break-even point (B/E 1) to the horizontal axis and read off the sales activity at which the concern breaks even. In this case it is 6,000 units.

Check:

		£
Sales	6,000 units at £4	24,000
Direct Cost at £2 per unit		12,000
Margin		12,000
All other Overhead (constant)		12,000
Profit/Loss		—

Now give the answer to (*b*) above. Erect a perpendicular from activity point 7,500 units on the horizontal axis to cut the profit zone. Measure the distance in the profit zone between sales line and total cost line. This gives £3,000.

Check:

		£
Sales	7,500 units at £4	30,000
Direct cost at £2 per unit		15,000
Margin		15,000
All other Overhead (constant)		12,000
Profit		3,000

Exhibit 48.10

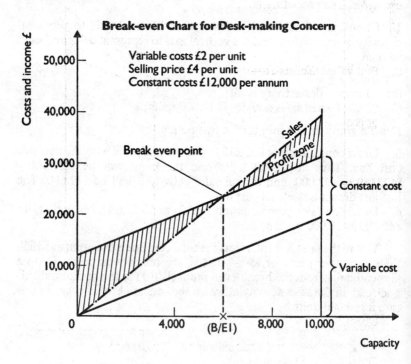

To answer question (*c*) above, draw a revised sales line from £0 at nil sales activity to £37,500 at 10,000 units activity, see Exhibit 48.11. This reveals:

1. a new break-even point (B/E 2) at 6,857 units approximately; and
2. a profit of £5,500 if 10,000 units are sold.

Check:

		£
Sales	10,000 units at £3·75	37,500
Direct Cost at £2 per unit		20,000
Margin		17,500
All other Overhead (constant)		12,000
Profit		5,500

Exhibit 48.11

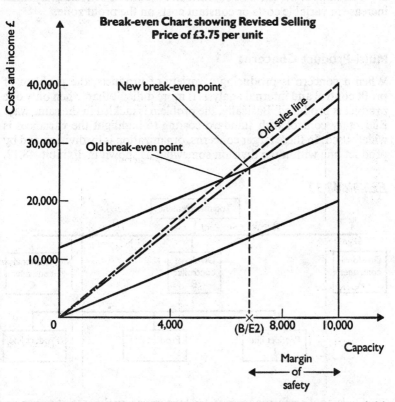

Break-even Chart showing Revised Selling Price of £3.75 per unit

Similarly, the effect of an increase in constant costs or variable costs can be plotted and their reaction evaluated on:

1. the profit zone; and
2. the break-even point.

The reader should now construct his own graphs and try to gauge the effect that various hypothetical decisions would have on the profitability and safety of the concern. Some of the points of interest are:

1. The angle of intersection: a narrow angle indicates that a considerable increase in sales activity must take place to obtain a sizeable increase in profits. A decision to increase capacity may bring with it the problems of increased factory constant costs and a different variable cost per unit.

2. The margin of safety: this is the distance from the present operating capacity (10,000 units in our case) to the break-even point (B/E 1 or B/E 2) compared with the total distance on the horizontal axis (0 to 10,000 units). In the first case (Exhibit 48.10) sales could drop 40 per cent to 6,000 units before the break-even point is reached.

3. The slope of the variable cost line and the effects of a relatively small increase in variable costs or constant costs on the profit zone.

Multi-Product Concerns

When a concern is producing a variety of products, the problem of profit control and internal analysis is more difficult than when only one product is produced. Basically, the problem is tackled in the same way. Budgetary control with standard costing to highlight the variances is widely used. In these larger concerns, organization is by division and by product line within the division somewhat as shown in Exhibit 48.12.

Exhibit 48.12

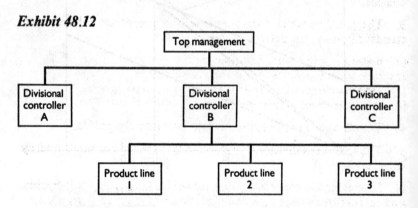

Divisional performance is tested by comparing the rate of return on the assets employed by each division. The general idea is that each division should earn a minimum acceptable return on investment, and all the ratios concerning the concept of return on investment discussed in the previous chapter are brought to bear at divisional level. Very considerable use of break-even charts and associated profit graphs are made by each division. In Exhibit 48.12, division B is responsible for three product lines. Intensive studies are made to define the contribution made by each different product to the overall margin earned by division B. The direct costing approach is essential in such cases and largely determines such questions as:

1. Favourable product mix.

2. Discontinuance of certain products in favour of others.

3. Decision to make or buy a product.

4. Absolute minimum selling price without incurring losses on manufacturing.

5. The effect on profit if one line is closed down, and so on.

Internal Analysis

From the foregoing discussions it will be appreciated that internal analysis has a somewhat broad meaning. It may be said to cover:

1. An analysis of the organization and its command structure.

2. A detailed analysis of the functions controlled by each section leader, manager, executive, controller with a view to responsibility accounting—that is, a man should be responsible for only those items under his control. The first two points are prerequisities for budgetary control.

3. The detail to which variances from the budget are subject: with standard costing, the detail covers at least—

(a) materials, as to usage and as to price;
(b) labour, as to efficiency and as to labour rates;
(c) variable overhead, as to efficiency and as to cost;
(d) sales, the effect of mix and price.

4. The effect of various alternative decisions on the profits.

5. The analysis of divisional performance in the light of assets used by those divisions.

6. Special studies concerning long-range planning, capacity increases, and early retirement of equipment in favour of more modern plant.

Since the turn of this century, accountants in industry have concentrated more and more on the matters discussed in this chapter. Business managers must have the right type of information available to them if they are to make the correct decisions. Weekly or monthly profit reporting is essential and the reports must be designed to yield the type of information required. The accent is on economic profit rather than accounting profit reporting. The disciplines of costing, statistics and economics are indispensable to the accountant who intends to make his mark in industry.

Exercises

Extra questions for this edition with answers, are questions 48.6, 48.7, 48.8, 48.9 and 48.10.

48.1A. On 1 February Year 1 J.K. started business as a sole-trader with capital in cash £8,000 and a loan for the purchase of initial stock for £2,000, from his uncle who traded in the same line of goods in the next town.

J.K. ran his business from premises which he rented at £200 a calendar month. He said, 'By doing all the work myself I shall save the wages, of about £7,200 a year, that I would have to pay someone else to run the business for me.'

At the end of the first three months of being in business on his own account, J.K. prepared the following:

Statement of Profit—1 February to 30 April, Year 1

	£	£
Sales (at cost plus 25%)		15,000
Opening Stock	2,000	
Purchases	14,000	
	16,000	
Less Closing stock at selling price	5,000	
	11,000	
Rent	400	
Purchase of Fixtures	700	
General expenses	240	
Insurance for one year—from 1 February Year 1	160	
Cash to uncle in full Repayment of Loan with Interest	2,020	
		14,520
Profit		480

J.K. did not regard a profit of £480 for three months' work as satisfactory but was undecided whether to sell the business or to continue a little longer in the hope that it would improve.

What information would you give J.K. in order to help him reach a decision? Your answer may, in part, take the form of a revised statement of profit.

48.2A. The Balance Sheet of Fulvia Ltd at 31 December Year 8, is given below:

	£		£
Share Capital:		Fixed Assets:	
Ordinary Shares of £1	8,000	Premises	5,000
Retained earnings	600	Equipment	2,000
Net Worth	8,600		7,000

		£	
Current Liabilities:		Current Assets:	
Creditors	400	Stock	800

Debtors		300	
Bank		900	
		—	2,000
	9,000		9,000

Fulvia is a private limited company—essentially a family affair—and annual profits before tax have been in the order of £4,000.

Required:

From the budget data and other pertinent details given you are to prepare:

(a) a forecast Income Statement for the three months ended 31 March Year 9.
(b) detailed monthly forecasts for Sales, Purchases, Debtors, Creditors, Overheads, Cash;
(c) a forecast Balance Balance Sheet at 31 March Year 9;
(d) a short statement as to why—when forecast profits are at an annual rate of some £8,000—the business bank account can move into an overdraft position in the short term.

Data:

Year 9	Sales forecast (all credit)	Mark-up on cost	Closing stock required at month end (at cost)	Overheads including advertising
	£		£	£
		To be a uniform rate of 50 per cent throughout		
Jan	1,500		2,000	1,000
Feb	3,000		3,000	300
March	6,000		3,000	300

Other pertinent detail:

1. Recipts-from-Debtors pattern is that they pay during the month following the month of sale;
2. Payments-to-Creditors pattern is that they are paid as to half the month's purchases during that month and the balance in the month following;
3. Payments-for-overheads pattern is that they are paid at the end of the month in which they occur;
4. Depreciation, Tax, Bad Debts, and Discounts are to be ignored.
5. The format of one of the detailed forecasts is given for your guidance:

	Jan	Feb	March	Summary
Purchases Forecast:	£	£	£	£
To meet forecast sales	x	x	x	x
Month-end stock required	x	x	x	x
Sub-total	x	x	x	x
Less beginning stock	x	x	x	x
Buy	x	x	x	x

48.3A. M. Nixon, a cabinet maker, started business on his own account on 1 January Year 1. He had no employees and decided that until he could expand his business he would concentrate on making and selling only one item, an 'antique' blanket chest. He contacted a number of furnishers and a department store in his home town and obtained some initial orders which he agreed to supply on one month's credit.

At the end of the first six months in business, Nixon prepared the profit statement below and was very pleased with the results it showed.

	£	£
Sales		1,900
Materials used	500	
Wage for self	1,500	
General expenses	200	
Selling expenses	100	
	2,300	
Less Stock of finished chests at 30 June year 1 (representing half the six months' output)	1,150	
Cost of sales		1,150
Profit		750

Nixon was a little concerned at the way his creditors were increasing and sought your opinion about his position.

On enquiry you found that Nixon spent approximately three-fifths of his time on production, one-fifth on administration and one-fifth on selling; half the general expenses were associated with production and half were of an administrative character; on the basis of Nixon's profit statement his balance sheet position at 30 June Year 1 was as shown below:

	£		£
Capital 1 Jan Year 1	1,000	Equipment at cost	
Profit for the half-year	750	1 Jan Year 1	620
	1,750		
Creditors	300	Stocks: Materials	100
		Finished chests	1,150
		Debtors	100
		Balance at bank	80
	2,050		2,050

What information and advice would you give Mr Nixon concerning his:

(i) profit for the half-year;
(ii) liquidity position at 30 June Year 1;
(iii) future prospects?

48.4A. The Board of a certain company are accustomed to being presented with

Operating Statements prepared on full absorption cost lines. The latest such Statement disclosed the following:

	Product Line A	Product Line B	Total
Sales (units)	50,000	100,000	
	£	£	£
Sales Income	250,000	800,000	1,050,000
Cost of sales	150,000	600,000	750,000
Gross profit	100,000	200,000	300,000
Other overhead absorbed	70,000	140,000	210,000
Net profit before tax	30,000	60,000	90,000

The plant is operating at full capacity, and the Board are considering a proposal to cut back production of Product A to 30,000 and thus make and sell an additional 15,000 units of Product B.

The company's cost accountant has advised against such change, but the Board are not satisfied and before making a decision call you in as outside consultant. You carry out an investigation culminating in the following re-drafted Operating Statement.

Operating Statement as Re-drafted by Consultant:

	Product A	Product B	Total
Sales (units)	50,000	100,000	
	£	£	£
Sales Income	250,000	800,000	1,050,000
Direct Costs	125,000	320,000	445,000
Contribution margin	125,000	480,000	605,000
Less fixed costs			515,000
Net profit before tax			90,000

Required:

Show—with workings—what would happen if the Board disregarded the advice of their accountant and went ahead with the proposal given above.

48.5A. At the beginning of the financial year the Florens Co Ltd started up a separate division to manufacture floral electrical humidiser units. During the first year of operations the division sold 45,000 humidisers at £6·00 per unit. At the end of the year, there were 5,000 finished units in stock, and 4,000 units in process that were complete as to materials but only 50 per cent complete as to labour and overhead costs.

The division reported the following costs debited to Work in Process Account during the year:

	£
Materials	86,400
Labour	78.000
Variable overhead	18,200
Fixed overhead	49,400

and also prepared the following schedule for selling and administrative overhead:

	Fixed	Variable per unit sold
	£	£
Selling expenses	27,200	0·40
Administrative expenses	19,000	0·80

The divisional Manager has prepared an operating statement for the first year's activity showing a divisional profit of £4,200, based on absorption costing principles.

The Group Financial Director (who is an advocate of direct costing) has pointed out to the Chairman that on a direct cost basis, the division did not generate sufficient margin to cover the fixed costs incurred for the year, and that a loss on operations has been sustained.

Required:

(a) Prepare an Operating Statement for the division's first year under absorption cost principles and showing a profit of £4,200. Enclose also supporting schedules for closing stock valuations.
(b) Prepare an Operating Statement for the division's first year such as the Group Financial Director had in mind, giving supporting schedules for closing stock valuations under direct costing principles.
(c) Explain the differences in profit reporting between the divisional Manager and the Group Financial Director for the division's first year activities.

48.6. Mr Heap sells razor blades and sculpture balloons on market days in Stockport, Levenshulme and Whaley Bridge.

(a) His razor blades cost him 10p per packet and he fixes his selling price so as to give him a gross margin of 37½ per cent per packet. What is his mark-up as a percentage?
(b) Heap pays 4p per packet of five balloons and marks them up 400 per cent per packet. What is his gross margin percentage?
(c) Will your answer to (b) above change if Heap sticks to his pricing policy and sells 114 packets of balloons at Levenshulme market on 6 January 19–7?
(d) If Heap's overheads are £3,990 for a full year's operations and he sells his razor blades and sculpture balloons in the mixture of one packet of blades to two packets of balloons, what is his break-even point in packets?
(e) Would you advise a friend to copy Entrepreneur Heap? If not, why not? Restrict your comments to Heap's business operation.

48.7. Mr A and Mr Z operate identical foundries, each producing the same manhole casting, but for different local authorities. They both started their foundries two years ago, and (astonishingly) have had identical sales and costs for both years as follows:

	Year 1	Year 2
Sales (Number of castings)	1,000	1,000
Selling price per casting	£350	£350
Sales (1,000 × £350)	£350,000	£350,000
Selling and Administration overheads	£25,000	£25,000

Production data:

Opening stock of castings	nil	nil
Closing stock of castings	nil	200
Castings produced	1,000	1,200
Total variable cost per casting	£220	£220
Fixed production costs	£60,000	£60,000

Although competitors, Mr A and Mr Z agreed to compare each other's financial results for the two years—under the auspices of the local Ironfoundry Association. The results were as follows:

	Year 1	Year 2
Mr A profit for the years	£45,000	£45,000
Mr Z profit for the years	£45,000	£55,000

Mr Z claimed that there was no error in his accounts although he showed £10,000 more profit in year 2 than Mr A, and that Mr A's Accountant must be wrong since both foundries had had exactly the same revenue and costs for the two years.

Required:

Draft the Manufacturing Accounts for both businesses using the costing philosophy followed by the Accountants for each business. Show that the Accountant for Mr A's business has NOT made an error and explain why Mr Z thinks that £55,000 is the 'right' figure for year 2.

48.8. The following statement has been handed to you with a request to consider the possiblity of eliminating product B—since this seems to be producing a 'loss' compared with product A.

Product	A	B	Total
	£	£	£
Sales	750,000	750,000	1,500,000
Total costs	650,000	800,000	1,450,000
	100,000	(50,000)	50,000

You ascertain from various cost studies that the 'fixed' cost element in the above total costs of £1,450,000 is as follows:

	£
Product A	225,000
Product B	75,000
	300,000

Required:

1. What is the probable effect of discontinuing product line B?
2. What other factors should be considered in a decision of this type?

48.9. Amarti Limited manufactures one product, the cost data for which is:

	£
Direct materials	2·50
„ labour	3·20
Variable overhead	1·00
Fixed overhead	2·00*
Unit total cost	8·70
Selling price	11·00
Unit profit	2·30 Before allowing salemen's commission of 10 per cent on selling price.

One of the sales representatives telephones in with the news that he has the chance of selling Z Limited 2,000 units at a special price of £8·00 per unit.

He is going to telephone back in one hour's time for a decision.

Required:
Prepare two answers to the request from the representative as follows:
(*a*) Yes, stating the effect of the decision.
(*b*) No, stating the cost of this decision and reasons.

*The fixed unit cost is based on an annual fixed cost of £400,000 and an output of 200,000 units.

48.10. The following accounting information has been supplied by the Cost Accountant of ARVI Productions Limited, which operates a factory with three production lines, X, Y and Z.

Product line	Sales	Total costs of operation	Profit/loss before tax
	£	£	£
X	200,000	164,000	36,000
Y	40,000	52,000	(12,000) loss
Z	160,000	162,000	(2,000) loss
	400,000	378,000	22,000

At a Board meeting, the Sales Director suggested closing down product line Y or Z or both. This action, he claimed, would affect total profits as follows:

		Revised total profit
		£
Close down product line Y	=	34,000
„ „ „ „ Z	=	24,000
Close down both product lines	=	36,000

The Personnel Director agreed with the Sales Director but thought that only product line Y should be closed down in view of the relatively small loss from product line Z.

The Managing Director had a particular pride in product Y since it was he who had done the market research which lead to the decision to start up this line in the first place. He was therefore reluctant to agree to this first proposition, and asked the Cost Accountant to identify the product variable costs contained in the above total costs of operation. These were supplied as follows:

	£
Product Line X	120,000
„ „ Y	42,000
„ „ Z	146,000

Required:
Evaluate the above proposals by the Sales Director and the Personnel Director, and (based on the information given) give *your* advice to the Board of Directors.

APPENDIX NO 48.1
Examinations at Stage Two Level

I trust that you will first of all read Appendix 27.1 which is concerned with Stage One level examinations. Everything that is said there is also relevant at Stage Two. What I want to add is concerned with the fact that the Stage Two examinations are at a more advanced level, and therefore other additional factors have to be borne in mind.

At this stage some examinations have rather more essay questions than is the case at stage one. Where essay questions are set then they are rather more difficult than those at the earlier stage, where most of the essay questions are simply asking you to repeat facts that you have learned already. They are mainly asking you for a brief definition of various accounting terms. When you reach stage two then the examiner is starting to look, not just for the ability to construct accounts from given information, but also a slightly deeper understanding of what accounting is all about. It is fairly rare at this stage for a particular essay question to be compulsory. There is usually a choice, so read the essay questions very carefully before deciding which to tackle. An examiner is trying to set differently worded questions from one year to another, so he won't want to set the question in exactly the same way as he did two years previously. The question may really be searching for the basic understanding, but he will try to word it so that the good student will still know exactly what the question is calling for, and the poor student may not understand it at all. You see, earlier in your studies the examination may have asked for answers in which rote learning (learning things by heart) played a much more important part. Now the examiner is setting questions where rote learning is not enough. It is therefore very important to see as many past papers as possible.

Although I have touched on the next point in Appendix 27.1 concerning the examinations for Stage One, I don't think that it can be repeated often enough. Before I get down to looking at it in detail I want you to read the following two questions, and then to sit back before reading further and think about the answers that you would give to them. By all means jot down the main points of your answers. Don't read further until you have done that; you could read straight on, but you will only be cheating yourself. After all I can't watch what you are doing.

Question 1. 'Describe how the charging of provisions for depreciation affect the retention of cash within a business.'

Question 2. 'Examine the reasons lying behind the choice of a particular method of valuing stock.'

Now let us look at your answers. I can tell you that, as an examiner myself, I have set both of these questions in the past in examinations sat by students in many parts of the world. I know therefore, only too well, how most of the students taking the examinations answered these questions.

In question 1 most students would in fact have started to write down everything that they knew about depreciation. They would describe the straight line method, the reducing balance method, and they may well use figures to illustrate how these methods work. Have you done just that? Well, you would have been awarded no marks at all. You simply did not read the question properly. Let us underline the key words to see what the question actually asked for.

Describe *how* the *charging* of provisions for *depreciation affect* the *retention* of *cash* within a business.
i.e.   how   charging   depreciation affect   retention   cash

This is therefore completely different from what most people read into it. The answer can be seen to be (briefly, although the examiner would expect a much fuller answer) concerned with the fact that if depreciation is charged then the profits recorded by the business will be smaller than they would have been if no depreciation had been charged at all. Because smaller profits are recorded then a firm would have the tendency to pay out smaller dividends, or in the case of a sole trader he would tend to take less drawings, and so the consequence of the charging of depreciation would tend to result in the leaving of more cash in the business.

In question 2 most students gave the following type of answer. They wrote about the various methods of valuing stock, such as FIFO, LIFO and Average Cost, and so on. Marks gained by such answers, I think you will have guessed by now, would be nil. Instead the key words in the question are:

reasons   choice   method valuing stock

It did not ask the candidate to describe the various methods of valuing stock. Instead it asked him why he should choose any one particular method. If you will read *Business Accounting 2*, Chapter 28, you will find part of the chapter headed 'Factors Affecting the Stock Valuation Decision'. That contains the type of answer which I wanted.

I hope the message that you should read the question carefully, then underline the key words to bring out the essential parts of the question, has got home to you. The advice is good for any subject, not just Accounting.

You should attempt the following two papers which have answers at the back of the book. Please note that the duration of one paper is $2\frac{1}{2}$ hours and the other is for 3 hours. There are also two further full papers without answers for practice.

(N.B. Full answers to these questions are to be found at the back of the book.)

The London Chamber of Commerce and Industry

BOOK-KEEPING
INTERMEDIATE STAGE

(Three hours allowed)

INSTRUCTIONS TO CANDIDATES

(*a*) All questions should be attempted.

(*b*) Marks may be lost by lack of neatness.

---

1. On 1 July 19–4, James Purdey of London, whose financial year ends on 31 October, sent on consignment to his agent Elmer Keith in Kentucky 100 cases of locks at £120 per case.

Purdey was to bear all expenses up to the time the goods reached the customer. Elmer Keith was entitled to a commission of 10 per cent and a *del credere* commission of 5 per cent.

Purdey paid delivery charges to the docks £96, freight £160 and insurance £44.

5 cases were lost in transit and on 31 August 19–4 Purdey received a cheque from the insurance company for £650 in full settlement of his claim.

On 31 October, James Purdey received an account sales from Elmer Keith showing that he had sold 75 cases on credit at £140 per case and had incurred a bad debt of £70. He had paid landing charges of £15, haulage from docks to his warehouse £42 and selling expenses of £25. A bill of exchange for the amount due was included with the account sales.

Required:

In the books of James Purdey, show:

(*a*) Consignment account
(*b*) Goods on Consignment account
(*c*) Elmer Keith's account.

(16 marks)

2. Arnold and Bennett, who were partners in a small manufacturing business, agreed to amalgamate with Colin and Dennis, who were partners in another similar business.

Their balance sheets at 31 December 19–5 were as follows:

	Arnold & Bennett £	Colin & Dennis £
Fixed Assets		
Land & Buildings	6,000	—
Plant & Equipment	4,500	5,800
Motor Vehicles	1,200	900
	11,700	6,700
Goodwill	4,000	—

Current Assets:	£	£		
Stocks	3,600		4,500	
Debtors	5,100		6.300	
Bank	900		1,700	
	9,600		12,500	
Less Current Liabilities:				
Creditors	3,800		4,700	
		5,800		7,800
		21,500		14,500

Capital Accounts:	£	£
Arnold	12,000	
Bennett	9,500	
Colin		7,000
Dennis		7,500
	21,500	14,500

Their profit and loss sharing ratios were:

Arnold & Bennett	3:2
Colin & Dennis	2:1

For the purposes of the amalgamation, it was agreed that certain assets should be revalued as shown below:

	Arnold & Bennett £	Colin & Dennis £
Land & Buildings	10,000	—
Plant & Equipment	3,800	6,400
Stocks	3,300	5,100
Goodwill	6,000	4,500

The other assets and liabilities were correctly valued.

It was also agreed that the profit sharing ratio in the new firm should be:

Arnold	4
Bennett	3
Colin	2
Dennis	1

Immediately after the amalgamation, goodwill in the new firm was to be eliminated.

Required:

(a) For each of the original businesses—
   (1) Partners' Capital Accounts
   (2) Revaluation Accounts

(b) For the new firm—

   (1) Partners' Capital Accounts
   (2) Balance Sheet after giving effect to all the transactions.

(30 marks)

3. Surethings Ltd was formed on 1 July 19–5, with an authorized capital of £850,000 of £1 ordinary shares, £650,000 of which was to be issued. The prospectus stated the terms on which applications would be accepted, viz.
Ordinary Shares to be issued at £1·20

   payable: 25p on application
         60p (including 20p premium) on allotment
         35p on first and final call on 30 September

Any excess application money is to be applied towards amounts due on allotment with any balance being refunded.

The issue of ordinary shares was heavily oversubscribed and the directors proceeded to allotment as follows, on 10 July:

Size of Application	Total Shares Applied for	No. of Shares Allotted
50 shares	2,000	nil
100 shares	5,000	5,000
over 100 to 500 shares	300,000	225,000
over 500 to 1,000 shares	400,000	240,000
over 1,000 shares	400,000	180,000
		650,000

All application money was received on 5 July 19–5. Money refundable was returned to applicants on 10 July, and all money due on allotment was received on 19 July. The call on the ordinary shares was made and all money due was received on 30 September.

Required:

(a) The journal entries, including cash, to record the above transactions, with narrations.

(b) A calculation of the amounts due or to be refunded on allotment of the ordinary shares.

(24 marks)

4. Westley Richards, who is in business as a hardware merchant, does not keep proper books, but merely makes notes of his cash transactions. He is now thinking of selling the business and needs accounts to be prepared for a potential purchaser. He gives you the following information for the year 19–5:

Summary of Cash Transactions

	£		£
In Hand 1 January 19–5	29	Paid into Bank	13,833
Shop takings	13,826	Staff Wages	2,534
Amounts paid by debtors	3,567	Payments to Suppliers	752
		Motor Van Expenses	265
		In Hand 31 December 19–5	38
	17,422		17,422

Analysis of Bank Statements

	£		£
Balance 1 January 19–5	862	Payments to Suppliers	11,086
Cash Paid in	13,833	Rent & Rates of Shop	750
		General expenses	442
		Shop Fixtures & Fittings	370
		Drawings	2,000
		Balance 31 December 19–5	47
	14,695		14,695

Assets & Liabilities	1 January 19–5	31 December 19–5
Debtors	628	576
Creditors	1,480	1,623
Shop fittings (cost £800) written down value	520	
Stock	1,856	1,919
Motor Van (cost £720) written down value	540	

Notes:

1. Depreciation of shop fittings is charged at 10 per cent, straight line method, on assets in use at the year end.
2. Westley Richards had taken goods costing £136 from the business for his own use.
3. Depreciation of the motor van is charged at 25 per cent, straight line method.

Required:

Prepare a Trading Account and Profit & Loss Account for the year ended 31 December 19–5, and also a Balance Sheet as at that date.

Note: Show your calculation of the capital at 1 January 19–5, and also details of any other calculations you have to make.

(30 marks)

(N.B. Full answers to these questions are to be found at the back of the book.)

The Royal Society of Arts Examinations Board

Single-Subject Examinations

Accounting

Stage II (Intermediate)
(Two and a half hours allowed)

SECTION A—All questions to be answered

1. The summarized accounts of Staghill Ltd for 19–5 are as follows:

Trading & Profit & Loss Account for 19–5

	£		£
Variable cost of sales	120,000	Sales	200,000
Depreciation	24,000		
Administration expenses	26,000		
Net profit	30,000		
	200,000		200,000

Balance Sheet 31 December 19–5

	£	£		£	£
Share capital		160,000	Fixed assets		
Profit & loss account		60,000	Cost		240,000
			Less depreciation		80,000
		220,000			160,000
Current Liabilities:			Current Assets		
General	20,000		Stock	50,000	
Dividend	20,000		Debtors	30,000	
			Cash	20,000	
					100,000
		260,000			260,000

The directors of Staghill Ltd propose to expand, and two plans for the year 19–6 are under consideration:

I   An increase of £100,000 in turnover. This will require an investment of £120,000 in plant with a life-expectancy of 10 years; variable costs will remain the same percentage of turnover as in 19–5; administration costs will increase by £7,000. It will be necessary to invest a further £20,000 in stock, debtors will rise proportionately to sales and general creditors will go up by £10,000.

II An increase of £200,000 in turnover. This will require an investment of £240,000 in plant with a life-expectancy of 10 years; variable costs will remain at the same percentage of turnover as in 19–5; administration costs will increase by £14,000. It will be necessary to invest a further £40,000 in stock, debtors will rise proportionately to sales and general creditors will go up by £20,000.

Staghill's bank is prepared to finance the development, but requires that the overdraft at the end of 19–6 shall not exceed £80,000.

Required:

(i) a calculation of the profit that can be expected in 19–6 under

(a) Plan I
(b) Plan II

(ii) a statement to show the amount of the overdraft at the end of 19–6 under

(a) Plan I
(b) Plan II

(iii) in the event of the overdraft at 31 December 19–6 exceeding £80,000 under either of the above proposals, a calculation of the additional period after the end of 19–6 that will be needed to bring it down to the required amount. Assume that the expectations for 19–6 extend into 19–7, etc., unchanged.

Note:

The dividend is to remain unchanged; ignore taxation and bank interest.

(34 marks)

2. Slipford owned a small block of furnished flats. Lingham, an estate agent, looked after the flats and rendered half yearly accounts to Slipford. The accounts for 19–5 were as follows:

	6 months to 30 June	6 months to 31 December
	£	£
Rent collected	5,536	5,088
Amounts collected from:		
electric meters	432	200
telephone meters	284	308
	6,252	5,596
	£	£
Rates paid	1,260	1,300
Electricity charges paid	404	282
Telephone charges paid	300	324
Management charges, including repairs and agent's commission	964	1,024
Cost of installing refrigerators (installed on 1.4.–5)	1,600	—
Paid to Slipford	1,200	2,800
	5,728	5,730

The agent's commission is at the rate of 10 per cent of the rents collected.

Slipford pays the full cost of electricity and telephone, and recovers the major part of the cost from the meters that are installed.

The value of the furniture and fittings in use on 1 January 19–5, after charging depreciation to that date, was £15,000. The annual depreciation charge is to be calculated at the rate of 10 per cent per annum on the written down value.

The following additional details are given:

	31 Dec. 19–4	31 Dec. 19–5
	£	£
Rent receivable in arrears	280	320
Telephone charges accrued	124	142
Electricity charges accrued	182	156

Required:

A statement of Slipford's net income from the property for the year 19–5.

Note:

The meters for electricity and telephone were cleared on the last day of each month. (22 marks)

3. Run and Walk are in partnership sharing profits in the ratio of 3:2 and the following trial balance was extracted from their books at 31 December 19–5:

Capital: Run		16,000
Walk		13,000
Sales		101,126
Purchases	71,443	
Debtors and creditors	9,437	6,321
Bad debts	328	
Provision for doubtful debts at 31 December 19–4		436
Rent and rates	1,060	
Lighting and heating	417	
Salaries and wages	9,592	
General expenses	1,330	
Motor vans at cost at 31 December 19–4	10,000	
Provision for depreciation of motor vans at 31 December 19–4		5,200
Motor expenses	1,048	
Freehold premises at cost	19,500	
Bank balance	1,855	
Stock in trade 31 December 19–4	11,236	
Drawings: Run	2,639	
Walk	2,198	
	142,083	142,083

You are given the following additional information:

(i) Stock in trade 31 December 19–5, £13,116.

(ii) Rates paid in advance 31 December 19–5, £80.

(iii) Lighting and heating due at 31 December 19–5, £116.

(iv) Provision for doubtful debts to be increased to £514.

(v) Depreciation has been and it to be charged on the vans at the annual rate of 20 per cent of cost.

(vi) During 19–5 Run used his private car for business purposes and is entitled to an allowance of £216 for this use.

(vii) Walk ordered goods for his own use at a cost of £107 and this amount was paid by the firm and debited to purchases.

Required:

A trading and profit and loss account for 19–5 and a balance sheet at 31 December 19–5.

(30 marks)

SECTION B: Answer EITHER question 4 OR question 5, not both.

4. It has been suggested that the purpose of capitalizing profit (issuing bonus shares) is to enable a company to obtain additional financial resources for expansion and development.

Discuss this view.

(14 marks)

5. Why is it necessary to provide a separate capital account for each partner? Explain how you would calculate the amount due to a partner on retirement or dissolution.

(14 marks)

THE LONDON CHAMBER OF COMMERCE AND INDUSTRY

Intermediate Stage

Book-Keeping

(Three hours allowed)

INSTRUCTIONS TO CANDIDATES

(*a*) All questions should be attempted.
(*b*) Marks may be lost by lack of neatness.

————

1. The following information is available for the year 19–6, from the books of a trading company:

	£
Sales Ledger debit balances 1 January 19–5	5,200
Sales	28,418
Cash Sales	1,226
Returns outwards	3,480
Discounts allowed	960
Cash received from debtors	22,670
Bad debt written off	90
Bills of exchange received from debtors	430
Bills of exchange discounted by bankers	350
Discount received	740
Bought ledger contras	1,570
Sales ledger credit balances 31 December 19–5	1,260
Returns inwards	1,830
Customer's dishonoured cheque returned by bank	87

Required:

Prepare the Sales Ledger Adjustment (or Control) Account as it would appear in the General Ledger for the year 19–5.

(16 marks)

2. The following balances were extracted from the books of Hale & Parker Ltd, at 30 September 19–5:

	£
Raw materials purchased	198,300
Factory expenses	5,460
Directors' fees	3,000
Stocks 1 October 19–4	
Raw materials	17,800
Work in progress (at prime cost)	4,600
Finished Goods (at transfer price)	15,400
Sales	460,000
Rates and Insurances	1,600
Direct wages	102,700
Repairs to plant and machinery	7,900
Repairs to buildings	3,700
Office salaries	28,400
Factory power	8,640
Carriage inwards	700
Premises—held on lease expiring in 10 years time on	
30 September 19–4—cost	54,000
Provision for depreciation of lease	36,000
Returns outwards	600
Discounts allowed	1,300
Bank interest—debit balance	2,600
Plant and machinery at cost	250,000
Provision for depreciation	150,000
Selling and distribution expenses	14,000
Unappropriated profit	5,400

Notes:

1. Finished stock is transferred from factory at factory cost plus 10 per cent.
2. Rates and insurances prepaid £400.
3. Stocks at 30 September 19–5:

	£
Raw material	12,600
Work in progress (at prime cost)	5,300
Finished goods (at transfer price)	25,300

4. Depreciation of plant and machinery to be charged at 20 per cent diminishing balance method.
5. 25 per cent of rates and insurance to be charged to the offices.

Required:

For the year to 30 September 19–5 prepare:

(*a*) Manufacturing Account, showing prime cost and factory cost.
(*b*) Trading Account.
(*c*) Profit and Loss Account—including an adjustment for the unrealized profit in stocks.

(30 marks)

3. P. Walther started in business on 1 January 19–5. His first year was quite successful as he made a return of 20 per cent on his year-end capital employed of £42,000.

Other information and ratios based on his year end balance sheet are:

1.	Depreciation for the year was £2,000 charged at 10 per cent on the fixed assets at the year end.	
2.	Current ratio	2:1
3.	Capital turnover' i.e. $\dfrac{\text{sales}}{\text{capital employed}}$	3
4.	Debtors to average monthly sales	2:1
5.	Quick ratio (Debtors plus bank to current liabilities)	1:1
6.	Stock turnover (there was no opening stock)	4
7.	Drawings for the year	£1,400
8.	General expenses for the year	£19,600
9.	The only current liabilities were trade creditors.	

Required:
(a) Trading and Profit and Loss Account for the year ended 31 December 19–5.
(b) Balance Sheet as at 31 December 19–5.

(26 marks)

4. Chilton Ltd decided to purchase a lorry from A. Sellers Ltd by means of a hire purchase agreement.

The cash price would have been £10,000. The hire purchase agreement provided for a deposit of 20 per cent to be paid on 1 January 19–1 and for three annual payments of £2,802 and a fourth payment of £2,803 on 31 December in each of the years 19–1 to 19–4.

Interest was charged at 15 per cent per annum on the balance outstanding at the beginning of each year.

Depreciation was charged at 20 per cent per annum straight line method.

All payments were made on the due dates.

Required:

Show the ledger accounts for the four years for:

(a) the motor lorry.
(b) A. Sellers Ltd.
(c) Hire Purchase Interest.
(d) Depreciation of motor lorry.
(e) Provision for depreciation of motor lorry.

Note: Calculations to be made to the nearest £.

(28 marks)

THE ROYAL SOCIETY OF ARTS EXAMINATIONS BOARD

Single-Subject Examinations

Accounting

Stage II (Intermediate)
(Two and a half hours allowed)

ALL questions in Section A and ONE question in Section B
are to be attempted.

SECTION A—ALL questions to be answered.

1. Bluebridge Ltd manufactures one product called plyston at its factory in London. The product is sold at a uniform price of £2 per unit throughout Great Britain; the unit cost of production remains unchanged during the period covered by this question.

The country is divided into five areas for sales purposes, and there is a district office with a resident manager in each area. All goods are despatched from the factory to the customer on the basis of each order placed with an area office.

The following data are extracted from Bluebridge's books covered the year 19–5.

	£
Raw material consumed	75,600
Factory wages	95,000
Factory expenses	29,400
Head office administration	20,000

	Area				
	1	2	3	4	5
	£	£	£	£	£
Sales	84,600	53,400	39,600	64,800	57,600
Rent and rates	6,000	2,000	1,600	1,200	800
Salaries	14,000	6,000	2,600	4,800	3,200
Delivery costs	422	534	594	1,296	1,734
Promotion expenses	2,000	5,000	2,400	6,000	7,000

There are no stocks of any kind held at either the beginning or at the end of the year.

Required:

(a) Revenue accounts for 19–5 designed in a manner which in your opinion provides the maximum amount of information for management and

(b) A discussion of the significant points disclosed by the accounts together with any recommendations you think appropriate.

(24 marks)

2. The balance sheet of the Blowball Club at 31 December 19–4 is as follows:

	£	£		£
Accumulated Fund		48,920	Investments at cost	24,600
Creditors			Furniture & equipment at	
Bar purchases	2,040		cost less depreciation	15,200
Expenses	80	2,120	Bar stocks	4,100
			Bank balance	7,140
		51,040		51,040

A summary of the Club's bank account for 19–5 is as follows:

	£		£
Balance at 1.1.19–5	7,140	Bar purchases	40,380
Subscriptions received	6,200	Wages & salaries	8,420
Bar sales	53,300	Rent and rates	2,400
Interest on investments	2,080	General expenses	2,680
		Cost of new investments	13,000
		Balance at 31.12.19–5	1,840
	68,720		68,720

On 31 December 19–5, bar stocks were valued at £5,968 and £2,284 was owing for bar supplies; £124 was owing for expenses.

The owner of the building of which the club occupies a part proposes to sell it for £88,000; he has offered it to the trustees of the club and they are considering the proposal.

The investments held by the club could be sold for £40.160 and a member of the club has offered to lend £10,000 at 10 per cent per annum, for five years; the secretary of the club has approached the bank to negotiate an overdraft for the balance needed to complete the purchase of the building; the bank has asked to see the 19–5 accounts and wishes to have an estimate of the amount that will be available annually for repayment.

Part of the building is occupied by a second organization which pays its own rates and from which an annual rent of £100 is receivable. The club will remain liable for the rates on the part of the building it occupies amounting to £900 per annum.

There are no subscriptions in arrears or in advance; depreciation should be charged on the furniture and equipment at the rate of 10 per cent per annum on the opening value.

Required:

(a) a bar trading account and a profit and loss account for 19–5 and a balance sheet at the end of that year

(b) a calculation showing:

  (i) the maximum amount to be borrowed on overdraft, as at 1 January 19–6, to meet the cost of the building;
  and
  (ii) the annual surplus that will be available to meet the interest on the over-

draft and for repayment on the assumption that the 19–5 results are repeated in each of the following five years.

Notes:

(1) Ignore income tax.
(2) There was no capital expenditure during 19–5.

(34 marks)

3.   The trial balance of Laxdale Ltd at 31 December 19–5 was as follows:

	£	£
Share capital (100,000 shares of £1 each)		100,000
Share premium		50,000
10 per cent Debentures repayable 1990		30,000
Freehold buildings at cost	130,000	
Machinery at cost	55,000	
Provision for depreciation of machinery		
31 December 19–4		20,500
Stock in trade 31 December 19–4	22,642	
Purchases	110,841	
Sales		261,942
Rent and rates	3,580	
Administration expenses	12,921	
Manufacturing wages	67,242	
Office Salaries	21,148	
Bad debts	1,026	
Provision for doubtful debts		
31 December 19–4		962
Directors' salaries	10,000	
Debenture interest	1,500	
Debtors	28,668	
Creditors		12,112
Bank balance	25,481	
Profit and loss account		
31 December 19–4		14,533
	490,049	490,049

You are given the following additional information:

  (i) Stock in trade 31 December 19–5, £20,246.
 (ii) Rates paid in advance 31 December 19–5, £150.
(iii) Administration expenses due at 31 December 19–5, £624.
 (iv) Provision for doubtful debts at 31 December 19–5 to be £1,005.
  (v) Depreciation is to be charged on machinery at the annual rate of 10 per cent of cost.
 (vi) Debenture interest for the half year to 31 December 19–5 was paid on 1 January 19–6.
(vii) It is proposed to pay a dividend of £10,000 for the year to 31 December 19–5.

Required:

A trading and profit and loss account for 19–5 and a balance sheet at 31 December 19–5.

Note:

Ignore taxation.

(28 marks)

Section B—Answer EITHER question 4 OR question 5, not both.

4. Discuss the problem of profit measurement in relation to fixed periods of time such as a year.

(14 marks)

5. 'Accounting reports and statements should be based on historic cost because it is an objectively established fact.' Discuss this statement.

(14 marks)

49

Consolidated Accounts: Introduction

The owners of a company are its shareholders. The purchase of ordinary shares normally gives a person three main rights, these being proportionate to the number of shares held by him. These are:

(a) Voting rights.

(b) An interest in the net assets of the company. (Net assets means assets less liabilities.)

(c) An interest in the profits earned by the company.

Because of the voting rights the ordinary shareholder is normally entitled to vote at shareholders' meetings. It should be mentioned that there are some ordinary shares, known as 'A' shares, which do not have voting rights—the reader may wish to look at the stock exchange prices in his daily newspaper where he will find some shares where the name of the company has 'A' after it, these shares are non-voting ordinary shares. In addition, preference shares do not normally have full voting rights, their votes usually being restricted to where their dividends are in arrears or where their special rights are being varied. The reader should also realise that debentures carry no right to vote at general meetings.

At the shareholders' meetings the ordinary shareholder, by virtue of his voting rights, is able to show his approval or disapproval (in accordance with the number of shares owned by him) of the election of directors. The directors appoint the officers of the company and manage its affairs. Therefore any group of shareholders acting together, who between them own more than 50 per cent of the voting shares of the company, can control the election of directors and, as a consequence, they can control the policies of the company through the directors. This would also hold true if any one shareholder owned more than 50 per cent of the voting shares.

One company may hold shares in another company; therefore if one company wishes to obtain control of another company it can do so by obtaining more than 50 per cent of the voting shares in that company.

Holding Companies and Subsidiary Companies

A company, S Ltd, has an issued share capital of 1,000 ordinary shares of £1 each. On 1 January 19–6 H Ltd buys 501 of these shares from Jones, a shareholder, for £600. H Ltd will now have control of S Ltd because it has more than 50 per cent of the voting shares. H Ltd is called the 'holding' company and S Ltd is said to be its 'subsidiary' company.

Now just because the identity of S Ltd's shareholders has changed does mean that the balance sheet of S Ltd will be drafted in a different fashion. Looking only at the balance sheet of S Ltd no one would be able to deduce that H Ltd owned more than 50 per cent of the shares, or even that H Ltd owned any shares at all in S Ltd. After obtaining control of S Ltd both H Ltd and S Ltd will continue to maintain their own sets of accounting records and to draft their own balance sheets. In fact if the balance sheets of H Ltd and S Ltd are looked at, both before and after the purchase of the shares, then any differences can be noted.

Exhibit 49.1

(a) Before H Ltd acquired control of S Ltd.

H Ltd Balance Sheet as at 31 December 19–5

	£		£	£
Share Capital	5,000	Fixed Assets		2,000
Profit and Loss Account	2,000	Current Assets:		
		Stock-in-Trade	2,900	
		Debtors	800	
		Bank	1,300	
				5,000
	7,000			7,000

S Ltd Balance Sheet as at 31 December 19–5

	£		£	£
Share Capital	1,000	Fixed Assets		400
Profit and Loss Account	100	Current Assets:		
		Stock-in-Trade	400	
		Debtors	200	
		Bank	100	
				700
	1,100			1,100

(b) After H Ltd acquired control of S Ltd the balance sheets would appear as follows before any further trading took place:

H Ltd Balance Sheet as at 1 January 19–6

	£		£	£
Share Capital	5,000	Fixed Assets		2,000
Profit and Loss Account	2,000	Investment in		
		Subsidiary Company		600
		Current Assets:		
		Stock-in-Trade	2,900	
		Debtors	800	
		Bank	700	
				4,400
	7,000			7,000

S Ltd Balance Sheet as at 1 January 19–6

	£		£	£
Share Capital	1,000	Fixed Assets		400
Profit and Loss Account	100	Current Assets:		
		Stock-in-Trade	400	
		Debtors	200	
		Bank	100	
				700
	1,100			1,100

The only differences can be seen to be those in the balance sheets of H Ltd. The bank balance has been reduced by £600, this being the cost of the shares in S Ltd, and the cost of the shares now appears as 'Investment in Subsidiary Company £600'. The balance sheets of S Ltd are completely unchanged.

From the Profit and Loss Account point of view, the appropriation section of S Ltd would also be completely unchanged after H Ltd takes control. H Ltd would however see a change in its Profit and Loss Account when a dividend is received from S Ltd, in this case the dividends received would be shown as Investment Income on the credit side of the Profit and Loss Account. Remember that dividends payable are charged to the Appropriation section of the paying company's Profit and Loss Account, whilst dividends received are in the main part of the receiving company's Profit and Loss Account.

The Need for Consolidated Accounts

Imagine a shareholder of H Ltd receiving H Ltd's Balance Sheet and Profit and Loss Account annually. After H Ltd's acquisition of the shares in S then £600 would appear as an asset in H's Balance Sheet. As the shares of S Ltd are now not so readily marketable, remembering that over 50 per cent are owned by H Ltd, it would be normal to find the investment remaining at cost, i.e. £600. The Profit and Loss Account would show dividends received from S Ltd. The cost of the investment in S Ltd and the dividends received from S Ltd would be the only items referring to the subsidiary in the records of H Ltd.

Anyone investing in H Ltd is, because of its majority shareholding in S Ltd, therefore also investing in S Ltd as well. Therefore just as the other assets and liabilities change over the years in H Ltd and the shareholders are very much concerned with the changes, so also does the shareholder of H Ltd want to know about the changes in the assets and liabilities of S Ltd. He is not, however, a shareholder of S Ltd, and therefore is not automatically entitled to a set of final accounts of S Ltd annually. Correspondingly, if the situation was to stay put at that point, the shareholder of H Ltd would not get a proper accounting view of his investment. This is accentuated if in fact the holding company was one with 20 subsidiaries, owning a different percentage of the shares in each one, and with all kinds of inter-indebtedness and inter-company sales—all of which need special treatment as seen later in this book.

The only way that a shareholder in H Ltd can see clearly, in accounting terms, how his investment is progressing is for him to receive a consolidated set of the accounts of both companies showing the overall effect of his investment.

Different Methods of acquiring Control of one Company by Another

So far the acquisition of control in S Ltd was by H Ltd buying more than 50 per cent of the shares in S Ltd from Jones, i.e. buying shares on the open market. This is by no means the only way of acquiring control, so by way of illustration some of the other methods are now described.

(a) S Ltd may issue new shares to H Ltd amounting to over 50 per cent of the voting shares. H Ltd pays for the shares in cash.

(b) H Ltd could purchase over 50 per cent of the voting shares of S Ltd on the open market by exchanging for them newly issued shares of H Ltd.

Or, acting through another company:

(c) H Ltd acquires more than 50 per cent of the voting shares in S1 Ltd for cash, and then S1 Ltd proceeds to acquire all of the voting shares of S2 Ltd. S2 Ltd would then be a sub-subsidiary of H Ltd.

These are only some of the more common ways by which one company becomes a subsidiary of another company.

The Nature of a Group

Wherever two or more companies are in the relationship of holding and subsidiary companies then a 'group' is said to exist. When such a group exists then besides the Final Accounts of the Holding company itself, then to comply with legal requirements, there must be a set of Final Accounts prepared in respect of the group as a whole. These group accounts are usually known as 'consolidated accounts', because the accounts of all the companies have had to be consolidated together to form one Balance Sheet and one Profit and Loss Account.

Sometimes holding companies carry on trading as well as investing in their subsidiaries. There are however other holding companies that do not trade at all, the whole of their activities being concerned with investing in other companies.

Teaching Method

The method used in this book for teaching consolidated accounts is that of showing the reader the adjustments needed on the face of the consolidated balance sheet, together with any workings necessary shown in a normal arithmetical fashion. The reasons why this method of illustrating consolidated accounts has been chosen are as follows:

(a) The author believes that it is his job to try to help the reader understand the subject, and not just to be able to perform the necessary manipulations. He believes that, given understanding of what is happening, then the accounting entries necessary follow easily enough. Showing the adjustments on the face of the balance sheet gives a 'birds-eye view' so that it is easier to see what is happening, rather than trace one's way laboriously through a complex set of double entry adjustments made in ledger accounts.

(b) The second main reason is that this would be a much lengthier and more costly book if all of the double entry accounts were shown. It is better for a first look at consolidated accounts to be an introduction to the subject only, rather than be at one and the same time both an introduction and a very detailed survey of the subject. If the reader can understand the consolidated accounts shown in this book then he/she will have a firm foundation which will enable him/her to tackle the more difficult and complicated aspects of the subject.

50

Consolidation of Balance Sheets: Basic Mechanics I

This chapter is concerned with the basic mechanics of consolidating balance sheets. The figures used will be quite small ones, as there is no virtue in obscuring the principles involved by bringing in large amounts. For the sake of brevity some abbreviations will be used. As the consolidation of the accounts of either two or three companies, but no more, will be attempted, then the abbreviations will be 'H' for the holding company, 'S1' the first subsidiary company, and 'S2' the second subsidiary company. Where there is only one subsidiary company it will be shown as 'S'. Unless stated to the contrary, all the shares will be ordinary shares of £1 each.

It will make the problems of the reader far easier if relatively simple balance sheets can be used to demonstrate the principles of consolidated accounts. To this end the balance sheets which follow in the next few chapters will usually have only two sorts of assets, those of stock and cash at bank. This will save a great deal of time and effort. If every time a consolidated balance sheet was to be drawn up the reader had to deal with assets of Land, Buildings, Patents, Motor Vehicles, Plant and Machinery, Stock, Debtors and Bank balances, then this would be an unproductive use of time.

Rule 1

The first rule is that in consolidation like things cancel out each other. In fact 'Cancellation Accounts' are in fact what consolidation accounts are all about. It also helps the reader to see the issue more clearly if the consolidated balance sheet is constructed immediately after H has bought the shares in S. In fact this would not be done in practice, but it is useful to use the method from a teaching point of view.

Exhibit 50.1

100 per cent of the shares of S bought at balance sheet value.

H has just bought all the shares of S. Before consolidation the balance sheets of H and S appear as follows:

H Balance Sheet

	£		£
Share Capital	10	Investment in subsidiary S (A)	6
		Bank	4
	10		10

S Balance Sheet

		£		£
Share Capital	(B)	6	Stock	5
			Bank	1
		6		6

Now the consolidated balance sheet can be drawn up. The rule about like things cancelling out each other can now be applied. As can be seen, item (A) in H's balance sheet and item (B) in S's balance sheet are concerned with exactly the same thing, namely the 6 ordinary shares of S; and for the same amount, for the shares are shown in both balance sheets at £6. These are cancelled when the consolidated balance sheet is drafted.

H and S Consolidated Balance Sheet

	£		£
Share Capital	10	Stock	5
		Bank (£4+£1)	5
	10		10

Exhibit 50.2

100 per cent of the shares of S bought for more than balance sheet value.
H Balance Sheet

	£		£
Share Capital	10	Investment in subsidiary S:	
		6 shares (C)	9
		Bank	1
	10		10

S Balance Sheet

		£		£
Share Capital	(D)	6	Stock	5
			Bank	1
		6		6

Now (C) and (D) refer to like things, but the amounts are unequal. What has happened is that H has given £3 more than the book value for the shares of S. In accounting, where the purchase money for something exceeds the stated value then the difference is known as Goodwill. This is still adhered to in the consolidation of balance sheets. The consolidated balance sheet is therefore:

H and S Consolidated Balance Sheet

	£		£
Share Capital	10	Goodwill (C) £9—(D) £6	3
		Stock	5
		Bank (£1+£1)	2
	10		10

Exhibit 50.3

100 per cent of the shares of S bought for less than balance sheet value.

H Balance Sheet

	£		£
Share Capital	10	Investment in subsidiary S:	
		6 shares (E)	4
		Stock	5
		Bank	1
	10		10

S Balance Sheet

		£		£
Share Capital	(F)	6	Stock	5
			Bank	1
		6		6

H has bought all of the shares of S, but has given only £4 for £6 worth of shares at balance sheet values. The £2 difference is the opposite of Goodwill. Contrary to what many people would think, this is not 'Badwill' as such a word is not an accounting term. The uninitiated might look upon the £2 as being 'profit' but your knowledge of company accounts should tell you that this difference could never be distributed as cash dividends. It is therefore a 'Capital Reserve' and will be shown accordingly in the consolidated balance sheet. The consolidated balance sheet therefore appears as:

H and S Consolidated Balance Sheet

	£		£
Share Capital	10	Stock (£5+£5)	10
Capital Reserve (F) £6—(E) £4	2	Bank (£1+£1)	2
	12		12

Cost of Control

In fact the expression 'Cost of Control' could be used instead of 'Goodwill'. This expression probably captures the essence of the purchase of the shares rather than calling it goodwill. It is precisely for the sake of gaining control of the assets of the company that the shares are bought. However the expression 'Goodwill' is more widely used and is correspondingly the one that will be used through the remainder of this book.

(You can now attempt Exercises 50.1, 50.2, and 50.3)

Rule 2

This states that, although the whole of the shares of the subsidiary have not been bought, nonetheless the whole of the assets of the subsidiary company (subject to certain inter-company transactions described later) will be shown in the consolidated balance sheet.

This rule comes about because of the choice made originally between two possible methods that could have been chosen. Suppose that H bought 75 per cent of the shares of S then the balance sheets could be displayed in one of two ways, e.g.

H and S Consolidated Balance Sheet

	£		£
Share Capital of H	xxxx	Goodwill	xxxx
		Assets of H: 100 per cent	xxxx
		Assets of S: 75 per cent	xxxx
	xxxx		xxxx

H and S Consolidated Balance Sheet

	£		£
Share Capital of H	xxxx	Goodwill	xxxx
Claims of outsiders which		Assets of H: 100 per cent	xxxx
equal 25 per cent of the		Assets of S: 100 per cent	xxxx
assets of S	xxxx		
	xxxx		xxxx

It can be seen that both balance sheets show the amount of assets which H owns by virtue of its proportionate shareholding. On the other hand the second balance sheet gives a fuller picture, as it shows that H has control of all of the assets of S, although in fact it does not own all of them. The claims of outsiders comes to 25 per cent of S and obviously they cannot control the assets of S, whereas H, with 75 per cent, can control the whole of the assets even though they are not fully owned by it. The second balance sheet method gives rather more meaningful information and is the method that is actually used for consolidated accounts.

Assume that S has 6 shares of £1 each and that it has one asset, namely stock £6. H buys 4 shares for £1 each, £4. If the whole of the assets of S £6 are to be shown on the assets side of the consolidated balance sheet, and the cancellation of only £4 is to take place on the other side, then the consolidated balance sheet would not balance. Exhibit 50–4 shows this in detail before any attempt is made to get the consolidated balance sheet to balance.

Exhibit 50.4

H Balance Sheet

	£		£
Share Capital	10	Investment in subsidiary:	
		4 shares (bought today)	4
		Stock	5
		Bank	1
	10		10

S Balance Sheet

	£		£
Share Capital	6	Stock	6

Now as the 2 extra shares have not been bought by H then they cannot be brought into any calculation of goodwill or capital reserve. H has in fact bought 4 shares with a balance sheet value of £1 each, £4, for precisely £4. There is therefore no element of goodwill or capital reserve. But on the other hand the consolidated balance sheet per Rule 2 must show the whole of the assets of S. This gives a consolidated balance sheet as follows:

H and S Consolidated Balance Sheet

Share Capital	10	Stock (£5+£6)	11
		Bank	1

Quite obviously the balance sheet totals differ by £2. What is this £2? On reflection it can be seen to be the £2 shares not bought by H. These shares belong to outsiders, they are not owned by the group. These outsiders also hold less than 50 per cent of the voting shares of S, in fact if they owned more then S would not be a subsidiary company. The title given to the outside shareholders is the apt one therefore of 'Minority Interest'. As the whole of the assets of S are shown in the consolidated balance sheet then part of these assets are owned by the minority interest. This claim against the assets is therefore shown on the capital and liabilities side of the consolidated balance sheet. The consolidated balance sheet becomes:

H and S Consolidated Balance Sheet

	£		£
Share Capital	10	Stock (£5+£6)	11
Minority Interest	2	Bank	1
	12		12

This therefore is the convention of showing the whole of the assets of the subsidiary (less certain inter-company transactions) in the consolidated balance sheet, with the claim of the minority interest shown on the other side of the balance sheet.

Exhibit 50.5

Where less than 100 per cent of the subsidiary's shares are bought at more than book value.

H Balance Sheet

	£		£
Share Capital	20	Investment in subsidiary:	
		6 shares (G)	8
		Stock	11
		Bank	1
	20		20

S Balance Sheet

	£		£
Share Capital (I)	10	Stock	7
		Bank	3
	10		10

H has bought 6 shares only, but has paid £8 for them. As the book value of the shares is £6, the £2 excess must therefore be Goodwill. The cancellation is therefore £6 from (G) and £6 from (I), leaving £2 of (G) to be shown as Goodwill in the consolidated balance sheet. The remaining £4 of (I) is in respect of shares held by the minority interest.

H and S Consolidated Balance Sheet

	£		£
Share Capital	20	Goodwill	2
Minority Interest	4	Stock (£11+£7)	18
		Bank (£1+£3)	4
	—		—
	24		24
	=		=

Exhibit 50.6

Where less than 100 per cent of the shares in the subsidiary are bought at less than book value.

H Balance Sheet

	£		£
Share Capital	20	Investment in subsidiary:	
		7 shares (J)	5
		Stock	13
		Bank	2
	—		—
	20		20
	=		=

S Balance Sheet

		£		£
Share Capital	(K)	10	Stock	9
			Bank	1
		—		—
		10		10
		=		=

Seven shares of S have now been bought for £5. This means that £5 of (J) and £5 of (K) cancel out with £2 shown as Capital Reserve. The remaining £3 of (K) is in respect of the shares held by the minority interest and will be shown as such in the consolidated balance sheet.

H and S Consolidated Balance Sheet

	£		£
Shares	20	Stock (£13+£9)	22
Capital Reserve	2	Bank (£2+£1)	3
Minority Interest	3		
	—		—
	25		25
	=		=

(You can now attempt Exercises 50.6 and 50.7)

Taking over Subsidiaries with Reserves

So far, for reasons of simplification, the examples given have been of
subsidiaries having share capital but no reserves. When reserves exist,
as they do in the vast majority of firms, it must be remembered that they
belong to the ordinary shareholders. This means that if H buys all the
10 shares of S for £15, and S at that point of time has a credit balance of
£3 on its Profit and Loss Account and a General Reserve of £2, then
what H acquires for its £15 is the full entitlement/rights of the 10 shares
measured by/shown as:

	£
10 Shares	10
Profit and Loss	3
General Reserve	2
	15

This means that the £15 paid and the £15 entitlements as shown will
cancel out each other and will not be shown in the consolidated balance
sheet. This is shown by the balance sheets shown in Exhibit 50.7.

Exhibit 50.7

*Where 100 per cent of the shares are bought at book value when the sub-
sidiary has reserves.*

H Balance Sheet

		£		£
Share Capital		20	Investment in subsidiary:	
Profit and Loss		5	10 shares (L)	15
General Reserve		3	Stock	11
			Bank	2
		28		28

S Balance Sheet

		£		£
Share Capital	(M1)	10	Stock	9
Profit and Loss	(M2)	3	Bank	6
General Reserve	(M3)	2		
		15		15

H and S Consolidated Balance Sheet

	£		£
Share Capital	20	Stock (£11+£9)	20
Profit and Loss	5	Bank (£2+£6)	8
General Reserve	3		
	—		—
	28		28
	=		=

The cost of the shares (L) £15 is cancelled out exactly against (M1) £10+(M2) £3+(M3) £2 = £15. These are therefore the only items cancelled out and the remainder of the two balance sheets of H and S are then combined to be the consolidated balance sheet.

Exhibit 50.8

Where 100 per cent of the shares are bought at more than book value when the subsidiary has reserves.

H Balance Sheet

	£		£
Share Capital	20	Investment in subsidiary:	
Profit and Loss	9	10 shares (N)	23
General Reserve	6	Stock	7
		Bank	5
	—		—
	35		35
	=		=

S Balance Sheet

		£		£
Share Capital	(01)	10	Stock	15
Profit and Loss	(02)	4	Bank	2
General Reserve	(03)	3		
		—		—
		17		17
		=		=

H paid £23 (N) for the entitlements (01) £10+(02) £4+(03) £3 = £17, so that a figure of £6 will be shown in the consolidated balance sheet for Goodwill.

H and S Consolidated Balance Sheet

	£		£
Share Capital	20	Goodwill	6
Profit and Loss	9	Stock (£7+£15)	22
General Reserve	6	Bank (£5+£2)	7
	—		—
	35		35
	=		=

Exhibit 50.9

Where 100 per cent of the shares in the subsidiary are bought at below book value when the subsidiary has reserves.

H Balance Sheet

		£		£
Share Capital		20	Investment in subsidiary:	
Profit and Loss		6	10 shares (P)	17
General Reserve		9	Stock	10
			Bank	8
		35		35

S Balance Sheet

		£		£
Share Capital	(Q1)	10	Stock	16
Profit and Loss	(Q2)	8	Bank	5
General Reserve	(Q3)	3		
		21		21

H has paid £17 (P) for the benefits of (Q1) £10+(Q2) £8+(Q3) £3 = £21. This means that there will be a Capital Reserve of £21−£17 = £4 in the consolidated balance sheet, whilst (P), (Q1), (Q2) and (Q3) having been cancelled out will not appear.

H and S Consolidated Balance Sheet

	£		£
Share Capital	20	Stock (£10+£16)	26
Profit and Loss	6	Bank (£8+£5)	13
General Reserve	9		
Capital Reserve	4		
	39		39

Exhibit 50.10

Where less than 100 per cent of the shares are bought in a subsidiary which has reserves, and the shares are bought at the balance sheet value.

H Balance Sheet

		£		£
Share Capital		20	Investment in subsidiary:	
Profit and Loss		17	8 shares (R)	24
General Reserve		8	Stock	15
			Bank	6
		45		45

S Balance Sheet

		£		£
Share Capital	(T1)	10	Stock	21
Profit and Loss	(T2)	5	Bank	9
General Reserve	(T3)	15		
		30		30

The items (R) and the parts of (T1), (T2) and (T3) which are like things need to be cancelled out. The cancellation takes place from the share capital and reserves of S as follows:

	Total at acquisition date	*Bought by H 80 per cent*	*Held by Minority Interest*
	£	£	£
Share Capital	10	8	2
Profit and Loss	5	4	1
General Reserve	15	12	3
	30	24	6

The amount paid by H was £24, and as H acquired a total of £24 value of shares and reserves the cancellation takes place without there being any figure of Goodwill or Capital Reserve. The consolidated balance sheet therefore appears:

H and S Consolidated Balance Sheet

	£		£
Share Capital	20	Stock (£15+£21)	36
Profit and Loss	17	Bank (£6+£9)	15
General Reserve	8		
Minority Interest	6		
	51		51

Partial Control at a Price not Equal to Balance Sheet Value

In Exhibit 50–10 the amount paid for the 80 per cent of the shares of S was equal to the balance sheet value of the shares in that it amounted to £24. Very rarely will it be so, as the price is normally different from balance sheet value. If an amount paid is greater than the balance sheet value then the excess will be shown as Goodwill in the consolidated balance sheet, whilst if a smaller amount than balance sheet value is paid then the difference is a Capital Reserve and will be shown as such in the consolidated balance sheet. Using the balance sheet figures of S in Exhibit 50.10 then if H had paid £30 for 80 per cent of the shares of S then the consolidated balance sheet would show a Goodwill figure of £6, whilst if instead £21 only had been paid then the consolidated balance sheet would show £3 for Capital Reserve.

When the acquisition of two subsidiaries brings out in the calculations a figure of Goodwill in respect of the acquisition of one subsidiary, and a figure for Capital Reserve in respect of the acquisition of the other subsidiary, then the net figure only will be shown in the consolidated balance sheet. For instance if H had acquired two subsidiaries S1 and S2 where the calculations showed a figure of £10 for Goodwill on the acquisition of S1 and a figure of £4 for Capital Reserve on the acquisition of S2, then the consolidated balance sheet would show a figure for Goodwill of £6. Given figures instead of £11 Goodwill for S1 and £18 Capital Reserve for S2 then the consolidated balance sheet would show a Capital Reserve of £7.

The final Exhibit in this chapter is a composite one, bringing in most of the points already shown.

Exhibit 50.11

Where two subsidiaries have been acquired, both with reserves, full control being acquired of one subsidiary and a partial control of the other subsidiary.

H Balance Sheet

	£			£
Share Capital	40	Investments in subsidiaries:		
Profit and Loss	50	S1 10 shares	(U)	37
General Reserve	10	S2 7 shares	(V)	39
		Stock		22
		Bank		2
	100			100

S1 Balance Sheet

		£		£
Share Capital	(W1)	10	Stock	19
Profit and Loss	(W2)	12	Bank	11
General Reserve	(W3)	8		
		30		30

S2 Balance Sheet

		£		£
Share Capital	(X1)	10	Stock	42
Profit and Loss	(X2)	30	Bank	18
General Reserve	(X3)	20		
		60		60

With the acquisition of S1 H has paid £37 for (W1) £10+(W2) £12+(W3) £8 = £30, giving a figure of £7 for Goodwill. With the acquisition of S2 H has given £39 for 7/10ths of the following: (X1) £10+(X2) £30+(X3) £20 = £60×7/10ths = £42, giving a figure of £3 for Capital Reserve. As the net figure only is to be shown in the consolidated balance sheet then it will be Goodwill £7−Capital Reserve £3 = Goodwill (net) £4.

H and S1 and S2 Consolidated Balance Sheet

		£		£
Share Capital		40	Goodwill	4
Profit and Loss		50	Stock (£22+£19+£42)	83
General Reserve		10	Bank (£2+£11+£18)	31
Minority Interest:				
3/10ths of (X1)	3			
3/10ths of (X2)	9			
3/10ths of (X3)	6			
		18		
		118		118

Now work through Exercises 50.10 and 50.11.

Exercises

50.1. The following balance sheets were drawn up immediately H Ltd had acquired control of S Ltd. You are to draw up a consolidated balance sheet.

H Balance Sheet

	£		£
Share Capital	200	Investment in S:	
		100 shares	110
		Stock	60
		Bank	30
	200		200

S Balance Sheet

	£		£
Share Capital	100	Stock	80
		Bank	20
	100		100

50.2. You are to draw up a consolidated balance sheet from the following balance sheets of H Ltd and S Ltd which were drawn up immediately H Ltd had acquired the shares in S Ltd.

H Balance Sheet

	£		£
Share Capital	6,000	Investment in S Ltd:	
		3,000 shares	2,700
		Fixed Assets	2,000
		Stock	800
		Debtors	400
		Bank	100
	6,000		6,000

S Balance Sheet

	£		£
Share Capital	3,000	Fixed Assets	1,800
		Stock	700
		Debtors	300
		Bank	200
	3,000		3,000

50.3. Draw up a consolidated balance sheet from the following balance sheets which were drawn up as soon as H Ltd had acquired control of S Ltd.

H Balance Sheet

	£		£
Share Capital	100,000	Investment in S Ltd:	
		60,000 shares	60,000
		Fixed Assets	28,000
		Stock	6,000
		Debtors	5,000
		Bank	1,000
	100,000		100,000

S Balance Sheet

	£		£
Share Capital	60,000	Fixed Assets	34,000
		Stock	21,000
		Debtors	3,000
		Bank	2,000
	60,000		60,000

50.4A. H Ltd acquires all the shares in S Ltd and then the following balance sheets are drawn up. You are to draw up a consolidated balance sheet.

H Balance Sheet

	£		£
Share Capital	42,000	Investment in S Ltd	29,000
		Fixed Assets	5,000
		Stock	4,000
		Debtors	3,000
		Bank	1,000
	42,000		42,000

S Balance Sheet

	£		£
Share Capital	24,000	Fixed Assets	12,000
		Stock	6,000
		Debtors	4,000
		Bank	2,000
	24,000		24,000

50.5A. Draw up a consolidated balance sheet from the balance sheets of H Ltd and S Ltd that were drafted immediately the shares in S Ltd were acquired by H Ltd.

H Balance Sheet

	£		£
Share Capital	80,000	Investment in S Ltd:	
		63,000 shares	50,000
		Fixed Assets	18,000
		Stock	5,000
		Debtors	4,000
		Bank	3,000
	80,000		80,000

S Balance Sheet

	£		£
Share Capital	63,000	Fixed Assets	48,000
		Stock	6,000
		Debtors	5,000
		Bank	4,000
	63,000		63,000

50.6. H Ltd acquires 60 per cent of the shares in S Ltd. Balance Sheets are then drafted immediately. You are to draw up the consolidated balance sheet.

H Balance Sheet

	£		£
Share Capital	4,000	Investment in S Ltd:	
		1,200 shares	1,500
		Fixed Assets	900
		Stock	800
		Debtors	600
		Bank	200
	4,000		4,000

S Balance Sheet

	£		£
Share Capital	2,000	Fixed Assets	1,100
		Stock	500
		Debtors	300
		Bank	100
	2,000		2,000

50.7. H acquires 95 per cent of the shares of S Ltd. The following balance sheets are then drafted. You are to draw up the consolidated balance sheet.

H Balance Sheet

	£		£
Share Capital	8,000	Investment in S:	
		2,850 shares	2,475
		Fixed Assets	2,700
		Stock	1,300
		Debtors	1,400
		Bank	125
	8,000		8,000

S Balance Sheet

	£		£
Share Capital	3,000	Fixed Assets	625
		Stock	1,700
		Debtors	600
		Bank	75
	3,000		3,000

50.8A. H buys 66⅔ per cent of the shares in S Ltd. You are to draw up the consolidated balance sheet from the following balance sheets constructed immediately control had been achieved.

H Balance Sheet

			£
Share Capital	2,300	Investment in S:	
		600 shares	540
		Fixed Assets	1,160
		Stock	300
		Debtors	200
		Bank	100
	2,300		2,300

S Balance Sheet

Share Capital	900	Fixed Assets	400
		Stock	200
		Debtors	240
		Bank	60
	900		900

50.9A. After H Ltd acquiring 75 per cent of the shares of S Ltd the following balance sheets are drawn up.

H Balance Sheet

Share Capital	6,000	Investments in S Ltd:	
		1,200 shares	1,550
		Fixed Assets	2,450
		Stock	1,000
		Debtors	800
		Bank	200
	6,000		6,000

S Balance Sheet

	£		£
Share Capital	1,600	Fixed Assets	800
		Stock	400
		Debtors	250
		Bank	150
	1,600		1,600

50.10. Immediately after H Ltd had acquired control of S1 Ltd and S2 Ltd the following balance sheets were drawn up. You are to draw up a consolidated balance sheet.

H Balance Sheet

	£		£
Share Capital	10,000	Investments in subsidiaries:	
Profit and Loss Account	6,500	S1 Ltd (3,000 shares)	3,800
		S2 Ltd (3,200 shares)	4,700
		Fixed Assets	5,500
		Current Assets	2,500
	16,500		16,500

S1 Balance Sheet

	£		£
Share Capital	3,000	Fixed Assets	2,200
Profit and Loss Account	400	Current Assets	1,300
General Reserve	100		
	3,500		3,500

S2 Balance Sheet

	£		£
Share Capital	4,000	Fixed Assets	4,900
Profit and Loss Account	1,000	Current Assets	2,100
General Reserve	2,000		
	7,000		7,000

50.11.

H Balance Sheet

	£		£
Share Capital	10,000	Investment in subsidiaries:	
Profit and Loss Account	2,000	S1 Ltd (1,800 shares)	4,200
General Reserve	1,400	S2 Ltd (2,000 shares)	2,950
		Fixed Assets	4,150
		Current Assets	2,100
	13,400		13,400

S1 Balance Sheet

	£		£
Share Capital	3,000	Fixed Assets	3,500
Profit and Loss Account	1,200	Current Assets	2,500
General Reserve	1,800		
	6,000		6,000

S2 Balance Sheet

	£		£
Share Capital	2,000	Fixed Assets	1,800
Profit and Loss Account	500	Current Assets	1,400
General Reserve	700		
	3,200		3,200

50.12A. Immediately after H Ltd had achieved control of S1 Ltd and S2 Ltd the following balance sheets are drawn up. You are to draw up the consolidated balance sheet.

H Balance Sheet

	£		£
Share Capital	15,000	Investment in subsidiaries:	
Profit and Loss Account	2,000	S1 4,000 shares	6,150
General Reserve	3,300	S2 6,000 shares	8,950
		Fixed Assets	3,150
		Current Assets	2,050
	20,300		20,300

S1 Balance Sheet

	£		£
Share Capital	4,000	Fixed Assets	5,300
Profit and Loss Account	1,100	Current Assets	1,200
General Reserve	1,400		
	6,500		6,500

S2 Balance Sheet

	£		£
Share Capital	7,000	Fixed Assets	6,000
Profit and Loss Account	1,400	Current Assets	3,450
General Reserve	1,050		
	9,450		9,450

50.13A. The following balance sheets of H Ltd, S1 Ltd and S2 Ltd were drawn up as soon as H Ltd had acquired the shares in both subsidiaries. You are to draw up a consolidated balance sheet.

H Balance Sheet

	£		£
Share Capital	11,000	Investment in subsidiaries:	
Profit and Loss Account	1,000	S1 3,500 shares	6,070
General Reserve	2,600	S2 2,000 shares	5,100
		Fixed Assets	2,030
		Current Assets	1,400
	14,600		14,600

S1 Balance Sheet

	£		£
Share Capital	5,000	Fixed Assets	4,800
Profit and Loss Account	900	Current Assets	2,400
General Reserve	1,300		
	7,200		7,200

S2 Balance Sheet

	£		£
Share Capital	2,000	Fixed Assets	2,800
Profit and Loss Account	1,400	Current Assets	900
General Reserve	300		
	3,700		3,700

51

Consolidation of Balance Sheets: Basic Mechanics II

In the last chapter the consolidation of balance sheets was looked at as if the consolidated balance sheets were drawn up immediately the shares in the subsidiary had been acquired. However, this is very rarely the case in practice, and therefore the consolidation of balance sheets must be looked at as at the time it actually takes place, i.e. at the end of an accounting period some time after acquisition has taken place. Correspondingly, the balance on the profit and loss account of the subsidiary, and possibly the balances on the other reserve accounts, will have altered when compared with the figures at the date of acquisition.

In chapter 50 the Goodwill, or Capital Reserve, was calculated at the date of acquisition, and this calculation will stay unchanged as the years go by. It is important to understand this. Say for instance that the calculation was made of Goodwill on 31 December 19–3 and that the figure was £5,000. Even if the calculation was made one year later, on 31 December 19–4, then the calculation must refer to the reserves, etc., as on 31 December 19–3 as this is when they were acquired, and so the figure of Goodwill will still be £5,000. This would be true even if 5 years went by before anyone performed the calculation. In practice therefore, once the figure of Goodwill has been calculated then there is absolutely no need to re-calculate it every year. However, in examinations the Goodwill figure will still have to be calculated by the student even though the consolidated balance sheet that he is drawing up is 5, 10 or 20 years after the company became a subsidiary. This has to be done because the previous working papers are not available to an examinee.

It would be outside the law and good accounting practice for any company to return its capital to the shareholders, unless of course special permission was granted by the court. Similarly, if a holding company was to pay its money in acquiring a company as a subsidiary, and then distribute as dividends the assets that it had bought then this is tantamount to returning its capital to its shareholders. This can best be illustrated by a simple example.

H pays £15 to acquire 100 per cent of the shares of S, and the share capital of S consists of £10 of shares and £5 profit and loss account. Thus to acquire a capital asset, i.e. ownership of S, the holding company has parted with £15. If the balance of the profit and loss account of S was merely added to the profit and loss balance of H in the consolidated balance sheet then the £5 balance of S could be regarded as being distributable as cash dividends to the shareholders of H. As this £5 of reserves has been bought as a capital asset then such a dividend would be the return of capital to the shareholders of S, and to prevent this the balance of the profit and loss account of S on acquisition is capitalized, i.e. it is brought into the computation as to whether there is goodwill or capital reserve and not shown in the consolidated balance sheet as a profit and loss account balance. On the other hand the whole of any profit made by S since acquisition will clearly belong to H's shareholders as H owns 100 per cent of the shares of S.

Exhibit 51.1

Where the holding company holds 100 per cent of the subsidiary company's shares.

H acquires the shares on 31 December 19–4. The balance sheets one year later are as follows:

	£		£
Share Capital	20	Investment in subsidiary:	
Profit and Loss	12	10 shares bought 31/12/19–4 (A)	18
		Stock	11
		Bank	3
	32		32

S Balance Sheet as at 31 December 19–5

		£		£
Share Capital	(B)	10	Stock	14
Profit and Loss:	£		Bank	2
As at 31/12/19–4	(C) 5			
Profit for 19/19–5	(D) 1			
		6		
		16		16

The shares were acquired on 31 December 19–4, therefore the calculation of the Goodwill or Capital Reserve is as the position of those firms were at that point in time. Thus for (A) £18 the firm of H obtained the following at 31 December 19–4, Shares (B) £10 and Profit and Loss (C) £5 = £15. Goodwill therefore amounted to £3. The profit of S made during 19–5 is since acquisition and does not therefore come into the Goodwill calculation. The figure of (D) £1 is a reserve which belongs wholly to H, as H in fact owns all of the shares of S. This (D) £1 is added to the reserves shown in the consolidated balance sheet.

H Consolidated Balance Sheet as at 31 December 19–5

	£		£
Share Capital	20	Goodwill	3
Profit and Loss (H£12+S£1)	13	Stock (£11+£14)	25
		Bank (£3+£2)	5
	33		33

Exhibit 51.2

Where the holding company holds 100 per cent of the shares of the subsidiary and there is a post acquisition loss.

H Balance Sheet as at 31 December 19–5

		£		£
Share Capital		20	Investment in subsidiary:	
Profit and Loss:	£		10 shares bought 31/12/19–4 (E)	19
As at 31/12/19–4	7		Stock	10
Add Profit 19–5	6		Bank	4
		13		
		33		33

S Balance Sheet as at 31 December 19–5

		£		£
Share Capital	(F)	10	Stock	9
Profit and Loss:	£		Bank	2
As at 31/12/19–4	(G) 4			
Less Loss 19–5	3			
		1		
		11		11

In calculating Goodwill, against the amount paid (E) £19 are cancelled the items (F) £10 and (G) £4, thus the Goodwill is £5. The loss (I) has been incurred since acquisition. A profit since acquisition, as in Exhibit 51.2, adds to the reserves in the consolidated balance sheet, therefore a loss must be deducted.

H Consolidated Balance Sheet as at 31 December 19–5

	£		£
Share Capital	20	Goodwill	5
Profit and Loss (£13—(I) £3)	10	Stock (£10+£9)	19
		Bank (£4+£2)	6
	30		30

Exhibit 51.3

Where the holding company acquires less than 100 per cent of the shares of the subsidiary and there is a post acquisition profit.

H Balance Sheet as at 31 December 19-5

	£	£
Share Capital	20	Investment in subsidiary:
Profit and Loss:	£	8 shares bought 31/12/19-4 (J) 28
As at 31/12/19-4	10	Stock 7
Add Profit 19-5	8	Bank 3
	— 18	
	38	38

S Balance Sheet as at 31 December 19-5

	£	£
Share Capital	(K) 10	Stock 28
Profit and Loss:	£	Bank 2
As at 31/12/19-4	(L) 15	
Add Profit 19-5	(M) 5	
	— (N) 20	
	30	30

H has given (J) £28 to take over 80 per cent of (K)+(L) i.e. 80 per cent of (£10+£15) = £20. Therefore Goodwill is £8. The profit for 19-5 (M) £5 is also owned 80 per cent by H = £4, and as this has been earned since the shares in S were bought the whole of this belongs to the shareholders of H and is also distributable to them, therefore it can be shown with other Profit and Loss Account balances in the consolidated balance sheet.

80% [margin annotation]

The Minority Interest is 20 per cent of (K) £10+(N) £20 = £6. It must be pointed out that, although the holding company splits up the profit and loss account balances into pre-acquisition and post-acquisition, there is no point in the Minority Interest doing likewise. It would however amount to exactly the same answer if they did, because 20 per cent of (K) £10+(L) £15+(M) £5 still comes to £6, i.e. exactly the same as 20 per cent of (N) £20+(K) £10 = £6.

H Consolidated Balance Sheet as at 31 December 19-5

	£	£
Share Capital	20	Goodwill 8
Profit and Loss (H £18+£4)	22	Stock (£7+£28) 35
Minority Interest:		Bank (£3+£2) 5
(Shares £2+Profit and Loss £4)	6	
	48	48

If there had been a post-acquisition loss then this would have been deducted from H's balance of Profit and Loss Account £18 when the consolidated balance sheet was drawn up.

(Before reading any further attempt questions 51.1, 51.2 and 51.4)

Exercises

51.1. H Ltd buys 100 per cent of the shares of S Ltd on 31 December 19–5. The balance sheets of the two companies on 31 December 19–6 are as shown, you are to draw up a consolidated balance sheet as at 31 December 19–6.

H Balance Sheet as at 31 December 19–6

	£	£		£
Share Capital		10,000	Investment in subsidiary:	
Profit and Loss Account:			4,000 shares bought	
As at 31/12/19–5	1,500		31/12/19–5	5,750
Add Profit for 19–6	2,500		Fixed Assets	5,850
		4,000	Current Assets	2,400
		14,000		14,000

S Balance Sheet as at 31 December 19–6

	£	£		£
Share Capital		4,000	Fixed Assets	5,100
Profit and Loss Account:			Current Assets	1,500
As at 31/12/19–5	800			
Add Profit for 19–6	1,800			
		2,600		
		6,600		6,600

51.2. H Ltd buys 70 per cent of the shares of S Ltd on 31 December 19–8. The balance sheets of the two companies on 31 December 19–9 are as follows. You are to draw up a consolidated balance sheet as at 31 December 19–9.

H Balance Sheet as at 31 December 19–9

	£	£		£
Share Capital		50,000	Investment in S Ltd:	
Profit and Loss Account:			7,000 shares bought 31/12/19–8	7,800
As at 31/12/19–8	4,800		Fixed Assets	39,000
Add Profit for 19–9	9,200		Current Assets	22,200
		14,000		
General Reserve		5,000		
		69,000		69,000

S Balance Sheet as at 31 December 19–9

	£	£		£
Share Capital		10,000	Fixed Assets	8,400
Profit and Loss Account:			Current Assets	4,900
As at 31/12/19–8	1,700			
Less Loss for 19–9	400			
		1,300		
General Reserve				
(unchanged since 19–5)		2,000		
		13,300		13,300

51.3A. H Ltd bought 55 per cent of the shares in S Ltd on 31 December 19–6. From the following balance sheets you are to draw up the consolidated balance sheet as at 31 December 19–7.

H Balance Sheet as at 31 December 19–7

		£		£
Share Capital		30,000	Investment in S Ltd:	
Profit and Loss Account:	£		2,750 shares	4,850
As at 31/12/19–6	900		Fixed Assets	13,150
Add Profit for 19–7	600		Current Assets	13,500
		1,500		
		31,500		31,500

S Balance Sheet as at 31 December 19–7

		£		£
Share Capital		5,000	Fixed Assets	4,600
Profit and Loss Account:	£		Current Assets	3,100
As at 31/12/19–6	700			
Add Profit for 19–7	500			
		1,200		
General Reserve		1,500		
(unchanged since 19–3)				
		7,700		7,700

51.4. H buys shares in S1 and S2 on 31 December 19–4. You are to draft the consolidated balance sheet as at 31 December 19–5 from the following:

H Balance Sheet as at 31 December 19–5

	£	£		£
Share Capital		40,000	Investments:	
Profit and Loss Account:			S1: 6,000 shares	8,150
As at 31/12/19–4	2,350		S2: 8,000 shares	11,400

Add Profit for 19–5	5,200	Fixed Assets	21,000
	7,550	Current Assets	12,000
General Reserve	5,000		
	52,550		52,550

S1 Balance Sheet as at 31 December 19–5

	£	£		£
Share Capital		10,000	Fixed Assets	9,900
Profit and Loss Account:			Current Assets	4,900
As at 31/12/19–4	1,100			
Add Profit for 19–5	1,700			
		2,800		
General Reserve		2,000		
(same as at 31/12/19–4)				
		14,800		14,800

S2 Balance Sheet as at 31 December 19–5

	£	£		£
Share Capital		8,000	Fixed Assets	6,000
Profit and Loss Account:			Current Assets	4,000
As at 31/12/19–4	500			
Less Loss for 19–5	300			
		200		
General Reserve		1,800		
(same as at 31/12/19–4)				
		10,000		10,000

51.5A. H Ltd bought 40,000 shares in S1 Ltd and 27,000 shares in S2 Ltd on 31 December 19–2. The following balance sheets were drafted as at 31 December 19–3. You are to draw up a consolidated balance sheet as at 31 December 19–3.

H Balance Sheet as at 31 December 19–3

	£	£		£
Share Capital		200,000	Investments in subsidiaries:	
Profit and Loss Account:			S1 Ltd 40,000 shares	49,000
As at 31/12/19–2	11,000		S2 Ltd 27,000 shares	30,500
Add Profit for 19–3	16,000		Fixed Assets	90,000
		27,000	Current Assets	80,500
General Reserve		23,000		
		250,000		250,000

S1 Balance Sheet as at 31 December 19–3

	£	£		£
Share Capital		50,000	Fixed Assets	38,200
Profit and Loss Account:			Current Assets	19,200
As at 31/12/19–2	3,000			
Less Loss for 19–3	1,600			
		1,400		
General Reserve		6,000		
(as at 31/12/19–2)				
		57,400		57,400

S2 Balance Sheet as at 31 December 19–3

	£	£		£
Share Capital		36,000	Fixed Assets	31,400
Profit and Loss Account:			Current Assets	14,600
As at 31/12/19–2	4,800			
Add Profit for 19–3	3,400			
		8,200		
General Reserve				
(as at 31/12/19–2)		1,800		
		46,000		46,000

52

Inter-Company Dealings: Indebtedness and Unrealised Profit in Stocks

When a subsidiary company owes money to the holding company, then the amount owing will be shown as a debtor in the holding company's balance sheet and as a creditor in the subsidiary company's balance sheet. Such debts in fact have to be shown separately from other debts so as to comply with the Companies Acts. Such a debt between these two companies is however the same debt, and following the rule that like things cancel out, then the consolidated balance sheet will show neither debtor nor creditor for this amount as cancellation will have taken place. The same treatment would apply to debts owed by the holding company to the subsidiary, or to debts owed by one subsidiary company to another subsidiary company. The treatment is exactly the same whether the subsidiary is 100 per cent owned or not.

Exhibit 52.1

Where the subsidiary company owes money to the holding company.

H Balance Sheet

	£		£	£
Share Capital	20	Investment in subsidiary: 10 shares		10
Profit and Loss	6	Stock		13
Creditors	9	Debtors:		
		Owing from subsidiary (A)	4	
		Other debtors	7	
			—	11
		Bank		1
	35			35

S Balance Sheet

	£	£		£
Share Capital		10	Stock	6
Creditors:			Debtors	13

Owing to holding company (B)	4	Bank	3
Other creditors	8		
	—	12	
	22		22

H & S Consolidated Balance Sheet

	£		£
Share Capital	20	Stock (£13+£6)	19
Profit and Loss	6	Debtors (£7+£13)	20
Creditors (£9+£8)	17	Bank (£1+£3)	4
	—		—
	43		43

Unrealised Profit in Stock-in-Trade

It is possible that companies in a group may not have traded with each other. In that case the stocks-in-trade at the balance sheet date will not include goods bought from another member of the group. Again it is also possible that the companies may have traded with each other, but at the balance sheet date all of the goods traded with each other may have been sold to firms outside the group, and the result is that none of the companies in the group will have any of such goods included in their stock-in-trade.

However, it is also possible that the companies have traded with each other, and that one or more of the companies has goods in its stock-in-trade at the balance sheet date which have been bought from another group member. If the goods had been traded between members of the group at cost price, then the consolidated balance sheet would not be altered just because of a change in the location of stocks-in-trade. This means that it would not offend accounting practice by adding together all of the stock figures and showing them in the consolidated balance sheet, as the total will be the total of the cost of the unsold goods within the group.

Conversely, goods are usually sold between members of the group at prices above the original cost price paid by the first member of the group to acquire them. If all of such goods are sold by group members to firms outside by the balance sheet date then no adjustments are needed in the consolidated balance sheet, because the goods will not then be included in the stocks-in-trade. It would however be more usual to find that some of the goods had not been sold by one of the companies at the balance sheet date. so that company would include these goods in its stock-in-trade in its own balance sheet. Suppose that the holding company H owns all the shares in S, the subsidiary, and that H had sold goods which had cost it £12 to S for £20. Assume in addition that S had sold none of these goods by the balance sheet date. In the balance sheet of S the goods will be included in stock-in-trade at £20, whilst the profits made by H will include the £8 profit recorded in buying the goods for £12 and selling them for £20. Although this is true from each company's point of view, it most certainly is not true from the group viewpoint. The goods have not passed to anyone outside the group, and therefore the profit of £8 has not been realized by the group.

Going back to basic accounting concepts, the realization concept states that profit should not be recognized until the goods have been passed to the customer. As the consolidated accounts are concerned with an overall picture of the group, and the profits have not been realized by the group, then such profits should be eliminated. Accordingly the figure of £8 should be deducted from the profit and loss account of H on consolidation, and the same amount should be deducted from the stock-in-trade of S on consolidation. This cancels an unrealized inter-group profit.

If H had sold goods which had cost it £12 to S, a 100 per cent owned subsidiary, for £20, and S had sold ¾ of the goods for £22 by the balance sheet date then the picture would be different. H will have shown a profit in its profit and loss account for these sales of £8. In addition S will have shown a profit in its profit and loss account for the sales made of £7, i.e. £22 − ¾ of £20. The two profit and loss accounts show total profits of £8 + £7 = £15. So far however, looking at the group as a whole, these goods have cost the group £12. Three-quarters of these have been sold to firms outside the group, so that cost of goods sold outside the group is ¾ × £12 = £9, and as these were sold by S the profit realized by the group is £22 − £9 = £13. This is £2 less than that shown by adding up the separate figures for each company in the group. Thus the group figures would be over-stated by £2 if the separate figures were merely added together without any adjustment. In addition the stock-in-trade would be overvalued by £2 if the two separate figures were added together because the remaining stock-in-trade of S includes one-quarter of the goods bought from H, i.e. ¼ × £20 = £5, but the original cost of the group was ¼ × £12 = £3. The adjustment needed is that in the consolidation process £2 will be deducted from the profit and loss balance of H and £2 will be deducted from the stock-in-trade of S, thus removing any unrealized inter-group profits.

This could be expressed in tabular form as:

(a) Cost of goods to H	£12
(b) Sold to S for	£20
(c) Sold by S, ¾ for	£22
(d) Stock of S at balance sheet date at cost to S ¼ of (b)	£5
(e) Stock of S at balance sheet date at cost to H ¼ of (a)	£3
(f) Excess of S balance sheet value of stock over cost to group (d) − (e)	£2

(g) Profit shown in H profit and loss account (b) − (a) = £8	
(i) Profit shown in S profit and loss account (c) £22 − ¾ of (b) £15 = £7	

(*j*) Profit shown in the profit and loss accounts of H and S = (*g*)+(*i*)
= £15

(*k*) Actual profit made by the group dealing with outsiders (*c*) £22
less (¾ of (*a*) £12) £9 = £13

(*l*) Profit recorded by individual companies exceeds profit made by
the group's dealing with outsiders (*j*)−(*k*) = £2

The action needed for the consolidated balance sheet is therefore to
deduct (*f*) £2 from the stock figures of H and S, and to deduct (*l*) £2 from
the profit and loss account figures of H and S.

Exhibit 52.2

*Where the stock-in-trade of one company includes goods bought from
another company in the group.*

H Balance Sheet as at 31 December 19–3

	£		£
Share Capital	20	Investment in subsidiary:	
Profit and Loss Account: £		10 shares bought 31/12/19–2	16
As at 31/12/19–2 8		Stock-in-Trade	24
Profit for 19–3 (C) 18		Bank	6
— 26			
	46		46

S Balance Sheet as at 31 December 19–3

	£		£
Share Capital	10	Stock-in-Trade (D)	22
Profit and Loss Account: £		Bank	3
As at 31/12/19–2 6			
Profit for 19–3 9			
— 15			
	25		25

During the year H sold goods which had cost it £16 to S for £28,
i.e. recording a profit for H of £12. Of these goods two-thirds had been
sold by S at the balance sheet date. leaving one-third in stock-in-trade.
This means that the stock-in-trade of S (D) includes £4 unrealized
profit (⅓×£12). The figure of H's profit for the year (C) £18 also includes
£4 unrealized profit. When consolidating the two balance sheets £4
therefore needs deducting from each of those figures.

In Exhibit 52.2 the subsidiary has been wholly owned by the holding
company. The final figures would have been exactly the same if it had
been the subsidiary which had sold the goods to the holding company
instead of vice-versa.

H Consolidated Balance Sheet as at 31 December 19–3

	£		£
Share Capital	20	Stock-in-Trade	
Profit and Loss Account		(S £22−£4+H £24)	42
(S £9+H £8+£18−£4)	31	Bank (H £6+S £3)	9
	51		51

Partially Owned Subsidiaries and Unrealised Profits

So far the examples looked at have been those where wholly owned subsidiaries have been concerned. The situation can be different when the subsidiary is only partly owned.

In Exhibit 52.2 the unrealized profit in stock-in-trade was £4, and in that case the subsidiary was 100 per cent controlled. Suppose that in fact the ownership or shares was 75 per cent then there would be more than one possibility:

(a) (i) That £4 is deducted from the stock-in-trade figure in the consolidated balance sheet, and correspondingly £4 is deducted from the profit and loss account of H when it is consolidated, there being no adjustment for minority interest, or

(ii) That £4 is deducted from the stock-in-trade figure in the consolidated balance sheet. To correspond with this a proportion is deducted from the minority interest, in this case £4 × 25 per cent = £1, whilst the remaining holding company proportion of 75 per cent, £3, is deducted from H profit and loss account when consolidated.

(b) That the profit to be cancelled out be restricted to the proportion of control of the subsidiary. In this particular case the part of the profit to be cancelled out is restricted to 75 per cent, i.e. £3. This has to be deducted both from the stock-in-trade of S on consolidation and from the profit and loss account of H.

None of these methods is incorrect, and they are all in use. With (b) the view is taken that only part of the sale, in this case 75 per cent, is connected with the group, the other part of the sale of 25 per cent being to the minority interest and therefore this 25 per cent of profits can be said to be realized.

Obviously there are advocates for each of these methods. A student at his first acquaintance with consolidated accounts is more likely to want to master the basic mechanics, leaving the study of the suitability of certain methods until later in his course. The simplest to operate is certainly method (a) (i) and in point of fact it accords with the author's opinion of the best method. In using any of these methods the student should always indicate in his answer that he/she realizes that more than one method could have been used. An asterisk against this part of the answer with a brief note shown below the balance sheet is sufficient, but it is dangerous to omit such a note, as the specimen answer from which the examiner is marking may have used one of the other methods, and it would be quite easy for him to mark the answer as wrong if a note was not appended.

Exhibit 52.3

Where the stock-in-trade of one company includes goods bought from another company in the group, and the holding company does not have 100 per cent of the shares in the subsidiary.

H Balance Sheet as at 31 December 19–6

		£			£
Share Capital		20	Investment in subsidiary:		
Profit and Loss Account:	£		8 shares bought 31/12/19–5		16
As at 31/12/19–5	3		Stock-in-Trade		25
Profit for 19–6	19		Bank		1
	—	22			
		—			—
		42			42

S. Balance Sheet as at 31 December 19–6

		£		£
Share Capital		10	Stock-in-Trade	27
Profit and Loss Account:	£		Bank	3
As at 31/12/19–5	5			
Profit for 19–6	15			
	—	20		
		—		—
		30		30

Included in the stock-in-trade of S at 31 December 19–6 are goods bought by H for £10 and sold to S for £15. S had not sold any of these goods before 31 December 19–6.

H and S Consolidated Balance Sheet as at 31 December 19–6

	Methods				Methods		
	(ai)	(aii)	(b)		(ai)	(aii)	(b)
Share Capital	20	20	20	Goodwill	4	4	4
Profit and Loss Account:				Stock-in-Trade:			
(ai) (S 80% × 15+H 3+19−5)	29			(ai) (25+27−5)	47		
(aii) (S 80% × 15+H 3+19−4)		30		(aii) (25+27−5)		47	
(b) (S 80% × 15+H 3+19−4)			30	(b) (25+27−4)			48
Minority Interest:				Bank	4	4	4
(ai) (Shares 2+P/Loss 20%×20)	6						
(aii) (Shares 2+P/Loss 20%×20 = 4−1)		5					
(b) (Shares 2+P/Loss 20%×20 = 4)			6				
	—	—	—		—	—	—
	55	55	56		55	55	56

Exercises

52.1. You are to draw up a consolidated balance sheet from the following details as at 31 December 19–9.

H Balance Sheet as at 31 December 19–9

	£		£
Share Capital	2,000	Investment in subsidiary:	
Profit and Loss Account:		1,000 shares bought	
	£	31/12/19–8	2,800
As at 31/12/19–8	1,500	Fixed Assets	1,100
Profit for 19–9	2,200	Stock	1,200
	3,700	Debtors	2,100
General Reserve	800	Bank	200
Creditors	900		
	7,400		7,400

S Balance Sheets as at 31 December 19–9

	£	£		£
Share Capital		1,000	Fixed Assets	1,200
Profit and Loss Account:			Stock	900
As at 31/12/19–8	950		Debtors	1,400
Profit for 19–9	1,150		Bank	300
		2,100		
Creditors		700		
		3,800		3,800

During the year H had sold goods which had cost £150 to S for £240. None of these goods had been sold by the balance sheet date.

At the balance sheet date H owes S £220.

52.2. Draw up a consolidated balance sheet as at 31 December 19–4 from the following:

H Balance Sheet as at 31 December 19–4

	£	£		£
Share Capital		20,000	Investment in subsidiary:	
Profit and Loss Account:			6,000 shares bought	
As at 31/12/19–4	6,500		31/12/19–3	9,700
Loss for 19–5	2,500		Fixed Assets	9,000
		4,000	Stock	3,100
Creditors		3,800	Debtors	4,900
			Bank	1,100
		27,800		27,800

S Balance Sheet as at 31 December 19–4

	£	£		£
Share Capital		10,000	Fixed Assets	5,200
Profit and Loss Account:			Stock	7,200
As at 31/12/19–4	3,500		Debtors	3,800
Profit for 19–5	2,000		Bank	1,400
		5,500		
Creditors		2,100		
		17,600		17,600

At the balance sheet date S owes H £600.

During the year H sold goods which had cost £300 to S for £500. Three-quarters of these goods had been sold by S by the balance sheet date.

52.3A. Draw up a consolidated balance sheet from the following details as at 31 December 19–8.

H Balance Sheet as at 31 December 19–8

	£	£		£
Share Capital		100,000	Investment in subsidiaries:	
Profit and Loss Account:			S1 30,000 shares	
As at 31/12/19–7	14,000		bought 31/12/19–7	39,000
Add Profit for			S2 25,000 shares	
19–8	9,000		bought 31/12/19–7	29,000
		23,000	Fixed Assets	22,000
General Reserve		2,000	Stock	26,000
Creditors		9,000	Debtors	13,000
			Bank	5,000
		134,000		134,000

S1 Balance Sheet as at 31 December 19–8

	£	£		£
Share Capital		30,000	Fixed Assets	22,000
Profit and Loss Account:			Stock	11,000
As at 31/12/19–7	8,000		Debtors	8,000
Less Loss for			Bank	3,000
19–8	5,000			
		3,000		
General Reserve		4,000		
(as at 31/12/19–7)				
Creditors		7,000		
		44,000		44,000

S2 Balance Sheet as at 31 December 19–8

	£	£		£
Share Capital		30,000	Fixed Assets	21,000
Profit and Loss Account:			Stock	9,000
As at 31/12/19–7	1,200		Debtors	7,000
Add Profit for			Bank	1,000
19–8	1,800			
		3,000		
Creditors		5,000		
		38,000		38,000

At the balance sheet date S2 owed S1 £500 and H owed S2 £900.

During the year H had sold goods costing £2,000 to S1 for £2,800. Of these goods one-half had been sold by the year end. He had also sold goods costing £500 to S2 for £740, of which none had been sold by the year end.

52.4A. You are to draw up a consolidated balance sheet as at 31 December 19–3 from the following:

H Balance Sheet as at 31 December 19–3

	£	£		£
Share Capital		300,000	Investment in subsidiaries:	
Profit and Loss Account:			S1 75,000 shares bought	
As at 31/12/19–2	22,000		31/12/19–2	116,000
Less Loss for			S2 45,000 shares bought	
19–3	7,000		31/12/19–2	69,000
		15,000	Fixed Assets	110,000
General Reserve		7,000	Stock	13,000
(as at 31/12/19–2)			Debtors	31,000
Creditors		23,000	Bank	6,000
		345,000		345,000

S1 Balance Sheet as at 31 December 19–3

	£	£		£
Share Capital		75,000		
Profit and Loss Account:			Fixed Assets	63,000
As at 31/12/19–2	11,000		Stock	31,000
Add Profit			Debtors	17,000
for 19–3	12,000		Bank	3,000
		23,000		
Creditors		16,000		
		114,000		114,000

S2 Balance Sheet as at 31 December 19–3

	£	£		£
Share Capital		80,000	Fixed Assets	66,800
Profit and Loss Account:			Stock	22,000
As at 31/12/19–2	12,800		Debtors	15,000
Less Loss for			Bank	4,000
19–3	2,400			
		10,400		
General Reserve		6,400		
(as at 31/12/19–2)				
Creditors		11,000		
		107,800		107,800

At the balance sheet date S1 owed H £2,000 and S2 £500, and H owed S2 £1,800.

H had sold goods which had cost £2,000 to S2 for £3,200, and of these goods one-half had been sold by S2 by the year end.

53

Consolidated Accounts: Acquisition of Shares in Subsidiaries at Different Dates

Up to this point the shares bought in subsidiary companies have all been bought at one point in time for each company. However, it is a simple fact that shares are often bought in blocks at different points in time, and that the first purchase of shares in a company may not give the buyer a controlling interest.

For instance, a company S has an issued share capital of 100 ordinary shares of £1 each, and the only reserve of S is the balance of the profit and loss account which was £50 on 31 December 19–4, and two years later on 31 December 19–6 it was £80. H buys 20 shares on 31 December 19–4 for £36 and a further 40 shares on 31 December 19–6 for £79. There are two possibilities open when calculating pre-acquisition profits, and therefore Goodwill or Capital Reserve. These are:

(*a*) To calculate these on the basis of shares bought as at the date of each purchase, i.e. as at 31 December 19–4 and 31 December 19–6.

(*b*) To calculate them on the basis of the shares held when control was achieved, i.e. as at 31 December 19–6.

This would give different answers which are now shown.

	£	£
Method (*a*)		
Shares bought 31/12/19–4	20	
Proportion of Profit and Loss Account as at 31/12/19–4: 20 per cent × £50	10	
	—	30
Shares bought 31/12/19–6	40	
Proportion of Profit and Loss Account as at 31/12/19–6: 40 per cent × £80	32	
	—	72
		102

	£	£
Paid 31/12/19–4	36	
Paid 31/12/19–6	79	
	—	115

Goodwill therefore £115—£102 = £13

Method (b)

Shares bought	60	
Profit and Loss Account of subsidiary of which control achieved 31/12/19–6: 60 per cent × £80	48	
	—	108

Paid 31/12/19–4	36	
Paid 31/12/19–6	79	
	—	115

Goodwill therefore £115—£108 = £7

There does not seem to be any doubt but that method (a) would be preferable for examination purposes. In fact both methods are used in practice. It would seem that method (b) would be preferred in practice where the shares bought prior to control constituted a relatively small part of the issued share capital, especially if in the earlier stages eventual control was not visualized. On the other hand where the purchases are all part of an overall plan to gain control of the company then method (a) is preferred.

In addition it has been conveniently assumed so far that all shares have been bought exactly on the last day of an accounting period. This will just not be so, most shares being bought part way through an accounting period. Unless specially audited accounts are drawn up as at the date of acquisition there is no up-to-date figure of Profit and Loss Account as at the date of acquisition. As this is needed for the calculation of Goodwill or Capital Reserve the figure has to be obtained somehow. Naturally enough specially audited accounts would be the ideal for the purpose of the calculation, but if they are not available a second-best solution is necessary. In this instance the Profit and Loss balance according to the last balance sheet before the acquisition of the shares is taken, and an addition made (or deduction—if a loss) corresponding to the proportion of the year's profits that had been earned before acquisition took place. This is then taken as the figure of pre-acquisition profits for Goodwill and Capital Reserve calculations.

Exhibit 53.1

Calculation of pre-acquisition profits, and Goodwill, where the shares are bought part way through an accounting period.

H bought 20 of the 30 issued ordinary shares of S for £49 on 30 September 19–5. The accounts for S are drawn up annually to 31 December. The balance sheet of S as at 31 December 19–4 showed a balance on the Profit and Loss Account of £24. The profit of S for the year ended 31 December 19–5 disclosed a profit of £12.

	£	£
Shares bought		20
Profit and Loss Account:		
Balance at 31/12/19–4	24	
Add Proportion of 19–5 profits before acquisition 9/12 × £12	9	
	33	
Proportion of pre-acquisition profits		
20 shares owned out of 30, ⅔ × £33		22
		42

Paid for shares £49
Therefore Goodwill is £49—£42 = £7

Exercises

53.1. On 31 December 19–4, S Ltd had Share Capital £40,000 and Reserves of £24,000. Two years later the Share Capital has not altered but the Reserves have risen to £30,000. The following shares were bought by H Ltd 10,000 on 31 December 19–4 for £23,500, and on 31 December 19–6 14,000 for £31,000. Assuming that this completed an overall plan to gain control of the company you are to calculate the figure of Goodwill/Capital Reserve for the consolidated balance sheet as at 31 December 19–6.

53.2A. On 31 December 19–6, S Ltd had Share Capital of £400,000 and Reserves of £260,000. Three years later the Share Capital is unchanged but the Reserves have risen to £320,000. The following shares were bought by H Ltd 100,000 on 31 December 19–6 for £210,000 and 200,000 on 31 December 19–9 for £550,000. This completed the plan to take control of the company. Calculate the figure of Goodwill/Capital Reserve for the consolidated balance sheet as at 31 December 19–9.

53.3. H Ltd bought 50,000 of the 80,000 issued ordinary £1 shares of S Ltd for £158,000 on 31 August 19–8. S Ltd accounts are drawn up annually to 31 December. The balance sheet of S Ltd on 31 December 19–7 showed a balance on the Profit and Loss Account of £36,000. The profit of S Ltd for the year ended 31 December 19–8 showed a profit of £42,000. Calculate the figure for the Goodwill/Capital Reserve to be shown in the consolidated balance sheet as at 31 December 19–8.

53.4A. On 1 January 19–1 S Ltd had a Share Capital of £300,000, a Profit and Loss Account balance of £28,000 and a General Reserve of £20,000. During the year ended 31 December 19–1 S Ltd made a profit of £36,000, none of which was distributed. H Ltd bought 225,000 shares on 1 June 19–1 for £333,000. Calculate the figure of Goodwill/Capital Reserve to be shown in the consolidated balance sheet as at 31 December 19–1.

54

Inter-Company Dividends

(a) Not from Pre-Acquisition Profits

These dividends are paid by one company to another. They will therefore be shown in the receiving company's own Profit and Loss Account
as Investment Income, with a subsequent increase in its final Profit and
Loss Appropriation Account balance and an equivalent increase in the
bank balance. From the paying company's own accounts point of view,
it has shown the dividend as a charge against its own Profit and Loss
Appropriation Account, thus reducing the final balance on that
account, and when paid there will be a reduction of the bank balance. If
the dividend has been proposed, but not paid, at the accounting year
end then it will be normal for the proposed dividend to be shown as a
current liability in the subsidiary company's balance sheet, and as a
current asset on the holding company's balance sheet as dividend owing
from the subsidiary.

From the consolidated balance sheet point of view (making an
assumption about pre-acquisition profit shown in detail later) no
action is needed. It is a past event which is automatically cancelled
when drafting the consolidated balance sheet as they are like things.

(b) If Paid from Pre-Acquisition Profits

In chapter 51 the company law principle that dividends should not be
paid out of capital was reiterated. To prevent this happening the pre-
acquisition profits were capitalized and brought into the Goodwill or
Capital Reserve calculation. A company cannot circumvent the principle by buying the shares of a company, part of the purchase price being for the reserves of the subsidiary, and then utilizing those reserves by
paying itself dividends, and consequently adding those dividends to its
own profits and then declaring an increased dividend itself. The next
two exhibits are drawn up to illustrate this.

Exhibit 54.1

Dividends paid from post-acquisition profits.

H buys 100 per cent of the shares of S on 31 December 19–4. In 19–5 S pays a dividend of 50 per cent = £5 which H receives. To simplify matters the dividend is declared for 19–5 and paid in 19–5.

H Balance Sheet as at 31 December 19–5

	£	£		£
Share Capital		20	Investment in subsidiary:	
Profit and Loss Account:			10 shares bought 31/12/19–4	23
As at 31/12/19–4	7		Stock	11
Add Profit for 19–5	8		Bank	1
(including dividend of £5	—	15		
from S)				
		—		—
		35		35
		=		=

S Balance Sheet as at 31 December 19–5

	£	£		£
Share Capital		10	Stock	19
Profit and Loss Account:			Bank	7
As at 31/12/19–4	12			
Profit for 19–5	9			
Less Dividend paid to				
H	5			
	—	4		
		16		
		—		—
		26		26
		=		=

The dividend is £5 out of profits made since the acquisition of £9. The dividend can be treated as being from post-acquisition profits, and can therefore be shown in the Profit and Loss Account of H as Investment Income and so swell the profits of H available for dividend purposes.

H Consolidated Balance Sheet as at 31 December 19–5

	£		£
Share Capital	20	Goodwill (£23−£10−£12)	1
Profit and Loss Account:		Stock (H £11+S £19)	30
(H £7+£8+S £4)	19	Bank (H £1+S £7)	8
	—		—
	39		39
	=		=

Exhibit 54.2

Dividends paid from pre-acquisition profits.

H Balance Sheet as at 31 December 19–4

	£		£
Share Capital	20	Investment in subsidiary:	
Profit and Loss Account	11	10 shares bought 31/12/19–4	23
		Stock	7
		Bank	1
	—		—
	31		31
	═		═

S Balance Sheet as at 31 December 19–4

	£		£
Share Capital	10	Stock	14
Profit and Loss Account	7	Bank	3
	—		—
	17		17
	═		═

H Consolidated Balance Sheet as at 31 December 19–4
(immediately after acquisition)

	£		£
Share Capital	20	Goodwill (H £23—S £10—	
Profit and Loss Account	11	S £7)	6
		Stock	21
		Bank (H £1+S £3)	4
	—		—
	31		31
	═		═

The consolidated balance sheet already shown was drafted immediately after acquisition. The following balance sheets show the position one year later. It is helpful to remember that the calculation of goodwill does not alter.

H Balance Sheet as at 31 December 19–5

	£	£		£
Share Capital		20	Investment in subsidiary:	
Profit and Loss Account:			(£23 originally calculated less	
As at 31/12/19–4	11		dividend from pre-acquisition	
Add Profit for 19–5*	8		profits £7)	16
(*does not include the	—	19	Stock	18
dividend from S)			Bank	5
		—		—
		39		39
		═		═

S Balance Sheet as at 31 December 19–5

	£	£		£
Share Capital		10	Stock	8
Profit and Loss Account:			Bank	2
As at 31/12/19–4	7			
Add Profit for 19–5*	0			
Less Dividend paid	7			
		10		10

*For simplicity the profit of S for 19–5 is taken as being exactly nil.

H Consolidated Balance Sheet as at 31 December 19–5

	£		£
Share Capital	20	Goodwill	6
Profit and Loss (P £19)	19	Stock	26
		Bank	7
	39		39

It will be noticed that when a dividend is paid out of pre-acquisition profits it is in fact a return of capital to the holding company. Accordingly the dividend is deducted from the original cost of the investment; it is a return of the purchase money rather than be treated as Investment Income of the holding company. A common practice of many examiners, or 'trick' if you prefer to call it that, would have been to treat the receipt as investment income instead of as a refund of capital. Thus the balance sheet of H as at 31 December 19–5 in this exhibit would have read 'Profit and Loss Account £26' instead of 'Profit and Loss Account £19', and the Investment would be shown at £23 instead of £16. This means that the examiner really wants the examinee to adjust what is in fact an incorrect balance sheet, so that the only way is to adjust the holding company's balance sheet before proceeding with the consolidation of the balance sheets of H and S.

Proposed Dividend at Date of Acquisition of Shares

Quite frequently there will be a proposed dividend as at the date of the acquisition of the shares, and the holding company will receive the dividend even though the dividend was proposed to be paid from profits earned before acquisition took place. The action taken is similar to that in Exhibit 54.2, in that it will be deducted from the price paid for the shares in order that the net effective price is calculated.

Exhibit 54.3

Shares acquired in a subsidiary at a date when a proposed dividend is outstanding.

H Balance Sheet as at 31 December 19–3

	£	£		£	£
Share Capital		20	Investment in subsidiary:		
Profit and Loss Account:			10 shares bought 31/12/19–2	22	
As at 31/12/19–2	4		*Less* Dividend from		
Profit for 19–3	5		pre-acquisition profits	6	
	—	9		—	16
			Stock		11
			Bank		2
		29			29

S Balance Sheet as at 31 December 19–3

	£	£		£
Share Capital		10	Stock	19
Profit and Loss Account:			Bank	4
As at 31/12/19–2 (after deducting the proposed dividend of £6	5			
Add Profit for 19–3	8			
	—	13		
		23		23

H Consolidated Balance Sheet as at 31 December 19–3

	£		£
Share Capital	20	Goodwill (see workings below)	1
Profit and Loss Account:		Stock	30
(H £9 + S £8)	17	Bank	6
	37		37

Calculation of Goodwill

	£	£
Paid		22
Less Shares taken over	10	
Less Profit and Loss balance at 31/12/19–2	5	
Less Dividend paid from pre-acquisition profits	6	
	—	21
Goodwill		1

Proposed Dividends

When a dividend is proposed by a company it will be shown as a current liability in its balance sheet. This is just as true for a subsidiary company as it would be for a company which is not controlled by another company. It is common practice for the holding company to show a proposed dividend from a subsidiary for an accounting period as being receivable in the same accounting period. Thus the subsidiary will show the proposed dividend as a current liability and the holding company will show it as a current asset. However, as this is merely another form of inter-indebtedness the amounts owing must be cancelled out when drawing up the consolidated balance sheet. Where the subsidiary is owned 100 per cent by the holding company then the two items will cancel out fully.

When the subsidiary is only part-owned there is the question of the minority interest. The cancellation of the part of the proposed dividend payable to the holding company is effected, and the remainder of the proposed dividend of the subsidiary will be that part owing to the minority interest. This can be dealt with in two ways, both acceptable in accounting:

(a) The part of the proposed dividend due to the minority interest is added back to the minority interest figure in the consolidated balance sheet.
(b) To show the part of the proposed dividend due to the minority interest as a current liability in the consolidated balance sheet.

It must be borne in mind that nothing that has been said refers in any way to the proposed dividends of the holding company. These will simply be shown as a current liability in the consolidated balance sheet.

Method (b) would seem to be the better method. For instance, when considering the working capital or liquidity of the group it is essential that all current liabilities due to external parties should be brought into calculation. If the proposed dividend soon to be paid to persons outside the group was excluded, this could render the calculations completely invalid.

Exhibit 54.4

Where a subsidiary has proposed a dividend, and there is a minority interest share in the subsidiary.
   This will be shown using method (b) just described.

H Balance Sheet as at 31 December 19–3

	£		£
Share Capital	20	Investment in subsidiary:	
Profit and Loss Account	11	6 shares bought 31/12/19–1	17
Proposed dividend (of the		Stock	19
holding company)	9	Proposed dividend receivable	
		from S	3
		Bank	1
	40		40

S Balance Sheet as at 31 December 19–3

	£		£
Share Capital	10	Stock	23
Profit and Loss Account	15	Bank	7
Proposed Dividend	5		
	30		30

Note: At the date of acquisition of the shares on 31 December 19–1 the profit and loss account balance of S was £10, and there were no proposed dividends at that date.

H Consolidated Balance Sheet as at 31 December 19–3

	£	£		£
Share Capital		20	Goodwill (see workings below)	5
Profit and Loss Account			Stock	42
(see workings below)		14	Bank	8
Minority Interest:				
Shares	4			
Profit and Loss 2/5ths	6			
		10		
Current Liabilities:				
Proposed dividends of				
Holding Company	9			
Owing to Minority				
Interest	2			
		11		
		55		55

Workings:	£	£	£
Profit and Loss Account:			
H's Profit and Loss balance			11
S's Profit and Loss balance		15	
Less Owned by Minority Interest: 2/5ths × £15	6		
Less Pre-acquisition profits at 31/12/19–1 bought by holding company: 3/5ths × £10	6		
		12	
			3
			14

Goodwill:			
Paid			17
Less Shares bought		6	
Less Pre-acquisition profits 3/5ths × £10		6	
			12
			5

If method (a) had been used then the consolidated balance sheet would be as shown except for Minority Interest and Current Liabilities. These would have appeared:

	£	£
Minority Interest:		
Shares	4	
Profit and Loss	8	
	—	12
Current Liabilities:		
Proposed Dividend		9

Exercises

54.1. The following balance sheets were drawn up as at 31 December 19–7. The person drafting the balance sheet of H Ltd was not too sure of an item and has shown it as a suspense item.

H Balance Sheet as at 31 December 19–7

	£	£		£
Share Capital		50,000	Investment in subsidiary:	
Profit and Loss Account:			20,000 shares bought	
As at 31/12/19–6	8,000		31/12/19–6	29,000
Add Profit for			Fixed Assets	40,000
19–7	11,000		Current Assets	5,000
		19,000		
Suspense*		5,000		
		74,000		74,000

*The suspense item consists of the dividend received from S in January 19–7.

S Balance Sheet as at 31 December 19–7

	£	£		£
Share Capital		20,000	Fixed Assets	17,000
Profit and Loss Account:			Current Assets	10,000
As at 31/12/19–6*	3,000			
Add Profit for				
19–7	4,000			
		7,000		
		27,000		27,000

*The balance of £3,000 is after deducting the proposed dividend for 19–6 of £5,000.

54.2A. The balance sheets of H Ltd and S Ltd were drawn up as at 31 December 19–4 as follows:

H Balance Sheet as at 31 December 19–4

	£	£		£
Share Capital		400,000	Investment in subsidiary:	
Profit and Loss Account:			100,000 shares bought	
As at 31/12/19–3	39,000		31/12/19–3	194,000
Add profit for			Fixed Assets	250,000
19–4*	64,000		Current Assets	59,000
		103,000		
		503,000		503,000

*The profit figure for 19–4 includes the dividend of £20,000 received from S Ltd for the year 19–3.

S Balance Sheet as at 31 December 19–4

	£	£		£
Share Capital		100,000	Fixed Assets	84,000
Profit and Loss Account:			Current Assets	49,000
As at				
31/12/19–3*	11,000			
Add Profit for				
19–4	22,000			
		33,000		
		133,000		133,000

*The balance of £11,000 is after deducting the proposed dividend for 19–3 £20,000.

54.3. Draw up a consolidated balance sheet as at 31 December 19–9 from the following information.

H Balance Sheet as at 31 December 19–9

	£	£		£
Share Capital		80,000	Investment in subsidiary:	
Profit and Loss Account:			30,000 shares bought	
As at 31/12/19–8	14,000		31/12/19–8	47,000
Add Profit for			Fixed Assets	44,000
19–9	9,000		Current Assets	12,000
		23,000		
		103,000		103,000

S Balance Sheet as at 31 December 19–9

	£	£		£
Share Capital		40,000	Fixed Assets	36,000
Profit and Loss Account:			Current Assets	21,000
As at 31/12/19–8	4,000			
Add Profit for				
19–9	7,000			
		11,000		
Proposed Dividend for				
19–9		6,000		
		57,000		57,000

The proposed dividend of S has not yet been brought into the accounts of H Ltd.

54.4A. The balance sheets of H Ltd and S Ltd are as follows:

H Balance Sheet as at 31 December 19–4

	£	£		£
Share Capital		500,000	Investment in subsidiary:	
Profit and Loss Account:			120,000 shares bought	
As at 31/12/19–3	66,000		31/12/19–3	230,000
Add Profit for			Fixed Assets	300,000
19–4	41,000		Current Assets	75,000
		105,000		
		605,000		605,000

S Balance Sheet as at 31 December 19–4

	£	£		£
Share Capital		200,000	Fixed Assets	203,000
Profit and Loss Account:			Current Assets	101,000
As at 31/12/19–3	51,000			
Add Profit for				
19–4	13,000			
		64,000		
Proposed Dividend for				
19–4		40,000		
		304,000		304,000

The proposed dividend of S has not yet been brought into the accounts of H Ltd.
Draw up the consolidated balance sheet as at 31 December 19–4.

55

Consolidated Balance Sheets: Sundry Matters

Preference Shares

It should be remembered that preference shares do not carry voting powers under normal conditions, nor do they possess a right to the reserves of the company. Contrast this with ordinary shares which, when bought, will give the holding company voting rights and also a proportionate part of the reserves of the company.

This means that the calculation of Goodwill or Capital Reserve on the purchase of preference shares is very simple indeed. If 9 Preference Shares of £1 each are bought for £12 then Goodwill will be £3, while if 20 Preference Shares of £1 each are bought for £16 then the Capital Reserve will be £4. The amount of Goodwill or Capital Reserve on the purchase of preference shares is not shown separately from that calculated on the purchase of ordinary shares, instead the figures will be amalgamated to throw up one figure only on the consolidated balance sheet.

Preference Shares owned by the minority interest are simply shown as part of the minority interest figure in the consolidated balance sheet, each share being shown at nominal value.

Sale of Fixed Assets between Members of the Group

There is obviously nothing illegal in one company in the group selling items in the nature of fixed assets to another company in the group. If the sale is at the cost price originally paid for it by the first company, then no adjustment will be needed in the consolidated balance sheet. Rather more often the sale will be at a price different from the original cost price. The inter-company unrealized profit must be eliminated in a similar fashion to that taken for the unrealized profit in trading stock as described in Chapter 52.

If the fixed asset is shown at its cost to the group in the consolidated balance sheet rather than at the cost to the particular company, then obviously the depreciation figures on that fixed asset should be adjusted to that based on the group cost rather than of the cost of the particular company.

Exhibit 55.1   H Balance Sheet as at 31 December 19–6

	£	£		£	£
Share Capital		100	Investment in S:		
Profit and Loss Account:			50 shares bought 31/12/19–5		95
As at 31/12/19–5	30		Fixed Assets	78	
For the year 19–6	40		*Less* Depreciation	23	
	—	70		—	55
			Current Assets		20
		170			170

S Balance Sheet as at 31 December 19–6

	£	£		£	£
Share Capital		50	Fixed Assets	80	
Profit and Loss Account:			*Less* Depreciation	20	
As at 31/12/19–5	20			—	60
For the year 19–6	25		Current Assets		35
	—	45			
		95			95

During the year H Ltd had sold a fixed asset which had cost it £20 to S Ltd for £28. Of the figure of £20 depreciation in the balance sheet of S, £7 refers to this asset and £13 to the other assets. The rate of depreciation is 25 per cent. The £8 profit is included in the figure of £40 profit for 19–6 in the balance sheet of H.

This means that the figure of £8 needs cancelling from the asset costs in the consolidated balance sheet and from the Profit and Loss Account balance. In addition the figure of depreciation needs adjusting downward, from the £7 as shown on the balance sheet of S, to the figure of £5, i.e. 25 per cent depreciation based on the cost of the asset to the group. This in turn means that the figure of profit for S £25 needs increasing by £2, as, instead of the expense of £7 depreciation there will now be a reduced expense of £5. The consolidated balance sheet becomes:

H and S Consolidated Balance Sheet as at 31 December 19–6

	£		£	£
Share Capital	100	Goodwill		25
Profit and Loss Account:		Fixed Assets	150	
(H £70−£8+S £25+£2)	89	*Less* Depreciation	41	
			—	109
		Current Assets		55
	189			189

Revaluation of Fixed Assets

The consolidated balance sheet should give a picture that is not clouded by the method of drafting consolidated accounts. The consolidation process is looked at from the point of view that the holding company acquires shares in a company, and thereby achieves control of that company, and, in addition, it is recognized that the reserves are also taken over. It has been seen previously that the economic view is that of taking over the assets of another company, after all one does not buy such shares so that one possesses the share certificates, rather it is for the assets which are taken over and used. The consolidated balance sheet should therefore give the same picture as that which would have been recorded if, instead of buying shares, the assets themselves had been bought directly.

If, therefore, the fixed assets as shown in the balance sheet of the subsidiary were really valued at more than that figure when acquisition took place, then it would be better if the value of the fixed assets in the consolidated balance sheet was to be shown at that figure.

Such a revaluation can either be recorded in the separate accounts of the subsidiary companies themselves, or alternatively it can be brought into the workings when the consolidated balance sheet is drawn up.

It can be seen that, failing attention to the above, some rather strange results can occur. For instance, if H buys all the 10 shares of S for £18 when the reserves are £5, then the Goodwill calculation normally is:

	£	£
Cost		18
Less share	10	
Less reserves	5	
		15
Goodwill		£3

However, H might have bought the shares of S because it thought that, instead of the value of £15 assets as shown on the balance sheet of S (represented on the other side of the balance sheet by Shares £10 and Reserves £5), the assets were really worth £17. In the eyes of H Ltd therefore it is giving £18 for physical assets worth £17 and the Goodwill figure is correspondingly £18−£17 = £1. Assuming that the difference is in the recorded value of fixed assets, then the consolidated balance sheet will be showing a wrong picture if it shows Goodwill £3 and Asset £15. The revaluation upwards of the fixed assets by £2, and the consequent reduction of the Goodwill figure by £2 will redress the view.

Where there are depreciation charges on the revalued assets then this also will need adjusting.

Exhibit 55.2

H Balance Sheet as at 31 December 19–6

	£	£		£	£
Share Capital		100	Investment in subsidiary:		
Profit and Loss Account:			30 shares bought 31/12/19–5		56
As at 31/12/19–5	20		Fixed Assets	80	
Add Profit 19–6	26		*Less* Depreciation		
	—	46	for the year	16	
				—	64
			Current Assets		26
		146			146

S Balance Sheet as at 31 December 19–6

	£	£		£	£
Share Capital		30	Fixed Assets	50	
Profit and Loss Account:			*Less* Depreciation		
As at 31/12/19–5	3		for the year	10	
Add Profit 19–6	21			—	40
	—	24	Current Assets		14
		54			54

At the point in time when H bought the shares in S the assets in S were shown at a value of £33 in the balance sheet of S. In fact however H valued the fixed assets as being worth £20 higher than that shown. The consolidated balance sheet will therefore show them at this higher figure. In turn the depreciation, which is at the rate of 20 per cent, will be £4 higher. The consolidated balance sheet therefore appears:

H and S Consolidated Balance Sheet as at 31 December 19–6

	£		£	£
Share Capital	100	Goodwill		3
Profit and Loss Account:	63	Fixed Assets		
(H £46+S £21—increased		(£80+£70)	150	
depreciation £4)		*Less* Depreciation		
		(£16+£14)	30	
			—	120
		Current Assets		40
	163			163

Exercises

55.1 From the following balance sheets and further information you are to draw up a consolidated balance sheet as at 31 December 19–8.

H Balance Sheet as at 31 December 19–8

	£	£		£	£
Share Capital		500,000	Investment in S:		
Profit and Loss Account:			200,000 shares		
As at 31/12/19–7	77,000		bought 31/12/19–7		340,000
Add Profit			Fixed Assets	300,000	
for 19–8	66,000		*Less*		
	——	143,000	Depreciation	100,000	
				——	200,000
			Current Assets		103,000
		643,000			643,000

S Balance Sheet as at 31 December 19–8

	£	£		£	£
Share Capital		200,000	Fixed Assets	210,000	
Profit and Loss Account:			*Less*		
As at 31/12/19–7	40,000		Depreciation	40,000	
Add Profit				——	170,000
for 19–8	32,000				
	——	72,000	Current Assets		102,000
		272,000			272,000

During the year H Ltd had sold a fixed asset, which had cost it £40,000, to S for £50,000. S has written off 20 per cent, i.e. £10,000 as depreciation for 19–8.

55.2A. From the following balance sheets and supplementary information you are to draw up a consolidated balance sheet as at 31 December 19–5.

H Consolidated Balance Sheet as at 31 December 19–5

	£	£		£	£
Share Capital		75,000	Investment in S:		
Profit and Loss Account:			10,000 shares bought		
As at 31/12/19–4	15,000		31/12/19–4		23,000
Add Profit			Fixed Assets	84,000	
for 19–5	23,000		*Less*		
	——	38,000	Depreciation	14,000	
				——	70,000
			Current Assets		20,000
		113,000			113,000

S Consolidated Balance Sheet as at 31 December 19–5

	£	£		£	£
Share Capital		10,000	Fixed Assets	26,000	
Profit and Loss Account:			*Less*		
As at 31/12/19–4	6,000		Depreciation	10,000	
Add Profit				——	16,000

for 19–5	7,000		Current Assets		12,000
	———	13,000			
General Reserve					
(as at 31/12/19–4)		5,000			
		———			
		28,000			28,000

During the year H sold a fixed asset to S. It had cost H £3,000 and it was sold to S for £5,000. S had written off £500 as depreciation during 19–5.

55.3

H Balance Sheet as at 31 December 19–7

	£	£		£	£
Share Capital		150,000	Investment in S:		
Profit and Loss Account:			60,000 shares bought		
As at 31/12/19–6	44,000		on 31/12/19–6		121,000
Add Profit			Fixed Assets	90,000	
for 19–7	33,000		*Less* Depreciation		
	———	77,000	for year	24,000	
				———	66,000
			Current Assets		40,000
		———			———
		227,000			227,000

S Balance Sheet as at 31 December 19–7

	£	£		£	£
Share Capital		60,000	Fixed Assets	70,000	
Profit and Loss Account:			*Less* Depreciation		
As at 31/12/19–6	17,000		for year	7,000	
Add Profit				———	63,000
for 19–7	14,000		Current Assets		28,000
	———	31,000			
		———			———
		91,000			91,000

When H Ltd bought the shares of S Ltd it valued the fixed assets at £95,000 instead of the figure of £70,000 as shown in the balance sheet of S.

Draw up a consolidated balance sheet as at 31 December 19–7.

55.4A.

H Balance Sheet as at 31 December 19–5

	£	£		£	£
Share Capital		80,000	Investment in S:		
Profit and Loss Account:			30,000 shares bought		
As at 31/12/19–4	27,000		31/12/19–4		53,400
Add Profit			Fixed Assets	60,000	
for 19–5	11,000		*Less* Depreciation		
	———	38,000	for year	6,000	
				———	54,000
			Current Assets		10,600
		———			———
		118,000			118,000

S Balance Sheet as at 31 December 19–5

	£	£		£	£
Share Capital		30,000	Fixed Assets	40,000	
Profit and Loss Account:			*Less* Depreciation		
As at 31/12/19–4	8,000		for year	4,000	
Add Profit					36,000
for 19–5	9,000		Current Assets		11,000
		17,000			
		47,000			47,000

When H Ltd took control of S Ltd it valued the fixed assets at 31/12/19–4 at £50,000 instead of £40,000 as shown.

Draw up the consolidated balance sheet as at 31 December 19–5.

56

Consolidation of the Accounts of Vertical Group of Companies

A vertical group can be said to be one in which a holding company has a controlling interest in a subsidiary, then that subsidiary has a controlling interest in a sub-subsidiary. This can be extended further in a vertical chain of downward holdings.

As an example H Ltd might own 90 per cent of S1, and S1 in turn owns 60 per cent of S2. This means that H owns 90 per cent of 60 per cent of S2 = 54 per cent. In that case H owned more than 50 per cent of the sub-subsidiary S2. In point of fact the eventual ownership of the holding company might be less than 50 per cent, as follows, H Ltd owns 60 per cent of S1 which in turn owns 75 per cent of S2. This means that H owns 60 per cent of 75 per cent of S2 = 45 per cent. In both of these cases consolidated accounts will have to be prepared including both S1 and S2. The fact that in the second case H Ltd controlled less than 50 per cent of S2 is immaterial. The holding company subsidiary relationship exists where the sub-subsidiary is a subsidiary of the subsidiary of the holding company, and all such companies need to be incorporated in the consolidated accounts.

There are in fact two different methods of consolidating the accounts. The first method follows the reasoning already given in this chapter which involves computing the holding company's interest in the sub-subsidiary company and taking that percentage of the capital and reserves of that company into the consolidation process. The second method recognizes the fact that if there are three companies H, S1 and S2, then S1 by law, because S2 is its subsidiary, must produce a consolidated balance sheet of S1 and S2. The technique therefore is to consolidate first the balance sheets of S1 and S2, and when that is done the balance sheet of H is then consolidated with the consolidated balance sheet of S1 and S2.

The recommended practice for students would be to use the first method. It is certainly simpler to apply, and it is finding increasing favour in practice. Given the necessarily simple type of examples in a basic text-book there does not in fact seem to be a great divergence of difficulty between the two methods, but this would not be so in more complicated examples.

Method A. Computation of the Holding Company's Indirect Interest

Exhibit 56.1

The following are the balance sheets of H Ltd, S1 Ltd and S2 Ltd.

H Balance Sheet as at 31 December 19–5				
	£	£		£
Share Capital		40	Investment in S1 Ltd:	
Profit and Loss:			8 shares bought 31/12/19–4	41
As at 31/12/19–4	24		Stock	53
Add Profit for 19–5	36		Bank	6
	—	60		
		——		——
		100		100
		══		══

S1 Balance Sheet as at 31 December 19–5				
	£	£		£
Share Capital		10	Investment in S2:	
Profit and Loss:			15 shares bought 31/12/19–4	25
As at 31/12/19–4	5		Stock	8
Add Profit for 19–5	10		Bank	2
	—	15		
General Reserve				
(as at 31/12/19–4)		10		
		——		——
		35		35
		══		══

S2 Balance Sheet as at 31 December 19–5				
	£	£		£
Share Capital		25	Stock	44
Profit and Loss:			Bank	16
As at 31/12/19–4	15			
Add Profit for 19–5	20			
	—	35		
		——		——
		60		60
		══		══

The control of the companies can be summarized as:

	S1 Ltd	S2 Ltd
Group	80%	60%
Minority Interest	20%	40%

The proportion of S2 owned by the group can be seen to be 80 per cent of 75 per cent = 60 per cent, with the remainder 40 per cent held by the minority interest.

H and S1 and S2 Consolidated Balance Sheet

	£		£
Share Capital	40	Goodwill	17
Profit and Loss:		Stock (£53+£8+£44)	105
(H £60+S1 £18+S2 £12)	80	Bank (£18+£6)	24
Minority Interests	26		
	146		146

Workings:

	£	£	£
Cost of Shares to Group: in S1 Ltd		41	
in S2 Ltd 80% of £25		20	
		—	61
Less Nominal Value of shares held:			
In S1 Ltd	8		
In S2 Ltd 60% of £25	15		
	—	23	
General Reserves S1 Ltd 80% of £10		8	
Profit and Loss Account:			
In S1 Ltd 80% of £5	4		
In S2 Ltd 60% of £15	9		
	—	13	
		—	44
Goodwill per Consolidated Balance Sheet			17

Minority Interests:			
In S1 Ltd: Shares 20% of £10	2		
Profit and Loss 20% of £15	3		
	—	5	
General Reserve 20% of £10		2	
In S2 Ltd: Shares 40% of £25	10		
Profit and Loss 40% of £35	14		
	—	24	
		—	31
Less cost of shares in S2 to minority interest of S1, 20% of £25			5
Minority Interest as per Consolidated Balance Sheet			26

Method B

This method first consolidates the balance sheet of S1 with that of S2. After this the resulting consolidated balance sheet of the S1 and S2 group is then consolidated with the balance sheet of H. The figures that are used are the same as for Exhibit 56.1.

Exhibit 56.2

S1 and S2 Consolidated Balance Sheet as at 31 December 19–5

	£		£
Share Capital	10	Stock (£8+£44)	52
Profit and Loss Account:		Bank (£2+£16)	18
(S1 £15+S2 £15)	30		
Capital Reserve	5		
General Reserve	10		
Minoriiy Interest			
(25% of £25+£35)	15		
	—		—
	70		70
	══		══

H and S1 and S2 Consolidated Balance Sheet as at 31 December 19–5

	£		£
Share Capital	40	Goodwill (£21—£1¼)	19¾
Profit and Loss Account		Stock (£53+£52)	105
(see below)	80	Bank (£13+£6)	19
Minority Interest (see below)	23¾		
	—		—
	143¾		143¾
	══		══

	£	£
Goodwill (remember this is calculated as at 31/12/–4)		
Cost		41
Shares	8	
Profit and Loss 8/10ths × S1 £5	4	
General Reserve 8/10ths × £10	8	
	—	20
		—
Goodwill on acquisition by H of S1		21
Less Capital Reserve on acquisition by S1 and S2		1¼
		—
		19¾
		══

Minority Interests	
General Reserve 2/10ths of £10	2
Shares of S1	2
Profit and Loss S1 and S2 2/10ths of £30	6
Minority Interest per consolidated balance sheet of S1 and S2	13¾
	—
	23¾
	══

Profit and Loss Account		
H Balance Sheet		60
Per consolidated balance sheet of S1 and S2 8/10ths of £30	24	
Less Pre-acquisition profits of S1 (there was a £5 balance at		
acquisition date) 8/10ths of £5	4	
	—	20
		—
		80
		══

It can be seen that the only differences between the methods are the amounts of the minority interest and of the goodwill calculated on consolidation.

Exercises

56.1. From the following balance sheets you are to draft a consolidated balance sheet for the group of H, S1 and S2. Use Method A as described in the chapter.

H Balance Sheet as at 31 December 19–7

	£	£		£
Share Capital		100,000	Investment in S1:	
Profit and Loss Account:			9,000 shares bought	
As at 31/12/19–6	15,000		31/12/19–6	23,000
Add Profit for			Fixed Assets	99,000
19–7	22,000		Current Assets	25,000
		37,000		
General Reserve		10,000		
		147,000		147,000

S1 Balance Sheet as at 31 December 19–7

	£	£		£
Share Capital		10,000	Investment in S2:	
Profit and Loss Account:			3,500 shares bought	
As at 31/12/19–6	7,000		31/12/19–6	6,000
Add Profit for			Fixed Assets	22,000
19–7	16,000		Current Assets	5,000
		23,000		
		33,000		33,000

S2 Balance Sheet as at 31 December 19–7

	£	£		£
Share Capital		5,000	Fixed Assets	6,000
Profit and Loss Account:			Current Assets	3,000
As at 31/12/19–6	1,000			
Add Profit for				
19–7	3,000			
		4,000		
		9,000		9,000

56.2A. From the following balance sheets prepare a consolidated balance sheet for the group H, S1 and S2. Use Method A as per the chapter.

H Balance Sheet as at 31 December 19–9

	£	£		£
Share Capital		200,000	Investment in S1:	
Profit and Loss Account:			16,000 shares bought	
As at 31/12/19–8	43,000		31/12/19–8	39,000
Add Profit for			Fixed Assets	200,000
19–9	36,000		Current Assets	40,000
		79,000		
		279,000		279,000

S1 Balance Sheet as at 31 December 19–9

	£	£		£
Share Capital		20,000	Investment in S2:	
Profit and Loss Account:			7,000 shares bought	
As at 31/12/19–8	6,000		31/12/19–8	13,000
Add Profit for			Fixed Assets	16,000
19–9	4,000		Current Assets	4,000
		10,000		
General Reserve				
(as at 31/12/19–8)		3,000		
		33,000		33,000

S2 Balance Sheet as at 31 December 19–9

	£	£		£
Share Capital		10,000	Fixed Assets	10,500
Profit and Loss Account:			Current Assets	5,500
As at 31/12/19–8	1,000			
Add Profit for				
19–9	5,000			
		6,000		
		16,000		16,000

57

Consolidated Profit and Loss Accounts

The consolidated profit and loss account is drawn up to show the profit (or loss) of the whole of the companies in the group, treating the group as a single entity. If all of the subsidiaries are owned 100 per cent, and there are no inter-company dividends or unrealized profits in stock, then it is simply a case of adding together all of the separate profit and loss accounts together to form the consolidated profit and loss account.

If on the other hand there is a minority interest in the subsidiary company/companies, then the whole of the profits of the separate companies are brought into account first of all, the whole of the corporation tax is deducted, and from the resultant figure the minority interest's share is deducted, leaving as a residual the profits after tax which belong to the group.

Exhibit 57.1

	H Ltd	S Ltd
	£	£
Profits for the year before Taxation	2,000	1,500
Less Corporation Tax	800	600
Profits for the year after Tax	1,200	900

H owns 80 per cent of the shares of S Ltd

This means that the minority interest are entitled to 20 per cent of the profits of S Ltd after tax has been deducted, i.e. 20 per cent of £900 = £180. The consolidated profit and loss account therefore appears as:

	£
Consolidated Profits for the year before Taxation	3,500
Less Corporation Tax	1,400
Consolidated Profits for the year after Taxation	2,100
Less Minority Shareholders' Interest	180
Group Profit for the year	1,920

Appropriation of Group Profits

Once the group profit has been found then the appropriations out of that profit can be shown. It must be remembered that all entries referring to the dividends paid or proposed by S Ltd will be completely eliminated for the purposes of the consolidation. However, the dividends paid and proposed by the holding company itself will be shown in the consolidated profit and loss account. This can best be seen in Exhibit 57.2.

Exhibit 57.2

	H Ltd		S Ltd	
	£	£	£	£
Profits (before showing dividend receivable from S Ltd as revenue)		2,000		
Profits				1,200
Add Dividend receivable from S Ltd		200		
Net Profit (profits before tax)		2,200		1,200
Less Corporation Tax	900		450	
Proposed Dividends	500		200	
		1,400		650
Unappropriated Profits for the year		800		550

If S had been owned 100 per cent by H then the consolidated profit and loss account would appear as:

	£
Consolidated Profits for the year before Taxation (£2,000+£1,200)	3,200
Less Corporation Tax	1,350
Group Profits for the year after Taxation	1,850
Less Appropriations:	
Proposed Dividends	500
Group Unappropriated Profits for the year	1,350

On the other hand if S had been only partly owned, say 80 per cent, by H then the figures would appear as in Exhibit 57–3.

Exhibit 57.3

	H Ltd		S Ltd	
	£	£	£	£
Profits (before showing dividend receivable from S Ltd as revenue)		2,000		
Profits				1,200

Add Dividend receivable from S Ltd		160	
		—	
Net Profits (profits before taxation)		2,160	1,200
Less Corporation Tax	900		450
Proposed Dividends	500		200
	—	1,400	— 650
Unappropriated Profits for the year		760	550

This means that the minority interest are entitled to 20 per cent of (£1,200 profits less £450 tax) £750 = £150.

The Consolidated Profit and Loss Account will appear as:

	£
Consolidated Profits for the year before Taxation	3,200
Less Corporation Tax	1,350
	—
Consolidated Profits for the year after Taxation	1,850
Less Minority Shareholders Interest	150
	—
Group Profits for the period	1,700
Less Appropriations:	
Proposed Dividends	500
	—
Unappropriated Profits carried forward to next year	*1,200

*Note: this can be reconciled with the figures per the separate companies accounts as follows:

	£	£
Per the Consolidated Profit and Loss Account		1,200
Minority Shareholders' Interest	150	
Less 20 per cent of Ordinary Dividend		
(included in the figure of £150 on the line above)	40	
	—	110
Per the Separate Accounts £550+£760		1,310

Any transfer to Consolidated Reserves will be:

(*a*) Those of the Holding Company, plus
(*b*) The Group's share of the Subsidiary's Transfers to Reserves.

These can be seen in Exhibit 57.4.

Exhibit 57.4

	£	£	£	£
		H		S
Profits (before dividend receivable from S)		3,000		
Profits				2,000
Add Dividend Receivable from S		300		
		3,300		2,000
Less Corporation Tax	1,400		800	
Proposed Dividend	1,000		400	
Transfers to General Reserve	550		600	
		2,950		1,800
Unappropriated Profits carried forward to next year		350		200

H Ltd owns 75 per cent of the shares of S Ltd		
Consolidated Profits for the year before Taxation		5,000
Less Corporation Tax		2,200
Consolidated Profits for the year after Taxation		2,800
Less Minority Shareholders' Interest		300
Group Profits for the year		2,500
Less Appropriations:		
Proposed Dividend	1,000	
Transfers to General Reserve (£550+¾ of £600)	1,000	
		2,000
Unappropriated Profits carried forward to next year		*500

*Reconcilable with separate Profit and Loss Accounts:			
Per Consolidated Profit and Loss Account			500
Minority Shareholders' Interest		300	
Less 25 per cent of Ordinary Dividends (included in the figure of £300 on the last line)	100		
Less 25 per cent of transfer to General Reserve (25 per cent of £600)	150		
		250	50
Per the Separate Accounts (£350+£200)			550

Exercises

57.1. From the following draw up the consolidated profit and loss account for the year ended 31 December 19–6.

	£	£	£	£
		H		S
Profits		80,000		30,000
Add Dividend receivable from S		4,500		
		84,500		

Less Corporation Tax	35,000		14,000	
Proposed Dividend	30,000		6,000	
		65,000		20,000
		19,500		10,000

H owns 75 per cent of the shares in S.

57.2A. Draw up a consolidated profit and loss account from the following for the year ended 31 December 19–8.

		H		*S*
	£	£	£	£
Profits		550,000		200,000
Dividend receivable from S		36,000		
		586,000		
Less Corporation Tax	254,000		98,000	
Proposed Dividend	180,000		60,000	
		434,000		158,000
		152,000		42,000

H owns 60 per cent of the shares of S.

57.3A. The following are summarized balance sheets of North Ltd, South Ltd, and West Ltd at 31 December 19–6.

	North Ltd	*South Ltd*	*West Ltd*
	£	£	£
Issued Share Capital (£1 Ordinary Shares)	100,000	25,000	15,000
Profit and Loss Account at 31 December 19–4	44,000	7,000	6,000
Net profit (loss) 19–5	16,500	2,400	(3,000)
Net profit (loss) 19–6	18,000	3,600	(1,200)
6 per cent debentures	—	5,000	—
Current liabilities	11,500	4,000	2,600
	190,000	47,000	19,400
Fixed assets	115,000	27,000	14,000
Current assets	31,000	9,000	5,400
25,000 ordinary shares in South Ltd at cost	39,000	—	—
10,000 ordinary shares in West Ltd at cost	—	11,000	—
£5,000 6 per cent debentures of South Ltd at cost	5,000	—	—
	190,000	47,000	19,400

North Ltd acquired its shares in South Ltd on 31 December 19–4, and South Ltd acquired its shares in West Ltd on 31 December 19–5.

The profit and loss account of South Ltd at 31 December 19–4 had been debited with a proposed dividend of £2,500. The dividend was paid on 1 March 19–5, and was included in the net profit of North Ltd for the year 19–5. No other dividends have been paid or proposed by any of the companies in the relevant years.

South Ltd issued the 6 per cent debentures on 1 July 19–6. The accrued interest for the six months to 31 December 19–6, has been deducted in the calculation of the net profit of South Ltd for 19–6, and has been included in the current liabilities of South Ltd, but no entry has been made in the books of North Ltd for the interest due on the debentures.

Prepare the consolidated balance sheet of the group at 31 December 19–6.

Give a short summary of your calculations for all items in the consolidated balance sheet, except share capital, fixed assets and current assets.

Ignore taxation.

(*Institute of Bankers*)

57.4A. The summarized balance sheet of Expansion Ltd, Flourish Ltd, and Growth Ltd at 31 December 19–0 were:

	Expansion Ltd	Flourish Ltd	Growth Ltd
	£	£	£
Issued Share Capital (£1 Ordinary Shares)	120,000	200,000	300,000
Profit and Loss Account	63,000	13,000	59,000
Proposed Final Dividends	30,000	12,000	5,000
9 per cent debentures	80,000	200,000	300,000
	293,000	425,000	664,000
200,000 shares in Flourish Ltd at cost	240,000	—	—
180,000 shares in Growth Ltd at cost	—	252,000	—
Sundry Assets *minus* Current Liabilities	53,000	173,000	664,000
	293,000	425,000	664,000

Details of profits and dividends for 19–9 and 19–0 are shown below:

	Expansion Ltd	Flourish Ltd	Growth Ltd
	£	£	£
Profit and Loss Account 31 December 19–8	48,000	31,000	
Net Profit 19–9	23,000	18,000 (not relevant)	
Less Dividends for 19–9:			
Interim paid July 19–9	—	(15,000)	
Final paid Feb. 19–0	(15,000)	(5,000)	
Profit and Loss Account 31 December 19–9	56,000	29,000	83,000
Net Profit 19–0	37,000	34,000	21,000
Less Dividends for 19–0:			
Interim paid July 19–0	—	(38,000)	(40,000)
Final proposed	(30,000)	(12,000)	(5,000)

Profit and Loss Account, 31 December
19–0   63,000   13,000   59,000

In the above statement, dividends have been credited to net profit of the relevant company when, and not before, the dividends were received.

All debenture interest has been appropriately deducted in the calculation of net profit and there were no share issues in the relevant years.

On 31 December 19–8, Expansion Ltd acquired its shares in Flourish Ltd and, on 31 December 19–9, Flourish Ltd acquired its shares in Growth Ltd. Both acquisitions were 'ex dividend', so that dividends declared prior to acquisition can be ignored.

Required:
(a) The consolidated balance sheet of the group at 31 December 19–0. It is important that you submit your calculations of all items in the consolidated balance sheet. Ignore taxation.

(b) Brief comments on what you considered to be the advantages or disadvantages (to a user of the accounts) of the information which would be shown in the consolidated accounts, compared with accounts for Expansion Ltd alone.

57.5A. The summarized balance sheets of E.S.T. Ltd and its two subsidiary companies, H.R.D. Ltd and S.N.W. Ltd, at 31 December 19–7, were as under:

E.S.T. Ltd

	£		£
Issued Share Capital		Fixed Assets	85,000
(150,000 Ordinary Shares		Current Assets	62,000
of £1 each)	150,000	16,000 Ordinary Shares	
Profit and Loss Account	26,800	in H.R.D. Ltd at cost	
Current Liabilities	38,000	*less* dividend for 19–5	19,800
		30,000 Ordinary Shares in	
		S.N.W. Ltd at cost	48,000
	214,800		214,800

H.R.D. Ltd

	£		£
Issued Share Capital		Fixed Assets	18,000
(20,000 Ordinary Shares		Current Assets	14,750
of £1 each)	20,000		
Profit and Loss Account:			
Balance at £			
31/12/19–5 5,500			
Less Dividend			
for 19–5 2,000			
———			
3,500			
Net Profit, 19–6 1,500			
———			
5,000			

Less Net Loss, 19–7	1,250		
		3,750	
Current Liabilities		9,000	
		32,750	32,750

S.N.W. Ltd

		£		£
Issued Share Capital			Fixed Assets	31,000
(30,000 Ordinary Shares			Current Assets	16,200
of £1 each)		30,000		
Profit and Loss Account:	£			
Balance at 31/12/19–6	7,000			
Net Profit, 19–7	4,200			
		11,200		
Current Liabilities		6,000		
		47,200		47,200

E.S.T. Ltd acquired the shares in the subsidiaries as follows:

Date		Price £
31 December 19–5.	12,000 shares in H.R.D. Ltd	15,000
31 December 19–6.	4,000 shares in H.R.D. Ltd	6,000
31 December 19–6.	30,000 shares in S.N.W. Ltd	48,000

For the purpose of determining the price of the shares in S.N.W. Ltd, the fixed assets of that company were valued at £5,000 in excess of the amount at which they stood in the books. The fixed assets were not written up in the books of S.N.W. Ltd, and, in the accounts of that company for 1967, depreciation was charged at 10 per cent of the book amount. In the consolidated accounts, the fixed assets of S.N.W. Ltd are to be brought in at their valuation at the date of acquisition of the shares, less depreciation, for the year 19–7, at the rate of 10 per cent of that amount.

You are required to prepare a consolidated balance sheet, as on 31 December 19–7.

Show your calculations.

Ignore taxation.

(Chartered Institute of Secretaries and Administrators)

57.6A. The following are the trial balances of A.T.H. Ltd, G.L.E. Ltd, and F.R.N. Ltd as on 31 December 19–8.

	A.T.H. £	G.L.E. £	F.R.N. £
Ordinary Share Capital (shares of £1 each, fully paid)	100,000	30,000	20,000
7 per cent Cumulative Preference Share			

Capital (shares of £1 each, fully paid)	—	—	5,000
Profit and Loss Account—balance at 31/12/19–7	15,600	6,000	1,900
Current Liabilities	20,750	15,900	18,350
Sales	194,000	116,000	84,000
Dividend received from G.L.E. Ltd	1,200	—	—
	331,550	167,900	129,250
Fixed Assets	45,000	29,000	25,000
Current Assets	46,000	27,500	22,500
24,000 Ordinary Shares in G.L.E. Ltd at cost	33,700	—	—
20,000 Ordinary Shares in F.R.N. Ltd at cost	21,250	—	—
Cost of Goods Sold	153,000	87,000	63,000
General Expenses	32,600	22,900	18,750
Dividend for 19–8, paid on 31/12/19–8	—	1,500	—
	331,550	167,900	129,250

A.T.H. Ltd acquired the shares in F.R.N. Ltd on 31 December 19–6, when the credit balance on the profit and loss account of F.R.N. Ltd was £700, and acquired the shares in G.L.E. Ltd on 31 December 19–7. No dividend was paid by either A.T.H. Ltd or G.L.E. Ltd for the year 19–7.

No dividend has been paid by F.R.N. Ltd for the years 19–6, 19–7 and 19–8 and none is proposed. The directors of A.T.H. Ltd propose to pay a dividend of £7,000 for 19–8.

The sales of G.L.E. Ltd for 19–8 (£116,000) include £1,000 for goods sold to F.R.N. Ltd and this amount has been debited to purchases account in the books of F.R.N. Ltd. All these goods were sold by F.R.N. Ltd during 19–8.

Required:

A consolidated trading and profit and loss account for the year 19–8 and a consolidated balance sheet as on 31 December 19–8 (not necessarily in a form for publication).

Ignore depreciation of fixed assets and taxation.

(Chartered Institute of Secretaries and Administrators)

57.7A. You are required to prepare a consolidated profit and loss account for the year ended 31 December 19–0, suitable for incorporation in the published accounts of A Limited, which will not include a separate profit and loss account for the holding company

	A Ltd	B Ltd
	£	£
Profit and Loss Account, balance at 1/1/19–0	36,000	15,000
Trading Profit	71,000	40,000
Dividends (gross) from B Ltd		
Preference	5,400	—
Ordinary	7,500	—
	119,900	55,000

Depreciation	12,000	4,000
Debenture Interest	10,000	—
Directors' Emolument	7,000	3,000
Taxation	22,000	15,000
Dividends Paid:		
6 per cent Preference 30 June	—	3,000
31 December	—	3,000
Ordinary:		
Interim 30 June	12,000	5,000
Final 31 December	12,000	5,000
Profit and Loss Account, balance at 31/12/19–0	44,900	17,000
	119,900	55,000

The following information relates to share capital:

	A Ltd	B Ltd
	£	£
Ordinary Shares of £1 each fully paid	400,000	200,000
6 per cent Preference Shares of £1 each, fully paid		100,000
Shares in B Ltd held by A Ltd:		
Ordinary Shares acquired 1/7/19–0		150,000
Preference Shares acquired 1/1/19–0		90,000

Income and expenditure are deemed to accrue evenly throughout the year. All dividends are payable out of the current year's profits. The directors of B Ltd resigned on 1 July 19–0 and were replaced on that day by directors of A Ltd who are to receive the same remuneration as the former directors.

(*Institute of Cost and Management Accountants*)

58

Accounting for the Results of Associated Companies

In January 1971 the Institute of Chartered Accountants in England and Wales issued its first statement of standard accounting practice. This was concerned with investments in companies which were either 50 per cent owned or less than 50 per cent owned by the investing company. Where a company is more than 50 per cent owned then it will be a subsidiary company and the rules which govern consolidated accounts, as explained in the last few chapters, will apply. With the investments in other companies then before 1971 these have normally been brought into the investing company's accounts only by virtue of the amount of the dividends received or receivable at the accounting date, and the cost of the investment has been shown in the balance sheet. This accounting standard brought in another form of company, an 'Associated Company'.

The Definition given of 'Associated Company' was as follows:

A company (not being a subsidiary of the investing group or company) is an associated company of the investing group or company if:

(a) the investing group or company's interest in the associated company is effectively that of a partner in a joint venture or consortium.

or

(b) the investing group or company's interest in the associated company is for the long term and is substantial (i.e. not less than 20 per cent of the equity voting rights), and, having regard to the disposition of the other shareholdings, the investing group or company is in a position to exercise a significant influence over the associated company.

In both cases it is essential that the investing group or company participates (usually through representation on the board) in commercial and financial policy decisions of the associated company, including the distribution of profits.

The accounting standard states that the consolidation procedure normally used for subsidiaries should be extended to associated companies. Since the Companies Act 1948 has required the preparation of group accounts normally in the form of consolidated accounts there had been two important developments. Previous to 1948 subsidiary companies had been the main way by which companies had conducted an important part of their business through the medium of other companies. Since then there has been the growing practice of companies to conduct parts of their business through other companies (frequently consortium or joint venture companies) in which they have had a substantial but not controlling interest. The other is the importance which investors have come to attach to earnings, as distinct from dividends, the price/earnings ratio and earnings per share. As investors have become more sophisticated they have realized that the dividends themselves tell only part of the story, what is also of importance is how much has actually been earned in profits during the period.

This has meant that, if a company had subsidiaries and what are now defined as associated companies, then the results of each subsidiary for both dividends and profits would be brought fully into the consolidated accounts. The associated companies results could merely be shown by virtue of dividends received or receivable and the cost of the investment. Thus a full view of subsidiaries was given but only a partial view, very often a totally misleading one, was given of the associated companies. The accounting standard of 1971 is to correct such poor reporting by putting associated companies on what really is the same basis as for subsidiary companies.

Of course a holding company will already have to prepare consolidated accounts for itself and its subsidiaries, and Exhibit 58.1 shows how the consolidated profit and loss account could be adjusted in respect of the associated companies. On the other hand, where a company has no subsidiaries, but it has one or more associated companies, then it will have to adapt its profit and loss account, suitably titled to incorporate the additional information. For an example of this see Exhibit 58.2.

The investing group or company should give particulars of the names of and its interests in companies treated as associated companies, and of any other companies in which it holds not less than 30 per cent of the equity voting rights but which are not treated as associated companies.

Exhibit 58.1

Example of consolidated profit and loss account for a company with subsidiaries.

Consolidated profit and loss account of an investing company and subsidiaries, incorporating results of associated companies.

		£
Turnover (of the investing company and subsidiaries)		x
		=
Operating profit (after charging depreciation and all other trading expenses of the investing company and subsidiaries)		x
Share of profits less losses of associated companies		x
		—
Profit before taxation		x
	£	
Taxation:		
Investing company and subsidiaries	x	
Associated companies	x	x
	—	—
		x
Minority Interests		x
		—
Profit after taxation before extraordinary items		x
Extraordinary items (group proportion after taxation, after deducting minority interests and including share of associated companies' items)		x
		—
Profit attributable to members of (the investing company) (See note)		x
Dividends		x
		—
Net profit retained		* x
		=
	£	
By the investing company	x	
By subsidiaries	x	
In associated companies	x	
	—	
	* x	
	=	

Note: Of the profit attributable to members of the investing company, £—is dealt with in the accounts of the investing company.

Exhibit 58.2

Example of profit and loss account for a company without subsidiaries.
Profit and loss account of an investing company incorporating results of associated companies.

		£
Turnover (of the investing company)		x
		$=$
Operating profit (after charging depreciation and all other trading expenses of the investing company)		x
Share of profits less losses of associated companies		x
		—
Profit Before Taxation		x
	£	
Taxation		
Investing company	x	
Associated companies	x	
	—	x
		—
Profit after taxation before extraordinary items		x
Extraordinary items (investing company and share of associated companies' items) after taxation		x
		—
Profit attributable to members of the investing company comprising:		* x
	£	
Profit of the investing company	x	
Profits retained in associated companies	x	
	—	
	* x	
	$=$	
Dividends		x
		—
Net Profit Retained		** x
		$=$
	£	
By the investing company	x	
In associated companies	x	
	—	
	** x	
	$=$	

APPENDIX NO 58.1
Examinations at Stage Three or Higher Level and also Professional Foundation Level

First, you must read everything that I have written in Appendices 27.1 and 48.1, for the advice that I have given there is still relevant, and will be so throughout any accounting examination.

Stage three and higher level examinations, and professional foundation examinations, do ask rather more than the two earlier stages. Rather than 'Can the student actually prepare the accounts, plus perhaps a little extra' type of approach, these examinations now become more of 'Can the student think like an accountant does'. This means that you have got to be able to arrive at solutions to problems which very often will be set in an unfamiliar style. In real life many business problems crop up to which the answer cannot be found in a textbook. This does not necessarily mean that the textbooks are incomplete; life itself is so complex and varied that it would be impossible for a textbook to be written covering so many possibilities. Business changes rapidly, and what you learn in your studies are the basic tools which will help you to solve business problems in accounting terms. The actual use of these tools in a particular situation has to be left to you.

This does not mean that there will not be any questions asking the basic questions on accounting, such as the preparation of final accounts, etc. They will still represent the bulk of the examination, but questions will normally be set in addition which will attempt to test how good you are at thinking like a good accountant is expected to think. Examiners do find it very difficult to come up with completely novel questions, and so quite often he/she will set a question dressed up rather differently so that simple rote learning will be insufficient. Very often this will mean leaving out figures that can be deduced. At the simplest level this would mean leaving one item, that of Capital, from the trial balance, and you are required to deduce that the figure needed is that required to make both sides of the trial balance agree.

Quite a few questions will be concerned with the interpretation of accounts. You should always remember that accounting does not give the full story of a business. For instance, if I was asked to lend money to a business I would find the past accounts of some use. But I would be very much concerned with what the plans were for the future. The future prospects and the problems and benefits facing the company would be of more interest to me than what has happened in the past. Of course we should learn lessons from what has happened in the past, but that is only part of the story.

As an examiner myself I have often set questions involving interpretation of accounts. I have frequently added an extra part to the question, 'If you could interview the managing director, what questions would you like to ask him about the business?' Lamentably very few candidates ever contemplated asking him about the business plans for the future. It does not mean that I would accept his plans as being reasonable or attainable. That is where the story from his accounts in the past would help me assess the likelihood of his plans being achieved. Accounting ratios would be of considerable use here.

You should look behind and beyond the figures. For instance, it is of extreme importance to know the relationship between a business, its customers and its suppliers. A business which has one very large customer could well be in serious difficulties if that firm were to cease business with it. Similar problems arise with suppliers. Therefore in interpreting accounts in examinations show some imagination as to what might happen in the real world. Your examiner will be suitably impressed.

At this stage the competition from other students is becoming much more fierce. Anyone passing these examinations is putting one foot on the ladder to a well-paid job. Whereas, at an earlier stage, the examiner would be reasonably tolerant towards your efforts, he expects much more of you from now on.

I wish someone would invent a better saying than 'Practice makes Perfect'; in any case it isn't entirely true. There is enough truth in it however, in that the more practice you have at tackling accounting questions then the better your performance will become. Many students with high intelligences have failed simply because they disregarded such advice. Other less able students have slogged their way through such practice and passed the examinations.

Besides the exercises attempted on a regular basis throughout your course, it is also an essential part of your training for your examinations that you should attempt full examination papers. I have therefore included two full papers from each of the following:

London Chamber of Commerce—Higher Stage.

Association of Certified Accountants—Foundation.

Institute of Cost & Management Accountants—Foundation.

Chartered Secretaries & Administrators—Financial Accounting I.

Full answers to one of the papers from each of these bodies is given at the end of the book. The second paper for each examination is given for further practice.

By all means do not limit your attempts to the papers for your own examining body. These papers are of a very similar standard. It will be of little use to you to decide which examination would be the easiest to pass. That depends entirely on the leniency or strictness of the examiners for each body. A pass mark of 50 per cent, where the examiner is being generous, may be quite easy to obtain. In another examination, where the examiner is being strict, a pass mark of 50 per cent may be quite difficult to achieve. It is therefore the standards set by the examiners which determines the difficulty of the examination, and these cannot readily be judged by the appearance of the examination paper.

Avail yourself therefore of the fact that there are four full papers with answers given at the end of the book. Work through all of them if you can possibly find the time.

THE LONDON CHAMBER OF COMMERCE AND INDUSTRY
Higher Stage

(Full paper—answers shown at the back of the book.)

Accounting
(3 Hours Allowed)

Candidates should attempt **all** questions in Section A, and **any two, but not more than two,** questions in Section B.

SECTION A—Answer all three questions.

1. PQ Ltd was incorporated on 1 April 19–6 with an authorized capital of 150,000 ordinary shares of £0·40 each to acquire as at 1 May 19–6 the partnership business of P and Q who shared profits and losses in the ratio 3:2.

The balance sheet of P and Q at 1 May 19–6 was as follows:

	£		£	£
Capital: P	18,000	Plant at cost		22,500
Q	14,000	*less* depreciation		5,500
	32,000			17,000
Creditors	7,500	Stocks		16,200
Bank overdraft	4,500	Debtors	12,000	
		less provision	1,200	
				10,800
	£44,000			£44,000

The assets and liabilities were taken over at the following valuations:

	£
Plant	19,000
Stock	15,500
Debtors	12,000 (less a provision of £600)
Creditors	7,500

The Bank overdraft was discharged by the partners.

The purchase consideration was £10,500 in cash and 80,000 shares in PQ Ltd valued at par. Any cash remaining in the partnership bank account after realization was to be divided equally between the partners.

On 1 May PQ Ltd issued a further 60,000 shares at a premium of £0·20 per share, and £10,000 of 10 per cent debenture stock at £96 per 100. On 4 May the Company purchased the freehold property occupied by the partnership from Q, the owner, for £25,000 paid in cash, and paid £1,100 formation expenses.

Required:
(1) (a) Partnership realization and capital accounts recording the above.
(b) State the *number* of shares received by each partner.

(Sub-total: 11 marks)

(2) Balance sheet of PQ Ltd, immediately after the completion of the above transactions.

(Sub-total: 11 marks)

(Total: 22 marks)

2. The following financial statements refer to two companies in the same industry. All figures are in £ thousands.

Revenue statements for the year to 31 March 19–6.

	AB Ltd		CD Ltd	
	£	£	£	£
Sales		500		300
Stock 1.4.19–5	58		125	
Purchases	384		270	
	442		395	
Stock 31.3.19–6	42	400	195	200
		100		100
Advertising and selling	54		20	
Administration	5		18	
Loan interest	1	60	12	50
		40		50
Taxation		20		25
		20		25
Proposed dividend		15		10
		5		15

Balance sheets at 31 March 19–6.

	AB Ltd	CD Ltd		AB Ltd	CD Ltd
	£	£		£	£
Ordinary shares	75	350	Fixed assets (net)	93	345
Retained profits	25	150	Stock	42	195
			Debtors	25	100
	100	500	Bank	1	60
Debentures	10	120			
Tax payable 1.1.19–7	20	25			
Proposed dividend	15	10			
Creditors	16	45			
	161	700		161	700

Required:

Calculate for each company the following (use ratios or percentages as appropriate).

(1) Gross profit to sales
(2) Net profit to sales
(3) Return on equity interest
(4) Return on capital employed
(5) Dividend cover
(6) Gearing ratio
(7) Current ratio
(8) Quick asset (or acid test) ratio
(9) Average stock turnover
(10) Creditors' turnover
(11) Debtors' turnover

Note:

Marks will be awarded for correctness of principle rather than arithmetical accuracy. Therefore workings should be shown.

(22 marks)

3. The following balances were extracted from the ledger of Manufac Ltd at 30 June 19–6.

	Dr £	Cr £
Stocks 1 July 19–5: Raw material	18,000	
Work in progress	16,450	
Finished goods	28,200	
Purchases of raw material	103,100	
Manufacturing wages: direct	77,000	
indirect	16,000	
Factory rent, rates and insurance	5,400	
Office rent, rates and insurance	2,200	
Machinery repairs	1,640	
depreciation	12,500	
Office wages, salaries and other expenses	14,400	
Salesmen's salaries and commission	19,160	
Advertising	16,000	
Motor vehicle repairs	2,250	
depreciation	4,400	
Directors' remuneration	12,000	
Auditors' fees and expenses	1,500	
Debenture interest	3,000	
Sales		303,500
Dividends on trade investments		1,600

	£
Stocks at 30 June 19–6: Raw material:	22,500
Work in progress:	13,200
Finished goods:	34,000

The sales director earns £4,000 per annum, all other directors are employed on administration. Office expenses are to be classed 50 per cent selling, 50 per cent administration. The motor vehicles are used entirely for selling and distribution of finished goods.

Required:
(1) A manufacturing, trading and profit and loss account for the year to 30 June 19–6 for management purposes, i.e. not for publication, clearly showing the following:
(i) Cost of materials consumed, (ii) cost of goods manufactured, (iii) cost of goods sold, (iv) gross profit, (v) selling expenses, (vi) administrative expenses, (vii) net profit.

Note: Work in progress and finished goods are valued at full manufacturing cost.

(Sub-total: 20 marks)

(2) (a) Raw material stocks have been valued on the FIFO basis, stock levels have been constant throughout the year and prices have been rising steadily. If the LIFO basis had been used, would profit be higher or lower?
(b) If finished goods stocks had been valued at prime cost instead of full cost is it likely that profit would be higher or lower for the year to 30 June 19–6?

(Sub-total: 4 marks)

(Total: 24 marks)

Section B—Answer any two questions

4. Redeb Ltd issued £100,000 of 10 per cent debentures at par during 19–8, redeemable at a premium of £4 per £100 nominal 20 years later on 30 September 19–7, unless repurchased by the Company in the open market before that date.

Interest is payable on 31 March and 30 September each year, and the first repurchases occurred during the accounting year ended 31 December 19–5, when Redeb Ltd bought £24,000 (nominal) on 1 September for £22,600 (ex interest) and £12,000 (nominal) on 31 October for £11,300 (cum interest).

The directors do not intend to establish a debenture redemption reserve out of profits, but any gains or losses on repurchase are to be transferred to general reserve.

Required:
The ledger accounts in the books of Redeb Ltd necessary to record the above transactions, including the half-yearly interest payments, for the year to 31 December 19–5. You are *not* required to show the cash account or profit and loss account.

Note: Ignore tax.

(16 marks)

5. The following are the balance sheets and revenue accounts of X, a sole trader, for 19–4 and 19–5.

Balance Sheets—31 December

	19–4 £	19–5 £		19–4 £	19–4 £	19–5 £	19–5 £
Capital at 1 Jan.	22,500	21,000	Property, at cost		8,000		8,000
Profit	3,500	6,000	Plant: cost	11,000		12,500	
			depreciation	7,000	4,000	8,600	3,900
	26,000	27,000					
Drawings	5,000	5,500	Stock		7,500		10,000
			Debtors		3,000		5,000
	21,000	21,500	Bank		3,500		100
Loan from wife		2,500					
Creditors	5,000	3,000					
	£26,000	£27,000			£26,000		£27,000

Revenue Accounts

	19–4 £	19–5 £
Sales	24,000	27,000
Cost of goods sold	18,000	18,000
Gross profit	6,000	9,000
Overhead expenses (including depreciation)	2,500	3,300
Profit on sale of plant	—	(300)
Net Profit	3,500	6,000

The plant sold during 19–5 had a book value at the date of sale of £400, and had originally cost £1,000.

X had become increasingly concerned during the last few months of 19–5 at his worsening bank balance and he finds it difficult to understand why it should have fallen by £3,400 in a year in which sales and gross profits have increased.

Required:

A sources and uses of funds statement, explaining the decrease in the bank balance during 19–5.

(16 marks)

6. H Ltd was incorporated on 1 January 19–5 with an authorized issued and fully paid capital of £10,000. On 10 January the company purchased 500 kg of material A at £20 per kg and subsequent purchases and sales were as follows, all transactions being for cash:

	Purchases: kg	Cost price per kg	Sales: kg	Selling price per kg
		£		£
1 March			300	25
1 May	400	30		
1 August			500	35
30 December	400	40		

The company's operating expenses (wages, transport, etc.) amounted to £6,000 for the year.

At 31 December 19–5 there were 500 kg of material A in stock with a net realizable value of £42 per kg.

Required:

(a) A valuation of stock at the end of 19–5 on a basis generally accepted as correct for accounting purposes.

(Sub-total: 3 marks)

(b) A revenue account for the year and a balance sheet at 31 December 19–5.

(Sub-total: 7 marks)

(c) Briefly discuss the following statement in the light of your answer to parts (a) and (b), and if you agree with the statement suggest methods by which its recommendation could be effected:

'In times of rising prices it is desirable to measure separately the proportion of total profit for a year due solely due to rising replacement costs of stock.'

(Sub-total: 6 marks)

(Total: 16 marks)

THE LONDON CHAMBER OF COMMERCE AND INDUSTRY
(Full paper—without answers)

Accounting
(3 Hours Allowed)

Candidates should attempt **all** *questions in Section A and* **any two, but not more than two,** *questions in Section B.*

SECTION A—Answer all three questions

1. State Securities Ltd is an investment trust whose accounting year ends on 31 December. The following data relate to its dealings in 12 per cent Treasury Stock, on which interest is paid half-yearly on 31 March and 30 September.

19–4
1 March	Bought £6,000 nominal, ex. div. for £6,348
1 June	Bought £8,000 nominal, cum. div. for £8,360
1 November	Sold £3,500 nominal, cum. div. for £3,982

19–5
1 May	Bought £4,000 nominal, cum div. for £4,486
1 September	Sold £14,500 nominal, ex div. for £15,480

Required:

(1) Write up the investment account for the accounting years to 31 December 19–4 and 19–5, valuing the securities held at the end of 19–4 on the FIFO basis. (Sub-total: 18 marks)

(2) Which amounts would be different, and by how much, if stock at the end of 19–4 were valued on the average cost basis? (Sub-total: 3 marks)

(Total: 21 marks)

2. N. Hawk, a sole trader, extracts a trial balance from his ledger at 31 March 19–6, which fails to agree. The difference is entered in a suspense account, and the trial balance, after the preparation of the Trading account, appears as under:

	£	£
Hawk: Capital at 1.4.19–5		29,500
Drawings	8,550	
Gross profit		13,360
Expenses (including depreciation)	5,820	
Fixed assets at cost less depreciation	19,440	
Stock	4,560	
Sales ledger control	9,144	
Purchases ledger control		6,321
Bank	2,127	
Suspense		460
	£49,641	£49,641

In addition to the two control accounts, which are an integral part of the double entry system, memorandum debtors' and creditors' ledgers are kept. The balances on these ledgers at 31 March 19–6 amounted to:

| Debtors' ledger | Dr | £10,545 | Cr | £ 422 |
| Creditors' ledger | Dr | 41 | Cr | 6,810 |

On investigation the following are discovered:

(1) The sales day book total for January 19–6 has been under-added by £1,000.

(2) A receipt of £759 from a debtor T. Dove has been credited to the personal account of another debtor, R. Dove.

(3) H. Sparrow, a debtor, paid £280 cash for goods sold to him on credit, being allowed discount of £20. Subsequently he returned the whole of the goods and was sent a credit note for £280, the latter amount being entered in the sales returns day book.

(4) S. Thrush, another debtor, overpaid £35 and was later repaid this amount. The cheque for repayment was posted to Thrush's personal account but not entered in the control account.

(5) W. Warbler is both a customer and a supplier and has accounts in both personal ledgers. A balance owing by him of £47 was correctly transferred to his account in the creditors' ledger but the book-keeper sought to adjust the control accounts by debiting sales ledger control and crediting purchases ledger control with £47.

(6) Warbler later paid the £47 and this was correctly posted to his account in the creditors' ledger, but included in the total receipts posted to Sales Ledger Control.

(7) An invoice for £376 for goods supplied to P. Martin was correctly entered in the sales day book, but posted to his personal ledger account as £367. He has not yet paid the invoice.

(8) Total purchases for June 19–5, £12,833, had been entered in the purchases ledger control account as £12,338, but correctly posted to purchases account.

Required:

(a) Journal entries to deal with items (1) to (8) above. Narrations are not required. (Sub-total: 12 marks)

(b) N. Hawk's balance sheet at 31 March 19–6 after all errors in the books have been corrected. (Sub-total: 9 marks)

(Total: 21 marks)

3. Outremer Ltd has grown rapidly over the last three years and is now planning to request credit facilities from its bank. The following sales forecasts have been made for 19–6 and 19–7:

	£'000s
July 19–6	60
August	60
September	120
October	180
November	240
December	120
January 19–7	120
February	60

The selling department believes that 10 per cent of each month's sales will be cash sales, the remainder will be paid during the *second* month following the sale (e.g. credit sales in July 19–6 will be paid for in September).

The total labour and raw material costs for each month, including £6,000 per month for indirect labour, are as follows (payment being made in the following month)

	£'000s
August 19–6	30
September	42
October	294
November	102
December	78
January 19–7	30
February	36

All finished goods are sold at prime cost plus 50 per cent: finished goods stocks are valued at prime cost, there is no work in progress and since materials are processed immediately on purchase there are no material stocks.

Other monthly charges are administrative salaries: £9,000, factory rent: £3,000, depreciation: £12,000 and miscellaneous expenses: £1,000. Corporation tax on the profits of the preceding year will be paid on 1 January 19–7. No other receipts or payments will occur.

The company's balance sheet at 1 September 19–6 is expected to show the following position (all figures in £'000s):

Share capital	100	Fixed assets at cost *less* depreciation	148
Retained profits	149	Stock at prime cost	50
Corporation tax	42	Debtors	108
Creditors	30	Bank	15
	£321		£321

Required:
(a) A monthly cash budget for the period September 1976 to February 19–7 showing the maximum bank overdraft required.   (Sub-total: 12½ marks)

(b) A budgeted trading and profit and loss account for the same period, and a budgeted balance sheet at 28 February 19–7.   (Sub-total: 13½ marks)

Note:
Ignore corporation tax on the profits arising during the budget period, and bank interest.

(Total: 26 marks)

4. The following are the balance sheets of H Ltd and S Ltd on 31 March 19–6.

H Ltd

	£'000s		£'000s
Share capital	1,000	Fixed assets	760
Profit and loss	350	Investment in S Ltd., cost	300
Current liabilities	143	Stock	293
		Other current assets	140
	1,493		1,493

S Ltd

	£.000s		£'000s
Share capital	540	Fixed assets	414
Profit and loss	40	Stock	150
Current liabilities	62	Other current assets	78
	642		642

H Ltd acquired 60 per cent of the issued capital of S Ltd when the *debit* balance on the latter company's profit and loss account was £25,000.

H Ltd's stock includes £50,000 purchased from S Ltd at cost plus 25 per cent, and S Ltd's stock includes £30,000 purchased from H Ltd at cost plus 20 per cent.

Required:

Consolidated balance sheet at 31 March 19–6. (16 marks)

5. The following is the draft profit and loss account for C Ltd for the year to 29 February 19–6.

	£	£
Trading profit		35,700
Depreciation	5,500	
Auditors' remuneration	1,200	6,700
Profit before tax		29,000
Corporation tax		7,250
Profit after tax		21,750
Proposed dividend (£0·03 per share)		3,000
Profit retained this year		18,750
Retained profits at 1 March 19–5		10,000
Retained profits at 29 February 19–6		£28,750

On investigation you find that the depreciation charged relates entirely to vehicles bought on 1 March 19–4 for £110,000. In the year of purchase these had been depreciated at a rate of 35 per cent per annum on the reducing balance basis, but the directors have now decided that the depreciation policy should be changed to the straight-line method at 20 per cent per annum as from the date of purchase, and the above account is intended to reflect that change of policy.

In the draft balance sheet at 29 February 19–6, fixed assets are shown:

	£	£
Motor vehicles at cost		110,000
Less depreciation to 28.2.19–5		
(@ 35%)	38,500	
Depreciation to 29.2.19–6		
(2 × 20%) − 35%)	5,500	44,000
		66,000

Required:
(1) Redraft the above profit and loss account in accordance with recognized accounting principles, showing clearly the correct figure for profit after tax.

(Sub-total: 11 marks)

(2) Calculate
    (*a*) earnings per share
    (*b*) dividend cover
according to the original accounts shown above *and* according to your redrafted account.

(Sub-total: 5 marks)

Note:
The charge for corporation tax (£7,250) will *not* be affected by any adjustments you may make in order to answer part (1).

(Total: 16 marks)

6. A Ltd and B Ltd were both incorporated on 1 January 19–5, each with authorized capital of £10,000 in ordinary shares which were issued at par, for cash, and fully paid.

During the year to 31 December 19–5 the following transactions took place:

19–5
10 January	A Ltd and B Ltd each purchased 5,000 shares in G Ltd, a very large mining company at a total cost of £10,000 to each company.
30 June	G Ltd paid a dividend of £0·15 per share.
15 July	A Ltd sold all its shares in G Ltd for £20,000, and placed the proceeds on deposit account.
15 December	A Ltd again purchased 5,000 shares in G Ltd this time at a total cost of £20,000.
31 December	A Ltd and B Ltd had each incurred administrative expenses, during the year, of £600, and A Ltd had received interest on deposit account of £650.

The market value of G Ltd's shares at 31 December 19–5 was £4.20 each.

Required:

(1) Revenue accounts for the year to 31 December 19–5 and balance sheets at that date for A Ltd and B Ltd, in accordance with recognized accounting principles. Profits on sales of investments can be treated as revenue profits.

Note: You should present your answer in columnar form.

(Sub-total: 7 marks)

(2) Comment on the results shown by the statements you have prepared. How accurately do you feel they reflect the relative performance of the two companies?

Note: Ignore taxation.

(Sub-total: 9 marks)

(Total: 16 marks)

ASSOCIATION OF CERTIFIED ACCOUNTANTS
(Full paper with answers)

Foundation Examination—Part A Paper 1
Accounting 1

Time allowed—3 hours
Answer FIVE questions only
Section A—ONE question (question 1) which is compulsory
Section B—TWO questions selected from questions 2, 3, and 4.
Section C—TWO questions selected from questions 5, 6, and 7.

SECTION A   (Compulsory question)

1. Smith and Jones formed a partnership on 1 April 19–4, sharing profits and losses in the ratio 2:1. The partnership was formed to manufacture and sell a new type of tin-opener developed and patented by Smith. Smith contributed capital of £8,000 and Jones of £5,000, and it was agreed to pay interest on capital of 6 per cent per annum. As Jones had the business acumen, it was agreed that he was to be responsible for most of the day-to-day work of the partnership, and therefore was to receive a salary of £1,000 per annum.

The initial capital was paid into a bank account. The partnership acquired a a ten year lease of suitable business premises for £6,000. The manufacturing process was relatively simple, and involved stamping out a plastic mould and inserting the patented cutting and opening device which was made under licence by Blades Ltd. The machines for producing the plastic moulds cost £5,000, and were to be paid for on an instalment basis of 10 quarterly payments of £500. This machinery, made by Synthetics Ltd was estimated to have a working life of 5 years.

Sales made through mail order were on a cash basis and all such cash received was paid immediately into the bank. Some local retailers collected the tin-openers for themselves and were allowed a trade discount of 20 per cent (on the normal price of £1) and a cash discount of 5 per cent if the accounts were settled promptly. These local sales provided a cash float from which some miscellaneous payments were made by cash. These were:

Wages	£600
Postage	2,582
Petrol and Oil	248
Motor Repairs	170

At the end of March 19–5, the partnership had £48 cash in hand.

A summary of the bank statements for the year to 31 March 19–5 showed:

Deposits	£
Capital introduced	13,000
Other bankings	23,590

Payments	
Lease	6,000
Blades Ltd (Purchases)	5,400
Purchases of plastic	3,800
Synthetics Ltd	2,000
Gas and electricity	150
Van (bought 1 July 19–4)	800
Insurance	150
Wages	1,500
Packaging material	1,627
Advertising	620
Telephone	760
Drawings—Smith	2,140
—Jones	1,520

A cheque sent out on 31 March 19–5 for electricity (£35) had not been cleared by the bank.

Of the tin-openers sold during the year, 5,000 were sold to local retailers, and of these 4,800 had been paid for by the end of the year and had been allowed the appropriate trade and cash discounts.

The insurance included £40 for motor insurance which expired on 30 June 19–5. Blades Ltd were owed £250 at 31 March 19–5.

At 31 March 19–5, the partnership had stock valued at £660.

Required:

(a) Prepare a Cash Account and Bank Account for the period ended 31 March 19–5. (6 marks)

(b) Prepare a Trading and Profit and Loss Account for the period ended 31 March 19–5 and a Balance Sheet as at that date. State clearly (by way of notes) any assumptions you make. (16 marks)

(c) Advise the partners on the success (or otherwise) of their first year of business. (6 marks)

(28 marks)

SECTION B (Answer TWO questions from this section)

2. The following list of balances was extracted from the books of the Howton Company Ltd at 31 December 19–4.

	£	£
£1 Ordinary Shares		150,000
8% £1 Preference Shares		50,000
7% Debentures		100,000
General Reserve		65,000
Land and Buildings at cost	111,000	
Plant and Machinery at cost	382,000	
Undistributed Profit at 1 January 19–4		35,000
Share Premium Account		20,000
Stock at 1 January 19–4	35,000	
Sales		290,000
Discounts allowed and received	3,200	4,600
Debtors and Creditors	48,000	27,000
Provision for Depreciation—Plant and Machinery		85,500
Bank	7,500	
Carriage inwards	1,100	
Purchases	165,000	
Suspense Account		400
Wages	23,500	
Lighting and heating	2,900	
Office salaries	8,600	
Debenture Interest	7,000	
Directors' Fees	12,800	
Interim Dividends		
Ordinary (5%)	7,500	
Preference (4%)	2,000	
Provision for Doubtful Debts		1,500
General Expenses	11,900	
	£829,000	£829,000

Inspection of the books and records of the company yields the following additional information.
  (i) On 31 December 19–4 the company issued bonus shares to the Ordinary Shareholders on a 1 for 10 basis. No entry relating to this has yet been made in the books.
 (ii) The authorised share capital of the company is 200,000 £1 Ordinary Shares and 50,000 8 per cent £1 Preference Shares.
 (iii) Stock at 31 December 19–4 was valued at £41,000.
 (iv) The suspense account (£400) relates to cash received for the sale of some machinery on 1 January 19–4. This machinery cost £2,000 and the depreciation accumulated thereon amounted to £1,500.
 (v) The directors, on the advice of an independent valuer, wish to revalue the land and buildings at £180,000, thus bringing the value into line with current prices.
 (vi) Wages owing at 31 December 19–4 amount to £150.

(vii) Depreciation is to be provided on plant and machinery at 10 per cent on cost.

(viii) General expenses (£11,900) includes an insurance premium (£200) which relates to the period 1 April 19–4 to 31 March 19–5.

(ix) The provision for doubtful debts is to be reduced to 2½ per cent of debtors.

(x) The directors wish to provide for:
   (1) A final ordinary dividend of 5 per cent.
   (2) A final preference dividend.
   (3) A transfer to general reserve of £15,000.

Required:
Prepare, *in vertical form*, the Trading and Profit and Loss Accounts of the Howton Company Ltd. for the period ended 31 December 19–4 and a Balance Sheet as at that date. Ignore taxation.   (20 marks)

3.   The balance sheet of J. Thompson, a sole trader, as at 31 March 19–5 was as follows:

J. Thompson
Balance Sheet as at 31 March 19–5

Capital at 1 April 19–4		£18,900	Land and Buildings		
Profit for the year			(at valuation)		£15,500
ended 31 March,			Machinery (cost)	£13,000	
19–5	£4,500		*Less* Depreciation	7,500	
Less Drawings	1,500				5,500
		3,000			
Creditors		6,300	Stock at cost	5,700	
Overdraft		2,700	Debtors	4,200	
					9,900
		£30,900			£30,900

Further investigation reveals the following information:

(i) The closing stock includes damaged goods which, although they had cost £100, have an estimated sale value of £75.

(ii) Debtors include £200 in respect of a customer who has gone bankrupt. A doubtful debt provision of 2½ per cent is also required.

(iii) The machinery was acquired five years ago, and is being depreciated down to its scrap value on a straight line basis over eight years. A more realistic estimate indicates that the life span will be 10 years.

(iv) The land and buildings were revalued in December 19–4 by Mr Thompson. The original cost was £13,500 and the surplus was credited to the profit and loss account for that year.

(v) Wages owing at 31 March 19–5 amounted to £95, but this has not been reflected in the accounts.

(vi) Charges for the bank overdraft, amounting to £80, have not been recorded in the accounts.

(vii) In arriving at the profit for the period, a salary of £1,000 paid to Mr Thompson had been deducted as an expense.

(viii) £200 rent owing to Mr Thompson for the letting of part of his business premises had not been received, and no entry had been made in the books in respect of this item.

Required:
(a) Prepare journal entries to reflect such corrections as you consider necessary.
(12 marks)

(b) Draw up a statement of revised profit for the period, and prepare a new balance sheet as at 31 March 19–5. (8 marks)

(20 marks)

4. The Alway Social Club had the following assets and liabilities as at 31 March 19–5.

Assets	£
Clubhouse (at cost)	8,400
Equipment (cost £2,300)	1,200
Bar Stocks	400
Rates prepaid	100
Insurance prepaid	35
Subscriptions in arrears	16
Cash at Bank	980
Cash in Hand	10

Liabilities	
Creditors for bar purchases	800
Subscriptions in advance	8
Electricity account owing	30

The treasurer seeks your assistance in preparing a forecast Income and Expenditure Account for the period ending 31 March 19–6 and a Balance Sheet as at that date, and supplies you with the following information.

(i) The club has 300 members, and it is intended to raise the subscriptions from the current £4 per annum to £5 per annum. The members who have paid in advance will be allowed subscriptions at the old rates. It is anticipated that the members currently in arrears with their subscriptions will pay the arrears during the coming year.

(ii) Extensions to the clubhouse are planned which will cost an estimated £1,500. Of this sum it is anticipated that £1,000 will be paid during the year.

(iii) Some of the club's sports equipment (which cost £250 and has a written down value of £100) will be sold for an estimated £50, and replaced with new equipment costing £340. All equipment is depreciated on a straight line basis over four years, and none of the equipment is more than three years old.

(iv) Bar purchases are made monthly on credit and paid for in the month following delivery. It is anticipated that the same volume of business—which is fairly constant on a monthly basis—will be done during the coming year, but that costs will rise by 25 per cent from 1 April 19–5. Bar stocks are normally held at the level of one half of one month's purchases. The bar makes a gross profit margin of 20 per cent on all sales. Bar sales are for cash which is banked daily. The bar steward, who is paid £100 per month, receives a commission of 5 per cent of the gross profit for the year. This is paid with his final wage cheque.

(v) The club runs monthly social evenings, and charges members £1 per head admission. An average of 200 members attend each of these evenings. Expenses usually amount to 70 pence per head.

(vi) Other expenditure is estimated at:

Insurance	£80
Bar Licence	50
Rates	500
Heat and Light	250
Miscellaneous	70

The rates are paid on 1 July in respect of the following twelve months, and the insurance payment is for the period 1 October 19–5 to 30 September 19–6. All payments are made by cheque, except for the miscellaneous expenses which are paid from the imprest cash fund, which is reimbursed immediately.

Required:

(a) Prepare the estimated bank account for the year ending 31 March 19–6.

(6 marks)

(b) Construct an estimated Bar Trading and Profit and Loss Account for the year ending 31 March 19–6.

(4 marks)

(c) Prepare an Income and Expenditure Account for the year ending 31 March 19–5, and a Balance Sheet as at that date.

(10 marks)

(20 marks)

SECTION C (Answer TWO questions from this section)

5. A retailer commenced business on 1 January 19–5 with a capital of £500. He decided to specialize in a single product line and, by the end of June 19–5, his purchase and sales of this product were as follows:

Date	Purchases		Sales	
	Units	Unit Price (£)	Units	Unit Price (£)
Jan.	30	5·00	20	7·00
Feb.	—	—	5	7·20
Apr.	40	6·00	25	8·00
May	25	6·50	30	8·50
June	20	7·00	20	9·00
	115		100	

Required:

(a) Ascertain the retailer's gross profit for the period assuming that:

(1) stock is valued on a Last-in First-out (LIFO) basis

and

(2) stock is valued on a First-in-First-out (FIFO) basis.

(9 marks)

(*b*) Assuming that all purchases and sales are made for cash and that there are no other transactions for the period, draw up balance sheets as at 30 June 19–5 showing (1) stock valued on a FIFO basis and (2) stock valued on a LIFO basis. Comment briefly on the significance of these balance sheets.

(7 marks)

(16 marks)

6. Recently, three friends, tired of the pressures of business life, decided to seek their freedom and fortune gold-mining in South America. At the end of a year, the three friends, who had worked independently, compared the results of their activities. By a strange—yet happy—coincidence all three found that each had experienced precisely the same events, as summarised by the four transactions listed below:

(i) Commenced mining operations with capital of £5,000.
(ii) Mined and refined 50 ounces of gold at a cost of £3,000.
(iii) Sold on credit 40 ounces of gold at £100 per ounce (the normal market price).
(iv) Collected cash from debtors for 30 ounces.

Required:
(*a*) Prepare year end balance sheets which reflect the above transactions assuming that the three friends respectively recognize profit when:
   (1) the gold is produced;
   (2) the gold is sold;
   and
   (3) the cash is collected from debtors. (8 marks)

(*b*) Discuss the extent to which each of the above balance sheets may satisfy the criteria for revenue recognition. (8 marks)

(16 marks)

7. On 1 January 19–3, a manufacturer acquired two identical machine tools at a cost of £5,000 each, and a reprographic machine for the office at a cost of £2,000. The machine tools are depreciated at 20 per cent per annum on a declining balance basis, and the reprographic machine, which has an estimated residual value of £200 and a life of 6 years, is depreciated on a straight line basis. On 1 January 19–4 one of the machine tools was sold for £2,750, and a new one acquired for £8,000.

Required:
(*a*) Prepare the relevant asset accounts, the provision for depreciation accounts, and the sale of asset account, for the year ended 31 December 19–4.

(9 marks)

(*b*) The manufacturer, observing the sale of asset account and the cost of the new machine, notes that 'in future we must increase the depreciation rate because we underestimated the amount of cash needed to replace the asset'. Discuss this statement. (7 marks)

(16 marks)

ASSOCIATION OF CERTIFIED ACCOUNTANTS
(Full paper—without answers)
Foundation Examination—Part A Paper 1
Accounting 1
Time allowed—3 hours
Answer FIVE questions only:
ONE question from Section A (which is compulsory) which carries 30 marks
TWO questions from Section B (two from three) each of which carries 21 marks
TWO questions from Section C (two from three) each of which carries 14 marks
Number of questions on paper—7
All workings should be shown

Section A (Compulsory question)

1. (a) The following balances have been extracted from the books of the
Nemesis Company Limited as at 30 September 19–7:

	£
Creditors	6,300
Sales	80,000
Land at cost	18,000
Buildings at cost	38,000
Furniture and fittings at cost	22,000
Bank (credit balance)	6,000
Depreciation—buildings	6,000
—furniture and fittings	10,000
Discounts received	1,764
Unappropriated profit at 1 October 19–6	2,000
Provision for doubtful debts	816
Goodwill	16,400
Cash in hand	232
Stock at 1 October 19–6	14,248
Interim dividend on preference shares	600
Rates	2,124
Wages and Salaries	8,000
Insurance	1,896
Returns inward	372
General expenses	436
Debtors	12,640
Purchases	43,856
Debenture Interest	400
Bad Debts	676
5% Debentures	16,000
6% £1 Preference Shares	20,000
£1 Ordinary Shares	20,000
General Reserve	10,000
Share Premium	1,000

Additional information:
  (i) Stock on hand at 30 September 19–7 was £15,546.
 (ii) Insurance paid in advance—£100.
(iii) Wages owing—£280.

(iv) Depreciation is to be provided at 10 per cent on cost of buildings, and at 20 per cent on the written down value of furniture and fittings.

(v) Provision for doubtful debts is to be reduced to 5 per cent of debtors.

(vi) Debenture interest outstanding at £400.

(vii) The directors propose to pay a 5 per cent Ordinary Dividend and the final Preference Dividend, and to transfer £8,000 to General Reserve.

Required:

Prepare the Trading, Profit and Loss and Appropriation Account for the period ended 30 September 19–7 and a Balance Sheet as at that date.

(22 marks)

(*b*) Examine the accounts you have prepared in (*a*) above and then answer the questions below:

 (i) How did the Share Premium Account arise?

 (ii) How could the goodwill account have arisen?

(iii) What is the rate of return on net capital employed, and what is the significance of this figure?

(iv) Which of the reserves are capital reserves and which are revenue reserves, and what, in principle, is the difference between the two?

 (v) The company is relatively highly geared: what does this mean?

(8 marks)

(Total 30 marks)

SECTION B (Answer TWO questions from this section)

2. The following is a summary of the Ilkton Social Club's cash book for the year ended 30 June 19–7:

Payments	£	Receipts	£
Rent	625	Bar Sales	583
Rates	200	Entrance Fees	60
Lighting	182	Members' Subscriptions	2,220
Wages	760	Donations	350
Printing, Stationery	126		
General Expenses	79		
Creditors for bar purchases	430		
Improvements to Club House	388		
Repairs	310		

Additional information available from the records is as follows:

	30 June 19–6	30 June 19–7
	£	£
Creditors for—Wines and Spirits	190	130
—Printing	12	16
—Wages	27	38
—Lighting	21	37
Arrears of subscriptions	89	97
Subscriptions paid in advance	45	38
Bar Stock	148	123
Cash in hand	60	72
Cash at Bank	210	
Premises	7,500	
Fittings (net of depreciation)	1,740	

Depreciation on fittings is to be provided at 10 per cent on the reducing balance.

Required:

(a) A combined cash/bank account for the year ended 30 June 19–7, and

(b) an Income and Expenditure Account for the year ended 30 June 19–7, and a Balance Sheet as at that date.

(21 marks)

3. On 30 September 19–7 Alexander and Arnold completed their first year of trading in partnership. They shared profits and losses in the ratio Alexander $\frac{2}{3}$, Arnold $\frac{1}{3}$, and were entitled to 5 per cent per annum interest on capital. Arnold was also entitled to a salary of £1,490 per annum. They kept a debtors' ledger, a creditors' ledger for goods purchased, and a single entry record of all other transactions.

A summary of their cash transactions for the year ended 30 September 19–7, is given below:

Receipts:	£
Cash float for till	20
Cash sales	12,800
Receipts from debtors	44,900
Payments:	
Creditors—goods purchased	2,600
Drawings—Alexander	1,400
—Arnold	1,200
Lodgements with Bank	52,190

A summary of the partnership bank account for the year ended 30 September 19–7 is also available.

Bankings:	£
Capital paid in—Alexander	8,400
—Arnold	7,200
Banked from business	52,190
Cheques drawn:	
Premises	11,000
Cash float	20
Creditors for goods	50,200
Van	1,600
Sundry expenses	4,720

The partners also supplied the following details:	£
(i) Stock in hand at 30 September 19–7	6,000
(ii) Debtors at 30 September 19–7	5,400
(iii) Bad debts written off (already excluded from debtors balance)	200
(iv) Creditors at 30 September 19–7	3,000
(v) Depreciation is to be provided for the van at 10% on cost.	
(vi) Sundry expenses accrued	150

Required:
Prepare the Trading, Profit and Loss and Appropriation Account for the period ended 30 September 19–7 and a Balance Sheet as at that date.   (21 marks)

4.   (*a*) An inexperienced book-keeper has drawn up a trial balance for the year ended 30 June 19–7:

	DR	CR
	£	£
Provision for doubtful debts	200	
Bank overdraft	1,654	
Capital		4,591
Creditors		1,637
Debtors	2,983	
Discount received	252	
Discount allowed		733
Drawings	1,200	
Office furniture	2,155	
General expenses		829
Purchases	10,923	
Returns inwards		330
Rent and rates	314	
Salaries	2,520	
Sales		16,882
Stock	2,418	
Provision for depreciation of furniture	364	
	24,983	25,002

Required:
Draw up a 'corrected' trial balance, debiting or crediting any residual error to a Suspense Account.   (4 marks)

(*b*) Further investigation of the Suspense Account, ascertained in (*a*) above, reveals the following errors.

  (i) Goods bought from J. Jones amounting to £13 had been posted to his account as £33.

 (ii) Furniture which had cost £173 had been debited to the general expense account.

(iii) An invoice from Suppliers Ltd for £370 had been omitted from the Purchase Account, but credited to Suppliers Ltd account.

(iv) Sales on credit to A. Hope Ltd for £450 had been posted to the Sales Account, but not to the debtors' ledger.

 (v) The balance on the Capital Account had been incorrectly brought forward in the ledger, and should have been £4,291.

(vi) An amount of £86 received from A. Blunt, a debtor, in settlement of his account had been treated as a cash sale.

(vii) Discount allowed has been undertotalled by £35.

Required:
Prepare Journal Entries correcting each of the above errors and write up the Suspense Account.

(12 marks)

(c) There are several types of error which will not affect the balancing of a trial balance; these include errors of omission, commission and principle.
Explain what is meant by these terms and give an example of each.

(5 marks)
(Total 21 marks)

SECTION C (Answer TWO questions from this section)

7. (a) Distinguish clearly between the terms 'revenue' and 'receipt' and explain carefully what conditions must be satisfied before an accountant will recognize that revenue has been earned. (6 marks)

(b) Demonstrate by means of successive balance sheets (i.e. a new balance sheet drawn up after each transaction), the effects of the following transactions, assuming that revenue is recognized:
  (i) When cash is received; and
 (ii) When goods are invoiced.
A   Commence business with £50,000 cash
B   Buy premises for £20,000 cash
C   Buy stock on credit for £15,000
D   Pay business expenses in cash for £1,500
E   Sell stock which cost £8,000 on credit for £12,000
F   Pay creditors amount due
G   Collect cash (£9,000) on account from the debtors.

(8 marks)
(Total 14 marks)

Note: A suitable format for your answer to part (b) might be:

Trans-action Item	A	B	C	D etc.
Capital Profit Creditors				
Premises Stock etc.				

6. (a) The cash book of a business shows a favourable bank balance of £3,856 at 30 June 19–7. After comparing the entries in the cash book with the entries on the related bank statement you find that:
  (i) Cheques amounting to £218 entered in the cash book have not yet been presented for payment to the bank.

(ii) An amount of £50 entered on the debit side of the cash book has not been banked.

(iii) An amount of £95 has been credited by the bank to the account in error.

(iv) The bank has credited and then debited the bank statement with an amount of £48, being A. Jones' cheque which it forwarded on 1 July 19–7 marked 'insufficient funds—return to drawer'.

(v) Interest of £10 has been charged by the bank, but not yet entered in the cash book.

(vi) A cheque from a customer entered in the cash book as £88 had been correctly entered by the bank as £188.

Required:
(a) (i) Show the additional entries to be made in the cash book and bring down the corrected balance.

    (ii) Prepare a bank reconciliation statement. (8 marks)

(b) Explain the reasons for preparing a bank reconciliation statement.

(6 marks)

(Total 14 marks)

7. (a) Explain clearly what in principle determines which account balances should be transferred to (i) the Trading Account and (ii) the Profit and Loss Account. (4 marks)

(b) The following account is taken from the ledger of a retailer who keeps his own books of account.

Goods Account

	£			£
April 1 Balance	810	April 10 Sales		420
20 Purchases	336	28 Sales		370
29 Returns	16	May 2 Allowance on		
May 31 Purchases	410	defective goods		25
June 12 Purchases	380	15 Sales		580
30 Profit	203	18 Returns		40
		June 2 Stock (at cost)		
		taken for own		
		use		50
		30 Stock in hand		670
	2,155			2,155

Required:
Show by a series of ledger accounts how the recording of transactions could be improved to give more information as to the operation of the business and to facilitate a comparison with future periods. Explain briefly the purpose of each account. (10 marks)

(Total 14 marks)

THE INSTITUTE OF
COST AND MANAGEMENT ACCOUNTANTS
(Full Paper—with Answers)

Foundation Stage: Section A
Financial Accounting 1

Candidates should attempt FOUR QUESTIONS ONLY, all three questions from Section A and one from Section B.

In marking papers the examiners take into account clarity of exposition and logic of argument, effective arrangement and presentation, and use of concise and lucid English. Time allowed: 3 hours.

SECTION A

You are required to prepare the manufacturing, trading, profit and loss and appropriation accounts of H Limited for the year ended 31 December 19–5, and a balance sheet as at that date.

The trial balance of H Limited on 31 December 19–5 was:

	£	£
Ordinary shares of £1 each, fully paid		60,000
Share premium		5,000
General reserve		22,000
Profit and loss account, balance at 1 January 19–5		1,000
8% debentures, repayable in 15 years' time, secured on land and buildings		10,000
Land and buildings, at cost; and depreciation provision	40,000	9,000
Plant and machinery, at cost; and depreciation provision	60,000	34,000
Stock of materials	12,000	
Work-in-progress, at manufacturing cost	8,000	
Stock of finished products, at manufacturing cost	47,000	
Debtors and creditors	27,400	11,000
Provision for bad debts		1,400
Cash in hand and bank overdraft	100	21,500
Purchases of materials	100,000	
Purchases and sales of finished products	1,000	200,000
Manufacturing wages	8,300	
Manufacturing expenses	10,800	
Administrative expenses	22,500	
Selling and distribution expenses	37,000	
Debenture interest	800	
	£374,900	£374,900

Notes:
1. Stocks at 31 December 19–5 were:

	£
Materials	13,000
Work-in-progress	9,000
Finished products	51,000

2. Depreciation for 19–5 (not included in the trial balance) was £1,000 for land and buildings and £6,000 for plant and machinery.

3. Depreciation of land and buildings is to be apportioned between manufacturing, administration, and selling and distribution in the ratios of 60 per cent, 30 per cent and 10 per cent respectively.

4. Depreciation of plant and machinery is to be apportioned as follows:

	£
Manufacturing	5,000
Administration	800
Selling and distribution	200

5. Accrued and prepaid expenses at 31 December 19–5 were:

	Accrued	Prepaid
	£	£
Manufacturing wages	700	
Manufacturing expenses	500	100
Administration expenses	900	1,300
Selling and distribution expenses	1,400	200

6. A bad debt of £400 is to be written off and the provision for bad debts to be made equal to £1,700. These adjustments are to be regarded as selling and distribution expenses.

7. Provision is to be made for a corporation tax liability of £8,000 on the year's profits. This is to be regarded as a current liability.

8. Provision is to be made for a proposed ordinary dividend of £6,000.

9. A transfer of profit of £1,000 to general reserve is to be made.

(35 marks)

2. You are required to show:
(a) the correcting entries, in journal form (but without narratives), in respect of each of the mistakes mentioned below;
(b) the trial balance of the company at 31 December 19–5 after these corrections have been made.

A company's book-keeper has prepared a preliminary trial balance for the year ended 31 December 19–5 which is as follows:

	£	£
Ordinary share capital in £1 shares, fully paid		110.000
Retained profit, at 1 January 19–5		50.000
10% debentures		30,458
Debtors and creditors	77,240	60,260
Cash in hand and bank overdraft	1,000	5,036
Stocks and work-in-progress at 1 January 19–5	108,000	
Fixed assets at cost and depreciation provision at		
31 December 19–5	161,879	60,943
Depreciation for year	15,000	
Purchases and sales	300.297	400.000
Returns	4,370	4,630
Discounts allowed and received	9,760	6,740
Wages and salaries, net	12,146	
Payments of PAYE income tax	5,988	
Purchases of national insurance stamps, graduated		
pensions, etc.	4,766	
Creditors for PAYE at 1 January 19–5		900
Proceeds of sale of fixed assets		2,000
Rent, rates and insurance	18,036	
Postages, telephone and stationery	3,009	
Repairs and maintenance	2,124	
Advertising	4,876	
Packing materials	924	
Motor expenses	2,000	
Sundry expenses	1,000	
Debenture interest	4,000	
Capital surplus		6,478
Suspense account	1,030	
	£737,445	£737,445

When the book-keeper discovered that the preliminary trial balance did not balance he made it do so by opening a suspense account and entering the required amount on the appropriate side. A subsequent investigation showed that the following mistakes had been made:

1. 40,000 ordinary shares had been issued at a price of £1.25, and the proceeds credited to ordinary share capital account.

2. On 31 December debentures with a nominal value of £10,000 were purchased by the company on the open market for £9,542 and this amount was debited to the debenture account. It is considered that any surplus should be taken to capital reserve.

3. Bank charges of £1,000 have been completely omitted from the books. The bank account balance has not been reconciled.

4. Fixed assets with an original cost of £11,879 and accumulated depreciation of £10,943 have been sold for £2,000. This amount is shown as a separate item in the trial balance, and no entries have been made in the asset or depreciation provision accounts. Any surplus or deficit on sale should be taken to capital surplus.

5. Deductions of £6,088 for PAYE income tax and £1,766 for national insur-

ance, graduated pensions, etc., were made from employees' wages and salaries during the year. The company's contribution for national insurance, graduated pensions, etc., amounted to £3,000. No entries have been made for these items.

6.   In addition to allowing discount of £240 and receiving discount of £260, various debtors and creditors accounts amounting to £10,000 were set off by contra. No entries whatever have been made in respect of these items.

7.   Debtors amounting to £2,000 are bad and need to be written off.

8.   A debt of £1,000 written off as bad in a previous year has been recovered in full. The amount has been credited to the debtors account and deducted from the total of the other debtors.

9.   Goods returned from a debtor of £630 have been correctly entered in the debtors account, but by mistake were entered in the returns outwards journal.

10.   A payment for stationery of £234 was correctly entered in the cash book but debited in the ledger as £243.

11.   A payment of £76 for packing materials has been correctly entered in the cash book, but no other entry has been made.

12.   A payment of £124 for advertising has been debited to repairs and maintenance.

13.   A cheque payment of £26 for insurance has been recorded in all accounts as £62.

14.   A page in the purchase journal correctly totalled as £125,124 was carried forward to the top of the next page as £125,421.

All entries other than those given above are to be assumed to have been made correctly.

(35 marks)

3. From the information of bank transactions given below you are required to prepare a company's bank reconciliation statement at 31 December 19–5:

Company's Cash Book

19–5 December	£	19–5 December	£
2 Balance brought forward from previous page	985	2 D Limited	123
4 G & Company	3,041	2 M Corporation Ltd	402
4 P Limited	862	5 Wages	5,371
12 U & Sons	1,749	5 Petty Cash	89
12 P & Q	2,680	5 Q & Sons	326
12 N Associates	3,124	8 T Limited	48
15 A Limited	678	9 J & Sons	1,060
16 K & Company	2,413	12 Wages	5,288
16 X Limited	29	13 Petty Cash	73
22 J & Sons	1,840	13 Y Limited	145
24 S Limited	1,026	16 G & Company	36
24 XYZ Limited	3,003	19 Wages	5,197
24 R Electrical Limited	1,156	19 Petty Cash	81
30 Z Limited	2,331	22 U & Sons	247
31 C & Sons	704	22 S Limited	762
31 V Limited	85	22 B & Company	97
31 F Sons & Co Ltd	1,598	22 W & Sons	431
31 Balance carried forward	347	23 O Limited	158
		24 Wages	5,316
		24 Petty Cash	78
		29 H Limited	504
		29 N Associates	65
		30 M Corporation Ltd	120
		30 P & Q	234
		31 D Limited	1,145
		31 L Limited	93
		31 E Associates	162
	£27,651		£27,651

Statement of Company's Account from the Bank's Books

		Payments	Receipts		Balance
		£	£		£
December					
1					1,011
4	Sundry credit		3,903		
4	465267	26			
4	465272	402			4,486
5	465274	89			
5	465271	123			
5	465273	5,371		O/D	1,097
10	465276	48		O/D	1,145
12	465279	73			
12	Sundry credit		7,553		
12	465278	5,288			1,047
15	Sundry credit		678		1,725
16	Sundry credit		2,442		4,167
17	465275	326			3,841
19	465282	5,197			
19	465281	36			
19	465283	81		O/D	1,473
22	Sundry credit		1,840		367
23	465280	145			222
24	Sundry credit		5,185		
24	465285	762			
24	465290	78			
24	465289	5,316		O/D	749
29	465286	97		O/D	846
30	465288	158			
30	Sundry credit		2,331		1,327
31	Charges	531			
31	Sundry credit		2,387		
31	Dividends on Investment		1,608		
31	465291	504			
31	465293	120			4,167

(10 marks)

SECTION B

4. You are required to state, *briefly*:

(a) what you understand by 'depreciation';
(b) the reasons for making a provision for depreciation in balance sheets and profit and loss accounts;
(c) three accounting methods of providing for depreciation, with a description of each. What are the advantages and disadvantages of each method?

(20 marks)

5. You are required to state *briefly* what you understand by:

(a) the 'going concern' concept;
(b) the 'accruals' concept;
(c) the 'consistency' concept.

(20 marks)

THE INSTITUTE OF
COST AND MANAGEMENT ACCOUNTANTS

Foundation Stage: Section A
Financial Accounting 1

Candidates should attempt *three questions only*, both questions from Section A and one from Section B.

In marking papers the examiners take into account clarity of exposition and logic of argument, effective arrangement and presentation, and use of concise and lucid English.

Time allowed: 3 hours.

SECTION A

1. You are required for APF Limited, a company which manufactures and sells two products X and Y, to prepare in vertical and columnar form:

(*a*) manufacturing, trading and profit and loss accounts for products X and Y for the year ended 30 June 19–7;

(*b*) an appropriation account for the year;

(*c*) a balance sheet as at 30 June 19–7.

The trial balance of APF Limited at 30 June 19–7 was as follows:

	£	£
Ordinary shares of £1, issued and fully paid		
(authorized £800,000)		800,000
6% Preference shares of £1, issued and fully paid		
(authorized £200,000)		100,000
Share premium		150,000
Retained profits, at 1 July 19–6		441,000
Fixed assets, at cost £1,200,000	914,000	
Stocks at 1 July 19–6:		
materials	80,000	
work-in-progress:		
product X	34,000	
product Y	29,000	
finished products:		
product X	280,000	
product Y	150,000	
Debtors and creditors	306,000	90,000
Bad debts provision, at 1 July 19–6		12,500
Sales: product X (120,000 units)		1,200,000
product Y (180,000 units)		1,200,000
Purchases of materials	720,000	
Manufacturing		
wages:		
product X	100,000	
product Y	200,000	
Manufacturing expenses	208,000	
Creditor for royalties, at 1 July 19–6		62,000
Payments for royalties	391,000	
Administration expenses	139,500	
Selling and distribution expenses	214,000	
Cash at bank and in hand	290,000	
	4,055,500	4,055,500

The following information is given:
1.   Depreciation is to be provided on fixed assets at the rate of 10 per cent per annum on cost. Additions to fixed assets during the year amounted to £100,000, purchased on 31 December 19–6. The annual depreciation charge is to be apportioned among manufacturing, administration, and selling and distribution in the proportions of 8:1:1.

2.   During the year the cost of materials consumed was £300,000 for product X and £400,000 for product Y.

3.   Work-in-progress for both products was constant in quantity and value at the beginning and end of the year.

4.   Stocks of finished products were:

	1 July 19–6 in units	30 June 19–7 in units
Product X	40,000	20,000
Product Y	30,000	50,000

These stocks are to be valued at manufacturing cost (i.e. materials consumed, manufacturing wages, royalties, manufacturing expenses and the depreciation apportioned to manufacturing).

5.   Royalties of £2 per unit for product X and £1 per unit for product Y are payable on the quantities of products completely manufactured.

6.   Manufacturing expenses, including the apportionment of depreciation, are to be divided between the products in proportion to the number of completed articles transferred from the factory to the finished product stock. All products are transferred immediately on completion.

7.   Bad debts of £6,000 are to be written off and the bad debts provision is to be made equal to £15,000. These items are a selling and distribution expense.

8.   Administration expenses, including the proportion of depreciation, are to be divided between the products in proportion to the number of products sold.

9.   Selling and distribution expenses, including the proportion of depreciation, bad debts written off and any increase or decrease in the bad debts provision, are to be divided between the products in proportion to sales values.

10.   Prepaid and accrued expenses at 30 June 19–7 were:

	Prepaid £	Accrued £
Administration expenses	2,000	1,000
Selling and distribution expenses	1,000	7,000

11.   Provision is to be made for:

	£
Corporation tax on the year's profit	135,000
Preference dividend	6,000
Ordinary dividend	120,000

12.   Advance corporation tax on dividends is to be ignored.

(50 marks)

2. You are required to prepare for CDM Limited:

(a) trading, profit and loss and appropriation accounts for the year ended 31 March 19–7; and

(b) balance sheets as at 31 March 19–6 and 19–7.

CDM Limited is a retail shop which arrives at its selling prices by adding 33⅓ per cent to the cost of goods purchased for resale. Its position on the two dates was:

	31 March	
	19–6	19–7
	£	£
Issued ordinary share capital	70,000	70,000
Retained profit	9,000	
Sundry creditors	17,000	18,000
Creditor for taxation	5,000	
Proposed dividend	7,000	3,000
Fixed assets at cost	80,000	
Provision for depreciation of fixed assets	30,800	
Stock	28,000	29,000
Sundry debtors	24,000	20,000
Cash at bank	8,000	7,100
Provision for bad debts	1,200	1,000

The following information is given:

1. Cash payments made during the year were:
   (i) £117,100 to creditors for goods for re-sale;
   (ii) £10,000 for purchase of additional fixed assets;
   (iii) £4,900 for taxation;
   (iv) £14,500 in respect of dividends;
   (v) after allowing for cash received from debtors, the balance on the cash account represents the payment of business expenses.

2. Discount allowed amounted to £3,800, and the discount received to £2,900.

3. Bad debts written off during the year amounted to £1,700.

4. No accounts were settled by contra.

5. Depreciation of fixed assets during the year amounted to £8,700.

6. No fixed assets were sold during the year.

7. Taxation of £8,000 (inclusive of any adjustment of the previous years' liability) should be charged against the profit for the year. Advance corporation tax on dividends is to be ignored.

(25 marks)

Section B

3. From the following information you are required to show:

(a) the adjusted net profit of REB Limited for each of the years 19–4, 19–5 and 19–6;

(b) the weighted average annual profit of REB Limited during those years after adjustments; and

(c) the purchase price of the business of REB Limited.

On 31 December 19–6, AHD Limited purchased the business of REB Limited, the price being the amount on which the weighted average annual profit of REB Limited would represent a return of 20 per cent per annum.

The weighted average annual profit of REB Limited was to be taken as the weighted average of the net profits of the three years 19–4, 19–5 and 19–6, after making adjustments to the published profit figures of those years in respect of depreciation of plant and machinery and the valuation of stock-in-trade due to the application of different accounting principles. The weights to be applied were one for 19–4, two for 19–5 and three for 19–6.

The annual net profits of REB Limited as shown in the published accounts were:

	£
19–4	51,213
19–5	50,253
19–6	108,222

The plant and machinery was all purchased on 1 January 19–2 at a cost of £300,000, and the depreciation charged in the accounts was:

	£
19–4	24,300
19–5	21,870
19–6	19,683

It has been agreed between REB Limited and AHD Limited that depreciation should have been calculated at the rate of 10 per cent per annum by the straight line method.

The valuations of stock-in-trade were as follows:

	In published accounts	As adjusted
	£	£
At 31 December: 1973	76,771	69,571
19–4	73,908	59,808
19–5	71,260	75,160
19–6	91,420	68,620

(25 marks)

4. You are required for HST Limited to show:
(a) The journal entries for the transactions given below:
(b) the balance sheet as at 30 June 19–7.

The summarized balance sheet of HST Limited on 30 June 19–6 was as follows:

	Authorized	Issued and fully paid
	£	£
Share capital:		
Ordinary shares of £1 each	2,000,000	800,000
Reserves:		
Retained profit		207,000
		£1,007,000
Cash at bank, overdrawn		(550,000)
Other net assets		1,557,000
		£1,007,000

On 1 July 19–6, the company made a bonus issue of one ordinary share, fully paid, for every four held.

On 1 January 19–7, the company issued a prospectus inviting the general public to apply for 500,000 of the company's £1 ordinary shares at a price of £1.20 per share, payable £0.50 on application and £0.70 (including the premium) on allotment.

Applications were received for 900,000 shares by 7 January 19–7 and the directors dealt with these as follows:

 (i) applicants for 200,000 shares were allotted the full number of shares applied for;
 (ii) applicants for 600,000 shares were allotted half of the number of shares applied for; no money was returned to applicants, but the surplus on application was set off against the amount due on allotment;
 (iii) the remaining applicants received no allotment and their money was returned.

The full amount due on allotment was received on 31 January 19–7.

During the year to 30 June 19–7, the company made a net profit of £230,000. An improved cash at bank position arose, not only from the share transactions, but from trading results to the extent of £60,000.

No fixed assets were purchased or sold and no dividends were paid. Taxation is to be ignored.

(25 marks)

THE INSTITUTE OF CHARTERED SECRETARIES AND ADMINISTRATORS
(Full paper with answers)

Part 2
Financial Accounting 1

FOUR questions only to be attempted: Questions 1(A) and 3(A) are alternative to Questions 1 and 3 respectively.

Time allowed: 3 hours

1.   (Alternative to Question 1(A).)
 (i) Discuss the relationship between costs, expired costs and expenses in the measurement of profit and the valuation of assets, and
 (ii) 'A major objective of accounting for stocks is the proper determination of profit through the process of matching appropriate costs against revenues.' Evaluate the stock valuation assumptions of (*a*) first-in, first-out, (*b*) weighted average, and (*c*) last-in, first-out in the light of this objective during periods of steadily rising prices.

(25 marks)

1(A). (Alternative to Question 1.)
 (i) What is the working capital ratio?
 (ii) To what extent does it serve as an index of financial strength and stability?
 (iii) Discuss the factors which should be taken into account when evaluating the size of the working capital ratio.

(25 marks)

2. Following the preparation of the profit and loss appropriation account, the trial balances of B. K. Limited as at 30 September 19–5, and 30 September 19–6, respectively, were as follows:

	19–5		19–6	
	£	£	£	£
Cash at Bank	8,400		23,200	
Stocks at or below cost	27,000		37,000	
Debtors	25,000		36,200	
Provision for doubtful debts		900		1,500
Plant at cost	29,400		37,000	
Provision for depreciation on plant		14,800		18,600
Land and buildings at valuation	50,000		54,000	
Goodwill	22,000		22,000	
Creditors		10,800		17,200
*Dividends payable		5,600		11,000
*Provision for taxation		10,200		15,300
Authorized and issued share capital:				
9% Preference Shares of £1 each		80,000		80,000
Ordinary Shares of £1 each		30,000		30,000
*General reserve		5,000		14,000
Profit and loss appropriation		4,500		11,400
*Stock replacement reserve		—		6,400
*Asset revaluation reserve		—		4,000
	£161,800	£161,800	£209,400	£209,400

The following information is available:
(a) Dividends provided at 30 September 19–5 were paid in March 19–6.
(b) Tax assessed on profits earned for the year ended 30 September 19–5 amounted to £10,000 and was paid in April 19–6.
(c) An interim ordinary dividend of £2,000 was paid in May 19–6.

Required:
(i) A profit and loss appropriation statement for the year ended 30 September 19–6.
(ii) A balance sheet as at 30 September 19–6, showing clearly the capital employed, the working capital and the net asset value, and
(iii) Explain the purpose of each of the five items marked * in the trial balance.
(25 marks)

3. (Alternative to Question 3(A).)
T.B. purchased an existing business on 1 December 19–5 for the sum of £20,000. The assets acquired included: Premises £13,000, Fixtures and Equipment £1,400 and Trading Stock £3,600. He did not keep any accounting records in the first year but from documents produced by him the following facts were ascertained:
(i) All payments were made by cheque and all receipts banked immediately.
(ii) On 1 December 19–5, he opened a bank account in the sum of £1,200 and on 31 August 19–6 he deposited a further sum of £500 as working capital.
(iii) During the year he received £20,470 in respect of cash sales and payments from debtors. At 30 November 19–6 customers owed the sum of £1,656.

(iv) At the financial year end 30 November 19–6 he was not able to produce details of amounts paid to suppliers of goods during the year. The only information was a file of unpaid invoices from suppliers, which produced the amount owing to suppliers at 30 November 19–6 of £1,188.

(v) Payments made from his business bank account during the year included Rates £260, of which £52 was prepaid. Advertising £284, Fixtures and Equipment £220, Wages £1,568, General Expenses £386, Drawings £2,080, and £164 for household expenses.

(vi) At 30 November 19–6, the selling price of the trading stock was £6,400. T.B. normally expects to sell all goods which will produce for him a gross profit of 25 per cent on selling price. His closing bank balance was £884.

(vii) Fixtures and Equipment are to be depreciated at 10 per cent.

Required:
(a) A Summarized Cash Account for the year ended 30 November 19–6.
(b) The trading and profit and loss accounts for the year, and a balance sheet as at 30 November 19–6, and
(c) Comment on the first year of trading under the management of TB.

(25 marks)

3(A). (Alternative to Question 3.)
(a) Distinguish between internal check and internal audit, and outline the essential features of an internal control system.
(b) The extraction of the balances on the individual accounts in the Creditors' Ledger of G. X. Limited produced a total of £139,089. At the same date the balance on the Creditors' Ledger Control Account was £146,709. A subsequent investigation reveals the following errors:

(i) A credit balance of £472 had been incorrectly scheduled as a debit balance.
(ii) The following individual balances had been omitted from the list of balances as follows:
Debits £654
Credits £4,636
(iii) The Purchase Returns Day Book had been overcast by £4,000.
(iv) The debit side of the account of D.T. Limited in the Creditors' Ledger had been undercast by £184.
(v) R.S. Limited had been debited with £2,432 in respect of returns on purchases, but no entry had been made in the Purchase Returns Day Book.
(vi) A credit balance of £180 had been incorrectly scheduled as £810.
(vii) N.Y.'s account in the Creditors' Ledger is settled monthly by contra against the balance on his account in the Debtors' Ledger. His balance in the Creditors' Ledger at 31 July 19–6 was £2,888, and had been settled by a contra transfer. However, no entry had been made in the Control Account.
(viii) Discounts received in the sum of £2,128 for May 19–6 had been entered in the Cash Book and had been posted to the relevant personal accounts of creditors but no entry had been made in the Control Account.
(ix) An old credit balance in the Creditors' Ledger for £60 was set off against the relevant expense account in April 19–6. No entry in the Control Account had been effected in respect of the transfer.

Required:
A Statement bringing the total of the Creditors' Ledger Balances into reconciliation with the balance on the Creditors' Ledger Control Account.

(25 marks)

4. (*a*) C. K. Limited is considering the possibility of increasing profits by selling to new customers who will take longer to pay than the present average 1·5 months' credit extended to existing customers.

Upon investigation, it is revealed that the gross profit margin is 25 per cent and other expenses which vary with sales amount to 5 per cent of the value of sales. The following information on the various categories of debtors and their payment patterns are as follows:

Categories	Percentage of Debtors not expected to pay	Average time taken by debtors to pay
1	0	1·5 months
2	5	3 months
3	17·5	6 months
4	30	8 months
5	50	12 months
6	90	18 months

The Sales Manager has surveyed some possible customers and estimated that the following additional sales could be made:

Category	1	2	3	4	5	6
Amount (£)	10,000	24,000	36,000	10,000	5,000	4,000

Required:

A report on the profitability of accepting all, or any, of these additional sales indicating any additional factors which you feel should be taken into account.

(*b*) The following statements summarize the performances and asset positions of M.T., a sole trader, and L.X. Limited for the year ended 31 August 19–6.

	M.T. £	L.X. Limited £
Sales	50,000	50,000
Cost of sales	37,500	37,500
Gross profit	12,500	12,500
Operating expenses:		
Rent	—	1,500
Wages and salaries of employees	2,000	5,500
Other expenses	500	500
	2,500	7,500
Net profit	10,000	5,000

Net fixed and current assets at 31 August 19–6:

	M.T. £	L.X. Limited £
Freehold property, at cost, purchased in 1936	500	—
Cash	2,000	2,500
Other assets	47,500	47,500
	50,000	50,000

Both enterprises are essentially in the same line of business. The wages and salaries of L.X. Limited include a remuneration paid to E.B., managing director, of £3,500, other directors do not receive any remuneration.

Required:

A report comparing the performance results and business structure of the two enterprises.

(25 marks)

THE INSTITUTE OF CHARTERED SECRETARIES
AND ADMINISTRATORS

Part 2
Financial Accounting I

FOUR questions only to be attempted: Questions 1 (A) and 3 (A) are alternative to Questions 1 and 3 respectively.

Time allowed: 3 hours

(Alternative to Question 1 (A).)
1. 'There are three broad tests which are applied in the recognition of revenue:
  (i) the measurability test;
 (ii) the market transaction test, and
(iii) the performance test.'

Discuss the above statement, and provide examples of the recognition of revenue under different trading situations.

(18 marks)

1 (A). 'Four basic standards are recommended as providing criteria to be used in evaluating potential accounting information: relevance, verifiability, freedom from bias, and quantifiability.' Explain each of these four basic standards and provide an example of how each standard may play an important part in determining the valuation to be placed on unsold stock in trade.

(18 marks)

2. A practising consultant, you are approached by a recently established business enterprise. This enterprise is seeking financial accommodation from its bankers, who are prepared to provide overdraft facilities, but before final approval can be given the figure for maximum overdraft is required, and the time in the year when this will arise. The forecast cash balance at the end of the first period of trading is also required.

The following facts and forecasts are obtained from your client:

 (i) Trading will commence on 1 March 19-5, when £8,000 cash will be introduced into the business.

 (ii) Business premises costing £22,000 will be paid for at the commencement of trading. A mortgage of the business premises has been negotiated for the sum of £12,000, receivable on 31 March 19-5. This amount is to be repaid over ten years at quarterly intervals by equal instalments of capital plus interest at the rate of 12 per cent per annum on the balance outstanding at the end of each quarter. The first repayment plus interest will be made on 30 June 19-5.

(iii) A part of the premises will be let on a five year tenancy at £200 per calendar month (inclusive of property rates), payable quarterly in advance as from 1 April 19-5.

(iv) Sales are estimated at £8,000 per month for the first quarter, £12,000 per month for the second quarter, and thereafter £24,000 per month. All sales are on credit and will be paid for by the end of the month following that in which the sales have taken place.

(v) A minimum stock of goods to the value of £12,000 will be purchased in March 19–5 and will be maintained throughout the period.

(vi) Trade creditors will allow accounts to be settled in the month following that in which the goods are supplied.

(vii) Gross profit margin on cost is expected to be 25 per cent throughout the period.

(viii) Insurances are estimated to be £240 per annum payable on 1 March 19–5 in advance.

(ix) Property rates are estimated to be £360 per annum payable half-yearly in advance on 1 April and 1 October.

(x) Other business expenses are expected to be £1,000 per month to be paid at the end of the month following that in which they are incurred.

(xi) Private drawings are estimated to be £400 per month, except in the months of July and October when additional drawings of £200 in each month will be made.

Required:
(a) A monthly cash flow forecast for the period 1 March 19–5 to 31 December 19–5;
(b) Forecast Trading and Profit and Loss Account in respect of the above period,
(c) Forecast Balance Sheet as at 31 December 19–5; and
(d) Forecast Flow of Funds statement in respect of the above period, reconciling the opening and closing cash balances.

(35 marks)

3. (Alternative to Question 3 (A).)
(a) R is in business as a wine retailer, and on 30 April 19–5, his financial position was as follows:

	£		£
Capital	2,880	Motor van	450
Creditors	1,440	Stock	2,640
Bank overdraft	3,570	Debtors	4,800
	7,890		7,890

R has decided to offer his manager K a partnership in the business. It has been suggested that K should be invited to join R by accepting one of the following options:

(i) That R should be credited with £2,400 for existing goodwill, and that K should introduce cash equal to half the increased capital of R;

(ii) that K should pay to R £1,200 as a premium on entry as a partner, which will be retained in the business, and in addition K will introduce further cash equal to half the increased capital of R, or

(iii) that K should introduce £1,440 as capital, and that R should withdraw £900 cash in respect of existing goodwill.

Required:
The Balance Sheets which reflect each of the above suggestions, and a brief

report to K advising him which option to accept, with the knowledge that he will take a one-third share of profits.

(b) In the accounts of BD Limited the opening provision for Bad and Doubtful Debts is £4,000 but the financial manager decides that the closing provision is to be £3,000. You are required to answer the following questions that arise from the creation of this provision and its reduction:

(i) Why should a business create a Provision for Bad and Doubtful Debts?

(ii) Why should the financial manager wish to reduce this provision?

(iii) How will the reduction be shown in the accounts of BD Limited?

(iv) How will the amount of the new provision be shown in the Balance Sheet of BD Limited?

(25 marks)

3 (A). (Alternative to Question 3.)

Summarized financial information is available from SK (Retailers) Limited for the last three years, and is presented below:

	19–3 £000's	19–4 £000's	19–5 £000's
Credit sales	1,200	1,280	1,440
Cost of sales	720	780	892
Gross profit	480	500	548
Net profit	120	130	136
Current assets:			
Cash at bank	60	—	—
Debtors	160	200	300
Stock	240	300	440
Prepayments	10	20	20
Total current assets	470	520	760
Fixed assets:			
Land and buildings	816	1,068	1,744
Furniture, fittings and equipment	314	412	496
	1,130	1,480	2,240
Total assets	1,600	2,000	3,000
Current liabilities:			
Creditors	80	120	280
Bank overdraft	—	40	160
Dividends	60	60	76
Taxation	50	56	60
	190	276	576
Debentures	200	200	200
Shareholders' funds:			
Share capital (£1 shares fully paid)	1,200	1,500	2,200
Retained earnings	10	24	24
Total equities	1,600	2,000	3,000

Required:

(*a*) Computation of the following performance and solvency business indicators for the three years. End of year figures, rather than average figures, may be used where relevant.

 (i) Rate of return on capital employed.

 (ii) Net working capital.

(iii) Stock turnover.

(iv) Debtors collection period.

(*b*) Evaluate the working capital position in terms of its size, direction of change, and its composition over the three years.

(25 marks)

4.   HP Limited was incorporated in December 19–3 with an authorized share capital of £50,000 in ordinary shares of £1 each. On 1 January 19–4 all the shares were issued and paid for in full on that date. On 4 January 19–4 the company acquired PX Enterprises for a cash consideration of £38,000 paid over on the same day. The balance sheet of PX Enterprises as at 4 January 19–4 appeared as follows:

			£
Capital			25,460
represented by:			
Fixed assets:			
Land and buildings at cost			14,750
Fixtures and fittings at cost, less depreciation			4,000
Motor vehicles at cost, less depreciation			3,200
			21,950
Current assets:		£	
Stock at or below cost		7,750	
Debtors		4,200	
		11,950	
Less current liabilities:	£		
Creditors	5,600		
Bank overdraft	2,840		
		8,440	
			3,510
			25,460

The following additional information is available:

 (i) The fixed assets and stock were acquired at the values as disclosed in the balance sheet of PX Enterprises.

 (ii) The debtors and liabilities are not included in the acquisition.

(iii) During the year 19–4 sales amounted to £74,900, and purchases amounted to £58,100. On 31 December 19–4 trade debtors and trade creditors were £5,960 and £4,720 respectively.

(iv) Other business expenses during 19–4 were £7,300, including £210 unpaid on 31 December 19–4. Trading stock on 31 December 19–4 valued at or below cost was £8,740.

(v) Provision for depreciation is to be made at 10 per cent per annum on fixtures and fittings and 20 per cent on motor vehicles, based on the acquisition values.

Required:
(*a*) Trading and Profit and Loss Account for HP Limited for the year ending 31 December 19–4, and

(*b*) Balance Sheet in vertical form as at the same date.

(22 marks)

Answers to Exercises

28.1 (a) Year 1—Dr Stock 500 *add* Production Cost 1,600 *less* Stock 300, Gross Profit 1,200, Cr Sales 3,000.
Year 2—Dr Stock 300, Production Cost 2,800 *less* Stock 700, Gross Profit 600, Cr Sales 3,000.
Year 3—Dr Stock 700, Production Cost 1,600 *less* Stock 500, Gross Profit 1,200, Cr Sales 3,000.

(b) Year 1—Dr Stock 1,000, Production Cost 1,600 *less* Stock 600, Gross Profit 1,000. Cr Sales 3,000.
Year 2—Dr Stock 600, Production Cost 2,800 *less* Stock 1,400, Gross Profit 1,000, Cr Sales 3,000.
Year 3—Stock 1,400, Production Cost 1,600 *less* Stock 1,000, Gross Profit 1,000, Cr Sales 3,000.

(c) The production cost method (in this case) would be used.

(d) Different production levels.

28.2 (a) (i) $\dfrac{10,000}{60,000} \times (180,000+285,000+36,000+24,000+15,000 = 540,000)$
$= 90,000$

(ii) $\dfrac{10,000}{60,000} \times (180,000+285,000+15,000 = 480,000) = 80,000$

(b) Trading—Dr Factory Cost b/d 540,000 *less* Stock 80,000, Gross Profit 90,000, Cr Sales 550,000, Profit and Loss Dr Other Fixed Expenses 36,000, Other Variable Expenses 24,000, Net Profit 30,000, Cr Gross Profit 90,000.

(c) Trading—Dr Factory Cost b/d 540,000, Gross Profit 120,000, Cr Sales 660,000, Profit and Loss Dr: Other Fixed Expenses 36,000, Other Variable Expenses 24,000, Extra Advertising 5,000, Net Profit 55,000. Cr Gross Profit 120,000.

28.3 (a) FIFO (i) Aggregate 16,775; (ii) Article 1,375+450+4,800+2,800+ 5,400+500 = 15,325; (iii) Category 1,875+8,400+6,100 = 16,375.

(b) LIFO (i) Aggregate 16,775; (ii) Article 1,250+400+4,600+2,800+ 5,400+400 = 14,850; (iii) Category 1,650+8,100+6,100 = 15,850.

28.4 16,420 *add* Sales at Cost 584, Error Stock Extension 75, Stock Sheet Omitted 300, Goods Sent on Approval at Cost 260 = 17,639 *less* Sales Returns at Cost 68, Supplied for next year 180, Stock Sheet Overstated 30 = 17,361 Stock Figure.

28.5 31,410 *add* Sales at Cost 1,240, Goods Sent on Approval at Cost 320, Goods Agreed to be Returned at Cost 340, Undercast of Stock Sheet 50 = 33,360 *less* Returns at Cost 60, Goods Received for next year (840—360) 480, Goods held for Processing 360, Error in Sub-total 180, Overcast 100, Error in Extension 550 = 31.630 Stock Figure.

29.1 *Sinking Fund*—Cr 19–6 Profit and Loss 542·925, 19–7 Profit and Loss 542·925, Interest 27·145, 19–8 Profit and Loss 542·925, Interest 55·649, 19–9 Profit and Loss 542·925, Interest 85·578, 19–0 Profit and Loss 542·925, Interest 117·003. Dr Old Lease written off 3,000.
Investment Account—Dr 19–6 Cash 542·925, 19–7 Cash 570·070, 19–8 Cash 598·574, 19–9 Cash 628·503. Cr Sale of Investment 2,340·072.

29.2 *Loose Tools Account*—19–4 Dr Balance b/f 1,250, Cash 2,000, Wages 275, Materials 169, Cr Manufacturing Account 994, Balance c/d 2,700. 19–5 Dr Balance b/d 2,700, Cash 1,450, Wages 495, Materials 390, Cr Manufacturing account 1,695, Balance c/d 3,340. 19–6 Dr Balance b/d 3,340, Cash 1,890, Wages 145, Materials 290, Cr Manufacturing Account, 1897, Supplier 88, Balance c/d 3,680.

30.1 *Branch Stock Account*—Memo Column+Double Entry Column, Memo Column figures shown first—Dr Balance b/f 4,400: 3,300; Goods from Head Office 24,800: 18,600, Gross Profit (no memo) 5,850, Cr Branch Debtors 21,000: 21,000, Cash Sales 2,400: 2,400, Returns to Head Office 1,000: 750, Goods Stolen 600: 450, Profit and Loss Normal Wastage 100: 75, Branch Profit and Loss—Excess Wastage 152: 114, Balance c/f 3,948: 2,961.
Branch Debtors (no memo cols)—Dr Balance b/f 3,946. Branch Stock—Sales 21,000, Cr Bad Debts 148, Discounts Allowed 428, Bank 22,400. Balance c/f 1,970.

30.2 Branch Stock—Dr Balance b/f 3,600, Goods to Branch 32,460, Branch Debtors 354, Cr Returns 642, Branch Debtors 33,780, Balance c/d 1,962. Stock Deficiency 30. Branch Adjustment Account. Dr Branch Stock 107, Balance c/d (one-sixth of 1,962) 327, Stock Deficiency 30, Gross Profit 5,546, Cr Balance b/d 600, Branch Stock 5,410.
Branch Debtors Dr Balance b/d 2,575, Branch Stock 33,780, Cr Branch Stock (returns) 354, Cash 32,848, Discount Allowed 1,415, Balance c/d 1,738.
Branch Profit and Loss Dr Discount Allowed 1,415, Branch Expenses 4,027, Profit 104, Cr Gross Profit 5,546.

30.3 (*a*) Branch Current—Dr Balance b/f 20,160, Goods sent 23,160, Expenses paid 6,000, Net Profit 3,500, Cr Cash 30,000, Goods Returned 400, Balance c/d 22,420.
(*b*) Proof—Branch Assets *less* Branch Liabilities = Branch on Current Account. Indicates: Amount of money invested in Branch.

30.4 Trading—Dr Stock Head Office 3,571, Branch 1,206, *add* Purchases Head Office 37,276, Goods sent to Branch Head Office *less* 9,706, Branch *add* 9,706, *less* Stock Head Office 4,390, Branch 1,362, Gross Profit Head Office 12,062, Branch 4,162, Cr Sales Head Office 38,813, Branch 13,712. Profit and Loss—Salaries and Wages Head Office 5,116, Branch 1,612, Rent Head Office 1,547, Branch 536, General Expenses Head Office 418, Branch 418, Branch 74, Depreciation Head Office 940, Branch 320, Administrative

Expenses Head Office *less* 300, Branch *add* 300, Net Profit Head Office 4,341, Branch 1,320. Gross Profit Head Office 12,062, Branch 4,162.

Balance Sheet—Capital: Balance 1 July 19–5. 15,844 *add* Net Profit 5,661, *less* Drawings 4,800, = 16,705, Creditors 4,107. Fixed Assets 12,600 *less* Depreciation 1,260 = 11,340, Stocks 5,752, Debtors 1,293, Bank and Cash 2,427, Balance Sheet totals 20,812.

30.5 (a) Trading—Dr Stock Head Office 13,000, Branch 4,400, Purchases Head Office 37,000, Goods from Head Office, Branch 17,200, *less* Stocks Head Office 14,440, Branch 6,570, Gross Profit Head Office 21,440, Branch 10,970. Profit and Loss Dr Salaries Head Office 4,500, Branch 3,200, Administrative Expenses Head Office 1,440. Branch 960. Carriage Head office 2,200, Branch 960. General Expenses Head Office 3,200, Branch 1,800, Provision for Bad Debts Head Office 50, Depreciation Head Office 150. Branch 110. Manager's commission Branch 360, Net Profit Head Office 9,900, Branch 3,600, Cr Gross Profit Head Office 21,440, Branch 10,970, Provision for Bad Debts not required 20. Appropriation Account Dr Packer commission 900, Interest on Capital P 840, S 240, Balance divided P three-quarters 8,640, S quarter 2,880, Cr Net Profits b/d Head Office 9,900, Branch 3,600.

(b) *Balance Sheet*—Capitals P 14,000, S 4,000, Current Accounts Profits P 8,640, S 2,880, Interest on Capital P 840, S 240, Commission P 900, *less* Drawings P 2,500, S 1,200, = P 7,880, S 1,920, Creditors 6,200, Bank Overdraft 1,350, Manager's commission 120, Balance Sheet totals 35,470. Furniture 2,600 *less* Depreciation 1,110, = 1,490, Stock 21,810, Debtors 10,000 *less* Provision 830, Cash and Bank 3,000.

(c) *Branch Current Account*—Dr Balance b/f 6,800, Administrative Expenses 960, Profit 3,600, Cr Goods in Transit c/d 800, Cash in Transit c/d 2,400, Balance c/d 8,160. Balance proved Furniture 1,100 *less* Depreciation 460, Stock 6,570, Debtors *less* Provision 2,820, *less* Creditors 400, Manager's Commission 120, Bank Overdraft 1,350 = 8,160.

31.1 *Cases Stock Accountant*—Dr Stocks b/d Factory (600) 900, at Customers (4,000) 6,000, Cash Purchases (5,000) 10,000, Profit on cases service to Profit and Loss 34,525, Cr Sales (45) 100, Cases kept by Customers (800) 4,800, Profit on cases hire 34,000, Stocks c/d Factory (2,150) 3,225, at Customers (6,200) 9,300.

Cases Suspense Account—Dr Customers cases returned (14,000) 84,000, Cases kept (800) 4,800, Profit on cases hire 34,000, Balance c/d (6,200) 37,200, Cr Balance b/d (4,000) 24,000, Customers—Cases kept (17,000) 136,000.

31.2 *Cases Stock Account*—Dr Stocks b/d at Warehouse (9,600) 19,200, At Customers (6,100) 12,200, Purchases (18,000) 54,000, Profit to Profit and Loss 37,025, Cr Returned to Supplier (4,000) 11,610, Cash scrapped (3,500) 55, Deficit (420) no money, kept by Customers (5,800) 23,200, Profit on cases hire 47,600, Stocks c/d (4,800) 9,600, Warehouse (15,180) 30,360.

Cases Suspense Account—Dr Returned (43,100) 172,400, kept by Customers (5,800) 23,200, Profit on cases hire 47,600, Balance c/d (4,800) 19,200, Cr Balance b/d (6,100) 24,400, sent to Customers (47,600) 238,000.

32.1 Royalties—Debits 19–1 600, 19–2 800, 19–3 1,200, 19–4 1,400, Credits—transferred to Trading Account 19–1 600, 19–2 800, 19–3 1,200, 19–4 1,400.

Smoker—19–1 Cr Royalties 600, Short Workings 400, 19–2 Dr Cash 1,000, Cr Royalties 800, Short Workings 200, 19–3 Dr Cash 1,000, Short Workings 200, Cr Royalties 1,200, 19–4 Dr Cash 1,000, Short Workings 200, Cr Royalties 1,400, 19–5 Dr Cash 1,200.

Short Workings 19–1 Dr 400, 19–2 Dr 200, 19–3 Cr 200, written off to Profit and Loss 200, 19–4 Cr 200.

32.2 J.B. 19–3 Dr Cash 500, Cr Royalties 430, Short Workings 70, 19–4 Dr Cash 500, Cr Royalties 490, Short Workings 10, 19–5 Dr Short Workings 45, Cash 500, Cr Royalties 545, 19–6 Cash 525, Cr Royalties 525. Royalties—19–3 Dr 430, Cr Man 430, 19–4 Dr 490, Cr Man 490, 19–5 Dr 545, Cr Man 545, 19–6 Dr 525, Cr Man 525.

Short Workings 19–3 Dr JB 70, 19–4 Dr JB 10, 19–5 Cr JB 45, Written off to Profit and Loss 35.

32.3 Royalties—Debits all Shipton, Credits all Profit and Loss, 19–2 Dr 200, Cr 200, 19–3 Dr 400, Cr 400, 19–4 Dr 600, Cr 600, 19–5 Dr 500, Cr 500.

Shipton—19–2 Cr Royalties 200, Short Workings 300, 19–3 Dr Cash 500, Cr Royalties 400, Short Workings 100, 19–4 Dr Cash 500 Short Workings 200, Cr Royalties 600, 19–5 Dr Cash 400 Short Workings 100, Cr Royalties 500, 19–6 Dr Cash 400.

Short Workings—19–2 Dr S 300, 19–3 Dr 100, 19–4 Cr S 200 Profit and Loss, Short Workings written off 100, 19–5 Cr S 100.

33.1 *Motors Account*—Dr Vendor 6,000.

Vendor Account—Dr 19–3 J Cash 846, D 2,000, Balance c/d 3,566, Cr J Motors 6,000, D H.P. Interest 412. 19–4 Dr December Cash 2,000, Balance c/d 1,851, Cr January Balance b/d 3,566, December H.P. Interest 285, 19–5 Dr December Cash 2,000, Cr January Balance b/d 1,851, December H.P. Interest 149.

Depreciation Account—Cr 19–3, 600, 19–4, 540, 19–5, 486.

Balance Sheet 31 December 19–3—Motors 6,000, *less* Depreciation 600, *less* Owing on H.P. 3,566 = 1,834.

33.2 (a) Machinery—Dr XY 1,046. Provision for Depreciation Account—Cr 19–3, 105, 19–4, 94, 19–5, 85.

XY & Co. Account—19–3, Dr January Bank 300, December 300, Balance c/d 521, Cr Machinery 1,046, H.P. Interest (10 per cent of 746) 75, 19–4, Dr Bank 300, Balance c/d 273, Cr Balance b/d 521, H.P. Interest 52, 19–5 Dr Bank 300, Cr Balance b/d 273, H.P. Interest 27.

(b) *Balance Sheet* 19–3—Machinery at cost 1,046, *less* Depreciation 105, owing on H.P. 521 = 420.

33.3 (a) *Motor Vehicles Account*—Dr 19–4 June 30 H.P. Co. (UE) 850, 19–5, January 31 H.P. Co. (XA) 910, Cr 19–5 August 1 Disposal (UE) 850, 19–6 February 28, Balance c/d 910.

(b) *Provision for Depreciation Account*—19–5, August 1 Disposal (UE) 170, 19–6, 28 February, Balance c/d 364, Cr 19–5, 28 February, Profit and Loss Account (UE) 170, (XA) 182, 19–6, 28 February, Profit and Loss 182.

(c) *H.P. Co. Account*—Dr 19–4, June Cash (UE) 94, 19–5, January Cash (XA) 118, February Cash $(8 \times 24 + 1 \times 26)$ 218, July Cash (5×24) 120, August Cash 500, 19–6, February Cash (12×26) 312, Balance c/d 506, Cr 19–4, June Motors (UE) 850, 19–5, January Motors 910, February Profit and Loss Interest $(8 \times 3 + 1 \times 4)$ 28, August Profit and Loss Interest (5×3) 15, August Disposals 17, 19–6, February Profit and Loss Interest (12×4) 48.

(d) *Assets Disposal Account*—Dr 19–5, Motors 850, H.P. Co. 17, Profit and Loss 3, Cr Depreciation 170, Cash 700.

Workings—UE Cash Price 850, *less* Deposit 94 = 756+Interest 108 = 864 payable in 36 instalments, 24 per time. Interest content per instalment $\frac{1}{36} \times 108$ = 3. XA Cash price 910, *less* deposit 118 = 792, *add* interest 144 = 936 payable in 36 instalments, 26 per time. Interest content per instalment $\frac{1}{36} \times 144$ = 4.

33.4 *Trading*—Dr Purchases 60,000 *less* stock (50×60) 3,000 = 57,000, Provision unrealized profit and interest 21,280 (53,200/95,000 × 38,000) Gross Profit 16,720, Cr Sales at H.P. Prices 95,000, Profit and Loss Dr Rent 2,250, Wages 4,300, General Expenses 5,135, Net Profit 5,035, Cr Gross Profit 16,720.

Balance Sheet—Fixed Assets 5,000, Current Assets Stock 3,000, H.P. Debtors 53,200 *less* Provision Unrealized Profit and Interest 21,280 = 31,920, Bank 5,315, Balance Sheet totals 45,235. Capital—Balance 38,000+ Net Profit 5,035, *less* Drawings 2,000 = 41,035, Creditors 4,200.

35.1 *Bank Account*—Dr Application 20,000, Allotment (30,000 *less* excess applications 5,000) 25,000, First Call $(119,200 \times 0·25)$ 29,800, Second Call $(119,200 \times 0·375)$ 44,700, D. Regan $(800 \times 0·9)$ 720.

D. Regan Account—Dr Ordinary Share Capital 800, Cr Bank 720, Forfeited Shares 80.

Application and Allotment Account—Dr Ordinary Share Capital 45,000, Cr Bank 20,000 and 25,000.

Ordinary Share Capital Account—Dr Forfeited Shares 800, Balance c/d 120,000, Cr Application and Allotment 45,000, First Call 30,000, Second Call 45,000, D. Regan Shares Issued 800.

First Call Account—Dr Ordinary Share Capital 30,000, Cr Bank 29,800, Forfeited Shares 200.

Second Call Account—Dr Ordinary Share Capital 45,000, Cr Bank 44,700, Forfeited Shares 300.

Forfeited Shares Account—Dr First Call 200, Second Call 300, D. Regan 80, Transfer to Share Premium 220, Cr Ordinary Share Capital 800.

35.2 *Bank Account*—Dr Application $(32,600 \times 0·5)$ 16,300, Allotment $(20,000 \times 1·5$ *less* Excess Application Monies 5,000) 25,000, First Call $(19,900 \times 2)$ 39,800, Second Call $(19,880 \times 1)$ 19,880, B. Mills (120×4) 480.

Application and Allotment Account—Dr Bank Refunds 1,300, Ordinary Share Capital 40,000, Cr Bank 16,300, Bank 25,000.

First Call Account—Dr Ordinary Share Capital 40,000, Cr Bank 39,800, Forfeited Shares 200.

Second Call Account—Dr Ordinary Share Capital 20,000, Cr Bank 19,880, Forfeited Shares 120.

Ordinary Share Capital Account—Dr Forfeited Share 600, Balance c/d

100,000: Cr Application and Allotment 40,000, First Call 40,000, Second Call 20,000, B. Mills (reissue) 600.

Forfeited Shares—Dr First Call 200, Second Call 120, B. Mills 120, Transfer to Share Premium 160: Cr Ordinary Share Capital 600. B. Mills—Dr Ordinary Share Capital 600: Cr Bank 480, Forefeited Shares 120.

36.1 *Balance Sheet*—Fixed Assets 11,750, Stock 3,400, Debtors 1,400, Bank 11,100, Discounts on Debentures 160. Totals 27,810. Issued Capital 11,800, Capital Redemption Reserve Fund 1,200, Profit and Loss Account 5,810, 7 per cent Debentures 8,000, Current Liabilities 1,000.

Workings—Share Premium Account: 550+Premium on Shares Issued 90, *less* Premium on Shares Redeemed 750, *less* Debenture Discount written off 80, leaving 190 deficit written off Profit and Loss. Profit and Loss Account 7,200 *less* Shares Redeemed not covered by new Issue 1,200 and Debit Balance on Share Premium Account 190 = 5,810.

Bank 5,200+Debentures Issued at Discount 7,760+Shares Issued at a Premium 1,890, *less* Shares Redeemed at a Discount 3,750 = 11,100.

36.2 Redeemable Preference Share Capital Dr 20,000, Redeemable Preference Shareholders Cr 20,000. Profit and Loss Account Dr 2,000, Redeemable Preference Shareholders Cr 2,000. Redeemable Preference Shareholders Dr 22,000, Bank Cr 22,000. Profit and Loss Appropriation Dr 22,000. Capital Redemption Reserve Fund Cr 22,000.

36.3 (a)   (i) Bank Dr 15,000, Profit and Loss Dr 2,500, Investments Cr 17,500.

    (ii) Redeemable Preference Share Capital Dr 65,000, Premium on Redemption of Preference Shares Dr 4,875, Preference Shares Redemption Account Cr 69,875.

    (iii) Application and Allotment of Ordinary Shares Account Dr 39,375, Ordinary Share Capital Cr 31,500, Share Premium Cr 7,875.

    (iv) Bank Dr 39,375, Application and Allotment of Ordinary Shares Cr 39,375.

    (v) Preference Share Redemption Dr 69,875, Bank Cr 69,875.

    (vi) Profit and Loss Dr 33,500, Capital Redemption Reserve Fund Cr 33,500.

    (vii) Share Premium Account Dr 4,875, Premium on Redemption of Preference Shares Cr 4,875.

(b) *Balance Sheet*—Sundry Assets 346,000, Bank 14,500, Totals 360,500. Issued Share Capital 256,500, Capital Redemption Reserve Fund 33,500, Share Premium Account 3,000, Profit and Loss 10,000, Sundry Creditors 57,500.

Workings—Ordinary Shares to be Issued: Profit and Loss per Balance Sheet 46,000, *less* Loss on Investments 2,500 *less* Amount to be left 10,000 = Available for Redemption 33,500. Shares being Redemmed 65,000, therefore 31,500 Value to be Issued (63,000 shares of 0·5 each). Bank Balance—At Start 30,000 *add* Sale of Investments 15,000 *add* Issue of Ordinary Shares 39,375, *less* Redemption of Preference Shares 69,875 = 14,500.

36.4 Ordinary Share Capital Cr Balance b/f 75,000, Ordinary Share Applicants 25,000, Bonus Issue 50,000. Share Premium Account Cr Ordinary Share Applicants 6,250, Dr Redeemable Preference Shareholders 6,250. Redeemable Preference Share Capital Account Dr Redeemable Preference

Shareholders 25,000, Cr Balance b/f 25,000. Redeemable Preference Share-holders Account—Dr Cash 31,250, Cr R.P. Share Capital 25,000, Share Premium 4,375, Profit and Loss 1,875. Profit and Loss Dr R.P. Shareholders 1,875, Shareholders Part Bonus Issue 10,000. Cr Balance b/f 30,000. Ordinary Share Applicants Dr Ordinary Share Capital 25,000, Share Premium 6,250, Cr Cash 31,250. Shareholders Account Dr O.S. Capital 50,000, Cr General Reserve 40,000, Profit and Loss 10,000. In the Balance Sheet shown as 150,000 Ordinary Shares of £1 each 150,000. Profit and Loss Account 18,125.

36.5 (*a*) *Six per cent Debentures Account*—Dr Cash (5,000 bought at 99 for cancelling) 4,950, Sinking Fund—Profit on Cancellation 50, Cash (75,000 Debentures repaid at 101) 75,750. Cr Balance b/f 80,000, Sinking Fund Premium in Redemption 750.

(*b*) *Sinking Fund Account*—Dr S.F. Investment Loss 150, S.F. Investment Further Loss, 1,600, Debentures Account Premium on 75,000 repaid 750, General Reserve: Debentures Redeemed 80,000 and Balance of fund no longer needed 750. Cr Balance b/f 79,350, Debentures Account Profit on Cancelled Debentures 50, Cash Interest on S.F. Investments 3,850.

(*c*) *Sinking Fund Investments Account*—Dr Balance b/f 79,350, Cr S.F. Cash Sale of Investments (cost 5,650) 5,500, S.F., Loss on Sale of Investments 150. S.F., Cash Sale of Investments (cost 73,700) 72,100. S.F., Loss on Sale of Investments 1,600.

36.6 (*a*) *Six per cent Debentures Account*—Dr Cash (Interest) 3,600, Debentures Redemption (debentures bought for cancelling) (Capital) 10,000, Cash (Interest) 3,300, Debenture Redemption (debentures redeemed on maturity) (Capital) 110,000. Cr Balance brought forward (Capital) 120,000, Transfer of Interest to Profit and Loss 6,900.

(*b*) *Sinking Fund Investments*—Dr Balance b/f 117,490, S.F. Account Profit on Realization (10,050–9,750) 300, S.F. Account Profit on Realization 2,460. Cr Cash 10,050, Cash 110,200.

(*c*) *Sinking Fund*—Dr Premium on Redemption 2,200, Transfer to Reserve 125,200, Cr Balance b/f 117,490, Profit on Realization of Investments 300, Profit on Redemption 200, Income from Investment 6,950, Profit on Investments Realized 2,460.

(*d*) *Debenture Redemption Account*—Dr Cash 9,800, S.F. Account 200, Redemption (at 102) 112,200. Cr 6 per cent Debentures Cancelled 10,000, 6 per cent Debentures Redeemed 110,000, S.F. Account Premium 2,200.

37.1 *Trading*—Dr Stock 6,385 *add* Purchases 56,660, *less* stock 7,115, = 55,930, Gross Profit 14,400, Cr Sales 70,330, Profit and Loss Dr Wages and Salaries 6,420, Rates 220, General Expenses 4,040, Depreciation 560, Net Profit 3,160, Cr Gross Profit 14,400.

Balance Sheet—F.A. Goodwill 4,745 (Purchase price 20,000–assets purchased 15,170+85 Provision Bad Debts not required = 4,745) Property 7,500, Motors 2,800 *less* Depreciation 560, Furniture 770, C.A. Stock 7,115, Debtors 6,150, Prepaid Expenses 50, Bank 3,520 Balance Sheet totals 32,090. Share Capital 25,000, Profit and Loss 3,160, Creditors 3,930.

Workings—Purchase Price satisfied by: Cash 9,315, Bank Overdraft paid off 685, Issue Shares 10,000 = 20,000.

37.2 (*a*)   (i) Debits Stock 9,800, Debtors 11,550, Freeholds 25,000, Motors 3,600, Goodwill 10,000, Credits Creditors 7,950, Best 52,000. Debit Best 52,000, Credits Preference Share Capital 10,000, Cash 42,000.

(ii) Debit Ordinary Shareholders 50,000, Credits Ordinary Share Capital 40,000, Share Premium 10,000, Debit Cash 50,000, Credit Ordinary Shareholders 50,000.

(*b*)   *Profit and Loss Appropriation*—Dr Reserves 4,000, Preference Dividend 800, Proposed Dividend 4,800, Balance c/f 2,520, Cr Net Profit Distributable (16,240 *less* 4,120) 12,120.

Balance Sheet—Fixed Assets Goodwill 10,000, Freeholds 25,000, Motors 5,700, *less* Depreciation 1,425, Current Assets Stock 11,104, Debtors 14,306 *less* Provision Bad Debts 700, Cash and Bank 19,011, Preliminary Expenses 850, Balance Sheet totals 83,846. Issued Capital—Preference 10,000, Ordinary 40,000, Reserves—Pre-incorporation Profits 4,120, General (?) 4,000, Profit and Loss 2.520, Current Liabilities. Creditors 8,406, Proposed Dividend 4,800.

37.3 (*a*)   *Journal*—Dr Land, Buildings and Plant 115,000, Stock 9,000, Debtors 3,800, Goodwill 9,390, Cr Metals Ltd 137,000, Provision for Doubtful Debts 190, Debits Metals Ltd 137,000, Discounts on Debentures 500, Credits Share Capital 80,000, Share Premium 20,000, Debentures 12,500, Cash 25,000.

(*b*)   *Journal:*

(i) Dr Realization 86,200, Cr Goodwill 5,000, Stock 67,000, Stock 10,400, Debtors 3,800.

(ii) Dr Realization 2,000. Cr Debentures 2,000.

(iii) Dr Engineers 137,000, Cr Realization 137,000.

(iv) Dr Cash 25,000, Shares in Engineers Ltd 100,000, Debentures of Engineers 12,000, Cr Engineers Ltd 137,000.

(v) Dr Creditors 2,000, Cr Cash 2,000.

(vi) Dr Share Capital 50,000, General Reserve 18,000, Profit and Loss 9,000, Realization—Profit on Sale 48,800, Cr Sundry Members 125,800.

(vii) Dr Sundry Members 125,800, Cr Shares in Engineers 100,000, Cash, 25,800.

37.4 See workings later:

(*a*)   (i) A holder 1,000 shares in X 57,200÷50 = 1,144 shares.

(ii) A holder 100 shares in Y 12,800÷200 = 64 shares.

Assets—Goodwill X 5,000, Premises X 45,000, Y 17,000, Stock X 15,000, Y 1,575, Debtors X 6,650, Y 1,425, Bank X 4,850, Total Assets X 76,500, Y 20,000, *less* Bank Overdraft Y 1,000, Creditors X 5,000, Y 3,000, = X 71,500, Y 16,000. Shares issued to X 57,200 shares valued at 1·25 = 71,500, to Y 12,800 shares valued at 1·25 = 16,000.

(*b*)   Fixed Assets Goodwill 5,000, Premises 62,000, Current Assets Stock 16,575, Debtors 8,500 *less* Bad Debts. Provision 425, Bank 3,850, Balance Sheets totals 95,500. Issued Share Capital 70,000, Share Premium 17,500, Creditors 8,000.

37.5 Property B 44,800, G 14,400, Plant B 30,570, G 17,095, Stock B 11,100 *less* 10 per cent 1,110 = 9,990, G 8,950 *less* 10 per cent 895 = 8,055, Debtors B 8,800 *less* 12 per cent 1,100 = 7,700, G 6,400 *less* 12½ per cent 800 = 5,600, Bank B 43,680, G 25,330, Investment G 10,000, Goodwill (following notes)

B 16,840, G 12,200, *less* Creditors B 21,580, G 12,680, Net Assets B 132,000, G 80,000. Number of Ordinary Shares B 60,000, G 25,000, Value per share B 2·2, G 3·2. Workings—Calculation goodwill: Profits 19–4 B 17,450, G 10,760, 19–5 B 19,340, G 12,290, 19–6 B 21,470, G 14,450, *less* Investment Income G 1,800, *less* Standard Profit B 3 × 11,000 = 33,000, G 3 × 5,800 = 17,400, Adjusted Net Profit for three years B 25,260, G 18,300, Average Profit B 8,420, G 6,100, Goodwill two years purchase B 16,840 G 12,200. Calculation Standard Profit—Assets (Balance Sheet) B 131,580, G 80,680, *less* Investment G 10,000, *less* Creditors B 21,580, G 12,680, Net Assets B 110,000, G 58,000, Standard Profit 10 per cent B 11,000, G 5,800.

37.6 Profit and Loss—Dr Expenses Pre 3,840, Post 15,360, Directors' Post 600, Profit Pre 2,160, Post 8,040, Cr Gross Profit Pre 6,000, Post 24,000.

37.7 (*a*) B = pre-incorporation, A = after incorporation. Salaries of vendors B 1,695, Wages B 2,160, A 6,480, Rent B 215, A 645, Distribution B 480, A 1,200, Commission B 200, A 500, Bad Debts B 104, A 210, Interest B 990, A 660, Directors' Remuneration A 4,000, Directors' Expenses A 515, Depreciation—Motors B 400, A 1,500, Machinery B 125, A 450, Bank Interest A 168, Net Profit B 1,631, A 3,672, Cr Gross Profit B 8,000, A 20,000.

Workings—Distribution and Commission split on basis of sales. Depreciation—Motors To 31 March 19–5, 20% × 3 mos × 7,000+20% × 1 month × 3,000 = 400.

After 20% × 9 mos × 7,000+20% × 9 mos × 3,000 = 1,500.

Machinery—To 31 March 19–5. 10% × 5,000 × 3 mos = 125. After 10% × 5,000 × 9 mos+10% × 3,000 × 3 mos = 450.

(*b*) Transfer to a Capital Reserve.

(*c*) Charge to a Goodwill Account.

37.8 *Trading*—Dr Stock 4,294 *add* Purchases 19,678 *less* Stock 3,542, Gross Profit B 2,000, A 5,500, Cr Sales 27,930, Profit and Loss Dr Office Salaries B 416, A 1,248, Office Expenses B 60, A 180, Rent B 41, A 123, Directors' Salary A 1,500, Carriage Out B 44, A 121, Commission B 162, A 451, Preliminary Expenses A 156, Pre-incorporation Profit transferred to Goodwill 1,275, Balance c/f 1,721, Cr Gross Profit B 2,000, A 5,500.

Balance Sheet—Fixed Assets 12,500, Goodwill 3,725, Current Assets 10,120, Stock 3,542, Balance Sheet totals 29,887, Share Capital 25,000, Profit and Loss, 1,721, Current Liabilities 3,166.

Workings—Calculation Ratio between Pre- and Post-incorporation Sales: January 2, February 1, March 1 = 4, April to October 1 each November and December 2 each = 11. The Gross Profit, Carriage Outwards and Commission split in this ratio 4 : 11. The other expenses either post-incorporation or split on time basis 1 : 3.

Goodwill—Surplus purchase consideration 25,000 over Switch Capital Account 20,000 = 5,000 *less* Pre-incorporation Profits 1,275 = 3,725.

37.9 *Asset Basis*—Goodwill revalued 5,000+Other Assets 45,000 = 50,000, *less* Creditors 9,000 and Debentures 10,000 = Total Value of Shares 31,000.

Yield Basis. Average Profit 4,000. If this = 10 per cent then full value is 40,000.

37.10 Adjusted Profits 10—4—Profit 16,400+Motor Expenses saved 620, +Depreciation Overcharged 1,500, +Wrapping Expenses saved 420, +Bank Interest 180 = 19,120 *less* Extra Management Remuneration 1,500, Invest Income 290, Rents Received 940 = 16,390.

Adjusted Profit 19–5—Profits 23,920+Motor Expenses 660, Depreciation Overcharged 700, +Wrapping Expenses saved 480+Bank Overdraft interest 590+Preliminary Expenses 690 = 27,400 *less* Undervaluation Opening Stock 1,900, Extra Man Remuneration 1,500, Invest Income 340, Rents Received 420, Profit on Property 4,800 = 18,080.

Adjusted Profits 19–6—Profit 19,650+Motor Expenses saving 700+Depreciation Overcharged 60+Wrapping Expenses 510+Bank Overdraft Interest 740 = 21,660 *less* Extra Man Remuneration 1,500, Invest Income 480 = 19,680.

Average Profit 16,390+18,080+19,680 = 54,150÷3 = 18,050.

Purchase Price 4×18,050 = 72,200.

37.11(*a*) Net Assets Acquired at book value B 50,000, C 35,000, Goodwill (see Workings) B 8,125, C 6,875 = Total Purchase Consideration 100,000 *less* Nominal Value Shares Issued 80,000 = Share Premium 20,000. Distribution of shares to members of Box 80,000×58,125/100,000 = 46,500. Cox 80,000×41,875/100,000 = 33,500 shares Ratio of shares in Acquisition Ltd to former holdings: Box 46,500 for 31,000 previously held = 3:2.

Cox 33,500 for 33,500 held before = 1:1.

(*b*) *Balance Sheet*—Fixed Assets 74,000+Goodwill 15,000+Current Assets 86,000+Cash 25,000, Balance Sheet totals 200,000. Share Capital 100,000, Share Premium 25,000, Current Liabilities 75,000.

Workings—Goodwill 19–3 B 7,050, C 5,500, 19–4 B 8,800, C 6,400, 19–5 B 8,900, C 6,850, Average B 8,250, C 6,250, *less* Standard Profit (see following) B 5,000, C 3,500 = B 3,250, C 2,750. Goodwill B 2½×3,250 = 8,128, 2½×2,750 = 6,875.

Standard Profit: Share Capital Issued B 31,000, C 33,500, *add* Retained Profits B 19,000, C 1,500 = B 10 per cent of 50,000 = 5,000, C 10 per cent of 35,000 = 3,500.

38.1 Profit and Loss Dr Debenture Interest 3,600, Net Profit c/d 50,500, Cr Profits b/d 50,000, Debenture Interest Received 1,100, Dividends Received 3,000. Appropriation Account: Dr Corporation Tax 24,000. Dividend 21,000, General Reserve 5,000. Balance c/f to next year 10,370, Cr Net Profit b/d 50,500. Balance b/f from last year 9,870. Balance Sheet: Share Capital 70,000, Profit and Loss 10,370, Debentures 40,000. Corporation Tax owing 24,000. Income Tax owing (1,080−330) 750.

40.1 (*a*) (i) Freehold Premises Dr 49,000, Profit on Revaluation Cr 49,000.

(ii) Profit on Revaluation Dr 40,000, Ordinary Shareholders Cr 40,000.
Ordinary Shareholders Dr 40,000, Ordinary Share Capital Cr 40,000.

(iii) Furniture Dr 2,000, Shop Fitters Cr 2,000.

(iv) Bank Dr 13,750, Investments Cr 13,750, Profit and Loss Dr 1,250, Investments (loss) Cr 1,250.

(v) Redeemable Preference Share Capital Dr 24,000, Redeemable

Preference Shareholders Cr 24,000.

Redeemable Preference Shareholders Dr 24,000, Bank Cr 24,000.

Dr Profits and Loss 24,000, Cr Capital Redemption Reserve Fund 24,000.

(vi) Debentures Dr 16,000, Debenture Holders Cr 16,000.

Premium on Redemption Dr 320, Debenture Holders Cr 320.

Debenture Holders Dr 16,320, Bank Cr 16,320.

Profit and Loss Dr 320, Premium on Redemption Cr 320.

(b) Balance Sheet-Premises 120,000, Furniture 17,000 *less* Depreciation 5,000, Stock 43,200, Debtors 39,650, Bank (41,150+13,750−24,000− 16,320) = 14,580, Balance Sheet totals 229,430. Issued Shares 120,000, Capital Reserve 9,000, Capital Redemption Reserve Fund 24,000, Profit and Loss (37,000−1,250−320−24,000) 11,430, Current Liabilities 65,000.

40.2 (a) Preference Share Capital Dr 37,500, Ordinary Share Capital Dr 175,000, Capital Reduction Cr 212,500; Capital Reduction Dr 3,375, Ordinary Share Capital Cr 3,375: Share Premium Dr 40,000, Capital Reduction Cr 40,000: Provision for Depreciation 62,500 Dr, Capital Reduction Dr 72,500, Plant and Machinery Cr 135,000: Capital Reduction Dr 176,625, Profit and Loss Cr 114,375, Preliminary Expenses Cr 7,250, Goodwill Cr 55,000: Application and Allotment Dr 62,500, Ordinary Share Capital Cr 62,500: Cash Dr 62,500, Application and Allotment Cr 62,500.

(b) *Balance Sheet*—Property 80,000 *less* Depreciation 30,000, Plant 75,000, Stock 79,175, Debtors 31,200, Bank 11,500, Balance Sheet totals 246,875. Issued Capital Preference 112,500, Ordinary 90,875, Creditors 43,500.

40.3 (a) Realization—Dr Goodwill 20,000. Fixed Assets 100,000, Stock 22,000, Work in Progress 5,500, Debtors 34,000, Bank 17,500, Formation Expenses 1,000, Cr Budgets Ltd 143,150, Loss on Realization 56,850.

Sundry Shareholders—Dr Profit and Loss 40,000, Loss on Realization 56,850, Budgets Shares 73,150, Cr Ordinary Share Capital 120,000, Preference Share Capital 50,000.

(b) (i) To Debenture Holders—Cash 20,000+6 per cent Debentures 30,000, To Creditors—Cash 14,000, Shares 6,000, To Preference Shareholders—Arrears Shares 5,400, For Shares 7 for every 8: 43,750, To Ordinary Shareholders 24,000 shares 1 for 5 = 24,000. Total 143,150 Purchase Consideration.

(ii) Agreed Value Fixed Assets Stock 20,000, Work in Progress 5,500 Debtors 34,000, Bank 17,500, Fixed Assets (balance) 66,150 = Total 143,150.

(c) *Balance Sheet*—Fixed Assets 66,150, Stock 20,000, Work in Progress 5,500, Debtors 34,000, Bank (details follow) 104,350, Balance Sheet totals 230,000. Issued Share Capital 200,000, Debentures 30,000.

Workings—Bank 17,500+Shares Issued (200,000 *less* 79,150) 120,850 *less* paid to Debenture Holders 20,000 and Creditors 14,000 = 104,350.

40.4 (i) Preference Share Capital Dr 12,500, Capital Reduction Cr 12,500.

(ii) Ordinary Share Capital Dr 120,000, Capital Reduction Cr 120,000.

(iii) Capital Reserve Dr 16,000, Capital Reduction Cr 16,000.

(iv) Preference Shares Capital Dr 37,500, Ordinary Share Capital Dr 80,000 New Ordinary Share Capital Cr 117,500.

(v) Debenture Holders Dr 50,000, Debenture Cr 50,000, Cash Dr 50,000, Debenture Holders Cr 50,000.

(vi) Capital Reduction Dr 148,500, Goodwill, etc., Cr 70,000, Plant Cr 15,000, Furniture Cr 2,200, Profit and Loss Cr 61,300.

Balance Sheet Goodwill, 5,000, Plant 56,600, Furniture 2,000, Stock 56,950, Debtors 21,700, Bank 35,800, Cash 50, Totals 178,100, Ordinary Shares 117,500, Debentures 50,000, Creditors 10,600.

41.1 *Trading*—Dr Stock 29,145, Purchases 110,670 *less* Own Use 1,180 = 109,490, *less* Closing Stock 32,630, Gross Profit 54,795, Cr Sales 160,800, Profit and Loss—Dr Wages 16,328+Owing 220 *less* Own Use 420 = 16,128, Motor Expenses 5,895, Rates 1,217 *less* Advance 78 = 1,139, Bad Debts 770, Provision for Bad Debts 150, General Expenses 7,890, Directors' Remuneration 3,000, Depreciation Motors 3,600, Net Profit c/d 17,223, Cr Gross Profit b/d 54,795, Invest Income 1,000. Appropriation—Dr Preference Dividend 1,000, Ordinary Dividend 10,000, General Reserve 3,000, Balance c/f 10,177, Cr Gross Profit b/d 17,223, Balance b/f from last year 6,954.

Balance Sheet—Fixed Assets: Properties 89,600, Motors at cost 18,000 *less* Depreciation to date 12,360 = 5,640, Unquoted Investments 5,800, Current Assets Stock 32,630, Debtors 28,370 *less* Bad Debts Provision 750 = 27,620, Prepaid 78, Bank 8,179, Balance Sheet totals 169,547, Authorized Capital (note) Issued Capital Ordinary 100,000, Preference 20,000 Reserves—General 3,000, Profit and Loss 10,177, Current Liabilities Preference Dividend 500, Ordinary Dividend 10,000, Creditors 25,650, Wages owing 220.

41.2 *Trading*—Dr Stock 6,024, Purchases 61,450 *less* Returns 410 = 61,040, Carriage In 630, *less* Stock 7,434, Warehouse—Wages 1,800 Heating and Light 700, Rates 840, Repairs 567, Gross Profit 10,723, Cr Sales 75,210 *less* Returns 320 = 74,890.

Profit and Loss—Dr Office Salaries 1,000, Carriage Out 470, Rates—Office 120, Heating and Light 100, Repairs 81, Discounts Allowed 265, Advertising 120, Directors' Remuneration 2,400, Depreciation Fixtures 800, Office Equipment 90, Motors 500, Net Profit 4,897, Cr Gross Profit b/d 10,723, Discounts Received 120.

Appropriation—Dr General Reserve 1,000, Preference Dividend 400, Ordinary: Interim 1,000, Final 3,000, Balance c/f 1,817, Cr Net Profit b/d 4,897, Balance b/f last year 2,320.

Balance Sheet—Fixed Assets: Premises 15,000, Fixtures 8,000 *less* Depreciation 3,800 = 4,200, Office Equipment 900 *less* Depreciation 340 = 560, Motor Vans 4,000 *less* Depreciation 2,500 = 1,500, Current Assets Stock 7,434, Debtors 8,050, Prepaid 240, Bank 3,335, Balance Sheet totals 40,319, Share Capital—Authorized (note), Issued—Ordinary 20,000, Preference 5,000, Reserves Share Premium 2,000, General 3,000, Profit and Loss 1,817, Current Liabilities Creditors 5,120, Accrued Expenses 182, Proposed Dividend 3,200.

41.3 (A) 1. This would appear by note only. 2. The original cost and aggregate depreciation figures would be shown instead of a net book value. Assumed that depreciation charged for the year to 31 March 19-7. 3. If assumed that A and B will pay for the goods taken by them, then the debit may be included with debtors. *Add* 97 to A and B Ltd Stock figures. 4. Bank balance should reflect unpresented cheques, i.e. should show overdraft 460 and not debit balance 144. For the car the tax and insurance 40, 10 charged against profits and 30 c/f as prepaid. 5. Exclude from stock and treated as sale; 20 deposit already appears to have been treated as sale. 6. Write off bad debt. Provision for bad debts calculated on 1,420+160. 7. Accrue 25 debenture interest.

(B) Fixed Assets: Premises 3,200 *less* Depreciation 800 = 2,400, Plant 3,000 *less* Depreciation 1,500 = 1,500, Motor 460, Fixtures 300 *less* Depreciation = 200, Current Assets Stock 957, Prepaid 145, Debtors 2,001, Balance Sheet Totals 7,663, Share Capital 4,500, Profit and Loss 1,038, Debenture 500, Current Liabilities: Trade Creditors 810, Other Creditors 355, Bank Overdraft 460. Note: there is contingent liability of 150.

Workings—Profit and Loss Balance: 1,173+(5) Profit 40, *less* (4) Motor Expenses 10 and Bank Charges 26, *less* (6) Bad Debts 114, *less* (7) Debenture Interest 25 = 1,038. Stock 980+(3) 97 *less* (5) Stock Sold 120 = 957.

Debtors, 1,245+(3) A and B 500+(5) Stock Sold 160+(6) Credit Balances 210+Old Bad Debt Provision 65, *less* New Bad Debt Provision 79, *less* Bad Debt 100 = 2,001. (Assumed Provision Bad Debts 5 per cent not to include 500 due from directors.) Creditors 888 *less* (4) 78 = 810. Other Creditors 120+(6) 210+(7) 25 = 355.

41.4 *Trading*—Dr Stock 20,000, Purchases 70,000, *less* Stocks 15,000, Gross Profit c/d 23,300, Cr Sales 98,300, Profit and Loss—Dr Administration Expenses 6,000, Directors' Remuneration 3,200, Debenture Interest 300, Selling Expenses 7,000, Provision for Bad Debts 400, Depreciation—Buildings 500, Plant 4,000, Net Profit before Tax 3,600, Cr Gross Profit b/d 23,300, Discounts Received 1,700. Appropriation—Dr Corporation Tax 2,500, Dividends 1,500, Balance of Profits c/f 10,200, Cr Net Profit b/d 3,600, Balance of Profits b/f from last year 10,600.

Balance Sheet—Fixed Assets: Freehold Land and Buildings at cost 20,000 *less* Depreciation 5,000 = 15,000, Plant and Fixtures at cost 30,000 *less* Depreciation 8,000 = 22,000, Current Assets Stock 15,000, Debtors (*less* Bad Debts Provision) 7,600, Prepaid Expenses 2,000, Cash 5,300, Balance Sheet totals 66,900, Share Capital—Authorized (note), Issued 30,000, Profit and Loss 10,200, Debentures 5,000, Current Liabilities Creditors 15,400, Accrued Expenses 1,300, Proposed Dividend 1,500, Corporation Tax 2,500, Suspense Account 1,000. *Note:* There is a contingent liability of 2,000 in respect of bills discounted.

Memo Bad Debt—The 1,000 Current Liability difference on the Suspense Account will have to be traced.

41.5 *Trading*—Dr Purchases 50,660, *less* Stock 8,200, Gross Profit 19,280, Cr Sales 61,740, Profit and Loss—Dr Wages and Salaries 8,850, General Expenses 4,250, Discounts Allowed 670, Debenture Interest 300, Depreciation ($10\% \times 15,000 + 10\% \times 10,000 \times 6$ mos) 2,000, Net Profit 3,800, Cr Gross Profit 19,280, Discounts Received 590, Appropriation—Dr Preliminary Expenses written off 90, Balance c/f 3,710, Cr Net Profit b/d 3,800.

Balance Sheet—Fixed Assets 25,000 *less* Depreciation 2,000 = 23,000, Current Assets Stock 8,200, Debtors 7,450, Bank 5,560 = 21,210   Capital and Issue Expenses—Preliminary Expenses 270, Discounts on Debentures 120, Balance Sheet totals 44,600. Share Capital—Ordinary 20,000, Preference 8,000, Share Premium 400, Profit and Loss 3,710, Debentures 6,000, Creditors 6,340, Debenture Interest owing 150.

Workings—Bank: Dr Ordinary Shares 20,000, Preference Shares 8,400, Debentures 5,880, Receipts from Drs 53,620, Total 87,900, Cr Preliminary Expenses 360, Fixed Assets—1 January 15,000, 1 July 10,000, Creditors 43,730, Wages 8,850, General Exepenses 4,250, Debenture Interest 150, Balance c/d 5,560.

Purchases Control—Dr Cash 43,730, Discount Received 590, Balance c/d 6,340, Cr Purchases (difference) 50,660.

Sales Control—Dr Sales (difference) 61,740, Cr Cash 53,620, Discount Allowed 670, Balance c/d 7,450.

41.6 *Trading*—Dr Stock 2,610, Purchases 9,204, *less* Stock 2,986, Gross Profit 11,292, Cr Sales 20,120, Profit and Loss—Dr Wages 4,954, Rates, etc. (410–35) 375, Discount Allowed 76, Debenture Interest 180, General Manager's Salary 1,600, Provision for Bad Debts 165, Depreciation 300, Net Profit 3,642, Cr Gross Profit 11,292, Appropriation Dr Preliminary Expenses written off 180, General Reserve 1,000, Preference Dividend 560, Ordinary Dividend 800, Balance c/f 1,102, Cr Net Profit b/d 3,642.

Balance Sheet—Fixed Assets: Goodwill 5,000, Freehold Premises 8,000, Fixtures 3,000 *less* Depreciation 300 = 2,700, Current Assets Stock 2,986, Debtors 8,250 *less* Provision 165 = 8,085, Prepaid Expenses 35, Bank and Cash 3,169, Total Current Assets 14,275, Preliminary Expenses 360, Balance Sheet totals 30,335. Share Capital—Authorized (note), Ordinary 10,000, Preference 8,000, Share Premium 800, General Reserve 1,000, Profit and Loss 1,102, Debentures 3,000, Current Liabilities Creditors 4,543, Expenses owing (Wages 40+Debenture Interest 90+Salary 400) 530, Proposed Dividends 1,360.

41.7 *Profit and Loss*—Dr Wages 5,275, Office and Administration 9,267, Selling Expenses 4,072, Directors' Salary 3,000, Loan Interest 250, Loss on Investments 167, Depreciation—New Van 190, under provision old van 70, Net Profit c/d 3,784, Cr Gross Profit (note 2 of the question 104,300 *less* 78,225) 26,075, Appropriation—Dr Balance c/f to next year 6,165, Cr Net Profit b/d 3,784, Balance b/f last year 2,481.

Balance Sheet—Fixed Assets: Property 27,500, Motor Vehicle at cost 950 *less* Depreciation 190 = 760, Current Assets: Stock 8,412, Debtors (9,018+ 3,825) 12,843, Bank (4,980+33) 5,013, Balance Sheet totals 54,528, Issued Capital 40,000, Share Premium 1,000, Profit and Loss 6,165, Creditors 7,363.

41.8 (a) *Trading*—Dr Stock 276,946 *add* Purchases 458,832, *less* stock 303,484, Productive Wages 76,238, Gross Profit 242,514, Cr Sales 751,136, Profit and Loss Dr Salaries 37,872, Rent and Rates 14,728, Insurances 2,498, General Expenses 32,872, Provision Discounts on Debtors 30, Directors' Remuneration 18,000, Debenture Interest (gross) 1,680, Audit 500, Depreciation—Motorcars 1,744, Motor Lorries 4,548, Machinery and Plant 8,850, Office Furniture 590, Net Profit c/d 120,112, Cr Gross Profit b/d 242,514, Reduction in Bad Debts Provision 110, Investment Income (gross) 1,400, Appropriation—Dr Formation Expenses written off 6,292. Debenture Redemption Reserve 2,000,

Preference Dividend 6,000, Proposed Ordinary Dividend 40,000, Corporation Tax 34,000, Balance c/f 108,654, Cr Net Profit b/d 120,112, Balance b/f from last year 76,834.

Balance Sheet—Fixed Assets: Buildings 157,000 *less* Depreciation 56,800 = 100,200, Machinery 70,800 *less* Depreciation 33,644 = 37,156, Motor Lorries 22,740 *less* Depreciation 11,928 = 10,812, Motorcars 8,720 *less* Depreciation 4,576 = 4,144, Office Furniture 5,900 *less* Depreciation 2,722 = 3,178, Quoted Investments (M.V. 12,950 note only) 10,326, Current Assets: Stock 303,484, Debtors *less* Provisions 174,970, Bills Receivable 1,128, Cash and Bank 88,540, Total Current Assets 570,458, Loans to Directors 4,000, Discounts on Shares 8,000. Share Capital: Authorized and Issued 100,000 (Preference), 200,000 (Ordinary), Reserves—Capital Redemption Reserve 60,000, Debenture Redemption Reserve 2,000, Profit and Loss 108,654, Debentures 24,000, Current Liabilities Creditors and Accrued Expenses 167,010, Bills Payable 10,190, Proposed Dividend 40,000, Corporation Tax Payable 34,000, Income Tax 84.

(*b*) *Profit and Loss*—Profit for the year before taxation 120,112, (Following shown as notes Depreciation 15,732, Audit Fees 500, Debenture Interest 1,680, Directors' Remuneration 18,000, Quoted Invest Income 1,504), *less* Corporation Tax based on profit of the year 34,000 = Profits for the year after taxation 86,216, *add* Unappropriated Profits brought forward from last year 76,834 = Profits available for Appropriation 163,050. *less* Appropriations—Formation Expenses written off 6,292, Transfer to Debenture Redemption Reserve 2,000, Preference Dividend 6,000, Proposed Ordinary Dividend of 20 per cent 40,000 = Unappropriated Profits at 31 January 19–7 carried forward to next year 108,758.

41.9 (*a*) *Trading*—Dr Stock 14,444 *add* Purchases 134,163 *less* Stock 51,246, Royalties 1,800, Gross Profit 90,202, Cr Sales 189,363, Profit and Loss Dr Wages and Salaries 19,377, Delivery Expenses 1,549, General Expenses 3,563, Provision for Bad Debts 45, Debenture Interest 1,100, Directors' Remuneration 7,000, Depreciation—Machinery 13,675, Land and Buildings 12,750, Motors 5,800, Fixtures 420, Prev underprov on machine 35, Net Profit c/d 26,498, Cr Gross Profit b/d 90,202, Invest Income Unquoted Investments 565, Quoted Investments 1,045, Appropriation—Corporation Tax 7,000, Interim Dividend 10,000, Proposed Final Dividend 15,000, Debenture Redemption Reserve 1,000, Balance carried forward to next year 8,388, Cr Net Profit b/d 26,498, Balance brought forward from last year 14,890.

(*b*) *Profit and Loss*—Profit for the year before taxation 26,498. Following shown as notes: Depreciation 32,680, Debenture Interest 1,100, Directors' Remuneration 7,000, Investment Income—Unquoted 565, Quoted 1,045: *less* Corporation Tax based on profit of the year 7,000, = Profit for the year after taxation 19,498, *add* Unappropriated Profits brought forward from last year 14,890 = Profit available for Appropriation 34,388, *less* Proposed Dividend 25,000, Debenture Redemption Reserve 1,000 = Unappropriated Profits at 31 March 19–6. Carried forward to next year 8,388.

Balance Sheet—Fixed Assets: Land and Buildings 255,000 *less* Depreciation 87,110 = 167,890, Machinery 136,000 *less* Depreciation 45,415 = 90,585, Motors 29,000 *less* Depreciation 17,293 = 11,707, Fixtures 16,800 *less* Depreciation 6,670 = 10,130, Investments—Unquoted 3,000, Debentures held 7,490. (Market Value as note 8,211), Current Assets: Stock 51,246, Debtors *less* Provision Bad Debts 18,340, Capital and Issue Expenses, Preliminary Expenses 1,500, Balance Sheet totals 351,888, Authorized and Issued Share Capital 200,000, Reserves— Capital Redemption Reserve Fund 15,000, Debenture Redemption Reserve 4,500, Share Premium 5,000, General Reserve 5,200, Profit and Loss 8,388, Total Share Capital and Reserves 238,088, Debentures 11,000, Current Liabilities Creditors and Accrued Expenses 20,210, Corporation Tax 7,000, Income Tax 557, Proposed Dividend 25,000, Bank Overdraft 60,033.

Chapter 42

Apart from the missing *Profit and Loss Account* balance being 11,000 for question 1 there is no set answer for any of these questions. Reference should be made to the chapter for the possible layout of vertical accounts.

43.1 *Trust Ltd Consolidated Loan Account* (N stands for Nominal column, I for Income, C for Capital)—Dr Bank (N) 12,000, (I) 200, (C) 7,060, Dr Adjustment for 1 month's interest on sale of 3,000 *ex div* (I) 10, Investment Income Account (I) 420, Profit and Loss: Profit on Sale (C) 75, Cr Bank $\frac{1}{2}$ yrs interest on 12,000 (I) 240, Bank sale at 61 *ex div* (N) 3,000, (C) 1,830, Adjustment per contra (C). 10, Bank $\frac{1}{2}$ yrs interest on 12,000 (I) 240, Balances c/f (N) 9,000, (I) 150, (C) 5,295 *Abee Ltd Ordinary Shares Account*—Dr Bank Purchase (N) 2,000, (C) 4,000, Bonus Issue (N) 3,000, (C)—, Investment Income (I) 225, Profit on Sale to Profit and Loss (C) 500, Cr Bank Sale at £1 each (N) 2,500, (C) 2,500, Bank Dividend (I) 225, Balances c/f (N) 2,500, (C) 2,000.
Ceedee Ltd Ordinary Shares Account—Dr Bank (N) 5,000, (C) 3,875, Rights Issue (N) 2,500, (C)—, Investment Income (I) 625: Cr Bank Sale of Rights (N) 2,500, (C) 625, Bank Dividend (I) 625, Balances c/f (N) 5,000, (C) 3,250.
Note: as no details are given of periods covered by ordinary dividends they have therefore not been apportioned.

43.2 *Investment Account*—Dr Balance b/f (N) 6,000, (C) 7,200, Bonus Issue (N) 3,000, (C)—, Cash (N) 1,800, (C) 1,890, Profit and Loss (C) 765, Investment Income Account (I) 1,490, Cr Cash Sale of Shares (N) 1,000, (C) 1,965, Cash Sale of Rights (C) 210, Cash Dividend *less* tax (I) 600, Cash Dividend *less* tax (I) 294, Taxation Account (I) 596, Balance c/f at cost (N) 9,800, (C) 7,680.

44.1 (a) *Contract*—Dr Materials Issued 9,411, Materials Purchased 28,070, Direct Expenses 6,149, Wages 18,493, Charge for Administration Expenses 2,146, Plant Purchased 12,180, Accrued Expenses c/d Wages 366, Direct Expenses 49 = 76,864, Profit and Loss Account—Profit 4,050, Cr Balances c/f—Work in Progress 68,600, Stock of Materials 2,164, Plant at cost *less* Depreciation 10,150.
(b) *Calculation of Profit*—Work Certified (net after retentions) 64,170 *add* 10 per cent Retention Money (one-ninth of 64,170) 7,130 = 71,300, *less* Cost of Work Certified: Expenditure to date 76,864 *less* w.d.v. of Plant 10,150, Stock 2,164 = 64,550, making Profit on Work Certified 6,750. Two-thirds Profit on Work Certified 4,500 *less* represented by retention money 450 = Profit to be taken to Profit and Loss Account

4,050. Working. Depreciation. Plant cost 12,180. Annual Depreciation Charge one-fifth of 12,180 = 2,436 per annum. Depreciation Charge for 10 months = $\frac{10}{12} \times 2,436$ = 2,030. w.d.v. 10,150.

44.2 *Contract*—Year 1. Dr Plant 16,250, Materials 25,490, Wages 28,384, Direct Expenses 2,126, Gross Profit to Profit and Loss 8,200 Cr Work Certified 58,000, Plant c/d 10,250, Stock and Work in Progress c/d 12,200.

Contract—Year 2. Dr Stock and Work in Progress b/d 12,200, Plant b/d 10,250, Materials 33,226, Wages 45,432, Direct Expenses 2,902, Penalty 700, Gross Profit to Profit and Loss 15,390, Cr Work Certified 116,000, Sale of Plant 4,100.

Workings—Computation Gross Profit Year 1. Contract Price 174,000 *less* Actual Expenditure Year 1 25,490+28,284+2,126, +Estimated Cost of Plant (16,250−4,250) 12,000, Estimated Expenses Year 2:81,400 = Profit for year 24,600.

Using Formula given by question $\dfrac{52,200+5,800}{174,000} \times 24,600$ = 8,200.

45.1 *Working Capital*—31 December 19–3, 600; 31 December 19–4, 1,760. Increase 1,160.

Working Capital Flow Statement. Contribution from Trading: Net Profit 2,200+Depreciation Land 260+Depreciation Plant 200 = 2,660+Loan 1,000 = 3,660 *less* Drawings 1,500 and Plant Bought 1,000 = 1,160 Increase in Working Capital.

45.2 Invested in New Fixed Assets 2,800 *less* Depreciation 953 = Additional Balance Sheet Value of 1,847, also Cash at Bank was 1,360 compared with previous bank overdraft of 620, an improvement of 1,980, so that assets increased by 1,847+1,980 = 3,827. Conversely the stock fell by 1,620, and debtors by 1,860, also a loan of 1,500 was received and creditors increased by 1,297, so that these meant a worsening in the financial position of 6,277. Overall, therefore, the position worsened to the extent of 6,277−3,827 = 2,450. Part of this was caused by the drawings of the proprietor 1,810 and the remainder (2,450−1,810) 640 was due to the *trading loss* of 640 in the year.

45.3 Source and Disposition of Bank Funds. Cash at Bank 1 January 19–5 118,000, *add* Sources of Bank Funds: Share Capital Issued 50,000, Sale of Motor Vehicles 13,000, Cash Flow from Profits (see later) 192,100, Debentures Issued 150,000, Reduction in Cash Balance 200 = Sources Total 405,300, *less* Disposition of Bank Funds: Taxation Paid 29,000, Dividend Paid 21,000, Reduction in Creditors 108,800, Premises Bought 15,000, Plant Bought 29,000, Motor Vehicles Bought (see workings) 24,000, Investments at cost 65,000, Increase in Stock 34,400, Increase in Work in Progress 15,000, Increase in Debtors 180,100, Total Dispositions 521,300 = Cash at Bank 31 December 19–5 2,000.

Workings—Cash Flow from Profits: *Per* Accounts 89,600, *add* Back Depreciation Plant 16,000, Depreciation Motors 8,000, Taxation Charged 41,000, Dividend 17,500, General Reserve 20,000 = 192,100. Motor Vehicles Dr Balance b/f 45,000+Additions 24,000 (difference) Cr Disposals 18,000, Balance c/f 51,000.

Depreciation Motors: Dr Disposals 11,000, Balance c/d 26,000, Cr Balance b/d 29,000, Profit and Loss (difference) 8,000.

Taxation—Dr Cash 29,000, Balance c/d 44,000, Cr Balance b/d 32,000, Profit and Loss (difference) 41,000.

45.4 *Sources*—From operations Profit 2,877+Depreciation 1,164+Increase in Reserve 18 = 4,059 *less* Profit on Sale of Plant 30 *less* Profit on Sale of Subsidiary 18 = 4,011 *add* Sale of Plant 90+Sale of Investments 27+ Issue of Debentures ± Issue of Ordinary shares 183 = 4,383. Applications: Cash Dividends 1,731, Purchase of Plant 1,743, Increase in Goodwill 21, Purchase of Investments 156 = 3,651. Net Increase in Funds is 732.

45.5 *Bank Account Summary*—Dr Balance b/f 4,420, Receipts from Debtors: Opening Debtors 9,600, Others 4×18,000 = 72,000, Issue of Ordinary shares 6,250, Balance c/d 10,880, Cr Payments to Suppliers: Opening Creditors 9,330, Increase in Stock 8,020, Others 5×15,000 = 75,000, Administration Expenses: Owing at Start 600, Others 5×720 = 3,600, Wages 6,600.
Trading—Dr Stock 1 June 19–6, 11,980+Purchases (difference needed to balance the Trading Account) 98,020, *less* Stock 30 November 19–6 20,000, Gross Profit 18,000, Cr Sales 108,000. Profit and Loss: Dr Wages and Salaries 6,600, Administration Expenses 4,320, Depreciation 450, Net Profit 6,630, Gross Profit 18,000.
Balance Sheet—Fixed Assets 9,000 *less* Depreciation 450 = 8,550, Stock 20,000, Debtors 36,000, Balance Sheet totals 64,550. Issued Share Capital 15,000, Share Premium 1,250, Profit and Loss 21,700, Creditors 15,000, Administration Expenses owing 720, Bank Overdraft 10,880.

45.6 (*a*) *Cash Book* (before issue of shares to see amount needed)—January: Dr Balance c/d 122,600, Cr Buildings 40,000, Machinery 22,000, Fixtures 4,000, Payments for Goods 47,000, Overhead Expenses 9,600.
February: Dr Debtors 50,000, Balance c/d 117,200, Cr Balance b/d 122,600, Payments for Goods 35,000, Overhead Expenses 9,600.
March: Dr Debtors 50,000, Balance c/d 117,200, Cr Balance b/d 117,200, Payments for Goods 35,000, Overhead Expenses 15,000.
April: Dr Debtors 50,000, Balance c/d 111,800, Cr Balance b/d 117,200, Payments for Goods 35,000, Overhead Expenses 9,600.
May: Dr Debtors 50,000, Balance c/d 106,400, Cr Balance b/d 111,800, Payments for Goods 35,000, Overhead Expenses 9,600.
June: Dr Debtors 50,000, Balance c/d 101,000, Cr Balance b/d 106,400, Payments for Goods 35,000, Overhead Expenses 9,600.
The highest amount needed is 122,600 in January. Therefore shares to be issued = 122,600. Thus the closing bank balance will be 122,600 *less* 101,000 = 21,600.
Trading Dr Purchases (difference on the Trading Account) 222,000, *less* Closing Stock 12,000 = Cost of Goods Sold 210,000, Gross Profit 90,000, Cr Sales 300,000. Profit and Loss—Dr Overhead Expenses 63,000, Net Profit 27,000, Cr Gross Profit 90,000.
Balance Sheet—Fixed Assets Buildings 40,000, Machinery 22,000, Fixtures 4,000, Current Assets Stock 12,000, Debtors 50,000, Bank 21,600, Balance Sheet totals 149,600. Ordinary Shares 122,600, Profit and Loss 27,000.

45.13 Net Profit 9,600+Depreciation 3,800+Sale Fixed Assets 1,400+Decrease in Working Capital 200 = 15,000. Applied to Equipment 9,000+Taxation 6,000 = 15,000. Decrease in Working Capital made up Stock in Trade 1,400+Debtors 400 less Bank (1,000)+Creditors (1,000) = (200).

45.14 Cash Projection: January Dr Capital 9,000, Cr Expenses 800 Balance c/f 8,200. February Dr Nil Cr Creditors 4,500, Expenses 900, Fittings 500. Balance c/f 2,300 March Dr Nil, Cr Creditors 2,250, Expenses 800, Balance c/f (750) April Dr Debtors 3,000, Cr Creditors 2,250, Expenses 800, Balance c/f (800) May Dr Debtors 3,000, Cr Creditors 3,000, Expenses 800, Balance c/f (1,600), June Dr Debtors 4,000, Cr Creditors 3,000, Expenses 800, Balance c/f (1,400), July Dr Debtors 4,000, Cr Creditors 3,000, Expenses 800, Balance c/f (1,200), August Dr Debtors 4,000, Cr Creditors 3,000, Expenses 900, Balance c/f 1,100 September Dr Debtors 4,000, Cr Creditors 3,000, Expenses 800, Balance c/f (900) October Dr Debtors 4,000, Cr Creditors 3,000, Expenses 800, Balance c/f (700) November Dr Debtors 4,000, Cr Creditors 3,000, Expenses 800, Balance c/f (500), December Dr Debtors 4,000, Cr Creditors 3,000, Expenses 800, Balance c/f (300).

Profit and Loss: Sales 46,000, Cost of Sales 34,500, Gross Profit 11,500, Depreciation 100, Expenses 9,900, Net Profit before tax 1,600, Corporation tax 800, Net Profit after tax 800. Balance Sheet: Fixed Assets 500 less Depn 100 = 400, Current Assets Stock 1,500, Debtors 12,000, Total 13,900. Share Capital 9,000 P/L 800, Current Liabilities Creditors 3,000, Taxation 800. Bank overdraft 300, Total 13,900.

The return on opening capital of 9,000 is 8·9 per cent not including any interest in overdraft. Some replanning necessary to achieve 10 per cent.

46.1 Net Present Values—Firm A 3,732·55, Firm B 3,615·41, Firm C 3,519·39. Therefore offer by Firm C chosen.

46.2 (a) (i) *Payback:*
Should be calculated on the incremental cash flows, i.e. after adding back depreciation to profits after tax:

A	B	C
$1\frac{5}{7}$ years	2 years	$1\frac{3}{7}$ years

(ii) *Rate of Return:*

$$\frac{\text{Average Profit Net of Depreciation}}{\text{Average Capital}}$$

A $\frac{75}{150} \times 100 = 50\%$
B $\frac{75}{150} \times 100 = 50\%$
C $\frac{75}{150} \times 100 = 50\%$

(iii) *Net Present Value:*
Should be calculated on cash flows, i.e. after adding back depreciation to profits:

$$A \quad \frac{175}{(1\cdot10)} + \frac{175}{(1\cdot10)^2} + \frac{175}{(1\cdot10)^3} = 435$$

$$B \quad \frac{125}{(1\cdot10)} + \frac{175}{(1\cdot10)^2} + \frac{225}{(1\cdot10)^3} = 427$$

$$C \quad \frac{225}{(1\cdot10)} + \frac{175}{(1\cdot10)^2} + \frac{125}{(1\cdot10)^3} = 443$$

(*b*) Choice should be that indicated by N.P.V. method, i.e. project C.

   A full answer should back up this choice by enumerating the advantages of the discounting method and the shortcomings of 'payback' and 'rate of return'.

46.3 Present value of investments (*a*) 3,250 (*b*) 3,800 (made up of 5,800 *less* 2,000), *add* Present Value of maintenance (*a*) × 3·791 = 947·75 (*b*) × 3·791 = 568·65, *less* Residual value × 0·621 (*a*) 372·60 (*b*) 621·00, = (*a*) 3,825·15 and (*b*) 3,747·65. Therefore (*b*) is cheaper alternative.

46.4 Cost 26,485 *less* 20 per cent 5,297 = 21,188. Divide 21,188 by present value of annuity factor 10·594 = 2,000 per annum.

47.1 (i) For style see Chapter 42   (iii) 4·16 to 1
   (ii) 2 to 1   (iv) 76,000

47.2 (*a*) 20   (*d*) 13·8 approx.
   (*b*) 2½ to 1   (*e*) 16%
   (*c*) 8; 1½ months

47.3 (*a*)   (i) *Stockturn Case 6·3 times:* Box 32 times.
      (ii) *Case 1·33 months:* Box 0·8 months.
      (iii) *Creditor Ratio Case 2·4 months:* Box 1·5 months.
      (iv) *Current Ratio Case 2·91:* Box 1·8.
      (v) *Return on Equity Case 12%:* Box 16%.
      (vi) *Liquid Ratio Case 1·94:* Box 1·50.
      (vii) *Gross Profit % Case 12·5%:* Box 11·11%.
      (viii) *Working Capital Case 112,200:* Box 32,500.
      (ix) *Return on Total Assets Case 9·48%:* Box 12·41%.
   (*b*) No set answer.

47.11

	19–4	31 Dec	19–5
	£		£
Cost of sales × mark up on cost = gross margin			
£2,000,000 × 22½%	450,000		
£2,500,000 × 22½%			562,500
Actual gross margin reported	500,000		500,000
Discrepancy	+50,000		−62,000

REPORT:

   This should cover at least the following points:
1. Overvaluation of stock 31.12.19–4;
2. Undervaluation of stock 31.12.19–5;
3. 19–5 sales erroneously included in accounts for 19–4;
4. 19–4 purchases erroneously included in accounts for 19–5;
5. Defalcation of cash and/or stocks.

Points (1), (3), and (4) would automatically effect the adjacent year 19–5.

Note: The question can be used to deal with the 'cut-off' procedures when discussing the year end stocktaking and valuation procedures.

47.12

(a)

TABLE	Foodstores	Motor Cycles
1. $\dfrac{20}{100} \times 100$	20·0%	
$\dfrac{20}{115} \times 100$		17·39
2. $\dfrac{20}{500} \times 100$	4·0	
$\dfrac{20}{125} \times 100$		16·0
3. $\dfrac{500}{100}$	5 times	
$\dfrac{125}{115}$		1·09 times
4. $\dfrac{50}{50}$	1 to 1	
$\dfrac{75}{30}$		2·5 to 1
5. $\dfrac{20}{50} \times 100$	40·0%	
$\dfrac{20}{65} \times 100$		30·77%

(b) Accounting ratios are useful indicators but they must be used with care and discrimination. Uncritical reliance on ratios, without regard to the circumstances of the particular business or period in question, may often point to the wrong conclusions. In this question, some assumptions and an appreciation of the type of business each company is engaged in is essential when examining the ratios as calculated. Furthermore, one ratio should not be viewed in isolation from the others, otherwise an erroneous conclusion may be reached.

The motor-cycles concern is a *manufacturing* business (this is given in the question) and has higher current and liquid ratios than the food-stores business. This contrast is exactly what might be expected if the contrasting nature of the two businesses is taken into consideration. The sales for foodstores must be predominantly for cash and so the out-standing debtors at the year end will be small: also the stock will be turning over very fast and one might well expect the creditors at any given point in time to be greater than the stock. All this would point to a modest current ratio—but not necessarily a dangerous one. It would be wrong, therefore, to conclude that the foodstores business is financially more vulnerable than the motor cycles business.

Similarly, it would be incorrect to describe the motor-cycles business as inefficient merely because its assets turnover rate is only 1 compared with

5 achieved by the other business. The former can be expected to have a low stockturn rate and must carry substantial stocks of raw materials, and work in progress.

Again, a low profit margin coupled with a very high assets turnover rate can be expected from a chain of foodstores, with precisely the reverse factors for the other business. This is borne out by the ratios.

Without knowing the capital structure in detail for both concerns, it is difficult to set out the precise reason for the greater return earned for 'the shareholders' by the foodstores business. The simple deduction is that, despite the gearing that exists in the manufacturing company (loans £20,000—and there could be preference shares in issue) the foodstores business is able to operate on a lower permanent capital—all obtained from its shareholders—owing to the nature of its business.

47.13

	19–5	19–6

Gross margin ratio

$$\frac{159,300}{425,000} \times 100 \qquad 37 \cdot 5 \%$$

$$\frac{166,200}{500,000} \times 100 \qquad\qquad\qquad 33 \cdot 2 \%$$

Note: if the gross margin percentage for 19–5 had been maintained in 19–6, the gross margin would have been   £187,500
actual gross margin   166,200
                                                              ————
Shortfall 19–6   21,200
                                                              ————

REPORT (this should cover the following possible reasons for the difference in the ratio).
1. An increase in purchase prices without a corresponding increase in selling prices;
2. A reduction in selling prices to combat fall in demand;
3. Cash sales made but not recorded = theft of cash; and/or Credit sales made but not recorded through oversight and therefore not in the books.
4. Stock shortages due to pilfering/waste/inefficiency;
5. Absence of departmental accounting: the mark up is probably different for all three types of goods traded in (musical instruments, hi-fi equipment, and cassette tapes), and the *same average margin percentage* will only occur for both years, if exactly the same 'mix' of goods is achieved. There should be departmental accounting with separate mark-ups established for control purposes;
6. Overvaluation of stock in 19–5;
7. Undervaluation of stock in 19–6.
Note: this list of points is not exhaustive.
The basic recommendation that should be made is that stated in point 5—the establishment of departmental accounting; ancillary recommendations could include better control of pricing procedures and proper records of price changes, and the tighter control of stocks and recording of sales.

48.6 (*a*) $\frac{37\frac{1}{2}}{62\frac{1}{2}} \times 100 = 60\%$

[Check: cost 10p per pkt
mark up 6p

selling price 16p

$\frac{6}{16} \times 100 = 37\frac{1}{2}\%$]

(*b*) Cost 4p per pkt
mark up 16p (400%)

selling price 20p

$\frac{16}{20} \times 100 = 80\%$ Answer

(*c*) No. per cent relationship is the same irrespective of volume provided mark-up policy is maintained. But, £ margin generated per packet *varies directly* with the number of packets sold.

Illustration:	*1 packet*	*10 packets*
Cost	4p	40p
mark up	16	160
Sales revenue	20	200
Gross margin	$\frac{16}{20} \times 100 = 80\%$	$\frac{160}{200} \times 100 = 80\%$

(*d*)

	Blades	*Balloons*	*Total*
Number of pkts	1	2	3
Gross margin	6p	32p	38p

B/E $\frac{F}{CM}$ $\frac{£3{,}990}{£0.38} = 10{,}500$ Answer

	£
[Check: 10,500 pkts blades × 6p contribution	630
21,000 pkts balloons × 16p contribution	3,360
Total contribution	3,990]

(*e*) *Discussion:* Include the following:

1. 3 market days per week = 150 market days per year of 50 weeks.
2. B/E pkts are 10,500 / 21,000 } which must be sold in 150 market days.
   Heap must sell on the average 70 pkts of blades and 140 pkts of balloons on each market day: Is this realistic?
3. Does £3,990 include his salary? Can he sell balloons during Oct/Nov and Feb/Mar for example?

4. He relies on balloon sales to generate £3,360 margin, so that his 'product mix' includes heavy reliance on seasonal sales.
5. On the evidence, probably your friend should NOT be advised to copy Entrepreneur Heap.

48.7 Mr A

Manufacturing Accounts

		Year 1 £000's		Year 2 £000's
Variable costs 220 × 1,000		220	220 × 1,200	264
Closing stock		—	220 × 200 (1/6)	44
		220		220
Sales 350 × 1,000		350		350
Contribution margin		130		130
Fixed costs:				
Production	60			
Selling and admin.	25	85		85
Operating profit		45		45

Mr. Z

	Year 1 £000's		Year 2 £000's
Production costs:			
Variable costs 220 × 1,000	220	220 × 1,200	264
Fixed costs	60		60
	280		324
Closing stock	—	$\dfrac{200}{1,200} \times 324 \ (1/6)$	54
	280		270
Sales 350 × 1,000	350		350
Gross profit	70		80
Non-Factory overheads:			
Selling and admin.	25		25
Operating profit	45		55

Comment: Mr A's accountant follows the marginal (or direct, or variable) cost principles in drawing up the account. Mr Z's accountant adheres to the principle of absorption costing.

Both accountants are 'correct' but A carries stocks at marginal cost only, whereas Z included a proportion of factory production fixed costs in the closing stock carried forward at the end of year 2: thus

A   stock valuation   £44,000 for 200 castings
Z   ,,   54,000   ,,

and that is why Mr Z is showing a higher profit than Mr A. This is precisely why it is difficult for non-accounting managers to understand how it is possible to state increased profits *on the same sales effort* (all costs and revenues being constant) as a previous period.

Mr Z, from his remarks, obviously does not understand the difference between the two costing philosophies: but he may have a point in considering that his closing stock is 'worth more' than just its variable cost.

48.8

Direct cost Statement for current operations

Product	A	B	Total
	£000's	£000's	£000's
Sales	750	750	1,500
Direct costs	425	725	1,150
Contribution margin	325	25	350
All 'fixed' costs			300
Operating profit			50

Observations:

1. Product line B IS contributing to fixed costs: if production on this line is stopped the probable effect will be a reduction in profit of £25,000, thus:

Contribution from Line A	325
All 'fixed' costs—these will continue by definition	300
Forecast operating profit	25

This forecast depends on the principle and accuracy with which costs can be separated into variable and non-variable elements.

2. Some factors which should be considered in decisions of this sort are:
   (a) the accuracy of the analysis of costs into variable, semi-variable and non-variable elements, as mentioned above;
   (b) Are the products absolutely non-complementary? and can therefore Line B's production be completely stopped?
   (c) What effect will there be on
      Space
      Machine usage
      Occupational costs
   (d) Can the employees from Line B be used on other operations? Can, in fact, in the light of current labour law and problems the workers on Line B be dismissed? (Reference could be made to recent labour problems in the British Leyland organization and their decision to shut down the factory at Speke in 1978.)

48.9 (a) Answer Yes:

	Direct cost per unit
	£
Materials	2.50
Labour	3.20
Variable overhead	1.00
	6.70
Normal selling price	11.00
Normal contribution margin BEFORE commission	4.30

Contribution margin after commission of £1.10 per unit = £3.20

		£
Result of decision Yes:	Variable cost as above	6.70
	Add salesman's commission 10% of £8	0.80
		7.50
	Selling price	8.00
	Contribution per unit sold	0.50

Contribution £0.50 × 2,000 units = £1,000 profit on this sale if break-even has already been reached—otherwise £1,000 contribution generated by the sale towards fixed costs and profit.

(b) Answer No: This means *FOREGOING* a contribution of £1,000 in order to secure some other advantage(s). Some important points which could result in a No decision are:

(1) The fear of an erosion in the normal selling price of £11 per unit;

(2) The wish to discourage pricing competition;

(3) It may be possible to sell the 2,000 units at the normal price, thus generating £6,400 contribution instead of £1,000 (£4.30 minus £1.10 = £3.20 × 2,000);

(4) What is the breakeven point in units?

(5) How far are we through the year?

48.10 Accounting statement re-drafted on direct cost principles: and table of results under the various proposals:

			(in £000's)		Eliminate	
Product line	Sales Revenue	Variable costs	Contribu- tion margin	Line Y	Line Z	Lines Y and Z
X	200	120	80	80	80	80
Y	40	42	(2)	—	(2)	—
Z	160	146	14	14	—	—
Total contribution margin			92	94	78	80
Fixed costs			70	70	70	70
Operating profit			22	24	8	10

Evaluation: It is clear that the Sales Director and the Personnel Director have not correctly evaluated the situation. The problem is that the cost information is not in the form which would assist decision-taking. If a production line is closed down, which costs *still continue* because of their 'fixed' nature? The question is better posed: 'What costs are avoided if we close down the production line? and what revenues are lost?'

By drawing up the costing data on marginal lines, it is clear that Z *IS* contributing towards fixed costs and profit and to close this line down will reduce the profits from £22,000 to £8,000.

On the other hand, the sales revenue from line Y does not cover even its variable costs: there is thus an *outflow* of cash by keeping this line in production.

The Managing Director was right to challenge the proposal to close down line Z and the correct decision (all other things being equal) is to close down line Y only. This advice is based only on the information given by the question: there would be other important points to evaluate and if possible, quantify, before the decision is taken.

APPENDIX NO 48.1

London Chamber of Commerce + Intermediate Stage

1(a)

Consignment to Elmer Keith

19-4		£	19-4		£
Jul 1	Goods sent on Consignment	12,000	Aug 31	Bank: Insurance claim	650
Jul 1	Bank:		Oct 31	E. Keith: Sales	10,500
	Delivery Charges	96	Oct 31	Stock c/d (20 cases)	
	Freight	160		$20/100 \times 12{,}300^{*1} = 2{,}460$	
	Insurance	44		$20/\ 95 \times\quad 57^{*2} =\quad 12$	2,472
Oct 31	E. Keith:		Oct 31	Loss on consignment	335
	Landing Charges	15			
	Haulage to warehouse	42			
	Selling Expenses	25			
	Commission (15% of 10.500)	1,575			
		13,957			13,957

*1 Stock valuation based on cases sent and charges relevant to them, i.e. plus delivery, freight and insurance.

*2 Stock valuation limited to cases that reached the destination, i.e. 95, and for landing and haulage only.

(b)

Goods sent on Consignment

		19-4		£
		Jul 1	Consignment to E. Keith	12,000

(c)

Elmer Keith

19-4		£	19-4		£
Oct 31	Consignment: Sales	10,500	Oct 31	Consignment:	
				Landing Charges	15
				Haulage	42
				Selling Expenses	25
				Commission	1,575
				Bills Receivable	8,843
		10,500			10,500

2(a)

Books of Arnold & Bennett
Revaluation

19-5		£	19-5		£
Dec 31	Assets Reduced in value:		Dec 31	Assets increased in value:	
	Plant & Equipment	700		Land & Buildings	4,000
	Stock	300		Goodwill	2,000
	Profit on Revaluation carried to Capital Accounts				

	Arnold 3/5	3,000		
	Bennett 2/5	2,000	5,000	
			6,000		6,000

Capitals

19–5		Arnold	Bennett	19–5		Arnold	Bennett
Dec 31	Balances to new firm	15,000	11,500	Dec 31	Balances b/f	12,000	9,500
				Dec 31	Profit on Revaluation	3,000	2,000
		15,000	11,500			15,000	11,500

Books of Colin & Dennis
Revaluation

19–5			£	19–5		£
Dec 31	Profit on Revaluation carried to Capital Accounts			Dec 31	Assets increased in value	
	Colin 2/3	3,800			Plant & Equipment	600
	Dennis 1/3	1,900	5,700		Stocks	600
					Goodwill	4,500
			5,700			5,700

Capital

		Colin	Dennis			Colin	Dennis
19–5		£	£	19–5		£	£
Dec 31	Balances to new firm	10,800	9,400	Dec 31	Balances b/f	7,000	7,500
				Dec 31	Profit on Revaluation	3,800	1,900
		10,800	9,400			10,800	9,400

2(b)

Books of New Firm
Capitals (Names abbreviated to save space)

	A £	B £	C £	D £		A £	B £	C £	D £
Goodwill written off	4,200	3,150	2,100	1,050	Balances from old firms	15,000	11,500	10,800	9,400
Balances c/d	10,800	8,350	8,700	8,350					
	15,000	11,500	10,800	9,400		15,000	11,500	10,800	9,400

Arnold, Bennett, Colin & Dennis
Balance Sheet as at 1 January 19–6

Capital Accounts			Fixed Assets		
Arnold	10,800		Land & Buildings		10,000
Bennett	8,350		Plant & Equipment		10,200
Colin	8,700		Motor Vehicles		2,100
Dennis	8,350	36,200			
					22.300
Current Liabilities			Current Assets		
Creditors		8,500	Stocks	8,400	
			Debtors	11,400	
			Bank	2,600	22,400
		44,700			44,700

3(*a*)   *The Journal*

19–5		Dr £	Cr £
Jul 5	Bank	276,750	
	Application & Allotment		276,750
	Being receipt of application monies of 25p per share on 1,107,000 shares		
Jul 10	Application & Allotment	552,500	
	Ordinary Share Capital		422,500
	Share Premium		130,000
	Being 650,000 shares allotted in respect of 65p on application & allotment & 20p in respect of share premium		
Jul 10	Application & Allotment	500	
	Bank		500
	Being oversubscription in respect of applications being refunded		
Jul 19	Bank	276,250	
	Application & Allotment		276,250
	Being cheques received in respect of sums due on allotment		
date not known	First & Final Call	227,500	
	Ordinary Share Capital		227,500
	Being first & final call made of 35p per share on 650,000 shares		
Jul 30	Bank	227,500	
	First & Final Call		227,500
	Cheques received in respect of all shareholders in full settlement of the first & final call		

(*b*) The only cash refunded is that of 25p per share application monies received on 2,000 shares where size of application was 50 shares = £500.
Besides the £500 just mentioned, the excess of application monies was

Received 25p × 1,105,000	276,250
Less Application 25p × 650,000	162,500
∴ excess of application monies set against allotment is	113,750

4.

Westley Richards
Trading & Profit & Loss Account for the year ended 31 December 19–5

	£		£
Opening Stock	1,856	Sales	17,341
Add Purchases	11,845		
	13,701		
Less Closing Stock	1,919		
Cost of Goods Sold	11,782		
Gross Profit c/d	5,559		
	17,341		17,341
Staff Wages	2,534	Gross Profit b/d	5,559
Rent & Rates	750		
Motor Van Expenses	265		
General Expenses	442		
Depreciation:			
Shop Fittings	117		
Motor Van	180		
Net Profit	1,271		
	5,559		5,559

Balance Sheet as at 31 December 19–5

Capital	£		*Fixed Assets*		£
Balance as at 1.1.19–5	2,955		Shop Fittings	1,170	
Add Net Profit for the year	1,271		Less Depreciation to date	397	773
	4,226		Motor Van	720	
Less Drawings	2,136		Less Depreciation to date	360	360
	2,090				1,133
Current Liabilities			*Current Assets*		
Creditors	1,623		Stock	1,919	
			Debtors	576	
			Cash at Bank	47	
			Cash in Hand	38	2,580
	3,713				3,713

Workings: Capital 1.1.19–5

Assets:	Cash	29
	Bank	862
	Debtors	628
	Stock	1,856
	Motor van	540
	Shop Fittings	520
		4,435
Less Liabilities:		
	Creditors	1,480
		2,955

Sales Control

Debtors b/fwd	628	Cash Sales	13,826
Total Sales to Trading Account	17,341	Cash from Debtors	3,567
		Debtors c/f	576
	17,969		17,969

Purchases Control

	£		£
Cash Payments	752	Creditors b/f	1,480
Cheque Payments	11,086	Goods for own use (Drawings)	136
Creditors c/f	1,623	Purchases to	
		Trading Account	11,845
	13,461		13,461

Royal Society of Arts, Stage II + Full Answers

1(i)

Staghill Ltd

Budgeted Trading & Profit & Loss Account for 19–6

	Plan I £'000s	Plan II £'000s		Plan I £'000s	Plan II £'000s
Variable cost of sales	180	240	Sales	300	400
Depreciation	36	48			
Administration Expenses	33	40			
Net Profit	51	72			
	300	400		300	400
Proposed Dividend	20	20	Net Profit b/d	51	72
Balance to next year	91	112	Balance from last year	60	60
	111	132		111	132

(ii) N.B. from author. Probably the easiest way for a student is to draft the balance sheet for each year. The missing figure needed to make the balance sheet totals agree will be the bank balance or overdraft. This will be easier for most students than drafting cash flow statements.

Budgeted Balance Sheets at 31 December 19–6

	Plan I £'000s	Plan II £'000s		Plan I £'000s	Plan II £'000s
Share Capital	160	160	Fixed Assets		
Profit & Loss Account	91	112	Cost	360	480
			Less Depreciation	116	128
	251	272		244	352
Current Liabilities			Current Assets		
General	30	40	Stock	70	90
Dividend	20	20	Debtors	45	60
Bank Overdraft	58	170		115	150
(missing figures)					
	108	230			
	359	502		359	502

(iii) In Plan II the bank overdraft needs to fall £90,000 to bring it down to £80,000.

At the current rate of cash inflow, the following year would see:

		£
Cash generated from Sales		400,000
Less variable cost of sales	240	
Administration Expenses	40	280,000
		120,000

This means an inflow of £10,000 per month. However the dividend of £20,000 will be paid soon so that £90,000+£20,000 will be needed

$$= \frac{£110,000}{£10,000} = 11 \text{ months to bring overdraft to required amount}$$

2.

Slipford
Profit & Loss Account for the year ended 31 December 19–5

	£	£		£
Rates		2,560	Rent Receivable	10,664
Electricity	660			
Less Collected	632	28		
Telephone	642			
Less Collected	592	50		
Management changes		1,988		
Depreciation: Fixtures				
& Fittings		1,660		
Net Income		4,378		
		10,664		10,664

Workings:

Rent Receivable

Debtors b/f	280	Cash—½ year to 30 June	5,536
		Cash—½ year to 31 Dec	5,088
Profit & Loss A/c	10,664	Debtors c/f	320
	10,944		10,944

Electricity

Cash	404	Accrued b/f	182
Cash	282		
Accrued c/f	156	Profit & Loss	660
	842		842

Telephone

Cash	300	Accrued b/f	124
Cash	324		
Accrued c/f	142	Profit & Loss	642
	766		766

3.   **Run & Walk**
Trading & Profit & Loss Account for the year ended 31 December 19–5

	£		£
Opening Stock	11,236	Sales	101,126
Add Purchases (71,443 − 107)	71,336		
	82,572		
Less Closing Stock	13,116		
Cost of Goods Sold	69,456		
Gross Profit c/d	31,670		
	101,126		101,126
Salaries & Wages	9,592	Gross Profit b/d	31,670
Rent & Rates (1,060 − 80)	980		
Lighting & Heating (417 + 116)	533		
Motor Expenses (1,048 + 216)	1,264		
Bad Debts (328 + 78)	406		
General Expenses	1,330		
Depreciation: Motor Vans	2,000		
Net Profit c/d	15,565		
	31,670		31,670
Net Profit Shared:		Net Profit b/d	15,565
Run $\frac{3}{5}$	9,339		
Walk $\frac{2}{5}$	6,226		
	15,565		15,565

Balance Sheet as at 31 December 19–5

Capital				Fixed Assets		
Accounts:	Run	Walk		Freehold Premises		
Balances				at cost		19,500
1.1.19–5	16,000	13,000		Motor Vans at cost	10,000	
Add Share of				Less Depreciation		
Net Profit	9,339	6,226		to date	7,200	2,800
Add Car						
Allowance	216					22,300
	25,555	19,226		Current Assets		
Less Drawings	2,639	2,305		Stock	13,116	
	22,916	16,921	39,837	Debtors 9,437		
				Less Provision		
				for Bad Debts 514	8,923	
Current Liabilities				Prepayments	80	
Creditors		6,321		Bank	1,855	23,974
Accrued Expenses		116	6,437			
			46,274			46,274

4.   Issuing bonus shares does not raise anything in the way of cash funds. It is purely a book-keeping entry whereby various reserves are made non-returnable to the shareholders by being converted into share capital. See Chapter 40, first few pages, for a fuller discussion.

5.   Naturally a separate capital account has to be kept for each partner, because otherwise the financial relationships of the partners as between themselves would not be known. In the extreme case of a partnership with partners with equal shares of profits with equal amounts of drawings, then naturally whatever was left in the business would belong to them equally. Apart from this the financial relationships between them will vary. Separate capital accounts will reveal the changing relationships between them in financial terms.

For the calculation of the amounts due on dissolution see Chapter 24, *Business Accounting 1*.

50.1 Share Capital 200, Total 200: Goodwill 10, Stock 140, Bank 50.

50.2 Share Capital 6,000, Capital Reserve 300, Total 6,300: Fixed Assets 3,800, Stock 1,500, Debtors 700, Bank 300.

50.3 Share Capital 100,000, Total 100,000: Fixed Assets 62,000, Stock 27,000, Debtors 8,000, Bank 3,000.

50.6 Share Capital 4,000, Minority Interest 800, Total 4,800: Goodwill 300, Fixed Assets 2,000, Stock 1,300, Debtors 900, Bank 300.

50.7 Share Capital 8,000, Capital Reserve 375, Minority Interest 150, Total 8,525: Fixed Assets 3,325, Stock 3,000, Debtors 2,000, Bank 200.

50.10 Share Capital 10,000, Profit and Loss 6,500, Capital Reserve 600 (Goodwill S1 300, Capital Reserve 900 = Net Capital Reserve 600), Total 18,500: Fixed Assets 12,600, Current Assets 5,900.

50.11 Share Capital 10,000, Profit and Loss 2,000, General Reserve 1,400, Minority Interest 2,400. Total 15,800. Goodwill 350 (Goodwill S1 600, Capital Reserve S2 250 = Net Goodwill 350), Fixed Assets 9,450, Current Assets 6,000.

51.1 Share Capital 10,000, Profit and Loss H 4,000+S 1,800, Total 15,800: Goodwill 950, Fixed Assets 10,950, Current Assets 3,900.

51.2 Share Capital 50,000, Profit and Loss (H 14,000−S 400) 13,600, General Reserve 5,000, Capital Reserve 1,790, Minority Interest 4,110, Total 74,500: Fixed Assets 47,400, Current Assets 27,100, Total 74,500.

51.4 Share Capital 40,000, Profit and Loss (H 7,550+S1 1,020−S2 300) 8,270, General Reserve 5,000 Minority Interest (60% of 10,000+2,800+2,000) 5,920, Total 59,190, Goodwill 1,390 (S1 Cost 8,150−60% of 10,000+1,100 +2,000 = 290, S2 Cost 11,400−(8,000+500+1,800 = 1,100)), Fixed Assets 36,900, Current Assets 20,900.

52.1 Share Capital 2,000, Profit and Loss (H 3,700−90+S 1,150) 4,760, General Reserve 800, Creditors 900+700−220 = 1,380, Totals 8,940, Goodwill

850, Fixed Assets 2,300, Stock (1,200+900−90) 2,010, Debtors (2,100+1,400−220) 3,280, Bank 500.

52.2 Share Capital 20,000, Profit and Loss (H 4,000−50+S 60% of 2,000) 5,150, Minority Interest (40% of 10,000+5,500) 6,200, Creditors (3,800+2,100−600) 5,300. Totals 36,650. Goodwill 1,600, Fixed Assets 14,200, Stock (3,100+7,200−50) 10,250, Debtors (4,900−600+3,800) 8,100+Bank 2,500.

53.1 Shares bought 31/12/19−4. 10,000, Proportion Profit and Loss at 31/12/19−4 (25% of 24,000) 6,000 = 16,000: Shares bought 31/12/19−6. 14,000, Proportion of Profit and Loss at 31/12/19−6. (35% of 30,000) 10.500 = 24,500. Total 40,500. Paid 19−4 23,500+paid 19−6 31,000 = 54,500. Goodwill therefore 54,500−40,500 = 14,000.

53.3 Shares bought 50,000, (Profit and Loss, balance 31/12/19−7, 36,000, Add Proportion 19−8 profits before acquisition 8/12×42,000 = 28,000. Total 64,000. Of this proportion of pre-acquisition profits 50,000/80,000×64,000 = 40,000) 40,000, giving total 90,000. Paid for shares 158,000, therefore goodwill is 158,000−90,000 = 68,000.

54.1 Share Capital 50,000, Profit and Loss (H 19,000+S 4,000) 23,000, Total 73,000. Goodwill (Cost 29,000−20,000−3,000−Dividend 5,000) 1,000, Fixed Assets 57,000, Current Assets 15,000.

54.3 Share Capital 80,000, Profit and Loss (H 23,000+S $\frac{3}{4}$ of 6,000+$\frac{3}{4}$ of 7,000) 32,750, Minority Interest ($\frac{1}{4}$ of 40,000+11,000) 12,750, C/liabilities, Proposed Dividend 1,500, Totals 127,000. Goodwill (Cost 47,000−$\frac{3}{4}$ of 40,000 +4,000) 14,000, Fixed Assets 80,000, Current Assets 33,000.

55.1 Share Capital 500,000, Profit and Loss (H 143,000−10,000+S 32,000+2,000) 167,000, Totals 667,000. Goodwill 100,000, Fixed Assets 500,000−Depreciation 138,000, Current Assets 205,000.

55.3 Share Capital 150,000, Profit and Loss (H 77,000+S 14,000−2,500) 88,500. Totals 238,500. Goodwill 19,000, Fixed Assets 185,000 less Depreciation 33,500, Current Assets 68,000.

56.1 Share Capital 100,000, Profit and Loss (H 37,000+S1 90% of 16,000+S2 63% of 3,000) 53,290, General Reserve 10,000, Minority Interest (Shares in S1 1,000+Shares in S2 37% of 5,000: 1,850, Profit and Loss S1 10% of 23,000: 2,300, S2 37% of 4,000: 1,480, Less Cost of shares in S2 for minority interest of S1 10% of 6,000: 600) 6,030. Totals 169,320. Goodwill (Cost of shares to group, in S1 Ltd 23,000, in S2 Ltd 90% of 6,000: 5,400) 28,400, Less shares: In S1 9,000. In S2 63% of 5,000 = 3,150, Total 12,150, Profit and Loss in S1 90% of 7,000: 6,300. In S2 63% of 1,000: 630) 9,320, Fixed Assets 127,000, Current Assets 33,000.

57.1 Consolidated profits for the year before taxation 110,000, Less Corporation Tax 49,000 = Consolidated profits for the year after taxation 61,000 Less Minority Shareholders Interest 4,000, Group Profits for the period 57,000, Less Appropriations: Proposed Dividends 30,000, Unappropriated profits carried forward to next year 27,000.

L.C.C. Higher Stage Accounting: Full Paper

1. (1)(a)

Realization

Assets to be realized	£	P.Q. Ltd: Sale of	£
Plant (net)	17,000	net assets	50,000
Stocks	16,200		
Debtors (net)	10,800		
Profit on Realization			
P $\frac{3}{5}$	3,600		
Q $\frac{2}{5}$	2,400		
	—— 6,000		
	50,000		50,000

Capitals

	P £	Q £		P £	Q £
Bank	3,000	3,000	Balances b/f	18,000	14,000
Shares allotted	18,600	13,400	Profit on Realization	3,600	2,400
	21,600	16,400		21,600	16,400

(1)(b) P would receive 46,500 shares at 40p = £18,600
Q would receive 33,500 shares at 40p = £13,400

2. *P.Q. Ltd, Balance Sheet as at 4 May 19–6*

Share Capital:	£	Fixed Assets at cost:		£
Authorized		Goodwill		4,100
150,000 × 40p	60,000	Freehold Property		25,000
Issued		Plant		19,000
140,000 × 40p	56,000			48,100
Reserves:		*Current Assets*		
Share Premium	12,000			
	68,000	Stock	15,500	
Ten per cent Debentures	10,000	Debtors	12,000	
Current Liabilities:		less		
Creditors	7,500	provision	600 11,400	
		Bank*	9,000	35,900
		Discount on Debentures		400
		Formation Expenses		1,100
	85,500			85,500

* Bank: Issue of shares at premium £36,000 + Debentures at discount £9,600 less Formation Expenses £1,100, Payments to P & Q £10,500, Freehold Property £25,000 = balance remaining of £9,000.

A.B. Ltd	*C.D. Ltd*
(1) $\frac{100}{500} \times \frac{100}{1} = 20\%$	$\frac{100}{300} \times \frac{100}{1} = 33\frac{1}{3}\%$
(2) $\frac{40}{500} \times \frac{100}{1} = 8\%$	$\frac{50}{300} \times \frac{100}{1} = 16\frac{2}{3}\%$
(3) $\frac{20}{100} \times \frac{100}{1} = 20\%$	$\frac{25}{500} \times \frac{100}{1} = 5\%$
(4) $\frac{20}{110} \times \frac{100}{1} = 18\cdot18\%$	$\frac{25}{620} \times \frac{100}{1} = 4\cdot03\%$

(The term 'Capital Employed' has several meanings. There is no agreed terminology. I have taken one of the possible meanings.)

	A.B. Ltd	*C.D. Ltd*
(5)	$\frac{20}{15} = 1\frac{1}{3}$ TIMES	$\frac{25}{10} = 2\frac{1}{2}$ TIMES
(6)	10/100 1 to 10	120/500 6 to 25
(7)	$\frac{68}{51} = 1\cdot33$ TIMES	$\frac{355}{80} = 4\cdot43$ TIMES
(8)	$\frac{26}{51} = 0\cdot5$ TIMES	$\frac{160}{80} = 2$ TIMES
(9)	$\dfrac{400}{(58+42)\div2} = 8$ TIMES	$\dfrac{200}{(125+195)\div2} = 1\cdot25$ TIMES
(10)	$\frac{384}{16} = 24$ TIMES	$\frac{270}{45} = 6$ TIMES
(11)	$\frac{500}{25} = 20$ TIMES	$\frac{300}{100} = 3$ TIMES

3. (1)

Manufac Ltd

*Manufacturing, Trading & Profit & Loss Account
for the year ended 30 June 19–6*

	£		£
Stock of Raw Materials		Production cost of	
1.7.19–5	18,000	goods manufactured c/d	214,390
Add Purchases	103,100		
	121,100		
Less Stock Raw			
Materials 30.6.19–6	22,500		
Cost of Raw Materials			
Consumed	98,600		
Direct Wages	77,000		
Prime Cost	175,600		
Factory Overhead			
Expenses:			
Indirect wages	16,000		
Factory rent,			
rates etc.	5,400		
Machinery			
repairs	1,640		
Machinery			
depreciation	12,500	35,540	
		211,140	
Add Work-in-Progress			
1.7.19–5		16,450	
		227,590	

Less Work-in-Progress 30.6.19–6	13,200	
	214,390	214,390

	£		£
Stock of finished goods 1.7.19–5	28,200	Sales	303,500
Add Production cost goods manufactured	214,390		
	242,590		
Less Stock finished goods 30.6.19–6	34,000		
Cost of Goods Sold	208,590		
Gross Profit c/d	94,910		
	303,500		303,500

Administration Expenses:		Gross Profit b/d	94,910
		Dividends on trade investments	1,600
Office rent & rates 50%	1,100		
Office wages & salaries*	14,400		
Directors' remuneration	8,000	23,500	

Selling & Distribution Expenses:		
Salesmen's Salaries etc.	19,160	
Advertising	16,000	
Sales Director's salary	4,000	
Motor Vehicle Repairs	2,250	
Motor Vehicle Depreciation	4,400	45,810

* Not clear whether office wages and salaries should be split between selling and administration.

(2) (a) Lower
    (b) Lower

Financial Charges:		
Auditors' Fees & Expenses	1,500	
Debenture Interest	3,000	4,500
Net Profit		22,700
		96,510

	96,510

4.

Redeb Ltd
10 Per Cent Debentures

19–5		£	19–5		£
Sep 1	Debenture Redemption	24,000	Jan 1	Balance b/f	100,000
Oct 31	Debenture Redemption	12,000			
Dec 31	Balance c/d	64,000			
		100,000			100,000

Debenture Redemption

19–5		£	19–5		£
Sep 1	Bank	22,600	Sep 1	Debentures	24,000
Oct 31	Bank	11,300	Oct 31	Debentures	12,000
Dec 31	Debenture Interest*	100			
Dec 31	General Reserve	2,000			
		36,000			36,000

Debenture Interest

19–5		£	19–5		£
Mar 31	Bank	5,000	Jan 1	Accrued b/f	2,500
Sep 30	Bank	5,000	Dec 31	Profit & Loss	9,000
Dec 31	Accrued c/d	1,600	Dec 31	Debenture Redemption	100
		11,600			11,600

* Adjustment of interest portions of purchase prices.

5.

Sources & uses of bank funds statement
for the year ended 31 December 19–5

		£
Bank Balance at 1 January 19–5		3,500
Add Sources of bank funds:		
Loan from wife	2,500	
Sale of plant	700	
Cash effect of profits	7,900	11,100
		14,600
Less Uses of bank funds:		
Extra Plant	2,500	
Extra Stock bought	2,500	
Increased Debtors	2,000	
Reduced Creditors	2,000	
Drawings	5,500	14,500
Bank Balance at 31 December 19–5		100

WORKINGS:

Plant

	£		£
Balance b/d	11,000	Cash (plant sold)	1,000
Cash (difference)	2,500	Balance c/d	12,500
	13,500		13,500

Depreciation

Disposal	600	Balance b/d	7,000
Balance c/d	8,600	Profit & Loss	2,200
	9,200		9,200

Gross Profit		9,000
Less Overhead Expenses—	3,300	
Depreciation	2,200	1,100
Cash Flow from Profits		7,900

6. (a) Stock valued on FIFO basis

$$100 \times £30 = 3,000$$
$$400 \times £40 = 16,000 = £19,000$$

(b)

H. Ltd
Revenue Account for the year ended 31 December 19–5

	£		£
Purchases	38,000	Sales	25,000
Less Closing Stock	19,000		
Cost of Goods Sold	19,000		
Gross Profit c/d	6,000		
	25,000		25,000
Operating Expenses	6,000	Gross Profit b/d	6,000
	6,000		6,000

Balance Sheet as at 31 December 19–5

Share Capital		Stock	19,000
Authorized & Issued	10,000		
Bank Overdraft	9,000		
	19,000		19,000

(c) Little purpose is achieved by having one overall profit figure to mark the progress of a business during times of rising prices. The profit figure should be split between (i) the recorded 'profit' element shown which is due solely to rising replacement costs of stock and (ii), the ongoing profit earned by operating the business.

In the case above, the business is shown as having broken even for the year. The same volume of operations applies as at the start, that 500 kg of material is for sale. At the start £10,000 was sufficient to finance this, but now the business has to plunge into a £9,000 overdraft to do so. If this continues the business will be able to finance less and less, and thus could not be considered to be keeping on an even keel but to be descending towards liquidation.

One method, a simple one, would be to charge as the cost of sales the replacement cost, as at the time of each sale. Thus selling price and cost of goods sold would be on the same time scale. That figure would be used for gross operating profit, any excess would be in respect of rising prices.

Certified Accountants: Foundation Examination

1. (a)

Bank

	£		£
Capital Accounts:		Lease	6,000
Smith	8,000	Purchases (Blades Ltd)	5,400
Jones	5,000	Purchases: plastic	3,800
Sales: mail order	23,590	Synthetics: machinery	2,000
		Gas & Electricity	185
		Motor Van	800
		Insurance	150
		Wages	1,500
		Packaging Materials	1,627
		Advertising	620
		Telephone	760
		Drawings: Smith	2,140
		Drawings: Jones	1,520
		Balance c/d	10,088
	36,590		36,590

Cash

	£		£
Sales	3,648	Wages	600
		Postages	2,582
		Petrol & Oil	248
		Motor Repairs	170
		Balance c/d	48
	3,648		3,648

1. (b) The Final Accounts are shown in a vertical form as this method of display seems to be preferred by professional bodies.

Smith & Jones

Trading & Profit & Loss Account for the year ended 31 March 19–5

	£	£
Sales[1]		27,590
Purchases[2]	9,450	
Less Closing Stock	660	8,790
Gross Profit		18,800
Less Expenses:		
Wages[3]	2,100	
Postages	2,582	
Packaging Materials	1,627	
Advertising	620	
Gas & Electricity	185	
Telephone	760	
Motor Expenses	418	
Insurance	140	
Discounts Allowed	192	
Amortization of Lease[4]	600	
Depreciation: Machinery[5]	1,000	
Motor Van[6]	160	10,384
Net Profit		8,416
Appropriated: Salary for Jones		1,000
Interest on Capital: Smith	480	
Jones	300	780
Balance of profits: Smith $\frac{2}{3}$	4,424	
Jones $\frac{1}{3}$	2,212	6,636
		8,416

Balance Sheet as at 31 March 19–5

	£	£
Capitals: Smith	8,000	
Jones	5,000	13,000
Current Accounts:*[7] Smith	2,764	
Jones	1,992	4,756
Net Capital Employed		17,756

Represented by:

	Cost	Depreciation	
Fixed Assets:	£	£	£
Leasehold Premises	6,000	600	5,400
Machinery	5,000	1,000	4,000
Motor Van	800	160	640
	11,800	1,760	10,040

Current Assets:			
Stock	660		
Debtors & Prepayments	170		
Bank	10,088		
Cash in Hand	48	10,966	
Less Current Liabilities: Creditors		250	10,716
			20,756
Less Long Term Liability: Machinery			3,000
			17,756

Notes:
*[1] Local sales £4,800—Trade Discount £960 = £3,840—Cash Discount £192 = Cash received £3,648.
$200 \times £1 = £200$—Trade Discount £40 = Debtors £160.
Sales: Local £3,840+£160+Mail Order £23,590 = £27,590.
*[2] Purchases: Blades £5,400+Creditors £250+Plastic £3,800 = £9,450.
*[3] Wages: Cash £600: Bank £1,500 = £2,100.
*[4] Lease amortized over 10 years—straight line basis.
*[5] Machinery depreciated over 5 years—straight line basis, no scrap value assumed.
*[6] Motor van depreciated straight line, 5 years, no scrap value.
*[7] Current Accounts:

	Smith	Jones		Smith	Jones
	£	£		£	£
Drawings	2,140	1,520	Salary	—	1,000
Balance c/d	2,764	1,992	Interest	480	300
			Share of Profit	4,424	2,212
	4,904	3,512		4,904	3,512

(c) (i) On capital of £13,000 a profit of £8,416 has been made. This is a return of approximately 65 per cent, which seems quite good.
   (ii) Gross profit percentage 64 per cent: net profit 30 per cent.
  (iii) Only partners can decide whether profit division has resulted in a fair distribution.
  (iv) Business in a very liquid position. Could surplus cash be used profitably?
   (v) Partners to compare their performance in the business with alternative outlets for their cash and energies.

2. **Howton Company Ltd**
Trading and Profit and Loss Account for the period ended
31 December 19–4

	£	£
Sales		290,000
Opening Stock	35,000	
Purchases	165,000	
Carriage Inwards	1,100	
	201,100	
Less Closing Stock	41,000	160,100
Gross Profit		129,900
Provision no longer required		300
Discounts received		4,600
		134,800
Less Expenses:		
Wages	23,650	
Office salaries	8,600	
Lighting and heating	2,900	
Discounts allowed	3,200	
General expenses	11,850	
Loss on sale of machinery	100	
Depreciation of machinery	38,000	
Debenture interest	7,000	
Directors' fees	12,800	
		108,100
Net Profit		26,700
Undistributed Profits from last year		35,000
Profits Available for Distribution		61,700

Dividends Paid:	£	£
Ordinary Dividend of 5 per cent	7,500	
Preference Dividend of 4 per cent	2,000	9,500
Dividends Proposed:		
Final Ordinary Dividend of 5 per cent	8,250	
Final Preference Dividend of 4 per cent	2,000	10,250
Transfer to General Reserve		15,000
Undistributed Profit carried to next year		26,950
		61,700

Balance Sheet as at 31 December 19–4

	£	£
Authorized Share Capital		
200,000 Ordinary Shares of £1 each	200,000	
50,000 8% Preference Shares of £1 each	50,000	
Issued Share Capital:		
165,000 Ordinary Shares of £1 each	165,000	
50,000 8% Preference Shares of £1 each	50,000	215,000
Reserves:		
Revaluation Reserve	69,000	
Share Premium	5,000	
General Reserve	80,000	
Undistributed Profit	26,950	180,950
7% Debentures		100,000
Net Capital Employed		495,950
Represented by:	£	£
Fixed Assets		
Land and Buildings (at valuation)		180,000
Plant and Machinery (cost)	380,000	
Less Depreciation	122,000	258,000
		438,000
Current Assets		
Stock	41,000	
Debtors and Prepayments less provision	46,850	
Bank	7,500	
	95,350	

	£		
Less: Current Liabilities			
Creditors and Accruals	27,150		
Proposed Dividends	10,250	37,400	57,950
			495,950

3. (a)

		Dr £	Cr £
(i) Capital (Reduction in profit) Stock Being damaged stock valued at lower of cost or market.	Dr	25	25
(ii) (a) Capital (Reduction in profit) Debtors Being bad debt written off	Dr	200	200
(c) Capital (Reduction in profit) Provision for Doubtful Debt a/c Being $2\frac{1}{2}\%$ provision for doubtful debts.	Dr	100	100
(iii) (a) Machinery a/c Opening Capital Being Adjustment of over-provision of depreciation prior to April 19–4.	Dr	1,200	1,200
(b) Machinery a/c Capital (Increase in profit) Being overprovision of depreciation in current year.	Dr	300	300
(iv) Capital a/c (Reduction in profit) Capital a/c (Revaluation Account) Being Unrealized profit on revaluation of buildings.	Dr	2,000	2,000
(v) Capital (Reduction in profit) Wages accrued Being wages owing at 31 March 19–5.	Dr	95	95
(vi) Capital (Reduction in profit) Bank Account Being overdraft charges for the period.	Dr	80	80
(vii) Drawings (Capital a/c) Profit (Capital a/c) Being salary to owner treated as drawings.		1,000	1,000
(viii) Debtors a/c Capital (Increase in profit) Being rent due but not received.		200	200

(b)

Profit as per Balance Sheet		4,500
Add:		
Depreciation overprovision	300	
Salary to J. Thompson	1,000	
Rent due	200	1,500
		6,000

Less:

Provision for doubtful debts	100	
Stock deterioration	25	
Bad debt	200	
Unrealized profit on land and buildings	2,000	
Bank Interest	80	
Wages	95	2,500
Net Profit after revision		3,500

J. Thompson
Balance Sheet as at 31 March 19–5

	£	£		£	£
Capital at 1 April 19–4	20,100		Land and Buildings		
Revaluation of asset	2,000		at valuation		15,500
		22,100	Machinery at cost	13,000	
			Less Depreciation	6,000	7,000
					22,500
Profit for the year ended 31 March 19–5	3,500		Current Assets		
Less drawings	2,500	1,000	Stock	5,675	
			Debtors less provision	3,900	
			Rent owing	200	
Current Liabilities					9,775
Creditors	6,300				
Accruals	95				
Overdraft	2,780				
		9,175			
		32,275			32,275

4.

Alway Social Club
Estimated Bank Account

	£		£
Balance at 1 April 19–5	980	Purchases	11,800
Subscriptions—in arrears	16	Wages	1,200
current	1,490	Extension to Clubhouse	1,000
Equipment sales	50	Equipment	340
Bar sales	14,875	Social Expenses	1,680
Proceeds from socials	2,400	Commission	149
		Insurance	80
		Imprest Cash—Miscellaneous	70
		Rates	500
		Heat and Light	250
		Bar Licence	50
		Balance c/d	2,692
	19,811		19,811

(b) *Estimated Bar Trading and Profit and Loss Account*
for the year ending 31 March 19–6

	£	£	£
Sales			14,875
Stock at 1 April 19–5	400	12,400	
Add Purchases	12,000		
Less: Stock at 31 March 19–6		500	11,900
Gross Profit			2,975
Wages		1,200	
Commission		149	
Bar Licence		50	1,399
			1,576

(c) *Estimated Income and Expenditure Account*
for the year ending 31 March 19–6

	£		£
Rates	475	Subscriptions	1,498
Light and Heat	220	Profit on bar	1,576
Insurance	75	Surplus on social	720
Miscellaneous	70		
Loss on equipment	50		
Depreciation of equipment	597		
Surplus for the period	2,307		
	3,794		3,794

Estimated Balance Sheet as at 31 March 19–6

	£	£	Fixed Assets	£	£
Accumulated Fund at			Fixed Assets		
1 April 19–5		10,303	Clubhouse at cost	9,900	
Surplus for the year		2,307	Less amount owing	500	9,400
		12,610	Equipment at cost	2,390	
			Less depreciation	1,547	843
Current Liabilities					10,243
Creditors		1,000			
			Current Assets		
			Stock	500	
			Prepayment	165	
			Cash at bank	2,692	
			Cash in hand	10	3,367
		13,610			13,610

5. (a) Sales for both methods amount to £811. Found by units × unit price of sales and totalling.

  (1) Stock LIFO 5 of January Purchases × £5 each plus 10 of April Purchases × £6 each = £85.

  (2) Stock FIFO 15 of June Purchases × £7 each = £105.

Trading Accounts for the 6 months to 30 June 19–5

	LIFO	FIFO		LIFO	FIFO
Purchases	692.50	692.50	Sales	811.00	811.00
Less Closing Stock	85.00	105.00			
Cost of Goods Sold	607.50	587.50			
Gross Profit	203.50	223.50			
	811.00	811.00		811.00	811.00

(b)

Balance Sheets as at 30 June 19–5

	LIFO	FIFO		LIFO	FIFO
Capital 1.1.19–5	500.00	500.00	Stock	85.00	105.00
Add Profit	203.50	223.50	Cash	618.50	618.50
	£703.50	£723.50		£703.50	£723.50

Return on Capital Employed:

$$\text{LIFO} \qquad \frac{203.50}{500} \times \frac{100}{1} = 40.7\% \qquad \text{FIFO} \qquad \frac{223.50}{500} \times \frac{100}{1} = 44.7\%$$

Difference caused simply by stock valuation method.

When prices are rising LIFO gives better picture of profit, but balance sheet values outdated. FIFO is the reverse of this.

6. (a)

Balance Sheets
Profit recognized when
(i) Gold is Produced (ii) Gold is Sold (iii) Cash Collected

Stock	1,000	600	600
Debtors	1,000	1,000	600
Cash	5,000	5,000	5,000
	£7,000	£6,600	£6,200
Capital	5,000	5,000	5,000
Add Profit	2,000	1,600	1,200
	£7,000	£6,600	£6,200

(b) Usual method in use is (ii) when the gold is sold. Obviously both conservatism and objectivity would rule against method (i).

Method (iii) would normally be considered to carry conservatism too far.

However, if there is a doubt about collection of debtors a provision for doubtful debts will be made which will therefore go in the direction of method (iii).

Cost and Management Accountants—Full Paper

(To save space in this book, the final accounts are shown here in the two-sided form.)

H. Limited
Manufacturing, Trading & Profit & Loss Accounts
for the year ended 31 December 19–5

Stock of Materials		Production Cost of	
1.1.19–5	12,000	Goods completed c/d	123,800
Add Purchases	100,000		
	112,000		
Less Stock cf Materials			
31.12.19–5	13,000		
Cost of Materials			
Consumed	99,000		
Manufacturing Wages	9,000		
Manufacturing Expenses	11,200		
Depreciation:			
Land & Buildings	600		
Plant & Machinery	5,000		
Add Work-in-Progress			
1.1.19–5	8,000		
	132,800		
Less Work-in-Progress			
31.12.19–5	9,000		
	£123,800		£123,800

Stock of Finished Goods		Sales	200,000
1.1.19–5	47,000		
Add Production Cost			
Goods			
Completed b/d	123,800		
Purchases of Goods	1,000		
	171,800		
Less Stock Finished			
Goods 31.12.19–5	51,000		
Cost of Goods Sold	120,800		
Gross Profit c/d	79,200		
	£200,000		£200,000

Administrative Expenses:			Gross Profit b/d	79,200
General	22,100			
Depreciation:				
Land etc	300			
Plant	800	23,200		
Selling & Distribution				
Expenses:				
General	38,200			
Bad Debts	700			
Depreciation:				
Land etc	100			
Plant etc	200	39,200		
Debenture Interest		800		
Net Profit c/d		16,000		
		£ 79,200		£ 79,200

Corporation Tax			Net Profit b/d	16,000
Provision		8,000	Unappropriated Profits	
Transfer to General			from last year	1,000
Reserve		1,000		
Proposed Ordinary				
Dividend		6,000		
Unappropriated Profits				
carried to next year		2,000		
		£ 17,000		£ 17,000

H. Limited
Balance Sheet as at 31 December 19–5

Share Capital & Reserves			Fixed Assets	Cost	Depreciation	Net
Share Capital		60,000	Land & Buildings	40,000	10,000	30,000
			Plant & Machinery	60,000	40,000	20,000
				100.000	50,000	50,000
Reserves						
Share Premium	5,000					
General Reserve	23,000					
Profit & Loss	2,000	30,000				
		90,000	*Current Assets*			
			Stock of Materials	13,000		
			Work-in-Progress	9,000		
			Stock of Finished Goods	51,000		
			Debtors less provision	25,300		
			Prepaid Expenses	1,600		
			Cash in Hand	100	100,000	
8 PER CENT DEBENTURES						
repayable 1990 (secured)		10,000				
Current Liabilities						
Proposed Dividend	6,000					
Corporation Tax	8,000					
Bank Overdraft	21,500					
Accrued Expenses	3,500					
Creditors	11,000	50,000				
		£150,000			£150,000	

2. Ordinary Share Capital	10,000	
Share Premium		10,000
(2) Debenture	458	
Capital Reserve		458
(3) Bank Charges	1,000	
Bank Overdraft		1,000
(4) Depreciation: Fixed Assets	10,943	
Proceeds Sale of Fixed Assets	2,000	
Fixed Assets		11,879
Capital Surplus		1,064
(5) Wages & Salaries	6,088	
Creditor: PAYE 1.1.19–5	900	

Payments PAYE		5,988
Creditor PAYE 31.12.19–5		1,000
Wages & Salaries	4,766	
Purchases National Insurance etc.		4,766
(6) Discount Allowed	240	
Debtors		240
Creditors	260	
Discount Received		260
Creditors	10,000	
Debtors		10,000
(7) Bad Debts	2,000	
Debtors		2,000
(8) Debtors	1,000	
Bad Debts Recovered		1,000
(9) Purchases Returns	630	
Sales Returns	630	
Suspense		1,260
(10) Suspense	9	
Postages, etc.		9
(11) Packing Materials	76	
Suspense		76
(12) Advertising	124	
Repairs and maintenance		124
(13) Bank Overdraft	36	
Insurance		36
(14) Suspense	297	
Purchases		297

(b)   *Trial Balance—after correction as on 31 December 19–5*

	Dr	Cr
Ordinary Share Capital		100,000
Retained Profits 1.1.19–5		50,000
Share Premium		10,000
Ten Per Cent Debentures		30,000
Debtors & Creditors	66,000	50,000
Cash in Hand and Bank Overdraft	1,000	6,000
Stock and work-in-progress 1.1.19–5	108,000	
Fixed assets at cost, depreciation provision	150,000	50,000
Depreciation for year	15,000	
Purchases & Sales	300,000	400,000
Returns	5,000	4,000
Discounts Allowed and Received	10,000	7,000
Wages & Salaries	23,000	
Creditor PAYE at 31.12.19–5		1,000
Rent, Rates and Insurance	18,000	
Postages, Telephone & Stationery	3,000	
Repairs & Maintenance	2,000	
Advertising	5,000	
Packing Materials	1,000	
Motor Expenses	2,000	
Sundry Expenses	1,000	
Debenture Interest	4,000	
Capital Surplus		8,000

Bank Charges	1,000	
Bad Debts	2,000	
Bad Debts Recovered		1,000
	£717,000	£717,000

3.

A Company's Bank Reconciliation as on 31 December 19–5

Balance per Bank Statement (CR)		4,167	
Add Bank Charges not yet entered in cash book		531	
		4,698	
Less:			
Dividends not entered in Cash Book		1,608	
Unpresented cheques: J. & Sons	1,060		
U. & Sons	247		
W. & Sons	431		
N. Associates	65		
P. & Q.	234		
D. Ltd.	1,145		
L. Ltd.	93		
E. Associates	162	3,437	5,045
Bank Overdraft per Cash Book			£347

4. See Chapters 10 and 29 in *Business Accounting*.
5. See Chapter 7 in *Business Accounting*.

Chartered Secretaries and Administrators (Answers to Full Paper)

1. Essay answers given in brief fashion.

   (i) 'Costs' here means the total of the expenditure incurred to procure both goods and services for resale in a particular period.

     'Expired costs' refers to the part of the 'costs' which have been used up in producing sales for a particular period.

     The treatment of expenses in the valuation of stock will affect the profit shown, depending on whether an absorption or marginal approach is used to stock valuation. However, expenses which are concerned with administration, selling or distribution will never be taken into account in the normal run of firms. There are however rare cases of it being the custom for this to be done.

  (ii) See Chapter 28, but briefly,

     (*a*) FIFO will underestimate profit. The longer the goods have been in stock the greater this will be.

     (*b*) Weighted average will smooth out in part the fluctuations in the cost of goods, but where prices are rising rapidly it is still the smoothing out of out-of-date cost figures.

     (*c*) LIFO will relate better, but system fails when stock quantities are reduced.

1A. Briefly,

   (i) Ratio of Current Assets to Current Liabilities.

  (ii) Normally seen as an indicator of the ability of a firm to pay its creditors promptly, and therefore show liquidity and stability. A firm which fails to meet its bills promptly will soon lose its credibility. Most business dealings are based on the confidence and reliance that the other party to the deal will settle the account within a reasonable period. If serious doubt is raised then the firm may well find all of its sources of supply drying up, and will be unable to obtain credit. A very large percentage of firms going bankrupt or going into liquidation do so, not because they are not making profit, but because of lack of liquidity.

 (iii) What will be a reasonable figure for the ratio for a particular firm will depend on the type of business and how it is operated. Some firms have a very low rate of stockturn, e.g. a jewellers dealing in expensive jewellery. Other firms will have an extremely high rate of stockturn, for instance firms dealing in perishable goods, such as fruit. A firm selling bananas would soon have a lot of bad stock being dumped if its stockturn rate decreased considerably.

     Where a firm receives goods and sells them quickly for cash a high figure for the current ratio would be unnecessary. For instance, a newsagent who buys newspapers and sells them for cash later on the same day will not need such a high ratio as a publisher of accountancy textbooks who pays for the books and then sells them on credit over the next two or three years. The newsagent may work very well with a ratio of 1:1, whereas the publisher would possibly be forced out of business with a ratio that low.

2. (i)

B.K. Ltd
Profit & Loss Appropriation Account for the year ended 30 September 19–6

	£	£		£
Taxation for the year	15,300		Net Profit for the	50,400
Less Over-provision in previous year	200	15,100	year brought down (balancing figure)	
Transfer to General Reserve		9,000		
Transfer to Stock Replacement Reserve		6,400	Unappropriated Profit, brought forward from	
Dividends: Interim—Paid		2,000	last year	4,500
Final—Proposed		11,000		
Unappropriated Profits carried to next year		11,400		
		54,900		54,900

(ii)   *Balance Sheet as at 30 September 19–6*

			£
Fixed Assets			
Goodwill			22,000
Land & Buildings—at valuation			54,000
Plant at cost		37,000	
Less Depreciation to date		18,600	18,400
			94,400
Current Assets			
Stocks at or below cost		37,000	
Debtors	36,200		
Less Provision for Bad Debts	1,500	34,700	
Cash at Bank		23,200	
		94,900	
Less Current Liabilities			
Provision for Taxation	15,300		
Proposed Dividends	11,000		
Creditors	17,200	43,500	
Working Capital			51,400
Net Assets			145,800
Financed by:			
Authorized & Issued Share Capital:			
9 per cent Preference Shares £1 each			80,000
Ordinary Shares of £1 each			30,000
			110,000

Reserves:

Asset Revaluation Reserve	4,000	
Stock Replacement Reserve	6,400	
General Reserve	14,000	
Profit & Loss Account	11,400	35,800

Capital Employed		145,800

(iii) Dividends Payable. This represents the amount of dividend which the directors have proposed should be paid. They have to be approved by the shareholders at the annual general meeting. If passed the dividend is normally paid very soon afterwards.

Provision for Taxation. The amount which it is estimated will be payable for Corporation Tax based on the current year's profits.

General Reserve. Profits of earlier periods held back for general use in the business.

Stock Replacement Reserve. As stock absorbs more and more cash in times of rising prices, some profits have been set aside, instead of using them to finance payments of dividends.

Asset Revaluation Reserve. When fixed assets are revalued, any surplus cannot normally be regarded as profits available for dividend purposes. It should therefore be shown in a capital reserve account suitably titled.

3. (a)   *Cash Account: Year ended 30 November 19–6*

	£		£
Capital: Opening	1,200	Rates	260
Further	500	Advertising	284
Cash Sales & Receipts		Fixtures & Equipment	220
from Debtors	20,470	Wages	1,568
		General Expenses	386
		Drawings	2,244
		Suppliers (difference)	16,324
		Bank Balance c/d	884
	22,170		22,170

(b)   T.B.

Trading & Profit & Loss Account for the year ended 30 November 19–6

	£		£
Opening Stock	3,600	Sales (20,470+1,656)	22,126
Add Purchases (16,324+			
1,188)	17,512		
	21,112		
Less Closing Stock			
(6,400 × 75%)	4,800		
Cost of Goods Sold	16,312		
Gross Profit c/d	5,814		
	22,126		22,126

Wages	1,568	Gross Profit b/d	5,814
Rates	208		
Advertising	284		
General Expenses	386		
Depreciation	162		
Net Profit	3,206		
	5,814		5,814

Balance Sheet as at 30 November 19–6

Capital	£	Fixed Assets—at cost	£	£
Cash & Items Introduced*	21,700	Goodwill		2,000
Add Net Profit	3,206	Premises		13,000
	24,906	Fixtures	1,620	
Less Drawings	2,244	Less Depreciation	162	1,458
	22,662			16,458
Current Liabilities		*Current Assets*		
Creditors	1,188	Stock	4,800	
		Debtors	1,656	
		Prepayments	52	
		Bank	884	7,392
	23,850			23,850

* Cash £1,700 + Premises £13,000 + Fixtures £1,400 + Stock £3,600 + Goodwill (difference) £2,000 = £21,700.

(c) He expected a gross profit percentage of 25 per cent; it has in fact turned out to be just over 26 per cent.

Current ratio is over 6:1, an extremely high figure. Also high degree of liquidity.

Net Profit as a percentage of Capital Employed is almost 15 per cent.

4. (a) Briefly. The total net profit which will be made if all customers pay is equal to gross profit margin 25 per cent less 5 per cent expenses = 20 per cent. The following table can therefore be constructed:

Category	Profit if all pay	Possible loss because of non-payment	Expected net result
1	£10,000 × 20% = £2,000	£10,000 × nil % = Nil	£2,000
2	£24,000 × 20% = £4,800	£24,000 × 5% = £1,200	£3,600
3	£36,000 × 20% = £7,200	£36,000 × 17½% = £6,300	£900
4	£10,000 × 20% = £2,000	£10,000 × 30% = £3,000	(£1,000)
5	£5,000 × 20% = £1,000	£5,000 × 50% = £2,500	(£1,500)
6	£4,000 × 20% = £800	£4,000 × 90% = £3,600	(£2,800)

The categories 1, 2 and 3 are the only ones that are going to show profits after expenses.

The interest factor should also be taken into account. As category 1 has an average period of $1\frac{1}{2}$ months for credit then this is clearly reasonable. However, category 2 has 3 months and category 3 has six months. The costs of borrowing funds for the periods in question should therefore be taken into account. Depending on alternative uses for the funds of the firm, such interest factors could well mean that category 3 in particular would not be worthwhile. As the net profit is only £900 anyway, it is likely that the interest costs would exceed that amount. Much more information would be needed for the sums to be done referring to interest charges.

(b) Briefly. One can only contrast like with like. To do this the two sets of accounts should be put on the same basis. Nothing is charged in the accounts of MT, for the work put in by MT, whereas LX has £3,500 charged to it for the services of a person doing a similar job to MT. Therefore £3,500 should be deducted from the profit of £10,000 of MT.

A similar deduction for rent should be made. After deducting £3,500 for services and £1,500 for rent, the businesses will then both show exactly the şame figures in the Trading and Profit and Loss Accounts. The figure of £500 difference for cash in the balance sheet is not material, and therefore the two businesses can be regarded as the same in terms of results and structure.

APPENDIX NO 58.2

TABLE 1

Compound Sum of £1

Year	1%	2%	3%	4%	5%	6%	7%	8%	9%	10%
1	1·010	1·020	1·030	1·040	1·050	1·060	1·070	1·080	1·090	1·100
2	1·020	1·040	1·061	1·082	1·102	1·124	1·145	1·166	1·188	1·210
3	1·030	1·061	1·093	1·125	1·158	1·191	1·225	1·260	1·295	1·331
4	1·041	1·082	1·126	1·170	1·216	1·262	1·311	1·360	1·412	1·464
5	1·051	1·104	1·159	1·217	1·276	1·338	1·403	1·469	1·539	1·611
6	1·062	1·126	1·194	1·265	1·340	1·419	1·501	1·587	1·677	1·772
7	1·072	1·149	1·230	1·316	1·407	1·504	1·606	1·714	1·828	1·949
8	1·083	1·172	1·267	1·369	1·477	1·594	1·718	1·851	1·993	2·144
9	1·094	1·195	1·305	1·423	1·551	1·689	1·838	1·999	2·172	2·358
10	1·105	1·219	1·344	1·480	1·629	1·791	1·967	2·159	2·367	2·594
11	1·116	1·243	1·384	1·539	1·710	1·898	2·105	2·332	2·580	2·853
12	1·127	1·268	1·426	1·601	1·796	2·012	2·252	2·518	2·813	3·138
13	1·138	1·294	1·469	1·665	1·886	2·133	2·410	2·720	3·066	3·452
14	1·149	1·319	1·513	1·732	1·980	2·261	2·579	2·937	3·342	3·797
15	1·161	1·346	1·558	1·801	2·079	2·397	2·759	3·172	3·642	4·177

Year	12%	14%	15%	16%	18%	20%	24%	28%	32%
1	1·120	1·140	1·150	1·160	1·180	1·200	1·240	1·280	1·320
2	1·254	1·300	1·322	1·346	1·392	1·440	1·538	1·638	1·742
3	1·405	1·482	1·521	1·561	1·643	1·728	1·907	2·097	2·300
4	1·574	1·689	1·749	1·811	1·939	2·074	2·364	2·684	3·036
5	1·762	1·925	2·011	2·100	2·288	2·488	2·932	3·436	4·007
6	1·974	2·195	2·313	2·436	2·700	2·986	3·635	4·398	5·390
7	2·211	2·502	2·660	2·826	3·185	3·583	4·508	5·6209	6·983
8	2·476	2·853	3·059	3·278	3·759	4·300	5·590	7·206	9·217
9	2·773	3·252	3·518	3·803	4·435	5·160	6·931	9·223	12·166
10	3·106	3·707	4·046	4·411	5·234	6·192	8·594	11·806	16·060
11	3·479	4·226	4·652	5·117	6·176	7·430	10·657	15·112	21·199
12	3·896	4·818	5·350	5·936	7·288	8·916	13·215	19·343	27·983
13	4·363	5·492	6·153	6·886	8·599	10·699	16·386	24·759	36·937
14	4·887	6·261	7·076	7·988	10·147	12·839	20·139	31·691	48·757
15	5·474	7·138	8·137	9·266	11·974	15·407	25·196	40·565	64·359

Year	36%	40%	50%	60%	70%	80%	90%
1	1·360	1·400	1·500	1·600	1·700	1·800	1·900
2	1·850	1·960	2·560	2·560	2·890	3·240	3·610
3	2·515	2·744	3·375	4·096	4·913	5·832	6·859
4	3·421	3·842	5·062	6·544	8·352	10·498	13·032
5	4·653	5·378	7·594	10·486	14·199	18·896	24·761
6	6·328	7·530	11·391	16·777	24·138	34·012	47·046
7	8·605	10·541	17·086	26·844	41·034	61·222	89·387
8	11·703	14·758	25·629	42·940	69·758	110·200	169·836
9	15·917	20·661	38·443	68·720	118·588	198·359	322·698
10	21·647	28·925	57·665	109·951	201·599	357·047	613·107
11	29·439	40·496	86·498	175·922	342·719	642·684	1164·902
12	40·037	56·964	129·746	281·475	582·622	1156·831	2213·314
13	54·451	79·372	194·619	450·360	990·457	2082·295	4205·297
14	74·053	111·120	291·929	720·576	1683·777	3748·131	7990·065
15	100·712	155·568	437·894	1152·921	2862·421	6746·636	15181·122

TABLE 2

Present Value of £1

Year	1%	2%	3%	4%	5%	6%	7%	8%	9%	10%	12%	14%	15%
1	0·990	0·980	0·971	0·961	0·952	0·943	0·935	0·926	0·917	0·909	0·893	0·877	0·870
2	0·980	0·961	0·943	0·925	0·907	0·890	0·873	0·857	0·842	0·826	0·797	0·769	0·756
3	0·971	0·942	0·915	0·889	0·864	0·840	0·816	0·794	0·772	0·751	0·712	0·675	0·658
4	0·961	0·924	0·889	0·855	0·823	0·792	0·763	0·735	0·708	0·683	0·636	0·592	0·572
5	0·951	0·906	0·863	0·822	0·784	0·747	0·713	0·681	0·650	0·621	0·567	0·519	0·497
6	0·942	0·888	0·838	0·790	0·746	0·705	0·666	0·630	0·596	0·564	0·507	0·456	0·432
7	0·933	0·871	0·813	0·760	0·711	0·665	0·623	0·583	0·547	0·513	0·452	0·400	0·376
8	0·923	0·853	0·789	0·731	0·677	0·627	0·582	0·540	0·502	0·467	0·404	0·351	0·327
9	0·914	0·837	0·766	0·703	0·645	0·592	0·544	0·500	0·460	0·424	0·361	0·308	0·284
10	0·905	0·820	0·744	0·676	0·614	0·558	0·508	0·463	0·422	0·386	0·322	0·270	0·247
11	0·896	0·804	0·722	0·650	0·585	0·527	0·475	0·429	0·388	0·350	0·287	0·237	0·215
12	0·887	0·788	0·701	0·625	0·557	0·497	0·444	0·397	0·356	0·319	0·257	0·208	0·187
13	0·879	0·773	0·681	0·601	0·530	0·469	0·415	0·368	0·326	0·290	0·229	0·182	0·163
14	0·870	0·758	0·661	0·577	0·505	0·442	0·388	0·340	0·299	0·263	0·205	0·160	0·141
15	0·861	0·743	0·642	0·555	0·481	0·417	0·362	0·315	0·275	0·239	0·183	0·140	0·123
16	0·853	0·728	0·623	0·534	0·458	0·394	0·339	0·292	0·252	0·218	0·163	0·123	0·107
17	0·844	0·714	0·605	0·513	0·436	0·371	0·317	0·270	0·231	0·198	0·146	0·108	0·093
18	0·836	0·700	0·587	0·494	0·416	0·350	0·296	0·250	0·212	0·180	0·130	0·095	0·081
19	0·828	0·686	0·570	0·475	0·396	0·331	0·276	0·232	0·194	0·164	0·116	0·083	0·070
20	0·820	0·673	0·554	0·456	0·377	0·319	0·258	0·215	0·178	0·149	0·104	0·073	0·061
25	0·780	0·610	0·478	0·375	0·295	0·233	0·184	0·146	0·116	0·092	0·059	0·038	0·030
30	0·742	0·552	0·412	0·308	0·231	0·174	0·131	0·099	0·075	0·057	0·033	0·020	0·015

Year	16%	18%	20%	24%	28%	32%	36%	40%	50%	60%	70%	80%	90%
1	0·862	0·847	0·833	0·806	0·781	0·758	0·735	0·714	0·667	0·625	0·588	0·556	0·526
2	0·743	0·718	0·694	0·650	0·610	0·574	0·541	0·510	0·444	0·391	0·346	0·309	0·277
3	0·641	0·609	0·579	0·524	0·477	0·435	0·398	0·364	0·296	0·244	0·204	0·171	0·146
4	0·552	0·516	0·482	0·423	0·373	0·329	0·292	0·260	0·198	0·153	0·120	0·095	0·077
5	0·476	0·437	0·402	0·341	0·291	0·250	0·215	0·186	0·132	0·095	0·070	0·053	0·040
6	0·410	0·370	0·335	0·275	0·227	0·189	0·158	0·133	0·088	0·060	0·041	0·029	0·021
7	0·354	0·314	0·279	0·222	0·178	0·143	0·116	0·095	0·059	0·037	0·024	0·016	0·011
8	0·305	0·266	0·233	0·179	0·139	0·108	0·085	0·068	0·039	0·023	0·014	0·009	0·006
9	0·263	0·226	0·194	0·144	0·108	0·082	0·063	0·048	0·026	0·015	0·008	0·005	0·003
10	0·227	0·191	0·162	0·116	0·085	0·062	0·046	0·035	0·017	0·009	0·005	0·003	0·002
11	0·195	0·162	0·135	0·094	0·066	0·047	0·034	0·025	0·012	0·006	0·003	0·002	0·001
12	0·168	0·137	0·112	0·076	0·052	0·036	0·025	0·018	0·008	0·004	0·002	0·001	0·001
13	0·145	0·116	0·093	0·061	0·040	0·027	0·018	0·013	0·005	0·002	0·001	0·001	0·000
14	0·125	0·099	0·078	0·049	0·032	0·021	0·014	0·009	0·003	0·001	0·001	0·000	0·000
15	0·108	0·084	0·065	0·040	0·025	0·016	0·010	0·006	0·002	0·001	0·000	0·000	0·000
16	0·093	0·071	0·054	0·032	0·019	0·012	0·007	0·005	0·002	0·001	0·000	0·000	
17	0·080	0·060	0·045	0·026	0·015	0·009	0·005	0·003	0·001	0·000	0·000		
18	0·069	0·051	0·038	0·021	0·012	0·007	0·004	0·002	0·001	0·000	0·000		
19	0·060	0·043	0·031	0·017	0·009	0·005	0·003	0·002	0·000	0·000			
20	0·051	0·037	0·026	0·014	0·007	0·004	0·002	0·001	0·000	0·000			
25	0·024	0·016	0·010	0·005	0·002	0·001	0·000	0·000					
30	0·012	0·007	0·004	0·002	0·001	0·000	0·000						

TABLE 3

Sum of an Annuity of £1 for N Years

Year	1%	2%	3%	4%	5%	6%	7%	8%
1	1·000	1·000	1·000	1·000	1·000	1·000	1·000	1·000
2	2·010	2·020	2·030	2·040	2·050	2·060	2·070	2·080
3	3·030	3·060	3·091	3·122	3·152	3·184	3·215	3·246
4	4·060	4·122	4·184	4·246	4·310	4·375	4·440	4·506
5	5·101	5·204	5·309	5·416	5·526	5·637	5·751	5·867
6	6·152	6·308	6·468	6·633	6·802	6·975	7·153	7·336
7	7·214	7·434	7·662	7·898	8·142	8·394	8·654	8·923
8	8·286	8·583	8·892	9·214	9·549	9·897	10·260	10·637
9	9·369	9·755	10·159	10·583	11·027	11·491	11·978	12·488
10	10·462	10·950	11·464	12·006	12·578	13·181	13·816	14·487
11	11·567	12·169	12·808	13·486	14·207	14·972	15·784	16·645
12	12·683	13·412	14·192	15·026	15·917	16·870	17·888	18·977
13	13·809	14·680	15·618	16·627	17·713	18·882	20·141	21·495
14	14·947	15·974	17·086	18·292	19·599	21·051	22·550	24·215
15	16·097	17·293	18·599	20·024	21·579	23·276	25·129	27·152
16	17·258	18·639	20·157	21·825	23·657	25·673	27·888	30·324
17	18·430	20·012	21·762	23·698	25·840	28·213	30·840	33·750
18	19·615	21·412	23·414	25·645	28·132	30·906	33·999	37·450
19	20·811	22·841	25·117	27·671	30·539	33·760	37·379	41·446
20	22·019	24·297	26·870	29·778	33·066	36·786	40·995	45·762
25	28·243	32·030	36·459	41·646	47·727	54·865	63·249	73·106
30	34·785	40·568	47·575	56·085	66·439	79·058	94·461	113·283

Year	9%	10%	12%	14%	16%	18%	20%	24%
1	1·000	1·000	1·000	1·000	1·000	1·000	1·000	1·000
2	2·090	2·100	2·120	2·140	2·160	2·180	2·200	2·240
3	3·278	3·310	3·374	3·440	3·506	3·572	3·640	3·778
4	4·573	4·641	4·779	4·921	5·066	5·215	5·368	5·684
5	5·985	6·105	6·353	6·610	6·877	7·154	7·442	8·048
6	7·253	7·716	8·115	8·536	8·977	9·442	9·930	10·980
7	9·200	9·487	10·089	10·730	11·414	12·142	12·916	14·615
8	11·028	11·436	12·300	13·233	14·240	15·327	16·499	19·123
9	13·021	13·579	14·776	16·085	17·518	19·086	20·799	24·712
10	15·193	15·937	17·549	19·337	21·321	23·521	25·959	31·643
11	17·560	18·531	20·655	23·044	25·738	28·755	32·150	40·238
12	20·141	21·384	24·133	27·271	30·350	34·931	39·580	50·895
13	22·953	24·523	28·029	32·089	36·766	42·219	48·497	64·110
14	26·019	27·975	32·393	37·581	43·672	50·818	59·196	80·496
15	29·361	31·772	37·280	43·842	51·659	60·965	72·035	100·815

Year	28%	32%	36%	40%	50%	60%	70%	80%
1	1·000	1·000	1·000	1·000	1·000	1·000	1·000	1·000
2	2·280	2·320	2·360	2·400	2·500	2·600	2·700	2·800
3	3·918	4·062	4·210	4·360	4·750	5·160	5·590	6·040
4	6·016	6·362	6·725	7·104	8·125	9·256	10·503	11·872
5	8·700	9·398	10·146	10·846	13·188	15·810	18·855	22·370
6	12·136	13·406	14·799	16·324	20·781	26·295	33·054	41·265
7	16·534	18·696	21·126	23·853	32·172	43·073	57·191	75·278
8	22·163	25·678	29·732	34·395	49·258	69·196	98·225	136·500
9	29·369	34·895	41·435	49·153	74·887	112·866	167·983	246·699
10	38·592	47·062	57·352	69·814	113·330	181·585	286·570	445·058
11	50·399	63·122	78·998	98·739	170·995	291·536	488·170	802·105
12	65·510	84·320	108·437	139·235	257·493	467·458	830·888	1444·788
13	84·853	112·303	148·475	195·929	387·239	748·933	1413·510	2601·619
14	109·612	149·240	202·926	275·300	581·859	1199·293	2403·968	4683·914
15	141·303	197·997	276·979	386·420	873·788	1919·869	4087·745	8432·045

TABLE 4

Present Value of an Annuity of £1

Year	1%	2%	3%	4%	5%	6%	7%	8%	9%	10%
1	0·990	0·980	0·971	0·962	0·952	0·943	0·935	0·926	0·917	0·909
2	1·970	1·942	1·913	1·886	1·859	1·833	1·808	1·783	1·759	1·736
3	2·941	2·884	2·829	2·775	2·723	2·673	2·624	2·577	2·531	2·487
4	3·902	3·808	3·717	3·630	3·546	3·465	3·387	3·312	3·240	3·170
5	4·853	4·713	4·580	4·452	4·329	4·212	4·100	3·993	3·890	3·791
6	5·795	5·601	5·417	5·242	5·076	4·917	4·766	4·623	4·486	4·355
7	6·728	6·472	6·230	6·002	5·786	5·582	5·389	5·206	5·033	4·868
8	7·652	7·325	7·020	6·733	6·463	6·210	6·971	5·747	5·535	5·335
9	8·566	8·162	7·786	7·435	7·108	6·802	6·515	6·247	5·985	5·759
10	9·471	8·983	8·530	8·111	7·722	7·360	7·024	6·710	6·418	6·145
11	10·368	9·787	9·253	8·760	8·306	7·887	7·499	7·139	6·805	6·495
12	11·255	10·575	9·954	9·385	8·863	8·384	7·943	7·536	7·161	6·814
13	12·134	11·348	10·635	9·986	9·394	8·853	8·358	7·904	7·487	7·103
14	13·004	12·106	11·296	10·563	9·899	9·295	8·745	8·244	7·786	7·367
15	13·865	12·849	11·938	11·118	10·380	9·712	9·108	8·559	8·060	7·606
16	14·718	13·578	12·561	11·652	10·838	10·106	9·447	8·851	8·312	7·824
17	15·562	14·292	13·166	12·166	11·274	10·477	9·763	9·122	8·544	8·022
18	16·398	14·992	13·754	12·659	11·690	10·828	10·059	9·372	8·756	8·201
19	17·226	15·678	14·324	13·134	12·085	11·158	10·336	9·604	8·950	8·365
20	18·046	16·351	14·877	13·590	12·462	11·470	10·594	9·818	9·128	8·514
25	22·023	19·523	17·413	15·622	14·094	12·783	11·654	10·675	9·823	9·077
30	25·808	22·397	19·600	17·292	15·373	13·765	12·409	11·258	10·274	9·427

Year	12%	14%	16%	18%	20%	24%	28%	32%	36%
1	0·893	0·877	0·862	0·847	0·833	0·806	0·781	0·758	0·735
2	1·690	1·647	1·605	1·566	1·528	1·457	1·392	1·332	1·276
3	2·402	2·322	2·246	2·174	2·106	1·981	1·868	1·766	1·674
4	3·037	2·914	2·798	2·690	2·589	2·404	2·241	2·096	1·966
5	3·605	3·433	3·274	3·127	2·991	2·745	2·532	2·345	2·181
6	4·111	3·889	3·685	3·498	3·326	3·020	2·759	2·534	2·339
7	4·564	4·288	4·089	3·812	3·605	3·242	2·937	2·678	2·455
8	4·968	4·639	4·344	4·078	3·837	3·421	3·076	2·786	2·540
9	5·328	4·946	4·607	4·303	4·031	3·566	3·184	2·868	2·603
10	5·650	5·216	4·833	4·494	4·193	3·682	3·269	2·930	2·650
11	5·988	5·453	5·029	4·656	4·327	3·776	3·335	2·978	2·683
12	6·194	5·660	5·197	4·793	4·439	3·851	3·387	3·013	2·708
13	6·424	5·842	5·342	4·910	4·533	3·912	3·427	3·040	2·727
14	6·628	6·002	5·468	5·008	4·611	3·962	3·459	3·061	2·740
15	6·811	6·142	5·575	5·092	4·675	4·001	3·483	3·076	2·750
16	6·974	6·265	5·669	5·162	4·730	4·033	3·503	3·088	2·758
17	7·120	5·373	5·749	4·222	4·775	4·059	3·518	3·097	2·763
18	7·250	6·467	5·818	5·273	4·812	4·080	3·529	3·104	2·767
19	7·366	6·550	5·877	5·316	4·844	4·097	3·539	3·109	2·770
20	7·469	6·623	5·929	5·353	4·870	4·110	3·546	3·113	2·772
25	7·843	6·873	6·907	5·467	4·948	4·147	3·564	3·122	2·776
30	8·055	7·003	6·177	5·517	4·997	4·160	3·569	3·124	2·778

Index—Volumes 1 and 2